ADULTERY IN THE NOVEL

Rembrandt, *The Woman Taken in Adultery*. Reproduced by courtesy of the Trustees, The National Gallery, London.

ADULTERY

IN THE

NOVEL

CONTRACT AND TRANSGRESSION

TONY TANNER

THE JOHNS HOPKINS UNIVERSITY PRESS

BALTIMORE AND LONDON

Printed in the United States of America

The Johns Hopkins University Press, Baltimore, Maryland 21218
The Johns Hopkins Press Ltd., London

Originally published, 1979
Johns Hopkins Paperbacks edition, 1981

Library of Congress Cataloging in Publication Data

Tanner, Tony.
  Adultery in the novel.

  Bibliography: pp. 378-79
  Includes index.
  1. Fiction—18th century—History and criticism.
  2. Fiction—19th century—History and criticism.
  3. Adultery in literature. I. Title.
PN3352.A38T3   809.3'3   79-4948

          ISBN 0-8018-2178-9
          ISBN 0-8018-2471-0 (pbk)

for NADIA FUSINI

per sempre

Spare your arithmetic: never count the turns;
Once, and a million!
                                        —Shakespeare, *Cymbeline*

... for if a woman
Fly from one point, from which she makes a husband,
She spreads and mounts then like arithmetic;
One, ten, a hundred, a thousand, ten thousand.
                                        —Middleton, *The Changeling*

Marriage is but a ceremonial toy:
And if thou lovest me, think no more of it.
                                        —Marlowe, *Doctor Faustus*

Hail wedded Love, mysterious Law, true sourse
Of human ofspring, sole proprietie,
In Paradise of all things common else.
By thee adulterous lust was driv'n from men
Among the bestial herds to raunge, by thee
Founded in Reason, Loyal, Just, and Pure,
Relations dear, and all the Charities
Of Father, Son, and Brother first were known.
                                        —Milton, *Paradise Lost*

—J'ai tort, j'ai tort, disait elle. Je suis folle de vous entendre.
—Pourquoi? . . . Emma! Emma!
                                        —Flaubert, *Madame Bovary*

CONTENTS

PREFACE

———————•——————

This book is offered as an exercise in reading. It is not intended as a contribution to Comparative Literature, inasmuch as there is no attempt to cover or summarize the immense amount of writing on Rousseau, Goethe, and Flaubert, nor even to offer any comprehensive account of their work in relation to their own times and to other writers. This involved a decision not to include references to the copious secondary literature on these three writers. Thus, for example, there is no reference to the work of Starobinski on Rousseau, nor to the famous essay by Walter Benjamin on *Elective Affinities,* nor to the many famous works on Flaubert, such as those by J. P. Richard and Sartre (to mention only two of the more obvious). For many scholars, such a sin of omission will seem to be grievous, if not fatally irresponsible. One excuse would be that such secondary works are so well known that it would be pointless to offer summaries or recapitulations here. But the book is deliberately written "blind" because I wanted to try having my say in my own way, and, to avoid interruptions, decided to avoid the continuous reference (and deference) to other well known critics and critical works. Such a procedure—I am aware it can hardly be called a methodology—obviously has its risks, and courts certain kinds of criticism. I can only ask readers to consider what is there, rather than point out—what I am well aware of—all that is *not* there.

I have started with a general topic, or problem, namely the role played by the transgressive act of adultery in fiction, and have attempted to show what kind of texts resulted from an engagement with this problem in the work of some of the major bourgeois novelists. I realize that the very notion of the bourgeois novel raises many questions of definition and typology (not to mention dating), but rather than attempt any preliminary theory concerning the bourgeois novel, I have preferred to offer a detailed examination of three key novels (*La Nouvelle Héloïse, Die Wahlverwandtschaften,* and *Madame Bovary*), in the hope that some of the determining outlines of the bourgeois novel will emerge from that discussion. In the first chapter, I have tried to open up a number of different ways into a consideration of the topic, deliberately avoiding many of the standard procedures of literary/historical criticism; aiming at a multiplicity of possible perspectives—admittedly fragmentary and discontinuous—rather than aspiring to a sequential critical approach to the problem. The first chapter, then, is intended to be suggestive. The following three chapters attempt to show what a close reading of three absolutely crucial texts in this area brings to light. In a subsequent volume, I hope to provide much of the theory that may be felt to be missing in this volume, and to synthesize a number of suitable and rewarding approaches to the problem of adultery as it is examined and portrayed in nineteenth-century and early-twentieth-century fiction. The present volume thus stands as a kind of prolonged prologue (or preliminary discourse) to the discussion of what I take to be one of the most important features of the development of the novel as we know it, or knew it. (I would also like to think that the book contributed something to the debate concerning the problem of "marriage" and "the role of the woman" that engages us now perhaps more and more urgently, than ever it did before.)

This work was started during a stay at the Center for the Advanced Study of the Behavioral Sciences, a place offering such incomparable facilities for exploring and developing new ideas that anyone who has been there will know what I mean when I say that the opportunity offered by a year there simply made all the difference when it came to the development of my own work. Like many others, I can only record my gratitude for that opportunity and hope that the resultant work will go some small way to justifying it. I would also like to express my thanks and sense of indebtedness to a number of people, in addition to the indefatigably helpful staff at the Center. In different ways I have been helped greatly by, and learned a lot from, Ian Watt, Frank Kermode, Edmund Leach, Edward Said, Richard Macksey, Tom Bower, Stephen Heath, and Christopher Prendergast. There are many others with whom I have had the most profitable kind of conversations—not least the dedicatee—the positive results of which I am powerless to trace or assess. I also wish to record my gratitude to Christina Peutsch for her patient instruction as I was struggling to acquire some reading knowledge of German (any assertions concerning the meanings and nuances of certain German words in the section on Goethe I owe to her advice, though needless to say, any errors in the same area are all my own). Heather Jarman was both a scrupulous reader and typist of a final portion of the text, and I am very grateful for her help. I wish to express my special gratitude to Cynthia Foote who was both an impeccably scrupulous and extraordinarily helpful copy editor. Mary Lou Kenney was very helpful in the later stages of the preparation of the book. Finally I should add that William Sisler has proved to be an admirable, encouraging, and most amiable and helpful editor, and I can only hope that this volume is to some degree worthy of his efforts and The Johns Hopkins University Press.

ADULTERY IN THE NOVEL

1

INTRODUCTION

Contract and Transgression

There are few general propositions concerning the age to which we belong which seem at first sight likely to be received with readier concurrence than the assertion that the society of our day is mainly distinguished from that of preceding generations by the largeness of the sphere which is occupied in it by Contract. . . . Not many of us are so unobservant as not to perceive that in innumerable cases where old law fixed a man's position irreversibly at his birth, modern law allows him to create it for himself by convention; and indeed several of the few exceptions which remain to this rule are constantly denounced with passionate indignation.—Sir Henry Sumner Maine, *Ancient Law* (1861)

In transgressing the Law of Nature, the Offender declares himself to live by another Rule, than that of *reason* and common Equity, which is that measure God has set to the actions of Men, for their mutual security: and so he becomes dangerous to Mankind, the tye, which is to secure them from injury and violence, being slighted and broken by him.—John Locke, *Two Treatises of Government* (1690)

The novel, in its origin, might almost be said to be a transgressive mode, inasmuch as it seemed to break, or mix, or adulterate the existing genre-expectations of the time. It is not for nothing that many of the protagonists of the early English novels are socially displaced or unplaced figures—orphans, prostitutes, adventurers, etc. They thus represent or incarnate a potentially disruptive or socially unstabilized energy that may threaten, directly or implicitly, the organization of society, whether by the indeterminacy of their origin, the uncertainty of the direction in which they will focus their unbonded energy, or their attitude to the ties that hold society together and that they may choose to slight or break. More generally it may be said that many of the protagonists of novels either find their position fixed *too* irreversibly at birth and will struggle against that condition; or they become "dangerous to Mankind," or at least to the specific community of their operations, and will attempt to assert their right to live by another rule. In particular, although the eighteenth- and nineteenth-century novel may be said to move toward marriage and the securing of genealogical continuity, it often gains its particular narrative urgency from an energy that threatens to contravene that stability of the family on which society depends. It thus becomes a paradoxical object in society, by no means an inert adjunct to the family décor, but a text that may work to subvert what it seems to celebrate.

Since much of what I want to write about concerns an act of transgression that threatens the family—namely, adultery—I wish to juxtapose two more quotations from Maine and Locke that may be well known to philosophers and legal historians, but perhaps less so to readers of the novel.

The movement of the progressive societies has been uniform in one respect. Through all its course it has been distinguished by the gradual dissolution of family dependency and the growth of individual obligation in its place. The individual is steadily substituted for the Family, as the unit of which civil laws take account. . . . Nor is it difficult to see what is the tie between man and man which replaces by degrees those forms of reciprocity in rights and duties which have their origin in the Family. It is Contract. Starting, as from one terminus of history, from a condition of society in which all the relations of Persons are summed up in the relations of Family, we seem to have steadily moved towards a phase of social order in which all these relations arise from the free agreement of individuals . . . The status of the Female under Tutelage, if the tutelage be understood of persons other than her husband, has also ceased to exist; from her coming of age to her marriage all the relations she may form are relations of contract. So too the status of the Son under Power has no true place in the law of modern European societies. If any civil obligation binds together the Parent and the child of full age, it is one to which only contract gives its legal validity. The apparent exceptions are exceptions of that stamp which illustrate the rule. The child before years of discretion, the orphan under guardianship, the adjudged lunatic, have all their capacities and incapacities regulated by the Law of Persons. But why? The reason is differently expressed in the conventional language of different systems, but in substance it is stated to the same effect by all. The great majority of Jurists are constant to the principle that the classes of persons just mentioned are subject to extrinsic control on the single ground that they do not possess the faculty of forming a judgment on their own interests; in other words, they are wanting in the first essential of an engagement by Contract.[1]

The novel may be said to follow this "dissolution of family dependency and the growth of individual obligation" in most careful detail, albeit while manifesting fluctuant and ambivalent feelings concerning the phenomenon. And by the same token it may be said to have shown a fairly marked interest in just those figures who according to law are supposed not to "possess the faculty of forming a judgment on their own interests"—i.e., the child, the orphan, and the lunatic (adjudged or not adjudged), who possess the faculty of forming judgments outside the given law of their societies. Maine concludes this passage with a paragraph that is now part of the history of the theory of law, but which it will be well to have before us.

> The word Status may be usefully employed to construct a formula expressing the law of progress thus indicated, which, whatever be its value, seems to me to be sufficiently ascertained. All the forms of Status taken notice of in the Law of Persons were derived from, and to some extent are still coloured by, the powers and privileges of the Family. If then we employ Status, agreeably with the usage of the best writers, to signify these personal conditions only, . . . we may say that the movement of the progressive societies has hitherto been a movement *from Status to Contract.*[2]

But if *Status* implies that what you may *do* is conditioned by *where you are* in the family, then clearly there is no simple or easy or clear-cut move to a state in which a person is entirely free to define himself or herself by contract. Indeed the tensions between the two states is often near the center of many of the classic European novels. In particular, the freedom of the child (up to an indefinite age) could remain highly problematical. It all comes down to a matter of "power," and when Sir Henry Sumner Maine refers to "Patriarchal Power" and adds that "I feel sure that Power over children was the root of the old conception of Power,"[3] he does indeed point us to a central concern for the novel as it evolved—namely, the power of the father. It was of course a concern to thinkers prior to novelists, and for my example I am citing part of Locke's argument with Sir Robert Filmer whose work *Patriarcha* he scathingly attacks in his *Two Treatises of Government.* Having attacked

---

[1]Sir Henry Sumner Maine, *Ancient Law* (1861), chapter 5, "Primitive Society and Ancient Law."

[2]Ibid.

[3]Ibid., chapter 9, "The Early History of Contract."

Filmer's notion of "*Fatherly Power*," or "this strange kind of domineering Phantom, called *the Fatherhood*,"[4] he makes the following proposition:

> Be it then as Sir *Robert* says, that *Anciently*, it was *usual* for Men *to sell and Castrate their Children.* . . . Let it be, that they exposed them; Add to it, if you please, for this is still greater Power, that they begat them for their Tables to fat and eat them: If this proves a right to do so, we may, by the same Argument, justifie Adultery, Incest and Sodomy, for there are examples of these too, both Ancient and Modern; Sins, which I suppose, have their Principal Aggravation from this, that they cross the main intention of Nature, which willeth the increase of Mankind, and the continuation of the Species in the highest perfection, and the distinction of Families, with the Security of the Marriage Bed, as necessary thereunto.

He proceeds to show up the untenability of Filmer's contentions and concludes that chapter with the following words:

> Thus this *New Nothing,* that is to carry with it all Power, Authority, and Government; This *Fatherhood* which is to design the Person, and Establish the Throne of Monarchs, whom the people are to obey, may, according to Sir *Robert,* come into any Hands, any how, and so by his Politicks give to Democracy Royal Authority, and make an usurper a Lawful Prince. And if it will do all these fine Feats, much good do our Author and all his Followers with their Omnipotent *Fatherhood,* which can serve for nothing but to unsettle and destroy all the Lawful Government in the World, and to Establish in their room Disorder, Tyranny, and Usurpation.[5]

The power of the father is absolute, or it is a "new nothing"—I am extracting the terms from the particular argument Locke is conducting with Filmer to point to a problem that stands behind, or well inside, the works I wish to study. Both absolute power (Locke takes it to extremes by citing the example of the father devouring his own children) and the absence of power may threaten "the continuation of the Species," "the distinction of Families," and "the Security of the Marriage Bed." In particular, adultery can be seen as an attempt to establish an extracontractual contract, or indeed an anticontract that precisely threatens those continuations, distinctions, and securities that Locke outlines. How *really* free the individual is to contract for himself, is one of the matters that this work is attempting to engage. To take two examples from works about which I will have more to say, we see Clarissa's father attempting to exercise the kind of absolute power over her that would seem to be implicit in Filmer's work: "It is owing to the good opinion, Clary, which your father has of you, and of your prudence, duty, and gratitude, that

---

[4]John Locke, *Two Treatises on Government: First Treatise,* chapter 2, section 6.
[5]Ibid., chapter 6, sections 59, 72.

he engaged for your compliance, in your absence. . . . and that he built and finished contracts upon it, which cannot be made void, or cancelled."[6] The contracts are made *in her absence*, or, as we may rephrase it, in her father's eyes she is a veritable absence offering no impediments to any contracts he may choose to build and finish. By way of contrast, we may take the state of Edward in Goethe's *Die Wahlverwandtschaften* in which he dreams of new contracts while languishing in exile from his wife and thinking of the young Ottilie with whom he is in love. "Everything that happens between us becomes interlaced and mingled. Sometime we are signing a contract; there her hand and mine, her name and mine are joined; both cancel each other out and consume each other." ("Alles was mir mit ihr begegnet, schiebt sich durch und übereinander. Bald unterschreiben wir einen Contrakt; da ist ihre Hand und die meinige, ihr Name und er meinige, beide löschen einander aus, beide verschlingen sich.")[7]

Before leaving Locke, it is worth noting some of his other comments on the relations that ought to exist between parents (particularly the father) and their children, since these may prepare us for a consideration of how these ideal relations are shown to be the source of crucial problems in *Clarissa*. Thus, although he states his belief that all are born in "a *State of perfect Freedom* to order their Actions, and dispose of their Possessions, and Persons as they think fit, within the bounds of the Law of Nature" and later that "*every Man's Children* being by Nature as *free* as himself, or any of his Ancestors ever were, may, whilst they are in that Freedom, choose what Society they will join themselves to"; he concedes the following: "*Children,* I confess are not born *in* this full state of *Equality,* though they are born *to* it. Their Parents have a sort of Rule and Jurisdiction over them when they come into the World, and for some time after, but 'tis but a temporary one." The apparently easy shift from *in* to *to,* and the actual extent of that temporary sort of Rule and Jurisdiction, conceal problems that will exercise Clarissa for hundreds of letters. Similarly, when Locke defines Law as "not so much the Limitation as *the direction of a free and intelligent Agent* to his proper Interest,"[8] we can imagine, as many novelists were to do, actual circumstances between people in a power situation in which it is difficult to distinguish "limitations" from "directions," or in which what appears to one person to be the former will seem to another to be the latter. Locke is making a

---

[6]Samuel Richardson, *Clarissa Harlowe* (London: Everyman's Library, 1962), vol. 1, letter 20.

[7]Johann Wolfgang Goethe, *Kindred by Choice,* p. 133; Goethe, *Die Wahlverwandtschaften,* p. 102.

[8]John Locke, *Two Treatises on Government: Second Treatise,* chapter 2, section 4, chapter 6, sections 73, 55, 57.

distinction that in fact contains the elements of innumerable possible conflicts, whether between child and parent,[9] or the individual and society. Again, when he asserts that *"where there is no Law, there is no Freedom,"* and goes on to define Freedom as "a *Liberty* to dispose, and order, as he lists, his Person, Actions, Possessions, and his whole Property, within the Allowance of those Laws under which he is,"[10] we can immediately conceive how difficult such a theoretic liberty may be to procure in many individual cases. Thus Clarissa tries to dispose and order her Person, or body, according to her own scrupulous ethics and arguably ambivalent desires, only to have it violated while drugged; her Actions are either

[9]The intergenerational struggle is necessarily a particularly important one from the point of view of the novelist—if only because it is partly based on the ever-renewed tension between the need for support, models of growth, and direction on one hand and the desire for freedom, the discovery of one's own self, and an absence of limitation.

The freeing of an individual, as he grows up, from the authority of his parents is one of the most necessary though one of the most painful results brought about by the course of his development. . . . Indeed, the whole progress of society rests upon the opposition between successive generations. . . .

For a small child his parents are at first the only authority and source of all belief. . . . Small events in the child's life which make him feel dissatisfied afford him provocation for beginning to criticize his parents, and for using, in order to support his critical attitude, the knowledge which he has acquired that other parents are in some respects preferable to them. . . .

The later stage in the development of the neurotic's estrangement from his parents, begun in this manner, might be described as "the neurotic's family romance". . . . At about the period I have mentioned, then, the child's imagination becomes engaged in the task of getting free from the parents of whom he now has such a low opinion and of replacing them by others, occupying, as a rule, a higher social station. . . .

If we examine in detail the commonest of these imaginative romances, the replacement of both parents or of the father alone by grander people, we find that these new and aristocratic parents are equipped with attributes that are derived entirely from real recollections of the actual and humble ones; so that in fact the child is not getting rid of his father but exalting him. Indeed the whole effort at replacing the real father by a superior one is only an expression of the child's longing for the happy, vanished days when his father seemed to him the noblest and strongest of men and his mother the dearest and loveliest of women. He is turning away from the father whom he knows to-day to the father in whom he believed in the earlier years of his childhood; and his phantasy is no more than the expression of a regret that those happy days have gone. Thus in these phantasies the over-valuation that characterizes a child's earliest years comes into its own again. An interesting contribution to his subject is afforded by the study of dreams. We learn from their interpretation that even in later years, if the Emperor and Empress appear in dreams, those exalted personages stand for the dreamer's father and mother. So that the child's over-valuation of his parents also survives in the dreams of normal adults. (Sigmund Freud, "Family Romances," in *Collected Papers,* vol 5, pp. 74–78)

I shall have occasion to refer to the figure of the Father quite often in the course of this book, and we can see that many novelists are drawn to writing their own versions of what Freud nicely calls—"the neurotic's family romance."

[10]Locke, *Second Treatise,* chapter 6, section 57.

restrained by familial imperatives and prohibitions or coerced by Lovelace's plotting; her Possessions are effectively confiscated by her unforgiving family; while the Property that she does own (from her grandfather) is no effective use to her during her ordeal. Indeed it is only in death that she can fully exercise this fourfold freedom. Thus in her "Will" she says of her body that "I will not, on any account, that it be opened"; her action—choosing to die—is her own, beyond the control or retardation of anyone; her possessions are distributed "as she lists"; and her property she freely bequeaths to "my ever-honoured father." This power of disposition that she can now exercise comes to her because, as she defines herself, being dead—"I am nobody's."[11] If it is only in the unownable condition of death that she can find Locke's freedom, we must consider it a very ambiguous freedom indeed. And by that redefinition of herself as "nobody's," she effectively diminishes her once all-powerful father into what we might indeed call a "new nothing," since apart from some recorded signs and groans, his voice is silenced after her death. By "contracting" herself in one sense ("to draw together, concentrate; to narrow limits, shorten"), as she does to her own body and lifespan, she avoids the odious contract that would have been forced upon her. In what the OED gives as the etymological sense of the word *transgression,* she, in one sense, "passes over or beyond," as we say people have passed on. Later heroines will break their way out of intolerable contracts by a different mode of transgression, or "passing beyond" legally affixed boundaries.

I am not concerned here to go over the familiar ground of the history of theories of contract, but some statements by Rousseau might usefully be kept before us. Thus, in his *Social Contract,* he asserts that:

> Since no man has any natural authority over his fellows, and since force alone bestows no right, all legitimate authority among men must be based on covenants. . . . as each man's own strength and liberty are the chief instrument of his own preservation, how can he merge his with others' without putting himself in peril and neglecting the care he owes to himself? . . . This difficulty, which brings me back to my present subject, may be expressed in these words: "How to find a form of association which will defend the person and goods of each member with the collective force of all, and under which each individual, while uniting himself with the others, obeys no one but himself, and remains as free as before." This is the fundamental problem to which the social contract holds the answer.
>
> The articles of this contract are so precisely determined by the nature of the act, that the slightest modification must render them null and void; they are such that, though perhaps never formally stated, they are everywhere the same, everywhere tacitly admitted and recognized; and if

---

[11]Richardson, *Clarissa,* vol. 4, letter 146.

ever the social pact is violated, every man regains his original rights and, *recovering his natural freedom, loses that social freedom for which he exchanged it.* [My italics—and the italicized words point precisely to the problem faced by such contract breakers as adulterers.]

This formula shows that the act of association consists of a reciprocal commitment between society and the individual, so that each person, in making a contract, as it were, with himself, finds himself doubly committed, first, as a member of the sovereign body in relation to individuals, and secondly as a member of the state in relation to the sovereign. Here there can be no invoking the principle of civil law which says that no man is bound by a contract with himself, for *there is a great difference between having an obligation to oneself and having an obligation to something of which one is a member.* [12] [My italics—and again the italicized words point to a possible problem, namely, what happens when these two "obligations" are felt to be—experienced as—mutually exclusive?]

This is not the place to go into the curious contradictions contained within *The Social Contract,* nor the dissonance of many of its propositions with those in other works by Rousseau. A late quotation from *The Social Contract* illustrates the state of mind that Rousseau was in when he wrote it. "It is said that a people of true Christians would form the most perfect society imaginable. I see but one great flaw in this hypothesis, namely that a society of true Christians would not be a society of men. I would say, too, that this imagined society, for all its perfection, would be neither the strongest nor the most durable. Being perfect, it would be without *bonds of union; its ruinous defect would lie in its very perfection.*" [My italics.] "Man was born free, and he is everywhere in chains." Fine. But what is needed is not, apparently, a casting off of those chains in the interests of a recapturable feedom, but rather the transformation of those chains into "contracts" and "bonds of union." Otherwise there is the danger of the "ruinous defect" of "perfection." I will simply add one summary quotation from one of Rousseau's commentators, Maurice Cranston.

> And just as the Tutor is the dominant figure of *Emile* so does the Lawgiver become the dominant figure of *The Social Contract.* Indeed the Lawgiver repeats in the state the role that the Tutor performs for the individual. He is needed for the same reason; men left alone will be led by their own passions and folly into disaster; they need someone to save them from themselves.
>
> It is a bad thing to have a master; for that is the reverse of freedom. But it is a good thing to have a tutor, so long as we follow him willingly and gladly. For Rousseau the way to liberty is the path of voluntary submission. "The King is dead; long live the Lawgiver!" Is this, in the end, the battle

---

[12] Jean Jacques Rousseau, *The Social Contract,* trans. Maurice Cranston with an introduction (Harmondsworth, Middlesex: Penguin, 1968) pp. 53, 60, 62.

cry of the republic? Does Rousseau wish us to say: "Advise and control us, *O Législateur.* As long as we live we shall need you. We need you more than ever now that we are taking on the duties of self-government"?[13]

Some of these problems and contradictions will, I hope, become clearer in the discussion of *La Nouvelle Héloïse.*

We should notice where Rousseau is putting the emphasis—not on some hypothetical natural goodness that should allow men to live together in perfect bondless harmony. Rather he is trying to inculcate respect for the contracts and bonds that make up the very essence of society. Not masters and chains, certainly; but a Lawgiver / father figure and contracts with an absolute binding power. Not slavery, certainly; but respect (which is, of course, what parents demand from their children). There is nothing wrong with respect appropriately bestowed (of course, transformed into a victimlike servility, it simply becomes another form of slavery). Without it society would be chaos indeed. But it necessarily has another side to it.

"Respect is really nothing but a devious route taken by violence. On the one hand respect keeps order in the sphere where violence is forbidden; on the other it makes it possible for violence to erupt incongruously in fields where it has ceased to be permissible. The taboo does not alter the violence of sexual activity, but for disciplined mankind it opens a door closed to animal nature, namely, the transgression of the law."[14] Or to put it at its most succinct—contracts *create* transgressions; the two are inseparable, and the one would have no meaning without the other.

Adultery and the Novel

It is such an obvious and legible phenomenon that many of those nineteenth-century novels that have been canonized as "great"—and in varying ways to varying degrees are felt to contain the furthest reaching fictional explorations into their age—center on adultery, that, with some exceptions, few have thought it worth trying to take the matter further. Yet the implications of this very obvious generalization involve the very

[13]Ibid., 182–83, 49, 42–43.

[14]Georges Bataille, "The Enigma of Incest," in *Death and Sensuality: A Study of Eroticism and the Taboo* (New York: Walker and Company, 1962). Reprinted in *The Perverse Imagination,* ed. Irving Buchen (New York: New York University Press, 1970).

nature and existence of the great bourgeois novel, and the connections or relationships between a specific kind of sexual act, a specific kind of society, and a specific kind of narrative seem to me to be worth exploring a little further. This is what I am attempting to start to do in this book. Before considering a selection of specific texts, let me make some general observations concerning aspects of this topic.

Adultery as a phenomenon is in evidence in literature from the earliest times, as in Homer (and indeed we might suggest that it is the unstable triangularity of adultery, rather than the static symmetry of marriage, that is the generative form of Western literature as we know it). It is a dominant feature of chivalric literature; and it becomes a major concern in Shakespeare's last plays (see the following section, "The Stranger in the House"). It appears in such genres as Restoration drama as a sort of social game, just as it may be found in many contemporary novels. But it seems to me that adultery takes on a very special importance in the late-eighteenth- and nineteenth-century novel.[15] Thus in this volume, I am attempting to establish the groundwork for the kind of consideration of the topic that I consider most fruitful and revealing.

It is important to emphasize that it is the problem of transgressing the marriage contract that is at the center of the novels I wish to discuss. Earlier fiction, particularly in the eighteenth century, abounds in seduction, fornication, and rape, and it would be possible to show how these particular modes of sexual "exchange" were related to differing modes of economic exploitation or simply different transactional rules between classes or within any one class. Adultery is a very different matter. For one thing, it introduces an agonizing and irresolvable category-confusion into the individual and thence into society itself. Lover, mistress, whore—no matter how each may suffer from being thus categorized—are all at least recognized as having an existence and a definition that is not incompatible with the social terminology and economy within which they live. But the very word *adulteress* is close to a contradiction in a single term. *Adulteration* implies pollution, contamination, a "base admixture," a wrong combination. *Adulteress* points to an activity, not an identity; an unfaithful wife, and usually by implication a bad mother, is an unassimilable conflation of what society insists should be separate categories and functions. The wife and mother in one set of

---

[15]In addition to the novels discussed in this book, I have in mind such works as *Anna Karenina; Effie Briest* and *Beyond Recall; Le rouge et le noir; La femme de trente ans, La muse du département, Gobseck, La Duchesse de Langeais; Epitaph of a Small Winner* and *Dom Casmurro; The Scarlet Letter; The Awakening; The Age of Innocence; One of Our Conquerors; Orley Farm; Jude the Obscure; The Good Soldier; Lady Chatterley's Lover;* also some other English novels in which adultery is just, but sedulously, avoided—*Wuthering Heights; Jane Eyre; Daniel Deronda,* among others. I hope to discuss these, and other novels, in a subsequent volume.

social circumstances should not, and cannot be, the mistress and lover in another. It is well known how bourgeois society tends to enforce unitary roles on its members who then impose them on themselves. From the point of view of that society, adultery introduces a bad multiplicity within the requisite unities of social roles. From another point of view, we could say that the unfaithful wife is, in social terms, a self-canceling figure, one from whom society would prefer to withhold recognition so that it would be possible to say that socially and categorically the adulterous woman does not exist. Yet physically and creaturely she manifestly does, so she becomes a paradoxical presence of negativity within the social structure, her virtual nonbeing offering a constant implicit threat to the being of society. (The fact that it is almost inevitably the adulterous *woman* on which many nineteenth-century novels focus is itself a matter for later comment.) If society depends for its existence on certain rules governing what may be combined and what should be kept separate, then adultery, by bringing the wrong things together in the wrong places (or the wrong people in the wrong beds), offers an attack on those rules, revealing them to be arbitrary rather than absolute. In this way, the adulterous woman becomes the "gap" in society that gradually extends through it. In attempting to ostracize her, society moves toward ostracizing itself.

Related to this is the notable fact that in many of the novels I have in mind, the actual adulterous act (the initial act that makes of the woman an adulteress) is not described. This is by way of notable contrast with novels that preceded and succeeded them and cannot be simply ascribed to the prudishness of the bourgeois audience. The invisible, inaudible deed becomes a silence and an absence in the text that gradually spreads, effectively negating what *is* made audible and present. In the eighteenth-century novel, sexual activities are much more visible, often overtly related to considerations of money and class—there is little mystification, and one result of this is that sexuality in no sense threatens the structure of society or the institution of marriage. After the period I am discussing, the novel dealing with sexual matters may be said to mutate toward two extremes. One is represented by *Lady Chatterley's Lover,* in which the sexual activity is totally visible and audible and takes over the foreground of the novel. It almost doesn't matter that it is in fact technically adulterous love, and the idea that the novel acts as a critique of contemporary England (impotent mineowners, virile working-class people, etc.) seems to me to put the emphasis in the wrong place. For in this novel it is society itself that is receding into silence and non-Being, and the significance of adultery is drowned in the experience of physicality. Lawrence is attempting to redefine the very terminologies of contracts and relationships—a revaluation by rebaptism, in Nietzsche's terms. The other extreme may be found in Joyce, in whose work, as has been pointed out, there is no example of what might be called normal sexual intercourse and perversion is the usual mode of procedure. Here familial and social problems are absorbed into an ultimate exploration of "linguicity" (the word is Edward Said's).[16] My general suggestion is that we can see adultery as the gap, or silence, in the bourgeois novel that finally leads to its dissolution and displacement by postsocial fictional forms involving extreme states of physicality and / or linguicity (or Proustian solipsism). The bourgeois novel of adultery finally discovers its own impossibility, and as a result sexuality, narration, and society fall apart, never to be reintegrated in the same way—if, indeed, at all.

The way the bourgeois novel confronts the problem of adultery may be compared to the two strategies for dealing with adultery in the Bible. According to Old Testament Law, the adulterous man and woman are almost without exception to be excluded from society, canceled even to the point of execution. In the New Testament, Christ confronted with the woman taken in adultery makes the would-be lawgivers aware of her problematical reality, calling into question both the impersonal application of the law and the justification and rights of the would-be legislators. Effectively this implies the disintegration of society-as-constituted. (I shall return to these passages in more detail.) In the bourgeois novel we can find a strictness that works to maintain the law, and a sympathy and understanding with the adulterous violator that works to undermine it. (It is perhaps worth noting in passing that up to the end of the eighteenth century, adultery was an offense that could be, and still was, prosecuted in a court of law. In the nineteenth century, though the law remained in the books, it was, I gather, never publicly prosecuted in a court of law—i.e., it moves to the unspoken realm of those silent secondary laws of society, where the rules and the punishments are applied and meted out privately. This is another reason why adultery is one of *the* central problems for the bourgeois novel—unlike, for example, murder, which is arguably a greater threat to person, property, and law, but was never unspeakable in society and thus never undescribable in fiction.) What I have called the Old Testament and New Testament methods of confronting adultery may both be found operating within the same book, as I suggest they are in *Anna Karenina*. Indeed it is arguable that it is just such a tension between law and sympathy that holds the great bourgeois novel together, and a severe imbalance in either direction must destroy the form.

---

[16]In conversation, Edward Said suggested that there was a third alternative to the two I have sketchily outlined—the "hommes-femmes," as described by Proust. This would point to a kind of self-sealing narcissistic sexuality leading to the solitary solipsism of Proust's famous soundproof room and a life given over to endless *writing*.

What is implicit in all I have said so far is that marriage is *the* central subject for the bourgeois novel; not marriage as a paradigm for the resolution of problems of bringing unity out of difference, harmony out of opposition, identity out of separation, concord out of discord—as it is, for instance, in *A Midsummer Night's Dream*, where marriage is not only social but magical, mythical, metaphysical—but just marriage in all its social and domestic ramifications in a demythologized society. Or rather a society in which marriage *is* the mythology (at least the socially avowed one; it would be possible to say that money and profits made up a more secret mythology). Marriage, to put it at its simplest for the moment, is a means by which society attempts to bring into harmonious alignment patterns of passion and patterns of property; in bourgeois society it is not only a matter of putting your Gods where your treasure is (as Ruskin accused his age of doing) but also of putting your libido, loyalty, and all other possessions and products, including children, there as well. For bourgeois society marriage is the all-subsuming, all-organizing, all-containing contract. It is the structure that maintains the Structure, or System (if we may use that word, for the moment, to cover all the models, conscious and unconscious, by which society structures all its operations and transactions). The bourgeois novelist has no choice but to engage the subject of marriage in one way or another, at no matter what extreme of celebration or contestation. He may concentrate on what makes for marriage and leads up to it, or on what threatens marriage and portends its disintegration, but his subject will still be marriage. What he discovers, I will suggest, is that the bourgeois novel is coeval and coterminous with the power concentrated in the central structure of marriage. As bourgeois marriage loses its absoluteness, its unquestioned finality, its "essentiality," so does the bourgeois novel. On another level we may say that as the contact between man and wife loses its sense of necessity and binding power, so does the contract between novelist and reader. This contract is still binding in Goethe; it is abrogated in certain calculated ways by Flaubert (for example); it becomes extremely problematical in the work of the late James; and for Lawrence (and Joyce) we may say that the old contracts no longer have any force at all. In confronting the problems of marriage and adultery, the bourgeois novel finally has to confront not only the provisionality of social laws and rules and structures but the provisionality of its own procedures and assumptions.

The central importance of marriage makes it clear why it was adultery rather than seduction (or any of those other kinds of sexual behavior recorded, or imagined, in books like *My Secret Life*) that became such a crucial subject. The woman in the marriage situation becomes a paradigm for the problems of interrelating patterns. To put it very simply, the woman as a biological entity cannot be changed (putting aside for the moment the problems of cultural "sexing"); her organic determinants are given; the familial identifications of daughter and/or sister that are conferred on a female are not inherent qualities, but they are irremovable categorizations by the irreversible fact of consanguinity (this is Antigone's point about her relation to her brother in Sophocles' play). But the category of being a wife is in no sense given even in the most conventionally prearranged marriages. It is a totally social and cultural *arrangement,* and an arrangement on which society totally relies. It is at this point that we can see why so many problems of pattern converge on the figure of the wife. We may put it this way. Nature has her own patterns of seasonal and cyclical growth and decay, of mating impulses and fertilization processes; the family is a more stable and narrower pattern imposed on nature, while society is another pattern relating all the families according to intrafamilial and transfamilial rules. In a religious age, which the bourgeois age notionally is, there is also the possibility of inscrutable divine patterns too large for any one human mind to grasp in their totality, but of which at certain moments—for Levin, at the death of a brother, the birth of a child—a man or woman may feel he has caught a glimpse. As these divine patterns are institutionalized, they will tend to be translated as being supportive of the existing social patterns. To these the novelist adds his own pattern, not only to comprehend these various patterns but also to explore and illuminate the relationships, oppositions, and mediations between them.

The most important mediation procedure that attempts to harmonize the natural, the familial, the social, and even the transcendental is, of course, marriage. Thus, in a marriage you may participate in nature's pattern of coupling and breeding; but this can be incorporated within the existing interfamilial patterns and validated contractually by society. It can also be sanctioned by the church. Ideally, then, marriage offers the perfect and total mediation between the patterns within which men and women live. One may immediately discern a potential tension between differing time schemes here. For if nature works seasonally while God works through eternity, the family works by generational changes (each particular family has to disintegrate to make sure the family continues with different members), while society—and here I am thinking specifically of bourgeois nineteenth-century society—tends to believe in what Sartre calls the myth of its own "perenniality," or permanence and stasis. Set in any one of these patterns, the life span of the individual mortal can mean, and be felt to mean, different things. If the mediation of marriage works, then everything is, as it were, at rest, all the patterns moving harmoniously together. It is the bourgeois ideal (an ideal that precludes the envisaging of possible patterns of *historical* and *political* change). But if something happens to disturb this mediation, or rather all the mediations that center on marriage, or to make them unacceptable or impossible, then a person involved may experience that anxiety or "unhappy consciousness" that is a result of feeling he or she is participating in two or more irreconcilable patterns, with no means of mediating them any longer.

The figure of the wife ideally contains the biological *female,* the obedient *daughter* (and perhaps sister), the faithful *mate,* the responsible *mother,* and the believing *Christian,* and harmonizes all the patterns that bestow upon her these differing identities. But if the marriage starts to founder, then the different identities and roles fall apart or come into conflict, so that, for instance, the female cannot find herself in the wife, and the wife feels herself separating from the mother. As cultural anthropologists have shown, it can become impossible to participate in two different patterns, when they are experienced as such, without mediation. Then something or someone, or part of someone, has to give. In one way or another the person who registers this impossibility of participating in irreconcilable patterns will be compelled to seek some mode of extrication from at least one of them. What these modes might be, and to what extent such extraction is finally possible, the novels I wish to discuss will themselves explore. But it is now perhaps clear why adultery should be the main, if the undescribed, topic for the bourgeois novel. For without anything or anyone necessarily having changed place or roles (in social terms), the action of adultery portends the possible breakdown of all the mediations on which society itself depends, and demonstrates the latent impossibility of participating in the interrelated patterns that comprise its structure.

It may be objected here that the theme of cuckoldry is as old as literature and that cuckoldry in no way threatened the actual institution of marriage. It may also be objected that society learned to contain the ruptures implicit in adultery by the negative ritual of divorce. But in the first case, cuckoldry—or, for that matter, intermarital games in Restoration comedy—is conceived of as separate from the formal institution of marriage itself, which is unthreatened by wayward sexual behavior on the part of those thus contractually joined. There were so many other religious and social normative and constitutive patterns binding people together. It is only when marriage is seen to be the invention of man, and is felt to be the central contract on which all others in some way depend, that adultery becomes, not an incidental deviance from the social structure, but a frontal assault on it. Divorce is, of course, the main way in which society came to cope with adultery, but it is notable that, although the topic arises, in none of the novels I wish to consider does divorce occur, nor is it felt to offer any *radical* solutions to the problems that have arisen. It is as if the novelist realized that divorce was a piece of surface temporizing, a forensic palliative to cloak and muffle the profoundly disjunctive reverberations and implications of adultery. A third objection might be that within bourgeois society, partners could play the marriage game without believing in it, indulging in what we might call a cynicism of forms. This is a matter that James looks at in *Portrait of a Lady,* in which the Countess Geminini embodies such a cynicism. Isabel herself is caught between marriage as a theoretically and conceptually magnificient form, as evoked by Osmond, and the "ghastly form" she actually experiences and as it is described by Caspar Goodwood. What she cannot accept is the alternative that is exemplified in an extreme form by the withered, almost dehumanized figure of the Countess. Isabel is thus caught in an impossible crisis of forms, which is one reason why the ending seems so ambiguous or mystifying or evasive to many readers. But in running from the metaphorical sea of Caspar's kiss to the actual doorway of the lighted house, Isabel is avoiding the thing that is not named, but is all the more present for that—adultery, and the absolute annihilation of forms that it would imply for her.

City, Field, and Temple

22. If a man be found lying with a woman married to an husband, then they shall both of them die, *both* the man that lay with the woman, and the woman: so shalt thou put away evil from Israel.
23. If a damsel *that* is a virgin be betrothed unto an husband, and a man find her in the city, and lie with her;
24. Then ye shall bring them both out unto the gate of that city, and ye shall stone them with stones that they die; the damsel, because she cried not, *being* in the city; and the man, because he hath humbled his neighbor's wife: so thou shalt put away evil from among you.
25. But if a man find a betrothed damsel in the field, and the man force her, and lie with her: then the man only that lay with her shall die:
26. But unto the damsel thou shalt do nothing; *there is* in the damsel no sin *worthy* of death: for as when a man riseth against his neighbor, and slayeth him, even so *is* this matter:
27. For he found her in the field, *and* the betrothed damsel cried, and *there was* none to save her.

(Deuteronomy 22)

This formulation of the Mosaic law concerning adultery presupposes two discrete realms that can be absolutely differentiated—the city and the field. Within the city the prescriptions of the law extend to both sexes because theoretically everyone can be *heard*. Everyone and everyone's activities, in this case specifically their sexual activities, is contained and defined within the prevailing discourse. Language has total authority, and within it individuals have total responsibility. The architecture of the city—which includes not only buildings but the related edifices of law, rule, and custom, all of them interrelated by language—"architectures" the relationships between the sexes with complete explicitness and the wrongfully assaulted woman is obliged to "cry out" according to her categorization (damsel, virgin, betrothed unto an husband). There is no appeal against these categories, and transgression of the imperatives that organize the relationships between these categories is punished by death at the gate of the city, i.e., an irrevocable cancellation of the offenders' social and biological existence. The gate to the city becomes, among other things, that necessary gap in the wall discriminating social from nonsocial space, through which violators of the social space can be excorporated into nonbeing.

The same absoluteness of law does not obtain in the field, for although there is still voice, there is no community. Thus the responsibility of the man and woman becomes more problematical. The law begins to break in two as it tries to reach out to cover the actions of its temporarily displaced inhabitants. What we can witness here is the tendency of the law to fragment in its efforts to cope with relationships that take place outside its realm. Beyond the discourse of the city—or out of hearing— the bonds of social imperatives and constraints necessarily weaken, and force and passion may emerge with a new insistence as they disengage from the categories of the city. However, in Mosaic law there is still a refusal to give up control over what people do outside the city. There is a potential, though totally suppressed, difficulty here. By defining itself *as* a city, the city immediately creates nonsocial space outside it. This nonsocial space can of course be subjected to further differentiations. The field suggests a relatively domesticated area of nature adjacent to the city and controlled by it. It is quite feasible to expect to be able to make the laws of the city extend into the area around it that has been subjugated in a different way by agriculture. But once outside the city a whole new problem arises—that of distance and separation. The city by definition has limits; whatever falls outside the city ultimately has none. In terms of this Mosaic law the individual in the city cannot be either too far away or too near. He or she is theoretically perpetually present and equidistant to the rest of the community through a notional unbroken *audibility*. There is nothing too private that cannot instantly be transformed into the public realm by utterance. Nobody is out of earshot in the city.

It is otherwise in the field. Responsibility fades with distance—in this case for the woman only. But it would be possible to imagine yet greater distances where the definitions, nominations, and prescribed relationships between categories recede entirely. This is not envisaged by the Mosaic law, which operates here according to one rigid dichotomy—city and field. But the introduction of a third area, beyond the field, could have the effect of unstabilizing this opposition that strives to hold together the city and the field while recognizing their difference. Mosaic law can only operate as long as the basic model is binary and rigid, in which men and women are in the city *or* the field and nowhere else. As law it necessarily cannot afford to explore what might happen beyond the horizons of its authoritative categories. Nor can it allow the possibility of any space between the categories, for just as, in the strictness of this generic model, there is nowhere beyond the field, neither is there any area of indistinctness at the point at which they meet. The gate is the one punctuation mark, as it were, in a statement that attempts to contain and control the "illegal" sexual activities of all those born within the domain of the law. It is a statement of complete clarity that presupposes the immediate transparency of any action falling within its jurisdiction. The possible opacity of an unobserved, inaudible sexual relationship is denied, for although the law begins to divide as it moves out of the city into the field, it in no way modifies its categories or recognizes the possibility of different *kinds* of abrogation of the law. It asserts that there is finally only one law, just as there is only one language for both the city and the field. At this point two possible questions can be imagined arising from this paradigm. Supposing the damsel did not cry out and did not want to cry out, preferring to avail herself of the abandon of the field after the restriction of the city. And more generally, for those who go willingly, if secretly, into the field, is there any way back into the city?

27.   Ye have heard that it was said by them of old time, Thou shalt not commit adultery:
28.   But I say unto you, That whosoever looketh on a woman to lust after her hath committed adultery with her already in his heart. (St. Matthew 5)

Jesus went unto the mount of Olives.
2.   And early in the morning he came again into the temple, and all the people came unto him; and he sat down, and taught them.
3.   And the scribes and the Pharisees brought unto him a woman taken in adultery; and when they had set her in the midst,
4.   They say unto him, Master, this woman was taken in adultery, in the very act.

5. Now Moses in the law commanded us, that such should be stoned: but what sayest thou?

6. This they said, tempting him that they might have to accuse him. But Jesus stooped down, and with *his* finger wrote on the ground, *as though he heard them not.*

7. So when they continued asking him, he lifted up himself, and said unto them, He that is without sin among you, let him first cast a stone at her.

8. And again he stooped down, and wrote on the ground.

9. And they which heard it, being convicted by *their own* conscience, went out one by one, beginning at the eldest, *even* unto the last: and Jesus was left alone, and the woman standing in the midst.

10. When Jesus had lifted up himself, and saw none but the woman, he said unto her, Woman where are those thine accusers? hath no man condemned thee?

11. She said, No man, Lord. And Jesus said unto her, Neither do I condemn thee: go, and sin no more.

(St. John 8)

This time the question of law is grounded in a specific situation with an individual adulteress being presented in the temple—the offense is presented in a sacred setting, and the scribes and Pharisees intend to make her the object of a forensic debate. They invoke the Mosaic law, but Christ's response completely alters the terms and premises of the debate, for he *refuses to answer* and starts to *write* on the ground. Thus silence and writing introduce a gap in the monolithic generalities of the Mosaic law. When he does answer, it is not in terms of the law. He cuts across the impersonal prescriptions of the law with a personal statement to those who would like to see the law impersonally applied. That is, he relocates the obligations of judgment and punishment within those who regard themselves as the spokesmen of society. In doing so he makes law problematical. The details of his physical response are extremely significant. The scribes and Pharisees (society in this context) set up a situation in which the woman is brought forward as a classified object to be looked at and talked about; they have depersonalized her (a woman taken in adultery) and reified her (she is "set" in the midst). Christ refuses to look and, initially, refuses to talk. That is, he refuses to participate in this purely specular attitude to the woman and to discuss her as a category. By doing this he restores the full existential reality to the situation that society seeks to deny. By treating the woman as spectacle and category, the representatives of society attempt to alienate her from her own being and to separate themselves from her by adopting the role of being the community from which the woman by her offense has isolated herself. Christ refuses to participate in their discourse, and when he does speak it is to them directly. This has two effects. It thrusts them back into their own interiority (they are "convicted by their own *conscience*"), and it dissolves the group identity within which they have concealed themselves (they go out "one by one" as individuals, having arrived as "scribes and Pharisees").

In this way Christ disperses the social stare that petrifies the wrongdoer, just as he uncongeals the legal language that seeks to imprison her in a category. Effectively he desocializes the situation, so that when he looks up, the "accusers" are all gone and there is only the woman left with him in the otherwise empty temple. This is a subtler act than driving out the moneylenders, for this time Christ has banished the whole language and attitude of social "accusation" from the temple. He then speaks to the woman directly, as an individual, and without ignoring her deed he frees both her and it from the prevailing terminology of condemnation. He has restored the act to the individual, who must, indeed, take it away with her in her inner self—an inwardness that Christ also retired into when the scribes and Pharisees addressed him with the voice of society. His crucial gesture is to assert the *inaudibility* of that voice, an inaudibility not envisaged in the Mosaic law. That this gesture of inaudibility is made in the temple is of course significant. For the temple is both in society and, inasmuch as it is a sacred space, out of it. What Christ has done is enforce a reconsideration of the context in which the woman's act should be considered, and suggest a limitation of the existing social categories by moving that act into the inner realm of conscience. The temple thereby becomes a realm of a different order to those of the city and the field, a silent realm from which society gradually withdraws and where language itself finally gives back the deed to the doer of the deed, restoring to it that opacity and that problematic privacy that the Mosaic law sought to deny. (Just as in his statement in Saint Matthew, Christ points to the possibility of inner adultery that the law never reaches after.)*

---

*In this connection it is interesting to compare the frontispiece and jacket illustration for this book. Rembrandt's "The Woman Taken in Adultery" has more of a Mosaic feeling about it than Blake's watercolor on the same subject (pen and watercolor over pencil, to be precise). We notice the high gloomy spaces of the temple; the phallic columns looming through the dimness; the intimations of hierarchy in the architecture (starting with the steps and going up to higher levels), with male figures at every level, in a range of clothing—rags and armour, austere and sumptuous robes of sacred and secular offices, etc.—that indicates the hierachy within society itself; the woman on her knees and weeping in a traditional posture of contrition which is, as it were, demanded by the scenario; and the figure in the black robes (priest/death) offering the spectacle of the "guilty contrite woman" for Christ's comment. All these features suggest the presence of a powerfully juridical, authoritarian, and, of course, male-dominated society. And if there is a kind of majesty in the scene, there is also a distinctly Mosaic rigidity. The woman is "illuminated" but, one feels, more for purposes of cruel inspection than to indicate a blessed or enlightened state. Christ is admittedly the tallest figure in the painting—at least as far as the viewer is concerned, but it is impossible to discern any trace in his stance, or his

Using the terms suggested by this topographical model, it is possible to identify a recurring opposition or alternation of realms in the novel of adultery for which "the city" and "the field" provide generic equivalents. (These two realms need not of course be literal equivalents of city and field—they may be a house and a lake, or a settlement and a forest, for example, or a bedroom and a battlefield, a court and an orchard, the castle and the sea, etc.) This simple distinction suggests that there is an area that is inside society and one that is outside, where the socially displaced individual or couple may attempt to find or practice a greater freedom. Whether there is a genuine outside becomes a problem in the nineteenth century, when it comes to seem that the apparent outside is an illusion, a space already socialized in one way or another. This may then precipitate a hopeless quest for an area outside the outside, as it were (the problem for many of Ibsen's later protagonists, for example), or a weary return to the existing society. Both of these patterns of action are very clearly pursued by Anna Karenina, for instance. But in addition to the city and the field, "the temple" is also present in one form or another, in the general sense of a disturbed consciousness trying to locate itself in relation to these two realms—not in abstract sociolegal terms, but in the language, or silence, of personal experience. We could then see the bourgeois novel as a kind of secondary temple attempting to contain, dramatize, and analyze the city-field-temple tensions discernible in the society to which it addressed itself, thus attempting to become the better

---

features, or his gesture, of what he will do next, what reaction he will have. His face and bearing seem to indicate pity, but—as yet—nothing more. Rembrandt has evoked the scene at its stillest point, when the scribes and Pharisees have, as it were, set up their test case—staged it—and Christ has yet to respond in that disruptive and unexpected way that the Bible describes.

How different is the Blake depiction. Gone is the domineering, overbearing architecture and oppressive space of the temple; Rembrandt's fixed spectators, in all their visible difference of rank and status, are now a homogeneous mass struggling to get out of the temple; instead of the eyes being fixed on the woman, we see only the backs of heads—the erstwhile spectators are now fleeing, not looking. The woman is bound, but not weeping; and standing, if not proudly, then hardly penitentially. We are very much aware of her as a particular, very physical, sexually attractive woman (note the slightly disheveled hair—which manages to hint at insouciance and eroticism, even if it is evidence of a certain amount of rough handling by her captors). Christ dominates the left foreground (there are no levels) as he stoops—majestically—to write. His eyes are on the ground. The woman's eyes are on him. Instead of the passive spectacle she has become the active watcher, her hands bound, but her body flowingly alive in vestment and limb. The figures are not united or bound together in one scenario or theatricalized setting—Christ has already broken up the tyranny of the group, established gaps between the Pharisees, the woman, and himself—with the consequence that the woman seems to be close to her release, already in a state of separateness and freedom. And the whole foreground is dominated by the two supremely powerful figures of Christ and the woman. In all this, and much more, Blake's picture is not only indicative of his own distinctive reading of the Bible, but closer to the spirit of the New Testament account of "The Woman Taken in Adultery."

conscience of that society (or, in some cases colluding with its false conscience, or unconscience). In that temple there is sympathy for the antinomian impulses of the socially condemned, plus a recognition of the necessary structurings of laws of all kinds. This provides the necessary structural tensions. Sympathy dissolves, law upholds: you can't have a society without law, and you can't have a novel without sympathy (or empathy, or understanding, etc.). As the sense of the inadequacy and provisionality of the normative and prescriptive categories governing behavior increased, so did the temple of the great bourgeois novel begin to dismantle itself and turn into something else.

The Stranger in the House

Western literature as we know it starts with an act of transgression, a violation of boundaries that leads to instability, asymmetry, disorder, and an interfamilial and intertribal clash that threatens the very existence of civilization (as then known) itself. I refer, of course, to the abduction of Helen by Paris and the incredibly ruinous war that ensues, threatening, not only Troy, but all existing bonds that held together states, armies, families, lovers, friends. The conventions and rules dictating or circumscribing the practice of "hospitality" (which etymologically contains within it both guest and host, but also, from the Latin *hostis*, a stranger and potentially an enemy) were of course absolutely crucial for tribes and city-states, since a mutual recognition of these rules and rituals was the key way of avoiding rupture both within the tribe or state and at its boundaries. Thus, as anthropologists have amply demonstrated, from ancient times, tribes had ways of finely discriminating between enemy, alien, stranger; ally, friend, relation. The basic intention of the art of hospitality was to transform the *stranger* into a *guest,* thus defusing a potential threat to the established equilibria existing within the tribe or state. It was a strategy of accommodation by renomination, a virtual metamorphosing of the alien presence from the unknown by assimilating him (or her) into an allotted place within the family (or tribe, state, etc.). It was a ritual of dealienation, in order to mitigate or eliminate the potential danger of the arrival of the unknown "other" within the boundaries and precincts of the tribal territory, the city walls, the hierarchically stable household. For this to be effective, both guest and host had to observe the rules meticulously, of course; any deviation could instantly revive the possibility of some kind of disruption of the previous order, or some terrible retribution or vengeance to be visited on the transgressor— or both.[17]

But we should remember that the apparently positive, benign, and

[17]There is, of course, an extensive literature on this topic in both anthropology and linguistics. See, for example, the essay by Meyer Fortes entitled "Strangers" (pp. 229–53 in *Studies in African Social Anthropology,* ed. Meyer Fortes and Sheila Patterson [London and New York: Academic Press, 1975]). He is discussing this problem with reference to the customs and habits of the Tallensi, but many of his discoveries and observations have relevance in other cultural contexts. He starts by quoting from Georg Simmel: "To be a stranger is naturally a very positive relation; it is a specific form of interaction," and he goes on to describe how the Tallensi regard and treat different kinds of stranger. It is a matter of some importance, since "it is not impossible that a person presenting himself as an unknown stranger might in fact be a Being of the Wild or an evil tree or stone which has *ngalem* transformed itself into a human shape to test and tempt one. To refuse hospitality in such a case lays one open to the mystical attack that might result in madness." So the possible or "virtual enemy at the outset" should "at once or later be accepted as a welcome or at least tolerated guest." The wariness behind this code is indicated in such sayings and proverbs as: "When a stranger has gone there is not wanting trouble (to clear up)." Just as the Greeks distinguished between *Xenoi,* strangers who were nevertheless Greeks, and *Barbaroi,* foreigners who spoke another language, so do many African communities distinguish between what Fortes calls "the internal stranger, who comes from the same cultural and political community in the widest sense as the host group, and the external, foreign or alien stranger who may be left to live in peace segregated from the host group but is not permitted to become assimilated into the host group even in a client or other dependent status."

For some comments from a linguist we may turn briefly to Emile Benveniste and his long study: *Indo-European Language and Society* (trans. Elizabeth Palmer [Coral Gables, Fla.: University of Miami Press, 1973]). I shall run together some pertinent quotations from book 1, *Economy,* and from book 3, *Social Status:*

> The primitive notion conveyed by *hostis* is that of equality by compensation: a *hostis* is one who repays my gift by a counter-gift. Thus, like its Gothic counterpart, *gasts,* Latin *hostis* at one period denoted the guest. The classical meaning "enemy" must have developed when reciprocal relations between clans were succeeded by the exclusive relations of *civitas* to *civitas* (cf. Gr. xénos "guest" > "stranger"). Because of this Latin coined a new name for "guest": *hosti-pet-,* which may perhaps be interpreted as arising from an abstract noun *hosti* "hospitality" and consequently meant "he who predominantly personifies hospitality," is hospitality itself. But the meaning of Gothic *gasts* and OSl. *gostĭ* is "guest," whereas that of Latin *hostis* is "enemy." To explain the connexion between "guest" and "enemy" it is usually supposed that both derived their meaning from "stranger," a sense which is still attested in Latin. The notion "favourable stranger" developed to "guest"; that of "hostile stranger" to "enemy."
>
> In fact, "stranger, enemy, guest" are global notions of a somewhat vague character, and they demand precision by interpretation in their historical and social contexts.

The notion of a "stranger" necessarily requires, or assumes, the concept of a "friend." Thus, from book 3:

> In Germanic, the connexion which is still felt for instance between German *frei* "free" and *Freund,* allows us to reconstitute a primitive notion of liberty as the belonging to a closed group of those who call one another "friends." To his mem-

reconciliatory word *guest* still carried within it the sense of "stranger," the foreign, the extraordinary, even "enemy"—as though language itself recognized that the attempt to familiarize the alien presence could never be wholly sure of success—and there was always the possibility that the apparently domiciled, accommodated "guest" could revert to an enemy in the midst, and release a disruptive power that could have endless repercussions. Indeed, it could fairly be said that the failure to transform, tame, familiarize, or domesticate the ambiguous presence from "the outside" (another territory, another world—or just another house) is one of the permanently generative themes of Western literature—whether we think of the magician Medea in Corinth and her terrible revenge on her betrayer, Jason, or of the gypsy Heathcliff, welcome and unwelcome in the home of the Earnshaws, whose love for Catherine and temporary desire to be "civilized" turn, or return, once thwarted, into an unholy will to destroy the houses and even the inhabitants of the

---

bership of this group—of breed or of friends—the individual owes not only his free status but also "his own self": the derivatives of the term *swe*, Gr. idiótēs, "individual," Latin *suus* "his," but also Greek *étēs*, *hetaîros* "ally, companion," Latin *sodalis* "companion, colleague" show that the primitive *swe* was the word for a social entity, each member of which realizes his "self" only in the "inter-self."

. . . .

Each of the Indo-European societies is pervaded by a distinction founded on free or servile condition. One is born free or born a slave. In Rome we have the division between *liberi* and *servi*. In Greece, the free man, *eleutheros* . . . is opposed to *doûlos*.

. . . .

We grasp the social origins of the concept of "free." The first sense is not, as one would be tempted to imagine, "to be free of, rid of something"; it is that of belonging to an ethnic stock designated by a metaphor taken from vegetable growth. Such membership confers a privilege which a stranger and a slave will never possess.

And finally:

The notion of stranger is not defined in ancient civilizations by fixed criteria, as he is in modern societies. Someone born elsewhere, provided that he has certain conventional links, enjoys some specific rights, which cannot be granted even to the citizens of the country: this is shown by the Greek *xénos* "stranger" and "guest," that is to say the stranger who benefits by the laws of hospitality. Other definitions are at hand: the stranger is "he who comes from outside," Lat. *advena*, or simply "he who is outside the limits of the community," Lat. *peregrinus*. There is no "stranger" as such: given diversity of notions, the stranger is always a particular stranger, who carries a distinct status. In short, the notions of enemy, stranger, guest, which for us form three distinct entities—semantically and legally—in the Indo-European languages show close connections.

. . . .

It is always because a man born elsewhere is *a priori* an enemy that a mutual bond is necessary to establish between him and the EGO relations of hospitality, which would be inconceivable within the community itself. . . . Rites, agreements and treaties thus interrupted this permanent situation of mutual hostility which existed between peoples or cities. Under the protection of solemn conventions and by means of exchange arrangements, human relationships could develop, and as a result the words for agreements or legal status come to denote sentiments.

Earnshaw and Linton families. Other examples are virtually innumerable, but the root theme is the same: the *guest*, for whatever reasons and from whatever motives, reverts to the *stranger-enemy*, and threatens or destroys the host-structures that sought to "incorporate" him. He becomes, in every sense, he who will not be "taken in." And as a result, not seldom a terrible violence is born.

Let me return to the figure of Paris and his archetypal transgression of the rules of hospitality in the form of his seduction of Menelaus's wife, Helen, while he is visiting Sparta and his elopement with her to Troy. This "simple" act of adultery ultimately leads to the destruction of Troy and the near destruction of the Greeks. His puncture/punctuation of Helen's body and the bonds and boundaries of hospitality (the body politic), precipitates a prolonged period of carnage and turmoil on a scale that is virtually cosmic—it even sets the gods and goddesses to quarreling and discord. Aeschylus conveys the sense of the almost insane disproportion between the one act of adultery and abduction and the war that followed. But the breaker of the guest/host rules can have no sense of the havoc that will be caused by that one act of rupture. Thus, from *Agamemnon:*

> So drives Zeus *the great guest god*
> the Atreidae against Alexander:
> for one woman's promiscuous sake
> the struggling masses, legs tired,
> knees grinding in dust,
> spears broken in the onset.
> Danaans and Trojans
> they have it alike.
>
> > (Chorus, lines 60–67; my italics)

> This was Paris: he came
> to the house of the sons of Atreus,
> stole the woman away, and *shamed*
> *the guest's right* of the board shared.

> She left among her people the stir and clamor
> of shields and of spearheads,
> the ships to sail and the armor.
> She took to Ilium her dowry, death.
>
> > (Chorus, lines 399–406; my italics)

> Who is he that named you so
> fatally in every way?
> Could it be some mind unseen
> in divination of your destiny
> shaping to the lips that name
> for the bride of spears and blood,

Helen, which is death? Appropriately
death of ships, death of men and cities
from the bower's soft curtained
and secluded luxury she sailed then,
driven on the giant west wind,
and armored men in their thousands came,
huntsmen down the oar blade's fading footprint
to struggle in blood with those
who by the banks of Simoeis
beached their hulls where the leaves break.

(Chorus, lines 681–96)[18]

There are frequent references in the play to "the guest board shamed," and it is worth remembering that the house of Atreus had a long history of the guest board shamed in the elementally taboo ways. Thus, according to the legend, Thyestes seduced the wife of his brother, Atreus (adultery). In revenge, Atreus invited Thyestes to a feast and served him the flesh of his murdered children to eat (intrafamilial cannibalism). Thyestes fled in horror and cursed the house of Atreus, which indeed suffered numerous subsequent calamities. Thyestes became the father of Aegisthus by his own daughter Pelopia (incest). Aegisthus killed Atreus—who was the father of Agammnon and Menelaus. Agamemnon killed his own daughter in a dubious act of sacrifice, and Menelaus—married Helen. The story of taboo atrocities goes even further back, receding into the mist of the origins of Greek mythology and the time of the gods, since Cronos devoured his own children, a fate from which Zeus was only spared by his mother, Rhea. All these acts add up to a kind of compendium of the dreaded (and thus tabooed) deeds that threaten the very possibility of the existence of civilization itself, since, quite apart from the horror attendant on the deeds, cannibalism of one's own children negates generational continuity; incest not only involves a chaotic confusion of generations by sexuality bringing together precisely the two figures who should be kept apart when it comes to sexuality and mating, it also effectively refuses and nihilates that transaction, or interfamilial exchange of the daughter in marriage, on

[18]Aeschylus, *Agamemnon*, in *Aeschylus One*, trans. Richmond Lattimore (Chicago: University of Chicago Press, 1953). In this connection it is worth recalling Freud's essay on "The Antithetical Sense of Primal Words" and his quotation from the philologist Abel to this effect: "The original words with a double meaning separate in the later language into two with single meanings, while each of the two opposite meanings takes to itself a slight 'reduction' (modification) in the sound of the original root. . . . The essential relativity of all knowledge, thought, or consciousness cannot but show itself in language. If everything we can know is viewed as a transition from something else, every experience must have two sides; and either every name must have a double meaning, or else for every meaning there must be two names."

which society depends. It is the ultimate travesty of endogamy from which no healthy future can come. Adultery threatens all family bonds; while murder simply ends life altogether, with the murder of the daughter by the father being a particularly vivid demonstration of the past violently destroying the future. In all these cases, what we witness is a hopeless and destructive conflation of people and bodies that should remain separate and unviolated if the family, and by extension society itself, is to have any clearly defined ongoingness. They betoken the threat of a return to chaos and old night, with all distinction gone.

My interest in this book is primarily in the transgressive act of adultery, for reasons that I hope to make clear in due course. In particular I want to attempt to trace out some of the implications of the act of adultery as they are explored in a number of the great eighteenth- and, more importantly, nineteenth-century novels—implications affecting not only the writing of fiction but society itself. But it is instructive to make a few selective comments on adultery as it is depicted, and particularly as its results are drawn out, in earlier literature. Thus, remaining with the *Iliad* for a moment, it is sometimes forgotten how Helen feels after what we may take to be her initial infatuation (never mind what role the gods and goddesses are supposed to play in it) is over, and she finds herself living a daily life of misery in her "alien" surroundings. When Iris brings her the news that Paris and Menelaus are to fight a duel with herself as a prize for the winner, Helen's thoughts are not for her lover. "This news from the goddess filled Helen's heart with tender longing for her former husband and her parents and the city she had left." And to Priam, who has asked her to identify one of the Greek giants, she answers in a way that indicates the extent of her regret for her adultery and all that followed from it. "I wish I had chosen to die in misery before I came here with your son, deserting my bridal chamber, my kinsfolk, my darling daughter and the dear friends with whom I had grown up. But things did not fall out like that, to my unending sorrow. However, I must tell you what you wished to know. The man you pointed out is imperial Agamemnon son of Atreus, a good king and a mighty spearman too. He was my brother-in-law once, shameless creature that I am—unless all that was a dream." After Paris's dismal performance on the battlefield, from which he is only saved by Aphrodite—who finally rescues him by hiding him in a mist and transporting him to his "perfumed fragrant bedroom"—Helen refuses to go to him until she is forced to by threats from Aphrodite. She scorns Paris for his failure against Menelaus, but Paris merely answers in terms of his sexual desire and soon "the two lay down together on the well-made wooden bed." The bed is the opposite to the battlefield—private, secluded from the realm of action and history in a goddess-protected, ahistorical, nonsocial realm of pure desire. Paris is equally hated by both sides, but he cannot be found because he is literally not among the soldiers of the field. He is in fact invisible. "Not that if anyone had seen him he would have hidden him for love: they loathed him, all of them, like death."[19] Paris, indifferent to the terrible war he has caused and to his own inadequacies as a warrior, exists in a dreamworld apart, a realm of pure desire. Helen is drawn into that world, but it is an agonizing problem for her to ascertain just which part of her life is "a dream"—the previous existence she led among kith and kin in which her status was clear, orthodox, and validated; or her present sojourn in the unsanctified, unlocalized annex of adulterous pleasure and desire that she unwillingly shares with the guest-turned-traitorous-stranger who, with divine help on his side, has her in his power. Here indeed is a recurring problem for the woman who has committed herself to adultery, no matter what her subsequent regrets: which is the dream—the life she left or the new life she entered? And in which, if indeed in either, does she find or experience her real being as a woman? Is Anna Karenina most herself when she is immersed in "the dream of life" with her passionless but respectable husband, or when she steps out of society into a passional existence with Vronsky that indeed wakes her bodily, and feeds a physical hunger she hardly knew she had, but that finally leads to a sense of universal meaninglessness and her suicide from the end of a platform that offers nowhere further to go? *Helen* means "death"—in her case, death to others; and legend generously restores her to her husband and her home in Sparta. Later women, who transgress the marriage boundary into adultery but who are not the beneficiaries of the flexible recuperations available in legend, also find themselves intimate with death—but more usually it is their own.

Helen is named for death: Tristan is named for sadness. His undying passion for the legally prohibited person of Queen Iseult the Fair, "the golden haired," and his disinclination to have any physical contact with his own wife, Iseult of the White Hands, form the basis of a legend of chivalric adultery that is archetypal. The legend has been submitted to numerous analyses (especially by Denis de Rougement, whose work I shall refer to later), but some points may be made about it that are particularly relevant in this particular context. Two aspects of the tale are immediately noticeable: everything is externalized or physicalized. There are, for example, two Iseults, existing clearly in antipodes, the one attracting to herself all of Tristan's illicit desire, the other having the status of his lawful wedded wife to whom he owes prescribed obligations

---

[19]Homer, *The Iliad,* trans. E. V. Rieu (Harmondsworth, Middlesex: Penguin, 1950), pp. 67, 68, 74, 75, 76.

that he cannot fulfill. Thus the desired body belonging to another that is a source of constant stimulation is clearly opposed to the undesired body belonging by contract to Tristan and that never excites any desire for contact at all. In this manner, any possible ambiguities that might radiate from the single loved object are clarified by the literal splitting of the woman into two women, a process not unlike "the splitting of the ego"[20]). The other aspect is that everything is rendered in terms of action and locale; so that, for instance, Tristan and Iseult do not gradually draw together through mutual attraction, but accidentally drink a love potion, and, as Brangien says on discovering the results of her neglect: "Friend Tristan, Iseult my friend, for that bad ward I kept take here my body and my life for through me and in that cup, you have drunk not love alone, but love and death together."[21] Thus it is impossible to ascribe any guilt to their subsequent behavior. The passion-poison came from without. That this may only be a way of conveying a psychologically plausible sudden attraction is not to the point. Rather it makes it seem that Tristan and Iseult are helpless enactors of a force that entered them without their knowledge and against their conscious wishes. They do not fall in love; rather, love falls into them. With a vengeance, we may say.

Action is continual. Tristan's and Iseult's love is dramatized in terms of preventive obstacles, deterrents, and restrictions or banishings that have to be overcome—thus the many leaps, disguises, and devious strategies of communication that mark the action; and on the other side, the spyings, pursuits, and threats of physical punishment. Thus when King Mark, significantly enough, orders Tristan to leave his castle and not to "repass its moat or *boundaries*" (my italics), Tristan goes away, only to feel the urge to return more imperious than ever—"desire without redress bore him like a bolting horse towards the well-girdled towers which shut in the Queen." And always he can find some point of leakage or penetration in the castle through which he can reach Iseult, as when he finds a spring that runs from the outside orchard into the castle through the women's rooms, which he uses to send a message to Iseult

---

[20]In Freud the term refers to "the coexistence at the heart of the ego of two psychical attitudes towards external reality in so far as this stands in the way of an instinctual demand. The first of these attitudes takes reality into consideration, while the second disavows it and replaces it by a product of desire. The two attitudes persist side by side without influencing each other" (J. Laplanche and J.-B. Pontalis, *The Language of Psycho-Analysis*, trans. Donald Micholson-Smith [London: The Hogarth Press, 1973], p. 427.) In the externalized world of the legend, the splitting is not internal to Tristan; rather, there is the reality of his wife Iseult, which he effectively disavows by not treating her as a husband should; and there is the Iseult who, in a way, is both the product and producer of his "desire."

[21]*Tristan and Iseult*, as retold by Joseph Bédier; translated by Hilaire Belloc and completed by Paul Rosenfeld (New York: Pantheon, 1945), p. 65.

that, once again, enables them to renew their lovemaking. But in his endless compulsive return to the gravitational center of his desire, he is continually reapproaching the point of his own destruction. "Madman, will you for ever be seeking death?" asks a loyal friend. The answer is yes, because it is inseparable from forever seeking Iseult. He even returns to the castle dressed in rags, simulating madness, and living like a dog in a kennel—disguised so effectively that Iseult neither recognizes him nor believes that he is indeed Tristan. He endures all kinds of "banter and blows," but then "taking on his own form and beauty, he passed from his dirty hole to the chamber of the Queen." Whatever the prohibition or interdiction or downright hostile defense mechanisms around the Queen, Tristan becomes he-who-will-not-and-cannot-be-denied-access. His is that desire that will always find a way of bypassing the threatening censorship of the father figure (Mark), no matter what form it has to take, what devious strategies it must deploy, what metamorphoses and disguises it must have recourse to. Nothing can keep him from the body of his Queen, just as nothing can induce him to enter the body of his wife. Such a desire recognizes boundaries only as lines of demarcation to be transgressed. Morality never enters into it—it is beyond good and evil.[22]

Quite as significant as the actions in the book is the topography and variation of locale it specifies. In his youth Tristan is snatched from his native land and taken to sea (a realm and element that plays a large part in his life). He is set down on an alien shore after a terrible storm and is taken in by King Mark, who recognizes some unusual qualities in the boy (he is both expert hunter and harpist—as it might be, an Orpheus combined with an Achilles). He thus becomes that familiar figure, the stranger, guest, adopted son, who, despite his will to be loyal to King Mark, becomes the uncontainable enemy within the house. More than once in the course of his adventures he drifts on the sea, and it is of course at sea that he and Iseult first "give themselves up to love" (the significance of this intimate alliance between the sea and illicit passion will, I hope, become clearer in the course of this book). On land there are two clearly opposed areas, familiar enough from literature of all times. There is the castle, monolithic in its mute authority and manifesting the compelling or restraining strength of the father-king. Outside there is an orchard, a sort of middle ground where Tristan and Iseult also indulge their passion. Then there is the forest, or wild wood that has never been felled, to which Tristan and Iseult flee and where they start to live a "savage life."[23] Here they can literally disappear in high grass and be-

[22]Ibid., pp. 81, 82, 166, 235.
[23]Ibid., pp. 65, 114.

hind curtains of leaves—it is a completely nonsocialized area, out of historic time and beyond the reach of any royal edicts. They live in a green hut in a green shade. And even when they are discovered asleep by King Mark (with the sword lying between them), they seem to be untouchably remote, as though in some realm in which their adulterous love actually became a new form of chastity that cannot be disturbed.

As Mark's wife, Iseult had dwelt among frescoes, tapestry, jewels, and curtains on which were depicted all kinds of animals and beasts of the sea and field—a highly civilized but static life in which reality has been supplanted by dead images of itself, its bounding, fecund abundance replaced by glittering, inert representations (almost exactly as in Tennyson's *Palace of Art*). The forest, by contrast, offers the thing itself, nature in its utterly noncivilized state. And here, indeed, the lovers are happy. But not for long. The sign of possible dissatisfaction, interestingly enough, comes when they miss "the taste of salt" when eating the flesh of wild animals. Without going into Lévi-Strauss's theory of *The Raw and the Cooked,* we can see that the preparation and preservation and spicing of food was a very early sign of civilized life. A certain minor but noticeable savor has gone out of their life with their removal to the forest. In due course, other deprivations are noticed, as their fine bodies go thin from inadequate diet, and their courtly clothes turn into rags because of the briars. The marks of rank disappear, and so far from being queen and knight, they become more like babes in the wood. They cannot live in the ambiguous freedom of the wild wood forever, and it is not long before they find themselves separated—though with no ebbing of desire—she returning to the castle, he taking to the sea. But "apart the lovers could neither live nor die, for it was life and death together."[24]

The sea, castle and court, the wild forest—in each realm the lovers indulge their passion, but none offers any secure permanence (as, in a different way, neither did the bedroom, the city, nor the battlefield for Paris and Helen). This inevitably leads to a dream of some further realm, beyond all hostile force and restricting or debarring structures (or beyond a structurelessness that will finally not support them—the sea, the forest). Iseult speaks to Tristan of a mythical freedom in which all the scythes and gates and walls of prohibition vanish. The whole exchange must be quoted in full.

> And so she said one night: "Oh, Tristan, I have heard that the castle is fairy and that twice a year it vanishes away. So it is vanished now and this is that enchanted orchard of which the harpers sing. A wall of air girdles it on all sides; there are flowering trees, a balmy soil; here without vigil the

[24]Ibid., pp. 117, 183.

hero lives in his friend's arms and no hostile force can shatter the wall of air."

Even as she spoke, from the towers of Tintagel there resounded the bugles of sentinels announcing the dawn.

"No," said Tristan, "the wall of air already lies shattered and this is not the enchanted orchard. But, one day, friend, we shall go together to a fortunate land from which none returns. There, rises a castle of white marble; at each of its thousand windows burns a lighted candle; at each a minstrel plays and sings a melody without end; the sun does not shine there but none regrets his light: it is the happy land of the living."

But high on the towers of Tintagel the dawn illuminated alternate great blocks of vert and azure.

The alternation between a dream of some impossible realm of freedom (walls of air, a sunless realm of music and love) and the reality principle of their immediate, actual surroundings (the bugles, the castle towers, the rising sun) is rendered starkly clear. There is literally no enduring place in the world of social and natural cyclicity—in which day always follows night, the bugles summon to duty, and the towers loom with their impregnable power—where the adulterous lovers can find a locale, a realm of their own. The quest for, or dream of, such an impossible world apart recurs constantly in the novel of adultery—for all available areas of the given world ultimately seem inhospitable to the adulterous lovers. Thus, at the moment of their final separation, Iseult begs Tristan to take her to that "happy place" he once described, and he promises to take her to "the Happy Palace of the living."[25] Shortly afterwards they both die. The "Happy Palace of the living" in which no bugles sound, no walls separate and hinder, and no sun ever shines, can only be the land of the dead. This often turns out to be the alternative realm that the adulterous lover (or lovers) has to seek. So it often is in the nineteenth-century novel, and it is perhaps no accident that it was in that period, so devoid of heroic action, so nostalgic for the mythic time of knights and kings and queens and their great lives and great deaths, that the legend of Tristan and Iseult was often revived and recelebrated in literature[26]

---

[25]Ibid., pp. 83–84, 236.

[26]To take one example, it is worth noting that Matthew Arnold in his fragmentarily narrative poem "Tristram and Iseult" concentrates on the scene of the dying Tristram in the home of Iseult of Brittany. Thus the whole period spent by Tristram and Iseult of Cornwall indulging in what Arnold revealingly calls "a love they dare not name" (thus imposing a Victorian reticence on two lovers for whom it could not be more inappropriate), is referred to only glimpsingly in retrospect and during Tristram's feverish dreams. The poem is really a celebration of the domestic, wifely, and maternal qualities of Iseult of Brittany—"the sweetest Christian soul alive."

> Behold her here, the patient flower,
> Who possess'd his darker hour!
> Iseult of the Snow-White Hand

(and, of course, opera). What the happy land of the living meant for the bourgeois adulterer (and adulteress), where it might be sought, and whether it could be found are questions to be considered in due course.

The story of the love of Launcelot and Gwenyver, as recounted by Malory, continues the mode of chivalric adultery and arguably com-

---

> Watches pale by Tristram's bed.
> She is here who had his gloom,
> Where art thou who hadst his bloom?

Arnold's sympathies are all with the patient housewife:

> And is she happy? Does she see unmoved
> The days in which she might have lived and loved
> Slip without bringing bliss slowly away,
> One after one, tomorrow like to-day?

Arnold makes very free with the legend, as is entirely within his poetic rights, but what finally emerges is *both* a typically Arnoldian bitter outcry against the erosion of the ability to feel, brought about by

> this strange disease of modern life,
> With its sick hurry, its divided aims,
> Its heads o'ertaxed, its palsied hearts
>
> ("The Scholar-Gipsy")

and an excoriating attack on the folly and wastage brought about by strong feelings.

> No, 'tis the gradual furnace of the world,
> In whose hot air our spirits are upcurl'd
> Until they crumble, or else grow like steel—
> Which kills in us the bloom, the youth, the spring—
> Which leaves the fierce necessity to feel,
> But takes away the power—this can avail,
> By drying up our joy in everything,
> To make our former pleasures all seem stale.

. . . .

> And yet, I swear, it angers me to see
> How this fool passion gulls men potently;
> Being, in truth, but a diseased unrest,
> And an unnatural overheat at best.
> How they are full of languor and distress
> Not having it; which when they do possess,
> They straightway are burnt up with fume and care,
> And spend their lives in posting here and there
> Where this plague drives them; and have little ease,
> Are furious with themselves, and hard to please.
>
> ("Tristram and Iseult")

Where passion is concerned, for Arnold it seems equally bad to feel it or not to feel it. Nobody wins—all the time. Yet a preference for the demurely domesticated Iseult of Brittany is clear throughout, and it is indicative of Arnold's deep suspicion of erotic attraction and passion that he ends his poem with an account of Merlin, imprisoned through his own magic by the treacherous, faithless, seductive Vivian. The great legend of chivalric adultery becomes a tract on the joyless virtues of Victorian domesticity and the dangers of sexual passion.

pletes it. Many of the features are familiar but will bear recounting in this context. Thus Launcelot is the greatest of the knights of the Round Table and the one who also demonstrates the most "curtesy." He is the favorite "son" of the father figure, King Arthur, to whom he has done great service and has often rescued, and to whom he feels most loyal. This sense of devoted service extends to Arthur's wife Gwenyver and is reciprocated by a love that finally draws them into adultery. Again, the very obstacles put up to guard the queen only prove an incentive to Launcelot to penetrate her chamber. He pulls apart the iron bars at her window by sheer manual strength (thereby sustaining a bleeding wound that almost betrays him) and spends the night with the queen, who has, effectively, summoned him. "So, to passe uppon thys tale, Syr Launcelot wente to bedde with the quene and toke no force of hys hurte honde, but toke hys pleasaunce and hys lykynge untyll hit was the dawnyying of the day." Their secret relationship arouses the jealousy of various other knights, and in the concluding book—"The Most Piteous Tale of the Morte Arthur Saunz Gwerdon"—the results of the adultery are almost as catastrophic as they are in Homer. It starts with the spying and plotting of Sir Aggravayne, who is determined to catch Sir Launcelot with the queen and to kill him, maintaining that Launcelot is a traitor—though it is Aggravayne's plot that starts the chain of destruction that ensues. Sir Gawayne and Sir Gareth can immediately see the threat to the whole society of the Round Table that will ensue. "Alas! . . . now ys thys realme holy destroyed and myscheved, and the noble felyshyp of the Rounde Table shall be disparbeled." Notwithstanding the omens of danger, Launcelot goes to the queen's bedchamber on the night of the plot. Malory's comment on what went on between them reveals a delicacy of tone that we may well envy. Neither prurient nor mystifying, Malory will not commit himself to the details of an ultimate privacy. "For, as the Freynshhe booke syeth, the quene and sir Launcelot were togydirs. And whether they were abed other at other maner of disportis, me lyste nat thereof make no mencion, for love that tyme was nat as love ys nowadays." What we do hear passing between the queen and Sir Launcelot is conducted at a high level of decorous courtesy. She is his "speciall good lady" and he her "poure knyght" whose devotion serves both to rescue her (when Arthur threatens to burn her) and return her as Arthur's queen at the appropriate time. Whatever passes between him and the queen, he maintains that he comes to her "for no maner of male engyne," and with utmost sincerity, it would seem, he will fight anyone who impugns her honor and goodness. It almost seems like adultery refined to a high level of innocence and courtliness—but the disasters ensue. After killing all but one of the plotters, Launcelot recognizes that "now ys warre comyn to us all." King Arthur, who appropriately erough invokes the law in condemning his wife, nevertheless foresees with sadness the ultimate outcome: "for now I am sure the noble felyshyp of the Rounde Table ys brokyn for ever," and later "Alas, that ever I bare crowne uppon my hede! For now have I loste the fayryst felyshyp of noble knyghtes that ever hylde Crystyn kynge togydirs." The breaking of one bond (by adultery) portends the dissolution of all bonds. From then on, everything in Arthur's kingdom does, indeed, fall apart. Individual transgression leads ultimately to social disintegration.[27]

In fact, shortly before his death, King Arthur has a dream that effectively reveals the eventual outcome of all that has been happening to his Round Table (the binding circle, the ring—symbol of infinity, of what cannot be broken, of the "wedding" till death do us part: the Table—hospitality, the place of peaceful foregathering at which no one person has a hierarchically marked preeminence).

> So uppon Trynyté Sunday at nyght kynge Arthure dremed a wondirfull dreme, and in hys dreme hym semed that he saw uppon a chafflet a chayre, and the chayre was faste to a whele, and thereuppon sate kynge Arthure in the rychest clothe of golde that myght be made. And the kynge thought there was undir hym, farre from hym, an hydeous depe blak watir, and therein was all maner of serpentis and wormes and wylde bestis fowle and orryble. And suddeynly the kynge thought that the whyle turned up-so-downe, and he felle amonge the serpenties, and every beste toke hym by a lymme. And than the kynge cryed as he lay in hys bed.
> "Helpe! Helpe!"

Instead of the Round Table, the Wheel of Fortune—but, more to the point, the dream reveals the utter beastly chaos lying beneath the regal order of the Arthurian society, and how, with one inversion, all can collapse back into that nightmare cauldron of the serpent-infested primordial slime. The dream is shortly enacted in reality with that "last, dim, weird battle of the west" (as Tennyson described it in his own Victorian way [see "The Passing of Arthur" in *Idylls of the King*]), leaving thousands dead, while the king is taken back into the lake on the barge with a retinue of black-hooded ladies, all wailing and shrieking as at some apocalyptic conclusion to the world itself. After hearing of Arthur's death, Gwenyver becomes a nun and does great "penaunce," "as ever ded synfull woman in thys londe." When Launcelot visits her, she rejects him, blaming their love for all that has happened—"for thorow the and me ys the floure of kyngis and kynghtes destroyed." Thus, when no obstacles to their love ostensibly remain, they separate: "And they departed; but there was never so harde an herted man but he wold have

[27] *The Works of Sir Thomas Malory*, ed. Eugène Vinaver, vol. 3 (Oxford: Clarendon Press, 1947), pp. 1162, 1165, 1166, 1168, 1169, 1174, 1183.

wepte to see the dolour that they made, for there was lamentacyon as they had be stungyn with sperys, and many tymes they swouned." Thus, without even a final kiss, Launcelot takes himself away to his own penance and, as he leaves his "speciall good lady" for the last time, he utters the simple, unforgettable cry—"Alas! Who may truste thys world?" He dies shortly after Gwenyver, for there is no life left for them, whether in the bedroom, the court, the battlefield, or some other country. All have been effectively destroyed, and in effect ultimately destroyed, because of the adultery of the noblest knight and fairest queen of the land. The rich and unresolvable paradox of the most noble adulterer is perfectly caught when "syr Ector" makes his lament over Launcelot's body. He was "hede of al Crysten knyghtes," and "the curtest knyght that ever bare shelde!": but above all—"thou were the trewest lover, of a synful man, that ever loved woman."[28] Truest lover / sinful man—how can we resolve that apparent paradox? The answer is that we cannot—"for love that tyme was nat as love is nowadays."

> Adultery?
> Thou shalt not die: die for adultery! No....
> Behold yond simp'ring dame,
> Whose face between her forks presages snow,
> That minces virtue and does shake the head
> To hear of pleasure's name.
> The fitchew, nor the soiled horse, goes to't
> With a more riotous appetite.
> Down from the waist they are Centaurs,
> Though woman all above: But to the girdle do the gods inherit,
> Beneath is all the fiend's.
> There's hell, there's darkness, there is the
> sulphorous pit,
> Burning, scalding, stench, consumption; fie, fie, fie!
> pah, pah! Give me an ounce of civet; good apothecary, sweeten my
>   imagination....
>
> (*King Lear,* act 4, scene 6)

There is nothing like this obsessional overspill of language—with its half-deranged preoccupation with the sheerly physical, sexual aspect of the female body—in the chivalric mode. Lear's imagination has indeed been "unsweetened," and here it is centered upon a vision of abandoned universal promiscuity, and in particular the stench and random appetite that may originate from the female genitals: if the "face" belies the "forks" (legs), where can a man put his trust? Appearances conceal a filth of unbridled desire, and his sick imagination, strained to the uttermost,

[28]Ibid., pp. 1233, 1243, 1252, 1253, 1254, 1259.

threatens to collapse into hyperbolic gibberish as his distorted vision takes over his mind and his words. Since law bespeaks no fidelity, where is kindness to be found? As for authority—"a dog's obeyed in office" (act 4, scene 6); the whole apparel of the social world, which should signify degrees of rank, obligation, an allocated and faithfully enacted role in a stable hierarchy, is mere deception and disguise. "Robes and furred gowns hide all" (act 4, scene 6). Such tearing and excoriating rhetoric, almost vomiting out truths as it peels its way to the center of things, is unthinkable from a King Mark or a King Arthur as they sadly invoke the law and authority that condemns their adulterous wives to be executed. In Shakespeare the chivalric code is more often degraded and even destroyed, as in *Troilus and Cressida,* and where it does persist, it is as a "strain of rareness" (*Cymbeline:* act 3, scene 4) operating almost anachronistically in a world that seems to have no codes or honorable behavior at all.

For the middle and late Shakespeare one overriding concern was the fate of those "holy cords... Which are too intrince t'unloose," (*King Lear:* act 2, scene 2) and the operations of those human "rats" who simply bite through these cords. Those cords are all the sacred bonds of society and family that hold everything together in a possible harmony, and Shakespeare's imagination increasingly probed what happened when, out of whatever motives and from whatever sources, those bonds were contemptuously regarded as mere marks of bondage that were arbitrary and provisional, and could easily be broken or breached by someone who scorned their binding power, and cynically—or passionally—denied and betrayed them. If all the bonds are made a mere mockery and no centers hold, it is pointless to single out adultery as a particularly horrendous transgression. On the other hand, it may be that, as we have seen before, the act of adultery itself forebodes the breaking of other bonds to the point of social disintegration. There is a growing horror in Shakespeare of the giving of the word that as easily becomes the breaking of the word, so that we often encounter a crisis of utterance, where truth turns to asides or silence, and falsehood brazenly appropriates the central heard discourses.

> I'll take thy word for faith, not ask thine oath.
> Who shuns not to break one will sure crack both
> (Act 1, scene 2)

as Pericles tersely puts it. And from *spoken* to *broken* word, it is but the sliding of a couple of letters, or the smallest deviation of motive and intention. It is in *Pericles,* incidentally (rather than in *Hamlet,* as is usually maintained), that we come nearest to a sense of the feeling in Sophocles' *Oedipus Rex*—incest connected to a riddle and a terrible famine makes a clear if distant echo of the Oedipus scenario. It is worth noting that when Pericles guesses the answer to King Antiochus's riddle, which contains the mystifying revelation of his incest with his daughter, he pleads to be allowed to remain silent, in an extraordinary metaphor.

> It is enough you know; and it is fit,
> What being more known grows worse, to smother it.
> All love the womb that their first being bred,
> Then give my tongue like leave to love my head.

> (Act 1, scene 1)

The refusal to speak the unutterable, the inclination to smother it, is conceived of in terms of a kind of secondary incest, linguistic rather than physical, in which the tongue (the sexual organ of speech) desires to return to and remain in the womb of the mouth, not wishing to emerge and articulate in an atmosphere dominated by actual incest between the prime figure of authority (and thus the lawgiver) and his daughter—an absolute negation of the true role of the father-king, who should maintain, rather than desecrate, the basic familial relationships on which the larger family of the state depends.

Where incest leads to silence, a withholding of utterance, adultery can provoke an excessive loquacity, to the point of a rampant spillage of words, something like language as nausea. More to the point, or my point, language can *create* adultery when it does not in fact take place— its verbally evoked image working more powerfully on the speaker than any other countering evidence in the outside world. The problem of "evidence" in Shakespeare is a well-recognized theme, particularly when the imagination seizes on the wrong kind of evidence and will not be deflected or detached from the images and convictions it generates, until too late (or apparently too late) the truth breaks in on the sealed imagination and scatters its phantasms with the awful truth. Thus it is, in different ways, with Othello and the handkerchief, and his insistence on "ocular proof" when Desdemona's honour is, precisely, "an essence that's not seen": thus it is with Lear, who asks for the wrong kind of verbal proof in the first scene and disastrously fails to comprehend the integrity of Cordelia's silence: thus, too, it is with Macbeth, who puts his faith in the murkily and mephitically ambiguous prophecies of the witches. In each case they alone are truly "taken in" or "bewitched" by the wrong kind of evidence and either abdicate from all their other faculties of perception and reasoning, or hand them over to the service of their malfounded convictions. But in two of Shakespeare's last plays, in addition to the themes familiar from the corpus of his work—seeming and being, the potential misleadingness of all "garments" as opposed to a correct reading of "the body," the fanatical adherence to the wrong kind of evidence—there are two other preoccupations I wish to comment on that, at this point, I shall call simply "suddenness"[29] and "the perverse pleasure of mistrust" (the latter being related to the bewildering ability of the human mind to generate from within the evidence that torments it, in the absence of even a handkerchief to beguile or confuse it. In such a case the "magic" is now in "the web" of the mind, and a horrifying magic it is that can transform nothing, or an absence of evidence, into proofs of the vilest kind). It is in this connection that I wish to offer a few comments on *Cymbeline* and *The Winter's Tale*. And in both plays we shall find, once again, the disruptive effects of the stranger in the house.

Cymbeline starts with a reference to frowning ("You do not meet a man but frowns" [act 1, scene 1]), and this adequately anticipates the enormous mixture of confusion that is to ensue, until the final rush of clarifications. The first frown is a response to the odd phenomenon of the king's daughter (Imogen) marrying beneath herself in rank ("a poor but worthy gentleman") This man is Posthumus, whose name describes and suggests what his ontological and social position is, because his origin is not known and his genealogy uncertain ("I cannot delve him to the root"). He is thus somewhat like the figure of Tristan, for Cymbeline has taken him in and raised him like a son. Thus he is the first stranger in the house, who appears to cause dismay and disruption by marrying the king's daughter. For this he is promptly banished by the king, who inverts his previous affection, effectively trying to negate him. "Thou basest *thing,* avoid hence, from my sight!" (My italics. The adopted son is rejected as a "thing.") When Posthumus takes his departure from Imogen, the father literally interrupts their parting discourse—he comes in between. Imogen laments, in lovely words, that she had "most pretty things to say." But—

> Betwixt two charming words—comes in my father,
> And like the tyrannous breathing of the north
> Shakes all our buds from growing.
>
> (Act 1, scene 3)

It is a classic case of paternal interdiction. The father acts as a sterile force, attempting to blight a love-marriage that is already sealed by legal contract and marked by the exchange of a ring and a bracelet. Could the king but see it, theirs is a positive union, based on love and hiding no treachery, but he is blind (as the father and comparable figures in authority often are—I shall return to this in a later chapter) and also

---

[29]Cf. Nietzsche: "In the inner psychic economy of the primitive man, fear of evil predominates. What is evil? Three things: chance, the uncertain, the sudden" (*The Will to Power,* trans. Walter Kaufmann and R. J. Hollingdale [New York: Vintage Books, 1968], bk. 4, section 1019.)

unknowingly beset by poisonous plots being engineered by his second wife against him and on behalf of her stupid son, Cloten. The second stranger in the court is Iachimo.

> FIRST LORD. Did you hear of a stranger that's come to court tonight?
> CLOTEN. A stranger. and I not know on't?
> SECOND LORD. *(Aside)* He's a strange fellow himself, and knows it not.
>
> (Act 2, scene 2)

Strange, stranger, estranged, most strange—the play on these words is common in Shakespeare, particularly when the known and established world goes awry and is called into question. For where then is the true family / familiar to be reliably found?

Iachimo is the real stranger / enemy in the court, who has come to do mischief and create disunion, and it is to this figure and his curious malevolent power I wish to turn now. (It hardly needs mentioning that the whole play contains a reenacting of the *Othello* situation, with the Iachimo-Iago figure, the confusing use of objects to deceive trusting / jealous minds, the calumnied pure wife, and so on. But Shakespeare often returns to his preoccupations in different ways, to explore the particular phenomenon ever more deeply—here let us say it is the rapid onset of jealousy due to the calculating manipulations of a base but crafty mind. His interest in the intimate connection between trusting love and ferocious jealousy becomes ever more marked in the middle and late plays, particularly in the two plays I am briefly considering here. And *Cymbeline,* with its incredible synthesis of so many modes and concerns, is a much richer play than *Othello*—which the later play almost contains in précis, a kind of dramatic asyndeton taking the place of the detailed progress of *Othello*.) The dramatic time between Iachimo's goading Posthumus into betting on Imogen's virtue and his return to Rome with the illusory evidence that turns all of Posthumus's trust in Imogen into a bilious conviction of her adultery and betrayal, is very short—so short, indeed, that some critics have complained that the sequence of events is too rapid and unprepared for. But that is just the point. That it can take little to no time for strong emotions to reverse themselves into their opposite and that—frighteningly enough—the most reverent love can carry as its obverse side a ravenous will to mistrust and a readiness (or desire) to believe the worst. Our strongest feelings are not built on sand, but rather on their own opposites.

The trouble starts with one of those "contentions in public" in which Posthumus, having boasted of the superiority and fidelity of his wife Imogen, is drawn into Iachimo's wager that, given the opportunity, he can easily rob her of her virtue. The comment of Philario, a sensible bystander to the wager, is crucial. "Gentlemen, enough of this. It came in *too suddenly*" (act 1, scene 4; my italics). Such, exactly, is the precipitate onset of strong emotions: bypassing all the considerations and retardations of reason and reflection, they come on too suddenly. Almost immediately Posthumus offers the ring Imogen gave him as his stake in the wager, thus turning the symbol of their union and trust into a mere money equivalent in a betting match (Iachimo bets ten thousand ducats). Here already we have not only a secularization but a degradation of the sacred object, just as the holy person of the virtuous Imogen is reduced to her "bodily part," a possessible thing to be wagered over. Iachimo makes play with the equivalence of "she your jewel, this your jewel," thus effectively reducing both ring and woman to something like market commodities. So, as quickly as Posthumus had made an honorable *contract* with Imogen, he makes a dishonourable *covenant* with Iachimo, in an exchange that is really a debased travesty of the marriage vows. (*Contract*, containing *tractare*, "to handle," is, or should be, a much more strongly binding commitment than a *covenant*, a more ad hoc "coming together." In this case it is manifestly wrong to equate the latter with the former, or even to engage in the latter at all. Philario is again the reasonable voice that declares "I will have it no lay" (act 1, scene 4). "See better, Lear," says Kent (*King Lear*, act 1, scene 1), but "suddenness" means blindness, and the ensuing road to true vision is arduous and hard to find.) Like some other Shakespeare protagonists, Posthumus is confusing value and price, a confusion of values that translates itself into a convulsion of events.

Iachimo's cool, skeptical Machiavellian mind works differently. We are given an early clue when he and some others are discussing Posthumus, who is about to arrive in Rome. "But I could then have looked on him without the help of admiration, though the catalogue of his endowments had been tabled by his side and I to peruse him by items (act 1, scene 4)." Near the end of this magical play, Posthumus will awake to indeed find such a catalogue lying on his chest—a divine superscription on his body of his endowments, his real identity and intended achievements. But for the moment we may note that Iachimo's eye does indeed peruse by items and views the world—and people—as a catalogue of parts. He does not see the whole, but fragments the object of his vision, the better to master and manipulate it—hence missing the wonder of the rareness in the world (thus his refusal of admiration as an aid to vision) and disappreciating its totality, or the totality of an individual. It is a version of the empirical eye, working emotionlessly by parts, for maleficent, calculating ends. It is his perusal by items that works so efficiently in Imogen's bedroom, but not before he has tested her with insinuations about the promiscuous behaviour of Posthumus among the whores of Rome in words that are among the most lubricious that Shakespeare ever wrote. He pretends that he cannot understand why Posthumus (though he does not actually name him) should turn from one so fair as Imogen to the kind of copulating trash that (he all but asserts) now engages his appetite.

> Sluttery, to such neat excellence opposed,
> Should make desire vomit emptiness,
> Not so allured to feed.

> The cloyèd will—
> That satiate yet unsatisfied desire, that tub
> Both filled and running—ravening first the lamb,
> Longs after the garbage.

(Act 1, scene 6)

He suggests that Imogen should take her revenge, while (Posthumus) is "vaulting variable ramps."

Imogen rejects all this as the product of the "beastly mind" of a "saucy stranger," simply deflecting and ignoring Iachimo's flow of metaphors depicting the nauseating behavior of the lowest reaches of desire. And it is then that Iachimo, following an old tradition, pretends that he was just testing the loyalty of Imogen for his friend Posthumus. Thus all is forgiven, and he is welcomed into the court. At which point he asked the fateful favor of leaving the case of treasure ("a present for the Emperor") in her safe possession, because, he says, "I am something curious, being strange," which indeed means he is anxious because he is a foreigner, but can also mean exactly what it says—he is an enemy in the court who wishes to satisfy his curiosity, for what ends we already know. Imogen, ever-trusting, promises to keep the case in her bedchamber, saying "send your trunk to me," which has a double meaning she cannot be aware of. For that is exactly what Iachimo intends to do—i.e., send his *trunk* ("body") to her in a *trunk* ("case"). (*Trunk* also implies the main part of the human body, which is why the headless corpse of the luckless, fatuous Cloten is such an important object in the play. It is the most literal enactment of the fact that while Imogen "keeps her head," as we say, all around her others are losing theirs, not so literally as Cloten but in the sense of losing their faculties of true vision and ratiocination. For certain periods the play is thus a "headless world" [to use a phrase from Elias Canetti's novel *Auto da Fé*], which leads to endless failures of recognition as people tend to read others by bodies, and garments [which are endlessly changed and changeable], not seeing the true features of actual identity.)

Iachimo's speech in Imogen's bedroom is too well known to require much comment here. What *is* notable is that even he is first of all overcome with admiration before he remembers "my design." Thus to mitigate his sense of wonder at the beauty of the *whole* scene, he decides "I will write all down" and breaks the scene up into scripted details. Having itemized the "meaner moveables"—pictures, windows, furnishings, etc., he makes some "natural *notes* about her *body* . . . t'enrich mine *inventory*" (act 2, scene 2; my italics), having recourse to the specular, particularizing vision that is his habitual mode of appropriating the world. Thus he notes the mole on her breast while slipping off the bracelet that Posthumus gave her ("she your jewel, this your jewel"), interchangeable "vouchers" (since he has no hierarchical sense of values) that will work "to th' madding of her lord." Returning to Rome with all these "particulars" to "justify my knowledge"—(act 2, scene 4), he works readily on Posthumus's incomprehensibly vulnerable imagination, which is all too hospitable to the trivia of circumstantial evidence. He resists briefly until Iachimo produces the bracelet, at the sight of which he immediately capitulates to a virulent and generalized misogynistic mistrust, and hands over his ring to Iachimo.

> It is a basilisk unto mine eye,
> Kills me to look on't. Let there be no honor
> Where there is beauty; truth, where semblance; love,
> Where there's another man. The vows of women
> Of no more bondage be to where they are made
> Than they are to their virtues, which is nothing.
> O, above measure false!
>
> (Act 2, scene 4)

The good sense of Philario briefly prevails against this hopelessly premature conviction, but the tide of jealousy is rapidly rising to full flow and there is no possibility of an ebb. Posthumus asks for some "corporal sign"—again, evidence from the body, not the person—but as soon as Iachimo swears that he had the bracelet from her arm—as indeed he did, though without her cognizance (an obvious possibility that Posthumus does not stop to consider)—the jealousy renews its build-up, moving toward an ever more degrading, corporal vocabulary in his mounting loathing.

> No, he hath enjoyed her.
> The cognizance of her incontinency
> Is this. She hath bought the name of whore thus dearly.
>
> (Act 2, scene 4)

The latinate, more formal mode of utterance, soon gives way to a blunt colloquial physicality. Again rejecting Philario's reasonable speech of intercession, he says: "Never talk on't. / She hath been colted by him." When Iachimo slips in the detail about the mole on Imogen's breast, implying that he has plenty more to tell, Posthumus silences him with the unforgettable words: "Spare your arithmetic; never count the turns./ Once, and a million!" One act of adultery equals an infinity of such acts—Posthumus is away into the perverse pain/pleasure of hyperbolic revulsion, and nothing can stop him. He makes his exit with distinctly Othello-like bombastical threatening, verging on the edge of the collapse of coherent discourse.

> O that I had her here, to tear her limb-meal!
> I will go there and do't i' th' court, before
> Her father. I'll do something—
>
> (Act 2, scene 4)

"I'll do something"—the blind imprecisions of unfettered rage and nausea have taken over and obliterated the solemn vows of the marriage contract—"I do." Having formalized and internalized his image of Imogen as the type of adulterous traitorous woman, he can fulminate endlessly over that, quite swamping and negating any memories he might have of the real woman.

The response to Posthumus's deranged accusations is seen in Britain. He writes to Pisanio, his servant, giving orders to kill Imogen. Not for the first time in Shakespeare, the servant's response is more honorable than his lord's.

> How? of adultery? Wherefore write you not
> What monsters her accuse? . . .
>   Disloyal? No.
> She's punished for her truth and undergoes,
> More goddess-like than wife-like, such assaults
> As would take in some virtue. O my master,
> Thy mind to her is now as low as were
> Thy fortunes.
>
> (Act 3, scene 2)

Pisanio cannot fulfil Posthumus's cruel and insane orders, but instead sets in motion a plot of his own to save Imogen, from which evolves much of the remainder of the play. But Imogen's reaction to the letter Posthumus wrote to Pisanio—which he finally lets her read—is noteworthy in this context. She reads: "Thy mistress, Pisanio, hath played the strumpet in my bed, the testimonies whereof lies bleeding in me. I speak not out of weak surmises, but from proof as strong as is my grief and as certain as I expect my revenge." She then launches into her lament concerning the implications of Posthumus's cardinal, culpable, and by extension catastrophic failure of trust:

>   O,
> Men's vows are women's traitors! All good seeming,
> By thy revolt, O husband, shall be thought

Put on for villainy, not born where't grows,
But worn a bait for ladies. . . .
True honest men, being heard like false Aeneas,
Were in his time thought false, and Sinon's weeping
Did scandal many a holy tear, took pity
From most true wretchedness. So thou, Posthumus,
Wilt lay the leaven on all proper men;
Goodly and gallant shall be false and perjured
From thy great fail.

(Act 3, scene 4)

Launcelot and Gwenyver's adultery (if we may assume it to be such) finally brought about the disastrous collapse of the whole order of the Round Table. The potential results of Posthumus's failure of trust and his adultery-obsessed imagination, when none in fact occurs, presage a state of affairs less visibly disastrous than the ruinous battles in Malory's story, but arguably more insidiously undermining for society as a whole. For from his "great fail" could extend, by implication, a world in which virtue is regarded as vice, honest men deemed corrupt, being taken for seeming, and nature's own true coin dismissed as counterfeit. Such would be the world in which a mentally induced image of adultery displaces and negates the actual nonadulterous faithful woman living in the outside world. Such a hideous failure and perverse "dis-reading" of evidence could be a paradigm for a world in which all values are inverted and, indeed, nothing is but what is not—or what *is* only in the diseased-image–engendering mind. Posthumus makes a solemn contract with Imogen by swearing the marriage vows with her, only to show himself almost immediately willing to violate that contract in the most extreme way by having her murdered. Marriage is at the very heart of the customs that ensure the stability and continuity of society, and Posthumus threatens to blaspheme and destroy his marriage at the first hint that comes his way, while he is absent from Imogen. (It is only at the end that she is fully present to him, and he achieves full presence of himself to himself.) But, as Imogen says so memorably in another context—"The breach of custom / Is breach of all" (act 4, scene 2). Posthumus's behavior threatens the coming into existence of an un-customed or de-customed world—a chaos of blighted and bloodily broken bonds.

This is but a part of *Cymbeline,* to my mind one of the richest of Shakespeare's plays. In *The Winter's Tale* the part of the action concerned with the onset of Leontes's jealousy, and his certainty that his pure wife Hermione is an adultress, is even shorter, since the attack of perverse mistrust comes on even more suddenly, without the provocative hints of an Iago or a Iachimo or the ambiguous evidence of a handkerchief or a bracelet. It is *totally* unprepared for, a completely abrupt and arbitrary catastrophe of the mind that extends itself into the previous order and harmony of his court. We may compare the account in Shakespeare's main source, *Pandosto. The Triumph of Time*, by Robert Greene, which is, as the text announces at the beginning, concerned with jealousy. "Among al the passions wherewith humane mindes are perplexed, there is none that so galleth with restlesse despight, as the infectious soare of Jealousie." Here Pandosto (Leontes) *gradually* becomes suspicious of the relations between his wife, Bellaria (Hermione) and Egistus (Polixenes). And the latter two do spend time in secret intimacy with each other— albeit their conduct is quite honorable. But it is a *slow* provocation to Pandosto's imagination. "First, *he called to minde* the beauty of his wife Bellaria, the comeliness and braverie of his friend Egistus, thinking that Love was above all Lawes, and therefore to be staied with no Law: that it was hard to put fire and flax together without burning; that their open pleasures might breede his secrete displeasures. *He considered with himselfe* that Egistus was a man, and must needes love: that his wife was a woman, and therefore subject unto love, and that where fancy forced, friendship was no force. These and such like doubtfull thoughtes *a long time* smoothering in his stomacke, beganne at last to kindle in his minde a secret mistrust, which increased by suspition, grewe at last to be a flaming Jealousie, that so tormented him as he could take no rest." (My italics.) This is a cool, reflective and even rational process by comparison with Leontes's sudden inexplicable irruption, and what Shakespeare has most notably omitted is that "long time" referred to by Greene. In Leontes's case, the "flaming Jealousie" attacks him and takes him over in *no time at all*. There is no considering or calling to mind, just an immediate, total perceptual inversion and an upwelling nausea that generates its own self-convincing images of adulterous betrayal.

It starts, in fact, the minute Leontes has asked Hermione to persuade Polixenes to stay and she decorously gives her hand to their guest and old friend. His resolute misinterpretation of the gesture commences, appropriately, in an "aside"—the private utterance of the self to the self in public: "Too hot, too hot!/To mingle friendship far, is mingling bloods" (act 1, scene 2). And it continues with a quite gratuitous doubt whether his son Mamilius is really his—a masochistic playing with the absurd that begins to mark the degeneration of his speech, which collapses from the formal and kingly to a private semisequential muttering. Having generalized on the falseness of all women, he moves into a train of disordered thought of which the logic seems only comprehensible to him. And when Polixenes and Hermione make an innocent exit Leontes has convinced himself against all rational argument: "Gone already!/Inch-thick, knee-deep, o'er head and ears a fork'd one!" and his own discourse becomes more bawdy and indulges in a kind of inverted concupiscence, painfully, perversely, yet eagerly focusing on his wife's "slipperiness." He orders one of his lords, Camillo, to say that what *he* says is true, but once again the rational bystander-servant speaks the calm truth. "You never spoke what did become you less / Than this." In his ranting that follows Leontes reveals that the real world has been totally supplanted by the imaginings of his "diseas'd opinion." "Is whispering nothing?" he starts, and goes on to show how he has completely misinterpreted the courtly behavior of Hermione and Polixenes, and indeed has invented carryings-on that only exist in the fumes of his mind.

> is this nothing?
> Why, then the world and all that's in't is nothing;
> The covering sky is nothing; Bohemia nothing;
> My wife is nothing; nor nothing have these nothings,
> If this be nothing.
>
> (Act 1, scene 2)

He is negating the external world as total absence and emptiness—an ontological void: the only "something" is what he has misconceived in his phantasmagoria. The unspoken converse also holds, of course—because the behavior of Polixenes and Hermione does *not* signify anything amiss or disloyal, then it is Leontes and his world that are "nothing" in their complete unreality.

His ensuing behavior has precedents in the earliest drama. If anyone disagrees with his version of the truth, they are liars and traitors. A recognizable paranoia sets in: "There is a plot against my life, my crown; / All's true that is mistrusted" (act 2, scene 1)—thus reacted Oedipus when gainsaid, and thus Creon in *Antigone*. What Leontes cannot hear in his own discourse is the hidden truth of his words. There *is* a plot against his life, but it is his own: and Hermione, most mistrusted of all, is, indeed, true. But Leontes congratulates himself as being sole perceiver of the truth. "How blest am I / In my just censure, in my true opinion!" Hermione's first reaction is that it must be all "sport" on Leontes's part. But he retaliates first of all by making her a public spectacle—"You, my lords, / Look on her, mark her well"—and then goes on to abuse and degrade her as virulently as possible. "She's an adultress," he says twice, "a bed-swerver," "a traitor," and, denying every aspect of her rank, her character, her identity, he reduces her to a mere object: "O thou *thing*! / Which I'll not call a creature of thy place . . . (my italics) Her courteous answer indicates the possible enormity of what he is doing.

> Gentle my lord,
> You scarce can right me throughly then, to say
> You did mistake.
>
> (Act 2, scene 1)

The said word cannot be unsaid, nor the public accusation retracted. However, Leontes is so certain of "those foundations which I build upon" that he orders her to prison, and when the remaining lords try to penetrate his sealed mind with a sense of the wrongness he is committing, he literally rejects their words, insisting on the primacy of his own. "What! lack I credit?" he exclaims—in which case he will do without it, his "credence" being the only needful factor.

> Why, what need we
> Commune with you of this, but rather follow
> Our forceful instigation? Our prerogative
> Calls not your counsels; . . . the matter,
> The loss, the gain, the ordering on't, is all
> Properly ours.
>
> (Act 2, scene 1)

He is asserting the omnipotence of his own discourse, beyond the need of dialogue—in this mood, what he asserts to be, *is* so. Though to nobody else but himself. Again, when he alludes to the "proof" he has of the supposed adultery, his words give him away even while he thinks they are establishing the rightness of his cause. He refers to Hermione's and Polixenes's "familiarity."

> Which was as gross as ever touch'd conjecture,
> That lack'd sight only, naught for approbation
> But only seeing, all other circumstances
> Made up to the deed
>
> (Act 2, scene 1)

This can be interpreted in more than one way, but among other things, it reveals that his evidence is "circumstantial" and his proof merely "conjecture." Yet he resolves to send Hermione and her newborn baby to the fire. Before doing so, however, he holds a public court, of an improvised kind, effectively to make Hermione more of a spectacle and increase her degradation. He has sent to the oracle for confirmation, but he regards this as a mere formality. His speeches are a parody of forensic discourse, which simply hinge on the nonfact that obsesses him: that Hermione is an adultress. As she understandably says:

> Sir,
> You speak a language that I understand not:
> My life stands in the level of your dreams,
> Which I'll lay down.
>
> (Act 3, scene 2)

He is indeed generating a nonreferential discourse of his own that is quite unrelated to, and unchecked against, reality and all plausibility.

Thus the so-called court proceedings have nothing to do with "law," as Hermione observes:

> if I shall be condemn'd
> Upon surmises, all proofs sleeping else,
> But what your jealousies awake—I tell you,
> 'Tis rigour, and not law.

(Act 3, scene 2)

These last words come straight out of Greene, and in his work, Pandosto, like Leontes, is quite prepared to override Law and replace it with his word. "The king presently made answere, that in this case he might, and would, dispence with the Law, and that the Jury being once panneld, that should take his word for sufficient evidence, otherwise he would make the proudest of them repent it." In both works, then, we have the spectacle of the father-king asserting the absolute power of his Word, against all evidence, reasoning, protest, or anything else. This is the Word of the Father in its most terrifying form. When the oracle's verdict is delivered, exonerating both Hermione (Bellaria) and Polixenes (Egistus), there is a slight but significant difference in the way the two kings react. Pandosto *immediately* believes the oracle, but it is too late—his son and wife having fallen down dead. He is so shocked and repentant that he swoons and lies for "three dayes without speache." He has, indeed, lost his Word. Leontes, on the other hand—quite in the manner of Oedipus—is willing to deny and discount the sayings of the oracle: "There is no truth at all i'the oracle:/ The sessions shall proceed: this is mere falsehood." It is only when he hears that his son is dead and Hermione "dead" that he quite suddenly loses all his obsession with adultery and betrayal and realizes—"I have too much believ'd mine own suspicion." Greene's story ends with Pandosto's near-incest with his daughter and his subsequent suicide. Shakespeare's play ends with magic, restoration and rebirth: the "great difference" alluded to in the opening words of the play becomes a great harmony and family reunification; all the "wide gaps" of time (and between people), are to be annulled, sutured, and filled in, and the "disseverance" referred to in the last line of the play, and which has occurred in varying forms throughout, is transformed, retrospectively, into a long prologue to rejoinings and new unions and reunions. Such is the world of Shakespeare's last plays. But this is not to forget that the sudden, unprovoked onset of jealousy and a perverse obsession with imagined adultery, is nowhere more violently depicted by Shakespeare than in the first half of this play. I have said that there is no Iago or Iachimo to spark off this mental furnace, no ambiguous, unsettling guest to upset the status quo. There is no need for such a figure. Leontes the king is the *stranger / enemy* within his own court. Such a state of affairs is an ultimate nightmare, for the only permitted reality is his Word, and that omnipotent word speaks truly— and truly speaks—nothing. But it is a nothing that can annihilate his whole world, dispatching all sacred bonds to the fire of his own imagination. It takes Shakespeare's superior imagination both to confront and to cope with such a dire phenomenon.

Puns, Perversions, and Privations

It is my contention that whereas the ideal *belief* of bourgeois society was that it had effected a harmonious interrelationship of patterns of property and patterns of passion and feeling, and that it was in possession of a language that could both effectively mediate those patterns and stabilize the environment, the *knowledge* about that society as it began to emerge in the explorations of the novel was that in fact these patterns were all awry. With this knowledge the novel began to lose its innocence and realized that its own patternings were not simply reflections of social patterns but existed in a very problematical relationship to those patterns. I am suggesting in general that bourgeois society, more than any other, sought to establish its own stability within history (I am excluding the kind of timeless society considered by Mircea Eliade in *The Myth of the Eternal Return,* as well as societies sanctioned by some religious system on which they base their rhythms and renewals)—bourgeois society is, in this sense, post-Viconian society: the society that *knows* that it makes itself, even if it does not always know how, or always wish to know how. But as the novelists began to scrutinize this self-created, self-stabilizing, self-mythologizing society, they discovered a series of discontinuities and instabilities that effectively gave the lie to the bourgeois's image of his own society.

For purposes of contrast as well as comparison let me just cite the example of Petronius's *Satyricon.* Of course there is no nineteenth-century novel in any way like it, but in an extreme form the *Satyricon* demonstrates the kind of collapse and perversion or inversion of patterns and systems of relationships that, in a more indirect way, the novelist of bourgeois society was also discovering. I will not attempt to engage in any summary of the fragmented plot, for that is not the point. What is more important is, rather, the prevailing atmosphere, which is, to put it at its most simple, one in which sexuality, language, and economics have all gone wrong. The sexual perversions and confusions are well known—homosexuality, adultery, promiscuity coexist with impotence, scopophilia, and voyeurism, so that one model for society is that of a brothel maintained in part by eunuchs. Everything, and nothing, goes. In addition there is constant reference to the depraved state of language, which has lost its chastity. The text opens with a discussion of rhetoric and a complaint about the degeneration of language. "Action or language, it's all the same: great sticky honeyballs of phrases, every sentence looking as though it had been plopped and rolled in poppyseed and sesame.... By reducing everything to sound, you concocted this bloated puffpaste of pretty drivel whose only real purpose is the pleasure of punning and the thrill of ambiguity. Result? Language lost its sinew, its nerve. Eloquence died."[30] Complaints about atrocious puns are frequent throughout the book, and we may say that puns and ambiguities are to common language what adultery and perversion are to "chaste" (i.e., socially orthodox) sexual relations. They both bring together entities (meanings/people) that have "conventionally" been differentiated and kept apart; and they bring them together in deviant ways, bypassing the orthodox rules governing communications and relationships. (A pun is like an adulterous bed in which two meanings that should be separate are coupled together). It is hardly an accident that *Finnegans Wake,* which arguably demonstrates the dissolution of bourgeois society, is almost one continuous pun (the connection with sexual perversion being quite clear to Joyce). We may say that Petronius was fairly prescient in this matter. Economics I will come to a little later. For the moment I want to say a few words about Trimalchio's feast, and the importance of eating in general.

The meal—intrafamilial or hospitable—is obviously one of the central events and activities in the bourgeois home and thus in the novel related to it. We find nothing so extreme there as Trimalchio's feast, but that feast does reveal a kind of perversion and transformation and concealment of sources and materials that has its more muted analogues in the bourgeois novel. In general all the dishes are disguised as something else (just as people are constantly using disguise throughout—wigs, makeup, etc.). Nothing is what it seems. Bronze donkeys carry olives, black damsons and red pomegranates are arranged like flames over charcoal, a hen carved from wood reveals eggs that contain orioles; there is a hare tricked out with wings like a little Pegasus, gravy boats are shaped like satyrs with phalluses for spouts, a wild sow is clustered around with

[30]Petronius, *Satyricon,* trans. William Arrowsmith (New York: New American Library, 1960), p. 21.

pastry piglets sucking on her teats, there are quinces like sea urchins, pigs stuffed with sausages, and so on. In general the whole feast is an "atrocious pun" in which there is nothing natural (no *water* is served) and in which cooking is not simply a mode of preparation but has become a way of investing and conflating the realms of nature, manufacture, myth, and culture. Reality has, as it were, been extracted from everything, and there is no organizing reference point from which these realms could be differentiated. There is a similar confusion and conflation of learning in the conversation, as when Trimalchio refers to the picture on his goblet—"things like Daedalus locking up Niobe in the Trojan Horse." Though the confusion has its incidental significance. Thus, Daedalus made the wooden cow for Pasiphae, a kind of perversion of craft; Niobe is the mother mourning her dead children—the loss of family; while the wooden horse inside Troy is the classical example of a man-made container with the deceitful contents (men *inside* the horse is a culture/nature inversion)—the very model of Trimalchio's feast in which everything contains something else. The full implications of this perversion of substances is perhaps indirectly brought out by Trimalchio when he speaks of the Sybil of Cumae. "I once saw the Sybil of Cumae in person. She was hanging in a bottle, and when the boys asked her, 'Sybil, what do you want?' she said, 'I want to die.'"[31] At Trimalchio's dinner table death has been transformed into a silver skeleton with joints so that it can be twisted into obscene postures.

But if the feast celebrates an insane abundance, a plenitude gone wrong, a complete loss of meaning in sheer excess and perversion, both of form and of content, there is another side to it. For it is striking how quickly it all can turn to waste. In particular, things keep falling to the floor, which is, as it were, the one place from which Trimalchio averts his eyes. Thus, whenever he drops one of the balls he plays with, he never picks it up but simply takes another one—a very image of the consumer in a society based on disposability! Also, he likes jugglers, acrobats, tumblers on ladders, and condemns most other forms of entertainment as trash. It is as though, in every sense, he does not wish to examine the ground of his condition. But, just as a boy falls from the ladder, so handles snap, pitchers crash, tables collapse, and dishes fall to the floor, whence they must not be retrieved but, on Trimalchio's orders, "tossed back on the floor" and swept up as rubbish. The instant transformation whereby the furniture, accessories, and whatever is *on* the table are immediately reclassified if they fall to the ground, indicates the close

[31]Ibid., pp. 46, 59, 57.

connection between overabundance and rubbish in the society of Trimalchio. There is a similar degeneration of words and music and gestures in the entertainment offered at and around the table, just as the feast offers a degeneration into perverted sexual activities. They all collapse together. It is entirely appropriate that the feast ends in chaos. Trimalchio pretends to be dead (which is indeed where the feast has been tending), though here again pretense is offered as a way of evading the real thing. He orders the playing of a funeral march, which—by an appropriate act of mistranslation—is interpreted as an alarm signaling that the house is on fire, and the local firemen smash down the door and rush in with buckets and axes to do their job. "Utter confusion followed, of course."[32] But "utter confusion" is what has been revealed as the basic antistructure of the whole occasion.

The economic factor obtrudes noticeably on several occasions. There are hints, such as that conveyed by the fact that Trimalchio uses coins for one of his games and in his confession of a passion for silver. There are clearer references to his estate at Cumae, where slaves and money are alike hoarded. Slaves figure prominently at the feast, and the way in which their freedom and bondage are, as it were, played with reveals the extent to which they are treated as a species of currency. Trimalchio has more farms than he knows what to do with. At the same time he does not buy things in the ordinary way. In this, as in all other activities, he has gone beyond the normal rules of commerce and exchange. Instead he prefers to auction off what he might consider is spare among his properties and things. (When the ragseller—note—Echion considers a trade for the boy who shaves him, he thinks of "Barbering or auctioneering, or at least a little law." Where barbering is functional and removes a literal superfluity, the equation of law and auctioneering suggests more abstract ways in which to create values and other kinds of superfluity on which to live.) The most direct reference to the real economic situation is made by Ganymedes, who observes: "But nobody mentions the real thing, the way the price of bread is pinching. God knows, I couldn't buy a mouthful of bread today. And this damn drought goes on and on. Nobody's had a bellyful for years now . . . the fields are lying barren . . .";[33] this kind of discourse, however, is abruptly cut off, since its effect would be to put the whole occasion back into a social context, whence it has been deliberately extricated by a process of disguise and mystification exemplified in the cooking of the various dishes. Trimalchio's disinclination to look at the earth or the floor is not only related to

[32]Ibid., pp. 60, 44, 84.
[33]Ibid., pp. 55, 52–53.

his obsession with time and his fear of real death. It is part of his refusal to scrutinize the social conditions in which his hopelessly overprivileged position is grounded. Such a disinclination is also observable in the bourgeois novel, even if in less vivid forms.

Near the end of the feast a boy hands round a jar containing puns and conundrums. The pun in the jar may be taken with the Sybil of Cumae in the bottle as offering an indirect comment on the proceedings and the real inner condition of this society. For when all the goods have been unwrapped, all the containers opened, all the physical and mental appetites satiated with perverted forms, what is finally found at the center is one lingering trapped desire: "I want to die." Much more could be said about Trimalchio's feast of course, and I am only referring to it here as a kind of extreme paradigm of interrelated perversions of systems of relationships that occur less visibly and audibly in the bourgeois novel. But one more aspect of the book is worth mentioning here. At one point the action moves to Croton, which reveals in effect the reverse side of the economy earlier manifested at Trimalchio's feast. As an informant describes it: "Sirs, you are going to a place which is like a countryside ravaged by the plague, a place in which you will see only two things: the bodies of those who are eaten, and the carrion crows who eat them." In this town there are no fathers, for they are regarded as pariahs and only bachelors are honored. This points to an extreme negation of generation and continuity that is, indeed, present in one way or another throughout the book. The text ends as a fragment, but how suggestively! Eumolpus has made his will, in which he decrees that his beneficiaries can only inherit on condition that they eat his body. In defense of this stipulation he begins to cite precedents, and his speech, and the text, break off with the following. "And when a terrible famine struck Petelia, the people all became cannibals, and the only thing they gained from their diet was that they weren't hungry any more. And when Scipio captured Numantio, the Romans found a number of mothers cuddling the half-eaten bodies of their children in their laps. . . ."[34] This ultimate image of a society devouring its own products, its own human continuity, its own future, acts as silent comment on the self-annihilating society depicted throughout the book.

The social significance of eating is, of course, far too large a topic to be engaged here. But two comments from Mikhail Bakhtin's monumental work on *Rabelais and His World* are worth bringing in here.

> In the oldest system of images food was related to work. . . . Work triumphed in food. Human labor's encounter with the world and the

[34]Ibid., pp. 126, 165.

struggle against it ended in food, in the swallowing of that which had been wrested from the world.... It must be stressed that both labor and food were collective; the whole of society took part in them.... If food is separated from work and conceived as part of a private way of life, then nothing remains of the old images: man's encounter with the world and tasting the world, the open mouth, the relation of food and speech, the gay truth. Nothing is left but a series of artificial, meaningless metaphors.

Let us stress again... that banquet images in the popular-festive tradition... differ sharply from the images of private eating or private gluttony and drunkenness in early bourgeois literature. The latter express the contentment and satiety of the selfish individual, his personal enjoyment, and not the triumph of the people as a whole. Such imagery is torn away from the process of labor and struggle; it is removed from the marketplace and is confined to the house and private chamber (abundance in the home); it is no longer the "banquet for all the world," in which all take part, but an intimate feast with hungry beggars at the door.... It is a static way of private life, deprived of any symbolic openings and universal meaning, no matter whether it is represented as satire, that is, as purely negative, or as a positive state of well-being.[35]

Bakhtin's generalizations are perhaps extreme, but they force into focus the whole question of the meaning of the meal—beyond its nutritional function—in the bourgeois home. It can, I think, mean many subtler things than he indicates here, but the more general point is to note what, if any, significance the novelist locates or identifies in the meal (no significance at all is, of course, significant). In referring briefly to the *Satyricon,* I intended to offer a reminder of an extreme version of the degenerate or deformed feast. It is as though all the food in the world (except chaste bread and water) has been drawn together and subjected to concealing or distorting transformations for Trimalchio's table. Outside there is only famine, drought, plague, slaves, corpses, and crows. (This is not a literal account of the topography of the book, of course, but a comment on the topography of feeling it suggests.) Total abundance is offset by total privation. And in this total abundance, to stress it once more, sexual, linguistic, and economic relations are all perverted. The meal thus becomes a metaphor for all-embracing perversion—for what it ultimately bespeaks, in addition to the perversions I have mentioned, is a radical perversion in man's relationship to nature itself.

[35]Mikhael Bakhtin, *Rabelais and His World,* trans. Helene Iswolsky (Cambridge: M.I.T. Press, 1968), pp. 281–82, 301–2.

The City of the Nuptials

In Vico's study of the development of civil society, marriage is of course crucial, and it is worth recalling how elemental he regarded it to be in man's transition from chaos to order, which for Vico was also the shift from the nomadic to the settled state, from man as savage giant to man as articulate citizen. I will quote a passage at length:

504 Moral virtue began, as it must, from impulse. For the giants, enchained under the mountains by the frightful religion of the thunderbolts, learned to check their bestial habit of wandering wild through the great forest of the earth, and acquired the contrary custom of remaining hidden and settled in their fields. Hence they later became the founders of the nations and the lords of the first commonwealths. . . . Hence came Jove's title of stayer or establisher. With this impulse the virtue of the spirit began likewise to show itself among them, restraining their bestial lust from finding its satisfaction in the sight of heaven, of which they had a mortal terror. So it came about that each of them would drag one woman into his cave and would keep her there in perpetual company for the duration of their lives. Thus the act of human love was performed under cover, in hiding, that is to say, in shame; and they began to feel that sense of shame which Socrates described as the color of virtue. And this, after religion, is the second bond that keeps nations united, even as shamelessness and impiety destroy them.

505 In this guise marriage was introduced, which is a chaste carnal union consummated under the fear of some divinity. We made this the second principle of our Science, with its source in our first principle, which is divine providence. It arose accompanied by three solemnities.

506 The first of these solemnities was the auspices of Jove, taken from the thunderbolts by which the giants were induced to observe them. From this *sors*, or lot (signified by the auspices), marriage was defined among the Romans as *omnis vitae consortium*, a lifelong sharing of lot, and the husband and wife were called *consortes*, or lot sharers. . . . In this determinate guise and in this first time of the world arose the law of the gentes that the wife adopts the public religion of her husband. For the husbands shared their first human ideas with their wives, beginning with the idea of a divinity of theirs which compelled them to drag their women into their caves; and thus even this vulgar metaphysics began to know the human mind in God. . . .

507 From this most ancient origin of marriage came the custom by which women enter the families and houses of the men they marry. . . . Thus not merely must marriage have been from the beginning a union with one woman only, as it continued to be among the Romans . . . but it must also have been a union to last for life, as indeed remained the custom among a great many peoples. Hence among the Romans marriage was defined, with this property in view, as *individua vitae consuetudo,* unbroken companionship of life; and divorce was introduced very late among them.

. . . .

509   The second solemnity is the requirement that the women be veiled in token of that sense of shame that gave rise to the first marriages in the world. This custom has been preserved by all nations; among the Latins it is reflected in the very name "nuptials," for *nuptiae* is from *nubendo,* which means "to cover." . . .

510   The third solemnity—also preserved by the Romans—was a certain show of force in taking a wife, recalling the real violence with which the giants dragged the first wives into their caves. And by analogy with the first lands which the giants had occupied by taking physical possession of them, properly wedded wives were said to be *manucaptae,* taken by force.[36]

I am neither competent nor concerned to comment on the validity of Vico's social anthropology. Rather I want to stress the centrality of marriage in his vision of the emergence of man as a social rational being. The dark background from which social man emerged is always characterized for Vico by promiscuity and a liberty that was indistinguishable from bestiality: "the infamous promiscuity of things and women" is a recurring phrase in his considerations of the presocial state. It is marriage that enables men and women to pass naturally from the state of nature to that of culture; that is to say, it is marriage that comprehends that basically incomprehensible evolutionary gap between the mute isolate giant (we would say anthropoid) and the articulate socialized man.

554   And here it is worth reflecting how men in the feral state, fierce and untamed as they were, came to pass from their bestial liberty into human society. For in order that the first of them should reach that first kind of society which is matrimony, they had need of the sharp stimulus of bestial lust, and to keep them in it the stern restraints of frightful religions were necessary. Thus marriage emerged as the first kind of friendship in the world. . . . The Greek word for friendship, *philia,* is from the same root as *phileō,* to love; and from it is derived the Latin *filus,* son. *Philios* in Ionic Greek means friend, and mutation to a letter of similar sound yielded the Greek *phylé,* tribe.

Here again I am not concerned to pronounce on Vico's etymological explanations and connections. What is important is his sense that all those relationships that keep man in some sort of stable social structure of interrelations—lover, son, friend, tribe—derive from the same root,

[36] *The New Science of Giambattista Vico,* revised translation of the third edition (1744) by Thomas Goddard Bergin and Max Harold Fisch (Ithaca, N.Y.: Cornell University Press, 1968).

not only phonetically but historically or existentially, and that all relationships depend on and originate in a series of restraints.

More generally, marriage is connected to the emergence of man's ability to establish boundaries, which again is what distinguishes the human from the prehuman. Man is one who creates and guards confines. "The guarding of the confines began to be observed with bloody religions under the divine governments, for it was necessary to set up boundaries to the fields in order to put a stop to the infamous promiscuity of things in the bestial state. On these boundaries were to be fixed the confines first of families, then of gentes or houses, later of people, and finally of nations" (para. 982). The use of signs to establish boundaries, the use of objects to express ideas, and the use of money Vico sees to be interrelated activities that in turn can explain the interrelated origins of all sign systems. "All these truths will give us the origins of languages and letters, and thereby of hieroglyphs, laws, names, family coats of arms, medals, money, and of the language and writing in which the first natural law of the gentes was spoken and written" (para. 434). If human society begins with settlement and boundaries, then it begins with identification and division, and here again Vico sees a flood of interconnections, starting with a consideration of "family arms" "Again, a coat of arms was called by the Italian *insegna,* an ensign in the sense of a thing signifying, whence the Italian verb *insegnare,* to teach. They also call it *divisa,* device, because the ensigns were used as signs of the first division of the fields, which had previously been used in common by all mankind" (para. 486). There is a sense of a mythical moment of all-at-one-ness (for Vico's perpetual trilogical division of the stages of development of human institutions is atemporal and ahistorical, even if he does lay down a pattern according to which societies evolve and decline) when man can make boundaries, establish distinctions, and mark divisions all these activities being dependent on identifiable signs and identifiable families. This is the moment of exodus from that infamous promiscuity in which nothing is differentiated because all things are in common.

Once things and people and land become divided, then the problem is immediately posed of how they should be related. Hence the importance of contracts. Vico can just about envisage an ancient age in which men "take no cognizance of the contracts" (para. 570) and live off natural objects with no understanding of language or the use of money. Such people must have been, "so to speak, all body" (para. 570). But inasmuch as man makes divisions, he makes contracts and transactions, and for Vico these basic contracts are the use of money, the use of language, and marriage—all of which, we would now say, are forms of exchange. This is certainly not out of line with modern theories of social anthropology, but it is not my intention to attempt to assess Vico's contribution to that field. I want rather to give some sense of the vision of the central importance of marriage in the mind of this mid-eighteenth-century Enlightenment philosopher, because in his work there emerges the first full theory of the part played by marriage in human society *as it is created by the human mind* (which is of course his crucial and perhaps most original and influential insistence). It is only shortly thereafter that the novel will embark on a fictional exploration of this institution that I will suggest, finally laid bare its radical instability. If marriage is at the center, and the center cannot hold, what then? This too the novel turns its attention to, and by quoting at length from Vico I have only attempted to give some sense of how much else might be thought to be in danger if marriage fails, for what then happens to all those other *related* transactions and contracts by which and in which man himself is constituted as man? For Vico religion is the sanction behind marriage. "Hence, if religion is lost among the peoples, they have nothing left to enable them to live in society: no shield of defense, nor means of counsel, nor basis of support, nor even *a form by which they may exist in the world at all*" (para. 1109; my italics).[37] For nineteenth-century bourgeois society one might almost say that marriage sanctioned religion, and if it is in any way called into question or it disintegrates, then for those implicated and involved in its unstabilizing, the problem does indeed arise—is there another form by which they may exist in the world at all? That is the social problem that the novel concerned with adultery finally must confront; and at the same time it is a question it begins to ask with regard to its own *narrative* form.

Before ending this brief excursus into Vico, it is worth emphasizing just how vividly he imagined the chaos that preceded the emergence of marriage. "Chaos" is a "confusion of human seeds in the state of the infamous promiscuity of women" (para. 688). The ancient theological poets, says Vico, "imagined it as Orcus, a misshapen monster which devoured all things, because men in this infamous promiscuity did not have the proper form of men, and were swallowed up by the void because *through the uncertainty of offspring they left nothing of themselves.* This (chaos) was later taken by the physicists as the prime matter of natural things, which, formless itself, is greedy for forms and devours all forms" (para. 688; my italics). I will note only in passing that in the novel of adultery by a strange inversion form can become greedy for formlessness, and there are recurrent signs of a regressive quest for the unstructured or prestructured state. Chaos is a state in which there are no

---

[37] "*Without the Christian Faith,*' Pascal thought, 'you, no less than nature and history, will become for yourselves *un monstre et un chaos.*' This prophecy we have fulfilled. . . ." Thus Nietzsche in *The Will to Power* (bk. 1, section 83).

marriages, and hence no identification of offspring, and hence an inability to establish names. "The marriage ceremony identifies the father" (Vico cites the jurisprudential maxim *Nuptiae demonstrant patrem,* [para. 587]), and the father names as he commands the children. The plebeians were precisely those who "could not name their fathers" (para. 587) because "they could not contract solemn matrimony" (para. 987). This calculated deprivation did indeed render the plebeians aliens, inasmuch as they could not bequeath property either to kin directly or by testament, since they were not citizens. The right of citizenship was indistinguishable from the right to contract marriage. This leads Vico to a vivid reading of the famous shield of Achilles, from which I will, once again, quote at length.

682 (1) At the beginning there could be seen thereon the sky, the earth, the sea, the sun, the moon, and the stars. This is the epoch of the creation of the world.

683 (2) Thereafter were depicted two cities. In the one there were songs, hymeneals and nuptials: the epoch of the heroic families including only children born of solemn nuptials. In the other there were no such things to be seen; this represented the epoch of the heroic families with their *famuli,* who contracted only natural marriages with none of the solemn rites which surrounded heroic nuptials. . . .

684 (3) Then, in the aforesaid city of the nuptials, the shield showed parliaments, laws, trials, and punishments. This accords with the answer of the Roman patricians to the plebs in the heroic contests, declaring that nuptials, *imperium,* and priesthoods, on the last of which depended the science of laws and hence judgments, were all their own exclusive institutions since the auspices which constituted the chief solemnity of nuptials were theirs. For this reason *viri,* men (which meant among the Latins the same as heroes among the Greeks), was the term applied to husbands in solemn matrimony, to magistrates, to priests, and finally to judges. . . .

685 (4) The other city is under armed siege and the two cities prey on each other by turns; hence the city without nuptials (the plebs of the heroic cities) becomes a separate and hostile city. . . . The two cities, regarding each other as alien, carried on eternal hostilities against each other. . . .

The two cities represent many differences, but the crucial one is between those who live within the ceremony of matrimony and those who are excluded from it or have to exist outside it. For Vico this is first and foremost a version of history and the evolution of society, but the metaphors on the shield still have their power and relevance, as read by Vico. For in society as it was discerned until comparatively recent times (how we think of it now is an entirely new problem), the crucial difference was between those living in the City of the Nuptials and those living in the City without Nuptials. Of course it was possible to pass from the latter to the former—indeed much of the history of the novel is concerned with that transition or translation. But what happens to those who—if not literally, then metaphorically—leave the City of the Nuptials, violating the permanence that for Vico was a basic constituent of marriage, breaking up what should be "unbroken," negating the contracts on which the City is founded? Those who in a categorical sense return to the City without Nuptials? For this precisely is what the act of adultery involves, no matter how secretly it is conducted. Adultery challenges the City of the Nuptials with the unthinkable—its own impermanence and instability. To want to join the City is one thing, and many are the ceremonies of welcome that attend the moment of initiation. But to want to leave it, whether by thought, word, or deed, that is quite another. And when this happens, then an old truth reasserts itself in contemporary guise, and we are reminded that "the city without nuptials . . . becomes a separate and hostile city" and "the two cities, regarding each other as alien, carried on eternal hostilities against each other." That ancient enmity reappears in the nineteenth-century novel, in various muted forms and mutations, of course, but it is nevertheless there, as the novel of adultery reveals. And the problem is only compounded for those who discover that the City without Nuptials is now *inside* the City of the Nuptials; then the departure recoils on itself, and any hopes for an escape to the "outside" turn into new torments involved in being an alien within the City. This is at once both to exist and not to exist, to leave without departing, to be excluded without being removed and to be excommunicated while still remaining within the prevailing circuits of communication. It is to be discategorized without literally being displaced.

In one sense the City of the Nuptials "owns" everything, for as Vico reads the shield of Achilles, the City has appropriated all the important signs. To explain this, it is necessary to remember that Vico insists that the "auspices" are "the first principle of everything that we have discussed in this work" (para. 1050). Auspices derive from watching or studying the birds and interpreting the signs, and seems to be the root activity at the basis of human society for Vico.[38] In the first age, the age of god, "the gentiles believed they lived under divine governments, and everything was commanded them by auspices and oracles, which are the oldest institutions in profane history" (para. 31). As long as the ruling class (the nobles) retain the auspices (i.e., the meaning of signs), they also retain control over the laws that bind everyone: they keep them "in a secret language as a sacred thing" (para. 32). And in his section concerning "The Guarding of the Institutions" Vico spells out the full signifi-

---

[38]Cf. *Macbeth,* act 3, scene 4, in which Macbeth indicates his belief in "Augures and understood relations" as being able to bring forth "The secret'st man of blood."

cance of this. "We may understand from this how much discernment the embellishers of the Law of the Twelve Tables fixed in the eleventh table, the article *Auspicia incommunicata plebi sunto*—"The auspices shall be withheld from the plebs"—for on these originally depended all civil institutions both public and private, which were thus all kept within the order of the nobles. The private institutions were solemn matrimony, paternal power, direct heirs, agnates, gentiles, legitimate succession, testaments, and guardianships" (para. 985). If we translate this into the conditions obtaining in bourgeois society, we may say that it is the propertied class who retain the auspices and attempt to withhold them from the lower classes, only *auspices* may now be taken to imply the signs and laws that order and shape society. To put it another way, we may say that not only do the propertied classes own land, capital, and machinery, but they also own the discourses that serve to define and regulate the various strata and groups within society.[39] Just as, from another point of view, we can say that men owned the signs that defined women and determined their role and position in society. Revolution at one level is nothing more or less than a disappropriation of the signs hitherto owned by a privileged class, or a challenging of what Lacan calls "the master words of the city"—("les maîtres-mots de la cité"). The City without the Nuptials may be seen as that part of a society that has no access to the auspices, or no control over the signs. Thus, the struggle between the two cities takes on a significance that goes far beyond the right to have access to the marriage ceremony, for it involves a struggle over the source of social signification. And the result is not quite what Vico reads in the shield. For when two cities fight against each for long enough, there can only be one final outcome; they destroy each other. The hostilities may be very long but they are not eternal. Adultery ultimately

---

[39]Cf. Marx:

> The ideas of the ruling class are in every epoch the ruling ideas, i.e. the class which is the ruling material force of society is at the same time its ruling intellectual force. The class which has the means of material production at its disposal, has control at the same time over the means of mental production, so that thereby, generally speaking, the ideas of those who lack the means of mental production are subject to it. The ruling ideas are nothing more than the ideal expression of the dominant material relationships, the dominant material relationships grasped as ideas; hence of the relationships which make the one class the ruling one, therefore, the ideas of its dominance. The individuals composing the ruling class possess among other things consciousness, and therefore think. In so far, therefore, as they rule as a class and determine the extent and compass of an epoch, it is self-evident that they do this in its whole range, hence among other things rule also as thinkers, as producers of ideas, and regulate the production and distribution of the ideas of their age: thus their ideas are the ruling ideas of the epoch.

(*The German Ideology*, in Marx, *Selected Writings*, ed. David McLellan [Oxford: Oxford University Press, 1977], p. 176.)

involves a two-way cancellation—of those who commit it and of those who condemn it. For what the deed, in the context of bourgeois society, implicitly states is this: The victories of the City of the Nuptials may be many, as its force is unquestionably greater. But it cannot stand forever.

Let me conclude this section with a quotation from Shakespeare, one that, among other things, gives I think some insight into why he seems so obsessed with all kinds of maneuverings and games with rings in his plays.

> PRIEST: A contract of eternal bond of love,
> Confirm'd by mutual joinder of your hands,
> Attested by the holy close of lips,
> Strengthen'd by interchangement of your rings;
> And all the ceremony of this compact
> Seal'd in my function, by my testimony.
>
> (*Twelfth Night,* act 5, scene 1)

The priest's description of how a marriage is conducted indicates just how many ideas and conventions that are crucial to the upholding of society converge in that transaction. The vocabulary alone gives some sense of the range of interconnected social acts: contract, bond, confirmation, mutuality, joining, attestation, interchangement, ceremony, compact, testimony—these are the various versions of exchange and ratified relationship on which the social structure depends, and under the auspices of the priest in the marriage ceremony, they are conceived of as being eternally binding, a defying of the fluctuations of time. Hands and lips are exactly the two parts of the body that man uses in an attempt to take hold of the world, whether simply to establish contact or to appropriate and possess—at the most basic level by mancipation and eating, at the cultural level also by construction and articulation. The holding and kissing of the bride thus becomes an ideal paradigm of the most balanced way of entering into a contractual and mutual relationship with the socialized world that man inhabits, a paradigm that is symbolized by the man-made object of the ring, which among other things suggests a continuous circuit of exchange, not one based on opposition and hostile unconnectedness.

If the making of a marriage draws all these things together, then the breaking of a marriage must suggest a collapse back into a state of severance and separateness in which bonds and contracts do not hold, modes of joining and interchanging are rendered dubious, confirmation and testimony are no longer to be trusted, while mutuality fades and ceremony becomes an empty show, a matter of dress and gesture rather than sanction and ratification. In such a state of affairs the ring only emphasizes the state of cohabiting solitudes into which man and woman have fallen. Such a society would not be unlike the one Vico imagined that could not agree on a monarch (or, we might say, a single governing principle or source of authority—a common point of social belief such as, I am suggesting, the institution of marriage became for nineteenth-century society).

> **1106** ... For such peoples, like so many beasts, have fallen into the custom of each man thinking only of his own private interests and have reached the extreme of delicacy, or better of pride, in which like wild animals they bristle and lash out at the slightest displeasure. Thus no matter how great the throng and press of their bodies, they live like wild beasts in a deep solitude of spirit and will, scarcely any two being able to agree since each follows his own pleasure or caprice. By reason of all this, providence decrees that, through obstinate factions and desperate civil wars, they shall turn their cities into forests and the forests into dens and lairs of men. In this way, through long centuries of barbarism, rust will consume the misbegotten subtleties of malicious wits that have turned them into beasts made more inhuman by the barbarism of reflection than the first men had been made by the barbarism of sense.

By analogy we may say that if the marriage bond is rendered unstable— and that is the ultimate implication of adultery—then by extension nothing in society is truly "bonded," and the state of chaos envisaged here in graphic terms by Vico may recommence at the very center of the most civilized society. As though by some reverse mythical all-at-once-ness, society at its heart returns to that "infamous promiscuity of things and women" from which man, by means above all of the idea of marriage, first emerged into true social humanity.

Law and the River

The Mill on the Floss begins and ends with an embrace in the river. At the start it is an embrace between the river and the sea, a projection of the idea of a human union by the narrator on what is simply a continuum in nature. To conceive of an embrace, you must first have the idea of separation, reunion can only follow division—these are the problems of the human social world that the novel explores. At the end the embrace is between Maggie and Tom returning to the union of childhood as they drown. The oppositions within the book are suggested by the topography referred to in the title, the man-made structure adjacent to the undifferentiated fluidity of nature. This opposition is recapitulated in different forms, for the rigid vertical of the mill and the horizontal flow of the river offer an underlying paradigm for many tensions discerned in the narrative and experienced by the characters—tensions between the obligations of property and the importunities of passion; between familial and social bonds and ties and unanticipated and unpatterned private promptings of desire; between culture, law, and nature; ultimately between life and death. Many of these tensions center on the relationship between Maggie and Stephen, who, while not officially committed to other partners, feel themselves to be in different ways engaged; thus they are both partly bound and partly free, and this introduces a problematical space in which their struggle takes place. At this point I want to consider some aspects of the evolving morphology of this struggle as it is described by George Eliot, concentrating on details from book 6.

It opens with "A Duet in Paradise," a chapter title that, coming as it does after the book title "The Great Temptation" immediately sets up ironic expectations and produces a sense of unease, for the Temptation has a greater prominence than the paradisal interlude and thus promises to be the larger context. The harmony of that first chapter, a social harmony centering on what seems to be the eminently rational and suitable pairing of Stephen and Lucy, is made to seem precarious in advance, and we are of course aware of the single figure of Maggie, a figure in many ways imperfectly assimilated into the social patterns within which she moves. She stands slightly apart, watching the progress of the socially sanctioned courtship, reading it from the outside. An example of this is provided by her habit of playing with musical patterns *after* Lucy and Stephen—who sing together—have gone out. Maggie significantly delights in the "concord of octaves" more than melody, tasting "by abstraction the more primitive sensation of intervals." These intervals might be likened to the prescribed intervals between people that are supposed to produce the appropriate social harmony. Maggie has an abstract appreciation of these intervals, but experience will take her into a violation of them, into a problematical private melody that is pure dissonance to the social ear.

The attraction between Maggie and Stephen really commences when it is thought to be over and "the spell seems broken." At the dance when Stephen waltzes with Maggie, the process is effectively set in motion. The dance occupies a peculiar position in the range of social activities—a kind of licensed vertigo—that plays a crucial role in, for example, *Madame Bovary* and *Anna Karenina*. The effects on Maggie of the dance are to make her feel "a keen vibrating consciousness poised beyond pleasure or pain. This one, this last night, she might expand unrestrainedly in the warmth of the present, without those chill eating thoughts of the past and the future". While dancing they indulge in a long "mutual gaze" that seems to isolate them from the eyes of society. The important aspects of this gaze are the vivid consciousness, the sense of unrestrained expansion, and the momentary release from chronology it bespeaks; all, however, contained within the restraining area of the drawing room. The brief venture outside the room when they are alone and Stephen covers Maggie's arm with kisses has a very different quality. For Maggie it is like a "leprosy," contaminating the momentary happiness experienced while dancing. The return to the drawing room is accompanied by a conviction that "duty would be easy." But a fissure has been made in her rigid carapace of moral and social ideas, and this gap widens on the boat trip that they take together. This of course is the crisis of the book in terms of Maggie's experience. Prior to it Stephen pleads with her about the arbitrariness of "ties that were made in blindness," but the whole matter remains at the level of debate, since Maggie's habitual mode of thinking has not been altered. It is a contest of abstractions. But the chapter entitled "Borne along by the Tide," perhaps deliberately numbered "13," renders a very different kind of experience in which language is annulled and with it a grasp of the distinctions and intervals that are the separating and uniting rules of the society that Maggie inhabits.

The boat trip that brings Stephen and Maggie alone together—in itself a discordant conjunction in the eyes of society—comes about because of apparent problems of number and arrangement. All four of the people involved—Lucy and Stephen, Maggie and Philip—are in varying degrees in favor of the idea of going boating, and it is initially decided that they should go in threes, the men accompanying the women on different days. This arrangement is upset, and Maggie, expecting Philip, finds herself with Stephen. The boat trip is deliberately described in terms of a move from the city to the field, using the topographic metaphors I outlined in an earlier section, so that starting from within familiar territory and landmarks, Maggie suddenly finds that they have traveled so far they are "out of sight" of the known domain. "No village was to be seen". The journey on the gliding water induces a loss of volition and an exclusion of memory, and above all a temporary disinclination to participate in language and thought. All is passivity, silence, "absence". This absence is ambiguous. Earlier Maggie had been wondering whether life had to be a "self-imposed wearisome banishment" or whether it might not offer her the "fulness of existence" her "nature craved." The problem here is whether life within society offers only a negative existence, an absence, that prompts the consideration of whether some longed-for plenitude might be found outside of social prescriptions.

In the event, she finds that what might have looked like a fulness from within the city turns out to be another kind of absence once outside it. Stephen tries to persuade her that the choice has come "without their seeking," an attempt to displace responsibility from themselves onto the irresistible currents of nature. Maggie temporarily yields to this abdication of responsibility and allows herself to drift with the river, to succumb almost entirely to the "fatal intoxication" of the moment, almost allowing herself to be deprived of the right to make any choices. But the abandonment is not complete. "All yielding is attended with a less vivid consciousness than resistance; it is the partial sleep of thought; it is the submergence of our own personality by another. Every influence tended to lull her into acquiescence. . . ." The *partial* sleep of thought. Here indeed is the central anguish. While her contact with Stephen at the dance induced a more vivid consciousness, once outside the city that vividness is transformed into a torpor. Thought is almost entirely erased as its habitual modes of operating are dissolved in the atmosphere of dream induced by the river and the venture into extrasocial territory. But thought is not obliterated completely, and it is at this point that the relatively uncomplicated move from the city to the field is made problematical by the temple of conscience. The physical move yields to the torments of an interiority that cannot be wholly negated. The point at which thought approaches a degree-zero state is aptly accompanied by Stephen's insistence on covering Maggie with a cloak, as if to muffle any residual resistant consciousness. And shortly after this he takes her on board the Dutch ship and tries to reclassify her as "my wife." But although at this point she feels "entirely passive" and on board the ship she lapses into a state in which "nothing was distinct" and everything in her mind is "melting and dissolving" like the evening sky, she is aware that there are thoughts that will "presently avenge themselves for this oblivion." Oblivion is inevitably followed by "waking" (a rhythm that can be traced back to Euripides), and that is the title of the next chapter.

When she wakes up she finds herself alone, but memory has returned, and with it, dread. Memory can act as a faculty that denies the possibility of any radically new future by preempting the present with the admonishments and perceptual patterns of the past. It is the opposite of genuine hope. Thus for Maggie the temporal move into the future is a return to the past in which everything is the same except her relationship to it. Hence the feeling of dread. Everything is distant again in the old terms; in waking she is precipitated back into the language, and hence the concepts and classifications, that she had temporarily left behind. The tyranny of this established language is absolute, and the terror that Maggie feels results from her unarticulated sense that she must reinsert herself into a social discourse that will deny her any social identity. The dominance of memory over hope eliminates the possibility of conceiving of any alternative mode of action. Waking up, then, amounts to a reassumption of a vocabulary that effectively prescribes her own annihilation. Any other way is foreclosed: "she had rent the ties that had given meaning to duty, and had made herself an outlawed soul with no guide but the wayward choice of her own passion. And where would that lead her?—where had it led her now? She had said she would rather die than fall into that temptation. . . . Her life with Stephen could have no sacredness: she must forever sink and wander vaguely driven by uncertain impulses; for she had let go the clue of life—that clue which once in the far-off years her young need had clutched so strongly." Maggie wakens to social law and defines herself as "outlawed." This is very important, for it equates the wakeful state with the existing social state and thus with the truly real; outside this law, there is only dream and oblivion—not an *alternative* reality but a temporary absence of it. Other novelists—for instance, Tolstoi—can envisage the reverse of this proposition and imagine a person waking to a reality that is precisely what is not contained within the social law and that makes society seem unreal. For Maggie there is no reality outside of the ties that give meaning to duty. She herself cannot generate new meanings, for meaning itself is possessed by the past. For Maggie, "the field" is a semantic void, and so whatever the consequences, she can only struggle back to "the city," into a realm of law and meaning that will negate her as her brother Tom negates her. He is a dominant, socially orthodox male who is not only a property owner but an owner of the right to define, condemn, and dismiss—as he does Maggie. There is no conceivable possibility of her renaming him and the whole male-dominated society he represents. And this is the ultimate form of her plight; that she can no longer exist in either realm, for in fact she carries the voice of "the city," or Tom's voice, with her into "the field," and she can never fully escape its audibility, whether inside or outside her.

This is what Stephen has to confront as he tries to argue with Maggie, invoking "natural law" and pointing to the "hollowness" of "constancy without love." But Maggie keeps returning to the past and its binding patterns. She will admit of no reformulation of those patterns in the name of an alternative vocabulary. Hence the claustrophobia of the room in the inn where the debate takes place. Stephen can only walk back and forth, stamp his feet, sit down and get up again; while Maggie only blushes, presses her fingers together, glances at Stephen and away from him. They are really cramped up in the room of an old language from which, as far as Maggie is concerned, there can be no escape. All she can think of is going home, going back, reentering the past—"else I shall feel as if there were nothing firm beneath my feet." Her resolve then is based on an ontological anxiety as powerful, if not more so, than the social, religious, and moral scruples that bind her consciousness to the past. The people who compose the "abstraction, called society which served to make their consciences perfectly easy in doing what satisfied their own egoism," people as "rigidly fixed" in their narrow perspectives and inadequate vocabularies as Tom is, nevertheless comprise the realm that for Maggie constitutes true being. For her the possibility of a temporary widening of consciousness in "the field" could only be experienced as a loss of true consciousness. The "temple" of her mind finally turns out to be an adjunct of "the city," in which she can experience the most intense anguish but cannot reformulate the imperatives and definitions of the past. What is tragic in this position is that whereas Maggie withheld meaning from herself while in her extrasocial position with Stephen, she has meaning withheld from her by society when she returns to it—just as Tom refuses to let her into her old home. "You don't belong to me." It is the cruelest and most painful statement in the book, for ultimately she belongs to nobody else. He *is* the past that owns her.

Hence the ending of the book, entitled ambiguously "The Final Rescue," is ultimately a return to the "Boy and Girl" relationship of the first book. George Eliot describes Maggie's reception back into society, which is a general nonrecognition and condemnation mitigated by occasional individual kindnesses and loyalties and sympathies. But there is no real possibility of a future, and Maggie's cry to herself, "how long will it be before death comes," brings out the impossibility of her existence. The answer to her question is supplied with extreme promptness by the author, for almost immediately Maggie feels the first of the flood water in which she will meet her end. That flood is described with deliberate echoes of the first book of Genesis—"a perception that the darkness was divided by the faintest light, which parted the overhanging gloom from the immeasurable watery level below." But instead of the primal creation of the cosmos by God, who divides the sea from the sky by the land, these words presage the terminal dissolution of Maggie in a recovered and regressive union with Tom, as described by George Eliot; not the establishment of a divine order but the conclusion of a fictional one. But there is one other factor present at their death that is worth noting—the "huge fragments" of "wooden machinery" that have drifted loose from the wharves. For these fragments are parts of the industrial and economic dimension of society that can break loose and endanger the inhabitants of that society. Maggie and Tom die like the little children they once were, obliterated by both the waters of the earth and the machinery of the society of their age—in effect by the mill and the Floss. For Maggie this is the only way back: it is the ultimate return.

They sat mutely gazing at each other: Maggie with eyes of intense life looking out from a weary, beaten face—Tom pale with a certain awe and humiliation. Thought was busy though the lips were silent: and though he could ask no question, he guessed a story of almost miraculous divinely-protected effort. But at last a mist gathered over the blue gray eyes, and the lips found a word they could utter: the old childish—"Magsie".

Maggie could make no answer but a long sob of that mysterious wondrous happiness that is one with pain.

They have regressed to an almost prelingual state: she is not Maggie Tulliver now, nor even just Maggie, but "Magsie." This kind of regression, associated with water, I shall refer to as thalassic, following Sandor Ferenczi's use of the word in *Thalassa*—it is a significantly frequent feature in the novel of adultery. In this particular case the feeling at the end of the book is unmistakably incestuous. Whether or not one would allow that there is any unconscious double entendre in Tom's last words to Maggie— " 'It is coming, Maggie!' Tom said, in a deep hoarse voice, losing the oars, and clasping her"—the final paragraph of the book suggests a final orgasmic love-death more commonly associated with sexual lovers than with brother and sister. "The boat reappeared—but brother and sister had gone down in an embrace never to be parted: living through again in one supreme moment the days when they had clasped their little hands in love, and roamed the daisied fields together." This is not just Victorian sentimentality. There are cases when the bourgeois novel avoids adultery only by permitting and even pursuing something that is very close to incest.

The Drawing Room and the Railway

In *The Kreutzer Sonata* Tolstoi establishes a narrative situation in which a man, Pózdnyshev, gives his account of how he killed his wife, whom he considered guilty of adultery. The novella can be, and has been, read as Tolstoi's own statement of his extreme views on marriage and women. But such a version fails to take account of the narrative situation. The setting is a train going on a long journey, with people coming and going in and out of compartments as they get on and off. This suggests a model of certain forms of contemporary life, old ties and bonds easily loosened, the fragmentation of community and the diffusion of destination. In addition, natural routines and rhythms are disturbed; places flow together, artificial light replaces the stable alternations of night and day, and the changing group of people in the railway carriage are not related in any way except through random contiguity—a fortuitous aggregate, not a unit. The train journey produces wakefulness and contributes to feelings of nervousness and anxiety. As Pózdnyshev tells his story to the listening narrator, he chain-smokes and drinks very strong tea. His eyes wander from object to object, settling nowhere, and he evinces a compulsion both to remove himself from the sight of others and to tell his story.

In the carriage a debate commences concerning modern love and marriage, and a spectrum of attitudes is voiced by, among others, an emancipated woman, who speaks for the idea of modern marriage based on free choice instead of parental arrangement, and an old merchant, who—having admitted his own dissipation—suddenly attacks this idea and blames education for contributing to the ruin of marriage. He believes in the inflexibility of the old law and maintains that marriage should be based on the fear of the woman for the man. A lawyer participates in the discussion with a sort of bland neutrality, as though not believing in the merchant's notion of putting the institution before the individuals and accepting the new interest in divorce in Europe. Then a man, as yet unnamed, questions the terms being used. "What kind of love . . . is it that sanctifies marriage?" The lawyer translates the term into more legal language, adding that marriage should be based on a "natural attachment," while the lady says "Love is an exclusive preference for one above everybody else." This provokes the question—"a preference for how long?" Once the question of the duration of predilection is raised and marriage is deeternalized, as it were, then the whole institution becomes endlessly debatable—as the opening of Tolstoi's novella dramatizes. If not "forever and a day," then why not a day less than forever—or perhaps only just a day? (This problem of relating the fluctuating longevity of desire with the scripted bonds of a contract is one that is considered in detail in Goethe's *Die Wahlverwandtschaften*.) To the problem of "How long?" may be added the question of "How many?" "Out of a thousand men who marry . . . there is hardly one who has not already been married ten, a hundred, or even, like Don Juan, a thousand times, before his wedding,"[40] says Pózdnyshev, in which case the marriage contract loses the significance of its singleness, and thence its validity as a transaction. And where Pózdnyshev raises the problems posed by promiscuity before marriage, adultery raises the problem of the mathematics of transgression, a prob-

[40]Leo Tolstoi, *The Kreutzer Sonata,* in *Great Short Works of Leo Tolstoy,* trans. Louise Maude and Aylmer Maude (New York: Harper & Row, 1967), pp. 360, 361, 369.

lem nowhere so tersely formulated as in the agonized cry of Posthumus to Iachimo when he has been convinced of Imogen's infidelity. "Spare your arithmetic. Never count the turns. / Once, and a million." (This is to be the fate of Madame Bovary, who turns, and turns, and turns, until she enters a state of mortal vertigo.)

What Pózdnyshev is driving at is that it is impossible to ground the stability of marriage on any kind of voluntary response on the part of the individuals concerned. He also mocks the idea of a marriage based on "spiritual affinity" (and the problem of combining, or confusing, spiritual and corporeal affinities is at the center of Goethe's *Die Wahlverwandschaften*). The question—an eternal one, but one raised in a specifically acute form in the novels I shall be considering—is, just what, in terms of law, can bind the variant volatility of a committed pair? If it is not "something sacramental, a mystery binding them in the sight of God," as the lady claims, then it is all a matter of copulation, deception, and purchase, so runs Pózdnyshev's argument—men treat women as commodities, or as serfs or Jews, and they in turn transform themselves into objects and instruments of pleasure. The relationship is related to the market economy where, in Marxist terms, exchange values have replaced use values. Women spend much of their time in shops where they, as it were, absorb the commodity status of the objects they consume. Property considerations have taken the place of human recognitions. In Pózdnyshev's terms "real debauchery lies precisely in freeing oneself from moral relations with a woman with whom you have physical intimacy." In these conditions proximity only engenders hatred, marriage is a hollow space in society, an "abyss of misery and . . . horrible falsehood" that becomes a living hell for the partners. Thus, in place of a relationship there are two alien egotists forced to confront the antirelationship in which they are trapped and in which mating and hating have become inextricably intermixed—a condition that Richardson and Goethe and even James describe as "monstrous" ("Marriage then is what you call the monster?" *The Golden Bowl*). One result of existing in this state is the befogging of consciousness, whether by a compulsive immersion in household affairs or with cigarettes and alcohol. "Thus we lived in a perpetual fog, not seeing the condition we were in." Emma Bovary, too, finds that her mind enters a state of postmarital fog; and just as Pózdnyshev's "thoughts go round and round in a circle of insoluble contradictions,"[41] so do Emma's, and Flaubert spends much of his time tracing her ordeal by fog and circulation. Anna Karenina with her morphine and mobility is a similar case.

[41] Ibid., pp. 362, 393, 380, 414; Henry James, *The Golden Bowl* (New York: Popular Library, 1973), bk. 1, pt. 1, ch. 2, p. 19.

It is worth mentioning one other aspect of Pózdnyshev's intense disillusion with the "monstrosity" of marriage. In his revulsion from the pollution through contradiction of the marriage bed he speaks for the desirability of "brotherly relations with a woman." Indeed, in a variant reading in the lithographed version that was privately circulated in Russia, when Pózdnyshev sees his wife as a woman and a human being for the first time, namely when she is dying, it is added that he sees her as "a sister."[42] This desire to replace the problematical contract of man and wife with the intrafamilial union of brother and sister reveals a latent, if faint, yearning for an incestuous relationship to avoid an adulterous one. This is a matter that emerged in Rousseau's *La Nouvelle Héloïse*—in a particularly dramatic way, as I will describe—just as I have suggested it is detectable in *Mill on the Floss.*

This indictment of marriage in contemporary society is articulated by a person who has broken out of the institution through violence and madness. He is in a postmarriage realm in which all his human relationships have been cut or dissolved—even his children have been separated from him. He is thus in a void from which he can look back and see marriage and society in a different way from those still inside the institutions. He now sees "Everything reversed, everything reversed!" and while this means that his discourse on marriage is not privileged, there is a peculiar—if deranged—force in his deconventionalized, or postconventionalized, vision. Society now seems like an intricate "brothel" to him. Those things that we regard as maintaining the home or embroidering society—good meals, fine clothes, uniforms, ornaments, dances, social gatherings—are all seen as helping to precipitate large amounts of dangerous and polluting sensuality. Bourgeois marriage is now seen as an impossible contradiction in which the woman supposedly belongs to the man to produce and nurse his children but is also supposed to spend time and money on making herself attractive to society at large. This impossible combination of ownership, production, and salesmanship is related to the economic practice of society in which people are supposed to live both with each other as a social unit and against each other as individual competitors and entrepreneurs. What Pózdnyshev has seen is that the drawing room is in fact modeled on the market that is so scrupulously excluded from visibility. As a result he has become an inverted libertine, now considering the sexual act itself as unnatural. When it is put to him that without it the human race would cease to exist, he says, "But why live? If life has no aim, if life is given us for life's sake, there is no reason for living."[43] He is in the unhappy position of having a con-

[42]Tolstoi, *The Kreutzer Sonata,* pp. 367, 448.
[43]Ibid., pp. 365, 371, 377.

sciousness aware of its own absolute contingency; life has no meaning, but it permits suffering, brutality, exploitation, and irrevocable acts. He has become a voice without a context, a sleepless talker on an endless railway journey.

His story concerns his increasing estrangement from his wife, the nausea that followed sexual satiety, the rows that took the place of any reciprocity, the growing misery of proximity without mutuality, the growing impossibility of either staying together or finding ways to separate. But in describing how his wife started a flirtation with a musician who plays duets with her, and how this grew into a clandestine adulterous relationship, he reveals two interesting psychological traits. For one thing he found himself not only not repelling the suspected rival but actively drawing him closer, lavishing invitations and good meals on him, thus encouraging the presence that is supposedly a torture to Pózdnyshev. In a social life in which Pózdnyshev avails himself of all kinds of stimulants and intoxicants to numb himself to his real condition, the rival becomes the most indispensable intoxicant.

The second notable trait is his habit of projection. He notes every word, gesture, glance and "attributed them with importance." He fancies, surmises, and interprets. He is in fact creating the situation he considers to be evolving (cf. my comments on Shakespeare's late plays in "The Stranger in the House"). He is indeed half aware of this, but when he does come home and see them together, he is sure that reality and imagination have at last coincided. Or as we say, for him the imaginary has become the real. And this is how he wishes things to be. When he enters the scenario he has effectively invented, the musician runs away, and Pózdnyshev, without his shoes, does not pursue him because "I remembered that it is ridiculous to run after one's wife's lover in one's socks; and I did not wish to be ridiculous, but terrible." He wills himself into being taken over by rage, anger, and madness—out of the world of shoes and stockings and into a realm of increasing intensity of passion. For this is the point about his killing of his wife: It is the final intoxicant. The way he describes his stabbing her, feeling the "resistance of her corset" and then the "plunging of the dagger into something soft"[44] presents his action as an ultimate deformation of the sexual act. And this

---

[44]Ibid., pp. 402, 423, 424. It is worth noting what might be called the overvaluation of clothes, or the displacement of emotions onto garments, so frequent in nineteenth-century novels. What Pózdnyshev regards as conclusive evidence of the adultery is the sight of a man's coat in the hall, rather as Othello takes the handkerchief as sufficient "ocular proof" that his wife is a whore—though there is hardly any magic in the web of Trukhachevski's coat. It is as though a generalized sense of the primacy of vestments has infiltrated the passional flow, introducing stimulations, irritations, and hesitations into it. In Pózdnyshev's case a coat can take him too far, and footwear can hold him back.

is an indictment of bourgeois marriage even more severe than any he himself has articulated. In a society in which there is no available criterion of sufficiency, no concept of enough, then everything is potentially to be consumed. This extends from the market realm to the bedroom, and it includes the possibility of willing oneself to be consumed by ever more extreme feelings, as we say that a person is consumed with anger. To this end the partner may also be consumed, annihilated to feed an obsession, a hunger for ever more extreme sensations that arises out of the intolerable void of the marriage itself.

Pózdnyshev concludes his account by a description of visiting his wife on her deathbed. He enters still considering roles—shall he be magnanimous and forgive her?—and it is only when he looks at her that he actually *sees* her for the first time. "I looked at the children and at her bruised disfigured face, and for the first time I forgot myself, my rights, my pride, and for the first time saw a human being in her. And so insignificant did all that had offended me, all my jealousy, appear, and so important what I had done that I wished to fall with my face to her hand, and say: 'Forgive me,' but dared not do so." He does at last ask for forgiveness, but the dying woman is so totally alienated from him that she finally just does not recognize him. This is the moment of terrible waking, a very different waking from that of Maggie Tulliver, but also involving a return to reality. In this case, however, it is the first time he has actually seen his wife in her unique otherness. He has lived his whole life in estrangement from his real condition and the reality of other people, regarding her as a commodity or a positive or negative intoxicant—as though marriage had become another kind of factory for the reification of people, or an extension of the shop in which handing money over the counter could be gradually transformed into plunging a dagger into the body. The most moving part in the story is when he describes the moment that he realizes what he had actually done— stripped of all fantasy, obsession, and distorted appetites. "Only when I saw her dead face did I understand all that I had done. I realised that I, I had killed her; that it was my doing that she, living, moving, warm, had now become motionless, waxen, and cold, and that this could never, anywhere, or by any means, be remedied."[45] Only in this moment of true vision does Pózdnyshev see through to the nonsocial realities of life and death. The sight of his wife as a *corpse*—finally beyond use of any other kind of instrumentality—is a moment of complete demystification from which he can never recover. He is awake in an extreme desolation of consciousness. After the hell of the drawing room, with its fog of falsifi-

[45]Ibid., pp. 427, 428.

cations, he is now experiencing the torment of the railway carriage, left alone with the dreadful bleakness of truth.

This truth is such that it cannot be contained within any of the theories or beliefs advanced by the other representatives of society in the train—the merchant, who speaks for a kind of absolutism based on property and trade; the emancipated lady who speaks for the realm of ideas that have not been tested in practice; and the lawyer who speaks for a relativization of law that offers official secular sanction to the rearrangements that society finds desirable. In different ways they all live within "the city," but to the clarified gaze of Pózdnyshev, the modern city is now radically changed. He describes how he and his wife moved from the country to the town. "In town a man can live for a hundred years without noticing that he has long been dead and rotted away."[46] Where the peasant experiences necessity and thus finds justification for his conjugal relationships, the city dweller finds his life inessential, based on distractions and burdens. These do not provide a sense of justification but rather of anxiety. (This becomes an increasingly common state or condition in nineteenth-century fiction—and the exploration of it could be seen as culminating in Freud's long analysis of it in "General Theory of the Neuroses," part 3 of *Introductory Lectures on Psycho-Analysis*.) There is no longer any "conscience" but only "criminal law," which operates by hiding away unassimilable people in jails. This produces an atmosphere in which people experience illness—hysteria, abnormal symptoms—rather than guilt. It is as though people can no longer name or employ the mental and emotional energies that find themselves redundant or superfluous in the sphere of city life. The tendency is to narcotize these energies either by routine or by distraction—neither of which produces the experience of necessity.

In this connection the music the title refers to takes on its special significance. The Kreutzer Sonata is the piece played by his wife and the musician. It arouses Pózdnyshev's suspicions because of the effect it has on him. While he can understand socially functional music—a mass, a military march, even music for a dance—he finds himself disturbed by music listened to in a condition of pure passivity. The tension is caused by the felt contradiction of both being in a consumer role to the music and finding that it induces not so much an elevation of the soul as an extreme agitation of mind and body. One is drawn into the mood of the composer, but this transferred mood cannot issue in action. Such a blending is potentially dangerous, particularly as music is nonlingual and may thereby temporarily dissolve the codes and structures by which a society operates. What results then for Pózdnyshev, is a *sense* of "new

[46]Ibid., p. 394.

feelings, new possibilities," a new consciousness that has no possibilities for actualization and will therefore subside after the music is over, returning the listener to his ordinary life with a renewed sense of bitterness and dissatisfaction. Thus music—particularly romantic nineteenth-century music, which in various ways extols the projection of an individual's subjective mood—is dangerous to the extent that it suggests the possibility of new and exciting mergings and a sense of "agitation" and discontent with one's own established position and habitual range of feelings. Pózdnyshev, finding himself entering into the mood of the composer, imagines a comparable merging between his wife and the musician. From one point of view music can be seen as an adulteration of ordinary consciousness—a new and exciting relationship with the mood of another, which, however, can find no realization in the realm of society. It can thus easily suggest just such a new and exciting relationship on the *physical* level, a volatile venture into a socially unsanctioned area in which the social self dissolves in contact with the other to enjoy a temporary new body-consciousness, which, and the parallel is precise, can find no realization in the realm of society. From this point of view, both music and adultery, within the rigid confines of bourgeois society, offer the possibility of an extrasocial excitation that cannot be translated back into a way of life within society. Concerning what has been designated as socially nonfunctional music (in the story this is exemplified by Beethoven's sonata), Pózdnyshev says: "an awakening of energy and feeling unsuited both to the time and the place, to which no outlet is given, cannot but act harmfully."[47] This is an apt formulation for what the novel concerned with adultery sets out to explore—not this or that illicit coupling, but the fate of awakened energy "unsuited both to the time and the place."

The Great Game of Differentiation

In writing about kinship systems, Lévi-Strauss has been concerned to see how they act as a series of rules of exchange, and his ideas are too familiar in their general outline and too complex in detail to be recapitulated here. But his emphasis on the particular role played by marriage in

[47]Ibid., p. 411.

the establishing of exchange systems is worth bringing out in this context because I think it can throw some light on the significance of what happens to marriage when it is adulterated in nineteenth-century fiction. In the chapter on "Totem and Caste" in *The Savage Mind,* Lévi-Strauss starts by asserting that "the exchange of women and the exchange of food are means of securing or of displaying the interlocking of social groups with one another." (The importance of the "exchange of food" or, as we may now see it, the offering of food as hospitality, and the related importance of the exchange of gifts as set out in Marcel Mauss's classic work *The Gift,* are still in evidence in mutated forms in the bourgeois novel.) Lévi-Strauss emphasizes that the difference between these two basic forms of exchange is, however, crucial: "the perpetuation of the group can only be effected by means of women, and although varying degrees of symbolic content can be introduced by the particular way in which society organizes them or thinks of their operation, *marriage exchanges always have real substance, and they are alone in this.* The exchange of food is a different matter. . . . In the former, although it may be described in conventional terms which impose their own limits on it, what is in question is primarily a way of doing something. In the latter it is only a way of saying something." (My italics.) The substantial reality of the exchange of women is based on the fact that "women really bear children," and the child, unlike food, money, words, may be regarded as the nonsymbolic unit of production and exchange on which the ongoingness of society is based. It would be pointless here to attempt any summary of Lévi-Strauss's work on endogamous and exogamous rules operating in different tribes and groups, and the rules governing restricted exchange or generalized exchange of women. The more important emphasis is on the fact that women are a different *kind* of exchange object than the others that are used by castes or groups or larger organized units. "A fundamental difference exists between the women who are exchanged and the goods and services which are also exchanged. Women are biological individuals, that is, natural products naturally procreated by other biological individuals. Goods and services on the other hand are manufactured objects (or operations performed by means of techniques and manufactured objects), that is, social products culturally manufactured by technical agents." If this is the condition that obtains among savage tribes, we may imagine that in nineteenth-century industrial society, when both commerce and division of labor increased exponentially, the difference between women and goods and services becomes more problematical because the systems of exchange begin to blur into each other as, to use Marx's terms again, use values everywhere give way to exchange values.

As characterized by Lévi-Strauss, marriage is the ambiguous but cen-

tral model by which and through which man tries to establish the differentiations and symmetries that will permit him to think about his
ambiguous position in nature and culture. The problem is that to have
rules of exchange governing marriage, it is necessary to differentiate
between women and to establish different categories for them, whereas
all women belong to the same natural species.

> This is the trap reality sets for the imagination and men try to escape it by
> seeking real diversity in the natural order, which is . . . the only objective
> model on which they can draw for establishing relations of complementar-
> ity and co-operation among themselves. In other words, men conceive
> these relations on the model of their conception of the relations between
> natural species (and at the same time of their own social relations). There
> are in fact only two true models of concrete diversity: one on the plane of
> nature, namely that of the diversity of species, and the other on the cul-
> tural plane provided by the diversity of functions. The model illustrated by
> marriage exchanges, lying between these two true models has an ambigu-
> ous and equivocal character. Women are alike so far as nature is concerned
> and can be regarded as different only from the cultural angle. But if the
> first point of view is predominant (as is the case when it is the natural
> model which is chosen as the model of diversity) resemblance outweighs
> difference. Women certainly have to be exchanged since they have been
> decreed to be different. But this exchange presupposes that basically they
> are held to be alike. Conversely, when the other viewpoint is taken and a
> cultural model of diversity adopted, difference, which corresponds to the
> cultural aspect, outweighs resemblance. Women are only recognized as
> alike within the limits of their respective social groups and consequently
> cannot be exchanged between one caste and another. Castes decree
> women to be naturally heterogeneous; totemic groups decree them to be
> culturally heterogeneous. And the final reason for this difference between
> the two systems is that castes exploit cultural heterogeneity in earnest while
> totemic groups only create the illusion of exploiting natural heterogeneity.

In nineteenth-century bourgeois society it would be hard to identify
totemic groups and castes in the pure form in which Lévi-Strauss discusses them. But it will be recognized that a class structure may retain
both totemic and caste characteristics, and that these may be registered
in the attitude to women when it comes to the crucial transaction of
marriage. For at times resemblance outweighs difference (i.e., it is the
woman's biological properties that are emphasized) while at other times
difference outweighs resemblance (i.e., the woman's membership of a
particular social subgroup is the paramount factor). From society's point
of view the ideal marriage would combine and reconcile the two characteristics, for, to emphasize the proposition again, it is marriage that is at
the center of man's thinking about himself and his position in the world.
It is the key transaction in what Lévi-Strauss calls "true reciprocity."

True reciprocity results from the articulation of two processes: "the natural one which comes about by means of women, who procreate both men and women, and the cultural one which men bring about by characterizing these women socially when nature has brought them into existence." Marriage is that point at which procreation and categorization meet, and it signals the sense of achieving a possible harmony between the two. By the same token, the point at which marriage is threatened may be the one at which they begin to fall asunder.

Lévi-Strauss emphasizes the preeminence of the exchange of women (over the exchange of goods and services, or food and occupations) in the following way.

> Women are naturally interchangeable (from the point of view of their anatomical structure and the physiological functions) and in their case culture finds the field open for the great game of differentiation (whether this is thought of in a positive or a negative way and used therefore as a basis for exogamy on the one hand or endogamy on the other). Foods however are not altogether able to be substituted for each other. The game reaches its limits more quickly in this second domain. . . . This applies even more to occupational functions. Because they really are different and complementary, they allow the establishment of reciprocity in its truest form. On the other hand, they exclude negative reciprocity and so set bounds to the logical harmony of caste systems.

I will only point out here that interchangeability is what is said to mark the condition of alienated man in an industrial society. Lévi-Strauss is obviously working at a higher level of abstraction, at which it is true to say that one woman is more like another woman when it comes to procreative equipment than, say, cheese is like milk (though both have a common source), or than a barber is like a shoemaker. There is a declining scale of substitutability. But if there is a growing stress on individuation in a society, if there is an increasing emphasis on the uniqueness of each relationship, and an attempt to substitute a particular I-Thou intersubjective sense for the substitutability noted in Lévi-Strauss's scheme, then the potentiality for uncontainable tensions arising within the marriage relationship increases dramatically. (For a literature that still seems to be aware of this underlying interchangeability of women in the maintenance of the social structure, consider some of Shakespeare's comedies.) To put it for the moment very generally, the nineteenth-century wife could feel herself to be in a contradictory system in which she was both interchangeable and yet without substitute. Here again is a point at which the system could begin to yield to the contradictions that it has generated. And if the wife trangresses the contract that gives her social identity, she may find herself involved in a nightmare of *un*differentiations.

Lévi-Strauss isolates the "two main systems of differences to which men have had recourse for conceptualizing their social relations" and declares that "we must therefore recognize the system of natural species and that of manufactured objects as two mediating sets which man employs to overcome opposition between nature and culture and think of them as a whole. But there is also another means." He then recounts a North American legend common to several hunting tribes, which I will summarize. They say that at the beginning of time the buffaloes were ferocious and hostile, being not only inedible themselves (all bone), but capable of attacking and eating man. That is to say, the relationship between the hunters and the buffaloes was imagined as being exactly contrary to the one actually experienced by the living hunters, for the buffalo provided soft edible flesh for man and did not prey on him. Lévi-Strauss looks into the explanation of this complete transformation and finds at the center a strange marriage between a buffalo who has fallen in love with a girl who was the only female in an all-male community. For the marriage ceremony the men gather together and give presents, each one of which was to represent a part of the buffalo's body. Thus, in every case a man-made object (and thus one over which he has control) is made to stand for a part of the buffalo (over which he has no control)—e.g., a bow for the ribs, moccasins for kidneys, and so on. Lévi-Strauss comments, "The marriage exchange thus functions as a mechanism serving to mediate between nature and culture, which were originally regarded as separate. By substituting a cultural architectonic for a supernatural primitive one, the alliance creates a second nature over which man has a hold, that is, a mediatized nature. After these occurrences buffaloes become 'all flesh' instead of 'all bones' and edible instead of cannibal." Marriage thus is indissolubly connected with the creating of that "second nature," that "cultural architectonic" that allows man to operate within the potentially oppositional dualism of nature and culture. In this it achieves more than the other "mediating sets," as outlined above.

This is his conclusion:

> This confirms what I suggested above, namely, first that the "system of women" is, as it were, a middle term between the system of (natural) living creatures and the system of (manufactured) objects and secondly that each system is apprehended as a transformation within a single group.
>
> The system of living creatures is the only one of the three systems which has an objective existence outside man and that of functions the only one which has a completely social existence, that is, within man. But the completeness of each on one plane explains why neither is readily handled on the other. . . . Reciprocity is not therefore absolute in either case. It is, as it were, blurred and distorted at the periphery. Logically speaking, the rec-

iprocity of marriage exchanges represents an equally impure form since it lies mid-way between a natural and a cultural model. But it is this hybrid character which allows it to function perfectly. Associated with one or the other form, or with both, or present on its own, as the case may be, the reciprocity of marriage exchanges alone can claim universality.

As I have noted, we cannot expect to see the kind of diagrammatic clarity of Lévi-Strauss's models in the nineteenth-century novel any more than the novelists would have seen them so clearly in society. But in between the analysis of the system of living creatures that exists wholly in nature (let us say represented by Darwin) and the analysis of the system of functions and manufactured objects (carried out most magisterially by Marx), it was the system of women, as worked out in marriage rules and customs, to which the novelist most often addressed himself. And in discovering the potential and actual malfunctionings and failures of reciprocation within this impure form—which in an abstract model of social organization, functions perfectly—the novelist scrutinizing adultery was doing no less than showing the tenuousness of all those systems of mediation between nature and culture, as well as all the systems of exchange, on which society itself is based.

If society cannot be comprehended as a whole, as Lévi-Strauss would maintain, then it has to be approached as a series of rule-governed relationships between person and person, people and objects, etc. In a similar way the observing and participating mind cannot observe itself in its wholeness. Both mind and society are unconsciously structured. To summarize a point made by Harold Scheffler, most people usually have their "conscious models" of the what, how, and why of their actions. But these are not to be taken as the society as such; they are products of what Lévi-Strauss calls "secondary rationalization." Scheffler continues, "Neither the conscious or unconscious models nor the apparent statistical order in transactional relations may be said to constitute *the* structure of the society concerned. These various forms of order, like the anthropologists' representations of them, are not *the* structures itself: they are, all of them, only *variant expressions of structure,* which is, again, in Lévi-Strauss's view, the 'logic' or 'code' whereby the human mind operates." The same observation holds true for the novelists' representations, and it is worth bearing this in mind as we consider the bourgeois novel, which is itself a variant expression of the underlying structure of society even while it may operate as a critique of other variant expressions of it, a conscious model confronting and perhaps contesting other conscious models. It is when the novel seems to approach the hidden secrets of this underlying structure itself that it starts to threaten society in its entirety. It is this, I shall suggest, that the novel of adultery starts to do in a way, say, that novels aimed at specific social abuses never did. Scheffler makes another point about Lévi-Strauss's anthropology that is important for my topic. "Thus it might be possible to demonstrate, for example, that the 'rules of kinship and marriage,' the 'economic rules,' and the 'linguistic rules' of the same or different societies are all systematically interdependent. To do this, it would not be necessary to reduce each of these types of communication (of women, of goods and services, and of messages, respectively) or their rules to one another. We might instead find that the rules ordering or regulating these different types of communication are best conceived as variant expressions of one another." Scheffler notes that the incest taboo is, in Lévi-Strauss's view, essentially "a rule relating to "groups" and its effect is to establish relationships of exchange between them, thus literally creating society," which is always related to "a system of communication based on the exchange of women."

But more importantly he emphasizes that kinship is rooted both in nature and in the human mind, as I have tried to show Lévi-Strauss demonstrating. What Sheffler brings out is that it seems general among different peoples to think that "genealogical connections naturally entail certain normative social relationships between the person so connected (just as our 'fathers,' whose 'blood' we share, are 'naturally' affectionate toward and protective of us)." This becomes more problematical when you consider marriage, for what would it be natural for a woman to feel when she is related to the man not by blood but by a system of exchange? Marriage vows, suggests Scheffler, "require a certain amount of *normative* reinforcement precisely because they are not instinctual and have such enormous adaptive values. It is for these reasons, it would appear, that men so often and so strongly insist upon wedlock (which unites groups as well as individuals) as a precondition for the legitimate engendering of children while continuing to recognize, as observant men must, that it is not a natural precondition and therefore not one of the bases of kinship proper." Thus he maintains that "systems of kinship and marriage" are in fact discriminable "though apparently interdependent in all human societies." And, ultimately, it is the system of marriage that is the basis of society. This is perhaps only to come full circle, but in view of the possible connections between systems of exchange suggested by Lévi-Strauss and itemized by Scheffler, the importance of the point can hardly be overemphasized. Because if rules of marriage, economic rules, and linguistic rules are in some way systematically interdependent, then the breakdown of one implies the possible breakdown of all three. Thus, to spell it out, the failure of marriage as a binding form may either presage or be isomorphically related to the imperilment of the particular economic system in which it is embedded and to a possible crisis in the status and ownership of the accepted discourses. If the marriage contract is broken in some radical way, then economic contracts may become problematical, and the author may find that he is forced to break *his* "contract" with his readers. The crisis for the bourgeois novelist, we might say, was not a failure of contact but a failure of contract that involved all the systems of exchange in the society of which he was a member.

One effect of this is a move from the more realistic novel of contract and transgression that I am describing, to what might be called the novel of metaphor. What I mean by this somewhat cryptic formulation will, I hope, become clearer in the course of the work. But let me give one very simple example. In the three novels I shall be considering in detail, boating in one form or another plays a crucial part in the evolution, or devolution, of the narrative and is intimately related to the latent or actual instabilities within the marriage contract. But we may glance here at some later examples. In *The Kreutzer Sonata*, Pózdnyshev locates the moment of his fatal error when he was deceived into the trap of marriage as coming immediately after a boat ride ("One evening after we had been out in a boat . . . I suddenly decided it was she!"), and he more than once recurs to what he ironically refers to as "the satisfactory boating." Among other examples, there is the famous boating scene in *The Ambassadors,* though there it is ambiguously confused, or interfused, with art by Strether's pictorially prepared imagination. In *The Golden Bowl,* however, the boating is in the conversation: " 'We're certainly not, with the relation of our respective *sposi,* simply formal acquaintances. We're in the same boat'—and the Prince smiled with a candour that added an accent to his emphasis."[48] The metaphor is played with at some length, and in this it is typical of a novel in which almost everything takes place at the level of "image" (one of the key words in the book), which is the level at which the failed contracts have to be reconstructed and renegotiated; it is a level also of consciously fabricated lies both of utterance and repression—and this is the level at which the book has to be "read." I use quotes to indicate that reading has become interpretation in a new way, and the book has become radically ambiguous in a way in which the earlier novels I shall be considering seldom are. We don't know where the author is, and he does not know where we are—metaphors proliferate in the space created by that locational uncertainty. If it is objected that that uncertainty is nothing new and that we certainly cannot mark a definite date or text of its occurrence, I would argue that the conventions by which the author pretended to know his gentle or not so gentle reader operated well into the nineteenth century and were from the start

[48]Ibid., pp. 369, 372; James, *Golden Bowl,* bk. 1, pt. 2, ch. 15, p. 188.

available for varying degrees of play (Fielding, Sterne, Thackeray). But I shall attempt to isolate a new kind of subversion of those conventions in *Madame Bovary,* and I am suggesting that *The Golden Bowl* offers an exemplary case of how those same conventions are dissolved in a flow of metaphors that recognizes no constraints.

The Whence of Desire

Man's ignorance (*nescience*) of his desire is "less ignorance of what he demands, which can after all be defined or limited, than ignorance of *whence* he desires."—Jacques Lacan, quoted in *The Language of the Self*

Since desire, which is always involved in some way with the sense of in-completion, is an essential source of action in any social structure, which by its very nature tends toward a self-perpetuating stasis, it is necessarily a central topic of all literature. Desire in action reveals itself as energy, and energy encountering structure is the paradigmatic tension of much of our literature. No one set of remarks can begin to cover the role of desire in literature, or indeed the role of literature in desire, but for my present purposes it is necessary to recognize two works that have made important contributions to our comprehension of the mystery of the "whence of desire."

In his pioneering work *Love in the Western World,* Denis de Rougement noted that "to judge by literature, adultery would seem to be one of the most remarkable of occupations in both Europe and America." He shows how through the centuries passionate love has invariably taken the form of adultery, and he infers from this that there is some unappeasable hunger for misfortune, unhappiness, and death, which is not simply engendered by the institution of marriage but is involved in passion as such. In relishing literature based upon adultery, we are "constantly *betraying* how widespread and disturbing is our obsession by the love that breaks the law. Is this not the sign that we wish to escape from a horrible reality?" And what is the source of this sickness? "Must the institution of marriage bear the blame for it, or is there something fatal to marriage at the very heart of human longing? . . . It is obvious that Western Man is drawn to what destroys 'the happiness of the married couple' *at least as much* as to anything that ensures it." This in spite of the fact, or is it because of it, that "the word 'adultery' sums up one half of human unhappiness—renunciation, compromises, separations, neurasthenia, together with the irritating and petty confusion of dreams, obligations, and secret acquiescence." To attempt to account for this tenacity of the Western addiction to the idea of a passion that annihilates the legal institutions within which Western Man lives, and that finally destroys the self as well, Rougemont starts with an analysis of the "myth of adultery" in *Tristan and Iseult* and traces its mutations and dissolutions through to the present day. The myth both conceals and reveals its origin—it is a strategy of indirection by which the unsayable may be uttered within society: "*a myth is needed to express the dark and unmentionable fact that passion is linked with death,* and involves the destruction of any one yielding himself up to it with all his strength. For we have wanted to preserve passion and we cherish the unhappiness that it brings with it; and yet at the same time both passion and unhappiness have stood condemned in the sight of official morals and in the sight of reason." Different societies and ages project and contain this myth in different ways, as "the rules of chivalry literally 'contained' the passion of Tristan and Iseult": it has to be contained because in "being the passion that wants Darkness and triumphs in a transfiguring Death, it must represent, for any society whatsoever, a threat overwhelmingly intolerable."[49]

As Rougemont sees it, "the myth that has been agitating us for eight hundred years as spell, terror, or ideal is at one and the same time a passion sprung from dark nature, an energy excited by the mind, and a pre-established potentiality in search of the coercion that shall intensify it." Thus he points out how Tristan searches for arbitrary barriers, a "*deliberate obstruction*" that will intensify his passion, a passion that needs the *absence* of the loved one more than the presence. Rougemont's insight is so close to Freud's description of "obstacle love" that it is surprising he does not quote it, so I will.

It is easy to show that the value the mind sets on erotic needs instantly sinks as soon as satisfaction becomes readily obtainable. Some obstacle is necessary to swell the tide of libido to its height; and at all periods of history, wherever natural barriers in the way of satisfaction have not sufficed, mankind has erected conventional ones in order to enjoy love. This is true both of individuals and nations. In times during which no obstacles to sexual satisfaction existed, such as, may be, during the decline of the civilizations of antiquity, love became worthless, life became empty, and strong reaction formations were necessary before the indispensable emotional value of love could be recovered. In this context it may be stated that the ascetic tendency of Christianity had the effect of raising the psychical value

[49]Denis de Rougemont, *Love in the Western World*, pp. 3, 4, 8.

of love in a way that heathen antiquity could never achieve; it developed greatest significance in the lives of the ascetic monks, which were almost entirely occupied with struggles against libidinous temptation.[50]

The secret quest within the apparent quest for obstacles that will intensify and enhance love is, says Rougemont, "a love for obstruction *per se*. Now, it turns out that the ultimate obstacle is death and at the close of the tale death is revealed as having been the real end, what passion has yearned after from the beginning." And this is the unavowable basic or latent message of the myth under all its manifest or narrative content. "Unawares and in spite of themselves, the lovers have never had but one desire—the desire for death!" Such passion is necessarily antithetical to marriage, and, as Rougemont describes it, the breakdown of marriage was accelerated by trying to "*ground*" it "*in values elaborated by the morals of passion.*" As long as social limitations were strong, so there was a corresponding intensity in the passions that pushed against them seeking their own forms of transcendence. It is part of Rougemont's pessimistic view of modern times that, in his opinion, as there has been a decay in "institutional obstructions," so there has been a slackening of tension between passion and society. There is no longer any real conflict between them, and what results is a "mutual neutralization,"[51] and a loss of meaning on both sides. When a society ceases to care much about marriage, and all that is implied in that transaction, by the same token it will lose contact with the sense of intense passion. This would mean that the novel of adultery, as I have been describing it, would vanish—as indeed it has. A novel like John Updike's *Couples* is as little about passion as it is about marriage; the adulteries are merely formal and technical. Adultery, we may say, no longer signifies.

Denis de Rougemont thus sees the ultimate whence of desire as the death wish, inasmuch as it is a desire that is in fact a passion that attempts to transcend anything or anyone obtainable within the given social world. In *Deceit, Desire, and the Novel*, René Girard stresses the importance of the "mediator." For him the basic paradigm is provided by *Don Quixote*, in which Don Quixote desires according to the book, and to preestablished images. Thus desire becomes triangular and loses its autonomy. "From the moment the mediator's influence is felt, the sense of reality is lost and judgment paralysed." What he concentrates on is the loss of the "autonomy of desire" even while such autonomy is believed in by the one who desires. But the desirer in this triangular situation "cannot draw his desire from his own resources; he must borrow them from

[50]Ibid., pp. 11, 36; Sigmund Freud, "The Most Prevalent Form of Degradation in Erotic Life," p. 213.
[51]Rougemont, *Love in the Western World,* pp. 45, 36, 298, 290.

others." The mediator may be a book, a chosen model, or a rival, and may be external or internal to the situation or the individual, but either way we encounter "a desire *according to Another,* opposed to this desire *according to Oneself* that most of us pride ourselves on enjoying." A key difference exists between those who consciously choose to be disciples of a model on which or on whom they base their desires, and those who pride themselves on being "original." The latter do not realize or wish to confront the fact that their desires are internally mediated, and they subscribe to "the lie of spontaneous desire." It is the achievement of great novels to reveal the presence and operation of the mediator and its "privileged role . . . in the genesis of desire."[52]

"The Mediator's prestige is imparted to the object of desire and confers upon it an illusory value. Triangular desire is the desire which transfigures its object. *Romantic* literature does not disregard this metamorphosis; on the contrary, it turns it to account and boasts of it, but never reveals its actual mechanism." "We believe that 'novelistic' genius is won by a great struggle against these attitudes we have lumped together under the name 'romantic' because they all appear to us intended to maintain the illusion of spontaneous desire and of a subjectivity almost divine in its autonomy." Triangular desire is that desire that increasingly unwittingly is based on the Other, in whatever form the Other may take, and it amounts to "a desecration which gradually infects the most intimate parts of being."[53] In the unconscious copying of the Other, the experience of true otherness is finally and utterly lost. The true novelist will restore the reality of the Other in all its actuality and visibility—its im-mediacy.

Girard does allow for what he calls "ontologically healthy desire," which in his terms is that passion that moves directly to the object of its desire without any traffic with any kind of mediator. The passionate person is "distinguished by his emotional autonomy, by the spontaneity of his desires, by his absolute indifference to the opinion of Others. The passionate person draws the strength of his desire from within himself and not from others." "He is the only realist in a world of lies." Yet even for those who avoid the sickness of triangular desire, there is no lasting satisfaction in the possession of the desired object. Girard describes how the object is "desecrated by possession," which would seem to imply not only that no desire can ever be satisfied but that desire itself cannot come to rest, since each selected, or mediated, appointment turns into a disappointment. As Girard points out, this disappointment within the novel during the nineteenth century changes from a predominantly physical

[52]René Girard, *Deceit, Desire, and the Novel,* pp. 4, 6, 16, 23.
[53]Ibid., pp. 17, 28–29, 43.

one to a metaphysical one. "The 'physical' and 'metaphysical' in desire always fluctuate at the expense of each other. This law has myriad aspects. It explains for example the progressive disappearance of sexual pleasure in the most advanced stages of ontological sickness."[54] Girard's study leads him to Proust and Dostoevsky, logically enough, but we may see a related phenomenon in the novel of adultery as well, namely, the disappearance of pleasure in bourgeois society. Whether this can be ascribed to the insidious dominance of triangular desire is perhaps questionable, for it could be argued that desire is always mediated in some way, if only by the setting in which the two people who desire each other meet. (This is very important for the novel of adultery in which, while the act may not be described, the setting invariably is. One could almost say that the description has been displaced into the setting and must be read there.)

Denis de Rougemont located the origin of desire in the death wish (we are now speaking only of the Western world); concentrating mainly on the nineteenth century, René Girard identifies the unoriginality of the desire that regards itself as original and, with certain privileged exceptions, he locates the source of desire in the Other as mediator. I want briefly to consider some remarks of Jacques Lacan, who places the origin of desire in language itself. Two of his most famous observations occur in the essay "The Insistence of the Letter in the Unconscious." "The speaking subject, if he seems to be thus a slave of language, is all the more so of a discourse in the universal moment of which he finds himself at birth, even if only by dint of his proper name." This leads him on to an attack on the idea of the "transcendental subject" as presented by Descartes's formula, *cogito ergo sum*—"the philosophical *cogito* is at the center of that mirage which renders modern man so sure of being himself even in his uncertainties about himself"—and a pregnant rephrasing of it in the following terms: "I think where I am not, therefore I am where I think not." He amplifies this further: "I am not, wherever I am the plaything of my thought; I think of what I am wherever I don't think I am thinking." This is not so obscure as it may sound on first hearing, though it is, of course, a deliberately provocative extreme statement. But since when we do start thinking, we think in and with the discourses that were implanted in us but were none of our making, it does make an important kind of sense to point out that there is no prior fully constituted self that *then* engages in thinking; rather the self is to a large extent constituted in and through its engagement in the existing discourses and paradoxically, therefore, comes into being via a medium that is precisely not itself since it was there waiting as a system into which the self must fit.

[54]Ibid., pp. 141, 19, 140, 88, 87.

(We might even rephrase Lacan's rephrasing of Descartes and say that since often I speak where I am not, therefore I am where I speak not, for much of the real self may be found in the gaps, spaces, and silences when it is, for intermittent periods, not a slave of language.)

In asking the leading question—"Is what thinks in my place then another I?"—Lacan is insisting on what he calls "the self's radical ex — centricity to itself," which he takes to be one of Freud's most important discoveries.

> The radical heteronomy which Freud's discovery shows gaping within man can never again be covered over without whatever is used to hide it being fundamentally dishonest.
> Then who is this other to whom I am more attached than to myself, since, at the heart of my assent to my own identity it is still he who wags me?
> Its presence can only be understood at a second degree of otherness which puts it in the position of mediating between me and the double of myself, as it were with my neighbour.
> If I have said elsewhere that the unconscious is the discourse of the Other (with a capital O), I meant by that to indicate the beyond in which the recognition of desire is bound up with the desire of recognition.

Some of the initial difficulties apparent in such a statement may be clarified if we risk simplifying what Lacan makes deliberately elliptical and convoluted and say that while *other* with a lower case *o* means other people, *the Other* with a capital *O* is "the scene of the Word insofar as the scene of the Word is always in third position between two subjects." Or again, the Other is "the locus where there is constituted the *je* which speaks as well as he who hears it (speak)." There is both some connection and some confusion between the other and the Other, and it is worth going back to one of Lacan's earliest formulations concerning the problem of desire. "To put it in a nutshell, nowhere does it appear more clearly that man's desire finds its meaning in the desire of the other, not so much because the other holds the key to the object desired, as because the first object of desire is to be recognized by the other."[55] (It might be noted in passing that Girard's formulations at times seem very close to Lacan's, though he nowhere mentions him, and of course there need have been no question of direct influence.)

The phenomenon of desire is essential to man's existence as man. ("Servitude and grandeur in which the living would be annihilated, if desire did not preserve its part in the interferences and pulsations which

---

[55] Jacques Lacan, "The Insistence of the Letter in the Unconscious," pp. 135, 136. Lacan quoted by Wilden in *The Language of the Self*, pp. 269, 266; Lacan, *The Language of the Self*, p. 31.

the cycles of Language cause to converge on him, when the confusion of tongues takes a hand and when the orders interfere with each other in the tearing apart of the universal work.") In particular, desire is the crucial mediation point between need and demand. It was one of Lacan's early insistences that "'need' and 'demand' have a diametrically opposed sense for the subject, and to hold that their use can be confused even for an instant amounts to a radical failure to recognize the "'intimation' of the Word"[56] He amplifies the relation between need, demand, and desire in later works, and once again I avail myself of the comments of Anthony Wilden.

> The question is further delineated by Leclaire in "L'Obsessionel et son désir" (1959). After stating that "need aims at the object and is satisfied by it"; that demand "puts the other as such into question"; that it is "that sort of appeal to the Other" whose nature is "to open up on to a *béance* and to remain unsatisfied"; and that desire participates of both, he summarizes: [Desire] is the necessary mediation between the implacable mechanism of need, and the dizzy solitude of demand. . . .
> . . . Desire is proper to the Imaginary; it is to be conceived of *significative mediation of a fundamental antinomy.* Thus it participates in need insofar as it is relatively satisfied by an object, but only sustains itself insofar as it participates in demand by its perennially unsatisfied quest of the being of the Other, *locus of the signifier.*[57]

The matter is further clarified in a summarization by Laplanche and Pontalis of Lacan's seminars. "Desire is born from the split between need and demand. It is irreducible to need, because it is not in principle a relation to a real object which is independent of the subject, but a relation to the phantasy. It is irreducible to demand, insofar as it seeks to impose itself without taking language or the unconscious of the other into account, and requires to be recognized absolutely by him."[58] A person may experience a specific need that can be satisfied by an object. In the child's case this need will first express itself inarticulately (through crying or reaching), but the child will learn to translate inarticulate personally felt needs into articulate demands that must, however, be expressed in the impersonal medium of language. It is in this process of translation that desire has its origin. We *need* because we are in the flesh; we *demand* because we are in language; we *desire* because we are in, and split between, both. (cf. Vico, para. 1045: "To sum up, a man is properly

---

[56]Lacan, *The Language of the Self,* pp. 42, 60.

[57]Serge Leclair, "L'Obsessionel et son désir," *L'Evolution Psychiatrique* (1959), pp. 386–90, quoted by Wilden in Lacan, *The Language of the Self,* pp. 143–44 n. 143.

[58]Jean Laplanche and J.-B. Pontalis, *Vocabulaire de la Psychanalyse* (Paris: PUF, 1967), quoted by Anthony Wilden, "Lacan and the Discourse of the Other," in Lacan, *The Language of the Self,"* p. 189.

only mind, body, and speech, and speech stands as it were midway between mind and body.") Commenting and glossing on Lacan's central statement that "Man's desire finds its meaning in the desire of the Other" Anthony Wilden offers this explication.

> The Other is not a person, but a principle: the locus of the "law of desire," the locus of the incest-prohibition and the phallus. According to Lacan, the Other—mythically represented in Freud by the symbolic father of *Totem and Taboo*—is the only place from which it is possible to say, "I am who I am." The paradox of identity and autonomy which this involves—identical to or identified with what?—puts us in the position of desiring what the Other desires: we desire what the Other desires we desire. We therefore desire to TAKE THE PLACE of the Other in desire. When all is said and done, then, we do not desire objects; we desire desire itself. Desire is represented by the phallus, which is not an object, but a "signifier."[59]

Such a desire can never be satisfied; it would be like "trying to find a hole to fill up a hole," in Wilden's terms, but let me continue with his version of Lacan's distinction between need, demand, and desire.

> Need represents the level of "instinct" or "drive"; desire is unconscious and ineffable; demand is the metaphoric expression of the relationship between need (which can be satisfied) and desire (which cannot). The emergence of desire is directly related to language, both ontogenetically and phylogenetically. The human *infans* cannot avoid learning to translate his needs into demands, through the acquisition of language. But language is controlled by and learned from the Other, not by and from any particular other. The Symbolic order of language awaits the child at birth: he or she has to discover where one fits into it. . . . Not only may the child be already identified as an object of exchange in his parents' phantasies; he also has to find out where "I" fits into the social universe of communication and exchange he discovers. This is the fundamental "desire to know" and Lacan translates the "Who am I?" of Oedipus into "What am I there?" (in the discourse). Desire comes into the world because of the necessary relation with others that makes humans human; the child's helplessness to attend to his own needs results in the detour of need, through language, into demand and it is this detour which generates unconscious desire as a fundamental and unfillable "lack." . . . Unconscious desire, then, in Lacan's sense, is the result of our being "creatures at the mercy of language." It corresponds to a kind of hole or "lack of being" introduced into being BY LANGUAGE ITSELF.[60]

---

[59]Anthony Wilden, *System and Structure,* p. 23.
[60]Ibid., pp. 24–25.

As Wilden points out elsewhere, these ideas could be related to Sartre's notion of "lack of being" manifesting itself as "desire" in the *pour-soi*—"desire is a lack."[61]

The figure of speech that Lacan identifies with desire is *metonymy* (*metaphor* is "symptom"—the use of the terms is taken of course from Jakobson); inasmuch as *metonymy* implies the part for the whole, language is always giving us the part for the whole and is thus always making us aware of a gap between the signifier and what might be being signified. "And the enigmas which desire seems to pose for a "natural philosophy" . . . these amount to nothing more than that derangement of the instincts that comes from being caught on the rails—eternally stretching forth towards the desire for something else—of metonymy."[62] It is as if desire is inexorably liable to be split between "a refusal of meaning or a lack of being," to the "extent that it goes along with the 'rails of metonymy' already tracked in language itself, or attempts to annul itself by withdrawing from language and thus from meaning." That desire—which is "introduced into being by language itself"—might nevertheless ultimately crave some nonlingual or prelingual condition is an important paradox, which has some bearing on my subject. Lacan himself says, "I identify myself in language, but only by losing myself in it like an object."[63] Thus the desire to extract the "I" from language would at the same time be a sort of counterdesire to secede from identity and cease to be a differentiated object.

I want to derive one final point from Lacan's infinitely complex work. The self, of course, realizes itself in relationships with others, and this realization takes place in either the realm of the Imaginary or the realm of the Symbolic, or both. I am unable to grasp the consistent connections between these realms as described by Lacan, or transcribed by Wilden. But a certain important distinction does emerge that, even if it is not faithful to Lacan, is useful in the study I am about to embark on. In the realm of the Imaginary, the self realizes itself in terms of identifications and oppositions with others, and in this way becomes alienated from itself into an image or an object. It realizes itself as a series of imaginary fixations, and is, to use Lacan's terms, a "moi" based on "mirages and misconstructions." The relation between the "moi" and others is analogous to the slave-master relationship as first described by Hegel and which Lacan makes use of. Or the self may enter into the realm of the

[61]Jean-Paul Sartre, *L'Etre et le Néant* (Paris: Gallimard, 1943), p. 652, discussed by Wilden in Lacan, *The Language of the Self,* p. 137 n. 107.

[62]Lacan, "Insistence of the Letter," p. 137.

[63]Lacan, *Language of the Self,* p. 63.

Symbolic (which is governed by the Other, the phallus, the "signifier") and come to realize itself in terms of similarities and differences. The "Word" is indeed the Word of the Other, but it is only by learning to locate itself within the discourse of the Other and using the Word that the self can achieve any intersubjectivity with others, as opposed to a permanent imprisonment within his imaginary fixations. The contrast between "moi" and "je" is quite prevalent, certainly in the early Lacan. He gives as a key example the change from the "ce suis-je" of the time of Villon to the "c'est moi" of modern man. The implication is that modern society increasingly forces the individual to experience himself as "moi" rather than "je."[64]

Let me give two more comments from Lacan on this distinction, both from *The Language of the Self*. "The *moi* of which we speak is absolutely impossible to distinguish from the insidious Imaginary captures (*captations*) which constitute it from head to foot, in its genesis as in its status, in its function as in its actuality, by another and for another." And "It is in proportion to the sense that the subject effectively brings to pronouncing the '*je*' which decides whether he is or is not the one who is speaking. But the fatality of the Word, in fact the condition of its plenitude, requires that the subject . . . be the one who is listening as much as the one who is speaking. For at the moment of the full Word, they both take equal part in it."[65] (There is a reference here to Lacan's distinction between the empty word and the full word: put very crudely, the empty word is spoken by the "moi" as he is effectively not "the one who is speaking"—only the "je" can speak the full word.) Lacan's emphasis given here to the italicized words refers to an opposed state—defined as "madness" of one kind or another—in which the subject, or self, has no grasp of the Word and thus exists "in a Language without dialectic." "The absence of the Word is manifested here by the stereotypes of a discourse in which the subject, one might say, is spoken rather than speaking."[66] This is a kind of "madness" that many characters in the novels I wish to consider suffer from to some degree. The relationships between those who speak and those who "are spoken" is related to the

---

[64]Ibid., p. 44.

[65]Lacan, "Introduction au commentaire de Jean Hyppolite sur la *Verneinung*," *La Psychanalyse*, I (1956), p. 22 (Seminar of February 10, 1954), quoted by Wilden in *Language of the Self*, p. 147 n. 158; and "Discours de Jacques Lacan (26 septembre 1953)," *Actes du Congrès de Rome, La Psychanalyse*, I (1956), p. 204, quoted in Lacan, *Language of the Self*, p. 147 n. 156.

[66]Lacan, *Language of the Self*, p. 43. Cf. the distinction between a "they-self" and an "authentic Self" in the work of Heidegger, which Lacan is almost certainly familiar with:

The Self of everyday *Dasein* is the *they-self*, which we distinguish from the *authentic* Self—that is, from the Self which has been taken hold of in its own way. . . . As

relationships between individuals that are instigated by desire. Language, apparently so simple and there to use, becomes not only the arena for all kinds of problematical encounters but the agency and medium that brings *into being* the encounters, the problems, and the forms they take.

We may note here an apparently simple problem that nevertheless has far-reaching implications. The bourgeois family is obviously going to engage in language, but what is there to talk *about?* (This, as will be seen, is intimately involved with what they—particularly the wives—will do. For many of them become occupiers with no real occupation, and where the eighteenth-century novel could still to some extent focus on adventure and exploration, the bourgeois novel inevitably concerns itself more with problems of tenure and maintenance.) The ideal aim of the bourgeois family, as of bourgeois society, was simply to maintain the structure it has established, to rescue it from the contingency of its origins and invest it with permanence and thus to participate in society's myth of its own perenniality. Thus the energies of the family are ideally aimed at countering any slippage or shifting in the status quo, at resisting change, supplying lacks, filling up gaps, and denying unacceptable kinds of difference (in the sense that it aims at some kind of centralizing homogeneity of behavior, any kind of deviance being registered and proclaimed as alien). But language itself introduces gaps and lacks into conscious being, as we have seen, and as a phenomenon, it is rooted in difference, change, and shifting. Thus there is a potential paradox between the speaker who is an owner (in the bourgeois sense), for speaking presages desire and change, while ownership succumbs to the logic of inertia and permanence. Speaking is rooted in difference, while ownership is based on maintenance, i.e., repetition. To return to the simple question—what were the members of the bourgeois family to talk about in the home (which is the invariable setting for the bourgeois novel)? Not business or the factory, for that was precisely a vocabulary, as it was a phenomenon, that was to be excluded from the domestic space. All that is strictly "male" talk, and as such it only penetrates the home in attenuated and indirect forms. Talk might be about furnishing, decora-

---

they-self, the particular Dasein has been *dispersed* into the "they," and must first find itself. This dispersal characterizes the 'subject' of that kind of Being which we know as concernful absorption in the world we encounter as closest to us. (*Being and Time,* part 1, division 4, section 27)

Cf. also the distinction George Herbert Mead makes between the "I" and the "me," in *Mind, Self, and Society,* particularly the chapter "The Fusion of the "I" and the "Me" in Social Activities." Mead's work is still underrated in Europe, but it could quite conceivably have influenced Lacan.

tion, clothes, entertaining, etc., but these are precisely functions of the bourgeois home and thus the talk participates in the repetition of maintenance and routine, and the words themselves become part of the "property" that they are serving. Anything, any feeling or phenomenon that might threaten the structure was taboo (which is why, for example, Conventry Patmore's *Angel in the House* was so popular and George Meredith's *Modern Love* was execrated); the more general result of this was that the *meaning* of bourgeois life was not a subject for discussion— the more serious taboo was on the realm of ideas, except to the extent that ideas could be transformed into items for entertainment and decoration, and thus could be defused of their power to question and contest the living conditions of the speakers.[67]

One obvious topic for conversation, one might have thought, would be children. But here we encounter a curious phenomenon. For in many of the novels involving adultery, although there invariably are children, or at least a child, often there is curiously little interest in them or it, even on the part of the mother (or especially on the part of the mother). And the children themselves are seldom very notable presences; if anything, they seem to incorporate some sense of negativity, a weak hold on life, and a latent indifference to things that seems to have been transmitted to them from their parents (or more particularly their mothers). They become a pathetic kind of living evidence of the radical failure of marriage as a genuinely fruitful union and contract. One might almost call them antiproducts. (There are of course exceptions—most notably Pearl in *The Scarlet Letter.* I am here offering opening generalizations.) Among other things, they seem to indicate an exhaustion on the part of the parents (or again most usually the mother), an indifference to the whole generative and regenerative process. It is almost as if, while busily seeking to ground and ensure its own perenniality, life in bourgeois society loses its point. This is registered indirectly by the loss of interest by the indispensable perpetuator—the mother. The negative or reverse aspect of an inclination to adultery would seem to be a disinclination to maternity, and it might be a mistake to try and find an order of priority for these feelings or to attempt to relate them in a cause-and-effect sequence. It is all part of the decomposition of that unstable, supposedly unitary trinity—the wife-mother-lover.

[67]Thus in *The Kreutzer Sonata,* Pózdnyshev describes the intolerable ordeal of contriving nonsignificant conversation: "As soon as we thought of something to say and said it, we had again to be silent, devising something else. There was nothing to talk about. All that could be said about the life that awaited us, our arrangements and plans, had been said, and what was there more? Now if we had been animals we should have known that speech was unnecessary; but here on the contrary it was necessary to speak, and there was nothing to say, because we were not occupied with what finds vent in speech." Tolstoi, *Kreutzer Sonata,* p. 375. The necessity to speak—the nothingness to be said: we are not so far from Beckett as we might think.

There are many other topics that could not be spoken about—from intimate details of personal experience to doubts about received religious tenets. But one more taboo topic is important for my essay. The bourgeois family might talk about changing houses, or moving to another job, or transferring to another place. But it could not confront or engage with the possibility of a *radical* change in their way of life. The idea of a wholly alternative mode of existence was not to be considered. In brief, when it came to bourgeois society, you could to some extent change the content but not the form. Thus language is, as it were, as trapped and idle within the house as the wife who all too often was condemned to a circularity that could not be transcended. It is at such a point that a sense of a gap or lack in being introduced by language per se becomes especially acute. The bourgeois home turns out to be a hothouse of desire, in the sense in which we have been considering it. I will make one further observation at this stage. Within the novel, the characters can never use language to escape from or transform their existence. But the novelist himself—or more notably, herself—is in fact using language in another medium to escape from or transform his or her own situation in society. George Eliot as authoress effectively transcended her social condition in a way that none of her more or less suffering (and *almost*, once or twice, adulterous) female characters ever do. Paradoxically, then, George Eliot wrote her way out of her condition by writing about, among other things, women who found no such option for themselves. This prompts a further marginal observation at this stage. That the entry of the artist *into* the bourgeois novel in a dominant role is another mark of the decline of the bourgeois novel as such. To put it another way—Isabel Archer *might* go on to commit adultery; she *might* go on to be an artist. She has both the situation and the consciousness to make either (or both) possible. Her refusal to countenance either (within the novel as we have it) and her opting for some kind of *turning back* (including at one point a wish to have the insentience of an object of stone), is by the same token a refusal of the novel itself to break out of its condition. They both opt for a re-version rather than a per-version. In the later James, the figure of the artist, or artist-type, is increasingly common and important, and if adultery is not ubiquitous, it is nevertheless present in a way it never was for him in his earlier work. And by the same token he ceased to write bourgeois novels. We might say that *The Sacred Fount* combines both these topics and is at the same time the novel least accessible to bourgeois reading expectations. In this connection it is interesting to note that in *Ulysses* we have both the decomposition of the family—the father a voyeur masturbator, the wife an adulteress, the legitimate child dead—and a study of the composition of the dedicated artist. One is tempted to say that the emergence of the artist-as-hero is coincident with a sense of the family-as-ruin.

The bourgeois home is a hothouse of desire because it contains, confines perhaps is a better word, unoccupied language just as it does unoccupied women. The two facts are related. For if sexual realities and economic realities are to be excluded from the home, then so too, to a large extent, are linguistic realities. Not allowed an economic role in society, excluded in a number of ways from her full sexual reality, the bourgeois wife is left alone with language, not so much in its referential capacity but in its more dangerous and less controllable potentiality for introducing a generalized sense of lack that cannot be filled. A good example of the bourgeois wife in her most extreme form, and situation, is provided by the figure of Hedda Gabler, who is both prisoner and product of the bourgeois house—against procreation, destructive of truly "creative" products, burning Lovberg's manuscript as if it were a "child," bored with the home but too frightened of scandal to leave it. She is truly "unemployed," and her "desire" is purely a sense of lack that does not even translate itself into any actual adultery, but expresses itself as a growing negativity that finally extends to her own person. Until then she plays with words as she plays with guns, but so far from filling the sense of lack, they increase the sense of void until there is no social space left for her to inhabit. She retires into a private theatre of her own making and turns the gun against the word, blowing out her brains and thus annihilating the speaking, lacking, present-absent, protected, pointless object she has become.

In speculating about the whence of desire we find that it is possible to see it as connected to environment (which includes objects, food, clothes, architecture, money, as well as less tangible operative factors); to mediators, models, rivals of all kinds; to "others" as they constitute the family and society around the self, and the "Other" as it constitutes the locus of "the source of desire"; to language itself, whether the subject speaks or "is spoken"; and even to the death wish and the end to identity and difference. We must think perhaps of the diffuse genesis of desire and consider how novelists attempt to track out its operations and strategies in their complex, devious, and diverse manifestations.

The Triumph of the Will

For in the state of the families, which was extremely poor in language, the fathers alone must have spoken and given commands to their children and *famuli,* who, under the terrors of patriarchal rule . . . must have executed the commands in silence and with blind obsequiousness.—Vico, *The New Science*

The next chapter is intended to offer a detailed analysis of Rousseau's *La Nouvelle Héloïse,* but before embarking on that it would be misleading not to include a few remarks concerning the novel that most influenced him, namely, *Clarissa.* Albeit the main "battle" in this book is between aristocratic presumptions and high-bourgeois attempts at self-consolidation (I use the word *battle* advisedly, since the book starts and ends with duels—about which more later), and there is no question of adultery or even seduction, since the other "blood-letting" action in the book is the rape (almost totally concealed at the time of its happening, in the shortest letter in the book),[68] there are nonetheless crucial questions concerning "will," "authority," "law," and the family that it will be well to have before us before turning to Rousseau's novel.

With regard to the matter of *will,* there are four distinct manifestations of this ambiguous word (connoting at least intention, volition, aspiration, and desire). There is Clarissa's grandfather's will, which—no matter how much she attempts to disburden herself of the financial and property advantages it bestows on her (which *could* make her independent of her father, but that is unthinkable)—provokes a constant hostility toward her from the members of her family. This will is a *written* will inserted from death into the present (to be emulated by Clarissa when *she* dies) and thus not open to dialogue or question. Then there is the *spoken* will of the father, who "commands" but refuses to engage in dialogue with Clarissa—as does her brother, who dismisses her "whining vocatives" and "nothing-meaning vocatives," so that she is denied the right of personal address in her own family. There is also the rank *physical* will of Lovelace, unsanctioned lust. Finally, there is the basically silent, unwritten, nonphysical, *internal* will of Clarissa, which in the circumstances can only manifest itself as negation and refusal, struggling against the constraints of the family who would force her into a *loveless* marriage, and the seductions of *Lovelace* who would embroil her in unmarried sexuality. Thus she earnestly hopes that "my father will be pleased only to allow of my negative" and keeps reiterating that she wants only her "*negative*; not my *independence.*"[69] Ultimately of course

---

[68]Richardson, *Clarissa,* vol. 3, letter 29.

[69]Samuel Richardson, *Pamela* (London: Everyman's Library, 1961), vol. 2, letter 102; Richardson, *Clarissa,* vol. 1, letters 50, 51, 53, 80.

Pamela, in the novel bearing her name, explicitly claims that "the negative voice . . . belongs to the sex" (meaning her own). The struggle to own the "negative voice" is one of the more interesting aspects both of social history and within the history of the novel. The negative voice belongs, traditionally, to the Father, who not only had the rights of command over his children but the power of interdiction and prohibition. But, as we

she can only find release from all the impinging and hostile wills that center on her in the ultimate negative of life itself—death.

She is, then, assailed by the will in all its forms—written, spoken, physical—against which she can only pit the negating will of her spirit, or, indeed, soul. Thus the word recurs continually. "I am sometimes tempted to think that we may make the world allow for and respect us as we please, if we can but be sturdy in our wills, and set out accordingly"—an early hope that does not take into account an irrational family bent on using her to increase its property and riches, or the drugged potions that may be administered in a brothel. She soon realises that her family intend to "*suppose* me into their will" and that her father "*will* have no child, but an obedient one." Lovelace, characteristically boasts "I am no slave in my will," but Clarissa can later refer to "my *will too unviolated*," and Lovelace speaks wiser than he knows when he asks "what honour is lost, where the *will* is not violated, and the person cannot help it?" And it is because Clarissa can complain that "a will of my own has long been denied me" that she finally sacrifices her violated/pure body to her own written will, for as Miss Howe had written much earlier, and more prophetically than she could have realized—"wills are sacred things." When Clarissa's brother, rebuffed by Clarissa during one of his crude attempts at bullying enforcement, complains "How strong is will!" he unwittingly points to a central question of the book—who really has the strongest will?[70] The answer is certainly not Clarissa's father or Lovelace, about whom I now want to make some comments.

---

shall see, his hold on the negative voice, as on the commanding one, tends to grow detectably weaker through the whole period I shall be considering—and arguably beyond it as well. How the woman can move from a position in which she needs to hold on to her "negative" and become more positive or affirmative, is another, and related, question to be considered.

[70]Richardson, *Clarissa*, vol. 1, letters 5, 8; vol. 3, letter 46; vol. 4, letters 18, 154, 40; vol. 1, letters 27, 79.

In the writings of Marx, the notion of the "will" necessarily takes on an added and different meaning, or context—necessarily, given the changed society he was examining; this is worth recording here, in anticipation of a consideration of the novels of that society.

In actual history, those theoreticians who regarded power as the basis of right, were in direct contradiction to those who looked on will as the basis of right . . . If power is taken as the basis of right, as Hobbes, etc. do, then right, law, etc. are merely the symptom, the expression of other relations upon which State power rests. The material life of individuals, which by no means depends merely on their "will," their mode of production and form of intercourse, which mutually determine each other—this is the real basis of the State and remains so at all the stages at which division of labour and private property are still necessary, quite independently of the will of individuals. These actual relations are in no way created by the State power; on the contrary they are the power creating it. The individuals who rule in these conditions, besides having to constitute their power in the form of the State, have to give their will, which is determined by these definite conditions, a universal expression as the will of the State, as law—an expression whose content is always

Clarissa is caught between dehumanized and dehumanizing appetites for property and for pleasure. Her father's house is the very architecture of prohibition and interdiction, and though she is pulled out of it through a gate (perhaps unconsciously wishing to find a gap of escape), *consciously* she never intends to leave it without paternal permission. The father, indeed, serves only to prohibit or command—never to inquire into his daughter's preferences or needs. He has a "terrible voice," but I would note here that there is an element of compensation in this. For, although it is easy to overlook the hints we are given, he is a *sick* father. One quotation: Clarissa early on refers to "the torture of a gouty paroxysm" to which he is liable, and adds: "But my father was soured by the cruel distemper I have named, which seized him all at once in the very prime of life, in so violent a manner as to take from the most active of minds, as *his* was, all power of activity, and that in all appearance for life. It imprisoned, as I may say, his lively spirits in himself, and turned the edge of them against his own peace, his extraordinary prosperity adding to his impatiency." Thus his intemperate roaring, his invocation of his "will," the law, his "AUTHORITY" ("the tyrant word"), his refusal of any independence to his children, his general "unpersuadability" (a word applied by the family to Clarissa, but more properly applied to the father in his refusal to be dialogued with), can be seen as having psychosomatic or pathological origins. He utters curses and maledictions on Clarissa (later, it is true, to be recalled but by then too late for any earthly aid to her rehabilitation), but does not offer the true paternal protection that Clarissa needs and seeks, nor that forgiveness that is essential to whatever hopes she may have of recovering her physical well-being. More typically, while Clarissa seems to him disobedient and bent on her own independence (a mishearing of what she is really asking for—which is only not to be forced into a relationship in which she will be alienated from herself and merely used as an instrument for the

---

determined by the relations of this class, as the civil and criminal law demonstrates in the clearest possible way. . . . Their personal power is based on conditions of life which as they develop are common to many individuals, and the continuance of which they, as ruling individuals, have to maintain against others and, at the same time, maintain they hold good for all. The expression of this will, which is determined by their common interests, is law. It is precisely because individuals who are independent of one another assert themselves and their own will, which on this basis is inevitably egotistical in their mutual relations, that self-denial is made necessary in law and right, self-denial in the exceptional case, and self-assertion of their interests in the average case (which, therefore, not they, but only the "egoist in agreement with himself" regards as self-denial). The same applies to the classes which are ruled, whose will plays just as small a part in determining the existence of law and the State.

(*The German Ideology* in Marx, *Selected Writings*, ed. David McLellan [Oxford: Oxford University Press, 1977], pp. 183–84.)

acquisition of more property), he refuses even to see her or look at her, thus completely invalidating her by refusing her precisely the true look of recognition, and nullifying her existence. His wife speaks for him and the family when she says to Clarissa that they want her "heart" ("never say your *heart is free*"), and until she agrees to submit that interior organ of authentic preference and revulsion, everything she does or does not do is dis-interpreted as perversity, obstinacy, contradiction, opposition. Because the father owns the word, or discourse, of the house, he can distort terminologies and vocabularies at his pleasure (or displeasure), and Clarissa is not allowed to make her own case in her own words without having it perversely maltranslated according to her father's sick preconceptions—or simply his blind, unseeing, unhearing anger. Clarissa indeed wants only an honorable return to her "father's house" (the religious implications of this have often been commented on but are hardly essential to this family story), and more than anything else wants a "parental blessing" but "a blessing to *die* with; not to *live* with."[71] In life, she has been harshly and systematically unfathered and the only space she can seek out in which her heart, at least, can be her own is the grave.

With Lovelace, the justifications, intentions, and imperatives are, of course, quite other. For him the sword is higher or mightier than the law, just as rape and seduction are more to his taste—or felt to be more appropriate to his class—than marriage. As an "aristocrat," albeit an utterly immoral one, he despises and puts himself above all the sanctions and ceremonies that the bourgeoisie (no matter if it is the high bourgeoisie) cling to. He promises Clarissa the very "free will" that her family denies her, but for him "will" is so closely allied to "desire," or appetite, that it could be rephrased as the freedom to do whatever impulse prompts—which is not the freedom that Clarissa is seeking. (It is interesting that at one point he calls himself "a machine at last, and no free agent" as he develops his devious campaign against Clarissa, since, for all his rakish liberty, or libertinism, he is basically a machine of appetites, his freedom a simulating and self-deceiving swagger, himself a victim of uncensored appetites.) Part of his contempt for bourgeois proceedings can be seen in his mockery of the whole business of "contracts" as he tries to deceive Clarissa with a fake marriage license—he calls it "a good whimsical instrument". "Whimsical" is precisely what contracts were not for the bourgeoisie, but his action merely serves to underline his contempt for all those reciprocal legal obligations that structured the bourgeois way of life (so that, as we saw, a contract made in the absence of one of the contractees—in this case Clarissa—was felt to be authoritative and binding). Thus he is, as Clarissa can see, a principle or force of

[71]Richardson, *Clarissa*, vol. 1, letters 7, 5, 15, 56, 18, 20; vol. 4, letter 20.

molestation and violation, not just of her but of everything represented
by her family's—and her class's—way of life. His rape, like his wounding
of Clarissa's brother in the opening of the book (no matter how justified), represent a supralegal, or simply nonlegal, attack by force on a
class whose basic mores he despises. He neither goes to court nor goes
a-courting (in any genuine sense)—he employs force and draws blood.
The fact that after Clarissa's death, for him "the whole world is but one
great Bedlam" and he experiences a total loss of any sense of substance,
identity, and reality—"What's the world? What's anybody in it?"—
indicates not just grief, remorse, or even some kind of inchoate guilt and
regret feelings, but rather that he never respected the world or the
integrity of the other person, and so, rather like Peer Gynt, he is now
experiencing the world as a madhouse in which the Emperor of Self is
transformed into a slave of felt nothingness, adrift in a world of matter
which *is*, but does not *mean*. And when he complains that he is "misera-
bly absent from myself," we realize that he has reached an extreme point
of self-alienation.[72]

But there is one other aspect to the figure of Lovelace that it is important to note, namely, that without him there would be no novel. In
Richardson's opening paragraph (in the preface) he talks of Lovelace as
"glorying in his talents for stratagem and invention," and we are constantly being reminded that he is a "great plotter" and that "*newelty*, that
was the man's word, was everything with him." "Newelty" is novelty, and
what is a novel without "newelty" and plots? Plots, contrivances, in-
trigues, stratagems, inventions, these are words that make up a recurring
part of his vocabulary. During Clarissa's illness, he may curse his "*contriving genius*" and his "reptile motives,"[73] but to *contrive* is to invent, to
devise, even to imagine, and without his contriving energy being
inserted—or erupting into—the house of Clarissa's father, we would
have no story, or "newelty," but only that stasis of maintenance without
incident or deviation that the bourgeoisie sought to preserve. And as for
his reptile motives—what would *Othello* be without Iago? Lovelace is thus
the novelist within the novel, no matter how diabolical a one. He is the
source of disruption and molestation, of dark, plotting energy, that
makes the book, while marring the characters within it. He is, more
crudely, the sexual drive that initiates the narration, without which the
text would remain in a state of inert noncommencement.

More specifically, he is the disrupter of the family. Clarissa's touch-
ingly idealistic belief at the start that "in my opinion the world is but one
great family" will be reversed until it is clear that the family is more like a

[72]Ibid., vol. 1, letter 85; vol. 3, letters 18, 26; vol. 4, letters 136, 150.
[73]Ibid., vol. 1, letter 4; vol. 4, letter 109.

world of selfishness and atomistic nonrelationships. The first sentence in the first letter (from Miss Howe) refers to "the disturbances that have happened in your family," disturbances consequent upon the penetration of Lovelace into the household—an entry that starts in decorum and ends in blood, thus, in a way, anticipating the whole novel (cf. "The Stranger in the House," above). For, as we gather from the second letter (from Clarissa), since that event the family has been "*discomposed . . . in tumults.*" This *dis*composition (later to become a *de*composition), so far from being resolved into a renewed harmony, gradually turns the family into "an *embattled phalanx*," the battle lines being drawn up more against Clarissa, who cannot escape, than Lovelace, who is very much on the loose with his plots and reptile motives. As things get worse, even Betty, the maid, cries "what hurly-burlies are here, where all used to be peace and quietness." What we witness, in spite of, or indeed partly because of, the sick father's blind ranting, the brother's bullying, the sister's cruel jealousy, the mother's unmaternal compliance with the majority, is the disintegration of the family rather than its increasing consolidation and expansion (the bourgeois aim). Lovelace, indeed, wants totally to deny Clarissa's family and to take its place: "She has no father, no mother, no sister, no brother; no relations but me." But that relationship is precisely not a relationship—for Clarissa, no matter what unconscious attraction she may have felt for Lovelace at one time, there can be no relationship based on rape, deception, and coercion. She is, indeed, totally *unfamilied* by the time of her death, with no true relations at all. (This is why she states that "I am nobody's" in her will.) And while Lovelace, in a last demonstration of his unremitting physicality and desire to penetrate and get at the inside of Clarissa, wants her dead body to "be opened and embalmed," she asserts her will even after death, writing of her body that "I will not, on any account, that it be opened." Against the onsets and assaults of all around, she effects a total closure and disengagement from all ties—both those of consanguinity and those of bloody coercion. Not allowed either the freedom of her heart, or the privilege of her negative, she divorces herself from everyone. Her body was to be treated as property to be bartered or as an instrument of pleasure—again she avoids both of these fates by negativing her body, calling it "nothing." Meanwhile, after her death, her family effectively falls apart: "To see them hang their pensive heads; mope about, *shunning one another*; though formerly never used to meet but to rejoice in each other" (my italics).[74] The family in which the members shun each other is no family at all; instead of the world as family, we are closer to the family as Bedlam—not Lovelace's madhouse so much as a house of lost communi-

[74]Ibid., vol. 1, letters 8, 1, 2, 32, 79; vol. 4, letters 137, 136, 146, 147, 158.

cation, broken contacts, and a batch of moping isolates, lost in the solitudes of their various self-recriminations and sense of loss.

Clarissa, then, is helplessly involved in all the problems of law, authority, freedom, dependence/independence, contracts, transgressions, imposed ceremony and abductive force, family, money, property, rank,
title, sex, appetite—to name only the most obvious and besetting. Her
mother calls her "the *warm statue,*" and, given her situation, this is not so
much of a paradox, since she is still flesh and blood but cannot make a
move of her own that will not be cruelly misconstrued or viciously
abused. Her only hope is to remain still, just as her only conscious desire
is the right to her negative. What she refuses is to be "wedded to a
monster" (i.e., Solmes), though she will be raped by another monster (i.e.,
Lovelace). *Monster* is an important word, not used lightly, and I will
return to it later in the book. She is "determined not to litigate with her
father," that deformed incarnation of the law, anymore than she will plot
and fornicate with Lovelace, the reptilian despiser of the law. Since,
given the opposing pressures on her, there is nothing she can either do
or not do, she would "willingly run away from myself,"[75] but there is
literally no *where* for her to go—except the nowhere of death. Death,
indeed, she does seek, though she will not hasten it by actual suicide.
This may seem like a retreat into an extreme form of ascetic denial of the
flesh, a masochistic turning-against life and perverse repudiation of the
body. But before we pass judgment on Clarissa's will to die, we might
consider these words of Nietzsche, which conclude *The Genealogy of
Morals:*

> Until the advent of the ascetic ideal, man, the animal *man,* had no
> meaning at all on this earth. . . . Man, the most courageous animal, the
> most inured to trouble, does not deny suffering *per se:* he wants it, he seeks
> it out, provided that it can be given a meaning. Finally the ascetic ideal
> arose to give it meaning—its only meaning, so far. But any meaning is
> better than none and, in fact, the ascetic ideal has been the best stopgap
> that ever existed. Suffering has been interpreted, the door to all suicidal
> nihilism slammed shut. No doubt that interpretation brought new suffer-
> ing in its wake, deeper, more inward, more poisonous suffering: it placed
> all suffering under the perspective of *guilt.* . . . All the same, man had
> saved himself, he had achieved a meaning, he was no longer a leaf in the
> wind, a plaything of circumstances, of "crass casualty": he was now able to
> will something—no matter the object or the instrument of his willing; *the
> will itself had been saved* [my italics]. We can no longer conceal from our-
> selves what exactly it is that this whole process of willing, inspired by the
> ascetic ideal, signifies—this hatred of humanity, of animality, of inert mat-

[75] Ibid., vol. 1, letters 20, 17, 28, 55.

ter; this loathing of the senses, of reason even; this fear of beauty and happiness; this longing to escape from illusion, change, becoming, death, and from longing itself. It signifies, let us have the courage to face it, a will to nothingness, a revulsion from life, a rebellion against the principal conditions of living. And yet, despite everything, it is and remains a *will*. Let me repeat, now that I have reached the end, what I said at the beginning: man would sooner have the void for his purpose than be void of purpose. . . .[76]

Not all these words are applicable to Clarissa, of course, particularly given her beset and isolated condition. But it helps to remind us that through her asceticism, and her negative, her will *is* saved, and not only saved, but proved stronger than the more mundane, life-involved, egotistical, and perverted wills of the other characters. And in her isolated helplessness, her purpose—albeit for the void—proves to have more strength and determination than the self-seeking purposes of the characters plotting around her.

One friend she does have, Miss Howe, and Lovelace scornfully refers to Clarissa and Miss Howe as "the pretended *inseparables*"—an idea that Rousseau was to make much use of (is it a coincidence that the name H–arl–owe, contains Howe, the nominal closeness intimating some more creatural affinity?). But Miss Howe can only sympathize, not actively help. With all her virtues, Clarissa is indeed "an absolute mistress of the *should-be*," but in her position she has no control over the "is." There is, indeed, one memorable occasion when she rebuffs the ever-predatory Lovelace by holding a penknife (the female equivalent of a sword) to her bosom and invoking, yes, the law. "The LAW shall be all my resource: the LAW",[77] which effectively sends Lovelace into a retreat to the other end of the room. For while he is expert in dueling (which she is explicitly against), he is helpless against the blade turned inward, the rapist rendered impotent by the threat of suicide: the penknife—in this context—mightier than the sword.

Whether or not Clarissa is unconsciously attracted to Lovelace has been much written about, and some deep ambivalence in her attitude to him need hardly be disputed. By comparison with Solmes!—Even the most lukewarm statue would have registered the difference. But her idea of love is of course very different from his. For Lovelace "Love, that deserves the name, never was under the dominion of *prudence,* or of any *reasoning* power." But such an attempt to isolate love from all other faculties of the mind effectively reduces it to brief infatuation. (Not for

---

[76]Friedrich Nietzsche, *The Genealogy of Morals,* trans. Francis Golffing (New York: Doubleday, 1956) essay 3, section 28.
[77]Richardson, *Clarissa,* vol. 3, letter 24; vol. 4, letter 168; vol. 3, letter 53.

nothing does he have an idea of establishing very short-term marriages, so that people may indulge in, say, an annual change, according to their "honest desires." It is the act of commitment and the idea of lifelong lastingness in marriage that his ranging appetites and volatile temperament—"Besely seeking with a continuell chaunge"—abhor. This is an idea or problem already mentioned, and to be examined by Goethe.) But Clarissa, like a proper Jane Austen heroine, does believe that love, prudence and reason, and indeed many other faculties, can and should go together—and if she believes that reason and prudence should dominate, it is precisely because of the immoral snares set by a loveless Lovelace, or the misguided imperatives of a property-hungry family. She is indeed in a kind of social menagerie, with some of the animals uncaged and on the loose. Thus among the scraps of paper— some torn, some crossed out and thrown under her table—that Lovelace finds she has written after the rape, there is the famous Paper iii, in which her meandering and distracted mind seems half to release an unconscious sense of what has happened.

> A lady took a great fancy to a young lion, or a bear, I forget which. . . . She fed it with her own hand: she nursed up the wicked cub with great tenderness; and would play with it without fear or apprehension of danger . . . But mind what followed: at last, somehow, neglecting to satisfy its hungry maw, or having otherwise disobliged it on some occasion, it resumed its nature; and on a sudden fell upon her, and tore her in pieces. And who was most to blame, I pray? The brute, or the lady? The lady, surely! For what *she* did was *out* of nature, *out* of character, at least: what it did was *in* its own nature.

Apart from indicating that in some way she was responsible for some initial dalliance with Lovelace—for the secret correspondence does represent an attempt to find some point of leakage in the father's stronghold, through which some of her suppressed feelings, suitably transcribed, can find a means of egress and release—the paper raises the whole problem of what it is to be *in* or *out* of nature, and whether character can transcend nature or simply enact its drives and promptings. She blames herself, effectively, for falling out of character and into nature, at least nature as defined by Lovelace. For her there is a higher nature than that of animal-man (lion, bear, snake, brute, monster, etc.), and it is to that nature and her own real character that she reaspires with all her energies for the rest of her life. (Thus she dies an extremely spiritual death, effectively purified of the body altogether; while, by contrast, the death of the prostitute or brothel keeper, *Madam* Sinclair, which follows shortly after, is described in terms of sheer physicality, with every deformity and sickness of the body given in great detail. It is not at all like Clarissa's "blessed *departure*," but just a horrible collapsing of the flesh, which "for an experiment only" is to be "lanced and quartered" and perhaps to suffer "amputation"—it is, in a sense, a "natural" death, but nature disnatured terminating a natural/unnatural life.)[78]

And so the final "triumph" is Clarissa's. Her father had tried to triumph by invoking paternal law over his child's inclinations and disinclinations. Lovelace attempts to assert "the triumph of nature over principle," but finally recognizes that Clarissa is "the triumphant subduer"—triumphant through the power of her own inner will over the "natural" and social and familial "wills" to coerce her heart and violate her body. Too late Lovelace vows that "I will have no will but hers,"[79] and in his state of unreclaimed "nature," no matter how elegantly "laced" in the style and accoutrements of the aristocrat, he could never aspire to Clarissa's transcendent concept of the will. He is literally corrupt—his heart is not broken so much as just not there—for all his fine physique and power, humanly speaking he is a hollow man. Her triumph makes of her negative the most positive phenomenon in the book, and with it she effectively negates the "newelties" and plots in which people seek to make her play an imposed role. In this way she blocks the "novel" into which Lovelace is, as it were, trying to "write" her, or make her play a pre-scribed part. In that novel she is apparently all victim; it requires Richardson's more spacious and morally comprehensive novel to celebrate her triumph while describing her fate and death.

Having mentioned "writing," I want to mention one aspect of this novel written in letters quite apart from, or in addition to, the usual justification for the epistolary mode—"Much more lively and affecting-. . . must be the style of those who write in the height of a present distress, the mind tortured by the pangs of uncertainty (the events then hidden in the womb of fate), than the dry, narrative, unanimated style of a person relating difficulties and dangers surmounted, can be" etc.: see Author's Preface. At an early point, Clarissa starts criticizing her family, then quickly retracts—"But whither roves my pen?" We may surmise that when the body cannot "rove," then, by a process of displacement and compensation, the pen will. This kind of affective transference of bodily energy and drives into written ones is manifest throughout, most dramatically in Paper X, written after the rape, when her disordered memory of her body's violation is projected into a violation of the very order of the written text, so that the fragmented notes and literary quotations that flow into her mind are scattered at different angles over the page—all linear coherence gone, all mental ordering temporarily distracted. This, in fact, is the nearest we come to actually seeing the

[78]Ibid., vol. 3, letters 25, 26, 33; vol. 4, letters 139, 138.
[79]Ibid., vol. 4, letters 10, 109.

rape—the disruption of the written page masking but revealing the disruption of the body. In the final volume the references to the importance of writing increase. "Writing is all my diversion," says Clarissa, thus indicating that it is not just a time-filling recreation, but a mode of deflection, away from the body and into print. Later, to Lovelace, she makes the point quite clearly. "But a will of my own has long been denied me; and to avoid a greater evil, nay, now I may say, the greatest, I write." Thus writing becomes both defense and compensation, the freedom of the page making up for the imprisonment of the body. Indeed, she writes so much and so compulsively that she feels "I do amiss in writing so much," but the explanation follows immediately when she complains "Yet how this *body* clings! How it encumbers!" She is, as I have intimated, transforming her encumbering body into the release of writing. That she is well aware of the difference (body/print) is clear from Lovelace's complaint that he has not had a "pardon from her *lips,* which she has not denied me by *pen and ink.*"[80] 'Twixt pen and lip, not only many a slip (lips are more vulnerable than pens), but a crucial space or gap—or, better, a *distance,* so that the isolated writer is secure within her writing, whereas the speaker/listener has to negotiate (in Clarissa's case) the always possible dangers of physical propinquity. Thus part of her final triumph is to *write* her *will* (not just the document of bequest, but *will* in all senses of the word), since, physically speaking, she could never live it. *This* will, with all its positives and imperatives, cannot be negated or gainsaid.

Before completing these brief remarks on this arguably most seminal of English eighteenth-century novels, I want to draw attention to two quite separate quotations, the relevance of which will, I hope, become clearer in the course of the book. First an idea put forward by Clarissa:

> The suiting of the tempers of two persons who are to come together is a great matter: and there should be boundaries fixed between them, by consent as it were, beyond which neither should go: and each should hold the other to it; or there would probably be encroachments in both. To illustrate my assertion by a very high, and by a more manly (as some would think it) than womanly instance. If the boundaries of the three estates that constitute our political union were not known, and occasionally asserted, what would become of the prerogatives and privileges of each? The two branches of the legislature would encroach upon each other; and the executive power would swallow up both.[81]

I have alluded to the importance of "boundaries" as outlined by Vico, but the problems involved in combining both binding and "boundary-

---

[80]Ibid., vol. 1, letter 13; vol. 4, letters 4, 40, 75, 88.
[81]Ibid., vol. 1, letter 68.

ing" in marriage are problems which start to come distinctly to the fore in the novels I will be examining. It is a matter, to extract from Clarissa's illustration, of the politics of marriage—two become one, yet must, and necessarily do, remain two. Then there are the many others around them offering attractions and distractions, so that two may become three, four, any number at all, and union (dependent on bonds and boundaries) may be lost in a merging multiplicity in which not just executive power but the very sense of difference and relationship itself is swallowed up. Where and how do you draw those lines by which, and within which, passion may be satisfied, while legal contracts are honored and the sense of separate identity is maintained?

The other quotation is perhaps not so far from this problem as may at first appear. It comes from the Conclusion and concerns the upbringing, or downbringing, of Polly Horton, who leads a youth of dissoluteness and finishes up in a brothel. Her mother—who "debauched" herself on all kinds of "romances and novels, songs and plays, and those without distinction, moral or immoral"—was the first baneful influence:

> ... as miss grew up under the influences of such a directress, and of books so light and frothy, with the inflaming additions of music, concerts, operas, plays, assemblies, balls, drums, routs, and the rest of the rabble of amusements of the modern life, it is no wonder that, like early fruit, she was soon ripened to the hand of the insidious gatherer. At fifteen she owned she was ready to fancy herself the heroine of every novel and of every comedy she read, so well did she enter into the *spirit* of her subject: she glowed to become the object of some hero's flame; and perfectly longed to begin an intrigue, and even to be *run away with* by some enterprising lover. ...

In all this, her early years offer a direct antithesis to Clarissa's, and what starts as a failure to make any distinction in *reading,* ends up as a failure to make any distinction among sexual partners. As we say, her imagination knows no bounds—nor, later, will her body. It is Clarissa who realizes that bindings only make sense with the recognition of boundaries. Polly Horton's confused education, or rather diseducation, is much closer to Emma Bovary's—but that is a matter for a later chapter. Clarissa, the obedient child who would never *run away,* but has, as it were, to be tricked, dragged, and drugged, feels that her "character ... was lost," at least "in the eye of the world" (and no eye bestows a crueller gaze), "from the very hour I left my father's house."[82] This all-pervading sense of the dire consequences of leaving "the father's house"—no matter how tyrannical an abode it is—is central to Rousseau's novel, to which we may now turn.

---

[82]Ibid., vol. 4, conclusion; vol. 3, letter 87.

2

---◆---

ROUSSEAU'S *LA NOUVELLE HELOISE**

Le Bosquet Profané

The first embrace between Julie and Saint-Preux takes place in a "charming arbor" in a grove that lies close to the house in which Julie lives, Clarens. She herself selects the spot and prepares him with a tantalizing hint that mingles topographic specificity with promisory vagueness and ordained constraints. "Among the natural arbors which make up this charming place, there is one more charming than the rest, with which I am most delighted and in which, for that reason, I am reserving a little surprise for my friend . . . I must warn you that we shall not go together into the arbor without the inseparable cousin" (p. 51). ("Parmi les bosquets naturels que forme ce lieu charmant, il en est un plus charmant que des autres, dans lequel je destine une petite surprise à mon ami . . . je dois vous prévenir que nous n'irons point ensemble dans le bosquet sans l'*inséparable cousine*" [p. 33].)[1] The choice of an arbor for a secret rendezvous is appropriate enough, but I want to note that the spot that will be the location of their unlegalized sexual embrace (fornication of course—*not* adultery) is very near the house that Julie, effectively, will never leave—the house of her father. The insistence on having the *inseparable cousin* (Claire) present when she is to give Saint-Preux his "surprise" is indicative of Julie's wish somehow to combine intrafamilial love with extrafamilial passion: the cousin, as "cousin" is to be a mediator between filial devotion and female sexuality, between the father and the

---

*A shorter version of this chapter appeared as "Julie and 'La Maison Paternelle': Another Look at Rousseau's *La Nouvelle Héloise*," *Daedalus* 105, no. 1 (winter 1976): 23–46.

[1]Unless otherwise indicated, French and English quotations from Rousseau's novel within this chapter are from Jean Jacques Rousseau, *Julie ou la nouvelle Héloïse* (Paris: Garnier'Flammarion, 1967), and Rousseau, *Julie, or The New Eloise*, translated and abridged by Judith H. McDowell (University Park: Pennsylvania State University, 1968).

lover, between what is in the home and what is not in the home. As cousin she stands exactly in relation to Julie's family (in the restricted sense of parents and their children) as the arbor does to the house: that is to say, not actually inside it, but not totally outside it either, not completely unconnected and foreign. Arbors (and related topographical phenomena) play a frequent role in the long iconistic history of that topographical "middle ground" between culture and wild nature where the two may meet; and for Julie it is clear that her cousin represents a relational middle ground that she herself hopes to be able to maintain between daughter and lover. Of course it proves to be impossible; but the desire and attempt to keep everyone and everything together, connected, related, unsundered and inseparable—literally in one place, as well as emotionally, mentally, and even, at times, perceptually indistinguishable and merged—is the dominant drive in Julie's existence. She even wants to internalize the external, as it were, and enhouse the unhoused elements of existence. It represents a dream of *total* harmony, of complete incorporation and domestication that at the same time wishes to maintain that it is totally *natural;* as if to maintain that nature *is* culture and culture nature (not a relationship but an identity). The relationship of this complex and impossible dream to the developments in the thought of the Enlightenment is too obvious to need any comment. But in terms of sexual/familial relationships such a dream can lead to strange displacements or confusions. *La Nouvelle Héloïse* is indeed a novel above all else about love, but the powerful love relationship is between Julie and her father. Saint-Preux is an adopted child. The novel sedulously avoids adultery, but it is marked by all-pervasive feelings of incest (emotional and mental incest of course, though in one extraordinary episode, it is almost as if the father brutally rapes Julie. By comparison the most physical action of Saint-Preux to appear in the text is a feverishly excited manual exploration of Julie's clothes and underwear [in her absence], in an equally extraordinary incident of quite astonishing prurience). Julie's dream is, in certain important ways, a dream of total incest. The ultimate utter failure and collapse of this dream is a crucial prelude to the great novels of adultery that were to follow it.

What apparently happens in the arbor on that first occasion is that the inseparable cousin first asks Saint-Preux for a kiss with a contradictory air of what one might call droll imploring ("d'un air plaisamment suppliant" [p. 34]), and a cousinly embrace ensues. It is now Julie's turn (it is all rather like the kissing games played at children's parties, as if Julie wants to defuse sexuality by infantilizing it), and she bestows a distinctly uncousinly kiss on the understandably "surprised" Saint-Preux. She then returns to the arms of the inseparable cousin and proceeds to faint. It is small wonder that Saint-Preux registers a certain degree of mystification in the scene ("sans rien comprendre à ce mystère" [p. 34]), and we may adjudge it a considerable understatement when he subsequently refers to "the test of the arbor" (p. 55) (l'épreuve du bosquet" [p. 36]). He is immediately afterwards ordered by Julie to leave the house and travel, which—being the bemused, compliant figure that he is—he as promptly does. Shortly thereafter he refers to the "delirium" of the arbor ("ce délire qu'il éprouva dans le bosquet" [p. 55]). At this point Julie falls hysterically ill, and Saint-Preux is summoned back, and in the very next letter Julie tells the absent Claire that the moment of "crisis" has arrived and begs her to return to her ("la crise est venue" [p. 58]). From the next letter we infer that she has capitulated sexually to Saint-Preux—it can only have been in the arbor, and only because the inseparable cousin was indeed separate. Julie has yet to learn that there is no such thing as an inseparable person since separation is, not a function of, but a condition of, individual existence.

Very soon, we gather, Julie accepts the clandestine sexual relationship (it is not to my purpose to discuss the endless rhetorical twistings and turnings, changes and modifications, etc., that characterize her letters and that accompany her shifts in attitude to her relationship with Saint-Preux), though she still seems to want to keep it within the controllable arena of some kind of game, as appears from a provocative letter in which she writes, à propos of the coming evening, "I shall perhaps repeat the lesson of the arbor at Clarens. . . . we shall all three go into my cousin's room. There, my loyal vassal, on your knees before your lady and mistress, your hand in hers, and in the presence of her chancellor, you will swear faith to her and loyalty on every occasion. . . . This done, you shall have the accolade and be acknowledged as sole vassal and loyal knight" (pp. 91–92). ("Je recorderai peut-être la leçon du bosquet de Clarens . . . nous passerons tous trois dans la chambre de la cousine. C'est là, mon féal, qu'à genoux devant votre dame et maîtresse, vos deux mains dans les siennes, et en présence de son chancelier, vous lui jurerez foi et loyauté à toute épreuve. . . . Ce faisant, aurez l'accolade, et serez reconnu vassal unique et loyal chevalier" [p. 70].) I shall have more to say about this reenactment of decontextualized bits of "chivalry" (bedroom mediaevalism) in a spirit of would-be serious make-believe (or nostalgia / play). But it is worth noting that the relationship of Julie and Saint-Preux can never move beyond the stage of "game." The real world is under the dominion of Julie's father, and he simply will not grant Saint-Preux admission. Games of course can be as painful, bittersweet, ecstatic as you like, and the letters between Julie and Saint-Preux add up to one of the longest and most complete emotional "games" ever set down as literature. Julie's father never plays.

After the arbor the two lovers graduate, as it were, to the chalet, and I will turn to that next. But before doing so I want to consider the implications of the strange "ceremony" that is improvised and stage-managed by M. de Wolmar long after he and Julie are married and after Saint-Preux has been taken into the house as a friend / child. One day he takes them both to the very grove that had been both a "test" and a "lesson" and had variously offered surprise, mystery, and delirium: the grove where, writes Julie, all the misfortunes of her life began. Wolmar, it is made clear both by himself and by Julie, is a detached observer, indeed a cool voyeur of the emotions of others. But his behavior on this occasion is so "rational" as to partake of perversity, a perversity that decrees an act of what can only be called purification by profanation. He orders the once-young lovers to repeat the initial kiss. "Getting up, he embraced us and desired us to embrace each other too, in that place . . . in that very place where once before . . . I made no resistance to it. . . . The kiss was nothing like the one which had made the grove fearful for me. . . . As we returned to the road to the house, my husband took me by the hand and, pointing to that grove we had just left, he said, laughing, 'Julie, fear that refuge no longer. It has just been profaned' " (pp. 321–23). ("En se levant il nous embrassa, et voulut que nous nous embrassassions aussi, dans ce lieu . . . et dans ce lieu même où jadis . . . je n'en fis aucune difficulté. . . . Ce baiser n'eut rien de celui qui m'avait rendu le bosquet redoutable. . . . Comme nous reprenions le chemin du logis, mon mari m'arrêta par la main, et, me montrant ce bosquet dont nous sortions, il me dit en riant: 'Julie, ne craignez plus cet asile, il vient d'être profané' " [pp. 372–73].)

It is worth pondering a little on the implications of Wolmar's use of the word *profaned*. What is "profane" is that which is "outside the temple," and the verb *to profane* means to treat something sacred with irreverence or contempt, to defile or debase it. Thus the implication is that the unsanctified and illicit sexual embraces and kisses enacted by Julie and Saint-Preux had effectively sacralized the arbor for them: i.e., transformed it into a private sacred space, not recognized as such by society. The chaste and licit embrace that Wolmar forces them to enact under his eye (the husband / father, the source of social sanctions) desacralizes the arbor. What had been temporarily an emotional temple for them is thereby robbed of its privately bestowed aura. The arbor is once more, like any other piece of unsanctified nature, outside the temple. Wolmar, not a man given to excessive mirth, laughs when he makes his remark to Julie, and though the tone is one of benign reassurance, I think we can detect something quite different implicit in the whole proceeding. Because, although Wolmar can present his action as all part of a plan of rational reconciliation, it is effectively a retrospective invalidation of the love that had been experienced by Julie and Saint-Preux in the arbor.

The message is: Let us all be good friends in a rational way, each clearly recognizing his or her position and relationship vis-à-vis the others. The metamessage is: Because it is within my total power to decree just what the positions and relationships of all involved shall be, it is also within my power to annihilate your own past emotional experiences; whatever you may think you felt for each other, I am hereby cancelling it out. He is asserting his control of the dominant discourse.

What he describes as "profane" thereby becomes profane. He owns the language. Since Julie is all obedience with Wolmar (she is all commanding with Saint-Preux), she accepts both message and metamessage, though it transpires in a later letter written near death that her feelings for Saint-Preux have not been so totally eradicated *as she had been persuaded to believe* that they had. In life she tries to accept totally Wolmar's versions of everything, herself and her own emotional orientations included. Since Wolmar is very clearly a surrogate for Julie's own father, the implications of this slave / master relationship (which, underneath all the harmonious reasoning and apparent agreement *inter pares*, it essentially is), are far reaching indeed. I shall come back to this.

Un Chalet à la Ville

Just as it was Julie who appointed the initial embrace in the arbor, so, as she comes to some extent to accept the sexual relationship, she decrees their next venue—a remote chalet in the country near the source of the Vevaise. (I will note now that Saint-Preux is never allowed to initiate any meeting, decide on any venue, fix on any abode. His life is entirely shaped and directed by others, starting with Julie. In innumerable ways he is constantly being reminded of the complete helplessness of his social position, his entire dependency on others for just about everything, including his identity. There is one strange letter from Julie in which she upbraids him, at some considerable length, for indulging in what we infer to have been obscene language and perhaps swearing. There are also reports in other letters of outbursts of anger that are clearly tantrums. These are symptoms of the frustration of a child who is deliberately not being allowed to grow up.) This is how she outlines their proposed meeting at the chalet. Having described the setting, she refers to the remote village that "sometimes is used as a shelter for hunters but should only serve as a refuge for lovers" (p. 93) ("qui sert quelque-fois de repaire aux chasseurs, et ne devrait servir que d'asile aux amants" [p. 71]). We can notice here a sign of that strategy of accommodation by rebaptism that in various ways comes to dominate the novel (i.e., she renames the "repaire aux chasseurs" as "asile aux amants"; the significance of transforming a space connected with hunting into one dedicated to loving will not go unnoticed). Julie continues: "At the invitation of Monsieur d'Orbe, Claire has already persuaded her papa to go with some friends to hunt for two or three days in that area and to take along the inseparable cousins. The inseparables have others, as you know only too well. The one, representing the master of the house, will naturally do the honours of it; the other with less ceremony will do those of a humble chalet for his Julie, and this chalet sanctified by love, will be for them the temple of Cnidus" (p. 44). ("Claire a déjà persuadé à son papa qu'il avait envie d'aller faire avec quelques amis une chasse de deux ou trois jours dans ce canton, et d'y mener les inséparables. Ces inséparables en ont d'autres, comme tu ne sais que trop bien. L'un, représentant le maître de la maison, en fera naturellement les honneurs; l'autre, avec moins d'éclat, pourra faire à sa Julie ceux d'un humble chalet; et ce chalet, consacré par l'amour, sera pour eux le temple de Gnide" [p. 72].) Monsieur is the accepted suitor of Claire and is to be her husband. Thus he may represent "the master of the house," i.e., her father. This is the one position that Saint-Preux is never to be allowed to occupy; at most he will be a child of the house, never the master—never, that is, the father's representative. Saint-Preux can only do the illusory honors of the chalet, and necessarily with less "éclat" than the appointed representative of the master of the house, since one aspect of his helpless position is that he is permitted almost zero access to social *éclat* of any substantial kind whatsoever. He can hardly shine, because he can hardly show—hardly, in fact, appear at all. Thus the lovers are thrown back on private temporary improvisations, making chivalric courts out of bourgeois bedrooms and temples out of chalets. Since these "transformations" have no social validation, they must necessarily be entirely provisional and ephemeral. Building on nothing, Saint-Preux and Julie can only build nothing, and it is hardly surprising that one of Saint-Preux's torments is that he lives for a series of discontinuous and randomly spaced ecstatic moments ("instants") separated by voids of tedious intervals ("ennuyeux intervalles" [p. 74]). He is not permitted to experience anything additive or cumulative. Since he and Julie are not permitted to be coadunate in any socially recognized way, he is constantly falling into or being pushed into mere apartness—the other side of the house, the other side of the world—from which he is occasionally, unpredictably, and on perpetually changing terms none of his making, summoned back. It is almost as if outside the house of the master time loses its continuity and relatedness. Because of his excluded position Saint-Preux's experience is deprived of its "durée"; when he is allowed in, it is for the most part an illusory inclusion—a momentary contact in an improvised frame.

Given this limbo of nonbeing in which Saint-Preux is compelled to remain suspended for indefinite periods of time, it is hardly surprising to find him, in his suppliant tone, asking whether it might be possible to make a "pilgrimage to the chalet" (p. 103) ("faire un pèlerinage au chalet" [p. 78])—notice again the habitual disposition to sacralize the erotic. At the conclusion of one letter he reveals that in his mind the chalet has effectively taken over ontological priority from the moral beliefs and prescriptions with which he and Julie tend to be so excessively liberal in their earlier letters. "All the morality you have offered is very good, but whatever you may say, the chalet is still better" (p. 107) (". . . car toute la morale que tu m'as débitée est fort bonne; mais, quoi que tu puisses dire, le chalet valait encore mieux" [p. 82]). Better, presumably, because whatever other putative pleasures it might offer, it also allows him the sense of existing as an authentic and recognized individual, temporarily out of reach of the pervasive and aggressive nonrecognition of the father (Julie's father, but in this book he is *the* father—we are hardly aware of Saint-Preux having had any parents). But, as we have noted, the chalet itself is only a temporary piece of make-believe, which has no stability. They will always have to be looking for new "chalets." So much is clear in Julie's response. "Well then, my friend, always the chalet? Your heart lays excessive stress upon the idea of the chalet, and I clearly see that sometime I must make it up to you. But are you so attached to the places where you never were that one may not compensate you elsewhere, and could not love, which created the palace of Armida in the middle of a desert, be able to create a chalet for us in town?" (p. 107). ("Eh bien donc! mon ami, toujours le chalet! L'histoire de ce chalet te pèse furieusement sur le coeur; et je vois bien qu'à la mort ou à la vie il faut te faire raison du chalet. Mais des lieux où tu ne fus jamais te sont-ils si chers qu'on ne puisse t'en dédommager ailleurs, et l'Amour, qui fit le palais d'Armide au fond d'un désert, ne saurait-il nous faire un chalet à la ville?" [p. 82].) We realize from this for the first time that in fact Julie has not actually met Saint-Preux in the chalet. (Perhaps I speak only for myself, but for the most part, it is difficult—if not impossible—to work out just when and if and how often Saint-Preux and Julie do actually establish physical sexual contact; but this mystification is not part of my immediate subject.) She tantalizingly outlines the venue, then finds all kinds of pretexts for postponing the actual meeting—notably she invokes her feelings for her parents and sends Saint-Preux off on an errand of mercy to arrange the legal marriage of Fanchon Regard (an impoverished girl dependent on Julie) and Claude Anet. Here again we see Julie oscillating between a desire to act on her own sexual and passional feelings and an instinctive clinging to the family and legalized relationships. (To send Saint-Preux on an errand to procure for others what Julie and her father are making impossible for him is tolerably sadistic; however, if Saint-Preux was not a masochist at the start, he quickly becomes one, as indeed he needs to do to survive in a world in which all power is in the hands of the generic "other" and, as far as he is concerned, is wielded errantly, unpredictably, unreliably, often ruthlessly—if he shows any signs of recalcitrance or resistance to its dictates—and always absolutely.) The chalet/temple was a fantasy outlining a desire that at times seems as strong as a passion and at times so weak and timid as to be a velleity.

But Julie's phrase "a chalet in town" points to the paradoxical strategy to which they will have to have recourse. In general it implies that the unlegalized lovers must establish their own fantasy spaces (chalets) inside the socialized space within which they have to live (the town—and whether or not they could or would leave that social space for some "world elsewhere" is an important matter to which I will return). Inside these temporary private "chalets" the unsanctioned sexual embrace may be enjoyed, without any disturbance of—or departure from—the existing society. And the place that Julie decrees (as usual it is she who decides and ordains) will serve as a "chalet in town" could hardly be more revealing. For it is nothing less than the house of the father, to which I must now turn.

La Maison Paternelle

In the letter in which Julie explains the layout of the house and just when and where Saint-Preux should come to her, she is at considerable pains to stress the danger of the proposed encounter—more so than the bliss it may promise.

> No, my sweet friend, no, we shall not leave this short life without having tasted happiness for an instant. But yet remember that this instant is surrounded by the horrors of death; that to come is to be subjected to a thousand hazards, to stay is dangerous, to leave is extremely perilous. . . . Let us not deceive ourselves. I know my father too well to doubt

that I might see him stab you to the heart immediately with his own hand, if indeed he did not begin with me; for surely I should not be spared, and do you think that I should expose you to this danger if I were not sure of sharing it?

Still, remember that it is not a matter of depending on your courage. You must not think of it and I even forbid you quite expressly to carry any weapon for your defense, not even your sword. Besides, it would be perfectly useless to you, for if we are surprised, my plan is to throw myself into your arms, to grasp you strongly in mine, and thus to receive the deadly blow so that we may be parted no more, happier at the moment of my death than I was in my life.

(Pp. 121–22)

Non, mon doux ami, non, nous ne quitterons point cette courte vie sans avoir un instant goûté le bonheur; mais songe pourtant que cet instant est environné des horreurs de la mort; que l'abord est sujet à mille hasards, le séjour dangereux, la retraite d'un péril extrême.... Ne nous abusons point; je connais trop mon père pour douter que je ne te visse à l'instant percer le coeur de sa main, si même il ne commençait par moi; car sûrement je ne serais pas plus épargnée: et crois-tu que je t'exposerais à ce risque si je n'étais sûre de le partager. Pense encore qu'il n'est point question de te fier à ton courage; il n'y faut pas songer; et je te défends même très expressément d'apporter aucune arme pour ta défense, pas même ton epée: aussi bien te serait-elle parfaitement inutile; car, si nous sommes surpris, mon dessein est de me précipiter dans tes bras, de t'enlacer fortement dans les miens, et de recevoir ainsi le coup mortel pour n'avoir plus à me séparer de toi, plus heureuse à ma mort que je ne le fus de ma vie.

(P. 96)

The length of the quotation is necessary to reveal the main source of Julie's emotional excitement. Even a casual glance at the letter would give one the sense that it is hardly calculated to encourage the summoned lover; but a more careful reading reveals that the summons amounts to an emasculation. He is to bring *no* weapons—not even his sword. All those hazards and horrors and dangers she refers to apply to one thing: they are the aura or atmosphere of the "maison paternelle"— the terrible presence of the father. And it is clear that Julie's imagination is fixed much more on the "sword" of the father than of her lover. Her fantasies center on seeing her father stab the unarmed lover (no question of the father not having *his* sword to hand), then—it becomes clear—the root fantasy is of being stabbed by her father herself. That is the dreaded/desired penetration. Saint-Preux is invited into her bed, not so much to satisfy her love for him but rather to indulge her imagination of the aroused and irresistible father.

If this seems excessive, let me go on to justify my contention that the most physical contact or encounter actually described in the book is not between Julie and Saint-Preux but between Julie and her father. The extraordinary letter in which Saint-Preux describes his waiting moments in Julie's room prior to her arrival reveals him in the posture of a feverish fetishist. Quite apart from the awkwardness inherent in the epistolary mode, the letter conveys the excitement of a man who derives his sensual satisfactions from associations. Since to all intents and purposes he has been forbidden to have direct access to the body of Julie, since he is summoned in swordless secrecy, it is hardly surprising that his feelings should have been displaced from the person, whom he constantly sees but is as constantly debarred from, to her accessories. So it is that he seems to be deriving his most sexual excitement from rummaging through her clothes, which he itemizes almost while fingering them. "All the parts of your scattered dress present to my ardent imagination those of your body they conceal" (p. 122). ("Toutes les parties de ton habillement éparses présentent à mon ardente imagination celles de toi-même qu'elles recèlent" [p. 97].) The excitement mounts until he is passionately kissing the whalebone of her corset, which has taken the imprint of her breasts. At this stage he is clearly on the point of involuntary orgasm or masturbation. Then—and we should not attribute this to the exigencies and constraints of the epistolary mode—he seeks relief in writing. "What good fortune to have found ink and paper! I am expressing my feelings in order to temper their excess; I moderate my ecstasy by describing it" (p. 123). ("Quel bonheur d'avoir trouvé de l'encre et du papier! J'exprime ce que je sens pour en tempérer l'excès; je donne le change à mes transports en les décrivant" [p. 97]). To a modern reader this moment is comic indeed; but in fact it has far-reaching reverberations. Saint-Preux is indeed forced away from the body of the loved other, and into writing, an inherently solitary activity. *Donner le change* is effectively to sidetrack or put off, as when putting dogs on the wrong scent, and for Saint-Preux to state that he is putting his emotions on the wrong scent or track by describing him gives us a clear picture of his position and behavior, which clarifies not only his position in Julie's room at that particular moment, but his position in the whole society throughout the book. He epitomizes the man who is forced to deflect and pervert his feelings into writings—hence, among other things, the extraordinarily long and often seemingly semantically depleted letters he writes. They are a kind of onanism, and for him, it is clear, there are many times when what matters is not *what* he is writing but *that* he is writing. It is almost all he is permitted to do by the rules that determine all the relationships in the society in which he lives. As the moment approaches for Julie's arrival, Saint-Preux seems almost on the verge of impotence. He thinks he hears a noise and immediately wonders whether it is Julie's cruel father ("ton barbare père" [p. 97]), as well he might, after her encouraging letter, and then as the door opens and he actually sees her—"c'est elle! c'est elle!" (p. 97)—he would seem to be about to collapse, indeed to be collapsing to the degree that collapsing is compatible with letter writing. "My heart, my feeble heart succumbs to so many agitations!" (p. 123). ("Mon coeur, mon faible coeur, tu succombes à tant d'agitations!" [p. 97].) In all seriousness, a reader might very well wonder whether that feebleness was not impairing other organs as well. And the feebleness of the lover is in direct correlation to the power of the father.

I don't think that it is in any spirit of disappointed prurience that I maintain that after the conclusion of this letter there is no *sense* of any real sexual connection and experience between Saint-Preux and Julie. It is indeed almost as if it never happened. What very certainly does happen and takes a vivid position in the text is Julie's father's attack on her, and their subsequent embrace. Again I must quote at length, since, among the hundreds of thousands of words exchanged by the lovers in letter, this is the one brute act that asserts a total dominance over the inferior power of the word. The episode takes place shortly after Lord Bomston, the English aristocrat, has offered to bestow a fortune and an estate on Saint-Preux, thereby hoping to qualify him as an acceptable suitor in her father's eyes. Julie's father dismisses the idea with angry contempt, for reasons to which I will return; but as a result of all the rational persuasion that people are bringing to bear on him—what, after all, *can* he have against the marriage after Lord Bomston's offer?—his irrational anger mounts until he turns on his own wife, who cannot understand his pathological insistence on rank and title as prime considerations when it comes to acceptable suitors: "'Learn,' he said, 'that it is an insult to the honor of a house to dare to solicit an alliance without a title for obtaining it'" (p. 142). ("Apprenez," dit-il, "que c'est offenser l'honneur d'une maison que d'oser en solliciter l'alliance sans titre pour l'obtenir" [p. 117].) The father's anger increases until he is, as it were, almost out of language and incapable of lexical control—"he kept saying the same things over a hundred times and yet changed the subject every moment" (p. 142) ("lui faisait redire cent fois les mêmes choses et changer à chaque instant de sujet" [p. 117])—and he starts to abuse Saint-Preux so insultingly that finally Julie makes the eminently rational objection that a man who deserved so many insults and disparaging remarks could hardly hold any danger for her. This is a good deal too rational for the wild and incoherent father, and he turns and spills his rage on the person at whom it has really been aimed all along.

At that moment, my father, who thought he felt a reproach in these words and whose fury awaited only a pretext, flew upon your poor friend. For the first time in my life I received a blow; nor was that all, but giving himself up to his fit of passion with a violence equal to the effort he was making, he beat me mercilessly, although my mother had thrown herself between us, covered me with her body, and received some of the blows which were intended for me. In shrinking back to avoid them, I stumbled, I fell, and my head struck the leg of a table, which caused it to bleed.

(P. 143)

A l'instant, mon père, qui crut sentir un reproche à travers ces mots, et dont la fureur n'attendait qu'un prétexte, s'élança sur ta pauvre amie: pour la première fois de ma vie je reçus un soufflet qui ne fût pas le seul; et, se livrant à son transport avec une violence égale à celle qu'il lui avait coûtée, il me maltraita sans ménagement, quoique ma mère se fût jetée entre deux, m'eût couverte de son corps, et eût reçu quelques-uns des coups qui m'étaient portés. En reculant pour les éviter, je fis un faux pas, je tombai, et mon visage alla donner contre le pied d'une table qui me fit saigner.

(P. 118.)

The attack could hardly be more sexual, albeit specific inadmissible incestuous lust has been translated, or distorted, into a violent anger that is permitted to the father simply because he is the father. The fact that at one point he is hitting Julie and her mother indifferently adds to the clarity of just what kind of passional energy he is releasing. Psychoanalysts refer to the figure of the mother and father copulating as "the combined object" in the eyes of the child. Here the wife and daughter form another "combined object" in the eyes of the father—eyes dazed with lustful anger, angry lust. And it is only when he has, as it were, drawn blood that the father's orgasmic eruption is over, and "the triumph of anger" finished. ("Ici finit le triomphe de la colère" [p. 118].)

There follows the reconciliation. Before describing it, Julie discusses "paternal dignity" ("la dignité paternelle") and makes the assertion that "a father's heart feels that it is made to pardon and not to have need of being pardoned" (p. 143). ("Le coeur d'un père sent qu'il est fait pour pardonner, et non pour avoir besoin de pardon" [p. 118].) All this points to the fact that for this family/society, all power, both to punish and to pardon, flows in one direction—*from* the father, not to him. In this way he directly and indirectly controls, one might say owns, the permissible reciprocities of all those in any way connected to him. What has Saint-Preux to offer that can compete with this power? The answer, or one answer, would have to be "words," or more generally the pleasures and persuasions of language. But the father has no need of language; he can just reach out and take what he wants. Thus Julie's account of the scene after the climax—a scene pervaded with a distinctly postcoital silence and exhaustion—continues. The father does not speak to her ("il ne me parla point" [p. 118]), but after dinner, as Julie and her parents are gathering round the fire, this is what happens.

I was going to get a chair in order to put myself between them, when, laying hold of my dress and drawing me to him without saying anything, he placed me on his knees. All this was done so suddenly and by a kind of quite involuntary impulse that he was almost regretful the moment afterwards. However, I was on his knees, he could no longer push me away, and what was more discomposing, he had to hold me clasped in his arms in this embarrassing position. All this was done in silence, but now and then I felt his arms press against my sides and heard a rather poorly stifled sigh. I do not know what false shame prevented these paternal arms from giving themselves up to these sweet embraces. A certain gravity which he dared not abandon, a certain confusion which he dared not overcome put between the father and his daughter this charming embarrassment that modesty and passion cause in lovers. . . . I saw, I felt all this, my angel, and could no longer hold back the tenderness which was overcoming me. I pretended to slip; to prevent myself, I threw an arm around my father's neck. I laid my face close to his venerable cheek, and in an instant it was covered with my kisses and bathed with my tears. I knew by those which rolled from his eyes that he himself was relieved of a great sorrow. My mother shared our rapture. Only sweet and peaceful innocence was wanting in my heart to make this natural scene the most delightful moment of my life.

(Pp. 143–44)

J'allais prendre une chaise pour me placer entre eux, quand, m'arrêtant par ma robe, et me tirant à lui sans rien dire, il m'assit sur ses genoux. Tout cela se fit si promptement, et par une sorte de mouvement si involontaire, qu'il en eût une espèce de repentir le moment d'après. Cependant, j'étais sur ses genoux, il ne pouvait plus s'en dédire; et, ce qu'il y avait de pis pour la contenance, il fallait me tenir embrassée dans cette gênante attitude. Tout cela se faisait en silence: mais je sentais de temps en temps ses bras se presser contre mes flancs avec un soupir assez mal étouffé. Je ne sais quelle mauvaise honte empêchait ces bras paternels de se livrer à ces douces étreintes. Une certaine gravité qu'on n'osait quitter, une certain confusion qu'on n'osait vaincre, mettaient entre un père et sa fille ce charmant embarras que la pudeur et l'amour donnent aux amants; . . . Je voyais, je sentais tout cela, mon ange, et ne pus tenir plus longtemps à l'attendrissement qui me gagnait. Je feignis de glisser; je jetai, pour me retenir, un bras au cou de mon père; je penchai mon visage sur son visage vénérable, et dans un instant il fut couvert de mes baisers et inondé de mes larmes; je sentis à celles qui lui coulaient des yeux qu'il était lui-même soulagé d'une grande peine: ma mère vint partager nos transports. Douce et paisible innocence, tu manques seule à mon coeur pour faire de cette scène de la nature le plus délicieux moment de ma vie!

(P. 119)

I want to stress again that nothing remotely comparably physical in contact is ever evoked as occurring between Julie and Saint-Preux. More than that, we may note from her ecstatic description of this "moment" that by a potentially perverse inversion of roles, it is no longer the father who is an interfering obstacle between the daughter and lover, but rather the lover who, by his violation of the girl's "innocence," is the source of a contaminating self-reproach in the otherwise blissful relationship between the daughter and the father. With the beaming mother looking on, this truly does offer a spectacle or scene that is pervaded with latent—and not so latent—incestuous feelings. (I am not so foolish or out of the world as to imagine that there is really no such thing as a family quarrel and a joyful reconciliation, but only transformed incestuous to-ings and froings; but here the physical detailing is so excitedly minute in a way that is so absent from Julie's letters to Saint-Preux that it seems to me permissible to perceive the scene and the attendant emotions it aroused in terms of barely controlled incest.) Julie revealingly goes on to add: "For myself, as I told him, I should think myself only too happy to be beaten every day for this reward, and there was no treatment so harsh that a single caress from him could not efface from my heart" (p. 144). ("Pour moi, je lui ai dit, et je le pense, que je serais trop heureuse d'être battue tous les jours au même prix, et qu'il n'y a point de traitement si rude qu'une seule de ces caresses n'efface au fond de mon coeur" [p. 119].) After this, what chance has Saint-Preux? He may be her lover, but more importantly, he is not, and cannot replace, her father. The lover's words are powerless beside the father's arms ("bras paternels"). Julie herself notes that a "revolution has taken place within me" (p. 145) ("quelle évolution s'est faite en moi" [p. 120])[2] and asks Claire a key question. "It seems to me that I look with more regret upon the happy time when I lived tranquil and content in the bosom of my family, and that I feel the weight of my fault increase along with that of the blessings it has caused me to lose. Tell me, cruel one! Tell me if you dare, is the time of love gone, no longer to return?" (p. 145). ("Il me semble que je tourne les yeux avec plus de regret sur l'heureux temps où je vivais tranquille et contente au sein de ma famille, et que je sens augmenter le sentiment de ma faute avec celui des biens qu'elle m'a fait perdre. Dis, cruelle, dis-le-moi, si tu l'oses, le temps de l'amour serait-il passé, et faut-il ne se plus revoir?" [p. 120].) The answer to this question in one very real sense is yes, and from this point, with no matter what delays, hesitations, and resistances, Julie turns her passional energies toward reachieving a kind of total family structure or situation that will reproduce in extended

---

[2]"évolution" is translated as "revolution" by Judith McDowell—a less drastic or dramatic word would be more suitable.

form the happy family circle that Saint-Preux so very imperfectly penetrated and, for a brief time, almost broke.

The morning after this scene is enacted, Julie's father comes to her
while she is in bed and reaffirms that he has decided who is to be her
husband, and that this decision is unalterable. "You know . . . the husband I have decided upon for you. I made that known to you as soon as I
returned and I shall never change my mind in this matter" (p. 144).
("Vous savez . . . à qui je vous destine; je vous l'ai déclaré dès mon ar-
rivée, et ne changerai jamais d'intention sur ce point" [p. 119].) He also
forbids her to see or speak to the unnamed "homme" who may have the
audacity to think he could be considered as his possible "gendre" (son-
in-law). The father does not name Saint-Preux because, in his terms, he
does not have a name. (I will return to this denial or withholding of the
name. It is also connected to the father's subsequent willingness to regard Saint-Preux as his superior on one condition—"Since he has been
certain that I could not become a member of his family, there is no kind
of civility he does not show me, and provided that I may not be his
son-in-law, he would willingly put himself beneath me" (p. 359). ("Depuis qu'il est sur que je ne saurais lui appartenir, il n'y a sorte d'honneur
qu'il me fasse; et pourvu que je ne sois pas son gendre, il se mettrait
volontiers au-dessous de moi" [p. 458].) *Appartenir,* "to belong to" . . . as
long as Julie's father never has to own Saint-Preux as his substitute (the
son-in-law who possesses the daughter), that is, as long as he may con-
tinuously disown him, he will willingly make any other concession; and
we may note the subjunctives and conditionals, which are appropriate
for the area of relationship to which the father indeed lays down the
conditions, in a very literal "if-then" way. If Saint-Preux tries to see you
again, then I will kill him. If Saint-Preux will never seek to be my son-in-
law, then I will confer an honorable extrafamilial existence on him. This
latter concession takes place during the great dream of harmony toward
the end of the book, to which I will return. The father is not only bitterly
contemptuous of Saint-Preux's nameless condition, he also hates him
even more "for the outrages he caused me to commit, and I shall never
forgive him for my violence" (p. 145) ("pour les excès qu'il m'a fait
commettre, et ne lui pardonnerai jamais ma brutalité" [p. 120]). The
father may enjoy his "excès" and indulge his "brutalité," and may then
blame them on the impotent young man who has dared to love his daughter. This is not only psychologically acute and many-layered in its implications; it is a superb example of the total injustice, or nonjustice, of the
power of the father. His brutality is his own and he may wield it; the
blame for it he feels magisterially free to bestow *on* the despised other,
who is in effect the secondary victim *of* it. (Effectively emasculated by the
daughter and banished on pain of death by the father, it is no wonder

that Saint-Preux's sense of ontological security should be so very minimal and uncertain! All things, and most people, seem to conspire to negate him after his brief sexual "entry" into the family. He is, indeed, a "guest-stranger" in the house, but too impotent to be really disruptive.) At the same time, then, as he is getting rid of Saint-Preux forever as a possible *gendre,* the father is decreeing who *will* be allowed to marry his daughter and enter the bed on which he is himself, at the moment, sitting—that is, after his orgasmic assault on Julie, the father reasserts his power to name his substitute, or rather surrogate (an older man, like himself, but so rational and passionless—the father is all unreason and passion—as not to be sensed as a true rival for the physical/sexual feelings of the daughter). As Julie writes to Claire in a lament that is also a submitting—"my father's command is precise; my lover's danger is certain" (p. 145) ("l'ordre de mon père est précis, le danger de mon amant est certain" [p. 120]). After this Julie feels a kind of illness and confusion that attend her recognition of and compliance with the orders of the father. All her friends and relations conspire to constrain Saint-Preux and to persuade him to leave, and after two more letters from Claire, he is helped into a carriage in an understandably hysterical and enfeebled condition and is packed off into the void.

There are two more points concerning this remarkable letter that I wish to make (and by way of explaining the detail into which I have gone concerning this one letter, I should perhaps say that I regard it as the single most important letter in the whole book—letter 63 in the first part). After what is, as I have tried to show, effectively a decisive capitulation to the will and orders of the father, Julie indulges in some of her earlier feelings for Saint-Preux, asking Claire to tell him not to despair or give up hope (though on what he could conceivably base any hope it is hard to see) and reiterating an earlier belief that Heaven made them for one another. "Yes, yes, I am sure of it; we are destined to be united . . . is not such assurance firmly rooted in our hearts? Do we not feel that they are inseparable and that we no longer have but one between us?" (p. 146). ("Oui, ou, j'en suis sûre, il nous destine à être unis . . . l'assurance n'en est-elle pas au fond de nos âmes? Ne sentons-nous pas qu'elles sont indivisibles, et que nous n'en avons plus qu'une à nous deux?" [p. 120].) Julie calls Claire her inseparable; from Saint-Preux she feels indivisible; and her dreams, fantasies, and aspirations all tend to the one article of faith that all the people she loves or cares for are "destined to be united"—"le bosquet," "le chalet à la ville," and her cousin's habitation are, as it were, somehow to be reclaimed and, after necessary purifications or modifications, to be brought together and contained in "la maison paternelle." What becomes of this dream of all-embracing unity is a matter for a subsequent section of this chapter. Here I simply want to insert the formulation, well established among some psychologists, that the father is, among other things, *he who separates*. In the Oedipal situation it is he who separates the mother from the child, thus standing as the obstacular presence preventing the child from returning to a state of blissful unseparated oneness with the mother that is, they say, a primal desire and fantasy. In this particular case we may say that it is the father who separates Julie from the desired sexual partner and lover. But more than that, it is the father who institutes and introduces all those divisions and separations and distances that the child has to both negotiate and employ as he grows up and out and into the world—spatial (who and what goes where), legal (who and what may and may not be related—as Julie's father at the same time names her husband and bans her lover), and linguistic (the source of the names and the namings of people and things).[3] Thus the father, as a presence is the source of all those separations and divisions that ultimately derive from the prohibition of an incestuous return to undifferentiated oneness with the mother (that fathers as specific individuals may, and indeed do very frequently, commit incest goes without saying, but that is another matter). Julie's dream of total union is a projection into the future of a totally regressive urge. What she has to learn, though she resists it in every way she can, is that the world is a place of separations and divisions. Or, to put it another way, you may curl up in the arms and on the lap of the father for ecstatic moments, but you can't do it forever.

The second point concerns the postscript, and its very delegation to that subsidiary area of the letter is itself significant, since in this way it is, as it were, separated from the otherwise blissful aspects of the paternal beating and embrace. I will quote it in full. "P.S. After I had written my

---

[3]This is of course a vast subject with a great deal of well-known work written about it—from Freud to Lacan and Melanie Klein, to name only three obvious writers who have engaged this topic of the role of the father in child development. For a felicitous and brief summary of just this one point I have tried to make here, I will quote from an article by Michel Foucault entitled "Le 'Non' du Père."

Melanie Klein puis Lacan ont montré que le père, comme tierce personne dans la situation oedipienne, n'est pas seulement le rival haï et menaçant, mais celui dont la présence limite le rapport illimité de la mère à l'enfant, auquel le fantasme de la dévoration donne la première forme angoissée. Le père est alors celui qui sépare, c'est-à-dire qui protège quand, prononçant la Loi, il noue en une expérience majeure l'espace, la règle et le langage. D'un coup sont données, la distance tout au long de laquelle se développe la scansion des présences et des absences, la parole dont la forme première est celle de la contrainte, et le rapport enfin du signifiant au signifié à partir duquel va se faire non seulement l'édification du langage mais aussi le rejet et la symbolisation du refoulé.

(*Critique,* no. 178 [March 1962] pp. 195–209)

I will have more to say about this article. For translation, see note 6, below.)

letter, I went into my mother's room and there became so ill that I was compelled to return to my bed. I even perceived ... I fear ... ah, my dear! I quite fear that my fall yesterday may have some consequence more disastrous than I had thought. Thus all is finished for me; all my hopes abandon me at once" (p. 146). ("Après ma lettre écrite, j'ai passé dans la chambre de ma mère, et je me suis trouvée si mal que je suis obligée de venir me remettre dans mon lit: je m'aperçois même ... je crains ... Ah! ma chère je crains bien que ma chute d'hier n'ait quelque suite plus funeste que je n'avais pensé. Ainsi tout est fini pour moi; toutes mes espérances m'abandonnent en même temps" [p. 121].) Although pregnancy is never mentioned and this shy allusive hinting is a deliberate kind of mystification, one does not have to read too hard between the lines, or rather along the dots, to infer that Julie has suffered some kind of miscarriage. This is borne out by a letter shortly afterwards in which Claire is describing how she persuaded Saint-Preux to leave. After all his pleadings have failed, he raises one further and final "objection."

> He spoke to me of the condition you suspected yourself in, swearing that he would rather die a thousand times than abandon you to all the dangers that were about to threaten you. I took care not to tell him of your accident; I simply told him that your expectation had again been mistaken and that there was no longer any hope.
> "Thus," he said to me, sighing, "there will remain no living memorial of my good fortune. It was disappeared like a dream that was never real."
> (P. 153)

> Il m'a parlé de l'état où tu soupçonnais être, jurant qu'il mourrait plutôt mille fois que de t'abandonner à tous les périls qui t'allaient menacer. Je n'ai eu garde de lui parler de ton accident; je lui ai dit simplement que ton attente avait encore été trompée, et qu'il n'y avait plus rien à espérer. "Ainsi, m'a-t-il dit en soupirant, il ne restera sur la terre aucun monument de mon bonheur; il a disparu comme un songe qui n'eut jamais de réalité."
> (P. 127)

Thus it is clear that in his assault on his daughter, the father also killed the prospective child she would have had from her lover. It is as though such is his power and his anger that he can reach into the latent future and eradicate a life that has already been engendered. In this way he effectively cancels the fertility of the lover—annuls the potency of his inseminations and leaves him and his life sterile. Saint-Preux is quite right to claim that his "bonheur" has disappeared like a dream, leaving no earthly monument, for the one unmistakably concrete evidence and fruit of his union with Julie has been blotted out. In this way such physicality as their relationship enjoyed is rendered effectively nonexistent. The father has attacked that, to him unacceptable, reality and has rendered it unreal—as though it had never *been* real. As we have seen his surrogate Wolmar do, the father can also reach into the past and eliminate a sexuality concerning his family that had neither his sanction nor his license. Such a father is indeed close to the awesome figure dominating the primal horde in Freud's vision of the powers of the primitive father.

Although Julie feels torn by having to choose between lover or father ("Veux-je suivre le penchant de mon coeur, qui préférer d'un amant ou d'un père" [p. 140]), she has already made the choice, or rather there was never any real chance of her abandoning the father for the lover. This is made very clear when Lord Bomston offers what would appear to be a perfect solution for the two lovers. Having attempted in vain to argue against the irrational prejudices of her father, and in vain having offered to make Saint-Preux both propertied and wealthy, this inexhaustible source of rational beneficence offers what would seem to be an impossibility—the legitimization of their passion in a new country. It is too obvious to require any emphasis to see that Lord Bomston acts and wishes to act as a father figure for the two young lovers; what should be noted is that he is trying to compensate for the blind irrationality of the real father by being the incarnation of *rational* paternity. Julie's father works with fists, threats, and interdictions; Lord Bomston, with kindness, praise, and facilitations. Thus he writes to Julie to invite her to join Saint-Preux in England—a very mythical England drawn from an atlas of imagined wish-fulfillments. He writes as a votary of love, romantic and passional love rather than familial devotion, and urges Julie to be true to what he believes to be the emotional condition of her heart: "l'état de votre coeur" (p. 138). Since, he argues, this condition cannot be altered there is only one thing to do: "you must make it legitimate" (p. 167) ("c'est le rendre légitime" [p. 138]). He then describes a beautiful estate he has in Yorkshire, with a fine old mansion, grounds with a river running through, an ample self-supporting economy, peaceful inhabitants, and a complete absence of "hateful prejudices" ("l'odieux préjugé"). It is indeed "a happy country" ("cette heureuse contrée")—familiar from pastoral-utopian modes, dream geographies, and golden-age literature since time immemorial. And, he tells Julie, it is all yours. ("Cette terre est à vous, Julie, si vous daignez l'habiter avec lui" [p. 138].) It is, one might say, the ultimate invitation to two young lovers, kept apart by parental edict. "Come, unique pattern for true lovers. Come, charming and faithful couple, and take possession of a place made to serve as the refuge of love and of innocence" (p. 167). ("Venez, modèle unique des vrais amants, couple aimable et fidèle, prendre possession d'un lieu fait pour servir d'asile à l'amour et à l'innocence" [p. 138].)

Whether there is or can be such a place may be said to be a question, or a quest, pervading literature of all ages. The important aspect in this context is that it offers not only ideal setting, subsistence, and so on but also, and most particularly, a *legitimization* that has been withheld by the real father. If Julie accepted the invitation, she would be acknowledging that there could be an alternative source for legitimization of her relationships to her father, and indirectly asserting that not all authority and sanctions come from the father, that there is a space, a law, and a language beyond his jurisdiction. Lord Bomston's final appeal would seem to be irresistible. "The tyranny of an obstinate father will plunge you into the abyss, which you will recognize after your fall ... you will be sacrificed to the chimerical distinction of rank" (p. 168). ("La tyrannie d'un père intraitable vous entraînera dans l'abîme qui vous ne connaîtrez qu'après la chute ... vous serez sacrifiée à la chimère des conditions" [p. 139].) But just at this point Rousseau interrupts with a footnote. "The chimerical distinction of rank! This is an English lord who is speaking in this way! Must not all this be fictitious? Reader, what do you say about it?" (p. 168). ("La chimère des conditions! C'est un pair d'Angleterre qui parle ainsi! et tout ceci ne serait pas une fiction! Lecteur, qu'en dites vous?" [p. 139].) This is no place to recapitulate the implications and significance of the familiar device whereby the author enters his own text to point to its fictitiousness. What is notable about this particular interruption, or interpolation, is that it impugns the credibility of Lord Bomston's offer, rational and indeed very Rousseauistic though his sentiments and beliefs are. What Rousseau is effectively marking with his marginal murmur of incredulity is, not the fictitiousness of his work, but the essential fictitiousness of Lord Bomston's offer. The "tyranny of the father" is real enough. It is that place of refuge for love and innocence, that "heureuse contrée" beyond all prejudices, that is, alas, only a fiction. We readers, don't we think so?

Of course Julie declines the invitation. To Claire she writes that although the idea of "conjugal fidelity" ("la foi conjugale") fills her with inexpressible delight, she could not be an "ungrateful and unnatural daughter" ("fille ingrate et dénaturée"), particularly in view of "the blind fondness of a doting father and mother" (p. 170) ("l'aveugle tendresse d'un père et d'une mère idolâtres" [p. 140]). To Lord Bomston she writes with lucid gratitude and absolute rejection. "You would offer two persecuted lovers a pleasant and secure refuge; there you would make their passion legitimate, their union sacred; and I know that under your proection I should easily elude the pursuits of an angered family ... you will deign to take the place of a father for me. Ah my Lord! Shall I deserve to find one, after having abandoned the one nature has given me?" (p. 176). ("Vous donnez une retraite agréable et sûre à deux amants persécutés; vous y rendez leurs feux légitimes, leur union solennelle; et je sais que sous votre garde j'échapperais aisément aux poursuites d'une famille irritée . . . vous daignerez me tenir lieu de père. Ah! milord, serai-je digne d'en trouver un, après avais abondonné celui que m'a donné la nature?" [p. 145].) There is more along this line as she imagines her remorse if she left her parents, and the conclusion is a ringing affirmation of what Julie knew all along, even if she did not know that she knew it—"I shall never desert my father's house" (p. 177) ("Je ne déserterai jamais la maison paternelle" [p. 146]). This declaration is reaffirmed to Saint-Preux some hundreds of letters later, when Julie, making use of a schizophrenic device by which she tries to combine the mutually exclusive lover and father, declares that she is his forever ("ta Julie sera toujours tienne" [p. 245]) but will never leave home. "Do not think that to follow you I shall ever abandon my father's house" (p. 251). ("Ne pense point que pour te suivre j'abandonne jamais la maison paternelle" [p. 246].) The "bosquet" and the "chalet" are insubstantial, dream-stuff; ultimate authority and ultimate reality reside in, and only in, "la maison paternelle."

La Parole du Père

All this might seem like something too much of the father, but the effects of his presence in this book (and the differing degrees of the father's absence in later works I shall be considering) is so crucial that a fairly careful consideration of his role and power is justifiable. The references to the father are not literally innumerable, but they are so plentiful as to give the impression of recurring constantly. The references range from references to his body—"le sein d'un père," "le cou de mon père," "les bras paternels," "la main de son père"—to descriptions of his temperament and will—"l'inflexible séverité de mon père," "les préjugés de ton père," "la volonté de mon père," "le discours de mon père," "la violence de ton père," "ton inflexible père," "la dignité parternelle," "des violences d'un père emporté," "la vanité d'un père barbare," "la défense de mon père," "l'esprit de votre père," "l'amour paternel," "les volontés d'un père," "la tyrannie de votre père," "la complaisance de mon père" (a good humor or obligingness of a somewhat debatable kind, since the condition of its existence is that the will of the father is obeyed in all things—it would be "abused" if Julie left the "maison paternelle," because then, of course, he would have to go too; as it happens, the world comes to Clarens, not the other way around). Recurrently this violent barbarous tyrant becomes, rather litanously, "le meilleur des pères," and after her marriage to Wolmar, Julie refers with grateful compliancy to "la bonne intention des pères" (p. 276) (good intentions that, she says, are guided by heaven). And, although he says very little (in effect he says only two things—Julie will not marry "that man"; Julie will marry Wolmar), there is above, or behind all—*la parole du père:* "la parole de cet homme inflexible est irrévocable" (p. 227). Not the words (Saint-Preux, we may say, has the words), but the Word. The Word is irrational, arbitrary, prejudiced, but it is inflexible, irrevocable, absolute. It is also, in Foucault's terms "la parole dont la forme première est celle de la contrainte." (See note 3.) Julie's most powerful experience of "la parole du père" is as an interdiction, a prohibition—"la défense du père." And after Julie's death, there is "la douleur d'un père infortuné."

In this context let us consider a little more closely the grounds of his utter rejection of Saint-Preux. An early hint, perhaps, occurs when we learn in a letter from Julie that her father is very content with her skill in everything "except heraldry, which he thinks I have neglected" (p. 63) ("au blason près, qui lui a paru négligé" [p. 42]). Inasmuch as the study of heraldry involves the tracing and recording of genealogies, it is devoted to a respect for the position, power, and prestige of long lines of the fathers and the names of the fathers; it also means a recognition of the *symbols* of that position and power—armorial bearings, coats of arms, and the like. As an object of study it has no use beyond that, no application to other aspects of life and learning; it involves no knowledge of history and has no educative potential. It is really a kind of fetishism, involving a prolonged and respectful meditation on the titles and trappings of the fathers. Another hint, a stronger and more obvious one, is given when we learn that Julie's father once killed a friend in a duel and some years later lost his only son, which he saw as a punishment for the deed. The paragraph is remarkable, for again it evokes very vividly the physical power, the bloodletting barbarity of the father, and I will quote it in full.

> You know that my father had the misfortune in his youth to kill a man in a duel. This man was a friend; they fought reluctantly, compelled by an absurd point of honour. The fatal blow which deprived one of his life robbed the other of his peace of mind forever. Since that time, painful remorse has never left his heart. Often we hear him cry and lament in private; he thinks he still can feel the blade thrust by his cruel hand into his friend's heart. In his nightmares he sees the pale and bloody body. Trembling, he gazes upon the mortal wound; he would like to staunch the

flowing blood; terror seizes him; he cries out; the frightful corpse does not cease pursuing him. Since five years ago when he lost the dear support of his name and the hope of his family, he has reproached himself with the death as if it were a just punishment from Heaven, who upon his only son avenged the unfortunate father whose son he had killed.

(P. 129)

Vous savez que mon père, dans sa jeunesse, eut le malheur de tuer un homme en duel; cet homme était son ami: ils se battirent à regret, l'insensé point d'honneur les y contraignit. Le coup mortel qui priva l'un de la vie otâ pour jamais le repos à l'autre. Le triste remords n'a pu depuis ce temps sortir de son coeur, souvent dans la solitude on l'entend pleurer et gémir; il croit sentir encore le fer poussé par sa main cruelle entrer dans le coeur de son ami; il voit dans l'ombre de la nuit son corps pâle et sanglant; il contemple en frémissant la plaie mortelle; il voudrait étancher le sang qui coule; l'effroi le saisit, il s'écrie; ce cadavre affreux ne cesse de le poursuivre. Depuis cinq ans qu'il a perdu le cher soutien de son nom et l'espoir de sa famille, il s'en reproche la mort comme un juste châtiment du ciel, qui vengea sur son fils unique le père infortuné qu'il priva du sien.

(P. 107)

That this is in a letter to Saint-Preux can hardly make him more sure of himself in his suit for Julie. But the key observation concerning the duel is that they were "compelled by an absurd point of honour."—"l'insensé point d'honneur les y contraignit." *Insensé* is "mad," "insane," literally without sense. The code behind this kind of point of honor—the content is not specified and is irrelevant—is irrational, arbitrary, and prejudiced, but (and by the same token) it is inflexible, irrevocable, absolute. That is to say it is exactly similar to the Word of the father as I have just described it. And its imperative asserts itself in the rent body and the flowing blood of a friend, just as the imperative of the Word of the father expresses itself in the beaten body and flowing blood of a daughter. The code and the Word are absolute *because* they are irrational, and vice versa. Their authority cannot be questioned because it cannot be questioned. Their power does not have to be sanctified, because theirs is sanctified, and sanctifying, power. The orders, edicts, and constraints of these powers can only be obeyed. The only alternative is to deny, destroy, or abandon the Code—and the father.

The connection between the duelling code and the Word of the father may be taken further. The Code issues an inflexible and irrevocable imperative to kill someone; the Word issues an inflexible and irrevocable imperative to marry someone (and thus of course not to marry another). Here a key difference emerges—the Code is directed toward death; the Word, inasmuch as it bestows the daughter in marriage (with procreational intentions quite disregardful of the girl's own feelings), is directed toward the continuity of families, and thus life. The duel and the marriage are two absolutely basic, and theoretically absolutely distinct, kinds of relationships. Using Gregory Bateson's terms,[4] I will refer to them as a symmetrical relationship and a complementary relationship. A symmetrical relation, as the word suggests, in one in which each partner attempts to do the same as the other (one of Bateson's examples is an arms race); in the duel each seeks to kill the other. In a complementary relationship, each partner does the opposite, but in a way that makes up an interdependency—Bateson's examples include assertiveness / submissiveness, exhibitionism / admiration, succording / dependence. A marriage is supposedly maintained by the asymmetrical male / female roles and contributions. By definition there is no "mutual irrelevance" in these relationships. If it works with flexibility, fluidity, and parity, the complementary relationship may be called a "reciprocal relationship"; when the asymmetrical roles become fixed and unalterable, the relationship is "complementary." Clearly, a marriage should ideally be a reciprocal relationship, though, just as clearly, it often tends to become a complementary one. Also one might want to concede, or indeed insist, that there are marriages that are effectively duels; and while it would be hard to suggest that there are duels that are really marriages, it may at least be noted that duels are often fights between close friends, and one might not want to exclude the possibility of the existence of a perverse erotic element in duelling. (The duellist who, for whatever motives, shoots his pistol in the air, or refuses to strike a fallen opponent, or whatever, has simply annulled the relationship by opting out of it. You cannot duel, any more than you can be married, on your own.) In this book the father has participated in the symmetrical, and mortal, relationship of the duel; and he is also concerned to constitute *on his own terms*, the complementary, and familially fruitful relationship of his daughter to the man of his choice (who, as I have said before, is his surrogate, a man who never formed any attachment before the imperative of the father was extended to him and he obeyed—"seconding my father's intentions" (p. 260), as Julie revealingly writes to Saint-Preux, ("secondant les intentions de mon père" [p. 272]). As father, he cannot conceive of the possibility of any other kind of relationship; that, for example, the children might be left alone to see whether they can work out reciprocal relationships with other children of their choice. In the novel Julie happily (or mostly happily) accepts the complementary relationship of her marriage to Wolmar and seems to adapt herself to it with a range of satisfactions and a minimum of discontents. In later novels we

---

[4]Gregory Bateson, *Steps to an Ecology of Mind* (New York: Ballantine Books, 1972). Passim, but see especially pt 2, "Form and Pattern in Anthropology."

shall see that the key problem can occur when an individual in a rigidified complementary relationship feels its disintegrative and deathward side (for such relationships can be as deadly as symmetrical ones) and turns to see whether it is possible to enter into and maintain a new, alive, relationship—at best, reciprocal; at least, sexual. Such is the novel of adultery; adultery is *specifically* dismissed as a possibility in this book. And it is so dismissed, effectively, because of the power of the father. Saint-Preux thinks that the socially unsanctioned, private bond or tie ("chaîne") that unites him and Julie "marks the extent of paternal power" (p. 243) ("est la borne du pouvoir paternel" [p. 239]). But in this book there are no limits to the "pouvoir paternel," or rather everything and everyone falls within those limits. The fate, and in varying ways the decline and even the disintegration, of that power is an essential aspect of the great bourgeois novels that were to follow.[5] But let me return to Julie's father's rejection of Saint-Preux.

Lord Bomston has not only offered to give Saint-Preux money and property; he has also attacked the pointless irrationality of Julie's father's attachment to the idea of a noble title as being indispensable in any potential husband for Julie. Thus Bomston—the cool, rational Englishman: "Nobility? An empty prerogative in a country where it is more injurious thjan useful. But he [Saint-Preux] has nobility even so, do not doubt it, not written in ink on old parchment but engraved on his heart in indelible characters. In short, if you prefer reason to prejudice, and if you love your daughter better than your titles, you will give her to him" (p. 138). ("La noblesse? Vaine prérogative dans un pays où elle est plus nuisible qu'utile. Mais il l'a encore, n'en doutez pas, non point écrite d'encre en de vieux parchemins, mais gravée au fond de son coeur en caractères ineffaçables. En un mot, si vous préférez la raison au préjugé, et si vous aimez mieux votre fille que vos titres, c'est à lui que vous la donnerez" [p. 113].) This argument carries a multiple sting, for in addition to putting the father in the position of valuing his titles more than

[5]Interestingly enough, dueling turns up in one of the last novels of adultery near the end of the nineteenth century—*Effie Briest*; here the "absurd point of honour" in fact is adultery. Dueling is also, of course, in evidence in Richardson's novels—and Rousseau himself writes against it in *The Social Contract*. The growing hostility toward dueling during the eighteenth century in France and England (to go not further afield) as society became more juridical, would offer very interesting material for a separate study. Richardson, in fact, became obsessed with the need to eradicate dueling—it is a recurring topic in *Sir Charles Grandison* in which Sir Charles asks: "Of what use are the Laws of Society, if magistracy may be defied.... Where, in short, is the evil to stop.... Lewis XIVth's edict against duelling was the greatest glory of his reign." In his concluding note, Richardson again returns to the topic, even quoting the Articles of War, which forbid dueling. But the duel continued to attract the interest of continental writers for over another century—see for instance the tales by Chekov, Conrad, and Alexander Kuprin, all entitled "The Duel," or Arthur Schnitzler's play, *Undiscovered Country*, in which dueling is an entirely absurd—but still lethal—code in an entirely corrupt society.

his daughter and esteeming an ink and parchment nobility more than a nobility of the heart, it attacks the substance of his own title. Here I will simply quote from the note provided by Judith McDowell as a gloss on the first point Bomston makes in the passage quoted above concerning the "empty prerogative" of the nobility of Julie's father. "Daniel Mornet provides the following explanation for this remark: Berne had conquered the Vaud region, after which all the Vaud nobility had been excluded from public office; since there was little commerce or industry in which they cared to engage, they were reduced to a life of idleness or expatriation" (p. 138). That is to say that Julie's father's noble title is *only* title, no longer referring to or connoting some kind of service or function in the land—as, Lord Bomston points out, noble titles usually do. This only serves to sharpen the focus on the *total* irrationality of the father's ferocious attachment to his name.

Here is part of his answer—or rather reaction, since Bomston's points are unanswerable. "What! My lord . . . can an honorable man like yourself even think that the last surviving branch of an illustrious family might lose or degrade its name by taking that of a nobody, without a home and reduced to living on charity??" (p. 138). ("Quoi, milord, dit-il, un homme d'honneur comme vous peut-il seulement penser que le dernier rejeton d'une famille illustre aille éteindre ou dégrader son nom dans celui d'un quidam sans asile et réduit à vivre d'aumônes?" [p. 113].) Since Bomston has just offered to bestow a home and money on Saint-Preux, the father's last two objections about him do nothing except reveal the father's wild impenetrability as he flails around trying to produce "reasons" for that which has no reasons and, as far as he is concerned, requires none. (He is forced into the business of producing reasons because Bomston has imposed the terms of the discourse with his notions and definitions of what is reasonable. Part of Julie's father's anger is a result of finding himself involved in a discourse whose premises he does not share, where he is totally lost, and in which he can only keep coming up against his own unreason.) For him it all comes down to the opposition—nom / quidam. *Quidam* is precisely some person, an unnamed individual, or, as Harrap's dictionary, puts it "Person (name unknown)." Julie's father refuses to recognize Saint-Preux as having what he would recognize as a name. Of course he does have one, just about— you can read a very long way into the book without finding out what it is; his letters are always "A Julie" or "Réponse" and so on—but it is one that the father effectively nullifies by his withholding of ratification. He is forced into the ontological category of *quidamity* (the word exists)— person (name unknown). Against that, the father upholds the name of the family—which is, of course, le nom du père—not this or that name in particular (indeed to be honest I cannot recall whether we ever learn his name or his title) but nominality as such and as he decrees it to be.

Because it is all he has, the father's unarticulated dread is twofold—of a daughter taken over by a quidam and of a world taken over by quidams, which would render his name, his role, his being, all alike meaningless.

In one of her initial rebellious outbursts, Julie writes to Claire, "But then has my father sold me? He considers his daughter as property, as a slave; he acquits himself at my expense! He purchases his life with mine! . . . cruel and unnatural father. Does he deserve . . . what! deserve? He is the best of fathers. He wants to marry his daughter to his friend, that is his crime" (p. 76). ("Enfin mon père m'a donc vendue! il fait de sa fille une marchandise, une esclave! il s'acquitte à mes dépens! il paye sa vie de la mienne! . . . Père barbare et dénaturé! Mérite-t-il . . . Quoi! mériter! C'est le meilleur des pères! il veut unir sa fille à son ami, voilà son crime" [pp. 57–58].) We notice that the rebellious moments are very short, and the guilty recoil into filial loyalty and devotion comes very quickly: even to write down the unthinkable paradox "père dénaturé" is a kind of blasphemy that must immediately be atoned for by a penitential rehearsal of, as it were, the established piety—"c'est le meilleur des pères." Similarly, she catches herself up as soon as she begins to entertain the notion of what a father "deserves." The dots in the letters are hers, as she falters before the concept that may not be entertained. As far as daughters are concerned—this is the ethos of Julie's house, not necessarily, of course, of all eighteenth-century European society—the father is not answerable to any kind of merits and rewards system. He simply is. And he speaks. And when necessary he acts. Nevertheless, her moment of rebellion contains flashes of genuine insight. As daughter, she *is* "marchandise," "une esclave," to be "sold" as he deems fit; she is part of that system of property exchange that centers on marriage, as outlined by Lévi-Strauss and others.[6] The furthest she gets in defying this condition is when, by an extension of the schizoid device I have mentioned above, she attempts to mediate between her feelings for Saint-Preux and her obedience to her father by promising the following to Saint-Preux. "I shall never marry you without the consent of my father, but I shall never marry anyone else without your consent" (p. 191). ("Je ne t'épouserai jamais sans le consentement de mon père, mais je n'en

---

[6]Julie is touching on, but only just touching on, a very dangerous topic here, which was to be explored and exposed at far greater, and more telling, length by writers like Marx, as when he refers to: "This latent slavery in the family, though still very crude, is the first property, but even at this early stage it corresponds perfectly to the definition of modern economists who call it the power of disposing of the labour-power of others" (*The German Ideology*, in Marx, *Selected Writings*, ed. David McLellan [Oxford: Oxford University Press, 1977], p. 168). Writing more generally of the family, John Stuart Mill asserted that: "If the family in its best forms is . . . a school of sympathy, tenderness, and loving forgetfulness of self, it is still oftener, as respects its chief, a school of wilfulness, overbearingness, unbounded self-indulgence, and a double-eyed and idealized selfishness, of which sacrifice itself is only a particular form. . . . The family is a school of despotism, in which the virtues of despotism, but also its vices, are largely nourished" (*The Subjection of Women*, ch. 2). Julie, like

épouserai jamais un autre sans ton consentement" [p. 159].) This would seem like a perfect device for putting herself in a permanent double bind, one result of which could easily be a very specific kind of schizophrenic catatonia in which the solution is to make no moves or responses at all. She breaks this impossible situation not, of course, by gainsaying the father, but by asking for her word back from her lover. "Restore to me, then, the freedom which I have pledged to you and of which my father will dispose" (p. 241). ("Rendez-moi donc la liberté que je vous ai engagée et dont mon père veut disposer" [p. 238].) The father proposes and the father disposes. The daughter gives everything back to him— her freedom, her body, her word. In this connection there is a curious and revealing little footnote by Rousseau at one point. Saint-Preux writes to her about receiving a letter "written by a hand which never wrote to any man but myself"—on which Rousseau comments, "One must, I think, except her father" (p. 134) ("écrite d'une main qui n'en écrivit jamais à d'autre homme"—"Il en faut, je pense, excepter son père" [p. 110]). Before she wrote to her lover, she wrote to her father. He is first in everyting, and to him the daughter returns everything except her virginity, which is, perhaps, the one thing that this particular father would not have allowed himself, in his august omnipotence, to take.

As Madame de Wolmar, Julie wants Saint-Preux to assume "a submissive and compliant manner with my father" (p. 295) ("un air soumis et complaisant avec mon père" [p. 321]), and as I have noted above, in the move toward general consensus and what I want to call *ensemblization* that dominates the later part of the book, even he comes round to respecting and admiring the father, despite what he rather nicely calls "la bizarrerie de ses préjugés" (p. 458) ("the singularity of his prejudices" [p. 359]). Bizarre indeed they are, and it is perhaps more than a happy accident that the etymology of that word not only involves the Italian *bizzarro*, "angry," but may also involve the Basque *bizarra*, "beard," thus suggesting a particular kind of male choler as well as the more general sense of the odd, singular, or whimsically strange. The prejudices are bizarre, but, as I have had occasion to stress, they are totally binding even on the father himself as well as on those within his jurisdiction. Julie, in her most distraught moment of conflicting urges and imperatives, attempts a kind of psychic fragmentation whereby she will let love dispose of her heart but allow her father to dispose of her hand (and her tears to flow to her cousin) "Let a father enslaved by his promise and jealous of a vain title dispose of my hand as he has pledged; let love alone dispose of

Clarissa, and many other children in fiction, has glimpsed the "school of despotism" in the family and its "latent slavery," but she prefers to revert to her commitment to regarding the family as a "school of sympathy." And it will be some time before a woman in literature recognizes overtly what Mill says so succinctly: "marriage is the only actual bondage known to our law. There remain no legal slaves, except the mistress of every house. . . ." (ch. 2)

my heart" (p. 251.) ("Qu'un père esclave de sa parole et jaloux d'un vain titre dispose de sa main qu'il a promise; que l'amour seul dispose de mon coeur" [p. 246].) Julie has complained that she is enslaved by her father; he in turn is *enslaved by his own word*—"esclave de sa parole." Thus the father is both the source and the slave of the Word. And there is a very important aspect of this double relationship he has to the Word. It is often noted in the book that Julie's father is blind as well as being irrational, given to foolish ideas and a general "bizarrerie" in his prejudices; there are references to his not knowing what is going on. It is as though he has the most power but sees the least. And this is not attributable to what he is by temperament so much as to *where* he is by role. That place, to use a phrase from Lacan, entails blindness ("cette place comportait l'aveuglement").

This comes from his famous "Seminar on 'The Purloined Letter,'" from which I wish to quote another paragraph.

> *Rex et augur,* the legendary, archaic quality of the words seems to resound only to impress us with the absurdity of applying them to a man. And the figures of history, for some time now, hardly encourage us to do so. It is not natural for man to bear alone the weight of the highest of signifiers. And the place he occupies as soon as he dons it may be equally apt to become the symbol of the most outrageous imbecility.
>
> Let us say that the King here is invested with the equivocation natural to the sacred, with the imbecility which prizes none other than the Subject.

In the world of this book, Julie's father occupies that role described by Lacan as bearing the "highest of signifiers," ("du plus haut des signifiants") and we may well feel, as most of the figures in the book do, that over the central issue he displays what at the time seems to be "outrageous imbecility," just that imbecility characterized by Lacan as being involved with being the supreme authority.

In all this, Rousseau's book is focusing on something quite extraordinarily crucial in the history of Western society. The Word of the father is, we have noted, bizarre but binding, not because of what it says, but because of where it comes from. The father is the ultimate sanction, the absolute "referential" in Lefebvre's sense of the term, the fixed point beyond rationality, *from* which flows power, *to* which can only flow obedience; the figure speaking a language of pure command and taboo, the source of nomination ("le nom du père") and prohibition ("le 'non' du père"). Because of the father and his inflexible command and irrevocable word, it seems as if the established institutions are secure and can endure; the momentary fissures of passion are blocked, and marriage, the family, and the whole way of life connected with these institutions as practiced in that society are celebrated as achieving an ideal of incorporative harmony and functioning with serene efficiency. The father makes the contracts, and the contracts hold. But, as we have noted, the Word of the father is even here in a very imperiled condition. His family name and title are becoming meaningless, based on functions, distinctions, and differences that were ceasing to exist. If the apparently "full" word of the father is listened to carefully and discovered to be in fact an "empty" word—what then? What becomes of all the dependence structures and binding contracts—not only between parents and children, husbands and wives, but between words and meanings, signs and things? With the nineteenth century—despite those grim images of the cruel authoritarian Victorian father such as Thomas Arnold—and indeed during the eighteenth century from around the time of Rousseau's novel (1761—but of course such phenomena have no date of origin), we are into a period in which the Word of the father and all that that implies (as outlined above) comes into question; and if it may be said that the Word in varying ways ceases to "enslave," it must also be added that it comes to be a problem to establish just what, if anything, it can hold together at all. Instead of the "nom du père" it could be said that there is a growing sense of the " 'non' du père," not in the sense of the paternal prohibition, but rather implying the absence of the father, or the father as absence. It is in this sense that Foucault uses the phrase in his essay concerning Hölderlin, "Le 'Non' du Père," to which I have referred above. The following quotation comes from the same article and follows directly on from the passage quoted in the earlier footnote.

> Ce n'est donc pas dans les termes alimentaires ou fonctionnels de la carence qu'il faut penser une lacune fondamentale dans la position du Père. Pouvoir dire qu'il manque, qu'il est haï, rejeté ou introjecté, que son image passe par des transmutations symboliques, suppose qu'il n'est pas d'entrée de jeu "forclos," comme dit Lacan, qu'en sa place ne s'ouvre pas une béance absolue. Cette absence du Père, que manifeste, en s'y précipitant, la psychose, ne porte pas sur le registre des perceptions ou des images mais sur celui des signifiants. Le non par lequel s'ouvre cette béance n'indique pas que le nom de père est resté sans titulaire réel, mais que le père n'a jamais accédé jusqu'à la nomination et qu'est restée vide cette place du signifiant par lequel le père se nomme et par lequel, selon la Loi, il nomme. C'est vers ce "non" qu'infailliblement se dirige la droite ligne de la psychose lorsque, piquant vers l'abîme de son sens, elle fait surgir sous les formes du délire ou du fantasme, et dans le désastre du signifiant, l'absence ravageante du père.[7]

---

[7]The following is a translation of the quotation from Foucault, part of which was quoted in note 3, above.

Lacan, following Melanie Klein, has shown that the father, as the third party in the Oedipal situation, is not only the hated and feared rival, but the agent whose presence limits the unlimited relationship between the mother and child and whose first, anguished image emerges in the child's fantasy of being devoured. Consequently, the father separates, that is, he is the one who protects when, in his proclamation of

Much of the material in the works I shall be considering takes place in the shadow of "l'absence ravageante du père," that father who, at the decisive moment in Julie's life was so "ravagingly" present for one last display of that blind, awesome fury and power that was perhaps in part provoked by a sense that that power was being in some indescribable way undermined and by the as-yet-unconscious dawning of an unformulable apprehension that it was on the verge of an irreversible decline, that, precisely the "nom du père" was in danger of giving way to the "'non' du père."

Elysium

At the end of part 3, Julie has decided on obedience to her father's orders and marries Monsieur de Wolmar. In a letter explaining her decision to Saint-Preux she declares that it is an error to think that "love is necessary to form a happy marriage" ("que l'amour est nécessaire pour former un heureux mariage"). On the contrary, the two are if anything opposed, mutually exclusive. "Love is accompanied by a continual uneasiness over jealousy or privation, little suited to marriage, which is a state

---

the Law, he links space, rules, and language within a single and major experience. At a stroke, he creates the distance along which will develop the scansion of presences and absences, the speech whose initial form is based on constraints, and finally, the relationship of the signifier to the signified which not only gives rise to the structure of language but also to the exclusion and symbolic transformation of repressed material. Thus it is not in alimentary or functional terms of deficiency that we understand the gap which now stands in the Father's place. To be able to say that he is missing, that he is hated, excluded, or introjected, that his image has undergone symbolic transmutations, presumes that he is not "forclosed" (as Lacan would say) from the start and that his place is not marked by a gaping and absolute emptiness. The father's absence, manifested in the headlong rush of psychosis, is not registered by perceptions or images, but relates to the order of the signifier. The "no" through which this gap is created does not imply the absence of a real individual who bears the father's name; rather, it implies that the father has never assumed the role of nomination and that the position of the signifier, through which the father names himself and, according to the Law, through which he is able to name, has remained vacant. It is toward this "no" that the unwavering line of psychosis is infallibly directed; as it is precipitated inside the abyss of its meaning, it evokes the devastating absence of the father through the forms of delirium and phantasms and through the catastrophe of the signifier.

(Michel Foucault, "The Father's 'No,'" in Foucault, *Language, Counter-Memory, Practice: Selected Essays and Interviews*, ed. Donald F. Bouchard, trans. Donald F. Bouchard and Sherry Simon (Ithaca, N.Y.: Cornell University Press, 1977), pp. 81–82.

of enjoyment and peace." (p. 261). ("L'amour est accompagné d'une inquiétude continuelle de jalousie ou de privation, peu convenable au mariage, qui est un état de jouissance et de paix" [p. 274].) This is a distinction of some considerable import, since it attempts to establish a separation whereby marriage is that state of "paix" that by definition excludes "inquiétude." Let us say that Julie is willing (thinks she is willing) to renounce "l'amour"—which, however we wish to think of it, involves, in her terms, "jalousie" and "privation"; the renunciation is made for the sake of "paix." But what, we may ask, will be the *content* of a "paix" from which, ideally, all "inquiétude" has been banished? If we consider that, in varying forms, human life and particularly human relationships consist of a dialectic or at least an alternation of what we may call, using Conrad's terms, "rest" and "unrest," then it would appear as if Julie is acceding to the attempt to turn life into continual "rest." The condition that most perfectly fulfills such an aspiration to vanquish and eliminate all "inquiétude" is, needless to say, death, and there is an ironic significance in the fact that Julie chooses to call her most cherished topographical creation—a strange kind of total garden—Elysium. As we discover, she knew very well that it originally referred to the abode of the blessed after death. To set up an ideal of marriage that consists of a relationship that establishes a state of life-minus-*inquiétude* has, then, some potentially disturbing implications.

After Julie's decision, there is nothing Saint-Preux can do except to write to his friend Lord Bomston suggesting that they commit suicide together, a proposal that, understandably enough, Lord Bomston is less than enthusiastic about, as his response indicates. So, after administering a good dose of paternal scolding to the "young madman" (p. 265) ("jeune insensé" [p. 291]), he sends him off to the East Indies as part of a trip round the world, and part 3 ends with the ever-obedient, and by now much-traveled, Saint-Preux setting off for "another hemisphere" (p. 268) ("un autre hémisphère" [p. 293]). So concludes the story of foiled young passion, the man departing for the unrest of exile and the girl pressed into the peace of marriage. But that is only half the book, and there are three more parts and over two hundred and fifty pages yet to come. What will they be about? This is not a frivolous question if you think that it is a truism that the majority of bourgeois novels either conclude with marriage (e.g., Jane Austen) or—if they start with marriage—inevitably go on to explore the very *inquiétudes* that are engendered by the married state. Since Julie's marriage is, in intention, to be devoid of all such *inquiétudes*, we may well wonder what awaits us, as readers, as we embark on book 4. Early on Julie had written to Saint-Preux, "I see, my friend . . . that love will be the great business of our lives" (p. 90). ("Je vois, mon amis . . . que l'amour sera la grande affaire de notre vie" [p. 68].) It is all very well to say that this love will now be transformed or rarified into spiritual or Platonic love, but there remains a more mundane and quotidian question. What are these characters going to *do*? With what other business will they busy themselves?

In the opening letter in part 4, the first thing Julie turns to is an attempt to annul the distinction between her cousin's house and her own by conflating them. "Do you not feel that thus to be alternately at your house and at mine is not really to be anywhere, and can you not contrive some means by which you may be at both at the same time?" ("Ne sens-tu pas qu'être ainsi alternativement chez toi et chez moi, c'est n'être bien nulle part, et n'imagines-tu quelque moyen de faire que tu sois en même temps chez l'une et chez l'autre?") And she reminds Claire of what they used to say as young girls—"Ah! If ever we are our own mistresses, no one will see us separated again" (p. 273). ("Ah! si jamais nous disposons de nous, on ne nous verra plus séparées" [p. 247].) As it happens, Claire's husband, another somewhat senior citizen, has recently died, so that Claire is effectively her own mistress and there is no reason why she should not merge her house with Julie's—not literally of course, but by leaving hers and coming to live in Julie's, which is, of course, *la maison paternelle*. Julie is embarking on her grand dream of rehousing the world in her home, the house of the father. The attempt at ultimate synthesis has begun. And one of her reasons for pressing Claire to join her in her home is worth noting. Something is lacking. Her husband is unresponsive ("il ne répond pas assez à ma fantaisie" [p. 298]) and his tenderness is too reasonable ("trop raisonable" [p. 298]); but Julie can hardly wish for an inrush of unreason, since that would be precisely to seek the very *inquiétude* she has chosen to leave behind. She refers to "all these voids" (p. 274) ("tous ces vides" [p. 248]), voids specifically left by her mother's death, and the death of Claire's husband, but more generally by the fact that as her children are yet too small for the kind of reciprocal love she needs, there is no one on whom she can lavish the full energies of her love and receive love in return. It is this role she wants to be filled by—her cousin, the inseparable. Yet clearly the void is one that can hardly be filled by a cousin—indeed it may be said to be an ontological void, but we do not need to go as far as that to comprehend what she is lacking. It is not necessarily Saint-Preux himself, but the passional irregularities, intensities, and reciprocities that can only be experienced in that *inquiétude continuelle,* together with the *jalousie* and *privation* that are a part of that *inquiétude*—all of which she has formally put behind her in choosing to reject him. It would seem that marriage has its privations as well as its peace; perhaps, even, it is its peace that is part of its privation.

Cousin Claire's response is to reaffirm her love for Julie and assert that Julie filled the void in *her* life left by the death of her husband, so it would seem that the cousins are attempting to fill each other's voids. Without wishing to suggest that this mutual aspiration indicates anything specifically perverse, there is no doubt that it is a form of emotional incest and does involve on the part of both the cousins the displacement of a considerable amount of suppressed sexual feeling. (Claire is adamant about never marrying again, and while Wolmar is undoubtedly alive, it is hard to associate his imperturbably grave demeanor and detached voyeurism with any erotic activity.) When Julie dies, Claire goes literally out of her mind ("hors de sens"), rolling about the floor mumbling incoherently and gnawing on the legs of chairs ("mordant les pieds des chaises" [p. 559]), a demonstration of an intensity of grief, indeed of sheer uncontrolled passion that is scarcely to be matched by any of the other signs of feeling in the entire book—perhaps only by the wild anger of Julie's father. It is the grief of "the inseparable," who finds herself at last truly and irrevocably separate; the response to a forced and final breaking of a bond so close and so deep that it seems to me to bespeak that primordial urge to merge back into intrafamilial oneness that goes under the name of incest. This is to anticipate the end, but I wish to consider first what it is Julie—or Julie-and-Claire—does while still alive. Having brought Claire into the house, Julie increases her plans for inclusion. Her husband writes a courteous and generous letter offering Saint-Preux his house ("il vous offre sa maison" [p. 311]). He accepts and is content to feel himself as being like the "child of the house" (p. 345) ("comme l'enfant de la maison" [p. 398]). The father, temporarily absent for a period because of involvement in a lawsuit (and one may imagine that he was often involved in such eristic errands, given his temperament), rejoins them. ("A long and troublesome law suit, nearly finished, will soon bring back the best of fathers into our arms" [p. 331]: "Un long et fâcheux procès prêt à finir va ramener dans nos bras le meilleur des pères" [p. 385].) Even Lord Bomston is brought in for a period, so that in a very real sense we may say that is indeed as if they are all there together in *la maison paternelle*—brought back from as far away as the East Indies and as near as the cousin's house, all united, and all so harmonious that Wolmar insists that Saint-Preux should embrace his wife, Julie, while Saint-Preux comes to love and respect the very father who ruined his life. Friction is at degree zero, and reconciliation and homecoming are everywhere. Everything is lovely in the garden—indeed, particularly in the garden, though things are pretty good in the house, too. But I will come to that in a moment. For now there is one other aspect of this drive to reunion, that ensemblization I mentioned earlier, to which I want to draw attention.

It concerns the move toward indistinguishability of Julie and Claire, particularly as mothers, a move that extends toward their children as well. It entails what at times amounts to an interchangeability of selves, so that the I-Thou disjunction/conjunction is dissolved. Thus Julie: "I feel that I doubly enjoy my little Marcellin's caresses when I see you sharing them. When I embrace your daughter, I imagine I am pressing you to my bosom. We have said a hundred times, as we see our little babies playing together, that our united hearts mix them, and we no longer know to which one of us each of the three belongs" (p. 274). ("Je sens que je jouis doublement des caresses de mon petit Marcellin quand je te les vois partager. Quand j'embrasse ta fille, je crois te presser contre mon sein. Nous l'avons dit cent fois; en voyant tous nos petits bambins jouer ensemble, nos coeurs unis les confondent, et nous ne savons plus à laquelle appartient chacun des trois" [p. 298].) Saint-Preux, writing about Claire's daughter Henriette, refers to her mothers: "I say her *mothers,* for to see the manner in which they act with her, it is difficult to distinguish the real one, and some strangers who arrived today are or seem to be still in doubt on the matter. In fact, both call her *Henriette* or *my daughter,* indifferently. She calls one *mama* and the other *little mama*" (p. 357). ("Je dis ses mères; car, à voir la manière dont elles vivent avec elle, il est difficile de distinguer la véritable; et des étrangers qui nous sont venus aujourd'hui sont ou paraissent là-dessus encore en doute. En effet, toutes deux l'appellent Henriette, ou ma fille, indifféremment. Elle appelle *maman* l'une, et l'autre *petite maman*" [p. 455].) And later he writes to Claire: "You are both more dear to me than ever, but my heart no longer distinguishes between you and does not separate the insepara- bles" (p. 367). ("Vous m'êtes toutes deux plus chères que jamais; mais mon coeur ne distingue plus l'une de l'autre, et ne sépare point les inséparables" [p. 468].) However, this same letter contains an account of a very ominous dream, to which I will return.

At the conclusion of part 5, Julie effectively suggests that Claire should marry Saint-Preux, and it is hard not to assume that, given their feelings of interchangeability (if not actual identicality), this would per- mit some vicarious indulgence in what might be expected to be the customary sexual embraces that would then legitimately ensue. "Ah cousin! What delight for me to unite forever two hearts so well formed for each other, who have been joined for so long in my own. Let them be even more closely joined in it, if possible. Let there be but one heart for you and me. Yes, my Claire, you will still serve your friend by indulging your love, and I shall be surer of my own sentiments when I shall no longer be able to distinguish between him and you" (p. 376). ("Ah! cousine, quel charme pour moi de réunir à jamais deux coeurs si bien faits l'un pour l'autre, et qui se confondent mieux encore s'il est possible; ne soyez plus qu'un pour vous et pour moi. Oui, ma Claire, tu serviras encore ton amie en couronnant ton amour; et j'en serai plus sûre de mes propres sentiments, quand je ne pourrai plus les distinguer entre vous" [p. 480].) The suggestion is firmly declined, but it testifies to an inclination to live in a kind of emotional blur in which her feelings can only be sure of themselves when they are no longer able, or constrained, to distinguish between their objects. From one point of view this desire to establish an inclusive happy-family mélange, in which, at least emotionally speaking, the various figures—cousin, lover, friend, father—are, as it were, heaped indistinguishably together, is an attempt to realize a dream of total harmony in which all the oppositional elements in human relationships—familial, passional—have been eliminated and all the different parties can come together to live forever and ever in peace and concord, never to part again. As Saint-Preux puts it, writing in the optative mood, if he can just see his friend Edward (Lord Bomston) happy, "we will all rejoin each other never to part again" (p. 361) ("nous nous rassemblons tous pour ne nous plus séparer" [p. 464]), though, as he notes in passing, if that state of perfect happiness was achieved, there won't in fact be much else for him to wish for, or to vow to do. Such a vision of human and humane harmony is from this point of view the acme of Enlightenment thought. From another point of view, Julie's dream (shared by others, but originating with her, or with her and Claire) involves an abandoning of distinctions, a loss of a sense of difference, which could be seen to point the way back to that "infamous promiscuity of things and women" that for Vico was the abhorrent state from which civilization had to emerge, that incestuous Ur-confusion we think of as the primordial region of chaos and old night. That, at its height, civilization should start to longingly look back (albeit obliquely and very indirectly) to the precivilized state from which it emerged is a phenomenon of some considerable implications. And that this incestuous dream is engendered in, and arguably engendered by, *la maison paternelle*—the paradigm locus of authority in society—is perhaps even more thought-provoking. The father, he-who-separates, produces a daughter who wishes to be she-who-brings-everyone-together-again. The rule of law engenders a dream of indistinguishability. Rousseau lays bare the outlines of a paradox that has more profound implications than he himself, perhaps, could guess.

Bringing people together is an activity, but scarcely a full-time one, and there remains the question of how people live in Julie's house and what they do. One answer is—they run the house, and tend the children. (Saint-Preux is brought back, among other things, to be their educator, a final flickeringly sadistic touch he accepts with the eager masochism that has become his regressive mode of existence.) In two letters Saint-Preux describes first the economy of the house ("l'économie de cette

maison") and then the garden. The first letter is inordinately long—
twenty-three pages—and outlines a domestic economy and mode of existence that amounts to a Utopian prescription for an impossibly ideal
high-bourgeois / low aristocracy way of life. It is a blueprint for a perfect
way of life that is so perfect in every detail as to be absurd, and worse.
For what one realizes in reading it is that there are degrees of harmoni-
zation that are intolerable. Because, when everything is so tidy and well-
regulated and balanced, you are suddenly confronted with the awesome
question—well what, after all, is it all about? I will quote, very selectively,
to give some small idea of the kind of perfection so enthusiastically and
admiringly outlined by Saint-Preux. The letter is to Lord Bomston.

> My Lord, what a pleasant and affecting sight is that of a simple and well
> regulated house in which order, peace, and innocence prevail.... Since
> the master and mistress of this house have fixed it as their residence, they
> have put to use all that formerly served only for ornament; it is no longer a
> house made to be seen but to be lived in.... There is not a single room in
> which one may not recognize that he is in the country and yet in which he
> may not find all the conveniences of the city.... Everywhere they have
> substituted the useful for the agreeable, and yet the agreeable has almost
> always prevailed.... All idle subtleties are unknown in this house, and the
> great art by which the master and mistress make their servants such as they
> desire them to be is to appear to their people as they are.... At the table,
> while strolling, in private, or before everyone, their language is always the
> same.... Even if no outside intrigues are allowed, no one is tempted to
> have any.... I have never seen an establishment in which self-interest was
> so prudently directed and in which it nevertheless was of less influence
> than in this house. All is done through affection. One would say that these
> mercenary souls are purified in entering this place of wisdom and har-
> mony.
>
> (Pp. 301-3)

> Milord, que c'est un spectacle agréable et touchant que celui d'une maison
> simple et bien réglée où règnent l'ordre, la paix, l'innocence.... Depuis
> que les maîtres de cette maison y ont fixé leur demeure, ils en ont mis à
> leur usage tout ce qui ne servait à l'ornement; ce n'est plus une maison faite pour
> être vue, mais pour être habitée. . . . Il n'y a pas une chambre où l'on ne se
> reconnaisse à la campagne, et où l'on ne retrouve toutes les commodités de
> la ville.... Partout on a substitué l'utile à l'agréable, et l'agréable y a pres-
> que toujours gagné.... Toutes ces vaines subtilités sont ignorées dans
> cette maison, et le grand art des maîtres pour rendre leurs domestiques tels
> qu'ils les veulent est de se montrer à eux tels qu'ils sont.... A table, à la
> promenade, tête à tête, ou devant tout le monde, on tient toujours le même
> langage.... Si l'on ne souffre aucune intrigue au-dehors, personne n'est
> tenté d'en avoir ... je n'ai jamais vu de police où l'intérêt fut si sagement

dirigé, et où pourtant il influât moins que dans celle-ci. Tout se fait par attachement: l'on dirait que ces âmes vénales se purifient en entrant dans ce séjour de sagesse et d'union.

(Pp. 329–52)

I have called this mainly a high-bourgeois dream because the stress is everywhere on the prudential, the utilitarian, the useful, the economical (another twenty pages or so of quotation concerning how they run the vineyards, treat the agricultural workers, teach the domestics, supervise the games and gatherings of the servants, arrange their Sundays, etc., etc., would only confirm this emphasis!); and there is that suspicion of "ornament" and of what is "subtle" and what is "agreeable," i.e., of that kind of aristocratic hedonistic self-gratification and aesthetic delight in certain kinds of abundance and excess and what transcends the "useful," that is a distinctly bourgeois trait. Of course it remains partly a lower aristocracy dream as well, given the extent of the estates, the numbers of workers, and the sense of rank and obligation to a whole chain of dependents. It is of course a magic house in which there are both the pleasures of the country and the amenities of the town; where there is stable hierarchy combined with a harmonious equality; where there is no subtlety because the minds of the inhabitants are drained of any disposition to deviousness (and wit!); where self-interest mysteriously turns into affection without losing the advantages of self-interest; where the profits of "venality" are retained and enjoyed, while those who benefit from it are "purified" of their venality; and where the language spoken, from the most intimate situations to the most public, is *always the same*.[8] Pondering existence in such a house, one doesn't know whether to say first "how utterly inconceivable" or "how ineffably boring." Everything is dominated by a "disposition à la concorde" (p. 346) that would quickly lose its sense of meaning, because the inhabitants would lose any of that sense of the always-possible discordancy in things, without which a "dis-

[8]This produces what Barthes calls "foreseeable discourse" ("Le discours prévisible"), of which he writes:

> Tedium of foreseeable discourse. Foreseeability is a structural category, since it is possible to give the modes of expectation or of encounter (in short: of *suspense*) of which language is the theater (this has been done for narrative); we might then establish a typology of the various kinds of discourse according to their degree of foreseeability. *Text of the Dead:* a litaneutical text, in which no word can be changed.
>
> (*Roland Barthes,* by Roland Barthes, p. 149)

This foreseeability characterizes not only the language spoken at Clarens but long sections of the novel itself (as it does Richardson's *Pamela* and *Clarissa*). It is all part of a strategy to extrude difference—in speaking, in writing, in living. As Barthes notes, the results can be very tedious, but the tediousness of the foreseeable text is only a reflection of the tedium of the foreseeable life.

position à la concorde" becomes a slack automatism: this because of the attempt to deny the existence of the "outside"—and therefore uncontrolled—world (the "au-dehors").[9]

One of the most common and basic sources of discord or dissonance in human arrangements is, needless to say, sexuality, with all its unpredictable eruptability, and this is very carefully monitored in the house of Clarens.

> To prevent any dangerous familiarity between the two sexes, they do not at all try to guide them by emphatic laws which they would be tempted to secretly infringe; rather, without appearing to be thinking about it, they establish customs more powerful than authority itself.... Following the admirable order that reigns here, they feel that in a well-regulated house men and women ought to have very little commerce between them . . . in a word, both converge on a common happiness by different routes; and this separation of tasks and cares is the strongest link in their union.... Madame de Wolmar's maxim is borne out very well by the example of her household; each person being, so to speak, with his own sex, the women there living very separated from the men. To prevent any suspicious meetings between them, her great secret is to keep both men and women continuously occupied; for their tasks are so different that it's only idleness that brings them together.
>
> (My translation; not translated in McDowell's abridgment.)
>
> Pour prévenir entre les deux sexes une familiarité dangereuse, on ne les gêne point ici par des lois positives qu'ils seraient tentés d'enfreindre en secret; mais, sans paraître y songer, on établit des usages plus puissants que l'autorité même.... Sur l'ordre admirable qui règne ici, ils sentent que dans une maison bien réglée les hommes et les femmes doivent avoir peu de commerce entre eux . . . en un mot, tous deux [men and women] concourent au bonheur commun par des chemins différents; et ce partage de travaux et de soins est le plus fort lien de leur union.... La maxime de Mme. de Wolmar [i.e., the idea just quoted] se soutient très bien par l'exemple de sa maison; chacun étant pour ainsi dire tout à son sexe, les femmes y vivent très séparées des hommes. Pour prévenir entre eux des

[9]We might compare this almost pathologically mechanical orderliness at Clarens with the regularity maintained at the house of Pamela and Mr. B. after their marriage (in *Pamela*). As one visitor notes, admiringly, it is "a heaven of a house: and being wound up thus constantly once a week, at least, like a good eight-day clock, no piece of machinery that was ever made is so regular and uniform as this family is." (vol. 2, letter 52) Lady Davers advises Pamela to be like "the master-wheel, in some beautiful piece of mechanism, whose dignified grave motions is to set a-going all the under-wheels, with a velocity suitable to their respective parts." (vol. 2, letter 9) The idea of the large household economy, dependent on a serving class and a proletariat, as a machine now strikes us rather differently— the clockwork regularity for us would more likely be replaced by the image of factory discipline, and the mechanization of the family would be likely to remind us of the insights of Marx.

liaisons suspectes, son grand secret est d'occuper incessament les uns et les autres; car leurs travaux sont si différents qu'il n'y a que l'oisivité qui les rassemble.

(Pp. 336-37)

Just what the servants really felt about this benign but despotic segregation we are not, of course, told. But notice what is considered to be the threat, and what the remedy. "Familiarité dangereuse," "commerce" between the sexes, and "les liaisons suspectes"—all these can be prevented by one strategy, the imposition of continual work. The only danger is—"oisivité"—idleness, that empty, unprofitable, private time that is withheld from the master, owner, overseer, whatever authority is programming the time and activities of those under it. It is time that has got away, so to speak, slipped the leash, and hence it is in that kind of uncontrolled time when other impulses, not repressed by incessant work or cowed by dominant and domineering customs ("usages"), may begin to feel their way out, and then there might occur *familiarité dangereuse* and *liaisons suspectes*, and indeed *familiarité suspecte* and *liaisons dangereuses*, and then who knows what would happen to this "séjour de sagesse et d'union," this house "bien réglée"? This is why the bourgeois has traditionally been apprehensive about idleness, if not for himself then certainly for those, or rather in those, who work for him—though more usually it was idleness itself, in all its forms (non-profit-making time) that was abhorrent to him. Hence, among other reasons, his dislike and suspicion of the aristocracy, who were, precisely, the idle class. Idleness threatens the whole structure of his way of life, just as Julie and her husband know very well that it would threaten the clockwork harmony of Clarens. But we can begin to sense the cost of that harmony based on unremitting toil and totally patterned and monitored activities. The inhabitants may be contented, but they can hardly be said to be alive. Clarens is, in a certain sense, a house of the dead. And, since the inhabitants seem to be happy, we may call it a house of the grateful dead. Which brings us to Elysium, but before commenting on that strange garden let me just note that we may compare Clarens to the constitution of Monsieur de Wolmar as described by Saint-Preux, transmitting to Lord Bomston Julie's distress at her husband's religious scepticism. "That man, so wise, so reasonable, so far from every kind of vice, so little subject to human passions, knows nothing of that faith which gives value to virtue and, in the innocence of an irreproachable life, he bears in the bottom of his heart the dreadful tranquillity of the unbeliever" (p. 348). ("Cet homme si sage, si raisonnable, si loin de toute espèce de vice, si peu soumis aux passions humaines, ne croit rien de ce qui donne un prix aux vertus, et, dans l'innocence d'une vie irréprochable, il porte au fond de son coeur l'affreuse paix des méchants" [p. 445].) He is as rationally and passionlessly organized and regulated as the house; both operate according to the same meticulous economy. And at the heart of both, we may infer, there is a dreadful tranquillity; in his case it is described, paradoxically, as the terrifying peace of the wicked (not just the unbeliever) as though a complete dedication to rational virtue has produced its opposite. Similarly the dreadful tranquillity of the house is the, to us, perverse result of a complete commitment to the rational ordering of every aspect of daily life, which produces, paradoxically, the dreadful peace of a daily death.[10]

[10]Whether or not it was intentional, the house, setting, and activities in the work of Marquis de Sade, particularly *Juliette,* offer an almost exact inverted parody of Julie's house, Clarens, with its totally regulated activities (Sade's subtitle—*les prospérités du vice*—certainly looks like a mocking inverted echo of Richardson's subtitle to *Pamela—Virtue Rewarded*). To take some observations from Roland Barthes's *Sade, Fourier, Loyola:*

> The enclosure of the Sadian site has another function: it forms the basis of a social autarchy. Once shut in, the libertines, their assistants, and their subjects form a total society, endowed with an economy, a morality, a language, and a time articulated into schedules, labors, and celebrations. Here, as elsewhere, the enclosure permits the system, i.e., the imagination. The nearest equivalent to the Sadian city will be the Fourierist phalanstery: the same attempt to establish in every detail a human internship sufficient unto itself, the same determination to identify happiness with a completed and organized space, the same eagerness to define beings by their functions and to regulate the entry into play of those functioning classes according to a detailed scenario, the same attention to instituting an economy of the passions, in short, the same "harmony" and the same utopia.
>
> (P. 17)

This also holds good for Clarens, and we might equally well compare and contrast Julie's garden with the "Gardens of the Société des Amis du Crime," constructed, not for bourgeois pleasure and repose, but for every possible infamy and the getting rid of victims. Sade's is a "highly coded society" (p. 25), but so is Julie's. "Sadian practice is ruled by a great notion of order: 'irregularities' are strenuously regulated, vice is unbridled but not without order (p. 27)"—so much could be said of Julie's house, except that there, *nothing* is unbridled, and instead of vice there is work, and a carefully monitored system of legitimate nonsexual "pleasures." "Juliette's imagination is eminently that of a bookkeeper"—and so is Julie's, though instead of planning a project for "the certain corruption . . . of the entire French population" (p. 29, n. 15) (as Juliette does), Julie plans rather to create a totally virtuous community under her jurisdiction. Instead of Sade's sequestered world of total crime and sexual perversion, Julie seeks to establish a no-less-sequestered world of total innocence and asexual good behavior. Barthes again:

> Yet on every page of his work, Sade provides us with evidence of concerted "irrealism": what happens in a novel by Sade is strictly fabulous, i.e., impossible; or more exactly, the impossibilities of the referent are turned into possibilities of the discourse, constraints are shifted: the referent is totally at the discretion of Sade, who can, like any narrator, give it fabulous dimensions, but the sign, belonging to the order of the discourse, is intractable, it makes the laws. . . .
> . . . The function of the discourse is not in fact to create "fear, shame, envy, an impression," etc., but to conceive the inconceivable, i.e., to leave nothing outside the words and to concede nothing ineffable to the world: such it seems is the keynote repeated throughout the Sadian city. . . .
>
> (Pp. 36–37)

To give some idea of the features of Elysium, I must again quote selectively from another extremely long letter in which this impossibly ideal garden, adjacent to the impossibly ideal house, is described in minute detail.

> For several days I had heard talk of this Elysium, about which they made a kind of mystery before me. . . . This place, although quite close to the house, is so hidden by a shady walk which separates them that it is visible

---

And such, if one thinks carefully about it, is the keynote of Rousseau's, or Saint-Preux's, description of Julie's ideal house and garden.

See also Barthes's comments in *Sade, Fourier, Loyola* on "The Family" in relation to Sade:

> To transgress the familiar interdiction consists in altering the terminological distinctness of the parental pattern. . . .
>
> The Family is defined on two levels: its "content" (ties of affection, society, gratitude, respect, etc.), at which the libertine mocks, and its "form," the network of nominative ties—and therefore combinatory ties—with which the libertine plays, which he recognizes the better to fake them and on which he brings to bear syntactical operations; it is on this second level that for Sade the original transgression occurs, the one that produces the intoxication of a continuous invention, the jubilation of incessant surprises: "He says he knew a man who had fucked three children he had had with his mother, whence he had a daughter he had married to his son, so that by fucking her he was fucking his sister, his daughter, and his daughter-in-law, and he was making his son fuck his sister and his stepmother." Thus transgression appears as a nominative surprise: to posit that the son will be the spouse or husband (depending on whether the father, Noirceuil, sodomizes his progeny or is sodomized by it) fills Sade with the same wonder as that which seizes the Proustian Narrator when he discovers that the Guermantes' Way and Swann's Way come together: incest, like time recaptured, is only a surprise of vocabulary.
>
> (Pp. 137–38)

This may all seem a long way from Julie's serenely ordered family home, yet a more careful consideration of Sade's world will bring to light a kind of distorted, nightmare mirror image of what must have been a version of Rousseau's ideal house and its activities and economies. In both, the network of nominative and combinatory ties is played with, and the terminological distinctness of the parental pattern is disturbed or threatened. And in both, blatant in Sade, repressed but detectable in Rousseau, is the actual or latent presence of the ultimate taboo act—incest.

There are, of course, no acts of sodomy or sexual perversion in Julie's novel (or house); indeed, we may fairly wonder if there is much sexuality at all—instead we have sentiment. But there is one thing that Sade's and Rousseau's books have in common: again, I quote Barthes on Sade: "Without formative speech, debauchery, crime, would be unable to invent themselves, to develop: the book must precede the book, the storyteller is the only 'actor' in the book, since speech is its sole drama" (p. 35). For "storyteller" read "letter writer," and we can say of *La Nouvelle Héloïse*, as we can of Richardson's *Pamela* and *Clarissa*, that ultimately writing is the only drama, in each the body is effectively written out by an almost uninterruptible flow of writing, sexuality being displaced onto, replaced by, script. Pamela and Clarissa are really far more worried about the possible loss of their *pen*, rather than their *men*—a substitution or replacement that bears some pondering over. But in all these letters that, as it were, will never stop, in this endlessly self-renewing, self-perpetuating writing, we do approach something like the decorporealization of narrative. It prefigures that state of fiction outlined by Barthes as follows: "What takes place in a narrative is from the referential (reality) point of view literally *nothing;* "what happens" is

from no part of the house. The dense foliage which surrounds it makes it impervious to the eye, and it is always carefully locked. I was no sooner inside and turned around than, the door being hidden by elders and hazel trees which permit only two narrow passageways on the sides, I no longer saw by which way I had entered, and perceiving no door, I found myself there as if fallen from the sky.

Entering this so-called orchard, I was struck by an agreeable sensation of freshness which the thick foliage, the animated and vivid greenness, the flowers scattered about on all sides, the murmur of a running brook, and the singing of a thousand birds brought to my imagination at least as much as to my senses; but at the same time I thought I saw the wildest, the most solitary place in nature, and it seemed I was the first mortal who had ever penetrated into this desert island. Surprised, impressed, ecstatic over a sight so little expected, I remained motionless for a moment, and cried out with involuntary enthusiasm, "Oh Tinian! Oh Juan Fernandez![11] Julie, the world's end is at your threshold!"

"Many people think the same of it as you," she said with a smile, "but twenty paces more presently leads them back to Clarens."

(Pp. 304-5)

Il y avait plusieurs jours que j'entendais parler de cet Elysée dont on me faisait une espèce de mystère.... Ce lieu, quoique tout proche de la maison, est tellement caché par l'allée couverte qui l'en sépare, qu'on ne l'aperçoit de nulle part. L'épais feuillage qui l'environne ne permet point à l'oeil d'y pénétrer, et il est toujours soigneusement fermé à clef. A peine fus-je au-dedans, que, la porte étant masquée par des aunes et des coudriers qui ne laissent que deux étroits passages sur les côtés, je ne vis plus en

---

language alone, the adventure of language, the unceasing celebration of its coming. ("Structural Analysis of Narratives") in *Image-Music-Text,* ed. and trans. Stephen Heath [Glasgow: Fontana/Collins, 1977] p. 124.) The importance to Sade of the physicality of writing, an importance that extends to other "epistolaromaniacs" in fiction—such as the ladies mentioned above—is well brought out in a final note on Sade by Barthes:

> Any detention is a system: a bitter struggle exists within this system, not to get free of it (this was beyond Sade's power), but to break through its constraints. A prisoner for some twenty-five years of his life, Sade in prison had two fixations: outdoor exercise and writing, which governors and ministers were continually allowing and taking away from him like a rattle from a baby. The need and the desire for outdoor exercise are easily understood (although Sade always linked its privation to a symbolic theme, obesity). The repression, obviously, as anyone can see, of writing is as good as censoring the book; what is poignant here, however, is that writing is forbidden in its *physical* form; Sade was denied "any use of the pencil, ink, pen, and paper." Censored are hand, muscle, blood. Castration is circumscribed, the scriptural sperm can no longer flow; detention becomes retention; without exercise, without a pen, Sade becomes *bloated,* a eunuch.

(P. 182)

[11]"Desert islands in the South Seas, celebrated in the voyage of Admiral Anson" (Rousseau). (Iles désertes de la mer du Sud, célebres dans le voyage de l'amiral Anson. [Note de Rousseau.])

me retournant par où j'étais entré, et, n'apercevant point de porte, je me trouvai là comme tombé des nues.

En entrant dans ce prétendu verger, je fus frappé d'une agréable sensation de fraîcheur que d'obscurs ombrages, une verdure animée et vive, des fleurs éparses de tous côtés, un gazouillement d'eau courante, et le chant de mille oiseaux, portèrent à mon imagination du moins autant qu'à mes sens; mais en même temps je crus voir le lieu le plus sauvage, le plus solitaire de la nature, et il me semblait d'être le premier mortel qui jamais eût pénétré dans ce désert. Surpris, saisi, transporté d'un spectacle si peu prévu, je restai un moment immobile, et m'écriai dans un enthousiasme involontaire: "On Tinian! O Juan-Fernandez! Julie, le bout du monde est à votre porte!"—Beaucoup de gens le trouvent ici comme vous, dit-elle avec un sourire; mais vingt pas de plus les ramènent bien vite à Clarens.

(P. 353)

Like the house, the garden offers impossible combinations and conflations. It offers all the delights of farawayness along with all the securities of home; it permits solitude twenty steps away from the communion of the house; it gives the exotic sensation of wildness, at the same time bestowing the solacing charms of a more pastoral, domesticated nature; it is the end of the world by the door of the house. It itself has a door, of course, but this interface and connecting point between Clarens and Elysium is effaced once the entrant has gone through, as though he had entered another order of space, perhaps even another dimension—we may call this the transcendence of adjacency. To itemize all the aspects of the garden that Saint-Preux enumerates would be somewhat exhausting, but certain features are worth pointing to. The first question that Julie asks of Saint-Preux is, as one might expect from a good bourgeois householder—"How much do you think it costs to put it in its present state?" (p. 305). ("Que pensez-vous qu'il m'en coûte pour le mettre dans l'état où il est?" [p. 353].) It turns out that she has managed things so prudently that this "metamorphosed orchard" (p. 306) ("ce verger ainsi métamorphosé" [p. 354]) cost her nothing, not perhaps the least of its merits in the economically minded eyes of its owners. What follows is an important part of that change in ideas of landscape gardening that reveals so much about the changing sensibility of the mid-to-late eighteenth century. Suffice it to say that Saint-Preux praises the absence of enforced order and symmetry (enough of that in the house, one might suppose) and what we can recognize as the cultivated naturalness that became an eighteenth-century ideal.

Indeed, interestingly enough, in place of the introduction of linear order into nature, it is the introduction of sinuosity into nature that Saint-Preux admires. For example, in the handling of the water (which, note, all comes from a gush of water at a place that was made by the

father—once again he is the source), the basic stream has been endlessly
divided up, deflected, made to diverge and brought together again, etc.,
to give the impression of many twisting little streams. "I saw, then, that it
had only been a matter of employing economy in making the waters twist
and wind" (my translation) ("Je vis alors qu'il n'avait été question que de
faire serpenter ces eaux avec économie. . . . [p. 355; my italics]), but the
French catches with perfect precision the combination of "économie"
and "faire serpenter" that I think is such a notable aspect of this historically very significant garden. "Cette eau si précieuse et si bien ménagée"
(p. 356),—and it is this management of nature in multiple winding forms
that I find so interesting. Similarly Saint-Preux says that they went down
"by a thousand turns" (p. 307) ("par mille détours" [p. 356]) to the
bottom of the orchard. Even allowing for his tendency to hyperbole, this
does sound like rather a lot of turns, even for Elysium! Later, Julie
explains, "The simulated irregularities of the winding paths are artfully
managed in order to prolong the walk, hide the edges of the island, and
enlarge its apparent size, without creating inconvenient and excessively
frequent turnings" (p. 311). ("Les sinuosités dans leur feinte irrégularité
sont ménagées avec art pour prolonger la promenade, cacher les bords
de l'île, et en agrandir l'étendue apparente sans faire des détours
incommodes et trop fréquents" [p. 359].) This is, as it were, to have the
attractions of extended space within a limited place, and the pleasures of
"turnings" without their inconvenience. Indeed just at what point a
"turn" may be felt to become inconvenient, or unbearable, is one of the
central questions in *Madame Bovary,* to which I will come in due course.
But here we may note again that the irregularité is "feinte" (sham) and
the "sinuosités" are "menagées." A "managed sinuosity" would be one
accurate, if awkward, way of describing a key feature of Julie's garden.

In addition to all the flowers, plants, shrubs, and trees, there are the
desirable natural inhabitants, birds in the air, fish in the water. It is
interesting to note how Julie enticed the requisite birds (coercion and
trapping and any enforcement are, of course, not allowed—unnatural).
She made sure that all the necessary "materials" ("des matériaux") for
nesting, and an abundance of "provisions" ("l'abondance des vivres")
were laid out readily available for them. Furthermore, they are protected from all their enemies, and they enjoy "uninterrupted tranquillity" (p. 309) ("l'éternelle tranquillité" [p. 357])—we may see in this a
kind of avian bourgeoisification, which enables the birds to enjoy their
own Clarens-in-the-woods! It is clear that they understand their part of
the contract, for they apparently do sing very readily for their supper
and indeed all their food and lodging. There is some even more scholas-
tic hairsplitting when it comes to the fish, for Saint-Preux contends that
they at least are a kind of "prisoner," since they were not originally in the

water, but he concedes Julie's point that as she in fact rescued them from the pan they are in a new sense, freed. The point is that it is all part of the attempt to manage nature in such a way as to efface all evidence of the managing: "nowhere do I see the slightest trace of cultivation," says Saint-Preux (p. 311) ("je ne vois nulle part la moindre trace de culture" [p. 359]). Walls are hidden, boundaries are blurred over, edges are concealed—all those linear markings that are evidence of man's presence in nature. Men can indeed walk in Elysium, but their footsteps are wiped out. ("I see no human footsteps," says Saint-Preux; "Ah," says Wolmar, "it is because we have taken great pains to efface them" [p. 311].) ("je n'aperçois aucun pas d'hommes—Ah! dit M. de Wolmar c'est qu'on a pris grand soin de les effacer" [p. 359].) What all this points to is the domestication of nature and space, so that they lose their wildness and limitlessness *without appearing to do so*. It amounts to the internalizing of the external, since whatever Julie and her husband want from the outside world—birds yes, bears no—is now safely on the inside, though, where desirable, still carrying its air of outsideness. Since this all costs nothing, we may agree that it was cheap at the price. But this domestication of the external was to have far-reaching effects and implications. By the end of the nineteenth century certain writers and characters had begun to take notice of a rather worrying phenomenon—namely, that there was no outside left.

We should note that it is very much Claire's garden, her creation as well as her fantasy. After showing Saint-Preux around, Julie asks him, "Are you still at the world's end?" and he answers, "No. . . . Here I am completely out of the world, and you have in fact transported me into Elysium" (p. 310). ("Etes-vous encore au bout du monde?"—"Non. . . . m'en voici tout à fait dehors, et vous m'avez en effet transporté dans l'Elysée" [p. 359].) As I have attempted to show, this end of the world or out of the world could hardly be more *in* the world, but they are dealing with an illusion or fantasy and they are well aware of the fact. Wolmar comments on Julie's name for the garden: "The pompous name she has given this orchard . . . truly deserves that raillery. Be modest in your praise of her childish games, and know that they have never entrenched in any way upon her duties as a mother" (p. 311). ("Le nom pompeux qu'elle a donné à ce verger . . . mérite bien cette raillerie. Louez modestement des jeux d'enfant, et songez qu'ils n'ont jamais rien pris sur les soins de la mère de famille" [p. 359].) This little exchange reveals a great deal. I noted before two phenomena that are repeated here. One was the strategy by which Julie tried to cope with the problematical drives of burgeoning sexuality by staging childish games (as in the arbor); the other was the attempt to improvise some space, not socially available, in which to find room for the expression of unsanctioned feelings, by renomination and make-believe (the bedroom as medieval court, the chalet as lover's home, etc.). Neither strategy worked for very long.

Here we see the same two activities, but oddly deployed in the opposite situation. Previously they were used in an attempt to cope with, or find space for, emotions and instinctual promptings that were outside the legitimate bondings of society. Now they are operating *within* the legitimate bond of marriage. That is to say, the "childish games" and the "pompous name" (or as we may more generally say, the attempt to elevate and metamorphose the given by the application of resonant and allusive nomenclature) are no longer ways of coping with premarital unlocalized feelings, but rather with marriage itself. The childish games and the pompous name *in no way,* it is stressed, infringe on "her duties as a mother." We may reverse this and say that Julie can perform her duties as a mother if she can be allowed her childish games with their pompous names. Duty, particularly the notion of family duty, became a very prominent and much-stressed virtue in the nineteenth century, as we very well know. What is interesting to note is that here we see very clearly one of the ways in which that duty was made bearable—by permitting those childish games and pompous names that become the very mark of bourgeois life in the nineteenth century (consider not only the cult of the child but the kind of desperate retrospective eclecticism whereby the literature and cultures of the past were raided for all kinds of styles, names, accoutrements, in architecture and domestic utensils, in art and literature itself—all of it extrinsic and basically ornamental). Julie is anticipating how countless middle-class Victorian and bourgeois families will survive, through a compromise whereby obligatory duty is made palatable by regressive fantasy, and regressive fantasy is justified by accomplished duty. But in this supposedly most reasonable and harmonious situation, things cannot be quite as perfect as the participants maintain if, after the fulfillments offered by marriage, Julie is still having recourse to strategies she had adopted to adjust to the prohibitions enforced prior to marriage.

I think something of this sense of the possibility of some profoundly hidden malaise may even be indicated in Julie's own explanation of the pompous name. She outlines her intention to bring her children up as gardeners in her metamorphosed orchard and imagines her anticipatory joy in simply strolling around in the shady walks prepared by their hands. Then: "In truth, my friend . . . days spent in this way suggest the happiness of the next life, and it is not without reason that in thinking of it I have given the name Elysium to those places" (p. 313). ("En vérité, mon ami, . . . des jours ainsi passés tiennent du bonheur de l'autre vie; et ce n'est pas sans raison qu'en y pensant j'ai donné d'avance à ce lieu le nom d'Elysée" [p. 364].) Julie's picture of her maternal bliss also bespeaks the kind of unemployment that was to beset many later bourgeois mothers, for the old question reasserts itself: if the well-ordered house, the fantasy garden, and children are supposed to be both the aim and justification of life, when you have achieved them—then what do you do? The conventional tacit answers—housework, gardening, and child rearing—were not to prove enough for a good many bourgeois wives in the society to come, which is one reason, I contend, why adultery becomes a paradigm for a large number of problems in nineteenth-century society and thus a key subject for novelists. It is not entirely clear that these answers are totally satisfactory for Julie herself, even if she thinks they are. For all the sweet serenity of her faith, and her belief in "le bonheur de l'autre vie," her words explaining her naming of the garden can be construed, without perversity, as revealing a latent death wish.[12]

It is, I said, very much Julie's garden. It is literally under her dominion in the sense that she is the keeper of the keys, and this leads to an odd little scene that is worth noting. There are four keys only. Her father has one, her husband a second, a trusted servant (Fanchon) who acts as her appointed superintendent, a third, and she herself the fourth. One of the facts that emerges in the long conversation Saint-Preux has with Julie and Wolmar in her garden is that she built it as a kind of expiation and substitute for the groves containing the famous *bosquet*, which lie on the other side of the house. Since her marriage she has never set foot in that place. It was in the bosquet that she gave up her virginity to Saint-Preux, or so we may assume; she then built a second "garden" to make up for that unsanctioned bestowal, and the symbolic connection between the garden and the womb has too long a history in iconology for us not to see some clear if unconscious sexual implication in this. This is reinforced by her handling of the keys. It is she and she alone who decides who can enter. When Saint-Preux begs to be allowed to have the privilege of borrowing Fanchon's key so that he can come in and feed the birds one day (a deed that seems to fill him with a somewhat disproportionate degree of anticipatory excitement!), Julie immediately gives him her own key. He accepts it, but with "a kind of reluctance. It seemed to me that I should have preferred to have Monsieur de Wolmar's" (p. 313). ("avec une sorte de peine: il me sembla que j'aurais mieux aimé celle de M. de Wolmar" [p. 364].) Given the very obvious phallic associations of keys, the fact that Julie immediately hands over her key to her ex-lover, who in

---

[12]A comparable sense of the latent existence of the death wish may be discerned in Richardson's Pamela, despite her apparently unmarred family happiness: it is much stronger in the helpless and much-beset Clarissa. In both, it is cast in Puritan terms—a heavenly home-going rather than a suicide or nihilistic denial of life.

turn would rather have been given the key of the husband, certainly suggests that there is something rather uneasy going on here, some kind of hidden and unexamined sexual malaise that has not so much been worked through as repressed or glossed over by the massive structure of rationalizations and orderings and regimentations that is represented by Clarens. More than this a sensible person will not say, since there is no more one can say. It's just that in all this rightness and harmony, something—indefinable but, I maintain, unmistakable—is somehow *wrong*. All is not well in Elysium, and the eternally blessed and blissful ones are not, perhaps, quite as happy as they think they are.

One further aspect of Saint-Preux's memorable introduction to Elysium deserves mention here. At one point in his letter Saint-Preux's long wave of praise for Julie peaks and crests and he exclaims: "My Lord, this incomparable woman is as dear a mother as she is a wife, as she is a friend, as she is a daughter, and, to the eternal torment of my heart, it is even thus that she was a mistress" (p. 313). ("Milord, cette incomparable femme est mère comme elle est épouse, comme elle est amie, comme elle est fille; et, pour l'éternel supplice de mon coeur, c'est encore ainsi qu'elle fut amante" [p. 364].) We have here a clear example of the multiplicity of roles that converge on the woman, to which I referred previously. In this case we notice that an equilibrium is established (if it really *is* established) between mother, wife, and friend by, as it were, banishing "lover" into the past tense—as we know that Julie did on getting married. We can readily imagine that a variety of disequilibriums might well occur if that suppressed or abandoned role were to reassert itself and make clamorous attempts to reenter the present tense to dispute the privileged mother-friend-daughter triad. In a letter to Claire Julie herself reveals the kind of strain imposed on the woman through this multiplicity of changing titles, and her lament has a curiously timeless quality about it, as though it is Woman herself recognizing with a kind of patient, accepting exhaustion the strangeness of her position in the world. "Ah! My dear, my poor heart has loved so much! It was exhausted so early that it grew old before its time, and so many diverse affections have so absorbed it that it has no room left for new attachments. You have seen me successively a girl, a friend, a mistress, a wife, and a mother. You know how all these titles have been dear to me! Some of these bonds are destroyed; others are relaxed" (pp. 273–74). ("Ah! ma chère, mon pauvre coeur a tant aimé. Il s'est épuisé de si bonne heure qu'il vieillit avant le temps; et tant d'affections diverses l'ont tellement absorbé, qu'il n'y reste plus de place pour des attachements nouveaux. Tu m'as vue successivement fille, amie, amante, épouse et mère. Tu sais si tous ces titres m'ont été chers? Quelque-uns de ces liens sont détruits, d'autres sont relâchés" [p. 298].) Julie is making clear her awareness that a woman is a point at which many titles meet, or rather a place where various titles are affixed. We are all to some extent venues of labels, but it is much more true of woman in general that she is the one who is labeled. For Julie, it has been an orderly, if tiring, progression of titles. It is when that order is not obtained and there is an imbrication of potentially contradictory titles that the trouble starts and the latent problematics of the position of woman-in-society, and thus by extension the problematics of society itself, begin to emerge.

The whole book is concerned with the business of titles and titling and, one could say, its relation to en-titling. While he is only her lover, Saint-Preux addresses Julie as "my wife" (p. 82) ("mon épouse" [p. 62]), as if to indulge in writing in the luxury of a title he will never be allowed to pronounce in public. Julie herself recognizes the paradox of their situation—that she is his but not his, he hers and not hers: "Until Tuesday then, my dear friend, my teacher, my penitent, my apostle. Alas! That you are not mine at all! Why must it be that with so many rights you lack only one title?" (p. 120). ("A mardi donc, mon aimable ami, mon maître, mon pénitent, mon apôtre: hélas! que ne m'es-tu point? Pourquoi faut-il qu'un seul titre manque à tant de droits?" [p. 95].) In asking this question, Julie is asking, perhaps, more profoundly than she knows. She realizes that she can give him her body, but cannot bestow the title of husband on him; he in turn is prevented from giving his name to her, so there is an asymmetry in the relationship, a frustration of exchange effected by the paternal prohibition. But Julie's question points to a problem that affects the whole structure of society, namely, what *is* the relationship between "titres" and "droits"? What happens when there is an imbalance between them or a dissonantal separation of them, so that there is an inequality between the two? And what does it say of a society if the power of the title is stronger than any right, so that Julie's "entitling" of Saint-Preux to penetrate her body, thus giving him rights over her, is powerless before that paternal decree that prevents Saint-Preux from entering her house and announcing that simple title—"mon épouse"? One way of looking at the history of western Europe since the American War of Independence and the French Revolution is to see it as a long rebellion of *rights* against *titles* in many different forms. But that is perhaps too large a subject to contemplate here.

The rational indefensibility of the power of the title is clear to Bomston, as we gather from his expostulations to Julie's father, already commented on. In a letter to Claire he speaks of the sacred law of nature ("la loi sacrée de la nature" [p. 135]) that can only be transgressed with impunity, "and which consideration for positions and ranks can repeal only at the cost of unhappiness and crime" (p. 164) ("que les considérations des états et des rangs ne peut abroger qu'il n'en coûte des malheurs et des crimes" [p. 136]). But once Julie has yielded to the Word—and titling—of the father, it is precisely such considerations of position (or station) and rank that sustain her. To her cousin she writes: "The rank of wife and mother elevates my soul" (p. 276) ("Le rang d'épouse et de mère m'élève l'âme" [p. 299]) and later refers to "the sweet title of wife" (p. 281) ("le doux titre d'épouse") [p. 308]). In her case, as it were, the rights have been handed over to the titles, and the sacred law of nature is now seen as running, not at variance with "considerations des états et des rangs," but rather in harmony with them. For her, a change of title or social station was her salvation (*title* of course extends to all forms of naming and describing, not simply aristocratic and marital titles). As her husband says to her, "You have acquired new force by changing your position. You are no longer that unfortunate girl who deplored her frailty as she yielded to it. You are the most virtuous of women, who knows no other laws than those of duty and honor" (p. 320). ("Vous en avez acquis de nouvelles en changeant d'état. Vous n'êtes plus cette fille infortunée qui déplorait sa faiblesse en s'y livrant; vous êtes la plus vertueuse des femmes, qui ne connaît d'autres lois que celles du devoir et de l'honneur" [p. 371].) Here again, this accurate observation carries far-reaching implications. If a change in position, or station or rank or title, can immediately change the category in which the individual is perceived by society (and by him or herself), so that the "unfortunate girl" becomes the "most virtuous wife," then it means that from the point of view of society it doesn't matter so much *what* you are as *where* you are—category precedes and predetermines essence as long as the members of that society accept this social way of thinking. As long as they do, then the organized constellations of positions and ranks and established taxonomies will hold, and *rights* will always defer to *titles.* But this raises the question of what will happen in such a society if women, some women (perhaps only one woman) no longer feel their souls elevated by the rank of mother, and when for such ladies the title of wife loses its sweetness? What will such women do, and what will that imply about the established pattern of categories that not only holds a society together but in a very real sense *is* that society? Such are some of the questions that will be raised by novels to be considered in due course.

Such questions are not raised, at least not directly, in this book, in which the title may be said to dominate. Related to this domination of the title is a phenomenon I shall refer to as the omnipotence of context, which is illustrated by Saint-Preux's reaction to Julie when he returns to her home after she is a wife and mother. In his description of his approach to the house he notes an interesting psychological sensation whereby "the world is ever divided for me into only two regions, where she is and where she is not. The first is extended when I am going away and grows smaller in proportion as I approach, like a place which I am never to reach. It is at present confined by the walls of her room" (p. 286). ("Le monde n'est jamais divisé pour moi qu'en deux régions: celle où elle est, et celle où elle n'est pas. La première s'étend quand je m'éloigne, et se resserre à mesure que j'approche, comme un lieu où je ne dois jamais arriver" [p. 313].) She is that inaccessible space—as vast as the universe minus Saint-Preux, as small as Julie minus the universe—at which he can never, ontologically, arrive. She is the space that defines his lack. However, he does corporeally reenter her house and this is what happens. He is then immediately introduced to her husband, and when they go into the house, she fetches her children and then embraces him again. "But what a difference between the first embrace and this one! I experienced it with surprise. It was a mother of a family whom I was clasping. I saw her surrounded by her husband and her children; this group was imposing . . . I felt myself forced to pay her a new kind of respect" (p. 289). ("Mais quelle différence du premier embrassement a celui-là. Je l'éprouvai avec surprise. C'était une mére de famille que j'embrassais; je la voyais environnée de son époux et de ses enfants; ce cortège m'en imposait . . . je me sentais forcé de lui porter une nouvelle sorte de respect" [pp. 315–16].) He is experiencing the power of the group, or *cortège*, which is a paradigm for the power of society as a whole. His own individual feelings and instincts are deflected, diffused, arrested, blocked, however one wants to put it, by this power of the *cortège,* so that he can no longer see the lover because he can only see the wife and mother. As long as this power of context survives, then there will be no question of adultery. Saint-Preux experiences this power again, this time as a mental image, when he goes alone into Elysium for his bout of bird feeding. It transpires (from the same letter describing Elysium), that he had intended to indulge in a kind of mental debauchery of just thinking of and imagining Julie as he had known her, as his lover, as an individual single girl. But he finds that he can no longer isolate her from the new *gestalt* into which she has been placed and which she has exhibited to him. "My Lord, I thought I beheld that woman, so charming, so chaste, and so virtuous, in the middle of that same group which surrounded her yesterday" (p. 314). ("Milord, j'ai cru voir cette femme si charmante, si chaste et si vertueuse, au milieu de ce même cortège qui l'entourait hier" [p. 365].) The power of the group is sufficient to monitor and determine the ways in which he thinks about Julie. This is power indeed, and we may say that as long as established contexts and configurations have such authority, then the institutions that compose them and that they compose are secure. As was noted, Julie repressed *l'amante* both in herself and in the person of Saint-Preux. With the literal return of the repressed lover, if the group structure is to hold, then the lover must undergo some kind of transformation—which he does, taking on the nonsexual protected role of the child. When the return of the repressed does not take such an abject and conciliatory form, the group structure is inevitably challenged and context begins to lose its omnipotence. Or rather socially ordained and prescribed contexts do—what then happens is that individuals try to invent and establish their own contexts. What degree of success they achieve is one of the matters to be considered in subsequent chapters.

The Dream of the Veil

I have noted already that adultery is specifically rejected in this novel. The exact terms of its consideration and rejection are important and should now be considered. Saint-Preux is writing to Julie from his "banishment" in Europe. Since his statement concerning adultery is central to the whole topic of this book, I will quote it in full.

> Listen to the one who loves you. Why should we alone try to be more prudent than all the rest of mankind, and with a childish simplicity pursue the imaginary virtues which everyone talks about and which no one practices? What! Shall we be better moralists than those crowds of philosophers with which London and Paris are peopled, who all laugh at conjugal fidelity and consider adultery as a game? Instances of it are not scandalous; it is not even permitted to find fault with it, and all reasonable people would laugh here at the man who through respect for marriage would resist the inclination of his heart. In fact, they say, is not an injury which consists only in opinion no injury at all when it remains secret? What harm does a husband receive from an infidelity of which he is unaware? With what obligingness cannot a woman make up for her faults?[13] What endearments does she not use to prevent or remove his suspicions? Deprived of an

[13]The footnote by Rousseau reads: "And where had the simple Swiss seen this? A long time ago women of spirit assumed more imperious airs. They begin by boldly establishing their lovers in the house, and if they deign to permit the husband there too, it is only as long as he behaves toward them with the respect he owes them. A woman who would conceal an illicit affair would cause it to be thought that she is ashamed of it and she would be dishonoured: not one reasonable women would take notice of her" (p. 253). ("Et où le bon Suisse avait-il vu cela? Il y a longtemps que les femmes galantes l'ont pris sur un plus haut ton. Elles commencent par établir fièrement leurs amants dans la maison; et si l'on daigne y souffrir le mari, c'est autant qu'il se comporte envers eux avec le respect qu'il leur doit. Une femme qui se cacherait d'un mauvais commerce ferait croire qu'elle en a honte, et serait déshonorée; pas une honnête femme ne voudrait la voir" [p. 248].)

imaginary good, he actually lives more happily, and this supposed crime about which so much stir is made is only one more thing which holds society together.

(Pp. 252–53)

Ecoute celui qui t'aime. Pourquoi voudrions-nous être plus sages nous seuls que tout le reste de hommes, et suivre avec une simplicité d'enfants de chimériques vertus dont tout le monde parle et que personne ne pratique? Quoi! serons-nous meilleurs moralistes que ces foules de savants dont Londres et Paris sont peuplés, qui tous se raillent de la fidélité conjugale, et regardent l'adultère comme un jeu? Les exemples n'en sont point scandaleux; il n'est pas même permis d'y trouver à redire: et tous les honnêtes gens se riraient ici de celui qui, par respect pour le mariage, résisterait au penchant de son coeur. En effet, disent-ils, un tort qui n'est que dans l'opinion n'est-il pas nul quand il est secret? Quel mal reçoit un mari d'une infidélité qu'il ignore? De quelle complaisance une femme ne rachète-t-elle pas ses fautes? Quelle douceur n'emploie-t-elle pas à prévenir ou guérir ses soupçons? Privé d'un bien imaginaire, il vit réellement plus heureux; et ce prétendu crime dont on fait tant de bruit n'est qu'un lien de plus dans la société.

(Pp. 247–48)

The society evoked by Saint-Preux here is familiar. It is the society of Restoration comedy, in which adultery is precisely a game that arguably has a conjunctive rather than a disjunctive effect, since everyone seems to know the rules. Not to know the rules is not to be a true initiate of that society. It is by definition an aristocratic society, and it would laugh at someone who suppressed impulse to protect marriage, because that would smack of the prudential bourgeois or trading classes that the aristocrat despised. To be seen to appear to be taking virtue seriously would be to be guilty of a kind of gaucherie or naiveté that would excite the ridicule of the witty and sophisticated aristocrats, who would disdain to be caught in such an awkward posture or to be heard to speak with such lugubrious seriousness. Needless to say, this is no very definitive description of Restoration or early-eighteenth-century society or any part of it, but that is the simplified model that Saint-Preux is transmitting to Julie in his doomed hope of persuading her to share one more gaudy night with him. Played in another spirit the game could easily turn perverse and ugly, as definitively demonstrated in Laclos's *Les Liaisons Dangereuses,* published twenty years after Rousseau's novel (1782), and obviously at any time in any society when virtues are considered chimerical because intangible, and infidelities harmless because unseen, the potential for a total collapse of values is there—a prospect that, for instance, occupied Shakespeare's imagination throughout his whole middle and later work. But where there were other rules and relationships and sanctions holding society together, the idle class, or part of it, could afford to consider adultery a kind of the game without endangering the structure of society. The matter is very different when we move into the bourgeois era and its novels, for then adultery is anything but a game—it is invariably a prelude to tragedy, if that word may be applied to any experience in the ninteenth-century novel. Rousseau's position as bespoken by the footnote is equivocal to say the least. He would seem to be patronizing Saint-Preux from a vantage point of superior, and more brazenly amoral, experience. While he may not be said to be detectably condoning the kind of shameless adultery he describes, he can scarcely be said to be discernibly condemning it, and his use of phrases such as "les femmes galantes" and "honnête femme" may as readily be read as registering admiration as indicating irony. Without stating that he has played the game, he is implying that he knows it very well. I am not, the author tells us, as naive and unexperienced as my rather simple character. (Perhaps it is this kind of equivocation between the sententious foreground commitment to virtue and the sly peripheral dalliance with a far-less-moral society that caused Voltaire to regard the enormous success of Rousseau's book as one of the scandals of the century.)

However, although Julie may certainly be regarded as "honnête," she is no "femme galante," and Saint-Preux doesn't have to wait long for a stern rebuke and the usual disproportionate punishment for such an immoral suggestion. In fact he doesn't have to wait at all, since the very next letter is from Claire telling him brusquely "Your mistress is no more" (p. 254) ("Votre amante n'est plus" [p. 249]). The next letter is from Julie herself, describing in what might seem to be cruel detail her wedding and asserting that this marriage is an "indissoluble tie" (p. 254) ("une chaîne indissoluble" [p. 249]), and this new "bond" ("lien"), once so feared, has now released her from what was a frightful servitude and has restored her to herself ("rendue à moi-même"). Everything is now changed between them ("Tout est changé entre nous"), but if he, Saint-Preux, has lost a lover, he has gained a faithful friend ("une fidèle amie"). None of this might be thought to be particularly consoling to Saint-Preux, but this is mild stuff indeed compared to Julie's reaction to his very reference to adultery. I must again quote at length, because where Saint-Preux's lines evoked a vanishing, or at least diminishing, aristocratic society (and arguably a fantasy or at least theatrical version of it, at that), Julie's words announce and define what is to be the orthodox bourgeois attitude to adultery.

What are they doing now—those lovers so tender-hearted, who burned with such a pure flame, who were so deeply aware of the value of honesty? Who could learn about it without weeping over them? Look at them, given over to crime. Even the idea of staining the marriage bed no longer arouses their horror . . . they contemplate adulteries! . . . How many centuries have been able to bring about this strange change? What length of time could destroy such a delightful memory, and cause the true feeling of happiness to be lost in one who once upon a time enjoyed it. Ah! if the first transgression is painful and slow, how quick and easy are the others. Oh, magic spell of the passions—in this way you bewitch reason, beguile wisdom and pervert nature before one notices it! One goes astray for a single moment of one's life, one turns aside just one step from the straight and narrow path—at once the unavoidable downward path of evil lures us away and ruins us: you fall into the abyss, and you wake up terrified to find yourself covered with crimes, though with a heart born to be virtuous. My dear friend, let us draw the veil again: do we need to see the terrifying precipice which the veil hides from us in order to keep us from approaching it?

(My translation)

Que font maintenant ces amants si tendres, qui brûlaient d'une flamme si pure, qui sentaient si bien le prix de l'honnêteté? Qui l'apprendra sans gémir sur eux? Les voilà livrés au crime. L'idée même de souiller le lit conjugal ne leur fait plus d'horreur . . . ils méditent des adultères! Quoi! Sont-ils bien les mêmes? Leurs âmes n'ont-elles point changé? . . . Combien de siècles ont du produire ce changement étrange? Quelle longeur de temps put détruire un si charmant souvenir, et faire perdre le vrai sentiment du bonheur à qui l'a pu savourer une fois? Ah! si le premier désordre est pénible et lent, que tous les autres sont prompts et faciles! Prestige des passions, tu fascines ainsi la raison, tu trompes la sagesse et changes la nature avant qu'on s'en aperçoive! On s'égare un seul moment de la vie, on se détourne d'un seul pas de la droite route; aussitôt une pente inévitable nous entraîne et nous perd; on tombe enfin dans le gouffre, et l'on se réveille épouvanté de se trouver couvert de crimes avec un coeur né pour la vertu. Mon bon ami, laissons retomber ce voile: avons-nous besoin de voir le précipice affreux qu'il nous cache pour éviter d'en approcher?"

(Pp. 259–60)

She returns to the topic even more warmly and vehemently further on in the same letter.

With regard to the so-called ties which adultery and infidelity can form between families, that is less a serious argument than an absurd and coarse joke which by way of answer only deserves contempt and indignation. The betrayals, quarrels, fights, murders, poisonings with which this licentiousness has covered the globe from time immemorial, sufficiently demonstrate what one might expect by way of peace and harmony between men from a tie based on crime. If some sort of society does result from this vile and despicable traffic, it is like a society of robbers, which it is necessary to destroy and annihilate to make legitimate societies secure.

(My translation)

A l'égard des liaisons prétendues que l'adultère et l'infidélité peuvent former entre les familles, c'est moins une raison sérieuse qu'une plaisanterie absurde et brutale qui ne mérite pour toute réponse que le mépris et l'indignation. Les trahisons, les querelles, les combats, les meurtres, les empoisonnements, dont ce désordre a couvert la terre dans tous les temps, montrent assez ce qu'on doit attendre pour le repos en l'union des hommes d'un attachement formé par le crime. S'il résulte quelque sorte de société de ce vil et méprisable commerce, elle est semblable à celle des brigands, qu'il faut détruire et anéantir pour assurer les sociétes légitimes.

(P. 266)

If Saint-Preux had the faintest vestige of a glimmer of hope left, it must surely have been extinguished at this point forever!

There are two notable features of the timing and the phrasing of this letter. It is as though the very fact of Saint-Preux's having brought up the subject of adultery finally and instantly precipitated Julie into the indissoluble tie of marriage, dropping the role of disturbed lover and *immediately* taking up or entering the role of virtuous wife. No gap is permitted; indeed it is as if marriage is used to preclude the possibility of any gaps and all the problems of fissures and interstices: contrast Nietzsche's defense and valuation of "the desires that create clefts"[14] (I will have more to say about this in considering *Madame Bovary*). Thus marriage must be a seamless whole and union—above all the gap caused by adultery is dismissed as effectively unthinkable. This leads to the second feature, namely, the violence of Julie's statement concerning adultery and adulterous unions. The first part of her disgusted repudiation of the very idea is couched in the fairly familiar terms of the topography of moral disaster—inevitable slopes, frightful precipices, chasms, and so on. Over all this, says Julie, let us allow the veil to fall once more; we do not need to look at it to avoid it. (That veil is to return in another form in a very surprising way.) At that point she turns to people and families that, as it were, conspire to agree to permit adulterous unions, and here her disgust is tinged with hysteria. She ascribes to such false unions the chaos of betrayals, quarrels, fights, murders, poisonings that have always littered human history. Such relationships do not form a society but rather a kind of antisociety, such as obtains among a band of brigands. And—and this is where the real bourgeois dread reveals itself—such antisocieties should be destroyed and annihilated to make legitimate societies ("les sociétés légitimes") secure. Here we see very clearly that bourgeois hatred of any kind of anti- or parody society that neither recognizes nor requires the kind of legitimizations that bind

[14]Friedrich Nietzsche, *The Will to Power*, trans. Walter Kaufmann and R. J. Hollingdale (New York: Vintage Books, 1968), bk. 1, section 32.

bourgeois society together. It is not a question of live and let live; it is a question of "détruire et anéantir" those who arrange and conduct their relationships in a different way. This hysterical extreme defense of marriage and attack on adulterous unions will be heard again, indeed in the very next novel I shall examine—Goethe's *Die Wahlverwandschaften*. Clearly such an extreme attack must involve some radical fear of the possible insecurity of the modes of union being defended. And, as I have tried to suggest, the "sorte de société" established by Julie sedulously avoids adultery only because it comes so very close to incest. To later figures trapped inside apparently seamless marriages, the kind of society or antisociety maintained by such outlaw groups as brigands will have a kind of appeal that Julie cannot, and dare not, imagine for one second.

But, as I have suggested, not everything is quite perfect at Clarens and in Elysium, and this brings me to Saint-Preux's nightmare—the dream of the veil. Saint-Preux has the dream after he has been established in Clarens but is setting out on a journey with Lord Bomston. In the dream he thinks he sees Julie's mother on her deathbed and Julie on her knees beside her, weeping and kissing her hands. Some remarks are exchanged, which conclude with the mother saying, "You will be a mother in your turn. . . ."

> She could not finish. . . . I tried to raise my eyes and look at her; I saw her no more. In her place I saw Julie. I saw her; I recognized her although her face was covered with a veil. I gave a shriek, I rushed forward to put aside the veil, I could not reach it, I stretched forth my arms, I tormented myself, but I touched nothing.
>
> "Friend, be calm," she said to me in a faint voice. "The terrible veil covers me. No hand can put it aside."

He has the dream three times. "Always the mournful sight, always that same appearance of death, always that impenetrable veil eluding my hands and hiding from my eyes the dying person it covered" (p. 365). ("Elle ne put achever. Je voulus lever les yeux sur elle, je ne la vis plus. Je vis Julie à sa place; je la vis, je la reconnus, quoique son visage fût couvert d'un voile. Je fais un cri, je m'élance pour écarter le voile, je ne pus l'atteindre; j'étendais les bras, je me tourmentais et ne touchais rien. "Ami, calme-toi," me dit-elle d'une voix faible: "le voile redoutable me couvre, nulle main ne peut l'écarter."

. . . Toujours ce spectacle lugubre, toujours ce même appareil de mort, toujours ce voile impénétrable échappe à mes mains, et dérobe à mes yeux l'objet expirant qu'il couvre" [pp. 466–67].)

One might speculate endlessly, and perhaps fruitlessly, about the interpretation of this dream. (How to read dreams *within* fiction is an interesting matter in its own right.) But that veil subsumes in very clear symbolic form a great deal; all that has indeed separated Julie from her lover, all that she has allowed to come between them, and all that she has interposed between them herself—the inseparable cousin (at the beginning), the word of the father, *la maison paternelle*, the *chaîne indissoluble* of her marriage, the rigid and powerful *cortège* in which she is fixed as the mother. All these have meant that when Saint-Preux has attempted to reach her, no matter how much he has stretched out his arms and tormented himself, he has always and inevitably (after the very brief and soon regretted affair during which, it would seem, he only once spent the night with Julie) touched—nothing. Because of that veil— "redoutable" and "impénétrable." It is also, of course, the bridal veil, which, worryingly enough, has turned into a shroud. So disturbing is the dream that Saint-Preux rushes to wake up Lord Bomston, who delivers the usual scolding ("you are worthless"—"vous n'êtes rien") and then drives Saint-Preux back to Clarens, where he can sneak a glimpse of Julie and tear away "that fatal veil which is woven in your mind" (p. 360) ("ce fatal voile tissé dans votre cerveau" [p. 467]). Ashamed as usual, Saint-Preux only pauses to hear the voices of Julie and her cousin coming from Elysium and returns to his travels quite happy, feeling that he has at least done the honor to himself as Edward's friend of "getting the better of a dream" (p. 367) ("de le mettre au-dessus d'un songe" [p. 468]).

But in a way it is the dream that has got the better of him, long before he had it, and in the event it is the dream that gets the better of them all, in a way that I will try to describe in the concluding part of this chapter. Claire, in her answering letter in which she urges them both to hurry back to their "little community" (p. 369) ("la petite communauté" [470]), registers her sense of the ominousness of the dream: "That veil! That veil? ... There is something indefinably sinister in it which disturbs me each time I think of it" (p. 369). ("Ce voile! Ce voile! ... Il a je ne sais quoi de sinistre qui me trouble chaque fois que j'y pense" [p. 470].) The implications of "ce fatal voile" for "la petite communauté" are indeed sinister, for they involve the unconfrontable and unthinkable fact of Julie's death and her disappearing into eternal untouchability.

Death by Water

Immediately after Monsieur de Wolmar has staged that strange ceremony of profaning the arbor (described at the beginning of this chapter), he announces his intention of going on a trip that will keep him away for a few days. He asks whether Saint-Preux would like to come with him or stay at Clarens with Julie (as Julie writes to her cousin, her husband seems "determined to drive me to the limit" [p. 322]—"semblait vouloir me pousser à bout" [p. 373]). Saint-Preux promptly states his preference for remaining, an answer that deeply pleases the perversely rational husband. However, the prospective situation disturbs Julie, and she communicates her anxieties to her cousin, registering her concern about her own latent instabilities. "Whatever you think of yourself, your mind is calm and tranquil, I am sure. Objects present themselves to it such as they are, but mine, ever agitated like a moving wave, confounds and disfigures them" (p. 324). ("Quoi-que tu penses de toi-même, ton âme est calme et tranquille, j'en suis sûre; les objets s'y peignent tels qu'ils sont; mais la mienne, toujours émue comme une onde agitée, les confond et les défigure" [p. 375].) Whether we decide to translate *âme* as "soul" or "mind," it refers to some absolutely central governing spirit or prime mover, and for Julie to say that hers is constantly agitated "comme une onde agitée" is to reveal an aspect of her character of far-reaching significance. For if she is watery at the center, fluid, labile, potentially "thalassic," then all the meticulous structuring and architecture of her life, starting from her complete submission to her father / husband (*he's* not fluid at the center—he is empty, a very different matter) and extending to the meticulous routinizing of life at Clarens, can be seen in another light. To some extent, perhaps a large extent, they may be motivated by a fear of internal dissolution, a kind of passional liquefaction in which she would lose herself and drown. By the time we reach the height of the Romantic era—however we wish to date it—we find many metaphors of yearning to dissolve and merge with the elements, other people, the universe, whatever. The "flow" seems to have lost its terrors and to have revealed its enrapturing allure. But for Julie it is still a source of worry. Her carefully constructed life may be seen as, in part, a dike erected against the possible flood tides within her, just as her marriage, as she clearly indicated, was not a way of releasing passion but of getting away from it. The problematical relationship (or opposition) between the dissolving liquefactions of passion and the binding structurations of marriage is at the very heart, or *âme*, of the great bourgeois novels of adultery.

Claire is not liquid, and she writes back promptly with some sensible-seeming advice to Julie. She reminds her that she loved as Eloise did and that, like her, she is now "pious" ("Cousine, tu fus amante comme Héloïse, te voilà dévote comme elle" [p. 376]). If Julie is worried about being alone with Saint-Preux, then make sure the children are always around, and go off for some excursions—boat rides, for instance. "You like boat rides; you deprive yourself of them for the sake of your husband who fears the water and for the children whom you do not wish to hazard on it. Take advantage of the time of this absence to indulge yourself in this amusement, leaving your children in Fanchon's care" (p. 326). ("Tu aimes les promenades en bateau; tu t'en prives pour ton mari qui craint l'eau, pour tes enfants que tu n'y veux pas exposer; prends le temps de cette absence pour te donner cet amusement en laissant tes enfants sous la garde de la Fanchon" [p. 379].) It is revealing indeed that Monsieur de Wolmar is frightened of water, but it is perhaps not exactly the most prudent possible advice to recommend the watery-centered Julie to go for boat rides with her former lover. Her justification that they will always be under the protection of the boatmen ("sous la protection des bateliers" [p. 379]), seems a little feeble. There are a large number of very important boat rides in the history of the novel; they figure prominently in the novel of adultery, as I shall have occasion to reiterate in different contexts. But the figure of the protective boatman is conspicuous by his absence. There may be boatmen, but they don't protect. And indeed, if the really dangerous waters are internal, it is hard to see how they could.

The excursion by boat is duly taken and described by Saint-Preux in a letter that concludes part 4. It is a trip laden with omen to say the very least—indeed it is effectively all omen, starting even from the base topography, for Julie's *house*, Saint-Preux reminds Lord Bomston, is "*not far from the lake*" (p. 332; my italics) ("Vous savez que la maison de Mme de Wolmar n'est loin du lac" [p. 386]), and "she likes being on the *water*" (p. 332; my italics) ("elle aime les promenades sur l'eau" [p. 386]). I have mentioned this basic house / water topography in an earlier section, and it could hardly appear more naturally than it does in Rousseau's book at the same time as it could hardly acquire more symbolic implications than it finally does. For Julie, householder and gardener supreme, is doomed to die by water. To select a few of the more notable details from this seminal boat-trip—Saint-Preux steers the boat into the middle of the lake, i.e., as far from the shore as possible; a gale blows up and soon the waves are terrible ("les ondes devinrent terribles" [p. 387]); the frail boat cannot resist them, and it is driven to the opposite shore. There it is impossible at first to find any shelter or a place to land, and Julie is seized with sickness and almost faints at the side of the boat ("Julie saisie du mal de coeur, faible et défaillante au bord du bateau" [p. 388]). Fortunately, she is "used to the water" (p. 333) ("elle était faite à l'eau" [p. 388]), and this condition does not last long. She then acts as a kind of lacustrine Florence Nightingale and goes around wiping brows and dispensing water and wine. There is just one moment when two planks are opened by a particularly deluging shock when it almost seems as though the boat might indeed founder, and the recorded reactions are revealing.

For an instant, two planks being partly opened in an impact which wet us all, she thought the boat broken to pieces, and in an exclamation from this tender mother, I distinctly heard these words: "Oh my children, must I see you no more?"

As for myself, whose imagination always exceeds the peril, although I knew the real state of the danger, I expected to see the boat swallowed up at any moment, that affecting beauty struggling in the midst of the waves, and the pallor of death dulling the roses of her cheeks.

(P. 334)

Un instant seulement deux planches s'étant entrouvertes, dans un choc qui nous inonda tous, elle crut le bateau brisé; et dans une exclamation de cette tendre mère j'entendis distinctement ces mots: "O mes enfants! faut-il ne vous voir plus?" Pour moi, dont l'imagination va toujours plus loin que le mal, quoique je connusse au vrai l'état du péril, je croyais voir de moment en moment le bateau englouti, cette beauté si touchante se débattre au milieu des flots, et la pâleur de la mort ternir les roses de son visage.

(P. 388)

Comment on Saint-Preux's morbid imaginings is redundant (notice he doesn't imagine trying to *save* her but only watching her drown!), though to the extent that they are perverse, it must be admitted that his treatment by society goes some long way to explaining why they should be so. (You surely can't be treated as a quidam in a hierarchical society for very long without some perversion of the imagination taking place.) But his vision of "le bateau englouti" and the lovers (former lovers, if you will) drowning together, is one that in varying forms may be said to have haunted the European imagination for well over the next century.

They do reach the shore safely, and at a place called Meillerie where Saint-Preux had spent a period of his life chafing away in enforced exile and carving Julie's initials and copious selections from the works of Petrarch and Tasso on a rock in a secluded spot in the mountains. He suggests a visit to this shrine of solitude and frustrated love, and she accompanies him. There he embarks on a prolonged speech about his feelings at that former time, and not surprisingly a certain amount of emotion is engendered on both sides. However, she finally cuts him short and gently leads him away. "Let us go, my friend. The air of this place is not good for me" (p. 336). ("Allons-nous-en, mon ami . . . l'air de ce lieu n'est pas bon pour moi" [p. 390].) On the way back in the boat he holds her hand and allows himself to drift into a reverie. This turns into a mood of such melancholy and then such torment that he is tempted to take hold of her and throw her with him into the water. "I was violently tempted to hurl her with me into the waves and end my long torments in her arms" (p. 338). ("Je fus violemment tenté de la précipiter avec moi dans les flots, et d'y finir dans ses bras ma vie et mes longs tourments" [p. 391].) To overcome this temptation he has to let go of her hand and go to the other side of the boat. When he has calmed down, he returns to her side and takes her hand again. He finds she is holding a handkerchief that is very damp. ("Elle tenait son mouchoir; je le sentis fort mouillé" [p. 392].) It is not trivial to mention these small domestic objects, because in the bourgeois novel they come to carry a large amount of signifying potential. Saint-Preux realizes that she has been crying and infers from this that she too has been thinking about their relationship and that the old feeling is still there. "Ah . . . I see that our hearts have never ceased to hear each other!" (p. 388). ("Ah! . . . je vois que nos coeurs n'ont jamais cessé de s'entendre!" [p. 392].) She concedes the truth of this, at the same time fortifying the prohibition on utterance and reference. "It is true . . . but let this be the last time that they will speak in this manner" (p. 338). ("Il est vrai . . . mais que ce soit la dernière fois qu'ils auront parlé sur ce ton" [p. 392].) They return home, red-eyed but calm. This episode constitutes what Saint-Preux refers to as a "crisis" that will, he hopes, restore him to himself ("la crise qui me rendra tout à fait à moi" [p. 392]). It is not entirely clear how much there is left of him to be restored to himself, given the long attritions of frustration, banishment, and refusal. But the episode does reveal that, despite what she might say in other contexts, Julie has opted for a life of protected repression. Clarens is Clarens and is dominant; but the water is still agitated and agitatable. And this alone points to a flaw in the overall apparent harmony.

Julie herself maintains that it is not repressed passion but purified passion, and this is the rarity of their relationship ("on étouffe de grandes passions; rarement on les épure" [p. 505]). She insists that they have managed to transform *amour* into *amitié* and that as a result they can "spend life together in fraternal familiarity and peaceful innocence" (p. 393) ("passer les jours ensemble dans la familiarité fraternelle et dans la paix de l'innocence" [p. 505]). Despite the length, or rather perhaps because of the length, at which they reassure and congratulate each other on these purifications and transformations, one registers both their precariousness and their latent perversity. To treat an ex-lover with fraternal familiarity because that falls within the bounds of the legitimate is, as I have suggested, to repress adulterous feelings only to allow them to be reinstituted as incestuous ones. It is a situation of uneasy equilibrium, which, in effect, can only wait for whatever will precipitate its inevitable disintegration—dangerous waters within, or without. In the event it is once again the external lake that precipitates a crisis, this time one that is terminal. On an expedition to the castle of Chillon on the lake, Julie's young son falls into the water, and she runs back like an arrow and throws herself in after him ("part comme un trait, et s'élance après lui" [p. 535]). The account of the accident is in a letter from Fanchon Anet, her closest attendant: "we had neither servants nor a boat there; it took time to get them out . . . the child is recovered, but the mother . . . the shock, the fall, the condition she was in . . . who knows better than I the dangers of such a fall! . . . She remained unconscious for a very long time. . . . From some orders she has given me, I see that she does not believe she will recover. I am too unhappy; she will not recover. Madame d'Orbe is more altered than she" (p. 395). ("On n'avait là ni gens ni bateau, il fallut du temps pour les retirer . . . L'enfant est remis, mais la mère . . . le saisissement, la chute, l'état où elle était . . . Qui sait mieux que moi combien cette chute est dangereuse! . . . Elle resta très longtemps sans connaissance. . . . Sur quelques ordres qu'elle m'a donnés, je vois qu'elle ne croit pas en revenir. Je suis trop malheureuse, elle n'en reviendra pas. Madame d'Orbe est plus changée qu'elle" [p. 535].) And it is that separated inseparable and much-changed cousin who informs Saint-Preux of Julie's death in brusque terms, which are indeed appropriate from someone stunned with grief, but which never-theless carry something of the tone of a reproach—as though it was somehow all his fault, both for loving her and for having the dream about the veil. "It is over. Imprudent, unfortunate man, unhappy dreamer! You shall never see her again . . . the veil . . . Julie is no more . . ." (p. 396). ("C'en est fait, homme imprudent, homme infortuné, malheureux visionnaire! Jamais vous ne la reverrez . . . le voile . . . Julie n'est . . ." [p. 535].) I have alluded before to the unusual intensity of feeling that the cousins express for each other, and it is with no intention of suggesting any actual sexual perversity that I point out that from the long account of Julie's dying, written by her husband, it transpires that not only will Claire not leave Julie's bedroom, but Julie invites her to share her bed ("couche dans mon lit" [p. 540]), while the tired husband is sent away ("l'on me renvoya" [p. 540]).

Saint-Preux is not heard from again, though we gather he is tem-porarily prostrated with grief. But enclosed with Wolmar's letter is a last letter from Julie to Saint-Preux that reveals that there was indeed some-thing wrong with her "project"—i.e., her dream of ensemblization. "We must give up our projects. All is changed, my good friend. . . . We dreamed of rejoining each other. *That reunion was not good.* It is Heaven's blessing to have prevented it, thereby, without a doubt, preventing mis-fortune" (p. 405; my italics). ("Il faut renoncer à nos projets. Tout est changé, mon bon ami. . . . Nous songions à nous réunir: cette réunion n'était pas bonne. C'est un bienfait du ciel de l'avoir prévenue; sans doute il prévient des malheurs" [p. 564].) This is tantamount to saying that adultery would have been inevitable (and for Julie, of course, death is far preferable to such a dishonor); but more, it is a revocation of the whole dream of union, or rather multiple reunion, itself. It does not work. As Julie reveals, there was a split between will and feeling that was permanently present. "This sentiment, nourished despite myself, was involuntary; it has cost my innocence nothing. Everything which was dependent on my will was devoted to my duty. If my heart, which was not dependent on it, was devoted to you, that was my torment and not my crime" (p. 405). ("Ce sentiment resté malgré moi fut involontaire; il n'a rien coûté à mon innocence: tout ce qui dépend de ma volonté fut pour mon devoir: si le coeur qui n'en dépend pas fut pour vous, ce fut mon tourment et non pas mon crime" [p. 564].) The House of Clarens, then, was built on repression and a secret torment. No wonder it was bound to fall.

In her last letter it is clear that Julie is still thinking in terms of some kind of total union of all her loved ones. "Would that I could invent still stronger bonds in order to unite all who are dear to me" (p. 406). ("Que ne puis-je inventer des noeuds plus étroits encore pour unir tout ce qui m'est cher" [p. 565].) But as Claire reveals in the last letter of the book, there is no union left, only despairing fragmentation and monadic misery. This letter effectively outlines the Fall of the House of Clarens, a fall, to my mind, of inestimable importance for the subsequent history of European literature. She writes to Saint-Preux: "you will see here only grief and sorrow; and perhaps our common affliction will be a solace for your own. In order to be given vent, mine needs you. I alone can neither weep, nor cry out, nor make myself understood. Wolmar understands me but does not respond to me. The sorrow of the unhappy father is buried within himself.... My children affect me but are incapable of pitying me. *I am alone amid everyone*" (p. 408; my italics). ("Vous n'y verrez que douleur et tristesses, et peut-être l'affliction commune sera-t-il un soulagement pour la vôtre. La mienne pour s'exhaler a besoin de vous. Moi seule je ne puis ni pleurer, ni parler, ni me faire entendre. Wolmar m'entend, et ne me répond pas. La douleur d'un père infortuné se concentre en lui-même.... Mes enfants m'attendrissent et ne savent pas s'attendrir. *Je suis seule au milieu de tout le monde*" [p. 566; my italics].) By the end of the letter, which is the end of the book, Claire, writing in a state of distracted discontinuity, reveals her sense of the utter void that has been left by Julie's death, and her desire to rejoin her inseparable cousin in the grave as soon as possible. "Confidence, friendship, virtues, pleasures, cheerful joys—the earth has swallowed all.... I hear a plaintive voice murmuring! ... Claire, oh my Claire, where are you? What are you doing far from your friend? ... Her tomb does not contain her wholly.... It awaits the remainder of its prey ... it will not wait long" (p. 409). ("Confiance, amitié, vertus, plaisirs, folâtres jeux, la terre a tout englouti.... j'entends murmurer une voix plaintive! ... Claire! ô ma

Claire! où es-tu? que fais-tu loin de ton amie?... Son cercueil ne la contient pas tout entière... il attend le reste de sa proie... il ne l'attendra pas longtemps" [pp. 567–68].) Perhaps when I stated earlier that the book was primarily about a love affair between father and daughter, I should have added: and between cousin and cousin. As far as the book is concerned, when Julie dies, Saint-Preux vanishes. But the most moving and significant statement in the whole letter is the one I have underlined. This enormous book is for the greater part concerned with an extensive dream of union whereby the family house can be extended and modified so as to contain within it everyone (and everything) that Julie loves in different ways; a dream of achieving a lasting tranquillity within which varying, and latently oppositional, relationships may be enjoyed in a kind of steady state of constant calm, friction degree zero. In a sense it is a dream of the world itself as one unchanging and contented family.[15] But there is that agitated water... and death. At the end, all the bonds have snapped; father, husband, cousin, children thrown back or turned in upon themselves, wandering around in a daze of misery without communication. Instead of the world as family, we have the family as isolation. "Je suis seule au milieu de tout le monde." There is a glimpse here of the unspeakable solitude at the heart of all relationships that every other page of the book has worked to transcend or conceal or deny. After the Fall of the House of Clarens, that glimpse was to increase until it would become the central focus of attention in some of the greatest of all the European novels of the nineteenth century.

[15]Richardson's *Sir Charles Grandison* is just such another dream. In the novel, characters are constantly stressing the desire to draw everyone into one big family. Where family ties do not exist, kinship terms are applied to incorporate others. "We are all of One Family, and will be forever," says Sir Charles. He even unites his extended English family to the Italian families in the book: not, note, by marriage, but by friendship—as so often there is no *real* affiliation or consanguinity in the new "relatives" who result from this endless process of "familialization." One should also note the numerous occasions on which people who are not relatives by blood are deemed so by an act of renomination. Strangers become "fathers," "mothers," "sisters," "brothers" by a sort of benign conspiracy of re-appellation. When the Italian girl Clementina calls Sir Charles her "brother" he notes "too clearly do I see the exclusive force of that last recognition." This is an insight not pursued, but of course all the terms of inclusion do precisely have an *exclusive* force. They remove the renamed person from the realm of sexuality. The inevitable result is a pervading sense of incest. In this connection consider the following remarks by Foucault: "since the eighteenth century the family has become an obligatory locus of affects, feelings, love; ... sexuality has its privileged point of development in the family ... for this reason sexuality is 'incestuous' from the start ... in a society such as ours, where the family is the most active site of sexuality ... incest ... occupies a central place; it is an object of obsession and attraction, a dreadful secret and an indispensable pivot"—all this arising out of what he calls "the affective intensification of the family space." (Michel Foucault, *The History of Sexuality* [New York: Random House, 1978], pp. 108–9.) It is just such an "affective intensification" that Richardson and Rousseau explored, or attempted to celebrate. Richardson contrives a "happy" ending of total familialization for *Sir Charles Grandison* (1753–54). Rousseau, writing just two or three years later, was more realistic—or prophetic.

3

GOETHE'S *DIE WALVERWANDTSCHAFTEN*

The Monstrous Rights of the Present

Thomas Mann referred to Goethe's novel as "that novel of the mystic dominance of nature over human psychology"; he also called it "the most daring and trenchant novel about adultery that the moral culture of the Occident ever produced." This in spite of the fact that the actual physical act of adultery does not take place. But if you take adultery in its larger sense of an improper conjunction, or the bringing together of things that law decrees should remain apart, then the novel does indeed explore this problem at every level as it occurs within bourgeois society. The book studies the effects on a hitherto stable household when the married couple, Edward and Charlotte, bring into the house an old friend of his, the Captain, and her niece Ottilie. Again it is the advent of strangers into the house (albeit friend and relation) that precipitates the disruptive action of the novel. It could be variously described as a study in the geometry of changing relationships, in the syntax of problematical arrangements within the grammar of middle-class society, or as the topography of shifting attractions and separations among four people. But we should note that the book itself contains talk of chemical experiments and geometry, discussions of books and handwriting, and the frequent use of old and new maps. That is to say that in addition to regarding the novel as a map, we must also note that it is a novel about people much involved in the activity of mapping. Among other things, it offers a topography of self-conscious topographers. This is important to bear in mind because in reading the book we should beware of thinking that we are interpreting a dimension of meaning of which the characters are unaware. It is the other way around. We become aware of the dimension of meaning that they inhabit. We are not interpreters; rather we are forced into a realization of the hermeneutics within which the characters move and have their being. What we might, as readers, consider too obvious, too significant, is a projection of the significances by which the characters define their existence and beyond which they cannot see.

Let me give a brief account of how this operates. The book starts with Edward and Charlotte working and walking and sitting in their garden. He is grafting new shoots onto young trees, which in turn precipitates a conversation considering the possibility of bringing new people into the house, or, as we say, "grafting" (p. 1) them onto the existing arrangement. The conversation takes place in an arbor ("Mooshütte"—literally a kind of moss-covered hut—p. 5), and is preceded by a consideration of the relative spatial amplitude of the arbor.[1] Is it cramped, or spacious enough for one or two more people? At the same time Charlotte makes Edward sit in a position so he can see the landscape through the doors and windows "as through a frame" (p. 2). Framing and grafting are two ways of ordering and rearranging nature through conscious control; and it is appropriate that within this setting Charlotte recalls how they were first of all linked through love, then separated because of Edward's father's "insatiable craving for property" (p. 5) ("aus nie zu sättigender Begierde des Besitzes" [p. 8]). She was in turn "bound" (p. 5) to a man she did not love. ("Meine Hand reichen musste" [p. 8].) "Bind" would be more appropriate for the translation of Edward's father's binding of Edward to a richer older woman—*verband* (p. 8). (In general we can see that from the beginning Goethe is gradually starting to incorporate the whole vocabulary of relationships into his text, the many different words we have for them, the different ways we make them—"giving one's hand" is a different activity from "binding," but they can both mean "marriage"—and the different significances we attribute to them.) They only became free to reunite after the deaths of their respective mates. Considerations of passion and property can separate and unite in different ways. At the moment they are enjoying a stasis in which property and feeling are at one. But the stasis by its nature provokes a desire for activity, to make changes, to build—hence Edward's desire to bring his old friend the Captain into the house, particularly because he is an able man "without occupation" (p. 3) ("geschäftlos" [p. 7]). Charlotte is more cautious, preferring to abide by earlier "plans and arrangements" (p. 5) ("unsern Planen, unsern Einrichtungen" [p. 8]). But once persuaded, she requests an invitation be also sent to her foster daughter, Ottilie. All these discussions can be related to the environment in which they take

---

[1]Unless otherwise indicated, German and English quotations from Goethe's novel within this chapter are from Johann Wolfgang Goethe, *Die Wahlverwandtschaften* (München: Deutscher Taschenbuch Verlag, 1972), and Goethe, *Kindred by Choice*, translated by H. M. Waidson (London: John Calder, 1960).

place and the other activities that accompany this way of life (grafting, tending, gardening, arranging, building, tidying, planning, and so on). The level of conscious discussion and decision is completely grounded in a specific social situation that to some extent speaks through them. In this connection the appearance of Mittler in the second chapter is of particular interest. He is an ex-minister who also mastered the law, then won money in a lottery and retired to a farm. His whole life's work has been dedicated to preventing divorce. He is a passionate "reconciler," and Goethe adds this comment on his name: "Those who are superstitious about the significance of names believe that the name of Mittler was the reason for his following this strangest of vocations" (p. 16). ("Diejenigen, die auf Namensbedeutungen abergläubisch sind, behaupten, der Name Mittler habe ihn genötigt, diese seltsamste aller Bestimmungen zu ergreifen" [p. 16].)

If we take Lacan's point that "The speaking subject, if he seems to be thus a slave of language, is all the more so of a discourse in the universal moment of which he finds himself at birth, even if only by dint of his proper name,"[2] we may say that the constraints and determinants on how the characters regard themselves and their activities, or on the terms in which they discuss possible patterns of behavior, reach back from the property they own, the objects that surround them, even to the names that they were given. Mittler, the compulsive upholder of the existing institutions, always arrives at situations from the outside, just as he is constantly galloping clumsily into other people's houses. He is entirely dependent on "preconceived notions." "Nobody was more dependent than he was on preconceived notions that had been hastily decided upon" (p. 138). ("Niemand war abhängiger von augenblicklich vorgefassten Meinungen als er" [p. 106].) He can only be and do his name.

This power of the name is evident in the central incident, or rather situation, in the book. It turns out that Edward and the Captain were both named Otto, but Edward (who has the more tenuous grasp on his own identity) willingly gave up his name to the Captain. The niece is named Ottilie and the wife, of course, Charlotte. Edward falls in love with Ottilie, while Charlotte and the Captain (Otto) are attracted to each other. In the event, the only adulterous sexual act takes place between the legitimately married Edward and Charlotte. He is thinking of Ottilie, she of the Captain, an unpleasant confusion of private hidden desires working within legitimate visible forms. The resultant child is named Otto, and it looks like the Captain and Ottilie. The name "Otto" is a palindrome, and the novel is full of "palindromic" tendencies. All this

[2]Jacques Lacan, "The Insistence of the Letter in the Unconscious," p. 114.

phonemic interechoing suggests not only similarities but a running together, the merging of disparate identities into one. Thus the names
suggest an inherently contradictory situation. Identity depends on separation and social identity on naming. Yet this configuration suggests a
reverse process, away from individuation, the many returning to one. It
is not enough for us to discern this paradoxical geometry of names—it is
indeed excessively legible; we must realize that this is a geometry
brought about by the participants, who thus find themselves acting out
the problematical counterdrives toward separation and merging that it
suggests.

We can see how this gradually works itself out by considering two
incidents not directly involving the characters in specific relationship but
in their relationship to their surroundings. When Edward writes to invite
the Captain, he asks Charlotte to add her approval. She had good handwriting, yet unexpectedly she spoils the paper with a blot of ink "which
annoyed her and became bigger, the more she tried to remove it" (p. 18)
("einem Tintenfleck, der sie ärgerlich machte und nur grösser wurde,
indem sie ihn wegwischen wollte" [p. 18]). After the signature of the
name, the blot that grows but means nothing—the calligraphic lapse is a
projection of the latent anxiety that will help to precipitate the ensuing
action. It is not a matter of an accident in the text that we from a loftier
position interpret as a symbol, thus transforming a contingency of experience for the characters into an essential attribute of his book for the
reader. These apparent accidents are exactly a part of the way these
particular characters, no matter with what degree of consciousness, write
the narrative of their lives. The later episode is concerned with the
landscaping that is their almost constant activity (being economically
independent, they have nothing else to do, and this of course is a key to
understanding their whole situation and what happens; they are released from certain kinds of socioeconomic conditions into a kind of play
and experimentation, not only with the composition and arrangement of
the garden and landscape but in the composition and arrangement of
themselves). They are looking at three pools, and the suggestion is made
(by a voice unnamed) that the three pools should be joined together into
one lake. The Captain, familiar with the old maps, replies that in ancient
times they did indeed compose one lake and that it would be quite
possible to unite them again (p. 71). ("Nun sollten nur noch, rief einer,
die drei Teiche zu einem See vereinigt werden.... Das liesse sich wohl
machen, sagte der Hauptmann: denn sie bildeten schon vor Zeiten einen
Bergsee" [p. 58].) Edward agrees, only asking that some trees that he
planted—"my" group of trees—be spared. ("Nur bitte ich meine
Platanen—und Pappelgruppe zu schonen, sagte Eduard..." [p. 58].)
Once again the suggestion is there in the landscape and the conversa-

tion. Awareness of individuation awakens memories of the ancient preindividual flow and suggests possibilities of putting aside identity and returning to a continuum. The trees suggest the stage of individuation on the evolutionary scale, but Edward's wish to save only his own trees reveals a kind of narcissism that ultimately manifests itself as a deep urge to lapse from social individuation altogether, as though the problems of the distance from the other that have to be negotiated in society become too exhausting for him. It is the Captain who comes to feel that the conversion of the three lakes into one is inadvisable, but by that time the suggestion has crystallized into a situation within which the characters are held.

The discussion concerning the possibility of transforming the three pools into one lake is immediately followed by a visit from a couple effectively living both separately (according to the letter of the law) and together (as arranged by the promptings of passion). This transfers the problem from the natural realm to the social. The Count and the Baroness have "to give the appearance of being separated, but their liaison continued" (p. 72). ("Sie mussten sich zum Scheine trennen, allein ihr Verhältnis blieb" [p. 59].) Mittler again appears to speak for the "indissolubility" ("unauflöslich")[3] of marriage, but he has removed himself

---

[3]His tirade at this point is a very good example of that kind of semihysterical defense of the abstract institution of marriage that I mentioned in connection with Julie's excessively violent attack on all those who do not accept the socially approved form of marriage.

"Anyone who attacks marriage," he cried, "anyone who undermines, through word or deed, this foundation of all moral society, will have to reckon with me. . . . Marriage is the beginning and the culmination of all civilisation. It makes the brutal man gentle, and the most educated man can have no better opportunity for demonstrating his humane spirit. It must be indissoluble; for it brings so much happiness that the individual instances of unhappiness cannot be taken into account. And what is this talk of unhappiness? . . . There are really no sufficient grounds for separating. The human condition is granted so much, both in pain and joy, that it is quite impossible to work out what the partners in a marriage owe to each other. It is an infinite debt, which can only be paid off in eternity.

(Pp. 74–75)

Wer mir den Ehstand angreift, rief er aus, wer mir durch Wort, ja durch Tat, diesen Grund aller sittlecher Gesellschaft untergräbt, der hat es mit mir zu tun. . . . Die Ehe ist der Anfang und der Gipfel aller Kultur. Sie macht den rohen mild, und der Gebildetste hat keine bessere Gelegenheit seine Milde zu beweisen. Unauflöslich muss sie sein: denn sie bringt so vieles Glück, dass alles einzelne Unglück dagegen gar nicht zu rechnen ist. Und was will man von Unglück reden? . . . Sich zu trennen gibt's gar keinen hinlänglichen Grund. Der menschliche Zustand ist so hoch in Leiden und Freuden gesetzt, dass gar nicht berechnet werden kann, was ein Paar Gatten einander schuldig werden. Es ist eine unendliche Schuld, die nur durch die Ewigkeit abgetragen werden kann.

(Pp. 60–61)

Schuld is perhaps an appropriately ambiguous word for a solid Protestant vision of marriage, since it means both "debt" and "guilt."

from the problematical flux of human relationships. His absolutism is based on a divorce from experience; within experience the problems of joining and separating are in constant flow. The Count and the Baroness—they are titles more than they are names—are "straight from the world of society" (p. 76). ("Die Neueintretenden, welche unmittelbar aus der Welt kamen..." [p. 62]); literally "from the world," and thus, one might say—allowing for the level of generality, verging on allegory, on which the book is conducted—they represent the distillation of "worldliness." It is worth noting that they come "unmittelbar"—direct or immediate, that is, without any mediation. They are precisely those who have no interest in the mediations so vociferously—and abstractly— asserted by Mittler. It is no wonder that he disapproves of them so vehemently and refuses to be in the same house with them. And where he is gauche and abrasive, they are at ease, showing no awkwardness, despite their socially compromised positions, but rather a contagious fluidity of manner and adaptive tract.

One of the Count's speeches concerning marriage should be quoted at some length and compared with the one by Mittler quoted in note 3, above.

> "We do so like to think that earthly things, and in particular marital ties, are really permanent, and, as far as this latter is concerned, we are misled by our comedies, which we see always being repeated, a desire that has been put off by the hindrances of illusions such as do not fit in with the way of the world. In comedy we see a marriage as the final fulfilment of several acts, and at the moment when it is attained the curtain falls and the temporary satisfaction it occasions lingers in our minds. In life it's a different matter; the play goes on behind the scenes, and when the curtain rises again, we would be glad not to see."

Charlotte comments that it cannot be quite as bad as all that, since some people who have left the stage are glad to return to it again at a later date. To which the Count replies:

> There's nothing to be said against that.... One is glad to take over a new role again, and when you know the world, you can see that in marriage too it is only this definite eternal duration amid so much that is transient in the world, that has something awkward about it. One of my friends whose good humour displayed itself in making suggestions for new laws maintained that every marriage should be undertaken only for a five-year period.
>
> (Pp. 77–78)

(This notion of a temporary or short-term marriage has been discussed in both Richardson and Tolstoi—a perennial problem.)

Wir mögen uns die irdischen Dinge, und besonders auch die ehlichen Verbindungen gern so recht dauerhaft vorstellen, und was den letzten Punkt betrifft, so verführen uns die Lustspiele, die wir immer wiederholen sehen, zu solchen Einbildungen, die mit dem Gange der Welt nicht zusammentreffen. In der Komödie sehen wir eine Heirat als das letzte Ziel eines durch die Hindernisse mehrerer Akte verschobenen Wunsches, und im Augenblick, da er erreicht ist, fällt der Vohang, und die momentane Befriedigung klingt bei uns nach. In der Welt ist es anders; da wird hinten immer fortgespielt, und wenn der Vorhang wieder aufgeht, mag man gern nichts weiter davon sehen noch hören. . . .

Dagegen ist nichts einzuwenden. . . . Eine neue Rolle mag man gern wieder übernehmen, und wenn man die Welt kennt, so sieht man wohl, auch bei dem Ehestande ist es nur diese entschiedene, ewige Dauer zwischen so viel Beweglichem in der Welt, die etwas Ungeschicktes an sich trägt. Einer von meinen Freunden, dessen gute Laune sich meist in Vorschlägen zu neuen Gesetzen hervortat, behauptete: eine jede Ehe solle nur auf fünf Jahre geschlossen werden.

(Pp. 62–63)

The Count speaks from, and for, and in terms of *die Welt. Bewegliches* is not so much "transient" as "that which moves," "mobile," and hence, potentially, unfixed, unstable. The world, for the Count, is the realm of the moving and movable, and that is why he discerns something *Ungeschicktes* in the institution of marriage, with its attempted and avowed fixities and permanencies—the word refers to something clumsy, in, say, a person's behavior if he is awkward in his movements and trips up, or if he says the wrong thing at the wrong time. It is a word that might very readily be applied to Mittler! The Count's attitude toward sexual and marital *mores* is identifiably aristocratic (it would be in line with the attitude of the world described by Saint-Preux in his letter to Julie about those societies in which adultery is recognized as a kind of game)—though the Count is not necessarily being cynical about attachments, only dubious about their power to act as the basis of a lifelong bond. He would like social laws and institutions to be as pliant and supple and adaptive as his own worldly manners—though whether that would be distinguishable from having no laws and bonds at all is not immediately clear. But this is why the bourgeois is suspicious of what I shall, for the occasion, designate as the aristocratic attitude toward sexuality and marriage. Charlotte is predictably disturbed by this conversation. "She knew full well that there is nothing more dangerous than an over-free conversation which treats a culpable or semi-culpable situation as if it were usual, general, and even praiseworthy; and surely anything that attacks the marriage union comes into this category" (p. 78). ("Sie wusste recht gut, dass nichts gefährlicher sei, als ein allzufreies Gespräch, das einen strafbaren oder halbstrafbaren Zustand als einen gewöhnlichen, gemeinen, ja löblichen behandelt; und dahin gehört doch gewiss alles, was die eheliche Verbindung antastet" [pp. 63-64].) By what metric the good bourgeois is to measure any deviation from his norms (At what point does the semiculpable shade into the demi-semiculpable?) is indeed a problem, for once outside his norms the slippery slopes of a fearful relativism are all around him. And by the same token, how can he (or she) decide at what point a conversation becomes—"gefährlich"? What is a permissible interesting talk, and what or when does it become "ein allzufreies Gespräch"? (*Allzufreies* carries a suggestion of looseness, too much liberty, of disputing limits.) Once again the problem recurs—What is the bourgeois family going to talk about? What can it afford to include; what should it work to debar? This indeed may be said to be a matter close to the center of this book.

Everything about the Count and Baroness—their clothes and appurtenances—bespeaks a completely socialized way of life and as such they are at the opposite extreme from Mittler, whose removal from all society was, however, made possible by a fortuitous win in a lottery (i.e., his words and his money come from different sources—hence, perhaps, his clumsiness of manner, since his life is imperfectly integrated and his aphorisms are based on a financial position of which the source is concealed and unexamined). So while they accept the social world and the rules governing appearances—including the appearance of being married to different people—they are quite prepared to manoeuvre within it to enable themselves to meet in private. They manipulate circumstances from the inside without changing the public names and categories. Thus it is that the Count persuades Edward to lead him to the wing in which the ladies are quartered. The men and women are notionally separated by particular arrangements of rooms; but within the architecture of the house there can be no absolute separation, and if there are locked doors and conventional lines of demarcation, there are also secret staircases that can subvert them; the directness of approach and retreat suggested by the uncomplicated linearity of the corridors[4] is countered by the deviousness of the spiral staircase up which Edward conducts the Count

---

[4]It is one of Lawrence Stone's main contentions in *The Family, Sex, and Marriage* that "The most striking change in the life-style of the upper classes in the seventeenth and eighteenth centuries was the increasing stress laid upon personal privacy." An important architectural aspect of this change was the introduction of the corridor into house plans of "the late seventeenth and eighteenth centuries, . . . which now allowed access without intruding upon privacy." (See chapter 6—"The Growth of Affective Individualism.") They also allowed access without disturbing legitimacy—any conditions set up to establish privacy are necessarily ambivalent in the uses to which they may be put. Goethe is clearly well aware of this, and of the whole significance of architecture and its effect on personal relationships.

to the Baroness. The amount of careful detail given to the architecture of the house is the reverse of gratuitous, for the house itself is a complex of contradictory possibilities. For every door expressing a taboo of no-passage, there is some other architectural feature suggesting possibilities of other modes of entry. It is a truism to note that the house is like the human body. More importantly, in this novel the house becomes a generative model of relationships, every consciously arranged separation suggesting new combinations by another route. Spaces and the connections between them become entirely problematic, and if more than two people are introduced into the house, all relationships become potentially volatile as people put themselves in different rooms or different chairs or, indeed, different beds. The house is thus like a code in which the inhabitants can formulate different messages according to where they position themselves, the syntax of their arranging. The point is that the code predetermines the kinds of messages that are possible, and in this case the code is the architecture. To pursue the metaphor further: passional energies that no longer feel identified and contained within the ties of the socially ordained relationships may indeed displace themselves from the rooms (categories) in which they ought to be at rest. But in so doing, they can only spell out illicit messages within the spatial code of the house. They cannot invent a new language.

This night maneuvering by the Count and all the thoughts and memories it arouses precede the central act of nonadulterous adultery between Edward and Charlotte. This seems to be one of the most important moments in the history of the European novel (inasmuch as it deals with the problems of human sexual-passional relationships), and I will consider it in some detail. Clearly the presence of the adulterous Count and Baroness in the house has had a stimulating effect on the latent nonconjugal feelings that are beginning to stir there. Mittler's comment on their presence is in this instance accurate. "Their nature is like yeast, which reproduces its own contagion" (p. 74). ("Ihr Wesen ist wie ein Sauerteig, der seine Ansteckung fortpflanzt" [p. 60].) After seeing the Count on his devious way to the Baroness's bedroom, Edward pauses outside Charlotte's bedroom, happens to hear a reference to Ottilie, and starts to think about her. "Edward was delighted to hear that Ottilie was still at her writing. 'She is being busy on my account!' he thought exultantly." ("Eduard hörte mit Entzücken, dass Ottilie noch schreibe. Sie beschäftigt sich für mich! dachte er triumphierend.") "Enclosed in upon himself through the darkness, he saw her sitting and writing in his mind's eye; he imagined himself approaching her, seeing her as she would turn round towards him; he felt an insurmountable desire to be close to her once more. But there was no way from here to the entresol room where she lived. Now as he found himself directly by his wife's door, a strange confusion took place in his soul; he tried to turn the handle, and the door was locked, he knocked softly, Charlotte did not hear" (p. 89). ("Durch die Finsternis ganz in sich selbst geengt sah er sie sitzen, schreiben; er glaubte zu ihr zu treten, sie zu sehen, wie sie sich nach ihm umkehrte; er fühlte ein unüberwindliches Verlangen ihr noch einmal nahe zu sein. Von hier aber war kein Weg in das Halbgeschoss, wo sie wohnte. Nun fand er sich unmittelbar an seiner Frauen Türe, eine sonderbare Verwechselung ging in seiner Seele vor, er suchte die Türe aufzudrehen, er fand sie verschlossen, or pochte leise an, Charlotte hörte nicht" [p. 72].)

Entzücken is a very strong word, implying ecstasy; it is what the mystics experience: for Edward to experience such ecstasy at this time and place upon hearing an apparently trivial detail about Ottilie seems disproportionate; it is as though there is more feeling foregathering in him than he is as yet aware of (passion is elsewhere described as building up pressure as in a vat).[5] He is outside his wife's door which is where, given the orthodox rules of the house, he most properly should be at this time of night. His imagination, however, is at dalliance with Ottilie, watching her, almost caressing her. But given the architectural layout of the house, he cannot gain physical access to her room, so he sends his imagination precisely where his body cannot go. On the other hand, his wife's door is locked, as though he is being temporarily debarred his legal right of access. In a sense he is for the moment almost nowhere and the German term "in sich selbst *geengt*" (p. 72; my italics) is a strange formulation that is appropriate to this awkward ontological moment of being both physically not in the room where he ought to be and mentally in a

---

[5]The comparison is a notable one and is worth quoting in full. "In general the normal way of life of a family. . . . has an extraordinary tendency to absorb a nascent passion like a vat, and a fair time can elapse before this new ingredient causes a noticeable fermentation and spills foaming over the edge of the vessel" (p. 55). ("Überhaupt nimmt die gewöhnliche Lebensweise einer Familie. . . . auch wohl eine ausserordentliche Neigung, eine werdende Leidenschaft, in sich wie ein Gefäss auf, und es kann eine ziemliche Zeit vergehen, ehe dieses neue Ingrediens eine merkliche Gärung verursacht und schäumend über den Rand schwillt" [p. 47].) In considering the possibility of establishing new geometries, or extending old ones, by the addition of new ingredients (the Captain and Ottilie), Edward and Charlotte had not considered the nongeometrical phenomenon of fermentation (*Gärung*)—diagrams do not contain "yeast"; people and the situations they are in do. The image of something within the house finally spilling and foaming over the edge is a very powerful one, conveying as it does not only a sense of all that the orderliness and "ordinaryness" of regular bourgeois life try to exclude from its house but the potent suggestion as well that the household itself is the very vessel, or vat (*Gefäss*), that can promote that secret, and ultimately ruinous, fermentation. The idea of certain elements or ingredients slowly building up and then erupting as a spillage that effectively destroys the household is conveyed again in the famous image in *Madame Bovary* concerning the rain that gathers in the choked gutters of the house: the householders are not aware of it until it breaks the walls and gushes through, a premonitory metaphor for the kind of passional spillage later to be enacted by Emma, even down to the literal spilling of champagne over the edge of the glass onto her rings.

room where he ought not to be. *Eng* is "narrow," and while the usual word for "to narrow down" is *einengen,* this somewhat cumbersome formulation—"in sich selbst geengt" (p. 72)—(perhaps unique to this context?) suggests that Edward is pressed down small into himself in a rather eerie way. This odd kind of momentary self-contraction or even self-erasure is accompanied or succeeded by a "strange confusion" (p. 89) in his soul: "eine sonderbare Verwechselung" (p. 72), where *Verwechselung* means to mistake one for another, not "to exchange," but to change too much and thus mix up and confuse. An erotic/mental blending is taking place in Edward's being that is a prelude to or symptom of an incipient loss of the faculties of differentiation that he is to experience.

Inside the marriage bedroom Charlotte is thinking about the Captain, particularly as the possibility of his leaving has just been brought up that evening. "It was he who filled the house with his presence and still gave life to the walks outside, and he was to go away, and all that was to become empty!" (p. 90). ("Er füllte noch das Haus, er belebte noch die Spaziergänge und er sollte fort, das alles sollte leer werden!" [p. 72].) For such an excellent housewife as Charlotte, this is indeed a worrying emotion. For if, despite all her objects and utensils, the furniture and decorations, the fruits and flowers, she feels her house will be empty on account of the absence of what is technically an illicit "other," then what does all that well-tended materiality that makes up her life signify? Indeed, what exactly makes for the experience of a full or an empty house may be said to be a crucial subject in the bourgeois novel. Charlotte, usually so composed, is so agitated that she weeps and abandons herself to her painful feelings. Edward, for his part, cannot leave the door ("konnte von der Türe nicht weg" [p. 72])—understandably enough, for where else, in his there/not there state in this full/empty house, can he go? He knocks for a third time, and Charlotte, hearing it, thinks it is the Captain, such is the potency of mental desire over the realm of the plausible and the actual. She then realizes that this is impossible, and asks who is there.

> "It's I."—"Who?" Charlotte replied, unable to distinguish the tone of the voice. In her imagination the Captain's figure stood before the door. Rather more loudly she heard "Edward!" she opened the door, and her husband stood before her. He greeted her in a joking manner. She could take up the conversation in a similar tone. He wrapped up the mysterious visit in mysterious explanation. "But I must confess to you the real reason why I've come," he said finally. "I have taken a vow to kiss your shoe this very evening."
>
> "You haven't thought of that for a long time," Charlotte said. "All the worse," Edward replied, "and all the better."
>
> (P. 90)

Ich bin's. Wer? entgegnete Charlotte, die den Ton nicht unterscheiden konnte. Ihr stand des Hauptmanns Gestalt vor der Tür. Etwas lauter klang

es ihr entgegen Eduard! Sie öffnete und ihr Gemahl stand vor ihr. Er
begrüsste sie mit einem Scherz. Es war ihr möglich in diesem Tone
fortzufahren. Er verwickelte den rätselhaften Besuch in rätselhafte
Erklärungen. Warum ich denn aber eigentlich komme, sagte er zulezt,
muss ich dir nur gestehen. Ich habe ein Gelübde getan, heute Abend noch
deinen Schuh zu küssen.

Das ist dir lange nicht eingefallen, sagte Charlotte. Desto schlimmer,
versetzte Eduard, und desto besser!

(Pp. 72–73)

I must confess immediately that whether his "vow" (and *Gelübde* is
very strong; it is what priests take) is a piece of shameless fetishism, or a
piece of old Bavarian gallantry not familiar to me, or part of some erotic
code or game between Edward and Charlotte, is not at all clear to me;
and just what Charlotte makes of Edward's last bit of gnomic banter I
cannot imagine. Whatever the case, kiss her shoe is very precisely what
he proceeds to do, and we are to infer that he did not stop at that
somewhat peripheral assuaging of his aroused desire. What is notable in
Goethe's depiction of this crucial moment is his description of how this
married couple, each of them thinking about another person and not
truly about the other, find it possible (*möglich*) to indulge in a
pseudocommunication based on jokes and mystification. What they, particularly Edward, are really doing is mystifying their own desires so that
they can find licit physical satisfaction with each other while indulging in
illicit thoughts about figures not present. Edward, as we have seen, was
in a state in which things (people, rather) are "confused" (*Verwechselung*);
Charlotte, similarly, cannot make out the voice outside her door because
of the confusion of her own imaginings—*unterscheiden* means to distinguish, and we find on both sides signs of that fading ability to differentiate that, I shall suggest, is intimately involved with the problematics of adultery in the bourgeois novel. For Charlotte it is a
momentary sensation, one from which she can struggle to recover; and
as it turns out she is, as it were, the survivor, whereas for Edward it is
part of an irreversible regressive tendency. But at this moment they both
capitulate to it, and so we come to one of the most important descriptions
of a sexual embrace in the whole history of the novel.

In the obscurity of the remaining lamp, inner attraction and imagination at
once asserted their rights over reality: Edward held only Ottilie in his arms,
it was the Captain who, more closely or more distantly, hovered at the
threshold of Charlotte's mind, and in this way the absent and the present,
strangely enough, were entwined in attractive and radiant confusion.

And yet the present will not be deprived of its monstrous rights. They
spent part of the night in all kinds of talk and levity which were all the freer
since the heart unfortunately had no part in them. But when Edward woke

the next morning in his wife's arms, the day seemed to him to be looking in upon him with foreboding; the sun seemed to him to be lighting upon a crime; he stole quietly away from her side, and when she awoke she found herself, strangely enough, alone.

(Pp. 91-92)

In der Lampendämmerung sogleich behauptete die innre Neigung, behauptete die Einbildungskraft ihre Rechte über das Wirkliche. Eduard hielt nur Ottilie in seinen Armen; Charlotten schwebte der Hauptmann näher oder ferner vor der Seele, und so verwebten, wundersam genug, sich Abwesendes und Gegenwärtiges reizend und wonnevoll durcheinander.

Und doch lässt sich die Gegenwart ihr ungeheures Recht nicht rauben. Sie brachten einen Teil der Nacht unter allerlei Gesprächen und Scherzen zu, die um desto freier waren, als das Herz leider keinen Teil daran nahm. Aber als Eduard des andern Morgens an dem Busen seiner Frau erwachte, schien ihm der Tag ahnungsvoll hereinzublicken, die Sonne schien ihm ein Verbrechen zu beleuchten; er schlich sich leise von ihrer Seite, und sie fand sich, seltsam genug, allein, als sie erwachte.

(P. 73)

The closing words of the first paragraph quoted are among the most important in the book, and a little more detailed consideration is warranted. *Verweben* is to interweave or intermingle, and it is the absent (*Abwesendes*) and the present (*Gegenwärtiges*) that weave themselves together in a promiscuous confusion, or mess (*durcheinander*) that is *reizend*—delicious, enticing, bewitching, tempting, stimulating—and *wonnevoll*—full of rapture, bliss, ecstasy. Since all good housekeeping must depend to some extent on keeping things apart and in their places, the kind of ecstatic untidiness caused by the merging of presence and absence suggested in these words must necessarily appear as a threat to the very idea of stability in marriage. The legitimized embrace is enjoyed only with the addition of those hovering absences that should, theoretically, not present themselves. I am not suggesting that no one before Goethe had ever observed or suggested that it is not an uncommon thing for a married couple to think of other people while making love. It is the context and placement of the insight that is crucial, for it has been promoted to what is, effectively, the core of the novel, suggesting not just that married sexual activity may effectively be adulterous sexual activity but that it may not in fact be possible to tell—or to keep—them apart. Inner attractions—*die innre Neigung*—not only obey no laws, social or even ethical, but it is possible that they ultimately do not answer to differentiating identifications. For a bourgeois society this really does represent an ultimate threat, and this I think is what Goethe saw and portrayed. (It is perhaps for this reason that Lord Byron called the book a mockery of marriage, though just how Lord Byron establishes an *assiette* that justifies him to condemn a work on those grounds is not immediately clear.)

Thus it is, Goethe continues in the first sentence of the following paragraph, "the present will not be deprived of its monstrous rights." *Ungeheures* is again a very strong word: *das Ungeheuer* is "the monster," *nicht geheuer* is "uncanny" or "haunted," and oddly enough, there is no positive *geheuer*—it is a thing, quality, an aspect of experience, a sensation, a feeling that is only defined by the negative—or, as we say, by an absence, something *not*—nicht, un. What are these monstrous rights of the present? Presumably the undeniable promptings of physical desire (no matter how overdetermined or confused the feelings that accompany them may be), which do not recognize the kind of respect for the past and obligation to the future that, preeminently, a wife and husband do, but that man himself—inasmuch as he recognizes himself as being to some extent an answerable continuity, with a past that is his and a future that will see the accomplishment of his acts, and inasmuch as he is a consciousness capable of retrospection and intention—inevitably *is*. Man is not monstrous, we may say, to the extent that he recognizes the social and moral compacts that extend through time. But what is a monster? Something extraordinary, unnatural, a prodigy, something that does not fit into the established taxonomies and classifications—the root is the Latin *monere*, "to warn," and was originally applied to divine portents or warnings. It is that which comes from outside what we think is the established order of things—our order, at any rate—and in some way threatens it. It warns us that *our* world is not *the* world, and that there are margins or fissures or gaps, or black holes, or other levels of being—whatever—through which or from which may issue things not dreamt of in our orthodoxies.

The "monstrous rights of the present" is thus a very worrying paradox, for since when did monsters have rights, and what is a monstrous *right*, since a right implies something recognized and even ratified by other people, so that we say that something is "within his rights"; but the *monstrous* is precisely that which is felt to be wrong, and we hardly say that someone is "within his wrongs," but rather outside or beyond his rights, which is surely the undelimitable realm of the monstrous. And if the present has these undeniable rights and we always live physically in the present (no matter what we want to say of our mental extensions and intentions back and forth—and sideways—through time), we are not in constant danger of being bemonstered? This was the word used by Albany to Goneril in *King Lear* (act 4, scene 2) ("Be-monster not thy feature"), and it is of course entirely appropriate, given the varying degrees of bestialization that Shakespeare was exploring as he considered how men and women may, so very quickly, relapse into the behavior we associate with the lower animals (all animals are ugly and mean in that play), indeed into behavior that transcends beneath that behavior and can only be associated with the behavior of animals as yet only imagined or heard of in rumor and legend—monsters. The timeless heath and the palaces of *King Lear* are one thing, but to introduce the idea of these monstrous rights into the daily routine of the good respectable bourgeois marriage is quite another, and it makes that marriage appear to be potentially a very different thing from the mythic values with which it is bestowed and the iconic associations and virtues that hover round it. This wife and husband spend their night in "talk and levity" (*Scherzen*— jokes, pleasantries) that are all the freer because the heart had no part (*Teil*—part, portion, component) in them. Such talk is free because it is not constrained by any considerations of expressing feeling or conveying truth. It is, precisely, language cut loose from all its obligations and it can sport around as freely—and this is where it becomes more disturbing— as freely as the married couple in their marriage bed. The marriage bed is supposed to be the center point of converging and binding mutual obligations, reciprocal undertakings, and so on. Yet it has somehow, here, turned into the opposite: not the place of the binding word, but the word unbound, with no obligations to meaning; not the place of a couple bound together by feeling, but, as it were, assorted by unfeeling, partly adrift in a legitimized ecstasy of loss of differentiation and partly tumbling around in a legitimized meaninglessness of sexuality devoid of heart. For that is the monster that Goethe has caught a glimpse of and put into his novel of these eminently reasonable (for the most part), kind, and responsible (for the most part) citizens. It is that monster that a marriage in which the heart has no part becomes. The heart is that absent presence, and that present absence, that can render marriage monstrous.[6]

---

[6]The history of the "monster"—the deviant, the "sport," the freak—is a very long one, of course, and is effectively inseparable from human attempts to classify the living world. François Jacob offers a convenient summary of some early aspects of the interest in monsters.

  Sixteenth-century descriptions of the living world are filled with all kinds of monsters. Entire books are devoted to them by Aldrovandus and Ambroise Paré and in each "History" of living organisms, of birds or of fish, fabulous and ordinary beings rub shoulders. These monsters always reflect what exists. None resembles nothing at all. None differs entirely from what can be seen at every turn. They simply do not resemble one single being, but two, three or more simultaneously. . . . Monsters always bear resemblances, but they are distorted resemblances which no longer correspond to the normal action of nature. The combinations and signs which can be deciphered no longer express the order of the world, but bear witness to the errors which can slide in. "Monsters are things which appear contrary to the course of Nature," observed Ambroise Paré. Contrary to the *course,* but not to the *forces* of nature, as nature does not make mistakes. . . . Each monster is the result of an iniquity and bears witness to a certain disorder: an act (or even an intention)

Part of the bliss of the confusion that this dark embrace offers is due to the temporary reprieve from the ordeal of differentiation and separation that Edward and Charlotte have been experiencing to different degrees. But the morning compounds the confusion with its sinister and paradoxical clarifications, so that the legal conjugal coming together now seems to be exactly the opposite, "a crime" (p. 92) ("ein Verbrechen" [p.

---

not in conformity with the order of the world. Physical or moral, each divergence from nature produces an unnatural fruit. Nature, too, has its morality.

(The Logic of Life)

(See also Jacob's comments on the change in 'status' of monsters in nineteenth-century studies of biology, and the examination of new problems of classification, also in chapter 2, "Organization.")

But in a number of ways, the monster in its many forms, becomes a decidedly nineteenth-century preoccupation. To take a few examples: we may note that in Mary Shelley's *Frankenstein* (1816), the "monster of my creation," as Frankenstein often refers to him, threatens his maker with the reiterated words: "*I will be with you on your wedding-night,*" and he takes his revenge by killing Elizabeth, thus literally destroying the marriage with his "monstrous" presence, having been denied what he claims to be his monster's right (i.e., to have a mate made for him). That there is a distinct sympathy for him in his utter isolation—"I am an outcast in the world for ever"—is, of course, part of the romantic tenor of the book. But a sympathy with, or at least an interest in, the "monstrous" more metaphorically conceived, can be discerned throughout the nineteenth century. The literal monster of Frankenstein speaks more prophetically than he could know when he cries "My reign is not yet over." The nineteenth century became interested in categories, classifications, and taxonomies of all kinds, an interest that, at the same time (and necessarily), provoked an interest in the "anomaly." Thus Edward Said notes—referring to Etienne Geoffroy Saint-Hilaire's *Philosophie Anatomiques: Des Monstruosités humaines* (1822), and the work of his son Isidore, which, together with the work of his father, resulted in *Histoire Générale et particulière des anomalies de l'organization chez l'homme et les animaux, ouvrâge comprenente des recherches sur les caractères, la classification, l'influence physiologique et pathologique, les rapports généraux, les lois et les causes des monstruosités, des varietés et vices de conformation, ou traité de teratologie* (1832–36): "Not only were Etienne and Isidore legatees of the tradition of 'romantic' biology passed down by Goethe among others, with their strong interest in analogy, homology, and organic Ur-forms among species, but they were also specialists in the philosophy and anatomy of monstrosity, teratology as Isidore called it, in which the most horrendous physiological aberrations were considered to be a function of internal degradation within the species life" ("Renan's Philological Laboratory" in *Art, Politics, and the Will: Essays in Honor of Lionel Trilling,* ed. Quentin Anderson, Stephen Donadio, and Steven Marcus [New York: Basic Books, 1977], pp. 55–98.)

Darwin, of course, was necessarily interested in the phenomenon of the monster, but he admitted it was difficult to distinguish between a monster and a variation. A monster may be a mutant, adapting to a new tomorrow. "At long intervals of time, out of millions of individuals reared in the same country and fed on nearly the same food, deviations of structure so strongly pronounced as to deserve to be called monstrosities arise; but monstrosities cannot be separated by any distinct line from slighter variations" (*The Origin of Species*). He also makes the rather tantalizing observation that "Domestic races often have a somewhat monstrous character," but this is not the place to summarize what Darwin writes about "Variation Under Domestication" (chapter 1 in *The Origin of Species*).

For a narrative dramatization of how the bourgeoisie reacted to the existence of human anomalies or monstrosities, see *Madame Bovary*. Many novelists in the nineteenth century were, of course, interested in monsters or the monstrous, in the sense that they were attracted to anyone/anything that was "anomalous," who/which crossed category lines, or threatened them, or were simply unclassifiable, or declassified—unfamiliar, or unfamilied.

73]), and in the morning, where there should be closeness and relationship there is solitude. The implications of this particular sensation are very far-reaching, for it means that law can engender criminality, or, to put it more extremely and worryingly, it implies the possibility that the legal may incomprehensibly turn into its supposed opposite and become the very thing it was formulated to prohibit and exclude. Similarly, the

---

Flaubert himself was very interested in "teratology," but more generally a novelist like Dickens was drawn to figures who were, in many different senses, monsters in comparison, or by contrast, with the more conventional figures surrounding them. Examples are plentiful and need not be adduced here; but I cannot resist one example from *Our Mutual Friend* (chapter 7, "Mr. Wegg Looks After Himself"), when Silas Wegg visits Mr. Venus, that expert of "the miscellaneous" who deals in, among other things, skeletal fragments of the human body. Silas Wagg wants to find out what he is "worth" to Mr Venus:

"Come! According to your own account, I'm not worth much,"

Wegg reasons persuasively.

"Not for miscellaneous working in, I grant you, Mr Wegg; but you might turn out valuable yet, as a—" where Mr. Venus takes a gulp of tea, so hot that it makes him choke, and sets his weak eyes watering: "as a Monstrosity, if you'll excuse me."

For a novelist like Dickens, "newelties" were necessarily more arresting and imaginatively challenging than "oldies," and if the newelty was also some kind of monster—well, so much the better for his "novels"! And the novel itself, with its mongrel origin, its variations and deviations, its generic unclassifiability, its unpredictable forms, its tendency to hybridization, is a kind of freak or sport of literature—a monster in its own right!

But apart from specific anomalies or monstrosities, the interest in all kinds of literal or metaphorical teratology spread into many discourses in the nineteenth century. As Michel Foucault indicates, the criminal in the nineteenth century came to be regarded as "a traitor, a 'monster.'" . . . Between the contractual principle that expels the criminal from society and the image of the monster "vomited" by nature, where is one to find a limit, if not in a human nature that is manifested—not in the rigour of the law, not in the ferocity of the delinquent—but in the sensibility of the reasonable man who makes the law and does not commit the crime?" (pp. 90–91). And again: "the criminal designated as the enemy of all, whom it is in the interest of all to track down, falls outside the pact, disqualifies himself as a citizen and emerges, bearing within him as it were, a wild fragment of nature; he appears as a villain, a monster, a madman, perhaps a sick and, before long, "abnormal" individual. It is as such that, one day, he will belong to a scientific objectification and to the "treatment" that is correlative to it." (*Discipline and Punish: The Birth of the Prison*, trans. Alan Sheridan [New York: Pantheon, 1977], p. 101.)

In a different area of study, Marx availed himself of the same word: "By turning his money into commodities that serve as the material elements of a new product, and as factors in the labour process, by incorporating living labour with their dead substance, the capitalist at the same time converts value, i.e., past, materialized and dead labour, into capital, into value big with value, a live monster that is fruitful and multiplies" (*Capital*, vol. 1, "The Production of Surplus Value." *See Marx: Selected Writings* ed. David McLellan [Oxford: Oxford University Press, 1977], p. 468). It is hardly surprising that Nietzsche makes tolerably frequent use of the word *monster*; he often quotes Voltaire:

> *Un monstre gai vaut mieux*
> *Qu'un sentimental ennuyeux.*

But at the end of *The Will to Power* (bk. 4, section 1067), he more seriously characterizes the world as monster: "This world: a monster of energy, without beginning, without end; a firm, iron magnitude of force that does not grow bigger or smaller, that does not expend

institution supposed to ensure companionship and mutuality produces isolation: "twoness" or "untogetherness."

This suggests a world of intolerable inversions and generates a new kind of singleness and apartness. Indeed, very shortly thereafter we read that the world is turned upside down for Edward. The occasion of this definitive feeling of inversion is worth noting. Ottilie has done some writing for Edward and brings it in for him to check. He notes that her handwriting in the early pages is her own, delicate and female (*weiblich*), then "the characters seemed to change and become easier and freer; but how surprised he was when he cast his eyes over the last few pages! "'Good heavens!' he cried, 'what's this? That's my handwriting!'" (p. 95). ("dann schienen sich die Züge zu verändern, leichter und freier zu werden; aber wie erstaunt war er, als er die letzten Seiten mit den Augen überlief! Um Gottes willen! rief er aus, was ist das? Das ist meine Hand!" [p. 75].) One does not have to be a scriptologist to recognize how much of an individual's interiority depicts itself in the individual's handwriting; utterly unique to each individual, his or her handwriting is the very sign and silhouette of the emotional being and temperament, the forever unfinished cartographic depiction of the lineaments of all his or her desires, satisfied and unsatisfied. The metamessage in Ottilie's script is that she is beginning to, as it were, cede her identity to Edward's, so that whereas Edward and Charlotte embraced only to discover their separation, Ottilie and Edward work in apparent separation only to begin to merge. It is as though in some strange way the passional flow has been

---

itself but only transforms itself; as a whole, of unalterable size, a household without increase or income; enclosed by "nothingness" as by a boundary...."

We have seen that novelists from Richardson to James have described marriage without love as a monster (cf. "Le mariage doit incessamment combattre un monstre qui dévore tout: l'habitude" Balzac: *Physiologie de Mariage* [pt. 1, ch. 5]). We may add here the unique story "The Murders in the Rue Morgue" by Edgar Allan Poe: we find a crime committed by an animal (in effect, a "monster") that the police cannot solve because, as Dupin says, the prefect of police has a way "*de nier ce qui est, et d'expliquer ce qui n'est pas.*" If, like a good bureaucrat, your thinking is dominated by established categories and classifications, then, by definition nothing can happen or be caused by an agent that falls outside these categories; but the criminal, as metaphorical or literal monster, is precisely that anomaly that the police-bureaucratic mind cannot envisage—it would rather, to translate Poe's words, "deny what is, and explain what is not." Thus, marriage, money, the crime, and the criminal can come to be regarded as monstrous if they do not fit into the theoretical tyranny of established classifications. Needless to say, the interest of the artist would necessarily fasten on those anomalies that were denied "existence" by the established authorities. It takes a Nietzsche to affirm that the world itself is such an anomaly.

In our own day, with science fiction, etc., we are back to literal monsters, but that is mainly for mere frisson. It is that nameless something—whether a bad marriage or an incomprehensible criminal—that monstrosity, which is some kind of per-version of nature as we have decided it is constituted and which looms and penetrates the unseen gaps in our self-stabilizing taxonomies, that presents the most profound threat and horror.

diverted from the bedroom to the page, for Ottilie's handwriting has more erotic power over Edward than Charlotte's body, and it is at this point that Edward embraces Ottilie. (*Züge* is, incidentally, a word of many connotations, so that it could imply that not only the characters of Ottilie's handwriting but also her features, characteristics, traits, sympathies, dispositions, inclinations, etc., begin to change and become easier and freer, as indeed the English *character* carries both the specific reference to written letters and the general reference to the whole complex of a person's emotional and conscious being.) "'You love me!' he cried, 'Ottilie, you love me!' and they held each other embraced. It would not have been possible to say who first clasped the other" (p. 95). ("Du liebst mich! rief er aus: Ottilie du liebst mich! und sie hielten einander umfasst. Wer das andere zuerst ergriffen, wäre nicht zu unterscheiden gewesen" [p. 75].) Again that crucial word *unterscheiden,* but this time it refers to a loss of distinction, or an inability to differentiate, that is welcome. The observation that it would not have been possible to say who first clasped the other indicates a very profound feature of this particular attraction, for it is a mark, not of a relationship based on symmetrical differences and reciprocities, but rather of one based on identity, and thus no relationship at all. There is no male initiative leading to female response, no dialogue of gestures, in this crucial moment of physical contact. It is as if each is losing himself in the other. Notice that Edward does not say "I love you, Ottilie," but rather "Ottilie, you love me." That there is something profoundly narcissistic in this relationship is of course its most significant aspect, but more important is just what the narcissism implies. Two want to become one and to be done with difference and separation. But two cannot become one. They can only become zero. And that is the latent but inevitable conclusion of this particular attraction. If this is a desire or drive that is engendered by the marriage, then there is indeed something monstrous about it, and nothing is but what is not. "From this moment on the world was turned upside down for Edward, he was no longer what he had been, nor the world what it had been" (p. 95). ("Von diesem Augenblick an war die Welt für Eduarden umgewendet, er nicht mehr, was er gewesen, die Welt nicht mehr, was sie gewesen" [p. 75].) *Umwenden* is "to turn inside out" or "to turn over," and what life is like in the bourgeois home when everything is just as it was and at the same time is *umgewendet* is what Goethe is to examine for the remainder of the book. Perhaps the most radical effect it has is summed up in Edward's words to Ottilie later on. "Why shouldn't I utter the hard words: this child was begotten in double adultery! It separates me from my wife, and my wife from me, whereas it should have united us" (p. 249). ("Warum soll ich das harte Wort nicht aussprechen: dieses Kind ist aus einem doppelten Ehbruch erzeugt! es

trennt mich von meiner Gattin und meine Gattin von mir, wie es uns
hätte verbinden sollen" [p. 191].)

In the same chapter (which, as I indicated, follows immediately on the
one describing the night Edward and Charlotte spend together), Charlotte for her part finds herself alone with the Captain in a boat and at the
conclusion of the trip allows herself to be kissed passionately. The kiss is
"*almost* returned" (p. 97) ("*beinahe* zurückgegeben" [p. 77]), and it is that
almost that denotes the basic difference between the relationship Charlotte has with the Captain and Edward's with Ottilie. For in that *almost*
lies all the felt constraints of the marriage vows, the restraining pauses
that law can put on passion. I will return to this kiss and the occasion, but
I want first to point to what follows, since it gives a very clear instance of
that kind of power of place and dominance of context that I have tried to
outline in connection with the influence of the architecture on its inhabitants. Charlotte returns to her bedroom. "But now she was standing in
her bedroom where she must have the feelings of being Edward's wife
and to regard herself as such" (p. 98). ("Nun aber stand sie in ihrem
Schlafzimmer, wo sie sich als Gattin Eduards empfinden und betrachten
musste" [p. 78].) Out on the lake she does not know quite what she is and
this disturbs her, but back in the house it is different. The site bespeaks
her classification and dictates her feelings. *Schlafzimmer* → *Gattin* → *musste.* Charlotte is adhering to the imperatives of the locale, and she does it
by literally reenacting the moment of her "wifing."

> As she had always been accustomed to be aware of her personality and
> to exercise self-control, it was not difficult for her now to come close to the
> desired equanimity by the exercise of serious thoughts; indeed she could
> not help smiling at herself when she thought of the unusual visit of the
> previous night. Yet a strange foreboding quickly came upon her, a joyfully
> anxious trembling that dissolved into pious wishes and hopes. Feeling
> moved, she knelt down and repeated the promise that she had made to
> Edward at the altar. Joyful images of friendship, affection and resignation
> passed through her mind. She felt inwardly refreshed. Soon sweet tired-
> ness seized her, and she went peacefully to sleep.
>
> (P. 98)

> Immer gewohnt sich ihrer selbst bewusst zu sein, sich selbst zu gebieten,
> ward es ihr auch jetzt nicht schwer, durch ernste Betrachtung sich dem
> erwünschten Gleichgewichte zu nähern; ja sie musste über sich selbst
> lächeln, indem sie des wunderlichen Nachtbesuches gedachte. Doch
> schnell ergriff sie eine seltsame Ahnung, ein freudig bängliches Erzittern,
> das in fromme Wünsche und Hoffnungen sich auflöste. Gerührt kniete sie
> nieder, sie wiederholte den Schwur, den sie Eduarden vor dem Altar ge-
> tan. Freundschaft, Neigung, Entsagen gingen vor ihr in heitern Bildern

vorüber. Sie fühlte sich innerlich weider hergestellt. Bald ergreift sie eine
süsse Müdigkeit und ruhig schläft sie ein.

(Pp. 77-78)

Having been disturbed by nascent passion, she seeks to reestablish tł
"desired equanimity" ("erwünschten Gleichgewichte") by, as it were,
turning herself into Edward's wife all over again; a not unfamiliar
psychic strategy whereby a feeling of harmony and security may be
sought for in repetition, the reinstitution into the problematical present
of some already established formula (or ritual, or vow, whatever) familiar from the past. Charlotte "did" (*getan*) her marriage vows or oaths
(*den Schwur*)—a rather odd formulation, since it is more usual to *ablegen*,
"lay down," or "take," an oath; but that is perhaps appropriate, since in a
sense it is an improvised pseudoritual, part of a mnemonic device for the
forestalling of any onset of any disequilibrating passion. It is in part a
reaction to that *seltsame Ahnung*—"strange foreboding"—and the somewhat paradoxical (and hence potentially confusing) *freudig bängliches
Erzittern*—"joyfully anxious trembling"—that temporarily seizes her. Her
stabilizing strategies also include the diversion of anxiety into piety, and
the cultivation of images of, among other things, renunciation (*Entsagen*), an important word for Goethe and, needless to say, an indispensable adjunct, or constituent, of the very concept of marriage, giving up all
others and cleaving unto one. If, however, the other no longer wishes to
be clung to, then inevitably the problems arise, and indeed the very
scene of Charlotte alone in her bedroom "doing" her vows conveys more
sense of solitude than of marriedness and suggests that the vows have, in
certain key aspects, become empty. But at this point Charlotte can still
induce that sense of sentimental content and that *süsse Müdigkeit* ("sweet
tiredness") that, rather than any high-pitched intensities of passion and
desire or pangs of longing and yearning, is what, one imagines, the good
bourgeois wife most likes to go to sleep feeling.

Country Living and Secret Passions

One other aspect of the architecture in the book should be mentioned
at this point. The four main characters are said to be in "circumstances
of country living and secret passions" (p. 76) ("ihrem ländlichen und

heimlich leidenschaftlichen Zustande" [p. 62]), being thus midway between the desocialized Mittler and the completely socialized Count and Baroness. On the surface level of country living, the main energies are directed to conscious planning and preservation at all levels. Charlotte makes a specialty of attempting to remove anything that might be harmful or "death bringing" (p. 31) ("tödliche" [p. 28]), the lead glaze on pottery, rust on copper vessels, and so on—just as she has transformed the graveyard into a pleasant place, with the gravestones removed and leant against the wall, and the mounds of individual graves leveled down. This is part of the bourgeois instinct to defer and deny death by concealing its marks and erasing the evidence of its continual encroachment. Similarly the two men, under the leadership of the Captain, set up a first-aid center because of the proximity of so many lakes, streams, and water constructions, and attempt to introduce order and cleanliness in the manner of the Swiss and to improve the estate—for instance, by erecting a proper communal wall to protect the village against the river. An insolent beggar intrudes on this benevolent planning, and they discuss methods both to depersonalize charity and to encourage beggars to leave the village by giving them exit money when they leave. This is all part of an attempt to tidy up, organize, contain and preserve. The socially unassimilable (the beggar) must be extruded: he must be deindividualized into a general category, which can then be dealt with administratively rather than confronted existentially in his unalterable individuality. Other figures help in this assault on the unclassified confusion of nture or the humanly unclassifiable that insists on obtruding itself within the social realm. For instance, the old gardener with his fear of "the limitless field of botany" (p. 213) ("unendlichen Felde der Botanik" [p. 163]) suggests this desire to work within manageable limits and distinctions, and the local boys are regimented into an army of gardeners. In addition to Mittler there are other maintainers of culture—controllers, tenders, and builders—such as the architect and the teacher. In the human realm as in the realm of botany and architecture, there is constant conservation and preservation work as well as the erection of new buildings, an overall attempt to keep clean a continuity of edifices and structures. One result of all this attempt to tidy up or repress or organize all the confusion that is felt to obtain in the limitless realm that lies beyond the boundaries of the particular culture of the moment is that the confusion returns in new forms right at the center of the bourgeois citadel—in the marriage bed of Edward and Charlotte.

Minds constantly conscious of the importance of surface architecture will inevitably become aware of depths. Thus Edward, aware that "walls and bolts separate" (p. 99) him from Ottilie ("Mauern und Riegel . . .

trennen uns jetzt" [pp. 78–79]), starts to imagine that "he could hear below the earth's surface the burrowing of busy animals to whom day and night are one" (p. 99) ("das wühlende Arbeiten emsiger Tiere unter der Erde vernehmen konnte, denen Tag und Nacht gleich sind" [p. 79]). And on the day of the laying of the foundation stone of the new building that they have planned together, the stonemason delivers a somewhat sententious speech. Holding his trowel and hammer and standing below ground level, where the stone will be layed, he says:

> "It is a serious concern, and our invitation to you is serious; for this solemn occasion is a matter of depths. Here inside this narrow, hollowed out space you do us the honour of appearing as witnesses to our secret work. . . .
>
> We could put into place without further ado this foundation-stone. . . . But here too there must be no lack of mortar, the binding medium; just as people who turn towards each other by nature are held together even better when they are cemented by law, so stones also, which fit together already by their shape, are combined even better by this unifying force. . . ."
>
> (P. 67)

> "Es ist ein ernstes Geschäft und unsere Einladung ist ernsthaft: denn diese Feierlichkeit wird in der Tiefe begangen. . . . Hier innerhalb dieses engen ausgegrabenen Raums erweisen Sie uns die Ehre als Zeugen unseres geheimnisvollen Geschäftes zu erscheinen. . . .
>
> Diesen Grundstein . . . könnten wir ohne weiteres niederlegen. . . . Aber auch hier soll es am Kalk, am Bindungsmittel nicht fehlen: denn so wie Menschen, die einander von Natur geneigt sind, noch besser zusammenhalten, wenn das Gesetz sie verkittet, so werden auch Steine, deren Form schon zusammenpasst, noch besser durch diese bindenden Kräfte vereinigt."
>
> (P. 55)

He continues with his interpretation of the significance of his work which is conducted in terms of the society that hires him and commissions his work. He works with conventional tools and materials and speaks with established precepts and tropes, and the two are interrelated. The idea of the foundations—which are both essential to the house and yet immersed in the undomesticated earth, both carefully built and then sedulously covered over—leads him to speak of the individual's awareness of his inner, buried secret intentions and acts. It provides a metaphor to think *with,* so it becomes uncertain as to whether the hidden part of the bourgeois mind containing memory, desire, and concealed intent "creates" the hidden foundations of the bourgeois house, or whether those foundations help to create that part of the bourgeois mind. Covert and secret work in the realm of architecture easily feeds back into a suggestion of comparable divisions within the people to whom the buildings belong. The proposition that we build as we are, now awakens the counterecho that in fact we are as we build; in constructing our houses we are also constructing a model of our minds, which we may then employ when it comes to thinking about the stratifications of consciousness we sense within us. Above all, it seems to me in the case of bourgeois society—oriented as it is around private property in which communal patternings can be replaced to some extent by personal choice in matters of design—it is possible to say that people do not so much put their heads into their houses as their houses into their heads.

In the atmosphere of determining suggestions and signs through which the main characters in the book move, I want to single out two more that may seem opposed, but in their ultimate effects prove not to be. I am referring to the influence of both man-made objects and the natural terrain. At the stone-laying ceremony a glass is drained and then thrown into the air. It is usually allowed to fall and break, but one of the workmen catches it, thinking of it as a happy omen. It has the initials E and O cut into it and was a glass made for Edward in his youth. He buys it from the workman—again the power of money—and clings to it as a sign with personal significance for him. "My fate and Ottilie's cannot be separated and we are not going to be brought to destruction. . . . Look at this glass! Our initials are carved in it. . . . I drink out of it every day so that I can convince myself daily that all relationships which fate has decreed are indestructible" (p. 136). ("Mein Schicksal und Ottiliens ist nicht zu trennen und wir werden nicht zu Grunde gehen. Sehen Sie dieses Glas! Unsere Namenszüge sind darein geschnitten . . . und ich trinke nun täglich daraus, um mich täglich zu überzeugen: dass alle Verhältnisse unzerstörlich sind, die das Schicksal beschlossen hat" [p. 104].) Mittler attacks this attempt to make everyday life portentous, but the more important point is the power of the returning object. Made for Edward as a youth, that is to say inserted into his immediate environment without his choice, the glass now returns as something of which he avails himself to give definition to his affective inner life. In this it may stand for all the objects that would surround such a childhood; starting off simply as things that a wealthy middle-class family can afford to purchase or to have made to amplify their domestic rituals, they are transformed into signs. As such they comprise a second discourse into which the child—Edward—is born and which, like language itself, speaks him as much as he speaks and uses it.

Another such object is the miniature of her father that Ottilie keeps round her neck on a chain. Pictures and paintings of various kinds are indeed conspicuous in this book, comprising a nonlingual order of representations about which more must be said. At this point I just want to refer to the incident when Edward and Ottilie are out walking. They walk from the castle gate down as near as they can come to the water; they then press along a path that is overgrown; soon they are, temporarily, lost among "thick undergrowth between moss-covered rocks" (p. 56) ("und sie fanden sich im dichten Gebüsch zwischen moosigem Gestein verirrt" [p. 47]). There is no *real* danger of getting lost—the terrain is all within the confines of the known—but in little it is a suggestive progress from the realm of the totally structured (castle gate) to that of the unstructured or uncharted (undergrowth and rocks), suggestive not so much for us as for them. For immediately following this venture, Edward asks Ottilie to remove the miniature of her father "not from your mind or your room," but "from your breast" (p. 57) ("entfernen Sie das Bild, nicht aus Ihrem Andenken, nicht aus Ihrem Zimmer . . . nur von Ihrer Brust" [p. 48]). His ostensible reason for this is that it might be dangerous for her, but in asking her to remove the image of her father from her physical presence (and note that he is well aware of room, mind, and body as being interrelated areas), he is effectively asking her to move beyond the area of rigid prohibitions centered in this society (as in most others) on the authority of "the father," into an area in which the instituted imperatives governing relationship are, temporarily, obliterated or out of sight. In response, Ottilie gives Edward the picture of her father, thus participating in the under-language of the occasion, for she is allowing Edward to replace the father and all that that figure implies. He understands. "He felt as if a stone had fallen from his heart, as if a barrier between himself and Ottilie had been removed" (p. 58). ("Ihm war, als wenn ihm ein Stein vom Herzen gefallen wäre, als wenn sich eine Scheidewand zwischen ihm und Ottilien niedergelegt hätte" [p. 49].) Shortly after this, when they are all discussing the best place to site the proposed summer house, Ottilie suggests building it at a point on a hill where it could be concealed, and they would not be able to see the castle and "the village and all the houses would be hidden" (p. 60) ("das Dorf und alle Wohnungen verborgen wären" [p. 50]). The advantage of this would be that they would find themselves "in a different, new world" (p. 60) ("einer andern und neuen Welt" [p. 50]). The idea of a new world out of sight of the existing architecture is a direct outcome of her earlier experience of the terrain and its inducement to elude the binding image of the father. Sometime later, when the stonemason asks people to contribute objects to be buried in the foundations of the new house, Ottilie finally puts in the golden chain on which her father's picture had hung. Here again, the idea of burying objects in the earth, raised to heightened significance by the interpretations of the stonemason, precipitates a gesture expressing the inclination to break the binding links with the past. But the language of that gesture is not Ottilie's own; it belongs to the chain, the stonemason, the architecture, and the terrain. At the end, when she is preparing for death, another "secret activity" (p. 280) ("eine heimliche Geschäftigkeit" [p. 213]), Ottilie packs up various precious objects in a casket, including the portrait of her father. In object language she is signifying a return to the past, to the primal authority from which she never really escaped. For a new world is a delusion in this excessively mapped and charted society—one can only be temporarily put out of sight, and such strategies of *concealment* are mute testimony to the recognition that the given order cannot be *changed*. The *transposition* of objects—picture and chain—leaves the society that *produced* those objects totally unaltered.

Having briefly considered the role played by household activities (topography, writing, gardening, etc.), names, architecture, objects and terrain, in determining the conceptualization of their social world by the main characters, one more element should be noted—water. In the landscape of the book, it is permanently present as that which can be dammed, or allowed to flow, but which itself cannot be mapped or differentiated. When Edward, Charlotte, and the Captain are at one point planning to cross the lake, Edward pushes off the boat and then jumps ashore to return to Ottilie. Charlotte is disturbed to find herself on "the uncertainly swaying element" (p. 96) ("dem schwankenden Element" [p. 76]), since, among other things, its suggests that they might travel "in any direction they might choose" (p. 96) ("in beliebiger Richtung" [p. 76]). It has a curious effect on her sense of reality—for she is in a realm that cannot be tended or tidied, cleaned or controlled, and some sense of nonrelatedness or not belonging induces a mood of sadness and fear. This produces the first fissure in her bourgeois consciousness, for although she asks to be put back on dry land, in the course of being translated from the "uncertainly swaying element" to the one where she is at home, she allows the Captain to kiss her "passionately" (p. 97) ("lebhaft" [p. 77]), and the moment is recognized as decisive. Competent and wakeful administrator as she is, she decides that they must change their situations, since they can't change their minds: "wenn wir den Mut haben unsere Lage zu ändern, da es von uns nicht abhängt unsere Gesinnung zu ändern" (p. 78)—*Lage* implying here their actual location and posture; hence her dislike of the water, where nothing and no one can be arranged. But Ottilie is drawn to it. Later on when Charlotte is pregnant and feeling fulfilled, she occupies herself happily around the house and garden. Ottilie by contrast has "lost everything" (p. 129) ("verlor alles" [p. 99]) and feels "an unending emptiness" ("eine unendliche Leere"), experiencing her life as "lack" ("Mangel") and "deprivation" ("Entbehrung").

She is drawn to the middle of the lake, where she reads travel books and dreams herself "into the far distance" (p. 130) ("träumte sich in die Fremde" [p. 100]), thinking of her absent friend (Edward). The lake thus becomes a place set over from the realm of housework, in which she has no part, for the house tells her only of her own emptiness. On the water she can fill that emptiness with images and dreams. Through book and revery the absent world becomes present, to compensate for a present world that for her has become absence. All of this is unrelated to the inherent properties of water; it is what water becomes for the house-bound mind—depending on your relationship to the house, it becomes a realm of unreality (Charlotte) or an alternative area, preferable to reality (Ottilie). That it is a realm in which people can literally drown is, of course, central to the book. Thus, at the celebrations to mark the opening of the house (and Ottilie's birthday), part of the crowd gathered to watch the fireworks fall into the lake, but only because the ground has been rendered insecure by the building of the dam—an irony basic to the book whereby, in attempting to put up barriers (at many levels), the custodians inadvertently create new possibilities for the collapsing of one element, or realm, or person, into another. Protective separation precipitates unplanned mergings. On this particular occasion the Captain saves one boy from drowning; like Charlotte, he is a person of the land and can rescue those in the water. By contrast, when Ottilie finds herself on the lake with Charlotte's baby—overexcited at a meeting with Edward and what seems like the possibility of their being able to come together—she unintentionally brings about its drowning. In trying to handle the oar, her book, and the baby, she falls and lets all three fall into the water. This is of a piece with her general inability to handle discrete orders of objects; indeed, her whole relationship to the object world is extremely tenuous. If this suggests her unaptness for the categories that separate people and things on the land, it also intimates her insecure grasp of the difference between the categories of life and death. It is as accurate to say that she finds her mode of existence on water, as it is to say that water finds its mode of existence in her. This is not to anthropomorphize an element but rather to note the kind of influential reciprocities that Goethe's novel suggests. If Ottilie finds her home on the water (as she effectively does), by an inversion of terms, the water finds its home in her. In the domesticated world depicted in this novel, the possibility of such inversions is part of the condition in which the characters live. Maps, names, houses, objects, terrain, and even the elements, all can take up house in those that have housed them. This, it seems to me, is one of the main points that Goethe is suggesting in his depiction of certain kinds of emerging high-bourgeois consciousness (as opposed to the completely socialized existence of the aristocracy living on simply as titles). For the country living of Edward and Charlotte and the Captain—and, by invitation if not by inclination, Ottilie—is not the same thing as the country house of the eighteenth-century gentleman or the retreat of the Horatian ideal. It is a new kind of totality: the world made by the bourgeois.

In calling it a totality, I wish to point to the fact that everything within it—land as well as house—can be arranged according to the disposition of the owners; and also to note that there is nowhere outside this world, ultimately, where life can be conducted on entirely different premises (the beggar and Mittler, for example, effectively inhabit nonsocial voids within society). This is revealed in such small recurring phenomena as the fact that although the four main characters may separate and go off in different directions in different combinations, they always find themselves coming together again. Death is, of course, the one outside or way out left, and both Ottilie and Edward do die in the course of the book— appropriately, as I shall try to suggest. But a certain tyrannous symmetry outlives them. The book starts with two; it is expanded to four; it returns to two. For the individuals involved, things are not the same. (At the end of the novel of adultery, "things can never again be as they were"—as Kate Croy says at the end of *Wings of a Dove*.) But the overall geometry survives them. It is as though no matter how many different paths the characters take—paths that may separate or come together, as described in the first chapter—they must inevitably return to the same places, no matter how different they may feel inwardly.

Combining and Separating

> When we reflect on nature, or the history of mankind, or of our own intellectual activity, the first picture presented to us is of an endless maze of relations and interactions, in which nothing remains what, where and as it was, but everything moves, changes, comes into being and passes out of existence—Engels: *Anti-Dühring*

The characters in the book are very aware, in theory at least, of the endless changes of relationships that constitute society and nature alike. In their own ways, along their own paths, they continually go apart and come together in different combinations, though within the limited and well-defined world in which they move, such changes of relationship are very circumscribed, and the tendency is always to return to their original positions. But in conversation and speculation they can range much wider, as they do in the long discussion in which the title phrase appears.[7] It starts with reference to "kinship" (p. 32) ("Verwandtschaften" [p. 29]) among people and thence to consideration of kinship among "inanimate things" ("leblosen Dingen"). As Edward says, "man is a true Narcissus; he likes to see his own reflection in everything" ("der Mensch ist ein wahrer Narziss; er bespiegelt sich überall gern selbst"). This is correct, but since he himself turns out to be completely narcissistic, the knowledge does not help him. The Captain continues the conversation by explaining that all living things have "connections" with one another ("einen Bezug auf sich selbst haben" [p. 30]). Bezug can mean reference as well as relationship, and the word implies some kind of reciprocity, though here the construction is self-reflexive and that standard translation "connections" does not, perhaps, quite convey the sense of the phrase that very loosely implies "every thing has a concern for itself"—thus suggesting that in their singularity and difference, things "will linger near to each other as strangers, and will refuse to bind themselves even after mechanical mixing and fricture like oil and water" (p. 34). ("Dagegen werden andre fremd nebeneinander verharren und selbst durch mechanisches Mischen und Reiben sich keineswegs verbinden; wie Öl und Wasser" [p. 31].) Mischen und Reiben are words that could well apply to the forced propinquities and muffled frictions taking place between the people in that very house. Clearly what is being touched on here is the very basis of culture, for things first have to be divided and then related in order to give any meaning and pattern to life (this is how the anthropologists interpret Genesis). The conversation moves from people to chemistry, where the same metaphors are employed. Among people you find different classes who stand opposed to each other, refusing to mix, like oil and water—Charlotte mentions the social classes: "the professions, the nobility and the third estate, the soldier and the civilian" (p. 35) ("die Stände, die Berufsbestimmungen, der Adel und der dritte Stand, der Soldat und der Zivilist" [p. 31]). But as Edward points out, society has ways of uniting what it has separated. "And what is more, just as those classes may be unified through customs and laws, so there are mediating factors too in our world of chemistry which can unite those

---

[7]The conversation on relationships is marked by two notable omissions—the relationships based on money and those based on the different modes of production in society; just the relationships that Marx was to study so intensely. "Besides calling capital a 'social production relation' (Verhältnis), Marx refers to money as a 'relation of production,' the mode of production itself as the 'relation in which the productive forces are developed' . . . His use of 'relation' as a synonym of 'connection' is more extensive still, with the result that Verhältnis probably occurs more frequently than any other expression in Marx's writing. . . ." (Bertell Ollman, Alienation [Cambridge: Cambridge University Press, 1971], p. 16). It occurs quite frequently in Goethe's novel as well, but eluding, and thus mystifying, the particular kinds of relations that Marx set out to demystify and clarify.

things which otherwise repel one another" (p. 35). ("Und doch, versetzte Eduard, wie diese durch Sitten und Gesetze vereinbar sind, so gibt es auch in unserer chemischen Welt Mittelglieder, dasjenige zu verbinden, was sich einander abweist" [p. 31].) Just how efficacious mediation may be when it comes to holding together people who have begun to repel each other is one of the inquiries of the book.[8]

As the discussion continues and examples are drawn from alkalies and acids and so on, what becomes clear is that the one topic—separation and relationship—is being explored on different metaphoric levels. In chemistry there are natures that grasp each other as though manifesting a "desire for unity" (p. 35) ("Eine entschiedene Vereinigungslust" [p. 31]); as Charlotte says, such natures would seem to be less like "blood relations" ("Blutsverwandte" [p. 32]), a nexus in which one finds onself without choice, and more like a "kindred of mind and soul" (p. 31) ("Geistes- und Seelenverwandte" [p. 32]). What is being opened up is the problem of relationships based on law, custom, and choice. "Elective affinities" ("die Wahlverwandtschaften") appear to operate in the realm of inanimate nature, as the Captain says in describing certain experiments. (The title itself poses a potential paradox, since *Verwandtschaften* are the family relationships, i.e., the ones you do not, in fact, and cannot choose [*wählen*]. Goethe's use of the word [and, outside of German eighteenth-century chemistry, the use of it would seem to be his alone or a reference back to his use of it] points exactly to the paradox of

---

[8]This whole conversation concerning attraction, separation, and displacement, is not, of course, unique to Goethe. In the field of science it had been a topic during the eighteenth century. I will simply quote François Jacob:

> What maintained the particles in place and bound them together to form a coherent universe was the force of attraction. This was not a component of the universe. It had no part in its construction but between all the constituent atoms of the universe it wove a network of dependencies giving cohesion to the world. It was the concept of gravitation that provided chemists with a force to replace the astral influences which, for the alchemists, had linked metals to stars and planets. When substances were blended, they did not remain inert but displaced one another. Thus between different bodies relations could be found which made them combine more or less readily. According to Geoffroy, when two substances with "some disposition to join together" were united, if a third appeared which had more affinity for one of them, it united with it "by making the other loose its hold." The force connecting certain corpuscles of different nature was called "affinity." It was no longer a magic principle, a virtue similar to those which alchemy attributed to substances. It was a property of bodies which could be measured by determining the order in which they displace one another.
>
> (*The Logic of Life*—chapter 1, "The Visible Structure")

The relevance of this to Goethe's novel is obvious, but perhaps we can say that he was the first writer to adopt and adapt these terms and problems from the realm of chemistry and apply them to the realm of human beings, so that, in a way, he wrote the first major novel dealing with attraction and displacement. (Geoffroy, incidentally, published his work in 1743, so it is quite possible that Goethe was familiar with it.)

marriage—that it is notionally a voluntary nonblood relationship that immediately becomes a binding blood relationship; the point of transformation is, as it were, indistinguishable, since it occupies no place or point in time; I am not simply referring to the conclusion of the actual ritual but more to a merging of categories that the parties undergo, a merging Goethe has marked by eliding the usually discrete and mutually exclusive words *choice* and *kinship*.) But as Charlotte points out, the union may be the result of the chemist who brought the materials together—"Opportunity occasions relationship" (p. 37) ("Gelegenheit macht Verhältnisse" [p. 33]). Speaking of such experiments, Edward notes that "the relationships are only interesting when they effect divorces" (p. 36) ("die Verwandtschaften werden erst interessant, wenn sie Scheidungen bewirken" [p. 32]), and that chemists used to be called "past masters in separation" (p. 36) ("Scheidekünstler" [p. 32]). In reply, Charlotte, thinking of the implications of the word *divorce* in the social realm, says, "Combining is a greater art and service. An artist in unification would be welcome for every occasion in the whole world." (p. 36) ("Das Vereinigen ist eine grössere Kunst, ein grösseres Verdienst. Ein Einigungskünstler wäre in jedem Fache der ganzen Welt willkommen" [p. 32]). The problem—once you move from the inanimate world dominated by natural laws and enter the social one in which law, custom, and choice are all operative in deciding 'divorces' and combinations—is that there is no control in advance on what may precipitate attraction or repulsion. Therefore, within the formulae laid down by society, many alterations of position may take place, though the formulae themselves cannot finally be changed. Charlotte wants to get beyond allegory, playing with the resemblances between the inanimate and the human realm, and to hold onto the uniquely human meaning of the words "kinship by choice." But the very phrase contains a paradox and potential disintegration, for what may be combined by kinship may be separated by choice. In the long discussion about the various experiments conducted in contemporary chemistry, the characters themselves are effectively creating the experiment in which they will be the materials.[9]

---

[9]The interest in "experiments," and the somewhat improvised use of them, is so important in this book, that it is worth noting some comments by Lukács, disputing Engels's ideas of the significance of "experiment."

> But Engels' deepest misunderstanding consists in his belief that the behaviour of industry and scientific experiment constitutes praxis in the dialectical, philosophical sense. In fact, scientific experiment is contemplation at its purest. The experimenter creates an artificial, abstract milieu in order to be able to *observe* undisturbed the untrammelled workings of the laws under examination, eliminating all irrational factors both of the subject and the object. He strives as far as possible to reduce the material substratum of his observation to the purely rational "product," to the "intelligible matter" of mathematics.

This conversation takes place between the three of them before Ottilie has arrived, and much of it concerns the problems of the interrelationships between three substances, which can then be resolved in a new way by introducing a fourth. The proposition is that two substances may exist in a stable combination; the introduction of a third may precipitate an instability whereby a new union excludes one of the initial substances. At which point the chemists can bring in a fourth to effect a further combination "so that no one goes empty away" (p. 38) ("damit keines leer ausgehe" [p. 33]). A comment on this by the Captain extends beyond the situation to suggest problems of patterning and relationships that touch not only on this novel but on many other bourgeois novels of adultery. Taking up Edward's comments on the chemist's experiments with four substances he says:

> "Yes, indeed! . . . these cases are in fact the most important and peculiar ones, where it is possible to describe attraction and relationship, this parting and uniting, so to speak in a really crosswise fashion where four substances, up to now linked together in two pairs, are brought in contact with each other, abandon their previous union and bind themselves together afresh. In this process of letting go and seizing, of fleeing and seeking, you really do believe you're seeing a higher destiny; you ascribe to such substances a kind of wishing and choosing and take the invented words 'kinship by choice' as wholly justified."[10]
>
> (P. 38)

> "Ja wohl! . . . diese Fälle sind allerdings die bedeutendsten und merkwürdigsten, wo man das Anziehen, das Verwandtsein, dieses Verlassen, dieses Vereinigen gleichsam übers Kreuz, wirklich darstellen kann; wo vier, bisher je zwei zu zwei verbundene, Wesen in Berührung gebracht, ihre bisherige Vereinigung verlassen und sich aufs neue verbinden. In diesem Fahrenlassen und Ergeifen, in diesem Fliehen und Suchen glaubt man wirklich eine höhere Bestimmung zu sehen; man traut solchen Wesen eine Art von Wollen und Wählen zu, und hält das Kunstwort Wahlverwandtschaften für vollkommen gerechtfertigt."
>
> (Pp. 33-34)

(Georg Lukács, *History and Class Consciousness: Studies in Marxist Dialectics*, trans. Rodney Livingstone [Cambridge, Mass.: The MIT Press, 1971], p. 132.)

In Goethe's novel, experiments tend to follow the description offered by Lukács and, at the conscious level, certainly emphasize observation and not praxis—though, as I am intimating, by a curious reversal, the experiments will effectively turn on the characters and experiment on them.

[10]Something of what the Captain is talking about—and what the characters find themselves involved in—is implied in the word *metathesis*, which refers not only to the transposition of sounds of letters in a word (cf. the relationships between their names I referred to above) but also, in chemistry, to a double decomposition, as when two compounds react with each other to form two other compounds. On one level, Goethe's novel may be said to incorporate a study of relational metathesis.

He then says that he cannot really explain this in words but will show it by actual experiments which are tangible and visible. "These creatures, that seem to be dead and yet are always inwardly prepared for activity, must be seen active before one's eyes and observed sympathetically in the way they seek each other out, attract, seize, destroy, swallow and consume one another, and after that emerge again from this most intimate union in renewed, novel and unexpected shape . . ." (p. 38). ("Man muss diese totscheinenden und doch zur Tätigkeit innerlich immer bereiten Wesen wirkend vor seinen Augen sehen, mit Teilnahme schauen, wie sie einander suchen, sich anziehen, ergreifen, zerstören, verschlingen, aufzehren und sodann aus der innigsten Verbindung wieder in erneuter, neuer, unerwarteter Gestalt hervortreten" [p. 34].) We may note that this is a good description of what we, as readers, do as we "watch" a novel in which the chemist-author arranges just such a human experiment for us. The matter is made more complicated by the discussion of the most suitable form of projection of such an experiment. The Captain says that you need to see the actual experiment, that ordinary words and technical terms give no adequate "picture" ("Vorstellung"). Edward then says that the relationships he is talking about can be expressed by letters. The Captain makes use of this "language of signs" (p. 39) ("Zeichensprache" [p. 34]), and he outlines a diagrammatics of contacts and relationships using the letters *A, B, C, D,* which Edward takes up and applies to their own situation: "let us look at this formula as a figure of speech from which we may deduce a lesson of immediate use" (p. 39) ("wollen wir diese Formel als Gleichnisrede betrachten, woraus wir uns eine Lehre zum unmittelbaren Gebrauch ziehen" [p. 34]). There are the *A, B, C,* and this obviously suggests the need for a *D* to complete the requisite "experiment" ("der Versuch"). Of course the irony, on one level, is that he regards himself and Charlotte as *A* and *B* and thinks of the Captain and Ottilie as *C* and *D*. Such would be the chemically and socially logical symmetry. As it transpires, the patterning arranges itself as *AD* and *BC,* but it is within the formula laid down in this conversation. The larger irony is that the participants are largely unaware to what extent they are, as it were, the victims and servitors of the very language of signs, formulae, figures of speech with which they are amusing or enlightening themselves. In ways they cannot perceive, they are their own experiment.[11]

[11]Obviously much has been written on this topic, but for a very clear and early statement referring to this process by which language, or more specifically conversation, *creates* situations, consider the following passage from the work of George Herbert Mead:

Symbolization constitutes objects not constituted before, objects which would not exist except for the context of social relationships wherein symbolization occurs. Language does not simply symbolize a situation or object which is already there in

In all this, the point is not simply that we are being prepared for the problematical relationships that are about to develop and alerted to the possibility that natural and human laws of combining and separating may be at odds. We should note the whole situation. This is a relaxed evening conversation within the security of the house. The characters draw on different kinds of discourse to develop the discussion; a whole range of signs are referred to or used, extending from iconic or object language (the idea of an actual visible experiment) to pictures through words to the algebraic abstraction of letters. This range is detectable throughout the whole book. Within various social situations and gatherings there are tableaux (in which people transform themselves into object language), pictures, books with illustrations, written letters, maps, and so on. Within the house, then, the characters can play, or experiment, with a range of different projections or signs. What this indicates is an excess of metaphor over experience. It is as though as actual lived experience decreases in its range—and how circumscribed is the actual life in this bourgeois world!—the compulsion to extend consciousness in the realm of metaphor increases, whether these metaphors are taken from chemistry, literature, myth, painting, or any other source. These metaphors then become part of the mental furniture that helps to determine the consciousness of those who play with them in their idleness. The idleness is important to stress. What I am pointing to is something very different from a character in a play or a book who uses metaphor in an attempt to understand and articulate an experience in which he is immersed. Macbeth is evil, perhaps, but in his speaking he is not idle. But in the bourgeois house of Goethe's novel, tableaux, pictures, discussions, and experiments are essentially used as distractions to fill up empty time. They are not functionally related to the conditions of the

---

advance; it makes possible the existence or the appearance of that situation or object, for it is a part of the mechanism whereby that situation or object is created. The social process relates the responses of one individual to the gestures of another, as the meanings of the latter, and is thus responsible for the rise and existence of new objects in the social situation, objects dependent upon or constituted by these meanings. Meaning is thus not to be conceived, fundamentally, as a state of consciousness, or as a set of organized relations existing or subsisting mentally outside the field of experience into which they enter; on the contrary, it should be conceived objectively, as having its existence entirely within this field itself. The response of one organism to the gesture of another in any given social act is the meaning of that gesture, and also is in a sense responsible for the appearance or coming into being of the new object—or new content of an old object—to which that gesture refers through the outcome of the given social act in which it is an early phase. For, to repeat, objects are in a genuine sense constituted within the social process of experience, by the communication and mutual adjustment of behavior among the individual organisms which are involved in that process and which carry it on.

(*Mind, Self, and Society*, p. 78)

characters' existence. The results of this are potentially far-reaching. Johann Gottfried Herder described human nature as "a texture for language." Bourgeois human nature, I suggest, becomes a texture for metaphor, or more generally for areas of signification that are not immediately functional within their living situation. Thus, images from chemistry, art, evolution, topography fill up the void time created by idleness; and since the characters do not set them to work, *they* set the characters to work. In this way the property owners become paradoxically owned by the metaphors they play with, or by the redundancy of signs and projections that they make use of during their leisure hours. In so doing, they effectively help to create the situations and patterns in which their unused energies will find formal expression.

A particularly notable example of this introduction of other constructs into the bourgeois setting is provided by the visiting English lord, who is a constant traveler. (He comes with a male companion while Edward and the Captain are away—two again becomes four.) Having lost interest in his own property, he has given himself over to restlessness, and the perpetual acquisition of pictures, curiosities, fragments of foreign information, and unusual anecdotes—these provide him with a second property of the mind, though he can no more settle in it than he could in his property in England. He is a collector without purpose, displaced from the role of an eighteenth-century gentleman but unable to adapt to a bourgeois mode of life. Thus he simply moves around gathering bits of the world in one place (with both his actual portable *camera obscura,* and the *camera obscura* of his memory) and exhibiting them in another. He is thus an unconscious agent for the kind of random dissemination of information without purpose that—although supposedly a desirable thing inasmuch as it extends the experience of the listeners or watchers—may have an incalculable disturbing influence by introducing dislocated fragments of foreignness into a closed setting. One result of this kind of peddling of vicarious experience is to turn the audience into passive consumers and voyeurs. Thus he shows the ladies a portfolio of pictures of the world amplified by his commentaries and "it gave them pleasure to travel through the world so comfortably, here in their solitude" (p. 220) ("Sie freuten sich, hier in ihrer Einsamkeit die Welt so bequem zu durchreisen" [p. 169]). But this kind of traveling without traveling—mental motion combined with physical inertia— instead of being educative (as we are still taught to believe), may effectively exacerbate the latent unrest of the audience without offering any true alternative avenues of action. Through pictures and words the world is transformed into a drawing-room commodity; the consuming consciousness may be glutted to no purpose, and what is left is once again a residue of images that cannot be applied to the current living situation. The lord's compulsive traveling has developed in him a need for constant change of "scene," just as he expects "fresh décor at the opera" (p. 222) ("wie man in der Oper immer wieder auf eine neue Dekoration wartet" [p. 171]) and moves from hotel to hotel so that he never has to worry about his own property or furniture or familiar objects. In this way he has severed all possibility of relationship between himself and the environment he is in—it is all scenery and décor—and thus he has made himself completely unessential, addicted to change that, since it can have no real significance for him, can have no end or fruition. In all this he is a negative image of what the bourgeois is striving for—the attempt to find significance in ownership, property, objects, and a maximum of organized routine within the house and grounds. It is an attempt at total stability set against a commitment to total restlessness. But the opposition is not so complete as it might seem. Where the traveler samples all contexts and domesticates himself in none, the bourgeois tries to isolate one context and see life in terms of this single model. But just as the traveling lord is glad of temporary hospitality— domesticity without the responsibilities of ownership, so the home owners are glad of temporary distraction—new experience without the ordeal of travel. They both want something for which they will incur no debts; it is a kind of complicitous swap testifying to a dangerous separation of human life into impossible aspirations towards complete stasis and endless motion. Sitting on his hosts' chairs, the traveling lord is providing dangerous furniture for the consciousness of his listeners.

In particular he introduces two paradigms that can only contribute to the latent unrest of his hosts, a novella and an experiment. The novella concerns a young couple who are initially supposed to get married, an arrangement favored by their respective families. But they rebel against this social planning and develop a destructive antipathy toward each other. They go their own ways, he into a successful career and she into an "official engagement" with an eminently suitable man. But having contracted this tie, she discovers that her resistance to her former friend had only been a form of concealed passion, so that she finds herself in a position where she is "indissolubly tied by society, family, fiancé, and her own assent' (p. 228) ("durch Welt und Familie, Bräutigam und eigene Zusage unauflöslich gebunden war" [p. 176]), while her natural inclinations urge her toward a quite different relationship. Seeing no way of effecting the change, she resolves to die, since if she cannot possess the man she wants, she can at least impose her dead "image" ("Bild") on his memory, and thus, as it were, possess his mind posthumously. The man arranges a boat trip for his old girl friend and her fiancé, and in the course of the trip the girl leaps into the water. The man jumps in to save her, "Water is a friendly element for those who are familiar with it and know how to treat it" (p. 230) ("Das Wasser ist ein freundliches Element für den, der damit bekannt ist und es zu behandeln weiss" [p. 177]), and brings her to dry land, away from all the people connected with their familiar social groups. There the girl, nearly dead, is undressed, and in her nakedness (without her social markings) she makes a direct passional appeal to the man, to which he responds. They then borrow some old wedding garments from a young couple in whose cottage they are resting, and in this "strange disguise" (p. 232) ("in ihrer sonderbaren Verkleidung" [p. 179]) they break the social ties they had formed and commit themselves to each other. It is as though only by changing their official vestments and confronting each other in a borrowed languge can they cut across the patterns to which they have committed themselves and come together in a new kind of engagement based on their own direct inclinations. "They had found their way from water to dry land, from death to life, from their family circle into a wilderness, from despair to rapture, from indifference to liking and passion, all in one moment . . ." (p. 232). (Sich vom Wasser zur Erde, vom Tode zum Leben, aus dem Familienkreise in eine Wildnis, aus der Verzweiflung zum Entzücken, aus der Gleichgütligkeit zur Neigung, zur Leidenschaf gefunden zu haben, alles in einem Augenblick" [p. 178].) Their new engagement is ratified when they return to society, and the mothers and fathers finally bestow their blessing on them. The whole story, with its central theme of a kind of thalassic regeneration allowing the couple to throw off the false relationships and roles decreed by their social position, and, through an archetypal rite of immersion / nakedness / new clothes find their true selves and bring their desires into alignment with a new social arranging, is in itself a kind of stereotype. Among other things, it is a classic pattern of comedies (as in Shakespeare), and as an aesthetic ordering it is too symmetrical and perfect to fit any specific social situationm. In fact it turns out that the story is a slightly "distorted" or "developed and decorated" (p. 234) version ("entstellt," "ausgebildet und ausgeschmückt" [p. 179]) of something that had happened to the Captain and a woman neighbor. It is thus close to the experience of Charlotte at least, and as such it is another disturbing pattern introduced into the house. It suggests a sequence of misarrangement followed by rearrangement, a misguided separation followed by totally felicitous combining, an achieved identity of passion and *law*, which is appealingly close to what the main participants in the novel think they desire but which only throws them back on the problems that the novella excludes. It is thus a metaphor of ideal congruence that tempts by its perfection and distrubs by its unrealizability. This simple novella contained within Goethe's complex novel provides an analogue for the situation in the novel in which simple metaphoric models are introduced into the complex consciousness of the characters, with ambiguous effects of imitation (if life could be like that) and alienation (what is wrong if life cannot be like that?). This is the latent torment caused by schematic simplifications of the partially relevant paradigm.

After the novella the lord conducts his experiment. It is based on the idea that there are "many connections and kinships which were at present concealed from us between inorganic materials, just as between organic and inorganic or organic and organic" (p. 236) ("sich gewiss noch manche Bezüge und Verwandtschaften unorganischer Wesen untereinander, organischer gegen sie und abermals untereinander, offenbaren würden, die uns gegenwärtig verborgen seien" [p. 181]). Since it transpires that Ottilie instinctively avoids a path below which it turns out there is a vein of coal, he proposes to conduct an experiment whereby an individual holds metals suspended by threads over other metals. He has his apparatus all ready, a small chest full of gold rings, iron ore, and other metals—again an example of his having collected fragments from various parts of the world that he can now use for a controlled experiment, which is also in part an evening distraction in the drawing room. When Charlotte holds the thread, there is no movement in the metals. When Ottilie does "the suspended object was agitated as if in a definite whirlpool; it turned, as the metals were changed underneath, now to one side, now to the other, at one time in circles, at another in ellipses, or else moved in straight lines" (p. 236) ("ward das Schwebende wie in einem entschiedenen Wirbel fortgerissen und drehte sich, je nachdem man die Unterlage wechselte, bald nach der einen, bald nach der andern Seite, jetzt in Kreisen, jetzt in Ellipsen, oder nahm seinen Schwung in graden Linien" [p. 181]). This would seem to indicate that whereas Charlotte is stable and "inner-directed," Ottilie is both extremely impressionable and susceptible to external forces and attractions. But to what extent it is a genuine scientific experiment, and what part Ottilie's own tremulous temperament might have played in introducing movement into the metals, is not established. She is in part enacting a theory that has already been suggested, or as we might say, she is taking on the role implied by the scientific novella that the lord and his friend have set up.

At this point we may consider the characters of the four protagonists as they emerge from the novel. Charlotte and the Captain share an instinct to arrange, preserve, control, and organize. They do in every sense bring things from water onto land, for while Charlotte is against the individuating reminders of death (the tombstones), she is totally in favor of maintaining the physical individuations of life, just as the Captain rescues the drowning body of the boy from the water and is ultimately against the merging of the three lakes. They are the appropriate masters of the house, and it is appropriate that toward the end Edward wants to give them "unrestricted authority to order everything relating to property, wealth; and materially desirable arrangements" (p. 247) ("Der Major und Charlotte sollten unterdessen unbeschränkte Vollmacht haben, alles was sich auf Besitz, Vermögen und die irdischen wünschenswerten Einrichtungen bezieht . . ." [p. 189]), as long as he can leave all responsibilities and just be with Ottilie. Two other characteristics are important. When Edward is trying to prevaricate at one point, Charlotte wants the matter "put into words" (p. 118) ("Warum sollen wir nicht mit Worten aussprechen" [p. 91]), for just as she and the Captain are the best at working with maps, so they prefer to clarify experience by dealing with it on the mapping level of language. Neither Edward nor Ottilie are quite at ease at this level. Also Charlotte is willing to accept "eternal separation" (p. 117) ("ewige Trennung" [p. 90])—and the word *Trennung*, with the multiple modes of severance and disconnection to which it can refer, occurs in many contexts and with increasing frequency throughout the book), while Edward says that his fate and Ottilie's "cannot be separated" (p. 136) ("Mein Schicksal und Ottiliens ist nicht zu trennen" [p. 104]). Since the level of language depends on separations, spaces, punctuations, it is related to the recognition that individuation is itself a state of separation, and though there may be the possibility of certain combinations, there can be no mergings. Everything in Edward tends in the opposite direction. He is spoiled; he cannot separate his papers according to subject (the Captain sorts out the mess): he has no gift for taxonomy at any level. This is related to a very uncertain hold on his own identity. There is one particularly significant moment when he registers his dislike of having someone look over his shoulder while he is reading; it puts him in a very uneasy situation between the otherness of the person and the otherness of the text. "What is written, the printed word, comes in place of my own thought and my own heart; and would I take the trouble to talk at all if a little window were fixed in front of my forehead or my breast so that the person to whom I wish to relate my thoughts and to offer my emotions in turn could already know a long time in advance what I was aiming at? When somebody looks over into my book, I always feel as if I were being torn into two pieces" (p. 32). ("Das Geschriebene, das Gedruckte tritt an die Stelle meines eigenen Sinnes, meines eigenen Herzens; und würde ich mich wohl zu reden bemühen, wenn ein Fensterchen vor meiner Stirn, vor meiner Brust angebracht wäre, so dass der, dem ich meine Gedanken einzeln zuzählen, meine Empfindungen einzeln zureichen will, immer schon lange vorher wissen könnte, wo es mit mir hinaus wollte? Wenn mir jemand ins Buch sieht, so ist mir immer, als wenn ich in zwei Stücke gerissen würde" [p. 29].) What he wants is to regress to some prelingual, pretextual, finally preindividuated mode of existence, where

there are no separating signs, but an impossible instantaneous copres-
ence of two-in-one—total identification instead of the mediations and
reciprocities by which individuals establish relationships.

When Ottilie arrives, the change in his role in the house begins. He
seems to get more childlike, he wastes money, he loses interest in the
property, he drinks more and in general loses his sense of moderation.
He is more excited by the fireworks display he puts on than in the more
laborious communications of social speech. Thus he tends to become
both eruptive and disintegrative, less interested in the steady continuities
of life than Charlotte and the Captain. He is drawn to any possible
"evidence" of merging and identity with Ottilie. He has headaches on the
right of his head, she on her left, so he says they will make nice
"counter-pictures" (p. 44) ("Gegenbilder" [p. 38]), as though this makes
them into mirror images. When he finds out that her handwriting is
exactly like his own (and, as previously noted, the style of handwriting is
always considered to be unique with each individual), "from this moment
the world was turned upside down for Edward, he was no longer what
he had been" (p. 95). ("Von diesem Augenblick an war die Welt für
Eduarden umgewendet, er nicht mehr, was er gewesen, die Welt nicht
mehr, was sie gewesen" [p. 75].) World and self are, for him, inverted,
reverted, even perverted. When he does attempt to separate himself
from Ottilie, he writes letters to himself in her name, which he then
answers in his own, and keeps the letters together—a narcissistic inversion of genuine epistolary communication. He also dreams about her
and himself. "Everything that happens between us becomes interlaced
and mingled. Sometimes we are signing a contract; there her hand and
mine, her name and mine are joined; both cancel out and consume each
other" (p. 133). ("Alles was mir mit ihr begegnet, schiebt sich durchund
übereinander. Bald unterschreiben wir einen Kontrakt; da ist ihre Hand
und die meinige, ihr Name und der meinige, beide löschen einander
aus, beide verschlingen sich" [p. 102].) *Verschlingen*, we may recall, is the
word the Captain uses to describe the mutually devouring animals in his
experiment.) It is the urge to cancel out the duality of self and other that
increasingly works through him, and after the death of the baby in the
lake and Ottilie's subsequent refusal to countenance the idea of any
legalized changes in the existing relationships, he himself turns towards
death, first of all seeking annihilation in war and then after Ottilie's
death simply by fading out of existence in his haste to join her. (He
declines the nourishment of both society and food.) Before their deaths
they withdraw completely from social relationships, seeking peace in
silent proximity. "Then they were not two people, but only one person in
unconscious complete easiness of spirit" (p. 276). ("Dann waren es nicht
zwei Menschen, es war nur ein Mensch im bewusstlosen vollkommen

Behagen" [p. 211].) There is no actual adultery between them, but the drive to annul differences and distances is a result of their inability to remain within the patterning that society has decreed for them. And any compulsion to make illicit remixings or reorderings within the existing framework is a version of "adultery." (The will to destroy or radically alter the framework would be revolutionary, but this is never considered in the bourgeois novel. Between adultery and revolution no alternative mode of existence is discovered as feasible.)

Ottilie is different from the other three characters in having no independent social status—she is a foster child, totally dependent on Charlotte. (Charlotte's own daughter Luciana provides a complete contrast with Ottilie.) We hear of her first from school, just as, in a different way, she is more herself in the privacy of her diary than in company. From her school reports we gather that she is not good at grasping "unconnected facts" (p. 26) ("das Unzusammenhängende" [p. 25]) and is not good at understanding connections and "relationships" (p. 26) ("die Mittelglieder" [p. 25])—middle, or intermediary, terms is a more precise translation). This pedagogic verdict is based on her "inability to grasp the rules of grammar" (p. 27). ("ihre Unfähigkeit die Regeln der Grammatik zu fassen" [p. 25]), her "lack of attention to political divisions" (p. 41) ("bei der Geographie vermisste man Aufmerksamkeit auf die politische Einteilung" [p. 36]) in geography, and a slowness in arithmetic. All this adds up to a failure to grasp the particular systems of divisions and relationships and the prevailing syntactical models in the society of the time. Instead she manifests an instinct for total empathy. Her grasp of "the whole ordering of things" (p. 45) ("die ganze Ordnung" [p. 39]) is intuitive rather than analytic. In both ways she operates at an inarticulate level at a remove from the people around her. She likes to serve, and she seems to wish to prolong the state of being a child. It is as though she has nothing of the potential bourgeois wife and mother in her. Compared with Charlotte, she is lacking in substance, shadowy, even transparent. It is this that seems to enable her to cede herself completely to another, as for instance she alone can completely blend with Edward's flute playings by an instinctive incorporation of his own particular way of playing music—shortcomings and all. (Charlotte can control her playing to keep up with Edward's erratic tempo, but she remains all the time outside of his music. Ottilie enters it as by a process of osmosis.) Where Luciana is full of crude animal energy, tearing up flowers in the garden and disrupting the household, Ottilie is drawn to stillness, a negation of energy. The opposition is made schematically clear by the contrast between Luciana's interest in monkeys (she keeps one as a pet) and delight in these "repulsive creatures which resemble human beings" (p. 166) ("vermenschlichten abscheulichen Geschöpfe" [p. 127]), but at a lower level (we are still dealing with a hierarchy of being rather than an evolutionary chronology), with Ottilie's ability to remain absolutely motionless in the religious tableau in which she plays the Mother of God. She is drawn to the higher forms.

At this point we may note that her relationship to the very idea of "form" is problematical. When the assistant from her boarding school sees her in the *tableau vivant*, he comments afterwards that he is uneasy about the combination of the sacred and the sensuous—adding that "the highest, most excellent quality of man is without form" (p. 194) ("das Höchste, das Vorzüglichste am Menschen ist gestaltlos" [p. 149]). Ottilie has noted in her diary that passions, whether faults or virtues, are "exaggerated forms." What Ottilie in fact writes is "Passions can be either faults or virtues, but they are exaggerated forms" (p. 169). ("Die Leidenschaften sind Mängel oder Tugenden, nur gesteigerte" [p. 129].) It is perhaps slightly misleading to use the translation "exaggerated forms" for *nur gesteigerte,* since the term means, rather, "enhanced" or "increased" (from *steigen,* meaning "to go up" or "to walk up"—or as we say of an incline that the road rises); so it might be better to say "only intensified." One can nevertheless see her as wishing to disengage herself from exaggerated forms into formlessness, which can only be death. In line with this is her liking for portraits, which enable you to hold the image of a person no matter whether he or she is absent or present. From this point of view, art provides a transformation of movement into stillness, body into image, life in an arrested form akin to death. (Charlotte dislikes portraits as pointing to something "distant and finished" [p. 146]—"etwas Entferntes, abgeschiedenes" [p. 112]. She is more interested in showing "reverence to the present" [p. 146]—"die Gegenwart recht zu ehren" [p. 112]—the incomplete, open-ended process in which she finds herself.) Ottilie is more at home in the chapel than in the house, for there she can meditate on images of older forms of worship. Her instinct is to regress both in time and space, to fade out of herself and her specific position in an historical-physical continuum. In a sense her inclination to merge with Edward is not a statement of sexual desire, but more of a metastatement concerning her wish to merge *out* of life altogether. Having broken her "rules" (p. 258) ("Gesetze" [p. 197]), she can turn to that "complete renunciation" (p. 261) ("das völlige Entsagen" [p. 199]) that she has been approaching indirectly throughout her life. She dedicates herself "to that holy power which . . . alone can protect us against those monstrous intruding forces" (p. 264). ("sie sich dem Heiligen widmet, das uns unsichtbar umgebend allein gegen die ungeheuren zudringenden Mächte beschirmen kann" [p. 202]. Note again the word *monster,* referring to the "monstrous evil"—"ungeheures Übel"— this is how Ottilie regards the indirectly fatal results of the illicit passion she and Edward felt for each other. In the bourgeois house there are, it would seem, more monsters than one might think.) The intruding forces are those passions and impulses without which there would be no combinations or fruitful relationships at all. *Life itself,* in its ongoingness and fluctuant embraces and separations, is an "exaggerated form" for Ottilie. She ultimately recedes from a world that she had hardly entered. She becomes an embodiment of a religious feeling, which is in effect a commitment to nonbeing, and her death is like a *tableau mort,* which draws people toward its beautiful stillness. In this it is directly opposed to the livingness of Charlotte's daughter Luciana, a figure of purely sensual, almost animal energy whose presence leads to "spoilt symmetry" (p. 212) ("die zerstörte Symmetrie" [p. 163]). Ottilie's death is an act of regained symmetry after the potential asymmetrical disturbances that would have been caused by adultery and divorce. But this time it is not the symmetry of art but the symmetry of death, the resolution of that "attractive and radiant confusion" experienced by Charlotte and Edward in their night of legitimate-adulterous embraces. Out of that confusion a child was conceived, but no new forms were engendered, and the only subsequent direction seems to be backwards to the unconfused inertia of the earth.

In isolating details of environment, incidents, and characters in this way, there is a danger of fragmenting the interlocking network of relationships that make up the totality of the book. It would in fact be possible to go through the book and find carefully encoded references to separating and combining, differentiation and merging or identification, building and disassembling, visible and secret activity, and so on, on every page. In addition, one can easily detect how the basic questions of movement toward and movement away from—i.e., affinity and aversion—are engaged on the four main levels of the inorganic, the botanical, the animal, and the human, to see what kind of isomorphism of relationships may connect these distinct categories. This in turn points to the all-inclusive problem of the very activity of taxonomy and categorization. For just as things have first to be separated to make identification and meaning and orientation in the world possible, and then to be related by certain laws so that the experienced world does not fall apart into monadic fragments; so individuals have first to be separated by family, class, tribe, etc., and then to be related by laws decreeing the class of the marriageable as distinct from the unmarriageable. This indeed is why marriage and language are so intimately connected, as the structuralists have taught us to recognize. In being so clear on all these matters, what Goethe's novel invites is, not further interpretation—which would indeed be redundant—but a recognition of certain conditions that effectively determine how social and passional relations can be *thought about.* In the world as portrayed in this novel, there is too much significance. What the characters need is a reprieve from excessive meaning. There is no space for new thought in this environment of interlocking things and concepts and activities that I have tried to evoke. In this totally formulated environment, all behavior is formularized; the formulas can be turned around but not evaded. This is borne out in one of Mittler's final injunctions. He attacks the negativity of the Ten Commandments, in particular the seventh, and expresses the wish that it could be rephrased as a positive exhortation: " 'Thou shalt not commit adultery' . . . how crude, how indecent! How different it would sound if it said, 'Thou shalt have reverence for the bond of marriage' " (p. 282). ("Du sollst nicht ehebrechen . . . wie grob, wie unanständig! Klänge es nicht ganz anders wenn es hiesse: Du sollst Ehrfurcht haben vor der ehelichen Verbindung" [p. 215].) But his insertion of this rearrangement of words comes at a point in the narrative that only underlines the poignant impotence of such verbal rearrangements, an impotence already discovered in all the other attempts at rearrangement in the book. Mittler's proposed formulaic difference would not make enough difference.

This leads to one final aspect of the book I wish to mention in this section. There is a tendency on the part of most of the characters to treat experience aphoristically. Mittler is at one extreme, and Ottilie in her diary is at the other. To take two examples from her diary, a rhetorical question and a statement. "How can character, that which is the peculiarity of each individual, be reconciled with manners?" (p. 182) ("Wie kann der Charakter, die Eigentümlichkeit des Menschen, mit der Lebensart bestehen?" [p. 140]); and "A man has only to declare himself free, and he feels himself at that moment to be limited. If he ventures to declare himself limited, he feels free" (p. 183). ("Es darf sich einer nur für frei erklären, so fühlt er sich den Augenblick als bedingt. Wagt er es sich für bedingt zu erklären, so fühlt er sich frei" [p. 140].)

From one point of view these verbal propositions can be extracted from the book and considered as general problems in isolation from specific experience. But it is precisely this characteristic that marks their unusability. We might say, for instance, that Jane Austen's novels depict figures essaying the difficult reconciliation of character and manners, and acting out an exploratory dialectic between freedom and limitation. But they do not articulate the problems to themselves in this abstract, generalized way. Once they become statements written in a diary, they take on the status of innutrient clarifications and contribute to that closure of alternative possibilities that is characteristic of the atmosphere of this novel. Here is another example, taken not from the privacy of a diary but from a conversation that occurs when Charlotte and the school assistant are discussing the changing attitude toward enclosure and expansion evinced by different generations. She evokes the time when the emphasis was all on walls, moats, drawbridges, fortifications, etc., and compares it to the present time when the emphasis is all on dismantling of walls and the filling in of moats (i.e., the general move toward erasure of marks of separation). "Nobody feels comfortable in a garden unless it looks like open country; nothing in it should remind us of art and compulsion; we want to draw breath in full, unconditional freedom. Can you then understand, my friend, that one could turn back from this state to another, the previous state?" (p. 206). ("Niemand glaubt sich in einem Garten behaglich, der nicht einem freien Lande ähnlich sieht; an Kunst, an Zwang soll nichts erinnern, wir wollen völlig frei und unbedingt Atem schöpfen. Haben Sie wohl einen Begriff, mein Freund, dass man aus diesem in einen andern, in den vorigen Zustand zurückkehren könne?" [p. 158].) The assistant, who revealingly initiated the conversation by commenting on the possibilities of intergenerational tension and difference between father and son, comments: "Why not . . . every state has its difficulties, the restricted as well as the uninhibited one. The latter take abundance for granted and lead to extravagant expenditure. As soon as there is a shortage, self-restriction is imposed once more. People who are compelled to make use of their land once more build walls round their gardens in order to ensure themselves of their produce" (p. 206). ("Warum nicht? . . . jeder Zustand hat seine Beschwerlichkeit, der beschränkte so wohl als der losgebundene. Der letztere setzt Überfluss voraus und führt zur Verschwendung. . . . Sobald der Mangel eintritt, sogleich ist die Sebstbeschränkung wiedergegeben. Menschen, die ihren Grund und Boden zu nutzen genötigt sind, führen schon wieder Mauern um ihre Gärten auf, damit sie ihrer Erzeungnisse sicher seien" [p. 159].) Here economic considerations—abundance, shortage—are fed into the conversation, thus producing a model of oscillating alternatives—parsimony, extravagance—which in turn yield a generalization that implicitly extends to passional relationships—restrictions (or repression), lack of inhibition. Here again, the clarification becomes a closure, as one vocabulary, by the subtle tyranny of analogy, extends its influence into other areas of experience, and the problems of how people feel become integrated into the consideration of how much they can afford.

This even extends to the question, which they go on to discuss, of whether there is any way of avoiding what seems to be this inevitable oscillation based on intergenerational conflict. The assistant suggests that the father should "raise his son to the level of joint-ownership" (p. 207). ("Der Vater erhebe seinen Sohn zum Mitbesitzer" [159].) Inasmuch as this might be a solution to the literal problem of how to avoid problems of opposed theories of landscaping, it sounds feasible enough.

But in the areas of human life, for which this specific problem is being used as a paradigm, it is far more ambiguous a suggestion, for it is tantamount to suggesting that you could make the present and past "joint-owners" of human beings, whose whole being is a constant movement from one to the other; and to the extent that the individual is owned *by* the past (as opposed to comprehending it in its pastness and its influence on the present), he cannot fully enter into possession of his own present. And this indeed is ultimately the condition of all the various figures in the book, a condition that is one of the central ironies in the bourgeois novel. The owners are owned by what they own (this extends from objects and property to concepts and formulae). The final irony is that in this world apparent awareness becomes a product of the moment and not a prelude to change. Thus Charlotte says, "As life pulls us along, we believe that we are acting of our own volition and that we are choosing our activity and our pleasures, . . . but, indeed, when we look at it more closely, they are only the plans and inclinations of the time" (p. 205). ("Indem uns das Leben fortzieht, versetzte sie, glauben wir aus uns selbst zu handeln, unsere Tätigkeit, unsere Vergnügungen zu wählen; aber freilich, wenn wir es genau ansehen, so sind es nur die Pläne, die Neigungen der Zeit, die wir mit auszuführen genötigt sind" [p. 158].) She is alluding to the way in which a generation can be dominated by a mere change in fashion, and changes in fashion unrelated to any other changes in society are in fact no change at all; they are mere changes in upholstery, and fashion becomes thereby the way in which the bourgeois conceals the radical stasis or reification of his existence from himself. Charlotte's reidentification of "volition" as subservience to fashion is an insight, but an insight that can effect no alterations in the patterns of action and thought in the given environment. Instead of releasing new constructive energy into the social environment, all these perceptions, insights, aphorisms, etc., effectively bind up energy so that it is imprisoned in articulate formulae whether these are deposited in a diary or given to the air in the course of a polite conversation. Not indeed that to articulate perceptions and ideas precisely is a negative undertaking: such an activity marks the greatest literature of the eighteenth century, the century to which Goethe is ultimately most committed. But context is the crucial factor here, and in the living context of the figures in this novel these formulations—irrespective of whether Goethe put many of his own neoclassic beliefs in Ottilie's diary—cannot intersect functionally and fruitfully with the environment, because in fact they are not rooted or grounded in that environment (hence their extractability: they can easily be taken out because they are at no point fixed in).

Pictures of Paternal Admonition

In connection with Richardson and Rousseau I had occasion to say a good deal concerning the figure of the father and his power. In Goethe's novel the father is not present, though we learn at the very beginning that it was on account of Edward's father's "insatiable craving for property" (p. 5) ("nie zu sättigender Begierde des Besitzes" [p. 8])—and *Begierde* is a very strong word, implying inordinate desire) that they were initially "separated" ("getrennt"); so once again we may say that in the past of the novel the father acted in his ancient role of "he who separates," and while Julie's father had a blind obsession with "name," Edward's father had a comparably blind, and equally lustful, appetite for "property"—name and property being, very obviously, the two principal adjuncts of the power of the father. But, as I said, that father is no longer present. Indeed the only real father among the protagonists is Edward himself, and he it is who most markedly regresses to the mental and emotional state and condition of a child, a reversal with potentially ominous implications for the sense of futurity and continuity of the family. But figures of the father do appear in Goethe's novel and in a most interesting and suggestive way.

One of the distractions suggested by the Count to occupy the time (as I have said before—what are these idle people going to *do* in the tidied, tended house and garden?) is the making of "tableaux vivants" (the German words used are *Nachbildung,* which implies a three-dimensional formation according to, or after, something else; and *natürliche Bildnerei* [pp. 135–36]). The idea is to "depict real, well-known pictures" (p. 177) ("wirkliche bekannte Gemälde vorzustellen" [p. 135]), using real people and actual settings. The three main pictures selected are as follows. The first is Van Dyck's Belisarius, which depicts a "blind general" (p. 177) sitting down ("den sitzenden blinden General" [p. 136]), while a young woman in the background seems to be counting out "generous alms" ("reichliche Almosen") into her hand in what could be construed as a simulation of charity, and another female figure is "really" ("wirklich") giving alms. Belisarius, may I remind you as I had to remind myself, was a Byzantine general who served under Justinian I. He had notable victories over the Persians; he saved Justinian's throne by putting down a revolt; he defeated the Vandal kingdom of North Africa, took Sicily, Naples, and Rome, and held Rome for a year against the Goths. He also saved Constantinople by driving a horde of Bulgars from its very walls. He was usually accompanied on his campaigns by his wife Antonia.

"There is no truth in the later legend of his being blinded and reduced to beggary."[12]

The second tableau is a copy of Poussin's picture of Ahasuerus and Esther. The story of Ahasuerus and Esther is to be found in the Book of Esther in the Old Testament and it concerns the mighty ruler of India and Ethiopia who so delights in the Jewish girl, Esther, that at her request he reverses plots and decrees aimed at exterminating her race. The tableau/picture concentrates on that moment when the young Esther is pleading before the king. "And Esther spake yet again before the king, and fell down at his feet, and besought him with tears to put away the mischief of Haman the Agagite, and his device that he had devised against the Jews" (Esther 8:3). So the tableau shows the "unconscious prostrate queen" (p. 178) ("ohnmächtig hingesunkene Königin" [p. 137]—*ohnmächtig* signifying complete powerlessness, literally in a faint—an interesting change from the biblical account in which she is actively supplicating on the ground before the king, who is, interestingly enough, described as the "Zeus-like king" [p. 178]) ("zeusgleichen König" [p. 137]), thus metaphorically fusing the primordial, omnipotent, mythic god/father with the Old Testament Oriental ruler of almost comparable secular power. For the third picture Byzantine-European history and mythic-sacred legend are left behind, and the actors move into a protobourgeois middle-class scene. This is Terborch's "Paternal Admonition" (p. 179) ("Väterliche Ermahnung" [137]), and who, asks Goethe, "is not familiar with Wille's magnificent print of this painting" ("und wer kennt nicht den herrlichen Kupferstich unseres Wille von diesem Gemälde?" [p. 137]). The reference to the familiarity of a print indicates that the picture had achieved far wider circulation than a single canvas could do, through the possibilities of mass cheap distribution of copies of it. Thus, we may infer, it could have become a sort of stereotype or cliché on the walls of many middle-class homes. (It is not hard to think of similar pictures in Victorian times or, indeed, our own, which become so much part of the visual vocabulary that programs us that we can hardly see them any more; they have become part of the familiar environment, having moved out of aesthetic space effectively into domestic space.) Since that familiarity is now lost to us (to me, at least, though I gather the original is still in Amsterdam), I will quote part of Goethe's description of the picture.

> A noble, knightly figure sits with one leg over the other and seems to be giving his daughter standing in front of him a talking-to. The latter, a magnificent figure in a white satin dress with abundant folds, is indeed only seen from behind, but her whole personality seems to indicate that

[12]*Encyclopaedia Britannica*, 1964, s.v. "Belisarius."

she is making an effort to restrain herself. The father's face and gesture make it clear that the admonition is not vehement and humiliating; and as far as the mother is concerned, she appears to be concealing a slight embarrassment by looking into a glass of wine which she is just about to drink up.

(P. 179)

Einen Fuss über den andern geschlagen, sitzt ein edler ritterlicher Vater und scheint seiner vor ihm stehenden Tochter ins Gewissen zu reden. Diese, eine herrliche Gestalt, im faltenreichen weissen Atlaskleide, wird zwar nur von hinten gesehen, aber ihr ganze Wesen scheint anzudeuten, dass sie sich zusammennimmt. Das jedoch die Ermahnung nicht heftig und beschämend sei, sieht man aus der Miene and Gebärde des Vaters; und was die Mutter betrifft, so scheint diese eine kleine Verlegenheit zu verbergen, indem sie in ein Glas Wein blickt, das sie eben auszuschlürfen im Begriff ist.

(P. 137)

Terborch was a Dutch painter of the seventeenth century (1617–81) and he was best known for his interiors of well-to-do middle-class life, so it is quite legitimate to see this picture as offering to some extent a distillation of aspects of bourgeois—or, as I said, protobourgeois—life. The father is "knightly" ("ritterlich") and this could mean that he was indeed a knight, a member of the lower aristocracy, but he operates as a bourgeois father, by which I mean the following. We see that it was legend that blinded the unbeatable General Belisarius, who could vanquish every noncivilized force in the world, Vandal, Goth, Bulgar—as though it was felt that such awesome power must inevitably have drawn down on it the wrath of the jealous gods as in the Greek myths. Ahasuerus was a ruler of such power that he could order the elimination of a race with the sign of his ring or save lives at whim with a touch of his golden scepter—a Zeus-like giver of life and death. But Terborch's "father"—not sitting in monolithic apartness like Belisarius, nor on a golden throne like Ahasuerus, but in a rather relaxed position in what we may take to be an easy (or relatively easy) chair—exerts his force, not through armies and sceptres, but "admonition" ("Ermahnung"). The phrase *ins Gewissen reden* more exactly refers to appealing to someone's conscience (*Gewissen*) and is more serious than "talking-to" might suggest. For it is not what we lightly call a "ticking off," but an attempt to awaken and enlist the moral feelings of another—to get them to see something from a particular moral perspective. And this, precisely, was how the bourgeois father attempted to wield power. There is a very noticeable and significant change here from the scene of Julie's father, floundering in furious irrationality, indifferent to matters of conscience, and simply beating the living daylights out of his daughter and, should she happen to come within range, his wife too. He made no appeals: he ordered and, when crossed, struck. In Terborch's picture the admonition is not *heftig,* which means "violent," "vehement," nor *beschämend,* "shaming" (rather than "humiliating," which is *demütigend,* though the difference is not, perhaps, very significant here). Violent and shaming, for him if not her, is just what Julie's father's assertion of paternal authority is, but, I suggested, perhaps part of that blind fury was due to a sense that that kind of paternal power was about to wane. The new weapon is to be conscience, with all that that can imply—whether a genuine attempt to inculcate what was felt to be an honorable ethical code, or the most exploitative kinds of moral bullying that can pass under its name. The atmosphere is not one of anger and blood but "embarrassment" ("Verlegenheit"; *Verlegen* means self-conscious, disconcerted, confused). And this, surely, was to be one of the most prevalent feelings generated by the middle-class home. Nothing is really disturbed (the father's legs are comfortably crossed), blows are not to be exchanged, voices should preferably not be raised. To impose his will the father works on that mysterious organ of self-admonition and self-recrimination, the conscience. The daughter, note, is seen only from behind, a faceless recipient, silent and motionless before the parental visage. But she is not, like Esther, prostrate and in a state akin to being in a faint ("ohnmächtig"). She is upright, a *herrliche* figure (literally, "like a lord"), and in fact is having to restrain herself. *Sich zusamennehmen* means literally to hold oneself together, whether in an attempt, say, not to cry, or in an effort not to say something that is clamoring for utterance. To hold yourself together is, by the same token, to hold something back—tears, words—and is precisely an effort of repression. In a home where things are repressed through the multiple strategies of conscience, the main sign of any unease or sense of potential or latent tensions is precisely *embarrassment,* which may be concealed with a glass of wine, or revealed in a stutter or a blush, but is the very presence in the air of the held-back, the rise of self-consciousness.

All these tableaux, then, represent in some form the presence of a dominating central male figure enthroned (or "enchaired") in a position of power, or at least (in the case of Belisarius) receiving alms and tribute, real as well as, perhaps, false. But this is, we may say, all in the tableaux. The peremptory and, if necessary, brutal, physically present father has been displaced from the home into art. And not quite directly into art, either. If you consider that the third tableau is an imitation of a print of a picture of a characteristic domestic scene, then we are seeing a copy of a copy of a copy. But then it gets more difficult, because in what sense is the domestic scene the original? There would be no point in attempting to pursue these old Platonic questions here, but I am concerned with a very specific aspect of the problem. We may say that Goethe has brought together in these three pictures something of a glossary of archetypes of male power, the power of the father in its most generic sense: mythic god, biblical emperor, invincible general, admonitory father. By the same token they have worked as stereotypes, whether through ubiquitous reading of the Bible or widespread diffusion of a print. So there is a sense in which the artistic (or pictorial-script-ural) figure takes ontological precedence and priority over the living father. How many fatherly admonitions must have been generated by Terborch's picture!

At a later stage, when they decide to do a tableau of the nativity play (in which Ottilie plays the Mother of God, a clear influence on her subsequent spirituality, indeed religiosity), there is an assertion that "in this case reality as a picture had particular advantage" (p. 190) ("hier hatte die Wirklichkeit als Bild ihre besondern Vorzüge" [p. 145]), though the condition or effect of these advantages is that everything and everyone in the picture is "held fast and petrified" (p. 190) ("festgehalten und erstarrt" [p. 146]). By unstated implication the transposition works two ways—in making reality into a picture ("Wirklichkeit als Bild"), they are making the picture into reality. When they depict the print of the Terborch painting, it is said that "without any question this living copy was far superior to the original painting" (p. 179) ("dass ganz ohne Frage diese lebendige Nachbildung weit über jenes Originalbildnis hinausreichte" [p. 137]), and by this point it is getting very hard to locate or even differentiate copies and originals. When the living copy is superior to the copy of the painting . . . this kind of Borgesian regress is perhaps all too familiar to us now, but it was certainly not in Goethe's time. And some of the implications are disturbing. To start with, this superiority and advantage is only secured by rigidification, "holding fast," and petrification (*erstarren* means to freeze in one's movements, and also to congeal, to harden, even to curdle), which, if extended from entertainment into life, is a mortal price to pay. Also, to the extent that in life the figures are turning reality into picture by turning picture into reality, it can mean that the roles, positions, distances and proximities between figures (power and love relationships, status in familial and social situations, in a word, the whole structuring of relationships), are all fixed in advance. The tableau vivant is only a static model of what the characters are engaged in in their daily lives outside the frame. They are simply in a large extent established pictures enacted through time. The real father has been replaced by the memory of a set of heteropaternal images that may be copied, lived back into.

This is why there is such a feeling of progression-as-regression at various levels in the book, whether in connection with the restoration of the old church that "grew back into the past" (p. 149) ("und die Kirche täglich auch . . . der Vergangenheit entgegen wuchs" [p. 114]) or with

Edward's and Ottilie's regression to childhood. The architect, for example, has his own collection of objects (like the visiting Englishman—collecting becomes an important and highly ambiguous activity at all levels in the period with which the novels I am discussing concern themselves): "for the most part they were of German origin; bracteati, double coins, seals . . . anything else of a comparable nature. *All these objects directed the imagination back to the past . . .*" (p. 149; my italics) ("Sie waren meistenteils deutschen Ursprungs: Brakteaten, Dickmünzen, Siegel und was sonst sich noch anschliessen mag. Alle diese Dinge richteten die Einbildungskraft gegen die ältere Zeit hin . . ." [p. 114].) In Ottilie's diary there is an entry noting that "there are many kinds of memorials and signs which draw us closer to those who are far away and dead" (p. 151) ("Es gibt mancherlei Denkmale und Merkzeichen, die uns Entfernte und Abgeschiedene näher bringen" [p. 115]), with the very significant accompanying comment, " 'To be gathered to one's father' is such a heartfelt expression" (p. 151) ("Zu den Seinigen versammelt werden, ist ein so herzlicher Ausdruck" [p. 115]—where *Seinigen* is not specifically "one's father," but more generally "one's own," which then prompts the consideration of to what extent the self is "owned" by its predecessors, the present owned by the past, life owned by death?). In connection with the chapel where Ottilie feels at home, she recalls the primitive idea that ancestors sat on thrones in caverns waiting for the living to die, and Ottilie is attracted to the idea of emulating that quiet and awesome patience.

One idea cherished by primitive people is solemn and can appear as terrible. They thought of their ancestors as sitting on their thrones in circles in great caverns, in silent communication. If a newcomer were worthy enough, they stood up and bowed welcomingly to him as he entered. Yesterday, as I was sitting in the chapel and saw a number of seats facing my own carved chair, this idea seemed to me quite a friendly and pleasant one. "Why can't I go on sitting here?" I thought to myself, "go on sitting here quietly and turned in upon myself, a long, long time, until at last my friends come and I stand up for them and show them their places with a friendly bow."

(P. 158)

Eine Vorstellung der alten Völker ist ernst und kann furchtbar scheinen. Sie dachten sich ihre Vorfahren in grossen Höhlen rings umher auf Thronen sitzend in stummer Unterhaltung. Dem neuen, der hereintrat, wenn er würdig genug war, standen sie auf und neigten ihm einen Willkommen. Gestern, als ich in der Kapelle sass, und meinem geschnitzten Stuhle gegenüber noch mehrere umhergestellt sah, erschien mir jener Gedanke gar freundlich und anmutig. Warum kannst du nichts sitzen bleiben? dachte ich bei mir selbst, still und in dich gekehrt sitzen bleiben, lange,

lange, bis endlich die Freunde kämen, denen du aufstündest und ihren
Platz mit freundlichem Neigen anwiesest.

(P. 121)

This idea of the seated dead silently waiting the inevitable arrival of
the living offers a vivid image of the authority of the past passively
preempting life in the present. This is not to say that the novel simply
depicts a mechanical backward-looking enactment of authoritative
models from the past. It is in the struggle, conscious and unconscious,
against these models, and among these signs and objects that transmit
fragments of the power of the past and the absent, that the dimension of
the novel comes into being. Edward and Ottilie are not simply passive
victims of a one-way determinism that reduces them to puppets, and the
Captain and Charlotte reveal different kinds of powers of resistance. By
the end of the novel Edward and Ottilie are dead and the future of the
Captain and Charlotte is not alluded to. (After the conclusion of the
English lord's novella of "The Strange Young Neighbours" ["Die wun-
derlichen Nachbarskinder"], we learn that there was a comparable incident in actual life that, in being transmitted by common talk and then
retold by a sensitive narrator, was both radically altered and profoundly
unchanged. "For the most part everything—and nothing—remains in
the end as it was" [p. 234]). ["Es bleibt zuletzt meist alles und nichts wie es
war" (p. 179).] We may apply these words to the conclusion of Goethe's
novel—and, I suggest, to the novel of adultery in general—and say that
by the end everything and nothing is as it was.) The individual characters
are indeed agents as well as actors, but they all inhabit a present that is
full of "pictures" and re-presentations of the past in many forms. In
striving for uniqueness and difference, they are unavoidably and inextricably involved in repetition and similarity.

In this connection Goethe offers an especially acute and profound
insight. When the spectators are looking at the first *tableau vivant,* there
is a general feeling that everything has been arranged so perfectly and
the figures and colors and settings are so suitable "that one might well
have believed that one was in another world, were it not that the presence of reality instead of appearance occasioned a kind of anxious feeling" (p. 178) ("dass man fürwahr in einer andern Welt zu sein glaubte;
nur dass die Gegenwart des Wirklichen statt des Scheins eine Art von
ängstlicher Empfindung hervorbrachte" [p. 136]). *Ängstlicher Empfindung* refers to a sensation of diffuse anxiety; it is not so strong as *die
Angst,* from which it is derived as an adjective, for the adjectival form also
acts as a diminutive. This kind of rather vague anxiety—not the dark
night of the soul, not some psychological or metaphysical crisis, but a
sense of unease of somewhat obscure origin—is the condition produced

by an incipient uncertainty as to the location of the real and the ontological status of what appears to the senses. The figures in the tableau vivant are in two contradictory places at once, since they are both in reality (the house) and in art (the picture). If what should be "appearance" (*der Schein*) is in fact the "real" (*das Wirklichen*)—then where or even what does this leave/make the spectator? In looking at the tableau vivant, which in its rigidity is also a *tableau mort*, the watcher might just begin to experience, perhaps unconsciously, an onset of category confusion—the leading edge of concern over just what picture-reality, life-death, he himself is participating in. When such unresolvable uncertainties take unobtrusive hold—not so powerful as to undermine the enthroned and privileged beliefs of orthodox consciousness, but somehow always potentially there like a mist hovering among the pillars of the mind—then this kind of unmelodramatic but pervasive "anxiety," originating from a variety of sources, becomes a habitual mode of existence. This, it seems to me, is another marked characteristic of the bourgeois novel, and it is no very great distance from the insights of Goethe to the labors of Freud.

4

FLAUBERT'S *MADAME BOVARY*

The Fog in Emma Bovary's Head

"Ah yes!" returned Félicité. "You're like old Guérin's daughter, the fisherman at Le Pollet, that I knew at Dieppe before I came to you. She was that wretched, you'd think to see her standing in the doorway there was a funeral pall hung up over the door. It seems she'd got a sort of fog in her head, the doctors couldn't do a thing with her, and no more could the *curé*. When she got it real bad she'd go off by herself long the beach, and the coastguard often used to find her there on his rounds. Stretched flat out on the shingle she'd be, crying her eyes out. . . . They say it went when she got married, though."

"But with me," replied Emma, "it didn't come on till I was married."[1]

(p. 122)

—Ah! oui, reprenait Félicité, vous êtes justement comme la Guérine, la fille au père Guérin, le pêcheur du Pollet, que j'ai connue à Dieppe, avant de venir chez vous. Elle était si triste, si triste, qu'à la voir debout sur le seuil de sa maison, elle vous faisait l'effet d'un drap d'enterrement tendu devant la porte. Son mal, à ce qu'il paraît, était une manière de brouillard qu'elle avait dans la tête, et les médecins n'y pouvaient rien, ni le curé non plus. Quand ça la prenait trop fort, elle s'en allait toute seule sur le bord de la mer, si bien que le lieutenant de la douane, en faisant sa tournée, souvent la trouvait étendue à plat ventre et pleurant sur les galets. Puis, après son mariage, ça lui a passé, dit-on.

—Mais, moi, reprenait Emma, c'est après le mariage que ça m'est venu.

(P. 154)

The "sort of fog" in the head of Guérin's daughter is imprecise, inde-

---

[1] Unless otherwise indicated, French and English quotations from Flaubert's novel within this chapter are from Gustave Flaubert, *Madame Bovary* (Paris: Gallimard, 1972), and Flaubert, *Madame Bovary,* trans. Alan Russell (Harmondsworth, Middlesex: Penguin, 1950).

finable, unamenable to the diagnoses and the remedies of the constituted secular and sacred authorities who can supposedly analyze and aid
the maladies of body and spirit. It is not something indistinct that can be
brought into focus with superior modes of definition—it is *indistinctness*
itself as a presence in the head. The effects of this malady of oppressive
interior indistinctness are notable. Standing in the doorway, she gives
the impression of having been transformed into a funeral pall, into cloth
("drap") that wraps up the dead body, so this fog can cause an apparent
loss of substance, a deformation or translation of flesh into material. As a
response to these attacks, she would make her way alone to the edge of
the sea, fall prostrate, and weep. This instinctive withdrawal from society
to the point where the land dissolves into the sea, accompanied by the
abandonment of the upright or vertical posture of the body and the
internal dissolving intimated by weeping, is an act of obvious archetypal
significance, a symbolic gesture of thalassic regression, and of devolution-
ary collapse, that indicates that life within the city, governed by the
rules of the fathers (note that this girl is not named, she is "la fille au père
Guérin"), has become insupportable, unlivable. Then the indistinctness
in the head prompts the body toward the undifferentiation of the sea, as
though it offered the only possible "cure": the name of the father contains the pun *guérir,* to "cure"—and this touches on the whole problem
of sickness and cure, which recurs in many contexts and is central to the
book. Who is to decide what is to be classified as sickness, and who is to
dictate what shall constitute a cure? In this little vignette it is quite clear.
For when the unnamed girl seeks some kind of cure for her unnamable
illness in a solitary movement toward the sea, she is found by *le lieutenant
de la douane*—coastguard, or literally lieutenant of customs—who is making his rounds ("faisant sa tournée"). It is almost as if it is his presence on
the beach that prevented her total abandonment to the sea, and the fact
that the guardian of the customs (to rephrase his title only slightly) is
always "making his rounds" suggests that it is precisely this motion, his
constant "circulation" as it were, that both prevents the girl's self-
annihilatory escape (he is effectively *between* her and the sea) and helps
to facilitate her restoration to society where the "cure" is completed by
her "marriage." Thus, in brief, her life is determined and defined by
three males—her father, the lieutenant, and the husband. Between
being daughter and wife she (simply "elle") suffers from the fog of
interior indistinctness. Her sickness must be connected to the vagueness
of her position in society; after being a daughter (and thus entirely
defined by the father—she was "la Guérine"), she exists on the threshold
("sur le seuil") in a sort of pronominal limbo. And indeed what will she
become when she crosses the threshold of her father's house? All the
problems of liminality, both those connected with crossing thresholds in

the stages of the individual chronological life and those involving literal and lateral movement from edifice to edifice within the governing architecture of society, are adumbrated in the girl's sad hovering on the threshold of her father's house, at which point ontologically she seems more like cloth than flesh. She is there, but what is she? Hence the fog in the head. And the flight to the beach. And the repudiation of human identity that is implicit in that most primitive of gestures, the negation of the upright position by an act of self-prostration. But the customs man finds her and . . . after her marriage the fog went away. She has been renamed, redefined, absorbed back into society. For if there is one thing that the guardians of society—including "le père," "les médecins," "le curé," and "le lieutenant de la douane"—seek either to check or to dispel, it is that nameless fog of indistinctness that threatens the whole edifice of consciousness of the individual and by implication the architecture of society itself. For one of the governing impulses in any society is, and must be, a terror of indistinctness. At its most extreme this can manifest itself as suppression of all deviation and diversity. But even in societies that may tolerate a very high degree of variety, something of that dread must still be there. "La Guérine" is thus cured by marriage. Her life story, as compressed in this one apparently casual paragraph, recapitulates a comparatively orthodox process of socialization and initiation, and her temporary sickness is the understandable result of the temporary nonidentity of adolescence. The fog in the head then can be seen as a by-product of that ontological lacuna in her life when she can no longer identify herself with her father but has not yet been initiated into a new identity as a wife. It is indeed a critical period of great sadness and may even produce suicidal moods. But, as we may say, she was rescued by "custom." This is indeed a conventional pattern of life in bourgeois or petit-bourgeois terms.

But what, then, of Emma, for whom marriage was not the cure but, much more worryingly, apparently part of the cause of that "manière de brouillard qu'elle avait dans la tête"? In trying to sense the connections between marriage and the fog in the head in the life of Emma Bovary I think we can begin to discover what Flaubert was doing in what is, after all, the most important and far-reaching novel of adultery in Western literature. Rather than trying to approach the problem of Emma Bovary directly, I want first to consider select aspects of the various men who in one way of another make up the male context within which she must articulate her life, or have it shaped and defined for her.

This will require a series of tentative steps that may not at first seem related to each other, but that are intended to open up the text in a way that will lay bare some of its most important lines of force, its most energetic intentions.

Charles Bovary Goes to School,
Drops His Cap, and Tries
to Say His Name

Why Emma's story should start with Charles Bovary's somewhat in-
auspicious entry into a schoolroom is a matter that prompts some careful
consideration. We should note, first of all, that the title of the book,
Madame Bovary, does not refer unequivocally to Emma, since there are
three Madame Bovarys[2] in the book and two of them, Charles's mother
and his first wife, are encountered in the first chapter. Emma is, initially,
Emma Rouault, and one of the matters the first chapter concentrates on
is the origin, or more accurately the transmission, of a name. Whatever
else he is, Charles is the bearer of the name of Bovary; it is not the least
of the burdens that he has to carry. (The name itself, of course, suggests
bovine qualities, indeed it could be said to contain both something of the
bullock and the cow since *bouveau* is "bullock" and *bouverie* is "cowshed."
The name can also be almost heard as Beau-voir-y, a latent cunning
irony given the marked absence of both beautiful views and perceptive
vision in the book—and it can hardly be a textual coincidence that the
Bovarys stay at a hotel in "la place Beauvoisine" (French—p. 290) on
their visit to Rouen to go to the theatre—an excursion that proves to be
the final undoing of Emma. It is not an idle exercise to point out the
presence of such latent puns and homonyms, as I hope to show in a later
section.) But the first thing he is described as carrying is a large desk ("un
grand pupitre" [p. 21]), and it is to his initial appearance in the book,
which is also his initial (and initiatory) appearance in the school, that I
want to turn.

The first word of the novel is *nous,* a nonspecific "we" that is dropped
after the first chapter. It would be possible to make endless speculations
about the implications of this, but whatever else we (as readers) understand by the *we* we read, the first scene reveals that *we* comprises the

---

[2]The phenomenon of "trebling" or "triplication," is deeply rooted in narrative and has
been identified by Vladimir Propp in his classic work, *The Morphology of the Folk Tale* (ed.
Louis A. Wagner, trans. Lawrence Salt, 2d ed., rev. [Austin and London: University of
Texas Press, 1968], p. 74). It is a recurrent phenomenon in the book. There are three
Madame Bovarys, there are three primary men (i.e., sexual partners) in Emma's life (as
there are three men in the life of "la Guérine"); when Rodolphe starts his seduction of
Emma at the Agricultural Show, he draws up three, not two, stools; she is buried in three
coffins; at her funeral there are three choristers, three batons, and her father sees three
black hens and promises three chasubles to the church; and the book itself is in three parts.
The phenomenon of triplication is, in this novel, related to the phenomenon of duplication, as I will suggest in another context.

staring, mocking, speaking, aggressive communality into which "le nouveau" is introduced. Charles is of course not named in the opening paragraph but is "a new boy dressed in 'civies'" (p. 15) "un *nouveau* habillé en bourgeois" [p. 21]). The word *nouveau* is italicized every time it occurs in the opening paragraphs, and while it of course implies "the new boy," it also has more unrestricted connotations meaning simply— the new. It is an adjective used as a noun, suggesting that this new presence is as yet only a quality and not an entity. That is to say that we (not "they," since we as readers, in possession of the language, are also implicated) are watching the introduction into the schoolroom of some unnamed "newness," a presence, an object, a phenomenon, that can be classified by its clothes, but as yet has no social identity. The schoolroom will do very well for a paradigm of society, since it is there that we study ("Nous étions à l'étude" [p. 21]) the texts and discourses that will constitute us (no matter how imperfectly) in later life. The Headmaster ("le Proviseur") who leads this *nouveau* into the classroom incorporates the male authority that sanctions the imposition of the particular forms of study and work ("l'étude" and "travail") of society. So, that entering "newness" is already encumbered with a desk, the epitomous object of the socializing and enculturating process. It is the first of many ambiguous containers and containing objects that we will encounter in the book. Carrying one's own desk is the ultimate secular inversion of Christ carrying his own cross. What we are watching is the painful insertion of "*le nouveau*" into "nous"; or, to put it another way, the incorporation or absorption of "*le nouveau*" by the "nous." This involves the placing of "*le nouveau*" in the "ranks," or rows and lines, by which a school operates (the master has to direct him toward the others, toward us—"le maître d'études fut obligé de l'avertir, pour qu'il si mît avec nous dans les rangs" [p. 22]). It is a difficult and harsh moment of transition, and as I shall suggest, it would seem to be intimately involved with the general trauma of entering language itself and the more specific trauma of nomination, which that process necessarily involves.

But before considering that part of the process, we must consider that famous cap that is given to us in such legible detail before we hear the name of the bearer of the cap. In a book in which we will everywhere encounter the primacy of clothes and garments of all kinds—particularly hats and shoes—over the wearers, it is entirely appropriate that we should be given a detailed account of how le nouveau was "habillé" before we learn how he has been named. But the cap has a special priority over any other garment in the book in the length and detail of its description, and this in itself is an exhortation to consider it very carefully. Certain features of the cap are very well known—for instance, that it contains elements of a fur hat, a lancer's cap, a bowler hat, an otterskin cap, and a night cap; this in itself suggests a deterioration in social roles, from the military and the hunting hat, down through the business hat, ending in the night cap, and there is no doubt that such degenerative hints are intended. But I want to look at the cap once again in its entirety. And the first thing that becomes apparent is that it is impossible to visualize this cap. It is *lisible* but not *visible*. It is as if, from the start, Flaubert is demonstrating that there can be written verbal constructs that the other senses cannot translate: language can create impossible objects that can be read and deciphered, but not seen and experienced. This potentially dangerous and disproportionate power of language over the senses is, in fact, a key part of Emma's dilemma. The cap itself is an assemblage of decontextualized quotations; a combination, or rather a weird tressage, of anomalous and incongruous fragments from other areas of experience; a cluster of signs taken from other fields of reference. The transposition of elements from the wild-animal kingdom and from the military ethos and business ethos to a schoolboy's cap is one obvious example of this, as though nature and history were dwindling into a random assortment of sartorial echoes. But there is even more going on in that "composite" cap ("une de ces coiffures d'ordre composite" [p. 22]), as begins to emerge when you try to figure out—literally—what is being described in the second long sentence dedicated to it. It requires quoting in full. "An oval splayed out with whale-bone, it started off with three pompons; these were followed by lozenges of velvet and rabbit's fur alternately, separated by a red band, and after that came a kind of bag ending in a polygon of cardboard with intricate braiding on it; and from this there hung down like a tassel, at the end of a long, too slender cord, a little sheaf of gold threads" (p. 16). ("Ovoïde et renflée de baleines, elle commençait par trois boudins cīrculaires; puis s'alternaient, séparés par une bande rouge, des losanges de velours et de poils de lapin; venait ensuite une façon de sac que se terminait par un polygone cartonné, couvert d'une broderie en soutache compliquée, et d'où pendait, au bout d'un long cordon trop mince, un petit croisillon de fil d'or, en manière de gland" [p. 22].) Brought together here in a very strange way—the cap is a nexus of incongruities!—are words of shape (oval, circular, lozenge, polygon, etc.) with words connected with construction (*renflée* implies "swollen" or "stretched out"; *boudins* is a particularly difficult word in this context, since it can mean "torus," "flange," "spiral," as well as "pudding"; *croisillon* refers to a "crosspiece" or "brace," etc.). These fairly firm, even rigid words of shape and construction are mixed in with words referring to all kinds of soft material (velvet, cardboard, even gold, which is a very soft metal), just as we have the firm bones of the largest animal in nature (*baleines*—"whale bone") conjoined in the same artefact with the soft fur of one of the reputedly most timid, the rabbit ("de poils de lapin"). The cap is a mélange of processed nature and produced material, of architecture and embroidery, and the most disparate shapes, qualities, and material converge in it. And there is one more aspect to the cap that is hard to define and isolate, since it shimmers evasively somewhere within the unfolding of this whole mélangerie, but it seems to me undeniably to be there. I can perhaps approach it indirectly by pointing out that the word *sac* is also used for the amniotic sac; the word *cordon* is also used for the umbilical cord; and the word *gland*, while undoubtedly meaning "tassel," as the standard translations indicate, is also used in anatomy to refer to the glans and is even now used colloquially to refer to the testicles (hardly surprising, since it also means acorn). What the cap seems to contain among all the other things mentioned is a fragmented recapitulation of the period in the womb and the birth process. These fragments, or echoes, are mixed in with the fragmentary references to animals existing at a much earlier evolutionary stage than man (whales, otters) and an animal renowned for its timidity and fecundity alike (the rabbit); with references to earlier professions and roles; and references to various shapes, containers, materials. Thus the cap is a tissue of ontogenetic, philogenetic, and epigenetic hints. It is exactly a composite object "ou l'on retrouve les éléments," not where you can *find* the elements or basic constituents, but where you can find them *again*—displaced from their original context, which range widely through time and space, and reappearing in vestigial bits in a particular garment, an irrational collation of shapes, textures and materials, a "casquette" that seems to carry within it barely distinguishable memories of immemorial realms and times but that now serves to contain the head of a schoolboy. The putting on of the cap thus represents a kind of second "birth" into a confusion of signs. If we accept that traditional initiation tends to fall into the three stages of baptism, chrism, and communion (confirmation), we can recognize that in this grotesque parody of initiation into the prevailing culture, the cap plays the chrismal role—when it is placed on the head, *le nouveau* is annointed with incoherence.

We have then these *two* objects at the start of the book: *Le nouveau*, unnamed, silent, frightened, volitionless, a piece of manipulable flesh—not yet defined, identified, human; and *la casquette*, a manufactured object that is an assemblage of displacements, not only from nature into clothing, but from thing to sign. Indeed it is only because everything has been transformed to the status of sign that the cap can be "written" at all. In the cap the whalebone has lost its whaleness, just as the hint of lancer's cap brings with it no martial echoes. Everything meets and merges at the level of *costume*. Whatever else the cap means, it bespeaks the homogenization of initially utterly disparate elements, and this is possible because these elements have been treated as disposable and displaceable signs. All cultures necessarily employ this process in some way or another, even if only by turning animals into food and skins into clothing, etc. The point about this cap, with the absurd miscellaneousness and unvisualizable overabundance of its signs, is that it operates here as the representative object of the kind of bourgeois culture Flaubert was writing about. This is the object that is put over the head of *le nouveau*; it sums up the enculturation process by which *le nouveau* is initiated into and prepared for the established society. Such an object, and all that it implies, instead of making for a clarification and enrichment of consciousness, works to produce its confusion and obfuscation. How it does this is one of the issues that the book explores.

The fact that "nous," the boys already established within the school, like to throw their caps under their seats and against the wall—to leave their hands freer—may indicate some initial disinclination to rest easy under the allotted headgear of their society. *Le nouveau* is certainly uncertain in his relationship with his cap, and his hold on it is of the most tenuous, as is made clear when the master tells them all to stand up and "he" stands up, letting his cap fall to the ground. ("Il se leva; sa casquette tomba" [p. 22].) When he tries to pick it up, his neighbor knocks it to the floor again with a blow of the elbow ("un coup de coude" [p. 22]—I will return to these words later on) and "he" is still fumbling for it when the master makes his pedantic joke—"Débarrassez-vous de votre casque" ("Disburden yourself of your helmet" in the Penguin translation, p. 16). Inasmuch as how and whether a person in that society can disburden him or herself of the helmet or hood that society has clamped over him or her becomes a basic concern of the book, the "joke" sends prophetic echoes through the following text. But at this point it serves as a prelude to the ordeal of nomination, or the traumatic entry into language, that *le nouveau* now has to undergo. Significantly, he does not know what to do with his cap—hold it, put it on his head, or put it on the ground. He leaves it lying on his knees, as yet having established no relationship with it. As long as *le nouveau* remains *le nouveau,* he will never comprehend what to do with the cap. For the essence of the cap is precisely to eliminate the *nouveauté* of *le nouveau* and turn it into part of the existing "nous." He will know what to do with his cap once he has entered the given circuit of discourse, which is why he first has to say his name in front of all the others, in front of "us." And in the ensuing description Flaubert compresses the painful stages by which *le nouveau* enters into *la condition linguistique.* It must be quoted in full.

> "Stand up and tell me your name."
> The boy stammered out some unintelligible noise.
> "Again!"
> The same halting syllables, smothered by hoots from the class.

"Louder! Louder!"

This time the new boy plucked up his courage, opened his mouth to an enormous width, brought out at the top of his voice, as if he were hailing someone, the word *Charbovari*.

(Pp. 116–17)

—Levez-vous, reprit le professeur, et dites moi votre nom.

Le *nouveau* articula, d'une voix bredouillante, un nom inintelligible.

—Répétez!

Le même bredouillement de syllabes se fit entendre, couvert par les huées de la classe.

—Plus haut! cria le maître, plus haut!

Le *nouveau*, prenant alors une résolution extrême, ouvrit une bouche démesurée et lança à pleins poumons, comme pour appeler quelqu'un, ce mot: *Charbovari*.

(p. 23)

The master's summons, a summons to verticality, to speech, to self-nomination, is a précis of the imperatives and exhortations by which the child, or *le nouveau,* is initiated into its social-linguistic identity.[3] And the three attempts to comply that *le nouveau* makes also offer a foreshortened paradigmatic enactment of the difficulties involved in this entry into language. At first he "articulates" in a mumbling voice an unintelligible name—"nom inintelligible." The choice of words is particularly interesting for *articuler* means "clear utterance," and what is uttered is indeed a "nom." But it is unintelligible to the listeners because of the mumbling voice, "voix bredouillante." It is as though *le nouveau* can talk perfectly clearly to himself but has not mastered the ability to participate in audible discourse. The voice dissolves into a mumble or stammer. This kind of failure or disintegration of speech implied in words like *bredouiller* and *balbutier* ("Stammer") occurs frequently throughout the book, and among other things we may detect in it some trace of the traumatic period spent on the threshold of speech (in it yet not in it, mastered by it yet not master of it) such as is here being described. It is a graphic reminder of how precarious our position is in language. The second attempt to obey the master's imperative results in a significant shift in the description even though it would seem to be a repetition of

---

[3]It could be said that in this scene Charles Bovary is being forcibly recruited into the dominant ideology of his class. Cf. Louis Althusser: "I shall then suggest that ideology 'acts' or 'functions' in such a way that it 'recruits' subjects among the individuals (it recruits them all), or 'transforms' the individuals into subjects (it transforms them all) by that very precise operation which I have called *interpellation* or hailing, and which can be imagined along the lines of the most commonplace everyday police (or other) hailing: 'Hey, you there!'" For that parenthetic "other" in this case read "school-teacher." See Althusser's whole essay on "Ideology and Ideological State Apparatuses" in *Lenin and Philosophy and Other Essays* (trans. Ben Brewster [New York: Monthly Review Press, 1972]).

the same noise. This time there is no "voix" but a "bredouillement de syllabes" that makes itself heard. The initiative seems to have passed from *le nouveau* (who in the first attempt was said to articulate) to a kind of inchoate speech-noise, or rather to something between the two. That is to say, it is not a voice saying a name, nor is it a totally nonsematic cry or jabber, but rather a kind of trembling of syllables ("syllabes"), a painful midway point between the private lalling of a young child and the full speech act, a point at which—following the implications of this description—the would-be speaker is not the controlling agent but rather the locus or venue where sounds and syllables foregather preparatory to transforming that venue into a public voice. At this point *le nouveau* is indeed more spoken, or rather half-spoken, than speaking. The pain involved in this period of transition is dramatized by the response of the listeners ("nous"), for those pathetic mumbling syllables trying to make themselves heard are covered or smothered by the hoots of the class ("couvert par les huées de la classe"). *Huées* ("hooting," "jeering," "booing," etc.), is a nonsemantic noise, but this time indicative, not of the helpless state of the infant (which means literally "without speech"), but of the aggression of "la classe"—or, we may say, society in its mob form, the mocking destructive roar of the deindividualized and thus dehumanized group. The fact that society both imposes the imperative to enter into language (the orders of the master) and can also, as it were, turn on language and negate it, nihilating individual articulation in a smothering communal noise, is a paradox that Flaubert puts before us at the very beginning of his book. We may refer then to the latent double humiliation in language—the painful ordeal of having to speak, and the continual risk of having your speech mockingly denied and erased by the surrounding others ("nous," "la classe," etc.).

The third attempt to obey the master ("Louder! Louder!") results in an almost orgasmic effort on the part of *le nouveau,* and the result this time is not a "*nom* intelligible" nor a "bredouillement de *syllabes*" but a "*mot*". It is, to be sure, a rather strange word, and I will come to that. But here again let us note just how Flaubert describes this climactic moment when *le nouveau* finally speaks an audible word. First of all it takes extreme determination, as though the whole being had to concentrate and come together to focus on this one act. Then the description of the opening of a mouth "démesurée" seems to anticipate many of the problems encountered later in the book. For while the word means simply "huge," it does also mean "beyond measure" or "unmeasured." A mouth beyond measure is a very suggestive paradox. Physically it is an impossibility; however big the mouth, it could still be "measured." But when the mouth is seen as the part of the body particularly involved with speech, then the word becomes very suggestive. Here we should note this: although the open mouth is a constant motif in the book (Charles dies with his mouth open) and is of course intimately connected with the whole problem of the satisfying of appetites and the vast amount of simple eating in the course of the narrative, it is in connection with the effort involved in *speaking* (i.e., not eating) that the mouth becomes an organ "beyond measure"—the unmeasurable dimension of the mouth is not primarily its hunger but its participation in language. That this unmeasurability might readily affect all the other appetites is of course a crucial aspect of the whole book. In a society where the dominant people live by *measure* of all kinds (number, law, finance—boxing, bottling, labeling—the world epitomized by Homais and his shop), the problems of "une bouche démesurée" may become acute, even unbearable. This will not be the case with *le nouveau*, but rather with the girl who takes on his name. Two other aspects of the description should be noted. First of all, there is something sexual about it: the full lungs (and Flaubert makes us vividly aware of differences in breathing, or what Dickens calls "the office of respiration," and its effects, throughout), then the release and the "throwing," or hurling, of the word, do suggest (through displacement or isomorphism, or something of both) that the final discharge of the whole being in a thrown word is in some way connected to the release in orgasm. The other point concerns the simile that Flaubert inserts— "comme pour appeler quelqu'un" (as if calling someone). Needless to say, there are no idle similes in this book, but this one brings more into the text than one might think at first glance. For in speaking, one is inevitably involved in "calling" someone. Here the multiple meanings involved in *appeler* are crucial, since it can refer both to calling out (hailing) and to naming and giving a term to. Once we are in language, we are forever "calling someone," calling for someone to help us, to love us, to answer us, and forever naming and labeling. It is as though in learning to speak, we first become fully aware of our own severance and state of separateness, so Flaubert carefully makes the first utterance of the word (in terms of this book) coeval with the need or compulsion to "call someone." And indeed in many ways they are one and the same act, since in speech there is always involved some element of a desire for connection, a reaching out, an attempt to join. And since the words we speak come from those around us, we are necessarily calling them in using their words. Once you move beyond unintelligibility and syllabic indeterminacy and gain the word, you are doomed forever to be calling someone. No one learns this lesson more thoroughly and painfully than Emma Bovary.

When *le nouveau* finally does erupt into speech, the first audible utterance is a word that is not a word, as the hysterical reaction of the class sufficiently indicates. It is worth examining with some care just what kind of word it is, and why it should arouse such derision. *Charbovari* is effectively a holophrastic utterance (i.e., the attempt to express a whole phrase or even sentence in a single word). What is missing is the gap between "Charles" and "Bovary." This may seem a rather slight and obvious point to make, but in fact many of the problems anatomized in the book may be said to be related to the difficulties involved in the managing or mastering of "gaps" of all kinds. At this point in the text, *le nouveau* has managed to master the single word, but he cannot handle the seriality of language, which depends on the competence to distribute and work with gaps. (Gap-incompetence would be one way of describing the ultimate source of Emma's malaise, but I will come to that later.) Holophrastic utterances characterize that stage of the child's life when it is passing from crying, babbling, and lalling into the sequential discourse of the family and society. It represents an attempt to get everything into one word, one utterance, one sound. In this it dramatizes the painful transition from crying to language. It is worth stressing how unerringly and with what economy and exactitude of detail Flaubert has redramatized in the opening pages of his book the various stages involved in the entry into language, finally focusing on the necessity to learn to insert gaps or holes into the continuum of uttered sounds in order to participate in social discourse (failure to do so results in annihilating mockery). The connection between this necessity and the onset of desire is very close; indeed, they are inextricable as Lacan (most recently) has sought to demonstrate in great detail. Using one or two of Lacan's terms we can see how Flaubert anticipates his insights. The initiation into the handling of gaps (or, in Lacan's terms, the hard lesson of being forced to divert immediate and total needs through the "defiles of the signifier," which both break up the specific needs and introduce previously nonexisting holes into the experience of the utterer), at the same time implants a "lack in being" in the speaker; this is a crucial phenomenon that Flaubert seems to have been uncannily aware of. If desire can be said to consist of "the presence of an absence of a reality," then we can see that this is certainly part of Emma's malaise.[4] If, in addition, that absent reality is nonspecific, but "the desire of a Desire" (a phrase used by Kojeve) then

---

[4]Jacques Lacan quoted by Anthony Wilden in *The Language of the Self*, p. 185; Lacan quoted by Wilden in *System and Structure*, p. 25; Lacan quoted by Wilden in *Language of the Self*, p. 193.

Flaubert is, of course, not alone among nineteenth century novelists in examining the problem of desire/absence/substitution. See, for example, *The Mayor of Casterbridge* by Thomas Hardy, in which we read—concerning Elizabeth-Jane—the following: "Yet her experience had consisted less in a series of pure disappointments than in a series of substitutions. Continually it had happened that what she had desired had not been granted her, and what she had been granted she had not desired." (*The Mayor of Casterbridge* [London: Macmillan and Co. Ltd., 1960], p. 180).

we may begin to appreciate the appropriateness of the metaphor of the fog in the head. Another of Kojeve's formulations is "the being of Language is the non-being of objects,"[5] which is too extremely metaphysical to be entirely appropriate in this context. But the realization that with the acquisition (imposed by preexisting others) of language, the child also acquires a sense of loss, of absence, a hole in being that can never be filled; that from one point of view, desire is another word for the gaps that are an indispensable and constitutive part of our speech acts as well as our writing acts, and that in one sense language *does* involve some degree of negation of objects or loss of grasp on the object world (it is an old saying that when the child acquires the word or the concept, he "loses" the thing)—all these realizations are present in vivid and compressed form in this opening incident in the novel, and they are crucial for everything that is to follow.[6]

In the incident as described by Flaubert, the "word" represents a basic cry of anguish, which is translated (diverted) under duress into a social utterance of the name. After the howls of derision that greet the first desperate holophrastic utterance of *le nouveau*, we note that the teacher effects the necessary separation of the composite word into two, thus literally "manging to take hold of the name of Charles Bovary" ("par-

---

[5]Alexandre Kojève, *Introduction à la lecture de Hegel*, p. 12, quoted by Wilden in *Language of the Self*, p. 193; Wilden on Kojève and Lacan in *Language of the Self*, p. 155 n. 186.

[6]In this connection it is worth noting that when children do learn to speak, they apparently literally lose a kind of cognition and mastery over the disposition, movement, and conservation of objects that they have prior to language: i.e., they do not exist in a buzzing booming chaos, but can in fact construe the world around them very clearly. The buzzing and booming chaos would seem to arrive with language, for in trying to solve problems of recognition, placement, conservation and so on by using words, they begin to get things wrong that they had previously got right. Cf. Jean Piaget in *The Construction of Reality in the Child* (trans. Margaret Cook [New York: Basic Books, 1954]):

> The adaptation of intelligence to these new realities, when speech and conceptual thought are superimposed on the sensorimotor plane, entails the reappearance of all the obstacles already overcome in the realm of action. That is why, despite the level reached by the intelligence in the fifth and sixth stages of its sensorimotor development, it does not appear to be rational at the outset, when it begins to be organized on the verbal-conceptual plane. On the contrary, it manifests a series of temporal displacements in comprehension and no longer only in extension, since in view of corresponding operations the child of a given age is less advanced on the verbal-conceptual plane than on the plane of action. In simpler terms, the child does not at first succeed in reflecting in words and concepts the procedures that he already knows how to carry out in acts, and if he cannot reflect them it is because, in order to adapt himself to the collective and conceptual plane on which his thought will henceforth move, he is obliged to repeat the work of coordination between assimilation and accommodation already accomplished in his sensorimotor adaptation anterior to the physical and practical universe.

(P. 361)

I am indebted to Dr. Thomas Bower for first explaining this phenomenon to me.

venu à saisir le nom de Charles Bovary" [p. 23]) by "having it pronounced and spelt and said over" (p. 17) or more literally, "dictated,
spelt, and reread" ("se l'étant fait dicter, épeler et relire" [p. 23])—three
activities that complete the enforced initiation into language: speaking
the name out loud, then breaking it down through spelling, then reading
it again. This is the process of repetition that is deeply involved in the
process of socializing the individual in such a society; it is part of the
method by which *le nouveau* is transformed into *Charles Bovary,* by which
the body is imprinted with the name (which then renders him
"holdable"—as we say that a name is someone's "handle") and the cap is
fitted over the head. After he has said his name, the first thing Charles
Bovary worries about is his cap, though as a newborn into language his
utterance is very faltering. "M-my c-cap . . ." (p. 17), or rather he lacks
the confidence to complete the word: "Ma cas . . . " [p. 23]). The
teacher's response is particularly significant, for he reacts to *le nouveau*
in two distinct but intimately related ways. He demonstrates angry, authoritarian imperiousness and then appeasing, consoling gentleness.
Thus he is "indigne" and speaks to everyone with "une voix furieuse"
and, focusing on Charles, orders him to write out twenty times "*ridiculus
sum,*" then "d'une voix plus douce," he reassures him that he will have his
cap back. The two utterances need to be seen in French. "Quant à vous,
le nouveau, vous me copierez vingt fois le verbe *ridiculus sum.*" "Eh! Vous
la retrouverez, votre casquette; on ne vous l'a pas volée" (p. 24). The new
one is both humiliated and somewhat comforted. The humiliation involves two processes. First of all he is being trained to define himself as
ridiculous or worthless in another language (the teacher withholds his
newfound name and recasts him as *le nouveau*); this reinforces the
strange self-alienating effect of *speaking* in the native tongue (it was
difficult enough to say "Charles Bovary") by making the figure define
itself in *writing* in a foreign (in this case, dead) language. It is extremely
efficient training in the exercise of self-reification and self-alienation, for
such a self will never know itself as other than an object to which he
obediently applies the imposed defining terms and names. (In Lacan's
terms, Charles Bovary is being prepared for a lifelong existence in the
realm of the imaginary, of "the other.") More significantly, the humiliation consists of *copying* the phrase twenty times. The importance of copying and repetition will emerge later on, but at this point we may note the
following features of this particular aspect of the punishment. Copying
devalues by repetition; continual identity of repetition ends in the annihilation of meaning; among other things, Charles is beginning a long
process of rendering himself meaningless. Learning, of course, requires
degrees of repetition, but in this particular case nothing is being taught,
even with the most crude pedagogical method, except how to start writ-

ing the self into oblivion. Charles Bovary's studies proper begin with self-negation as an institutionalized and supervised procedure. The process is backed up by anger. What emerges in the book is that the whole society itself is permeated with this kind of *compulsion to copy* that Charles learns at school as an exercise. The schoolroom is, among other things, the place where a kind of obsessive repetition is implanted in the child and copying is installed as a habit that may then extend into a way of life. It may be called a discipline in endless duplication. After this humiliation, the master's voice becomes quite gentle, and he reassures Charles that he will find his cap again ("retrouverez"—cf. *re-lire*—in this book things tend either to be done again, or undone: the prevalent prefixes are *re* and *dé*: the repetitive and the privative). It is as though Charles is ready to wear the cap properly, automatically, with no more confusion: he has been appropriately tamed and moulded for containment within the *casquette*. It is never referred to again and does not need to be, since from now on Charles wears the impossible cap of his culture (that insane salad of signs) permanently. He has learned to say his name, submitted to the exercise of self-negating copying, and re-found his cap. (A cap that was never lost, because it was both new ["neuve"] and the kind of costuming of consciousness that that society had prepared for him— and the likes of him in all the schools, for he is the generic *nouveau*.) With such a preparation he is ready to embark on the long somnolence of his life.

Two other aspects of his uneasiness within language should be noted, since they also anticipate, embryonically, problems that increase throughout the book.[7] Charles's behavior in school is exemplary; he is totally obedient, and industrious out of uncertainty. He looks up every word in the dictionary ("cherchant tous les mots dans le dictionnaire" [p. 24]), thus taking, or giving himself, more pain ("et se donnant beaucoup de mal" [p. 24]); it records an effort, made with quiet desperation, to incorporate what seems to be an alien substance. It is particularly significant that he learns the grammar but cannot employ the words with much combinatory style. The French is essential here: "s'il savait passablement ses règles, il n'avait guère d'élégance dans les tournures" (p. 24). Very literally, this could be translated as—if he knew his rules passably well, he

---

[7]A minor example of embryonic anticipations, or echoes, is the fact that while he is engaged in his first schoolwork, he is hit by an occasional ball of paper—"boulette de papier" (p. 24). This initial trifling torment is repeated in a new form just before his death when he feels "une boulette de papier" under his foot, which is how he discovers the love letters sent to Emma and thus begins his final period of suffering. Near both the start and the end of his life he is tormented with little balls of paper. That such echoes are quite deliberate is perfectly clear, and what Flaubert is doing will be considered later. Here it may suffice to point out that it is another form of copying and repetition—in Charles's life, in Flaubert's text.

had scarcely any elegance in his "turnings." Obviously, in the context, the primary meaning of *tournures* is "turns of phrase" or even "renderings." But *tournures* refers here to "turnings" in general; it also means the human figure (it appears in the next paragraph referring to the figure of his father), and it means turnings from a lathe. I will return to these and other implications of this crucial word further on. What is of great interest here is the opposition of *règles* and *tournures*: the first implies linearity, invariant or unvarying elements of procedure, directives and imperatives based on regulation and repetition; while the latter implies circularity (or curvature) or at least some partial deviation from everything straight and rule-dominated, if only the particular form of the human figure. We can see right away that Charles's whole existence is dominated by *règles* of all kinds, while Emma is constantly drawn towards *tournures* in many senses of the word (she is subject to giddiness—"étourdissements"—from the first). Moreover, the opposition between various kinds of straightness and of "turningness," or things and movements that are in some way turned (the ugliness of the phrasing is calculated to maintain maximum generality), is one of the organizing features of the book and reflects some basic tension and opposition in society and existence as described by Flaubert. Whether the latent opposition between *règles* and *tournures* can be maintained as a relationship (as it may be said to be in language, which depends equally on both), whether it must become a hostile opposition, or whether finally some curious third process supervenes whereby the rules are in some way turned and the turnings begin to reveal their permeation by rules— this is another matter that Flaubert explores in this novel. In view of my subject, it can be said that marriage in this society should be the paradigm for the ideal relationship between *règles* and *tournures*. The *règles* are the social sanctions and normative prescriptions contained explicitly and implicitly within the ritual and the contract (whereby, as a social category, all marriages are the same); the *tournures* are the unique individual variant elements, the particular human shaping and style of the relationship (whereby each marriage can be unique as a living experience). If marriage breaks down, a lot of other relationships break down with it—but this will become clearer in subsequent contexts.

The other aspect of Charles Bovary's anxiety within language that I wish to point to emerges when he is registered to study medicine and he goes to look at the syllabus. This makes *him* giddy ("lui fit un effet d'étourdissement" [p. 29]). Flaubert lists the various subjects—anatomy, physiology, pharmacy, etc., etc.—and concludes "all names of unknown import to him: doors into so many sanctuaries filled with an august obscurity" (p. 22) ("tous noms dont il ignorait les étymologies et qui étaient comme autant de portes de sanctuaires pleins d'augustes ténèbres" [p. 29]). We might say that Charles is here experiencing the "terror of terminology" (a phrase from William Gass). The terror is not that there is something specific and solid though yet unknown behind the doors of names, but rather that once through those doors you will find a majestic darkness—the phrase managing very powerfully to combine the sense of what is dark and insubstantial ("ténèbres") with a sense of something exalted, imperial, even sacred, having awesome powers, perhaps hinting at the frightening power of the Father, who is also the bestower of the name. Charles Bovary is here sensing something of that disturbing presence-absence that is inherent in language, and he flees from it—not literally, but by adopting a certain mode of existence that is described in the next paragraph. "He performed his daily little task like a mill-horse tramping round blindfold grinding away at he knows not what" (p. 22). ("Il accomplissait sa petite tâche quotidienne à la manière du cheval de manège, qui tourne en place les yeux bandés, ignorant de la besogne qu'il broie." [p. 29].) For the rest of his life, whatever he does and wherever he moves, Charles will "tourne en place," his capacity for true vision bound, bandaged, blindfolded forever, so that he will never have to confront those "augustes ténèbres" that he has sensed are hovering behind the doors of language—doors that he will never open. He turns from names to dominoes for relief, solid meaningless sign-objects that can safely be manipulated into certain rule-determined positions, and that have no threatening, disturbing darkness waiting behind them (tapping them on the table seems to him a precious act of freedom). As far as society is concerned he does become a doctor, but he is never a real doctor,[8] only a bad copy of one. (The "real" doctor, the "original" is Larivière of course—but he comes from another world, another level of reality.) What Charles Bovary really does is to take up a life of anxious blindness and graceless repetition, such as his schooling prepared him for. The loss of humanness, or the privation of participation in life, involved in such a process is immensely poignant, for Charles Bovary is—as Emma recognizes in some of the saddest words in the book—good: "tu es bon, toi!" (p. 409). Unfortunately he was never properly alive, never fully real. Yet this was the man, and the name, who were supposed to fulfill Emma, or fill in the gap in her life, to complete the incompleteness of her unmarried state. Given his education—and this surely is why Flaubert gives us the minute details of the opening scenes—such a person, such a copy, such a self-negated product can only serve to awaken

---

[8]To be precise, he only finally qualifies as an "officier de santé," i.e., a "health officer," though this distinction is somewhat obscured in the English translation by references to the "diploma" that Charles fails and then passes. But technically, Charles is never professionally a properly qualified doctor. Though that is the role he assumes, and is assumed to have.

more powerful feelings of unfulfillment, more painful gaps, a greater sense of incompleteness. Indeed, she finally comes to experience him, his "presence," as "nul," "néant"—one who is not one, the very body of nothingness. Thus part of the fog in Emma's head can be traced back to the schoolroom in which Charles Bovary was so traumatically and so destructively disciplined into nomination, repetition—and self-nihilation.

Following this minute description of these first decisive and determining moments in school, Flaubert proceeds to give details about the father and the mother and their respective notions about bringing up the boy Charles Bovary. It offers a composite process of at once both spoiling and neglecting the child. In a way, the habit of vague and mindless replication starts in the family, for the father has "un certain idéal viril de l'enfance" that is as vague and miscellaneous an assortment of incongruent fragments as the boy's cap (e.g., he tries to teach the boy to sleep without a fire, to drink rum, and to jeer at church processions), while the mother always tries to "drag" him after her ("le traînait toujours après elle" [p. 26]). It is worth noting that she cuts out carboard figures for him ("elle lui découpait des cartons"), since this is also an activity involved in producing copies in another material (and there was cardboard in his cap). The action of *découpage* is to become very important as the book develops. Similarly, she later chooses, or "cuts out," his house and his wife for him. In addition she pours her incoherent talk into him— stories, monologues without end, and what can perhaps best be translated as coaxing babblings ("chatteries babillardes [p. 26]). In this way she is projecting her own inner fragmentation onto him, but here again the French is necessary: "elle reporta sur cette tête d'enfant toutes ses vanités éparses, brisées" (p. 26). Note that it is *re-porta*, not just *porta*—i.e., a carrying over or forward, or a taking back; as I suggested, very little is *done for the first time* in this novel. And what is being carried over to the head of the child (the emphasis is important in view of the significance of the cap and what might be called the parodistic ritual of capping in the first scene) are what could be "ambitions" or "vanities," but also "futilities," that are scattered and broken. This scattering and breaking and many related modes of disassembling and diffusing recur in various forms throughout the book, and they are important activities and processes in a society that seems to live by strange assortments of random bits (as represented by the cap, but encountered in dozens of other ways). What seems to be lacking, not only in Charles Bovary's family upbringing but in the society at large, is any principle of integration, any genuine sense of a vital, organizing, centralizing thrust or push that might enable a growing child to emerge into a coherent, whole human being. Such a concept might itself seem to be suspiciously vague, but there can be no doubt about the relationship between fragmentation and dehumanization, or rather nonhumanization, in Flaubert's book. And it starts with the father and the mother.

There follow further instances of his education, which only serve to increase what may fairly be called the implanted incoherence in Charles Bovary's head. Lessons are short, haphazard, take place in shifting postures (standing up, slumped down half asleep), in random places (the vestry, the foot of a tree), and at confusing tempos (in a hurry, in a torpor), and are always inconclusive and interrupted, so that they are very accurately described as taking place in "odd moments," which are also *lost* moments ("aux moments perdus" [p. 26]). What he is really learning is inconsecutiveness, inconsistency, inconclusiveness. It is not a lost education but an education in loss. But while he is receiving this education of the mind, he is also moving and doing, and in a short space Flaubert covers a large range of different kinds of movement by almost listing or itemizing the way the young boy disports himself physically in his environment, or inserts himself into it: "vagabondait," "suivait," "chassait," "mangeait," "gardait," "fanait," "courait," "jourait," "suppliait," "aussi poussa-t-il comme un chêne" (wandered or ran wild, followed, chased, ate, guarded, tossed (hay), ran, played, begged—and grew like an oak). What we have here in very summary form is a spectrum of the different kinds of basic physical movement and actions that in various forms and contexts and combinations pretty well serve to cover all the different kinds of actions that will recur in the ensuing pages. Indeed it is a précis of life, or life in miniature. However, two activities are notably absent—making love (in whatever form, with whatever implications in the word) and sleeping. The matter of making love is encountered shortly after in this first chapter and then again throughout the whole book, *affecting all the other activities*; while sleeping, which is indeed a very prominent activity or nonactivity throughout the book, is brought in in a very interesting way. For while the child starts just by running wild ("vagabondait"), it is during his early bits of pseudoeducation that he falls asleep ("l'enfant s'endormait" [p. 27]). "Vagabonder" and "s'endormir" effectively contain all the other variant activities—they are the beginning and end of a day, a childhood, a life. Everything in between is the interlude of conscious existence, and the two words hover in the air throughout the book, centering on Emma but pervading the whole lexical atmosphere. And this is the notable aspect of the whole first chapter. Thus it is from one point of view a complete novel in little, a whole bildungsroman, a childhood, education, career, marriage—it only lacks a death. It is as though Flaubert is demonstrating that a life can be reduced to certain items of accounting (it could very well be described as the "account" of a life), which may be repeated on a different scale in different contexts, but these are also themselves repetitions. He is preparing us as readers for a novel concerning a mode of life that in a profound sense is without novelty.

Before leaving this first chapter and considering the life of the third Madame Bovary, I want to make three more observations. The first concerns the last appearance of the *nous* that started the book. Thus: "Il serait maintenant impossible à aucun de nous de se rien rappeler de lui" (p. 28) ("It would be impossible for any of us to remember the least thing about him now" [p. 21]). This "we," as I noted, involves us as readers as well as some nonspecific narrating entity and community, the plurality into which the singularity (only literally) of Charles Bovary is inserted. And apart from studying and staring, "we" do two particular things to Charles Bovary. We mock him, and we forget him. These are two ways of negating his existence. The child speaks, and it is as if he is calling for someone. We laugh and then fail to recall the child at all. This is the cruel reverse or ugly opposite of true community, and it is therefore appropriate that Flaubert should drop the traditional *nous,* having revealed what it does and how it now acts. In doing this, he is implying that there is no longer any true community and that the illusory contracts between people and between the writer and the reader have all failed; in the continuation/replication of the novel from chapter two onward, there is no more "nous." I would regard this as the most significant shift in narrative technique in the history of the novel, for its implications effectively influenced the whole subsequent development of the novel, and they are still with us today. Meaning and communication depend on (are a function of) what Saussure (in *Course in General Linguistics*) called "circuits" of discourse and on "context" (particularly as defined in the work of Gregory Bateson). If you cannot say "we," you cannot say or locate "I" and "you." With the vanishing of "we" in the book, the whole positioning of, and contextual relationship between, author, reader, and fictional figures becomes uncertain, unascertainable, and in this sense there truly is, by the end of the book, a complete loss of meaning. When Charles Bovary dies, there is no "we." His corpse is found by his daughter, and he is opened up by a doctor, Monsieur Canivet. "He opened up the body but found nothing" (p. 360). ("Il l'ouvrit et ne trouva rien" [p. 446].) That nothing is made up of all the nothings that his upbringing and education and subsequent life fed into him; it is the nothing that "we" make of him with our mocking and forgetting. It is not only Charles's body that is opened to reveal an emptiness, for we might fairly say that Flaubert has opened up a particular society and—"ne trouva rien."

The two other points about this first chapter concern love, apparently trivially but again in ways that will reappear and be replayed and reexperienced in different ways throughout the book. The first concerns

Charles's "passion" (in both languages) for dominoes. The place where he plays offers another distorted initiation: "It was an initiation into the great world, an attaining of forbidden pleasures; as he went in he put his hand on the doorknob with an almost sensual delight" (p. 23). ("C'était comme l'initiation du monde, l'accès des plaisirs défendus; et, en entrant, il posait la main sur le bouton de la porte avec une joie presque sensuelle" [p. 30].) But it is an initiation of a very important kind, an initiation into fetishism. I will comment on Freud's definition of fetishism subsequently, but here we may just note that first of all there is a "passion" attaching itself to little bits of dead black-dotted bone (as Flaubert describes the dominoes); then the "almost sensual joy" aroused by contact with the doorknob. Contact with the doorknob is sufficient to arouse anticipatory pleasure comparable in kind if not degree to contact with the dominoes themselves. This amounts to a perversity compounded by a kind of double fetishism. For if touching dead bits of bone (as opposed to the living body of another person) can arouse passion, and if then touching the knob of the door leading into the room where contact with the dominoes is possible can also give sensual pleasure, then there is theoretically and literally no limit to how far removed and deflected from the actual body of another person both passion and sensual pleasure may be. It could be that ultimately all sensual pleasure and passion might be attached to a single object, to the total exclusion of any human beings. An object like a doorknob. Or a napkin ring. I will return to this point later.

It is only after this perverted initiation that Charles Bovary encounters "l'amour" (and here again we notice the fragmentation, as though passion and sensual pleasure and love have been broken and scattered, disconnected, made into disparate phenomena—like his mother's futilities). We read that he learned how to make punch and finally came to know about, or learned about, love: ("sut faire du punch et connut enfin l'amour" [p. 30]). This is much more than an easy irony on Flaubert's part. In writing it this way, he is indicating not only the separating out of love from what might be thought of as its component features (passion, sensual attraction) but also its reduction thereby to what is an abstraction at the end of a curriculum that is the definitive parody of an education: an anticlimactic conclusion to the nonlearning that is Charles Bovary's preparation for his nonlife ahead. "Knowing" love and how to make punch are here rendered equivalent by proximity, as they have been rendered equivalent in Charles Bovary's experience. It would not take much to make them indistinguishable. And that too is one of the frightening possibilities explored in the book. The conjunction of "l'amour" with a pleasurable or palliative liquid recurs at the end of the first chapter (or the first novel within the novel, as I have

suggested), with the same potentially confusing, reducing, and equivalizing effect, when we read that his first wife (i.e., the *second* Madame
Bovary) "ended by asking him for a dose of medicine and a little more
love" (p. 25) ("et elle finissait en lui demandant quelque sirop pour sa
santé et un peu plus d'amour" [p. 32].) Here, in deliberately trivializing
and miniaturizing anticipatory form, are precisely the two hopelessly
confused "demands" or requests or "wants" that finally take over Emma's life and destroy it: specifically, requests made to Justin for the
medicine-poison and to Rodolphe and Léon for love they never had to
give, but more generally requests made to existence itself. It is yet
another terrible distortion that the adoring Justin complies with the
request for death out of love, while the men turn down her request for
love out of a kind of fearful egoism and insentience that is itself a form
of death in life. What happens to Emma is the final indictment of a
society in which equivalization and repetition have gone so far that it has
become almost impossible to distinguish its potions from its passions.

Monsieur Binet and His Lathe

Apart from the male relatives and lovers who impinge directly on
Emma's life, there are a number of other male figures who make up a
secondary environment around her and in many ways affect the shape
of her life as much as her more immediately proximate attachments.
These figures range from Monsieur Homais to the blind beggar, but one
of the most important is the strange figure of Monsieur Binet, who along
with Monsieur Homais is part of the first group the Bovarys encounter
when they arrive in Yonville-L'Abbaye and go to the local inn. His name
first occurs in the context of the timing of the evening meal, for the
landlady is horrified at the suggestion that Monsieur Binet might be kept
waiting. "There's not his like in the world for punctuality" (p. 87). ("Car
son pareil n'existe sur la terre pour l'exactitude" [p. 111].) This refers
specifically to his mania for punctuality, but the word *exactitude* has some
other relevant connotations. It covers the more general meanings of
exactness, exactitude, correctness, accuracy, etc., and it also refers to the
closeness of a copy. It is related semantically and phonemically to *exaction,* which is a word applied to the exaction of taxes. The relevance of
this is that Binet is a tax collector. (More specifically he is "an old soldier

now a tax collector" [p. 88] ["un ancien carabinier qui est percepteur" (p. 112)]; this is just one of many degenerative transformations throughout the book and all implicitly anticipated in Charles Bovary's cap.) And it is worth noting that there is a potentially very strange paradox in the landlady's pardonable exaggeration. Let me deliberately mistranslate what she says at this point and then try to explain why the paradox has such far-reaching implications.

Let us say, then, that she is also saying—this man, who is utterly dedicated to exact copying (i.e., everything done today must be exactly the same as it was yesterday) is without equal (or similar to comparable figures in the world). The weird miracle that is latent in this remark is the existence in the world of a person whose uniqueness lies in his total dedication to copying. How would such a figure come into being? What can be the origin of this total denial of originality? For this is certainly what Monsieur Binet's life is given over to. Everything must always be the same—things in the same place, meals at the same time, body in the same posture (as far as that is possible prior to actual death). Even his shoes have parallel swellings ("deux renflements parallèles" [p. 112]) where his toes turn up, as though even his body partook of his silent conspiracy to deny singleness and to commit the world to duplication and parallelism. This dedication is most clearly manifested in his hobby—turning napkin rings on a lathe: "He spent his time turning napkin rings on a lathe which he had at his house, and these he hoarded with all the jealousy of the artist and the possessiveness of the bourgeois" (p. 88). ("Il avait chez lui un tour, où il s'amusait à tourner des ronds de serviette dont il encombrait sa maison avec la jalousie d'un artiste et l'égoïsme d'un bourgeois" [p. 112].) Certain aspects of this hobby may be noted immediately. To start with, the napkin rings are entirely nonfunctional (he does not eat at home but in the inn). They simply fill up or encumber his house. They are from every point of view entirely valueless; indeed, they represent the reification of valuelessness. To be deliberately as simply literal as possible, a napkin ring is a material encirclement of nothing—it is not even like any kind of coinage with fiduciary markings. It is a manufactured hole. In this we may say that it represents the *symbolic* opposite of the wedding ring, which, as symbol, contains the most important contractual and linking significances society recognizes. As nonsymbolic *object,* however, the wedding ring is isomorphically identical to the napkin ring. One horror that the book explores is what happens when the wedding ring comes to mean as little as the napkin ring, part of the more general sense of disappearing distinctions that pervades the book. The related horror is the notion that the deformed energies of the artist and the bourgeois (jealousy and possessiveness) may combine in this manic *production* of nonmeaning, cluttering up not only the house but society and the world itself with these palpable things that are nonthings. It represents the ultimate fetishism when all the energy and passion that should find meaning in what is symbolized by the wedding ring transfers itself to focus on the napkin ring, which can only symbolize nothing: a shift from the procreational relationship of human beings to the solitary manufacture of nonfunctional holes.

The process is duplicated, repeated, endlessly, and it is this repetition that participates in that annihilation of individuality, difference, and meaning to which Monsieur Binet is unconsciously dedicated. He himself speaks very little, but the sound of his lathe pervades the village. (You can see "the lean profile of Monsieur Binet bending over his lathe, whose monotonous drone could be heard as far away as the Golden Lion" [p. 112] ["le profil maigre de M. Binet penché sur son tour, dont le ronflement monotone s'entendait jusqu'au *Lion d'Or*" (p. 142)]. *Ronflement* can be "whirring" or "humming" (it also phonetically echoes the *renflements* in his shoes), but it also means snoring—of which there is a great deal in this book, a book not so much of "the dead" as of "the sleepy." Snoring we may call the nonspeech of nonconsciousness, a drowning of semantic utterances in involuntary bodily noise. It is as though Binet is spreading a snoring throughout the community, eroding the distinctions of speech in the nonsemantic monotone of his lathe (a kind of *Dunciad* effect). When Emma is in the attic contemplating suicide after receiving Rodolphe's letter of rejection, the lathe seems to be calling her: "she had only to give way, to let herself go . . . And all the time the lathe went on whirring, like a voice furiously calling her" (p. 217) ("elle n'avait qu'à céder, qu'à se laisser prendre; et le ronflement du tour ne discontinuait pas, comme une voix furieuse qui l'appelait" [p. 272]). It acts here as a kind of antivoice summoning Emma to nonbeing, wordlessly telling her of the relief of abandoning the torments of individuation and identity. Indeed, in her state at this moment, with the air circling around in her empty head ("l'air circulait dans sa tête creuse") as though all consciousness has been hollowed out and the body vacated by the self, and whatever is still present of "Emma" poised on the very edge of the attic window as though she has all but abandoned the house (and all it implies) for the unsocialized space that is everywhere around her—at this moment the summons of the lathe takes on the tone of an imperious command. What in fact prevents Emma from capitulation to the narcotic imperative of the lathe is another voice from within the house. "—Ma femme! Ma femme! cria Charles" (p. 272). (The Penguin translation has "Emma! Emma!" [p. 217], but this misses the point that Emma is called back by a voice reminding her, not of her name, but of her role.) The human voice draws her back into her social definition and the call of the lathe is, at least temporarily, resisted. But the whirring is to continue throughout the book, and indirectly, Emma finally succumbs to all that is implied in the lathe and M. Binet's unceasing "work." By the endless repetitions of his lathe, he would indeed ultimately annihilate difference altogether and bring everything and everyone into irreversible sameness, a oneness not of the significant union of two but of the erasing of the distinctions between all. Monsieur Binet's lathe is one of the paradigm instruments of bourgeois society, filling the world with replicated voids. It is clear that Flaubert named him with care; *binet* is a kind of "save-all," but more importantly *biner* (which is phonetically identical with Binet) means "to duplicate" (as an intransitive verb—transitively it means "to dig ground a second time," "to hoe"). Monsieur Binet is exactly he who does things twice, the incarnation of the ultimately deadly drive to duplicate.

But there is more to the lathe than that, and now I can try to show why it has such an important influence on Emma's life. At one point, in the Golden Lion, Léon is complaining of his boring life. Binet says that he needs more amusement. Of what kind, asks Léon, to which Binet makes the unforgettable reply, "If I were you I'd get a lathe!" (p. 130). (Moi, à votre place, j'aurais un tour!" [p. 164].) Léon's objection that he does not know how to use a lathe also has a more general implication ("Mais je ne sais pas tourner" [p. 164].) At this point it is necessary to pause and emphasize the importance of these two words—*tour* and *tourner*. In addition to "lathe," *tour* covers a multitude of turnings and rounds, whether *le tour du monde* or *tour de cou* ("necklet"). It is a twist in the road, a turn of phrase, the contour or shape of a face, a turn of the head, a twist in the back. It is of course closely related to *tournure,* as I discussed the word in the previous section. Indeed, you can say that if you *tourner* on a *tour* you produce *tournures.* Put that way it sounds as though the whole process is a long tautology—which is exactly the point. The process of pointless repetition, the tendency to homogenize things and people, the elimination of distinction in monotone, is being reenacted or duplicated in the text by this sort of phonemic and semantic echoing, merging, moving together. Binet's hobby is solipsistic, masturbatory, yet it pervades society (he is after all the tax collector). He has fetishized tautology itself, and one way that Flaubert marks this is by showing the words in his text beginning to look at each other and discover similarities and repetitions that suggests the beginnings of some kind of ultimate perverse rapprochement among words themselves, not a marriage but a merging, meanings swallowing each other in hopeless circularity as Binet's lathe seems to swallow clear utterance in its insentient unvarying hum. This constitutes a further paradox: "sense" is involved in the quest for difference or change or originality—inasmuch as it is always some kind of deviation from the normative patterns—yet it is also perversely involved in bringing about the precisely opposite condition, namely, sameness through repetition. The search for change seems necessarily to accelerate the process of equivalization. It is one aspect of the dilemma discovered and enacted by Emma Bovary that she is forever "turning," seeking continual change, but the more she turns the more she finds she is more deeply immersed in sameness. When we read that "Emma had rediscovered in adultery all the banality of marriage" (p. 301) ("Emma retrouvait dans l'adultère toutes les platitudes du mariage" [p. 376]), we know that she is near to realizing the fatal futility of all her "turnings." It is as much as to say that she could no longer see the difference between a wedding ring and a napkin ring—the one has, effectively, turned into the other, and they have become indistinguishable at the level of significance. Such a loss of sense of difference would indicate that a total loss of any sense of meaning is imminent, which is indeed the real horror at the heart of Emma's experience.

This paradoxical combination of circular movement and accelerating sameness and immobility is a main feature of Emma's momentum in the book—the faster she runs, the more the same everything becomes; and when she runs fastest, she stops. Her involvement in all kinds of circular movement will be considered in a later section. At this point we may note that something of this paradox is represented in the figure of Binet himself. On the day of the Agricultural Show, Binet is present in his capacity of captain of the fire brigade, and he is described as a completely dehumanized object, an automaton. "He wore an even higher collar than usual today; and, buttoned tight into his uniform, the upper part of his body was so stiff and motionless that it seemed as if all the life in him had descended to his legs, which rose and fell with wooden exactitude as he marked time" (p. 144). ("Il portait, ce jour-là, un col encore plus haut que de coutume; et, sanglé dans sa tunique, il avait le buste si raide et immobile, que toute la partie vitale de sa personne semblait être descendue dans ses deux jambes, qui se levaient en cadence, à pas marqués, d'un seul mouvement" [p. 182].) The passage requires little comment in the present context. We can sense the connection between the endless turning of the lathe and this all-but-lifeless immobility; it is as though Binet has managed to erase all conscious and emotional life from himself through his dedication to the lathe, leaving only some vestigial automatic motor activity in the lowest portion of his body. This elimination of emotive, conative, and (almost) cognitive connection to the rest of the world is indeed all but complete. We are told that he does not meddle with other people's business ("Binet, qui ne se mêlait jamais des affaires d'autrui" [pp. 235-6]). He of course recoils from Emma in horror when she comes to him for help, and his absence from her funeral is specifically commented on by Homais ("Il remarqua de même que M. Binet s'était abstenu de paraître" [p. 433]). *Abstenir* is a verb to put with *biner* in considering his way of life, for ultimately what Binet is abstaining from is any trace of individual spontaneous feeling or thought. We gather that he occasionally suffers from hunger pangs ("des fringales" [p. 414]), but this indicates that the range of emotional and sexual desires and appetites experienced by such as Emma have contracted in him down to an irritating residual symptom for which an appropriate medicine can be prescribed. Effectively the cure (or palliative, rather) is indistinguishable from the radical cause of the sickness—the lathe serves as both.

All of this might make his little flirtation with illegality seem rather strange. The significant passage occurs when Emma is returning from a visit to Rodolphe and first of all sees a gun barrel sticking out of a tub, apparently aiming at her. Then a man leaps "out of the tub like a jack-in-the-box" (p. 178) (though here the French is more detailed than the standard English translation—"comme ces diables à boudin qui se dressent du fond des boîtes" [p. 223]: note the odd reoccurrence of the word *boudin* and the spelling out of the movement, "standing up at [from] the bottom of boxes"). This turns out to be Binet, and, we are told, there had been an official order, which he is ignoring, prohibiting duck shooting except from boats. "Monsieur Binet, despite his respect for the law, was at present on the wrong side of it" (p. 178). ("M. Binet, malgré son respect pour les lois, se trouvait en contravention" [p. 224].) In this he is of course related to Homais, who is also both a keen maintainer of bourgeois society and at the same time a slightly illegal practitioner. You could say that Flaubert is making the same kind of point made by Ibsen in *Pillars of Society,* showing that the pillars themselves are rotten and grounded in illegality. But in this instance the triviality of both the law and the transgression seem rather to point up the contrast between the almost meaningless bits and pieces of prohibition, interdiction, restriction, etc., that make up what Binet and his type regard as the Law and the more profoundly disturbing transgressions that Emma is involved in in her search for some notional reality and intensity of experience that may lie outside all man-made laws and may, perhaps, have laws of its own. Binet in his tub or at his lathe is too utterly desensitized and dehumanized to have any significant relationship to law at all, in obedience or contravention.

The moment when Emma actually confronts Binet directly with a plea for help, or some "scandalous proposition," comes of course at the climax of her increasingly desperate search for financial aid. She has literally been going round in circles at an increasing speed and has tried everything she can think of, when she makes a final dash to the tax collector. It is almost as though she has finally succumbed to the perverse power of the lathe and its deadly centripetal tug. It is worth noting how Flaubert transcribes the confrontation. He describes how two other ladies watch what is going on in Binet's garret, but they can scarcely hear a word that is spoken "à cause du tour" (p. 394); the lathe has almost achieved the total obliteration of language, just as it has achieved the total eradication of all feeling and responsive consciousness in Binet. Mainly the scene comes down to a physical request for help of the most basic kind: Emma takes hold of his hands. Whatever "abomination" she may or may not be proposing does not matter. What is clear is Emma's physical gesture of need and supplication and Binet's horrified recoil from her, as though he had seen a snake ("comme à la vue d'un serpent" [p. 395]). The reader may make as many associations with the word *snake* as he cares to, but whatever archetypal echoes may be felt to be operating, there is also the immediate sense of the horrified recoil of the completely reified, automatized, nonhuman servant of the lathe from the sensuous sinuosity of a still-alive individual female human being. The unpredictable turns of a snake's body in movement, no matter how disturbing they may be, are the direct opposite of the totally predictable (and therefore totally undisturbing) turnings of the lathe. They are the turns of life. What Binet really fears is everything that has not come under the domination of the lathe and all it stands for. We should note in detail how Flaubert describes him when Emma enters his garret: this is, after all, the last male to whom she is to appeal for help—apart from Rodolphe, who is elsewhere. Within the village, Binet is her last resort.

> He was alone in his garret, engaged in making a wood copy of one of those indescribable ivory carvings which are composed of crescents and spheres fitted one inside the other, the whole erect as an obelisk, and completely useless. And he was just starting on the last piece, the final touch! In the light and shade of his workshop . . . the wheels went whirring round. Binet was smiling, chin down, nostrils dilated—absorbed in one of those utter joys, belonging doubtless only to mediocre tasks, which entertain the mind with simple difficulties and satisfy it in a fulfilment where all aspiration ends.
>
> (Pp. 316–17)

> Il était seul, dans sa mansarde, en train d'imiter, avec du bois, une de ces ivoireries indescriptibles, composées de croissants, de sphères creusées les unes dans les autres, le tout droit comme un obélisque et ne servant à rien; et il entamait la dernière pièce, il touchait au but! Dans le clair-obscur de l'atelier . . . les deux roues tournaient, ronflaient; Binet souriait, le menton baissé, les narines ouvertes et semblait enfin perdu dans un de ces bonheurs complets, n'appartenant sans doute qu'aux occupations médiocres, qui amusent l'intelligence par des difficultés faciles, et l'assouvissent en une réalisation au-delà de laquelle il n'y a pas à rêver.
>
> (P. 394)

It is a description with devastating implications, clear to any reader. In this context I wish only to single out certain aspects of it. He is "en train d'imiter," and this is precisely the definition of his existence, for he is, as I said before, always engaged in copying. What he is copying is "indescriptible," a crazy, incoherent assemblage of shapes that looks like an obelisk but is as far from having the meaning of those ancient monuments as a napkin ring is from having the significance of a wedding ring. And of course it is completely useless. In all this it is related to Charles Bovary's cap and is, one might say, a typical product of a culture that initiates consciousness in such a way. In addition, he is reaching his goal, or aim ("but"). Here is another paradox. First of all, there is the problem of the source of the original in a life given over to copying; and second, there is the problem of having a goal, an objective and an end point, when your sole activity is repetition. For Binet there would seem to be no reason to start and no reason to stop, in every sense. He is a figure who would seem to be completely lacking in both ontological and teleological principles. Yet there he is. And what is more, he has achieved in his own way "un de ces bonheurs complets" and "une réalisation," "a fulfilment where all aspiration ends." In all this, his life is in many ways the opposite of Emma's who can never really find a *but* until she arrives at the chemist's shop for the poison; who tries to find some individual mode of being, though, as I shall indicate, she was hopelessly involved in repetitions from the start; and who never achieved a "bonheur complet" because, by definition, such a happiness was impossible for a being nurtured in incompleteness. Binet has found a way to get beyond dreaming; Emma is doomed to dream continually. Just how Binet has managed to achieve this contradictory and elusive condition is made clear by Flaubert, and the main factor is to be located there in the two wheels of his lathe, forever turning, and forever humming or snoring. What they are ultimately producing is the sleep of life. From *roue* comes "routine," and in the total routinization of existence, the lathe achieves its final success. It is no wonder that M. Binet never sells anything ("il ne vend rien" [p. 395]), because he never makes any thing. Or rather, he makes Nothing. And therein, frighteningly enough, lies his "bonheur complet."

The humming of the lathe recurs shortly afterward in a context that shows how subtly it has permeated Emma's existence. After Binet's rejection of her, Emma is seen (by the two town ladies) running toward the cemetery, which is indeed her *but*, as we can recognize by now. The text then changes its perspective so that after a gap we are given Emma's words directly, as though she has plunged back into earshot. These are the words ' "—Mère Rollet, dit-elle en arrivant chez la nourrice, j'étouffe! . . . délacez-moi" (p. 395). Emma's feelings of suffocation and her increasing need to be unlaced and unclothed fit into a pattern that I will discuss later. Here I want to point up the fact that her first word is "mother." It is of course titular as well—"Mère Rollet"— but it contains the helpless cry of the child that Emma has become. This is another process to which I will return later. After saying these words, Emma collapses on the bed and sobs (the exact combination of prostration and weeping described in the case of the girl on the beach with the fog in her head). As she says nothing more, "la mère Rollet" takes her spinning wheel and starts to spin linen or flax ("prit son rouet et se mit à filer du lin"). The next words are "—Oh! finissez, murmura-t-elle, croyant entendre le tour de Binet" (p. 395). This moment and Emma's drowsy confusion are exceptionally significant and merit detailed consideration. We may say that weaving and spinning are the archetypal activities associated with women, whether you want to think of Penelope at her loom or accept Freud's speculation when he writes: "People say that women contributed but little to the discoveries and inventions of civilization, but perhaps after all they did discover one technical process, that of plaiting and weaving."[9] In his book *Love's Body,* Norman O. Brown quotes Blake's lines from *The Gates of Paradise:*

> Thou'rt my Mother from the Womb,
> Wife, Sister, Daughter, to the Tomb,
> Weaving to Dreams the Sexual strife
> And weeping over the Web of Life.

In Blake's words, "every Female is a Golden Loom." For those who are interested in the kind of totalizing synthesis of archetypal references and associations that Norman Brown attempts, he pursues the significance of women and weaving at some length. I wish to make a more restricted point in this context. Emma has run from Binet at his lathe to "Mother" Rollet with her spinning wheel. She is not her real mother of course, just as it is impossible literally to go back in time. But it is possible to regress and rediscover that elemental need for the mother figure, which is what Emma experiences at this climactic moment of utter hopelessness. In her disarrayed state she hears the spinning wheel as Binet's lathe, which only compounds her nightmare. It is a confusion that signifies on many levels. One could say that in economic and industrial terms the *rouet* was indeed supplanted and replaced by the *tour* inasmuch as home and cottage industry were being replaced by the much more depersonalized machinery of the factory (in a related way we may note that Lheureux and all he stands for is replacing the old peasant lady, Le Roux, and all she stands for—I will return to this point). In a more local way we can say that everything implied in the drone of Binet's lathe, as I have tried to

---

[9]Sigmund Freud, "Femininity" (from *New Introductory Lectures*).

elicit it, has indeed permeated and effectively replaced the earlier (ontogenetically and philogenetically speaking) and much more comforting and creative noise of the mother at her spinning wheel. This degeneration of both the nature of the work and the role of the woman is taken to its third stage in the fate of Emma's daughter, for—we are told on the last page of the book—to earn her living, she is sent out to "une filature de coton" (p. 446): if the original mother was to be found at her spinning wheel, the modern daughter is forced to work in a cotton factory. The eclipse of the spinning wheel by the factory is the triumph of M. Binet's lathe, and we may note in passing that the dehumanizing of the male (as in Binet) always involves the degradation of the female. I say "in passing" because in a very important sense this phenomenon, and all the different manifestations it can take, is what the book is constantly concerned with. Emma's murmured anguished plea—"Oh! finissez"—is one of the saddest cries in the book, because it is inherent in the makeup of Binet's lathe that it never *really* stops, ever. And never will. Until existence itself has been transformed into napkin rings, serving no purpose, signifying nothing.

Before leaving this scene, it is worth noting that in her prostrate condition on the bed Emma sees another weaver—a spider: "a large spider crawling along a crack in the beam above her head" (p. 318). ("Elle contemplait . . . une longue araignée qui marchait au-dessus de sa tête, dans la fente de la poutrelle" [p. 396].) *Fente* covers such English words as crack, crevice, split, fissure, chink—it is also what Charles had in his clothes on his first day at school. It relates to a series of words for gaps and holes to which I will return. Here we may just note this. On its own level the spider encounters gaps in its environment that, if required, it can cover or negotiate with its natural ability to spin webs of natural thread. But for human beings there are more than topographical gaps—as I indicated in the first section of this chapter. Thus, for example, when Emma returns from the glamorous visit to the aristocratic château we read—"The visit to la Vaubyessard had made a gap in her life" (p. 69). ("Son voyage à la Vaubyessard avait fait un trou dans sa vie" [p. 88].) The experience produces a hole that was not previously there, the painful paradox of memory being that it contains residual traces of the content of the past that by the same token produce a sense of absence, loss, missingness in the present. In this way the gaps and the gap-creating processes introduced into consciousness by language itself (as outlined above) can be further compounded without limit, since every experience brings along with it another gap, or increases the ones already experienced. This is why desire is so intimately related with memory, as Freud made clear. Emma's problem, to put it in yet another simplifying way, is what to do about the accumulating "holes" in her conscious life, for there is no inborn human capacity to spin and weave that can naturally and spontaneously deal with these internal gaps in the way that the spider can negotiate the fissures of his environment. Recalling Binet's conversation with Léon, we may say that he has found one solution to the problem posed by the gaps of memory-desire: the lathe. Paradoxically, Binet fills any *trou* with his *tour*, which effectively produces manufactured *trous*. The phonetic repetitions, the words mirroring each other so that *tour* only requires the displacement of one letter to become *trou*, the odd and unstabilizing sense of apparently different phenomena merging into each other, are all surely important aspects of the experience of reading this book. After first committing adultery, Emma finds that nothing has changed, and yet for her it is as if something more considerable has happened than if the mountains had been moved or displaced ("se fussent déplacées" [p. 218]). "Displacement" is another crucial phenomenon in the book, as I will try to show. In this context, we can see the relevance of Emma's feelings to what is happening to the words in the text. From *trou* to *tour* requires the most minimal lexical displacement, which first of all may seem to change a great deal (the hole *transformed* into a lathe), but then has the opposite effect of decreasing our sense of distinction (there is no *difference* between the hole and the lathe). Just so, Emma thinks that the displacement of adultery will transform her life, and discovers that it changes nothing. In just how many subtle ways transformation and displacement can make for a very worrying loss of difference, Flaubert's text constantly makes us aware. Emma cannot fill the various *trous* in her life with a *tour*, yet she is constantly and increasingly involved in gaps and turnings until a reader begins to arrive at the awesome recognition that the gaps cannot be filled, and that all Emma can finally do is hand over her very being *to* those gaps. By increasing the rate of her own personal "turnings," she finally becomes all hole. The gesture with which she initiates the literal completion of this process offers a vivid physical paradigm for this process. She puts her hand in the blue jar, fills her hand with the white poison powder, and starts to eat it, cramming the gap of her mouth with that which will negate her entirely. When the process is complete—"elle n'existait plus" (p. 418).

After her death the problem of "gaps" remains, as Flaubert makes clear by an identical phrase repeated in very different contexts. When the workmen are putting the coffin containing the coffin containing Emma in the third coffin, they find that the outer one is too big and they have to fill up the space between with wool from a mattress—"il fallut boucher les interstices avec la laine d'un matelas" (p. 428). Just before the end of the book, Charles encounters Rodolphe who, in order to avoid any possible embarrassment, chatters on about irrelevant quotidian matters—"bouchant avec des phrases banales tous les interstices où pouvait se glisser une allusion" (p. 45). *Boucher* covers such meanings as occlude, fill up or stop a gap, block up a hole. It is the word used in the famous metaphor-omen with which Flaubert conveys so much of what is happening and is about to happen in Emma's life even prior to any actual adultery. "She did not know how on the terrace of a house the rain collects in pools when the gutters are choked; and she would have continued to feel quite safe had she not suddenly discovered a crack in the wall" (p. 113). ("Elle ne savait pas que, sur la terrasse des maisons, la pluie fait des lacs quand les gouttières sont bouchées, et elle fût ainsi demeurée en sa sécurité, lorsqu'elle découvrit subitement une lézarde dans le mur" [p. 143].) The conflating of the threat of accumulating water to the house and the threat of accumulating desire to the body is no mere arbitrary comparison or trope, as I will suggest when I discuss Emma's increasing "liquidation." Here we may say that the "lézarde dans le mur" is analogous to the "trou dans sa vie" and is connected to all those rents and crevices that are increasingly to make up her existence. Although the gutters can be stopped or blocked up—"bouchées"—the "trous" and "lézardes" in the life of the human organism cannot. Emma's life is a demonstration of the impossibility of the attempt. The close connection between *bouche* ("mouth") and *boucher,* so that the latter word suggests both the gap that seeks to be filled and the process of filling it (thus *bouchée* is "a mouthful"), is surely deliberately pointed to by Flaubert's text, and it would seem almost inevitable that she should die by the mouth, stuffing it with a powder of annihilation that will satisfy all appetites by destroying them. The repetition of the phrase "boucher les interstices" in those two different contexts after her death serves to extend our sense of the widespread nature of this activity, as though human existence was an ongoing and endless process of attempting to block up gaps. The fact that in one context workmen use wool to fill up the gaps in a sequence of coffins while in the other Rodolphe uses banalities to fill up the gaps in a conversation (or series of utterances) suggests that at all levels and using materials ranging from wool to words (two man-made products "spun" from nature), the need, or instinct, or desire is to "boucher les interstices." Since, it can be argued, human consciousness itself is the source of "discretization" introduced into the continuum of nature—and since, as has been stated before, language is inherently "interstitial"—the attempt is necessarily an impossible one. Whatever else he manufactures—wool and words—man is the creature who produces more gaps or interstices than can ever be filled, no matter what material may be employed in the attempt.

Rodolphe Fails to Distinguish

I have mentioned the extent to which duplication, triplication, repetition, and replication pervade the book. Binet is the central incarnation of this phenomenon, but it affects everyone and everything. Thus, to take just one small example, when Mlle. Rouault (i.e., Emma) works on her trousseau, she sends for part of it from Rouen and makes the rest of it "from borrowed patterns" (p. 38) ("d'après des dessins de modes qu'elle emprunta" [p. 49]). *Mode* of course carries many possible applications, from "fashion" to "mood." One question tacitly raised by the book is— what "modes" are *not* borrowed, whether it be modes of dress or modes of feeling and thought? But if everything is, in one sense, borrowed (as, for example, were all the elements that made up Charles Bovary's cap), this raises the problem of source or location of the original from which all the borrowings are made—unless everyone is always and everywhere only copying copies of copies of copies, which opens up the prospect of a dizzying infinite regression. The problem is most acute in the area in which individual feelings (which *in some sense* must be "original," if only in that they have their origin within one specific interiority: needless to say the shape and content of the feeling may be totally permeated with copies and borrowed patterns) have to be translated into speech that is nonoriginal, in that it is communal and based on certain tacitly agreed-on formulas for repetition. This problematical area is directly confronted by Flaubert in the famous passage on Rodolphe's boredom with women, a boredom based on the vicious logic of the lathe, whereby the more you make (or take) the more you render the same—only in this case the logic is operating in the realm of human beings and emotions. Rodolphe registers in an extreme form the devaluation implicit in all repetition. The passage must be quoted at length.

> He had listened to so many speeches of this kind that they no longer made any impression on him. Emma was like any other mistress; and the charm of novelty, gradually slipping away like a garment, laid bare the eternal monotony of passion, whose forms and phrases are for ever the same. Any difference of feeling underlying a similarity in words escaped the notice of that man of much experience. Because wanton or mercenary lips had murmured like phrases in his ear, he had but scant belief in the sincerity of these. High-flown language concealing tepid affection must be discounted, thought he: as though the full heart may not sometimes overflow in the emptiest metaphors, since no one can ever give the exact measure of his needs, his thoughts or his sorrows, and human speech is like a

cracked kettle on which we strum out tunes to make a bear dance, when we would move the stars to pity.

(P. 203)

Il s'était tant de fois entendu dire ces choses, qu'elles n'avaient pour lui rien d'original. Emma ressemblait à toutes les maîtresses; et le charme de la nouveauté, peu à peu tombant comme un vêtement, laissait voir à nu l'éternelle monotonie de la passion, qui a toujours les mêmes formes et le même langage. Il ne distinguait pas, cet homme si plein de pratique, la dissemblance des sentiments sous la parité des expressions. Parce que des lèvres libertines ou vénales lui avaient murmuré des phrases pareilles, il ne croyait que faiblement à la candeur de celles-là; on en devait rabattre, pensait-il, les discours exagérés cachant les affections médiocres; comme si la plénitude de l'âme ne débordait pas quelquefois par les métaphores les plus vides, puisque personne, jamais, ne peut donner l'exact mesure de ses besoins, ni de ces conceptions, ni de ces douleurs, et que la parole humaine est comme un chaudron fêlé où nous battons des mélodies à faire danser les ours, quand on voudrait attendrir les étoiles.

(P. 254)

Three different though closely related "languages" are identified here. There are the actual spoken utterances—"dire ces choses," "des expressions," "des phrases pareilles," "discours"—that make up "la parole humaine." Underneath this is what in this context may be called "le langage de la passion." The relationship between this "langage" and "la parole humaine" is the problematical relationship and tension between the momentary "nouveauté" of each individual utterance coming from specific lips in a particular situation, and "l'éternelle monotonie de la passion," which always has the same forms and "langage." Flaubert's use of that word is particularly paradoxical, since *langage,* while meaning "language," also implies the speech of an individual as opposed to the common language of a people or race, which would be *langue.* It is as though he can see the human individual caught in these two inextricable languages, one continually striving for *nouveauté* to express *dissemblance* (unlikeness, dissimilarity, difference), and the other constantly tending toward sameness ("les mêmes formes"), parity ("la parité des expressions"), alikeness ("des phrases pareilles"), monotony (a linguistic state in which there is "rien d'original"—which would finally be indistinguishable from the hum of Binet's lathe). Flaubert is here revealing one of the most poignant paradoxes of the situation of the speaking animal, who is, as it were, a physical locus where this two-way movement between "la dissemblance des sentiments" and "la parité des expressions" is constantly taking place, originality of feeling constantly and inevitably being transformed into the sameness and repetitions of language. The most poignant aspect of this situation is that it is precisely *in* the process of striving for expression that the originality of the feeling cedes to the equivalizing tendencies in language. Thus utterance itself constitutes loss of originality. The central paradox of our lingual condition is that it would seem as though we lose our feelings precisely when and because we try to communicate them, and while Rodolphe may think that "les discours exagérés" conceal "les affections médiocres," we might very well say that the reverse process takes place, and any exaggeration and intensity in the *affections* gets lost and destroyed in the mediocrity of the *discours*. Which is why Flaubert himself adds his own comment—"comme si la plénitude de l'âme ne débordait pas quelquefois par les métaphores les plus vides." The fullness is in the heart or soul; the emptiness is in the language. If speaking is spilling, spilling is losing. The more Emma tries to express her feelings, passions, desires, needs, sentiments, affections, the more she is doomed to encounter, not a metaphorical emptiness, but the emptiness of metaphors. The more she tries to become Emma, the more she becomes "la même," another phonetic echo involving a slight displacement that carries a multitide of implications. For if Emma, in trying to articulate whatever it is inside her that is her uniqueness, that makes her the one person she is and not someone else—her Emma-ness, let us say—discovers that she and the world around her are moving deeper and deeper into parity and similarity ("la même"-ness), this would imply that the passional quest for original expression can only and inevitably result in the opposite condition of eternal monotony. This is what is genuinely tragic in the experience of Emma Bovary. Her very capacity to feel doomes her to an increasing engagement with everything that serves to obliterate difference and *dissemblance* and to deny originality and individuality. The most "original" figure in the book is M. Binet—"son pareil n'existe sur la terre." And how has he achieved this condition of being without parallel, a condition that one feels Emma might have achieved? By "l'exactitude." Binet is unique in his commitment to repetition, Emma becomes repetitious (or suffers repetition) in her quest for originality. And Rodolphe—who is "full" ("plein"), not of feeling, but of "pratique" (practice, experience); who, unlike Binet, seems phallic, virile, potent, and loaded with all the machismatic equipment and ancillaries of ostentatious masculinity (whips, guns, hunting gear, cigars, etc.)—he in fact represents a terminal case of this condition that I have been trying to describe. "Il ne distinguiait pas!"; in context this refers to a specific failure to distinguish between unlikeness of feelings and parity of expressions, but this in turn is only the central failure of a disability that permeates his whole being. His life is quite as terrifyingly empty as Binet's, as any close examination of the passages describing it will reveal. He is precisely he who cannot distinguish and who

thereby increases the loss of difference in the world around him.[10] If
Binet is the active spirit of replication, Rodolphe is the incarnate force
denying and destroying distinction. Quite unconsciously and unbe-
knownst to each other they are both working toward the same end; and if
Binet treats his napkin rings as his love objects, we may just as well say
that Rodolphe regards his women as so many napkin rings. There is, in
fact, ultimately very little to choose between them.

I mentioned a third "language" implicit in this paragraph, which we
can locate in the simile of the falling garment. When Flaubert says that
for Rodolphe "le charme de la nouveauté, peu à peu tombant comme un
vêtement, laissait voir à nu l'éternelle monotonie de la passion," we are
given a new sense of the overwhelming significance of actual clothing in
the novel. Any reader will have noted the prolonged and meticulous
description of clothing that occurs throughout the book, not only all the
different kinds of footwear and headwear but complete outfits and en-
sembles. The words seem to hover longingly over details of dress, as
though they are as obsessed with clothing and material as the people
referred to in the book. And in a very important sense they are. By
comparison, the words spend comparatively little time engaging with the
physicality of the body, though certain *fragments* of the body—fingers,
nails, the neck, etc.—are indeed concentrated on, but as fragments, as
though the living body as a whole cannot be directly confronted in its
total nakedness. I hope to suggest that this is more than an adherence to
conventions governing what could be described in a novel, for what we
are witnessing is another kind of fetishistic displacement, both recorded
and enacted by the text, a displacement of passional or affective attention from the body onto clothes. It is the swish of Emma's skirt and the
creak of her boots that excite the men around her. I will give one small
and very clear example of this fetishistic displacement, which, I contend,
can be felt to be operating throughout the book, both in the words and in
what they refer to. One of the last men whom Emma goes to to seek help
is a lawyer, Maître Guillaumin. He starts to touch her and breathe heavily
and soon seizes her round the waist, even saying "je vous aime," a slob-

---

[10]This failure to distinguish, and loss of sense of difference (or indifference), affects
almost every figure in the book. It finally possesses, for instance, the apparently doting
Léon, who succumbs to another version of Rodolphe's boredom. "It bored him nowadays
when Emma suddenly started sobbing on his chest. Like those people who cannot endure
more than a certain dose of music, his heart grew drowsily indifferent to the clamour of a
love whose niceties he could no longer appreciate" (p. 301). ("Il s'ennuyait maintenant
lorsque Emma, tout à coup, sanglotait sur sa poitrine; et son coeur, comme les gens qui ne
peuvent endurer qu'une certaine dose de musique, s'assoupissait d'indifférence au vac-
arme d'un amour dont il ne distinguait plus les délicatesses" [je. 376].) Emma is receding
from "délicatesse" to "dose," from music to noise. I shall discuss some aspects of this
indifference in a later section.

bering, completely degenerate parody, a degraded précis of what might be regarded as the gradual steps toward intimacy in any true courtship (things are happening very quickly for Emma now; they are also getting smaller and meaner, part of a downward spiral to the slime). This provokes Emma into one of her most moving and dignified responses to the male world that has both encircled and abandoned her—"I am to be pitied . . . I am not to be bought!" (p. 315). ("Je suis à plaindre, mais pas à vendre" [392].) She leaves and the lawyer is stunned—"The notary was left dumbfounded, his eyes fixed on his beautiful embroidered slippers. They were a love gift; eventually the sight of them consoled him" (p. 315). ("Le notaire resta fort stupéfait, les yeux fixés sur ses belles pantoufles en tapisserie. C'était un présent de l'amour. Cette vue à la fin le consola" [p. 392].) I am not here concerned with Flaubert's own fetishism, but rather with his diagnosis of how prevalent fetishism is in all that he is describing. I will be returning to the subject of fetishism, but for the moment let me return to Flaubert's simile.

It was the charm of the novelty that, for Rodolphe, was falling like a garment, allowing the eternal monotony of passion to be seen naked. This is more intricate than it might at first appear to be. Obviously the simile suggests the undressing that precedes all lovemaking. It also suggests that the actual naked body of the other or the partner is the *source* of the monotony, a perverse reversal by which what should be the climactic moment of intimacy between two individuals confronting each other in their living, naked wholeness becomes a revelation of the eternal mono-tony (sameness, indistinguishability) of passion. This in turn implies that all the source of distinction, individuation, novelty, etc., has been transferred from the body to the dress. This we may call a metonymic displacement in the sense employed by Lacan. Thus in between *la parole humaine* with its empty metaphors, and the eternal monotone of the nonlingual language of passion, there is a language of *nouveauté* made up of a series of metonymic displacements from body to clothes. It is a hopeless, self-defeating language, which contains its own negation and impossibility. For the clothes have constantly to be changed and varied, but having provoked a momentary and illusory sense of *nouveauté* in the partner, they must be stripped off only to reveal the naked monotony and the monotonous nakedness of passion. Emma's life is a long dressing that turns into a long undressing. All the languages let her down, for ultimately she establishes no relationships—not through the metaphors of speech, nor the metonymies of clothes, nor the direct contacts of physical nakedness. None of the men around her really engages with her, though they may seem to respond to her words, touch her clothes, and to penetrate her body. She is taken and used in bits and pieces, as indeed she may be said to take and use herself. She is not

experienced in her entirety, just as her own entirety is not experienced
by her. What this notional entirety might be like, what a complete relationship of the whole Emma with another person might be if it could
have developed, it is of course impossible to imagine, any more than
Flaubert would try to describe what would be involved in satisfying un-
satisfiable desires ("Insatiate and satisfied desire, the tub/both full and
running" in Shakespeare's terms—*Cymbeline*, act I, scene 6). In the same
way it is ultimately pointless to try to "blame" anyone for what happens
to Emma (as she writes in her suicide note—*"Qu'on n'accuse personne"*
[p. 407]). What is so moving about this is that it is true that no one is to
blame, because no one feels real responsibilities for other people; no real
relationships seem to be possible; and fetishism, repetition, and insentience take the place of authentic interhuman contact. In a society that has
forgotten how to love, it is of no avail to try and locate the blame. But if
neither the men in the book nor the words of the book can confront the
whole Emma living, they can do so for Emma dying. The close detailing
by the words of what is happening to the entire body during Emma's
appalling death scene, paralleled by the dutiful attention of some of the
male figures in her environment, is felt to be in inverse proportion to the
inability to confront and describe her when she was living. This is, of
course, neither lack of sympathy on Flaubert's part nor a capitulation to
contemporary taboos. He is making us aware of an ultimate displacement from love—whatever that nebulous absence might be—to death,
which can be watched, noted, and transcribed very accurately indeed.

Of course all I have said in connection with this paragraph considering the three "languages" that seem ultimately to work together to make
for the annulment of authentic individual expression reflects on
Flaubert's own position. We may note that there is one other simile,
applied, not to *nouveauté*, but to *la parole humaine*; it is said to be "comme
un chaudron felé," a cracked cauldron, or "kettle." Instead of a garment,
this simile proposes a kitchen utensil, in which things are cooked and
thus, following Lévi-Strauss, transformed from nature into culture[11]: we
can see the aptness of this simile. But Flaubert twists it, and with a
sudden turn of incongruity he gives us the sense that as a utensil of
transformation, language itself has gone wrong. The cauldron is
cracked; furthermore, he states that we beat out tunes on it (but that is
not the function of a cauldron) to make bears dance (Bears? Where did
they come from, what are they doing here?), when we would like to move
the stars to pity. This dissonant shift in the development of the simile—
so that *la parole humaine* becomes a nonfunctioning cooking utensil im-

---

[11]See his "Culinary Triangle," in *New Society* (22 December 1966), pp. 937–40, in which
he considers cooking as a language.

possibly applied to the task of making melodies (which are nonsemantic), with the bizarre and absurd end result of making bears (nonlingual) dance—gives us a sense of all the deformations and distortions, both of means and ends, involved in the attempt to translate our "besoins," "conceptions," "douleurs," into language. It also shows that, in his attempt to translate into a written text that particular combination of needs, conceptions, and sadnesses that he has decided to name "Emma Bovary," Flaubert is aware that he himself is involved in a very special form of that absurd, futile, yet unavoidable procedure conjured up in that disjointed simile just outlined. Of course all fictional invention only pretends to be description or translation. There is no need to dwell on that well-established convention. But given all that Flaubert makes us aware of as being involved in living in and with and through *la parole humaine*, both speaking it and being spoken by it, internalizing its gaps, its deformations, its distortions and displacements, we are bound to consider—what can we ever know of this Emma Bovary whom he is pretending to describe or copy in words?

I will not pursue this topic further in this place, but instead I want to quote a passage from Nietzsche's *The Will to Power* (Book Two—177, p. 108) in which he is considering the relationship of Christianity to the figure who supposedly originated it.

> It is possible that the debt to Christianity ought not to be ascribed to its founder but to the finished structure, to the whole thing, the church, etc. The concept "originator" is so ambiguous it can even mean the accidental cause of a movement: the figure of the founder has been enlarged in proportion as the church has grown; but precisely this perspective of worship permits the conclusion that at some time or other this founder was something very uncertain and insecure, in the beginning. —Consider with what degree of freedom Paul treats, indeed almost juggles with, the problem of the person Jesus: someone who died, who was seen again after his death, who was delivered over to death by the Jews—A mere "motif": *he* then wrote the music to it—A zero in the beginning.[12]

The relationship outlined by Nietzsche between Paul as narrator and Christ as person is necessarily very different from the one between Flaubert and Emma, yet I think Nietzsche's insight can be applied. There is, of course, no particular historical human prototype for Emma Bovary—but Flaubert operates (in his own way) within the narrative convention which regards and describes characters *as if* they existed outside the pages of a novel. From this point of view we may say that Flaubert does treat the "life" and "person" of Emma Bovary with a great degree of freedom, may be said to juggle with them (even while he is

[12]Friedrich Nietzsche, *The Will to Power*, book 2, section 177.

imaginatively "creating" them). We have the finished book—"the finished structure, the whole thing"—but what do we know of that *she* who supposedly "originated" the book? It is, after all, in its way a kind of church erected to the memory and even the worship of its "founder," a founder who was, indeed, "something very uncertain and insecure, in the beginning." We have the music of Flaubert's text, and from it and within it we hear and infer the "motif" of Emma Bovary. But if we search harder and harder for that motif, exactly what happens is that we lose all sense of a founder, or "original" and "originating" person. Instead we confront—"a zero in the beginning."

Monsieur Homais Loses His Temper

We first encounter M. Homais shortly before the Bovarys do, in the Golden Lion, at the same time as we are introduced to M. Binet. One of his first comments is on M. Binet's lack of "imagination," clearly a faculty with which the chemist feels himself to be imbued. At the end of a series of remarks concerning the understandably engrossed and absorbed natures of remarkable men, he gives an example from his own life. "Why, in my own case—the times I've searched my desk for my pen to write a label, only to find in the end that I'd put it behind my ear!" (p. 89) ("Moi, par exemple, combien de fois m'est-il arrivé de chercher ma plume sur mon bureau pour écrire une étiquette, et de trouver, en définitive, que je l'avais placée à mon oreille!" [p. 113]). This is far from being one of Homais's more memorable fatuities, but I single it out because M. Homais is indeed he who writes labels, or the very spirit of labeling, spreading his platitudes over every aspect of human activity, forcing the world into the bottles and boxes of his shop, which are the external analogue of the accumulating rows and shelves of packets and blocks of decontextualized "information" in his mind. When Nietzsche writes of the will to reduce and equalize experience, his words apply very well to M. Homais. "Reduction of all events to the level of the man of the senses and the mathematician. It is a question of an inventory of human experiences—under the supposition that man, or rather the human eye and ability to form concepts, are the eternal witness of all things."[13] M. Homais would

[13]Ibid., book 3, section 640.

indeed reduce all human experience, all existence, to an inventory, which gives the illusion of complete knowledge and complete control. And although his career is founded in illegality—he is not qualified to practice medicine and has in fact once been summoned before the authorities and admonished—throughout the book the power and influence of Homais grow, and in the last paragraph, while Emma Bovary is nowhere, it is as though Homais is now everywhere. When he was called before the authorities, he had nightmare visions of himself in the "deepest of dungeons" and his bottles or "window jars" dispersed ("il entrevit des culs de basse-fosse . . . tous les bocaux disséminés" [p. 126]). As he increases in power within the community, he inverts the nightmare into a mode of operation and tries to put other people in various kinds of prison, just as he wants to have more and more of the world in his bottles. Prisons and bottles are two kinds of containers, and what is evident in Homais in an extreme form is that will to "contain" everything and everyone in order that everything and everyone may thus be safely "labeled." Something of the ambivalence of this drive is present in the very word *étiquette,* which means both a label and what we more generally infer from it—etiquette, formality, ceremony. It is as though good manners are related to good labels, but good labels somehow involve imprisoning and bottling. The treatment of knowledge as being contained and labeled in a vast inventory was of course explored even further by Flaubert in *Bouvard and Pécuchet,* and the rest, we may say, is an established part of the history of the development of modern literature.

But in this novel it is more interesting to see how Flaubert connects such an attitude to knowledge with what happens to Emma, for her place among labels and containers is very problematical and her relationship to the bourgeois inventory is very uncertain. It is characteristic both of the exponential growth of Homais's sphere of influence and of his relationship to human realities in general that he automatically applies himself to making suggestions for inscriptions for Emma's tombstone. For just as he is obsessed with medals and everything implied in the word *titres,* so he lives his life at the level of "inscriptions" and *etiquettes,* inserting or secreting them, with the irresistible force of some awesome machine, into every area of life—and death. Emma's inscription *does* give him some trouble. "For the inscription, Homais found nothing to beat 'Sta viator . . . Sta viator . . .' until at last he hit upon '. . . amabilem conjugem calcas,' which was adopted" (p. 356). The French implies something very significant in this uncharacteristic series of hesitations and gaps in what is usually the uninterrupted and uninterruptible flow of "appropriate" titles and labels from the mouth of M. Homais: "il se creusait l'imagination: il répétait continuellement: *Sta viator . . .*" (p. 441). *Se creuser* implies both "growing hollow" and hollowing out, and what is briefly suggested here is that what supersedes the demise and collapse or evacuation of imagination is—continual repetition. At the moment when his imagination fails, Homais suddenly becomes very like M. Binet, whose lack of imagination had earlier excited his derision. The will to label and the will to repeat momentarily seem very close. And of course we soon realize that what Homais regards as imagination is in fact only another form of repetition, not in the literal form of replicating napkin rings, but in the greedy absorption, adoption, and proliferation of clichés under the illusion of spreading knowledge. How dangerous such an activity can be we come to realize if we consider how important a role is played in the book by suggestions and ideas that come from M. Homais—his apparently benevolent knowingness is in fact a lethal ignorance, an active not-knowingness that mongers the unexamined and second hand stereotypes and in so doing deforms and distorts and destroys what it only purports to enlighten. In seeking to label life, M. Homais effectively turns life into labels, which turns out to be a very perverse activity indeed. (Not surprisingly, Homais is unbeatable at dominoes.) Yet labeling is precisely what is involved in *etiquette*, in the sense of those norms that regulate socially approved conduct. Whether in fact it is possible to have any society, or even any relationships, without labeling is a problem that continues to engage such psychologists or social anthropologists as Lacan, Erving Goffmann, K. Gergen, and R. D. Laing. The problems they consider are implicit in Flaubert's book and in the depiction of the rapidly accelerating and enlarging power of M. Homais, whose knowledge is rooted in an illegal absence of qualifications that *should* exclude him from practicing at all.

Yet by the end he is *the* power in his society. Where authority had once condemned him and his absence of qualifications, it now "respects" him ("l'autorité le ménage" [p. 446]—*ménager* having more of the connotations of handling him gently, or humoring him, or dealing tactfully with him); and the man who should never even have had a *clientèle* ("a practice") now has one that "grows like wildfire" (p. 361): "Il fait une clientèle d'enfer"—again Flaubert's words indicate how carefully they are chosen, for while this means colloquially "at top speed," it still reveals its more literal infernal origins. So while this statement does not mean, "He made a practice out of hell" it does not *not* mean it either! And that would suggest both M. Homais's ultimate achievement and the ultimate inversion that his rapid elevation in society represents. He is less a person than a toxic mental atmosphere that is pervading more and more of the world around it. M. Homais is the fog of pseudoinformation in the head of society. It is entirely appropriate that the book should conclude with the statement recording the fact that he has "just been awarded the Legion of Honour," not only because it is his unreality that has been acclaimed and rewarded by society, but because his life has been dedicated to the transference of life from its native conditions into his bottles, boxes, titles, inscriptions, and labels. The medal is simply the prestigious label awarded to the compulsive labeler for a lifetime's service to the activity of labeling. It is also completely meaningless, for while it is described as "la croix d'honneur," the cross no longer carries any religious force (and Homais is in any case a stereotyped atheist) and Honor has become an empty concept. It is a symbol that no longer symbolizes, and thus becomes its opposite—a sign recording loss of meaning, an absence of significance.[14]

Yet M. Homais seems to be a stickler for accuracy, as would appear on the one memorable occasion when he completely loses his temper. The placing of this scene is very important, for it indicates the kind of indirect connection between the increasing rapidity in the deterioration and destruction of Emma Bovary and the increasing rapidity in the growth of M. Homais's confidence and triump—a connection that may not at

---

[14]The ending of the novel that Flaubert decided not to use is, in its way, as significant as the one he did. Thus:

Le jour qu'il (l') reçue n'y voulut pas croire. Mr. X deputé lui avait envoyé un bout de ruban—le met se regarde dans la glace éblouissement.—. . . .

Doute de lui—regarde les bocaux—doute de son existence (délire. effets fantastiques, la croix répétée dans les glaces, pluie foudre de ruban rouge)—"ne suis-je qu'un personnage de roman, le fruit d'une imagination en délire, l'invention d'un petit paltoquet que j'ai vu naître/et qui m'a inventé pour faire croire que je n'existe pas/—Oh cela n'est pas possible, voilà les foetus. (voilà mes enfants, voilà, voilà)"

Puis se résumant, il finit par le grand mot du rationalisme moderne, Cogito, ergo sum.

The day he received it couldn't believe it. Mr X deputy had sent him a piece of ribbon—puts it on looks at himself in the mirror. vertigo.

Doubt about himself—looks at the drug bottles—doubt about his existence (delirium. fantastic effects. the cross repeated in the mirrors. torrent lightning flash of red ribbon)—"am I only a character in a novel, the fruit of a delerious imagination, the invention of a mere no-body which I have seen born and who has invented me to foster the belief that I do not exist/Oh, that's not possible. Look, there are the foetuses (there are my children, there, there)."

Then, summing himself up, he finished with the great dictum of modern rationalism: Cogito, ergo sum.

(Jean Pommier and Gabrielle Leleu, *Madame Bovary, nouvelle version* [Paris: J. Corti, 1949] p. 129.)

For a particularly interesting discussion of some of the implications of this unused ending, see the excellent article "Flaubert: Writing and Negativity" (*Novel*, spring 1975, pp. 197–213) by Christopher Prendergast (to whom I am indebted for drawing my attention to this suppressed ending in the first place). What has happened to that "grand mot du rationalisme moderne" since Flaubert's time is by now a familiar topic. But none of the attacks on the Cartesian formula would have surprised Flaubert, as is abundantly clear from his (tentatively) giving the words to Homais as a means of regaining a hold on his disintegrating identity—Homais, who does not really think and does not really exist except as a collection of stereotypes (including, of course, the Cartesian stereotype itself).

first be obvious, yet which seems to me an important part of the patterning of the book. The first chapter of book three records Emma's recommitment to adultery with Léon, the meeting in the cathedral, the famous
coach ride. The second chapter opens with her return to Yonville, when
she is immediately summoned to the house of M. Homais. As she enters
she notices an overturned armchair, and this turns out to be an appropriate symptom of what appears to be a state of unusual disorder. M.
Homais is shouting at the boy Justin, because Justin, in response to an
order to fetch another pan while the jam-making process was going on,
dared to take the key to M. Homais's "Capharnaum" and to venture into
that inviolable sanctuary in quest of an appropriate utensil. An explanation is given of the importance of the Capharnaum for M. Homais. It is
where he keeps all his professional utensils and supplies, and it is the
utterly private converse of his shop—the place where he concocts all his
pills, pellets, lotions, and potions. No one sets foot in it. It is the spatial
equivalent of an absolute interiority in which M. Homais is quintessen-
tially himself. Most notably, he spends hours up there engaged in "label-
ling, decanting, and re-tying" (p. 258): ("Souvent il y passait seul de
longues heures à étiqueter, à transvaser, à reficiler" [p. 324]). These
three words convey the essence of M. Homais's activity—he takes one
thing or substance from one place and puts or pours it into another
receptacle; he unties existing combinations of things and then ties them
up again in another way; and he puts labels on. Nothing is created;
everything is repackaged: nothing is truly known; everything is obses-
sively labeled. This is the secret of M. Homais's precarious yet ultimately
invulnerable power. So when the boy in his innocence goes into the
Capharnaum for a pan, it is felt by M. Homais not only as a violation and
a "monstrous irreverence" (p. 258) but also as some kind of nameless
threat to the secret center of his existence. His rage seems quite disproportionate to the slightness of the offense, for the starting point of his
anger is his outrage that Justin should have thought of bringing him a
pan that may be used in his chemical work, when he needed a pan for his
cooking work. Yet as he works himself up, the real source of his anger
becomes clear. He speaks for the importance of distinctions, thus *apparently* contrasting with Rodolphe, who failed to distinguish one woman
from another: "We must preserve certain distinctions, and not employ
for purposes little more than domestic, instruments intended for pharmaceutical use!" (p. 259): ("il faut établir des distinctions et ne pas employer à des usages presque domestiques ce qui est destiné pour les
pharmaceutiques!" [p. 325]). What particularly upsets M. Homais is the
fact that he keeps arsenic in a bottle next to the pan that Justin took, and
thus the poison might very easily have got mixed up with the jam
through the unwitting touch of an innocent hand belonging to a boy not

skilled in what Homais regards as his "art." The very thought of this provokes M. Homais to an outburst of incoherence that is extremely amusing, and amusing because it reveals the sense of utter confusion and chaos that underlies his superficial mastery of labeling and decant- ing. "All right, go ahead! smash! do your worst! Let loose the leeches! Burn the marshmallows! Pickle gherkins in the window-jars! Slash up the bandages!" (p. 259) ("Allons, va! ne respecte rien! casse! brise! lâche les sangsues! brûle la guimauve! marine des cornichons dans les bocaux! lacère les bandages!" [p. 325]). This outburst has something of the mad poetry of a bourgeois Lear, for it is a vision of wild disorder, albeit in the chemist's shop rather than on the cosmic heath. And Flaubert points up the importance of this sudden fissure in M. Homais's usually imperturb- able confidence and air of omnimastery and total control. In his anger Homais breaks into Latin and, writes Flaubert, he would have broken into Chinese or Icelandic if he had known either of these languages "for he was now at one of those crises in which the soul, like a storm-cleft ocean, gives a glimpse of all it contains, from the seaweed round its shores to the sand dredged up from its depths" (p. 260) ("car il se trouvait dans une de ces crises où l'âme entière montre indistinctement ce qu'elle enferme, comme l'océan, qui, dans les tempêtes, s'entrouvre depuis les fucus de son rivage jusqu'au sable de ses abîmes" [p. 326]). It is a crisis in which M. Homais sees the seething indistinct, unclassifiable, undifferentiated confusion that is within him, in which he dabbles and for which his apparently scrupulous care to distinguish between cooking and chemistry and to separate the domestic from the pharmaceutical is a profoundly inadequate strategy of mastery or masking. This man, ap- parently such a master of categories, who seems to know what should go where, and who has a suggestion for every occasion, an inscription for every gravestone, and a label for every bottle, is in fact a disseminator of that radical indistinctness that brims perpetually under his flow of un- questionable information and authoritative recommendation and ad- monition. What he purveys, whether in his shop or his words, is the very sand and seaweed of a mind awash with an ignorance that is indeed oceanic. If he is neurotic in his hysterical insistence on the importance of distinction and separation, it is because he fears that any slight departure from, or violation of, the total taxonomy that he has laid over existence will reveal this nightmare of ignorance and indistinctness and confusion that he carries within him. He labels everything because he knows noth- ing. (This is why his suggestions are so destructive.) He thinks that by writing *Dangerous* on a bottle of arsenic, he has controlled it. But when Emma Bovary decides to annihilate herself, she knows exactly where to come for the requisite substance. The label and the bottle only facilitate the expedition of her desire. Among other things, M. Homais is a figure who makes poison available in the name of progress. The actual powder that Emma stuffs into her mouth is only the most obviously fatal of his many toxic wares. Capernaum was where Christ preached salvation and healed the sick. M. Homais working so assiduously for power from his Capharnaum (which in French—as an ordinary noun—means a place of confusion, a place marked by a disorderly accumulation of objects), achieves precisely the reverse.

As he is angrily shaking Justin, a book falls out of the boy's pocket and Homais pounces on it and reads the title. "—*L'amour . . . conjugal!*" This provokes more clichés of paternal outrage and pseudoscientific sententiousness in a manner with which we are already familiar. There is a latent poignancy in the detail, however, for it could be said that Justin is the only male figure in the book who really loves Emma, *sees* her (wonderingly rather than lasciviously), values her, adores her, mourns her. But he is only a boy, not yet able to participate in a society that would seem to have gone some way toward turning "Married Love" into a base commodity—a dirty book to be read in secret. (Hence, incidentally, the *apparent* conventional adequacy, and *actual* absurd inappropriateness, of Homais's inscription for Emma's tombstone.) Justin's love is furtive, unallowed, and silent. It is a mute and pathetic reproach to every other kind of love expressed and enacted and permitted in the society around him. But it is not an alternative. It could hardly satisfy Emma in all her inarticulate longings. And by the time he is out of his adolescence and recognized by society as a sexually mature male, who knows but what Justin may have acquired that sort of fetishistic attitude to women shown by so many of the men in Emma's life? Books like *Married Love* will certainly help him in that direction! The conjecture is perhaps foolish, but Justin and his book serve as a linking point between Homais's crisis and Emma's irreversible recommitment to adultery.

(Flaubert's description of Justin's "love" is quite without irony. "She never dreamt that love [which had gone out of her life] pulsated so close at hand beneath that coarse shirt, in that youthful heart that had opened to the influence of her beauty" [pp. 227-28]. ["Elle ne se doutait point que l'amour, disparu de sa vie, palpitait là, près d'elle, sous cette chemise de grosse toile, dans ce coeur d'adolescent ouvert aux émanations de sa beauté" (p. 285).] There are very few "open hearts" in the book, and perhaps in Flaubert's vision it is a condition or gift—a generous and total openness to the other—that can scarcely outlast adolescence, for passive worshiping cannot be translated into an aspect of an active relationship without necessarily undergoing change. What it is that makes all the hearts close is another phenomenon explored by the book.)

Homais's original purpose for calling Emma to his house was to let her know that her father-in-law is dead. As it happens, he is so obsessed with his anger at Justin and the vision of disorder that comes in its wake, that he conveys the news entirely denuded of rhetoric and with what is, for once, an inappropriate bluntness. For us, however, Emma's presence at Homais's "crisis" offers the most suggestive juxtaposition, or rather superimposition, of two modes of experience, two realities. Homais's panic starts from a dread of mixing up the wrong things, the pharmaceutical contaminating the domestic. He is worried about any kind of "adulteration" (*adulterare*—"pollute," "to defile," etc.). Inside he is all confusion and mess; like the sea, his inner consciousness is totally adulterine. This is covered over by the pathological attention to labeling, decanting, and generally trying to put everything (and everyone) in its, or his, or her, place. It is Homais, above all, who would label Emma adulteress, although she does, of course, try the label on herself. Although Homais does not know it, she incorporates the phenomenon he most dreads. The wife has slipped her label to become a mistress, and the result is a polluting mixture that society calls, precisely, adultery. The Capharnaum is much more profoundly threatened by Emma just as she is, while Homais's misplaced anger and anxiety is deflected onto Justin. And the opposition is not a simple one. For marriage is itself a kind of labeling and re-tying and even decanting (the daughter is untied from the father to be retied to the husband and poured into a new bottle labeled *wife*). What Homais is doing in his Capharnaum is only an extreme form of the processes by which society is maintained (hence his connection with "étiquette"—in all senses of the word). Category divisions and separations are indeed crucial to the structure of any society, as is marriage, which is why adultery could have such worrying implications and be so feared and punished. But the category divisions, like the ceremony of marriage, must be felt to symbolize real and important aspects of, and relationships in, reality. If it all becomes *mere* etiquette, then the result is the kind of society where the only reality *is* labels, a society in which indeed M. Homais will triumph and where the growth of his practice is bound to increase exponentially. For he represents the totalization of labels achieved by the obscuring and ignoring of the actualities of unlabeled being. In a society where M. Homais's "étiquettes" are proliferating at such a rate, how and where can Emma Bovary find out who and what she is? While what she *is* threatens his taxonomies, what he *does* helps to destroy her being. If this might seem to overstate the nature of his influence and power, let us just briefly consider two of his suggestions and recommendations that might not seem to have any reference or relevance to Emma.

It is Homais who has read about a "marvellous new treatment for clubfeet" (p. 186), and it is he who persuades the totally ill-equipped Charles Bovary to undertake this undesirable and unfeasible operation.

It is with the chemist's advice ("avec les conseils du pharmacien" [p. 236]), that Charles has a special kind of box prepared for the operation. This box merits a moment's attention, for in many ways it is the central object of the book, just as Charles's cap is the opening object and Homais's medal is the final one (and it does occur almost exactly in the middle of the text): "he had a kind of box, weighing about eight pounds, constructed by the carpenter and the locksmith, with a prodigal amount of iron, wood, sheet-iron, leather, nails and screws" (p. 188): ("il fit donc construire par le menuisier, aidé du serrurier, une manière de boîte pesant huit livres environ, et où le fer, le bois, la tôle, le cuir, les vis et les écrous, ne se trouvent point épargnés" [p. 236]). This is another of those strange manufactured objects in this book that are composed of heterogeneous substances and signs forced into some new and incoherent assemblage that is both meaningless and menacing. Throughout the book, in fact, we can note recurrent references to all kinds of boxes, or boxlike containers, running from the biscuit tin in which Rodolphe keeps the letters he has received from women, to Emma's coffin, and including the various kinds and shapes and sizes of the rooms in which Emma finds herself—or rather tries to find herself. But this, we may say, is the ultimate or paradigm bourgeois box. It summarizes and contains in its structure and materials all the coercions and constraints of the society around Hippolyte. Flaubert is careful to state that everyone from the mayor down works on Hippolyte to persuade him to have the operation ("tout le monde l'engagea, le sermonna, lui faisait honte") [p. 236]— urging, preaching, and shaming being three basic social devices for enforcing obedience and conformity). It is a brutal box suggesting force, torture, punishment, mutilation, and imprisoning. It is with this piece of equipment that Charles, under Homais's guidance and acting for the whole town, will attempt to correct what Homais refers to as his "hideuse claudication" (p. 235) (hideous limp or "deformity" [p. 187]). There is indeed a conspiracy ("conjuration" [p. 235]) against Hippolyte, as he vaguely feels, and he gives in because of the decisive factor that "*it wouldn't cost anything*" (p. 187) ("*c'est que ça ne lui coûterait rien.*" [p. 236]). I will return to the shattering irony of those words in a later section. It is made very clear by Flaubert that Hippolyte's clubfoot is in fact the repository of his moral strength. At the end of a nonfetishistic, respectful scrutiny of this clubfoot, Flaubert asserts that "with long service it had developed as it were moral qualities of energy and endurance" (p. 188) ("des qualités morales de patience et d'énergie" [p. 236]). The unspoken irony is that he should, as it were, only be able to discover and identify these moral qualities in a clubfoot. And this is the deformity that Homais suggests should be corrected or removed.

Hippolyte is "fastened into the apparatus" (p. 189) ("dans le moteur mécanique" [p. 237]), and any reader will recall the hideous results of this outrageous and presumptuous attempt to eliminate the natural adaptation that the man had made to his unusual physical condition and to substitute a mechanical correction. Just as Homais refers to Hippolyte as "our famous strephopod" (p. 191) ("notre intéressant stréphopode" [p. 239]), so he can regard him as an object to be corrected in accordance with a norm established by the majority: the man's humanity vanishes in the label and in the machine alike. When Homais takes off the box they "laid bare a hideous sight," (p. 191) ("un spectacle affreux" [p. 240]). Their response is to put the limb back into the apparatus "clamping it still tighter to hurry things along" (p. 191) ("et en l'y serrant d'avantage, pour accélérer les choses" [p. 240]); with the terminal result, of course, that after much excruciating pain, Hippolyte loses his leg, and that repository of "moral qualities" (p. 188) he has accumulated there. These have been displaced, to be replaced with a wooden substitute. The painful audibility of that wooden leg, and all it bespeaks, reechoes through the remainder of the book. My point here is to emphasize that, as the "good woman" Madame Lefrançois says, it was Homais who had "started it all" (p. 193) ("Il était *la cause de tout*" [p. 242]). This mutilating box is connected to his labels and his bottles and his taxonomic clichés. What they all serve to do, in their varying ways, is to eliminate the anomalous, entrap the deviant, excise the asymmetrical, take hold of the vagrant multiplicity of the world and somehow force it all into controllable and constraining containers. This is not a case of the human mind introducing order into the randomness of nature; it is the inverse or perverse case of the human mind mindlessly but forcibly introducing deformation and constraining mutilation into the order of nature. "When am I going to get better? Make me well! It's awful! It's awful!" (p. 192) ("Quand est-ce que je serai guéri? . . . Ah! sauvez-moi . . . Que je suis malheureux! que je suis malheureux!" [p. 241]). Hippolyte's pathetic cry is one that in a different way is to be uttered by Emma. More generally, it is the outcry of "difference" against that cruel and life-denying will-to-sameness that is manifest in an extreme form in that box, or "moteur mécanique" (p. 189), an insane instrument constructed ultimately out of a mania to reduce all life to predictable formulae and manageable homogeneity. It is the grossest, but only the grossest, of the many "inventions" that may be traced back to the Capharnaum.

Homais's instinct to eradicate the anomalous shows itself again, even more nakedly, in his treatment of the blind beggar. Homais's first reaction to him is that such wretches should be "shut up and forced to work" (p. 310) ("On devrait enfermer ces malheureux, que l'on forcerait à quelque travail!" [p. 387].) He then attempts a ludicrous, fragmentary, and meaningless diagnosis of the beggar's affliction, guaranteeing that he can cure him—a promise as absurd as the idea of curing Hippolyte's clubfoot. But in the later stages, when the blind beggar's importunate presence becomes an embarrassing reminder of the worthlessness of his promised cure, Homais employs every available strategy against him— writing in the local paper inveighing against a return of the conditions of the Middle Ages, when beggars were permitted to display their diseases and sores in public places; invoking the vagrancy laws ("les lois contre le vagabondage" [p. 439]); and finally going to the lengths of inventing "anecdotes" that name the blind beggar as being the occasion of some accident or other. He manages to get him imprisoned ("il fit si bien, qu'on l'incarcéra" [p. 440]), but he is released, and both the beggar and Homais resume their activities. Flaubert summarizes: "It was a tussle. Homais won, his enemy being condemned to be detained for life in an institution" (p. 355). ("C'était une lutte. Il eut la victoire; car son ennemi fut condamné à une réclusion perpétuelle dans un hospice" [p. 440].) It is a fight between that which will not, or cannot, be contained within the operating categories and conventions of society (its etiquettes) and that which seeks to eradicate, to forcibly conventionalize, or to imprison forever whatever presumes to exist outside those categories and norms. Hippolyte is forcibly persuaded and shamed into the "moteur mécanique"; the blind beggar is condemned to "une réclusion per- petuelle dans un hospice." Each of these "curative" or concealing in- struments may be said to be "une manière de boîte" (p. 236), and they may in their different ways be traced back to Homais and the devices of his Capharnaum. "Il était *la cause de tout.*"[15]

In her own way Emma is as much of a social "deviant" as Hippolyte, as much of a wanderer and beggar as the blind man (in their different ways, they are both *vagabondant,* as the book makes clear). Indeed, her relationship to the blind man is particularly close, as I shall suggest later on. The difference is that Hippolyte's deformity and the blind man's affliction and sick condition are both clearly, physically visible. They may struggle, but they are an easy prey for Homais and all he stands for. But what would a Homais-society make of Emma, and what can Emma make of herself in a society rapidly being taken over by Homais? When Emma goes to his house, in the incident I have already described, she passes heaps of smoking jam; the ironic echo of smoking dung and the omen of sweetness that turns to excrement is clearly intended. But a particular detail is given. The heap outside the chemist's shop is much bigger than the others, "towering above the rest with that superiority which the

---

[15]Michel Foucault's work provides an exemplary historical-sociological-psychological background to Homais's treatment of the beggar—see *Discipline and Punish: The Birth of the Prison* (trans. Alan Sheridan [New York: Pantheon, 1977]) particularly part 4, "Prison."

kitchen stove must concede to the factory and individual caprice to public demand" (p. 257) ("qui dépassait les autres de la supériorité qu'une
officine doit avoir sur les fourneaux bourgeois, un besoin général sur
des fantaisies individuelles" [p. 324]). Homais is the central power of the
"officine" ("dispensary" more specifically than "factory") and he presumes to speak for, to represent, indeed to *be*, the "besoin général."
Emma is in various ways closer to the "fourneaux bourgeois," if scarcely
comfortable there, and she is enthralled in "fantaisies individuelles." It
is another fight, though this time not a conscious one as between Homais
and the blind beggar. And there can only be one outcome: which is why,
to say it again, at the end of the book Emma is nonexistent and Homais is
ubiquitous. It is a bitter but appropriate irony that it is Homais who
recommends and even urges Charles to take Emma to the theatre
("conduisez Madame au spectacle" [p. 289]), for it is that experience that
effectively initiates her into a life of "fantaisies individuelles" from which
there is this time no return. The timing is again important. After
Rodolphe abandons her, Emma is very ill for a long time; she is recovering gradually when Homais makes his suggestion to Charles that a visit
to the opera would be good for her. Once again we encounter another of
Homais's recommendations for a cure that will turn out disastrously.
Indeed, wherever he is concerned we may say that the cure turns out to
be the disease. What would or could or might genuinely cure what Emma
suffers from is the real problem posed by the book, which is itself a long
effort of true diagnosis. The person who puts up the strongest fight
against Homais is, not the blind man, but Flaubert himself, for his book
is written and directed against everything that emerges from that opposed center of bad alchemy and lethal noncreations, the Capharnaum.
It is Flaubert's text versus Homais' étiquettes—the one labeling and containing process over which Homais has no control. The labeler and
concealer is discovered and definitively labeled by a higher "inscribing"
power—Flaubert himself.

Fetishism—Castles of Cake, Pellets from the Seraglio, the Damascened Rifle

In connection with the phenomenon of fetishistic displacement that
pervades the society depicted by the book as well as the book itself, I

want to give three more examples. The cake at Emma's wedding that so impresses the guests is made up of three tiers. It has as a base a blue cardboard imitation of a temple complete with porticoes, colonnades, and stucco statuettes; on top of that is a "castle-keep in Savoy cake" (p. 41) ("un donjon en gâteau de Savoie" [p. 55]), with fortifications of almonds and raisins and so on; the top layer is a green meadow with lakes of jam and a Cupid ("un Amour") on a chocolate swing. One could say that this object is an implicit comment on the degeneration of society from the religious age, through the heroic age, finally evolving into the placid age of the pastoral-bourgeois. But of course the main feature of this object is that everything has been turned into cake. Just as all the varied signs and fragments that went into the making of Charles Bovary's cap were equalized and rendered meaningless by their transposition into the material and context of the cap, so the temple and the castle and even Amour itself are all reduced to the level of a rich dessert, a confectionary translation or displacement that robs them of their real significance by reconstituting them as a series of devourable references. (In the same way we find in the book napkins like bishop's miters and loaves like turbans reminiscent of the Gothic crusades—history, heroism, and religion have all been moved into the bourgeois kitchen and dining room, for cooking, serving, and decoration.) This is an example of what I mean by degenerative displacements or transformations. It is this process that underlies the whole description of Emma's early "education" in part one, chapter six, where Flaubert describes all the debased metaphors and images fed into Emma from a religious upbringing without any notion of real belief: bad novels, romantic stories, exaggerated painted plates, sentimental songs, and all the books and pictures that poured their stereotypes into Emma's head—not filling gaps, but causing them. This of course is part of the fog in Emma's head and has been often noted (as by Girard). What we should also note is that it serves inevitably to induce in Emma herself a certain kind of fetishism. Thus she starts to experience what amounts to an erotic thrill just by handling the books and watching the tissue paper float over the plates. "She thrilled as she blew back the tissue paper over the prints. It rose in a half-fold and sank gently down on the opposite page" (p. 51). ("Elle frémissait, en soulevant de son haleine le papier de soie des gravures, qui se levait à demi plié et retombait doucement contre la page" [p. 65].) This sensuous rising and falling of the soft white paper seems like a morphological prefiguration of the more overtly erotic risings and fallings of clothes, sheets, bodies implied or described in Emma's later sexual life (the smell of "damp sheets" is detectable in the setting of Emma's first appearance); it even suggests the kind of sensual inhaling and exhaling of breath of which she often becomes conscious both in herself and others.

One could see that one triggering stimulus in her later life might be traced to a fetishistic attachment to the childhood excitement at blowing back the tissue paper over pictures. Not exactly that she is trying to love by the book, but rather that she is trying to recapture an experience in the flesh that originated as a sensation caused by paper, and thus to rediscover in "love" the texture (even more than the text) of the book.

My second example occurs quite near the end, when Emma's disintegration is well advanced. We are told that she spends her days in her room, mentally benumbed and physically scarcely clothed, "occasionally burning some aromatic pellets that she had bought at an Algerian shop in Rouen" (p. 299) ("faisant fumer des pastilles du sérail qu'elle avait achetées à Rouen dans la boutique d'un Algérien" [p. 374]). Literally these are pellets of the seraglio, as though the essence of an oriental harem had been transformed (or "decanted") into a pill that can then be sold as a commodity in a shop that is itself an anomalous displacement (an Algerian shop in Rouen). The power behind this alchemical feat lies in the verb *acheter* of course, for money turns everything to transportable goods, so that there is seemingly no limit to the process by which the exotic from all realms and at all levels can be transplaced into the bourgeois domestic setting (witness the piece of coral in Emma's house).[16] I have alluded to this phenomenon of fragmenting the world, and moving it around as sample and spectacle, in connection with Goethe's novel. Flaubert reveals a society in which the process seems to permeate almost every area of activity. In this case these "pellets" also

---

[16]Money also can *transform* anything and everything, as Marx noted: thus, to give only one quotation:

> Money is the universal means and power, exterior to man, not issuing from man as man or from human society as society, to turn imagination into reality and reality into mere imagination. Similarly it turns real human and natural faculties into mere abstract representations and thus imperfections and painful imaginings, while on the other hand it turns the real imperfections and imaginings, the really powerless faculties that exist only in the imagination of the individual, into real faculties and powers. This description alone suffices to make money the universal inversion of individualities that turns them into their opposites and gives them qualities at variance with their own. As this perverting power, money then appears as the enemy of man and social bonds that pretend to self-subsistence. It changes fidelity into infidelity, love into hate, hate into love, virtue into vice, vice into virtue, slave into master, master into slave, stupidity into intelligence, and intelligence into stupidity.
>
> Since money is the existing and self-affirming concept of value and confounds and exchanges all things, it is the universal confusion and exchange of all things, the inverted world, the confusion and exchange of all natural and human qualities.
>
> ("On Money": *The Early Texts* in Karl Marx, *Selected Writings*, ed. David McLellan [Oxford: Oxford University Press, 1977] pp. 110–11)

This whole description of the "confusion and exchange of all natural and human qualities" is very appropriate to the world of Flaubert's novel, for as Emma experiences it, it is indeed an "inverted world," and the perverse power of money is made terribly clear.

serve to contribute to the fog in Emma's head; indeed it would seem that she bought them for that purpose, as if seeking to confound one sort of fog with another, or perhaps to compound all the fogs and fumes that seem subtly, then more obviously, to swarm upon her.

A rather different but related kind of displacement is in evidence when Emma goes to make her final appeal to Rodolphe, who turns her down with the explanation that he is a "bit short" ("gêné") himself. She says sarcastically how sorry she is for him and then looks around the room. "She let her gaze rest on a damascened rifle that glittered in a rack on the wall" (p. 323) ("une carabine damasquinée" [p. 401]) and starts to remark on the opulent objects that Rodolphe still retains in his "poverty." "When people are poor, they don't put silver on the butts of their guns! Or buy a clock inlaid with tortoise-shell! . . . or silver-plated whistles for their whips . . . or trinkets for their watches" (p. 323). Manifest in these objects are inappropriate and incongruous and totally pointless mergings of items and materials—a damascened rifle? What conceivable reason could there be for such an alogical collocation? Except that the rifle has ceased to be a genuine instrument to be used and has shifted into a fetish that can be decorated; and why put tortoiseshell on a clock ("une pendule avec des incrustations d'écailles" [p. 401]); and what on earth is a silver-plated whistle doing on a whip ("des sifflets de vermeil pour ses fouets" [p. 401])? Such questions could be answered in terms of the history of decoration, but in the terms of this book they seem to have the same origin in that incoherent assemblage of signs and materials that was manifest in that cap of "enculturation" that Charles Bovary holds onto so awkwardly during his initiation into the school and language of his society. The answer to Emma's protest is that it is precisely when people are "poor" that they indulge in the multiplying absurdities of displacement of materials and decorations and functions such as are exemplified in the objects in Rodolphe's room. This bespeaks a far-reaching impoverishment of feeling, emotion, spirit—whatever we might still mean by human and humane response to other human beings. It is the ultimate poverty, and Rodolphe is quite right in intimating that he is deep into it, much deeper than he thinks or could ever know. And the manifestation of this kind of poverty is, I suggest, visible in the fetishism implied by such an object as *une carabine damasquinée*.

I have been using *fetishism* in a general sense to denote that displacement of libidinal feeling from the complete sexual identity of the other (let us say the woman), to an ancillary object, some adjunct or appurtenance, or to some *portion* of the body (which being isolated from the living body, by drawing attention *away from* the whole to the part, takes on the status of a thing). The full sexual identity of the other is threatening, dangerous, unpredictable, and alive, and requires a commitment and engagement (and thus a risk) on the part of the one whose feelings are aroused. By contrast the "fetishized" objects are relatively safe, easily available, undemanding of reciprocity or commitment and thus allowing the person whose feelings have been aroused to remain in a passive, spectator/consumer relationship to the other (again, let us say the women—and here we should differentiate between transitional objects, which help to wean the child away from complete identification with the mother, and fetish objects, by which what is termed mature genital relationships are avoided so that the mutuality of love is never attempted). This kind of displacement of feeling onto decontextualized objects or fragments (the context would be the whole living woman) as substitutes or replacements, once it has been engendered, may take over increasingly large areas of the person's approach to life in general, and thus it can permeate an entire society's modes of feeling and dealing (thus misplaced emotion may lavish its loving attentions on a rifle instead of a person and produce the *carabine damasquinée*). At a certain indefinite point the fetish need not be in any way related to a woman or indeed women in general, so that the libidinal feeling does not, as it were, slide or veer away from, or stop short of, confronting the full sexuality of the woman to arrest itself in the security of an accessory object or an unsexual part, but can attach itself directly to objects. Thus I have called Binet's ecstatic devotion to his napkin rings a kind of extreme fetishism though there is no instance of his having transferred that feeling from any female object or femininity in general. However, in addition to this rather all-embracing use of the word, we do have Freud's essay, "Fetischism" (1927), and it is worth restating some of his ideas and insights here, since I think they are very relevant to Flaubert's depiction of what has happened to modes of sexual feelings and libidinal attachment in the society he describes. In the Standard Edition, the editor's note points out that in his earliest discussion of fetishism (*Three Essays*), Freud wrote that "no other variation of the sexual instinct that borders on the pathological can lay so much claim to our interest as this one," but did not go beyond maintaining that "the choice of a fetish is an after-effect of some sexual impression, received as a rule in early childhood." There are some intervening references to foot fetishism, but it is not until this famous essay that Freud introduces what the editors call a "fresh metapsychological development." It is this aspect of the essay that I wish to summarize here.

Freud starts by citing the case of a young man who "had exalted a certain sort of 'shine on the nose' into a fetishistic precondition." The explanation turned out to be that the boy had been brought up in an English nursery but had later come to Germany, where he forgot his mother tongue. "The fetish, which originated from his earliest childhood, had to be understood in English, not German. The 'shine on the nose' (in German *'Glanz auf der Nase'*)—was in reality a *'glance* at the nose.' The nose was thus the fetish, which, incidentally, he endowed at will with the luminous shine which was not perceptible to others." Freud goes on to maintain that "the meaning and the purpose of the fetish" in every instance he studied turned out to be the same. "When now I announce that the fetish is a substitute for the penis, I shall certainly create disappointment; so I hasten to add that it is not a substitute for any chance penis, but for a particular and quite special penis that had been extremely important in early childhood but had later been lost. That is to say, it should normally have been given up, but the fetish is precisely designed to preserve it from extinction. To put it more plainly: the fetish is a substitute for the woman's (the mother's) penis that the little boy *once believed in and*—for reasons familiar to us—*does not want to give up.*" (My italics.) Freud maintains that "the boy *refused to take cognizance of the fact of his having perceived* that a woman does not possess a penis" (my italics)—a refusal based on the ensuing fear of his own castration. What this amounts to in more general terms is no less than a strategy whereby new and threatening *knowledge* is overlaid by an earlier and comforting *belief.* In a crucial passage Freud differentiates this process from pathological repression. "If we wanted to differentiate more sharply between the vicissitude of the *idea* as distinct from that of the *affect,* and reserve the word *'Verdrängung'* ('repression') for the affect, then the correct German word for the vicissitude of the idea would be *'Verleugnung'* ('disavowal')." Freud explains further, "It is not true that, after the child has made his observation of the woman, he has preserved unaltered his belief that women have a phallus. *He has retained that belief, but he has also given it up.* In the conflict between the weight of the unwelcome perception and the force of his counter-wish, a compromise has been reached. . . . Yes, in his mind the woman *has* got a penis, in spite of everything; but this penis is no longer the same as it was before. *Something else has taken its place, has been appointed its substitute, as it were, and now inherits the interest which was formerly directed to its predecessor.*" (All my italics.) And while interest in the fetish increases "because the horror of castration has set up a memorial to itself in the creation of this substitute," so "aversion" [the German word *der Abscheu* implies even stronger feelings of both disgust and awe], which is never absent in any fetishist, to the real female genitals remains a *stigma indelible* of the repression that has taken place." One could thus conceive of how the two processes are mutually reinforcing, and an increased attachment to the fetishistic object(s) would both intensify and be intensified by a growing aversion to the actual genital identity of the woman. Irrespective of what a reader may think of Freud's unitary explanation of the source of all fetishism, we can, I think recognize that this process is ubiquitous in Flaubert's novel.

In his further comments on the choice of fetish objects (or "substitutes for the absent female phallus"), Freud maintains that it often seems that "when the fetish is instituted some process occurs which reminds one of the stopping of memory in traumatic amnesia. As in this latter case, the subject's interest comes to a halt half-way, as it were; it is as though the last impression before the uncanny and traumatic one is retained as a fetish." Thus fixing emotional regard on an object may be a deliberate way of *not* seeing the woman or the person; perception may in this way blockade its own processes with things. This too obtains in Flaubert's world.

Freud extends his discussion by describing the case of two boys who seem to have "failed to take cognizance" of the death of the "beloved father." It turned out that this was not so any more than the fetishist fails to take cognizance of the fact that women are "castrated." "It was only one current in their mental life that had not recognized their father's death; there was another current which took full account of that fact. The attitude which fitted in with the wish and the attitude which fitted in with reality existed side by side." This idea of the coexistence of two currents of thought avowing different and contradictory things and aims—one geared to "wishes" (*wunschgerecht*) and the other doing justice to "reality" (*realitätsgerecht*)—becomes increasingly common in later nineteenth-century thought and may be found, for example, in late Dickens, or William James, (*Dr. Jeckyll and Mr. Hyde* is a well-known popular version of this particular condition). The importance of Freud's formulation lies in the identification of a possible "splitting of the ego" involved in this process of acknowledgment/disavowal. "In very subtle instances both the disavowal and the affirmation of the castration have found their way into the construction of the fetish itself. . . . Affection and hostility in the treatment of the fetish—which run parallel with the disavowal and the acknowledgment of castration—are mixed in unequal proportions in different cases, so that the one or the other is more clearly recognizable." This uneasy combination of both acknowledgment (*die Anerkennung*) and affirmation (*die Behauptung*) with disavowal and denial (*die Verleugnung*)—whether or not we want to accept that it always ultimately involves the question of the female penis/castration—produces a fetishistic attitude to reality in general in which there is a constant attempt to substitute belief for knowledge. This may take many forms, including the substitution of a damascened rifle safely fastened on the wall—for Emma Bovary—sexual, dangerous, and mobile. "In later life, the fetishist feels that he enjoys yet another advantage from his substitute for a genital. The meaning of the fetish is not known to other people, so the fetish is not withheld from him: it is easily accessible and he can readily obtain the sexual satisfaction attached to it. What other men have to woo and make exertions for can be had by the fetishist with no trouble at all." Freud uses the word for traditional courtship, *werben* ("to woo"), and we may note how very little genuine wooing of that kind there is in *Madame Bovary*. Indeed is there any at all? Clothes and costumes woo each other more than people, another perverse displacement of the kind I have mentioned. And how much real "exertion" (*sich mühen* suggests travail, effort, and strain) is there in Flaubert's somnolent and idle world? Thus Charles Bovary's "wooing" of Emma is almost completely inarticulate. They are reported as having a conversation in which they each recall various childhood memories, but their most significant contacts as adults are restricted to a drink and a chance physical contact of chest and back while Emma is bending down to pick up Charles's whip, which, in a gesture that needs no further comment, she hands over to him. The actual proposal is avoided by Charles, and it is Emma's father who has to conduct whatever exchanges with Emma are necessary. The courtship in fact is reduced to an arbitrary sign that the father arranges and Charles can translate—i.e., instead of the man pleading his cause to the woman and winning her with his presence, his gestures, his words, we have Charles timidly waiting for forty-nine minutes outside the house while the father talks to the daughter, until the window shutter is pushed open and flat against the wall (the sexual implications of this sign are crudely and degradingly obvious)—"the shutter had been folded back, the hook was still rattling" (p. 38) ("l'auvent s'était rabattu, la cliquette tremblait encore" [p. 49]). The difficult and delicate persuasions traditionally involved in the language of love have been replaced by *l'auvent*; and the "work" of the suitor is conducted in summary form by the father: two more deteriorative displacements that fall within the "fetishised" atmosphere of the world of the book. It is indeed a society of fetishists.[17]

[17]It is also appropriate here to refer to Marx's writing on "The Fetishism of Commodities" (in *Capital*, volume one); indeed, it could be argued that there are possible and plausible relations between the fetishism described by Freud (concentrating on man's mystified "relation" to women) and that described by Marx (concentrating on man's mystified relation to his products), both emerging from the bourgeois-capitalist society that both men studied. I will quote one passage from Marx, noting that the mysteriousness of commodities was also clearly visible to Flaubert, who could see things relating to each other more purposefully than—and instead of—people.

A commodity is therefore a mysterious thing, simply because in it the social character of men's labour appears to them as an objective character stamped upon the product of that labour; because the relation of the producers to the sum total of their own labour is presented to them as a social relation, existing not between themselves, but between the products of their labour. This is the reason why the

Distance, Happiness, Blindness—Léon, Lheureux, et l'Aveugle

Shortly after her marriage to Charles, Emma succumbs to boredom ("ennui"—compared to a silent spider spinning or weaving its web in the shadow of the corners of her heart), and her mind disengages itself from the present into other tenses uncorrected by her immediate surroundings—speculative, hypothetical, conditional. Might she not have met another man... if, perhaps, could... what would her friends be doing now?... in this way her consciousness eludes the given of which it is a part and enters into the infinite realm of imaginary possibilities, the only constraint on the construction of which is that they shall be different from and negate the "now." It is a paradoxical procedure by which the bored (or desperate) mind tries to imagine precisely that which it does not know and has not experienced—for Emma, "that different life, that unknown husband" (p. 57) ("cette vie différente, ce mari qu'elle ne connaissait pas" [p. 74]). This is immediately before their visit to La Vaubyessard, a visit to another world that will indeed give her imagination a sense of another kind of life around which to organize her fantasies, and with which to both identify and exacerbate her discontents. But at the point to which I am referring, Emma's bored mind moves effortlessly and inevitably from imprecise hypothetical speculations about some unknown different life to memories of her own childhood, as though Flaubert could very clearly see the intimate subtle connections between discontent with the given, desire for difference, and reversion to memory. Emma thinks of the prize-giving days when she was looked at, admired,

---

products of labour become commodities, social things whose qualities are at the same time perceptible and imperceptible by the senses.... There is a physical relation between physical things. But it is different with commodities. There, the existence of the things *qua* commodities, and the value relation between the products of labour which stamps them as commodities, have absolutely no connection with their physical properties and with the material relations arising therefrom. There is a definite social relation between men, that assumes, in their eyes, the fantastic form of a relation between things. In order, therefore, to find an analogy, we must have recourse to the mist-enveloped regions of the religious world. In that world the productions of the human brain appear as independent beings endowed with life, and entering into relation both with one another and the human race. So it is in the world of commodities with the products of men's hands. This I call the Fetishism which attaches itself to the products of labour, so soon as they are produced as commodities, and which is therefore inseparable from the production of commodities.)

From Marx, *Selected Writings*, ed. David McLellan (Oxford: Oxford University Press, 1977), p. 436.

spoken kindly to by all "the gentlemen"; a nonproblematical prepubertal moment when she simply had to be a passive, pretty child sustained at the center of a circle of unthreatening masculine admiration and friendliness. But now she is Madame Bovary and—"How far away it all was!" (p. 58) ("Comme c'était loin, tout cela! comme c'était loin!" [p. 64]). From this point we may say that what is far will appeal to Emma more than what is near, that memory reconstitutes itself as desire, that in an impossible way she will be trying to displace herself from presence to distance, to bring herself near to the "far." Obviously there is a limit to the extent to which you can think yourself into distance, as Emma soon discovers in her post-La Vaubyessard fantasies. She can think herself out of Tostes, but it is difficult to think herself clearly into what is by definition the realm of the unclear—"After going some distance, there was always a vague blur where her imagination failed" (p. 70): ("Au bout d'une distance indéterminée, il se trouvait toujours une place confuse où expirait son rêve" [p. 90]). This is why she buys a map of Paris in an attempt to introduce some topographical precision and contour into her fantasies (another fetishistic displacement of feeling as she runs her sensitive finger over the map as if it was the paper landscape of love's own body). This is supplemented by a further diet of novels as she tries to extend the fictionalizing of her existence, using the memory of the Viscount as the center and referent points for her fantasies to exclude her awareness of the actuality of her husband.

All these desperate strategies of consciousness are engendered and constantly intensitified by one pain in many guises—the torments of proximity. They represent the self-defeating, self-destroying impulse to nihilate the present by the absent, and to lose the unbearable clarity and routinization of the near in the unknowable indistinctness and confusion of the far. Emma is making an impossible effort to shift ontological primacy from her physical life to her fantasy life. "The rest of the world came nowhere, had no proper status, no real existence. In fact, the nearer home things came, the more she shrank from all thought of them. The whole of her immediate environment—dull countryside, imbecile petty bourgeois, life in its ordinariness—seemed a freak, a particular piece of bad luck that had seized on her; while beyond, as far as eye could see, ranged the vast lands of passion and felicity" (p. 72). ("Quant au reste du monde, il était perdu, sans place précise, et comme n'existant pas. Plus les choses, d'ailleurs, étaient voisines, plus sa pensée s'en détournait. Tout ce qui l'entourait immédiatement, campagne ennuyeuse, petits bourgeois imbéciles, médiocrité de l'existence, lui semblait une exception dans le monde, un hasard particulier où elle se trouvait prise, tandis qu'au-delà s'étendait à perte de vue l'immense pays des félicités et des passions" [p. 91].) (Note here again the close phonemic and etymological entanglement of the words that parallels, indeed is part of, Emma's plight. Her thoughts "s'en détournait" from all that "l'entourait"—but can she ultimately "turn" *away* from everything that "turns" *round* her? In the middle of both words, as in the middle of her own life, there is that unavoidable *tour*.) Since the physical world of the present will not stay bracketed as a "freak" ("une exception dans le monde"), and *does* have *place précise* and is constantly asserting its *existence*, Emma cannot indefinitely cancel the near with the far. Instead she will engage in another pardoxical and ultimately self-destroying project; finding the far within the near, the *loin* in the *voisine*. And this is why her first attraction to Léon, for Léon seems to incorporate for Emma the attractions of the *loin* (it takes little to transform *Léon* into *loin*). He comes to stand for that desired impossibility—present farness.

Thus it is entirely appropriate that Emma does not have her first physical affair with Léon. Indeed their relationship is founded on incorporeality. Emma is first moved more by his shadow gliding past than by his bodily presence ("souvent elle tressaillait à l'apparition de cette ombre glissant tout à coup" [p. 139]). She likes to lie in bed and look at Léon as a memory, part of a scene to be recalled with that "lengthening of perspective that things attain in memory" (p. 115) "cet allongement de perspective que le souvenir donne aux objets" [p. 145]). Their reading is a coming together through signs and pictures of a nonpresent world (a fashion magazine serves as well as poetry). They wait for each other "at the bottom of the page" (p. 111) ("s'attendaient au bas des pages" [p. 141]) before they wait for each other in Rouen cathedral. They do establish a "kind of bond" (p. 112) ("une sorte d'association") through a constant commerce of books ("commerce continuel de livres" [p. 142]). We may indeed say that Emma turns from the repulsive contact of her husband's lips ("au contact de ses lèvres" [p. 328]) to the seductive images of Léon's books. (Again the words reveal the simple though decisive displacement and transformation that is taking place, for it is easy to turn from *lèvres* to *livres*. Once again the words are looking at each other, marking their similarities and noting their small differences.) Thus for a long time Emma prefers to seek out solitude so that she can "revel in his image undisturbed" (p. 120) ("afin de pouvoir plus à l'aise se délecter en son image" [p. 152]). As image he is both present and absent, an unstable compromise between near and far that cannot last indefinitely, and Emma's mental "delectations" can hardly fail to affect her bodily disposition. Her adultery is imaginary before it is physical. The image foreordains the fact. (Thus "des désirs adultères" are engendered by "la tendresse matrimonial" (p. 153); the marriage produces the image of what it is not, it is the negative to the positive of fantasy, and only later will the image attach itself to a man. In their origin adultery and adulterous desires are thus endo-marital rather than exo-marital, a proposition of some importance in consideration of the importance of marriage in the bourgeois novel.) And even though Emma does of course engage in a long physical relationship with Léon, he seems ultimately to lose all substance. At one point when her affair with Léon is effectively over and she is about to embark on her final round of desperate requests for help, she sits down by the walls of her own convent and once again reverts to memory. "The first months of her marriage, her rides to the forest, the Viscount waltzing, Lagardy singing, everything passed before her eyes once more; and Léon seemed suddenly as remote as the rest" (p. 294). ("Les premiers mois de son mariage, ses promenades à cheval dans la forêt, le vicomte qui valsait, et Lagardy chantant, tout repassa devant ses yeux. . . . Et Léon lui parut soudain dans le même éloignement que les autres" [p. 368].) Everything and everyone is equalized in this "même éloignement," and Léon, whose distinction was to seem to incorporate a certain quality of farness, and to compound suggestions of remoteness in his person, takes his place in the general indistinctness with which all things and people and memories are merging in Emma's mind. What remains of her relationship to him is more like a postmortem reflex. Thus she continues to write him love letters (following what Girard would call the mediating *idée* that this is what a woman does to her lover), but "as she wrote she saw another man, a phantom made of her most ardent memories, of the finest things she had read, of her most violent longings; who became in the end so real and so accessible that he set her thrilling with wonder, though she had no clear picture of him, for he receded like a god behind the abundance of his attributes" (pp. 301–2). ("Mais, en écrivant, elle percevait un autre homme, un fantôme fait de ses plus ardents souvenirs, de ses lectures les plus belles, de ses convoitises les plus fortes; et il devenait à la fin si véritable, et accessible, qu'elle en palpitait émerveillée, sans pouvoir néamoins le nettement imaginer, tant il se perdait, comme un dieu, sous l'abondance de ses attributs" [p. 376].) As Léon comes physically nearer and nearer to Emma, he loses his distinguishing quality of farness (for Emma his identity and reality were really his indistinctness, and distinctness paradoxically produces a loss of identity and reality). In his proximity to Emma, even his image finally vanishes, to be replaced by a true phantom, made up of memory, reading, and longing; a figure both accessible yet finally impossible to imagine, a "god" whose abundant attributes may be summed up in one word—absence. To the extent that Léon is subsumed into the world that for Emma, is *voisine*, he loses his potency for her as an image or locus of all that is *loin*. His place is inevitably taken by a phantom who seems more true and more real because he is composed of phenomena that by definition cannot be present. This is the great god

Lack, whom Emma truly worships and whose present-absence and accessible farness constitute an important part of the fog in Emma's head.

The man who insinuates his presence into Emma's immediate environment more persistently is Lheureux, who, indeed, visits her the evening after she has come to the conclusion that Léon is in love with her and as she is beginning to focus her discontent on unanswerable questions posed by the contrast between Charles and Léon "Oh, if only Fate had willed it . . . And why not? Why shouldn't it have been . . . ?" (p. 115) ("Pourquoi n'est-ce pas? Qui empêchait donc? . . . " [p. 146]). Lheureux is described as a tradesman or shopkeeper ("boutiquier") and a dealer in novelties ("marchand de nouveautés" [p. 146]). He is addressed by the text as "sieur" rather than "Monsieur," which would seem to be a deliberate debased foreshortening through the erosion or elimination of the personal pronoun. Even the formalities are in decline. For just as no one knows anything about Lheureux's past (what he has been formerly), so also he indeed "belongs" to nobody. He has no connections or relationships with anyone in the town; he is a gratuitous, pleonastic presence, an unnecessariness who subtly imposes himself on the town as a necessity. He is a bastard, self-synthesized product—"Gascon by birth and Norman by choice, he had grated upon his southern loquacity the cunning of the Cauchois" (p. 115) ("Né Gascon, mais devenu Normand, il doublait sa faconde méridionale de cautèle cauchoise" [p. 146])—another incongruous product, or "assembly" such as is prefigured by Charles Bovary's cap. Whether he has been a peddler ("porteballe") or some kind of moneylender ("banquier"), the one known fact about him is that he can do complicated calculations in his head that even frighten M. Binet ("des calculs compliqués à effrayer Binet lui-même" [p. 146]). In this he is like Homais, who does not produce anything, indeed does not know anything—but only decants, reties, and labels. Just so, Lheureux does and creates nothing; he is an intermediary calculator. Lheureux's rise to power may be said to be connected with the decline of the values and virtues and way of life represented by Catherine Leroux, the old peasant lady who is given a medal at the agricultural show. Just as Hippolyte's leg had its acquired "moral" qualities, so Catherine Leroux's drooping hands, knotted or twisted at the joints ("à articulations noueuses" [p. 204])—and thus, in a way, as "deformed" as Hippolyte's foot was— testify humbly to a lifetime of service and sustained hardships. From living among animals she has acquired their "mutisme" and "placidité." In all this we may say that she represents a kind of life and thus a range of values and characteristics directly opposed to Emma, who has no real work to do and never achieves the gifts—or reliefs—of *mutisme* and *placidité*. But in social terms the intimation is that the kind of existence connected with Leroux is being superseded by a way of life whose most distinctive apologist and advancer is Lheureux. Here again the slightly modified echo in the names seems to be deliberate. Leroux implies a russet-red color that is connected with the color of the earth (during the ride that will culminate in Emma's first adultery, the earth is described as "roussâtre" [p. 214]—"red-brown" [p. 171]), while Lheureux suggests that illusory kind of "happiness" that he intimates can be procured by buying his unwanted goods. It is another degenerative transformation, for while Leroux becomes a relic to be put on display at a fair, Lheureux comes out of nowhere to impose himself as a power in the economy of the town. "Happy" himself, he dispenses unhappiness to others, and he fastens on Emma unerringly as his first major potential victim.

How he does this is of course a clear part of the narrative line of the book. But it should be emphasized that he inserts himself, almost literally, into Emma's life through the "gaps" that have been made in it by such things as the memory of Le Vaubyessard and the image of Léon. What he is proposing, quite implicitly of course, is that Emma can fill the gaps of desire with materials and things. He is in fact the most dangerous seduction for Emma, for he works by trying to transform the vagueness and indistinctness of erotic-emotional desire into a specific greed for an infinity of unnecessary commodities. There is no more ruinous form of indirect exploitation. Uninvited but utterly insistent, obsequious but ruthlessly obstinate, Lheureux arrays his wares in front of Emma, another incoherent confusion reminiscent of that matrix of Charles Bovary's cap (one could see it as a kind of bourgeois Pandora's box out of which all the other absurd synthesized objects of the rest of the book flow, or as a base model from which an endless number of other objects can be generated)—Algerian scarves, English needles, straw sandals, embroidered collars, and "four egg cups carved out of coconut-shells by convicts" (p. 116) ("quatre coquetiers en coco, ciselés à jour par des forçats" [p. 147]). Her first reaction is to reject everything by saying there is nothing she needs or wants ("Je n'ai besoin de rien" [p. 147]). But Lheureux's method is precisely to attempt to create a sense of need where none previously existed (as I said, by tacitly soliciting the transference of unsatisfied erotic-emotional desires onto his palpable, though pointless, objects). He puts out more things and follows Emma's eyes "as they wandered irresolutely over his ware" (p. 116) ("le regard d'Emma qui se promenait indécis parmi ces marchandises" [p. 147]). This wandering indecision is the crucial instability in Emma that allows her to confuse *images* and "marchandises." Like the first Madame Bovary, who was always asking for "un peu plus," whether of love or of syrup, Emma will soon be unable to distinguish between kinds of needs, appetites, desires, and longings and will try increasingly to compensate for a dissatisfaction of the emotions with a satiation of *marchandises*. Once she

goes on to ask Lheureux—"Combien coûtent-elles" (p. 147)—she is effectively within his power, as he well recognizes when he predicts suavely
yet oddly menacingly, "We shall come to terms another time" (p. 117)
("nous nous entendrons plus tard" [p. 148]). So it is that throughout the
book Emma obtains more and more stuff from Lheureux, money as well
as clothes and other accessories, and we confront the painful paradox of
a woman who seems increasingly desirous of undressing with greater
urgency and speed yet at the same time is impoverishing and ruining
herself socially and economically through a largely pointless accumulation of useless material and costumery. Even when she goes to see him in
connection with her growing financial problems, he continues automatically to show her new dress material and "plusieurs marchandises
nouvelles" (p. 372). His office where she goes to plead with him is very
small and constricting, like so many of the places and spaces she finds
herself in, and his ledgers are protected by a "padlocked grating" (p. 296)
("une barre de fer cadenassée" [p. 370]), one of many grills and iron
objects that Emma encounters on her journeyings. I will comment on
this later, but it all contributes to the feeling of her getting herself further and further into a trap; there is something reminiscent of the box
used on Hippolyte's foot in that inner sanctum of ruthless "calculation,"
the office of "sieur" Lheureux (a comparison might also be made with
Homais's Carpharnaum—and even Binet's workshop—all bourgeois
interiors that in different ways serve to intensify the impossibility of
Emma's life). It should be noticed that it is of course M. Lheureux who
systematically organized Emma's financial ruin (he "undresses" her economically in his mind as Rodolph undresses her sexually—to both men
in different ways she shows herself as an exploitable object). One of the
ways he does this is to tempt her into borrowing money, then "passing on
her I.O.U.s" (p. 296). The French for this reveals a more incisive irony.
Emma accuses him of having promised "de ne pas faire circuler ses
billets" (p. 370). Such circulation may be seen as an extreme aspect of the
methods of circulation that were characteristic of bourgeois capitalist
society, though it would be exaggerating to suggest that the figure of
Lheureux is offered as a critique of the problems connected with the
sphere of circulation as opposed to the sphere of production. More
specifically, he has played his own lethal part in making Emma "circu-
late." He does this precisely to provide more capital for himself, and by
the end, through paper work of which she has no comprehension, she is
responsible for the accumulation of a capital sum for Lheureux. He
sends her round and round after money/materials, money/materials
until it is entirely understandable if she should be suffering from what in
the nineteenth century was called "la folie circulaire" (a form of manic-
depressive insanity). Other factors contribute to that *folie circulaire,* as I

will suggest, but it is important to note what a key role Lheureux plays in exacerbating Emma's condition. His rejection of her in her final extremity (when she can be of no further use to him) is more brutal than Rodolphe's—indeed, it is the most heartless rebuff she receives. There is just some slight poetic or rather "symmetrical" justice hinted at in the assertion that the one complaint Lheureux is troubled with is vertigo ("des vertiges"). Emma was, from the start, prone to giddiness, and her increasing turnings and circlings only aggravate the complaint. It is a giddiness connected with emotion and desire, with all the ambiguities and multiple connotations of these words, and it has its pathos as well as its follies. With Lheureux we witness the onset of another kind of vertigo, connected to the sphere of circulation in the broadest sense and deriving from pure, exploitative, unfeeling greed. His circulations have an even more damaging effect on human life than the napkin rings coming off M. Binet's endlessly turning lathe.

In this connection it is worth reminding ourselves of just how prevalent the emphasis is on circling of all kinds in many different spheres of life in this novel. That is to say, Emma is born into a circling world. Like the customs man (or coastguard), most figures in the book, in one way or another, are engaged in making their own kinds of rounds; in different contexts and changing modes, each one is seen *en faisant sa tournée*. These circlings range from the natural to the manufactured. Thus Emma's greyhound runs round in circles, and her meandering thoughts start to emulate this pattern of motion. "At first her mind roved aimlessly hither and thither, like her greyhound, which went circling over the grass.... Then gradually her thoughts took focus..." (p. 57). ("Sa pensée, sans but d'abord, vagabondait au hasard, comme sa levrette, qui faisait des cercles dans la campagne.... Puis ses idées peu à peu se fixaient" [p. 74]). This is part of a larger system of circlings that are, in some unstated but perceptible way, isomorphically or homologously related. But there are also crucial differences. The greyhound who, while still a pet, spends his time running round in circles, one day (during the move to Yonville) simply disappears, i.e., breaks out of the circle. This release or escape would seem to be possible only for an animal unburdened with consciousness and language. Emma's consciousness can never break out of the circle.

There is no one specific causal or determinative origin for her attraction (and compulsion) toward circular motion (as I tried to indicate in a previous section, it is inevitable that any life must be made up of varying combinations of, or oscillations between, *les règles* and *les tournures*). But the inclination to turn can be excited, aggravated, and given a distinctive set of associations and emotive qualities, by various specific turning motions and vortical activities made available by society, either offered as occasions of entertainment or imposed as patterns of work. One of the most influential vortical experiences in Emma's life is of course the waltz with the Viscount at Le Vaubyessard. "They started slowly, then got faster. They turned, and everything turned round them . . . " (p. 66). ("Ils commencèrent lentement, puis allèrent plus vite. Ils tournaient; tout tournait autour d'eux . . . " [p.84].) Emma experiences both extreme erotic excitement and extreme dizziness until she nearly falls and has to lean on his chest. We should note here once again the initiatory and controlling power of the male figure; in this case one having the awesome power vaguely implicit in the title *vicomte*. Here it is not love that makes the world go round but much more specifically the Viscount with his irresistible authority, skill, and command. He is the master of the waltz. Emma, we may say, is the one who is waltzed, for his is the guidance and hers is the vertigo. "Still turning, but more gently, he brought her back to her seat" (p. 66). ("Et puis, tournant toujours, mais plus doucement, il la reconduisit à sa place" [p. 84].) This particular kind of suave, assured power that pervades the atmosphere of the aristocratic sphere is echoed in little details itemized by Flaubert, such as the "whips and stirrups and curbs" that hang on the walls. With these instruments and equipment the aristocrats can dominate the bodies of their horses, accelerating them or holding them back as they please; it is just such a mastery over Emma's body and its movement that the Viscount exhibits in the waltz. And if Emma does learn to waltz so well, it is because she is initiated into the art by this very specific occasion. But waltzing is not a daily way of life, any more than the close embrace on the dance floor (their legs are intertwined) is a marriage bond. The kind of going round and round that is involved in the daily domestic routine of the bourgeois way of life in which Emma is effectively imprisoned is more appropriately symbolized by the endless circle of the wedding ring. The problem, and the impossibility, of combining the thrilling rotations of the waltz with the tedious repetitions implicit in the wedding ring is ineradicably implanted in Emma's life with this particular experience and further experience can only compound her sense of living among incompatible turnings—until all turnings come to seem the same.

In addition to the circling dog and the circling mind, and the vortex of the waltz, let me just cite three more circlings that are unobstrusively but definitely marked by the text. There is the minature drawing room on top of the barrel organ played by the swarthy itinerant who comes to Emma's window. It revolves to the tune of a waltz, thus offering a mechanical reduplication in miniature parodistic form of the memorable waltz scene Emma participated in at Le Vaubyessard: "dancers the size of your finger—women in pink turbans, Tyrolese peasants in jackets, monkeys in frock-coats, gentlemen in knee-breeches—went circling round and round amid armchairs, sofas and wall-tables" (p. 78) ("des danseurs hauts comme le doigt, femmes en turban rose, Tyroliens en jaquette, singes en habit noir, messieurs en culotte courte, tournaient, tournaient entre les fauteuils, les canapés, les consoles . . . " [p. 98]). The irony is obvious enough and even, one might say, quite traditional (the change of scale, the confusion of animal, human, and mechanical, are devices that can be found in eighteenth-century satire). But in terms of this book it is one more turning object in Emma's environment contribut- ing to the general pressure to make her move in circles in one way or another. For among other things, Emma confronts in her person the central problem of motion and direction. As a breathing, sentient, physi- cal being, she inevitably has energy *outwards* and *toward*—but toward *what* remains an ongoing problem, indeed torment. Yet she must move (or sleep) and when she moves, the conditioning pattern that is, as it were, laid down for her by figures and phenomena as various as her dog, Lheureux, and the barrel-organ toy, is invariably the circle. Emma is she who must *tourne*—perpetually. That society itself exists by various kinds of turning is emphasized by little reminders, such as the spectacle of the three men 'turning the big wheel of the Seltzer-water machine" at Bridoux's (p. 292) ("trois garçons qui haletaient à tourner la grande roue d'une machine pour faire de l'eau de Seltz" [p. 366]). This is a very obvious *roue*, indicative, if you like, of the kind of mindless repetitive labor demanded in an increasingly mechanized society. Subtler and more far-reaching aspects of all that is latent in that word may be seen when we consider Emma's movements in Rouen, perhaps the most im- portant "wheel" in her life, where she turns and turns so much that she may be said to have entered *Roue-n* still a wife but to leave it as a woman, generic, moving beyond social titles and labels and classifications, erod- ing herself in an irreversible capitulation to vertigo as a way of being in the world—or getting out of it.

Things that go round and round finally run down and stop.[18] This is one reason why there is so much somnolence, sleeping, and snoring in Flaubert's novel. Just where the society of this novel is heading Flaubert indicates very clearly in his account of the visit made by the Bovarys and friends to the new flax mill. "Nothing could have been less interesting than that object of interest. A large piece of waste ground, with some

---

[18]There is no need to go here into the obvious relevance of the laws of ther- modynamics: taking Levi-Strauss's terms we may say that Flaubert depicts a "steam engine" society rather than a "clock" society—i.e., one that is using up its energy and running down rather than one that is maintaining itself in an equilibrium by creating "the minimum of that disorder which the physicists call 'entropy.'" *Conversations with Claude Lévi-Strauss*, ed. G. Charbonnier, trans. John and Doreen Weightman (London: Cape, 1969), chapter 3, especially pp. 32–33.

already rusty driving-wheels scattered about among sand and gravel heaps, surrounded by a long quadrangular building riddled with little windows. It was still unfinished . . ." (p. 114). ("Rien pourtant n'était moins curieux que cette curiosité. Un grand espace de terrain vide où se trouvaient pêle-mêle, entre des tas de sable et de cailloux, quelques roues d'engrenage déjà rouilées, entourait un long bâtiment quadrangulaire que perçaient quantités de petites fenêtres. Il n'était pas achevé d'être bâti . . . " [p. 144].) How it looks before it is finished exactly anticipates how it will look after it is truly finished, not completed but exhausted. Some rusty wheels in an empty landscape—such indeed will be the most accurate memorial to the society depicted by Flaubert, the most appropriate comment on the variety of futile and finally self-destroying circlings that made up its organizing momentum. It is perhaps a final indication of Homais's position in this society that near the end he is described "enveloped" and "swathed" in a golden spiral of Pulvermacher's hydroelectric chains (p. 345). The French words have stronger and rather different connotations: "la spirale d'or sous laquelle il disparaissait" and in which his wife sees him "plus garrotté qu'un Scythe" (p. 441). "Garrotter" can hardly exclude the main meanings of being pinioned, even strangled, and added to the idea that Homais disappears inside the golden spiral, one might say that what seems to be his final triumph is also his lasting punishment. Apparently enthroned in a magical golden spiral, he is in fact a nonbeing (a not-there thing) in the total grip of a circle that opens up to extend through time (for that is what a spiral is)—and extends, we may add, forever. It is only one more paradox in the new relationship between the writer and his society that with regard to Flaubert's book we have to reverse his comment on the spectacle seen by his characters and say that nothing could be more interesting than that object of no interest (i.e., his society). The interest has moved conclusively, in Flaubert, from the referends to the referring—from world to text.

If Lheureux is a repellent presence and Léon, at least in the early stages of the book, an attractive absence, there is one figure who in an odd way combines something of both these characteristics, though the source of the repellent and "attractive" qualities are in his case quite different—I refer to the blind beggar. A blind person is almost literally a presence and an absence combined, and in a strange way it is as if Emma recognized some sort of relationship between herself and the beggar that is never made articulate—never, indeed, seen. The first description of his appearance needs to be quoted.

> A mass of rags covered his shoulders, his face was hidden by a battered beaver hat stuck on like an inverted bowl. When he removed this, he revealed where his eyelids should have been a pair of gaping holes all

stained with blood. The flesh was shredded into ribbons, discharging matter which had congealed in green scabs down to his nose. His black nostrils
twitched convulsively. To address you, he threw back his head with an idiot
laugh; and then his glaucous eye-balls, rolling in perpetual motion, shot up
towards his temples and knocked against the open sore.

(P. 278)

Un amas de guenilles lui recouvrait les épaules et un vieux castor défoncé,
s'arrondissant en cuvette, lui cachait la figure; mais, quand il le retirait, il
découvrait, à la place des paupières, deux orbites béantes tout ensanglantées. La chair s'effiloquait par lambeaux rouges; et il en coulait des liquides
qui se figeaient en gales vertes jusqu'au nez, dont les narines noires renif-
laient convulsivement. Pour vous parler, il se renversait la tête avec un rire
idiot; alors ses prunelles bleuâtres, roulant d'un mouvement continu, allaient se cogner, vers les tempes, sur le bord de la plaie vive.

(P. 348)

We note immediately that this is one of the most vivid physical descriptions we encounter prior to the detailing of Emma's dying (there is a
comparable emphasis on physicality in the account of Hippolyte's "operation"). It is as though the flesh only reveals itself in its deformities and
becomes visible only in its sickness (economic as well as bodily), when the
clothes are torn to shreds (or the operating box is taken off). As long as
Emma is, by the standards of her society, fairly healthy and well, she is
described much more in terms of her clothes than her bodily features.
Yet in many ways the blind man's features offer a perceptible mirror
image of what is happening to Emma internally and invisibly. He is the
physical image and incarnation of *lack* (*béance*), as may be seen when he
takes off his battered hat and reveals two bloody, gaping holes ("orbites
béantes tout ensanglantées"). This is, as it were, the hole (or lack) made
flesh, as well as the reverse, the body manifesting itself as a gap. This
paradoxical process is, as I have tried to suggest, one that Emma is
herself participating in, albeit under the concealment of the clothes and
houses that the beggar is excluded from. Emma is, in fact, the beggar *in*
society; for if the blind man plainly bespeaks penury, impoverishment,
sickness, deformity, mutilation, and the continual threat of being either
driven out or confined within, so in its own way does Emma's whole
life—though, as she is suffering from within the conventions while the
blind man is without, the phenomena referred to manifest themselves in
different forms. And whereas his flesh is literally shredding itself out
into bits and scarps ("lambeaux") it is notable that the verb used—
effiloquait—derives from *effilocher*, which is a word used mainly in connection with materials, meaning to ravel out, or break or tear; and although Emma seems to be accumulating more clothes, she is in fact
engaged in just such a process of unraveling herself, or cutting herself

up into bits. I will return to this, but here again the beggar's physical condition is described in such a way that we can register its metonymic relation to the experience that Emma is undergoing in her whole being. In the beggar's case, what is usually the center of the evidence of conscious sentient life—the eyes—have died, turned into a gap, while life goes on in the wounds ("la plaie *vive*"—my italics). This is, if you like, in part a reflection of the perversions perpetrated by this society—that, overall, there is more life to be found in the "wounds" than the "eyes." It certainly applies to Emma, of whom we might fairly say that she lives most intensely in the lesions in her experience. It is no wonder that while the blind beggar's physical appearance makes her shudder, his voice penetrates her whole being ("descendait au fond de l'âme") and for one notable quality—"it had a suggestion of remoteness that upset Emma" (p. 278) ("elle avait quelque chose de lointain qui bouleversait Emma" [p. 349]). The blind man's experience and knowledge of "lointain," stemming from the actualities of his experience and not from a mixed assortment of readings and memories, expresses itself in a voice that moves Emma more than any other voice in the book. It is surely with some unconscious fellow-feeling underneath her "disgust" that Emma throws the last of her money to the blind man who has been reduced to doing tricks by the orthodox society around him. Homais gives him some useless advice for a cure and a sou (and asks for some change!), and then Hivert tells him to put on his act: "tu vas nous *montrer la comédie*" (p. 388). No wonder if Emma both recoils, and throws to the beggar, with a gesture of deliberate, even theatrical, profligacy, all she possesses. For she must instinctively realize by now that she too is involved in doing tricks for pay (different tricks, different remuneration—but there is a similarity in the underlying principle and relationship), and that she too has been somehow compelled to "montrer la comédie," a comedy that will terminate in a physical condition of sickness and agonizing distortions not so dissimilar to the blind man's. It is, then, entirely appropriate that on her deathbed the last thing Emma hears is one of the blind man's songs—about a little girl who is bending down to gather up the harvest from the ground when the wind blew so hard that her petticoat flew away (which in a very reduced version is one account of Emma's life)—and equally appropriate that the very last word she says is—"L'Aveugle!" It is a cry of recognition in more than one sense, for you could say that Emma's last love affair is with the beggar, or more generally that in the figure of the blind man she finally sees a living reflection of her own life and what it has come to. The first words she is quoted as saying are, "Oh God, O God, why did I get married?" (p. 57) ("Pourquoi, mon Dieu! me suis-je mariée?" [p. 74]). Her last word is a kind of answer. Her existence among the men who make up the society in which she had to live her life and realize (or irrealize) herself has been, she finally recognizes, that of one who is in a radical sense blind, not because she lost her eyes but because she never learned and was never taught properly to *see*.[19] The last physical detail noted by the text establishes the strange rapprochement of Emma with the blind beggar, by the kind of deliberate echo in which the book abounds. Emma, dying, exhibits "la prunelle fixe, béante" (p. 418) ("Her eyes fixed, gaping" [p. 337]), just as l'Aveugle, living, had exhibited "deux orbites béantes." They are alike in their gaping lacks.

Who or What Is "Madame Bovary"?

What is now called the nature of women is an eminently artificial thing—the result of forced repression in some directions, unnatural stimulation in others. It may be asserted without scruple, that no other class of dependents have had their character so entirely distorted from its natural proportions by their relations with their masters; for, if conquered and slave races have been, in some respects, more forcibly repressed, whatever in them has not been crushed down by an iron heel has generally been let alone, and if left with any liberty of development, it has developed itself according to its own laws; but in the case of women, a hot-house and stove cultivation has always been carried on of some of the capabilities of their nature, for the benefit and pleasure of their masters.

—John Stuart Mill, *The Subjection of Women*

"For that name that fell from my lips—the name that fills my heart—is forbidden me. Madame Bovary: everybody calls you that! And it isn't your name, anyway, it's someone else's" (p. 168). ("Car ce nom, ce nom qui remplit mon âme et qui m'est échappé, vous me l'interdisez! Madame Bovary! . . . Eh! tout le monde vous appelle comme cela! . . . Ce n'est pas votre nom, d'ailleurs; c'est le nom d'un autre!" [p. 211].) These words are spoken by Rodolphe as he approaches the climax of his planned seduction of Emma Bovary and constitute a more decisive and undermining blow (or persuasive observation) than the clichés of longing and simulated pangs of helpless adoration that he pours out to Emma. To be

---

[19]*aveuglement* means "blindness," or by extension, "infatuation" or "delusion"—in which sense Emma is indeed "un aveugle," for all her bright and searching eyes.

sure, these clichés have an immense attraction to Emma, and she stretches out in them as if in a warm bath ("comme quelqu'un qui se délasse dans une étuve, s'étirait mollement et tout entier à la chaleur de ce langage" [p. 211]); the effect of relaxing liquefaction produced by the "warmth of his words" (p. 168) is all part of the slow but accelerating process of dissolution in which Emma is becoming engaged. But if she is starting to dissolve, and I will return to this phenomenon later, part of the reason—a very important part—is that there is no very clear definition available to her of who or what she is. Indeed from one point of view she is undefined, and thus unheld together, from the beginning. If she is, as I maintain, constantly perceived and appropriated in fragments, and if she herself seems to partake in this process of self-fragmentation, if she is, to take Lacan's word, *morcelée* (see note 20), it is because there is nothing to give her a firm and stable contour and identity that might bind and unify or organize all the bits that go under the name of Madame Bovary. For, as Rodolphe very accurately points out—though the implications are more devastating than perhaps even he could be aware of—Emma is forever bound to live under the "nom d'un autre." Since this is the inevitable lot of any woman who gets married, it may seem pointless to make this observation, and yet I think that Flaubert explored the implications involved in this process of nomination and renomination in a way that should provoke us to think again about a phenomenon we take so much for granted. I have already noted that there are three Madame Bovarys in the book; and since at the start of the book the third Madame Bovary is Emma Rouault, we may note that the process of becoming Madame Bovary involves a double replacement, one of title or classification (the *demoiselle* is transformed to *Madame*) and one of name (*Bovary* is substituted for *Rouault*). Thus the title of the book represents a complete obscuring of the girl's original name. It is a compound label that is imposed upon her. But more than that, it is a label imposed on a label. For Emma Rouault is also a mixture, participating in that latent contradiction involved in all naming. For if *Emma* is the girl's own name, *Rouault* is the name of the father. This point may seem too obvious to spell out, but it has implications worth pondering. It indicates that your name as far as society is concerned is made up of a part that is supposedly your own and designates your own self and a part that is by definition not your own and designates the Other, the father. The name of the father is a necessary part of the full name as far as society is concerned, if you are to have an identity. It provides, as it were, the context that gives the first name meaning. There is simply no way in which Emma could just be Emma. The basic truism that all naming, including the bestowing of a supposedly unique set of Christian, or first, names, is necessarily a reapplying of existing labels is not so important here. I am more concerned to point to Emma's problem in the social area or dimension of naming: can she find herself in the names, ranks, titles, classifications, and roles that society (starting with the family) bestow upon her?

When she is first referred to it is in the "discours" of the boy who leads Charles Bovary to the house of M. Rouault, and the text reports the word in italics—"sa *demoiselle.*" Thus it is quite accurate to say that Emma first appears as a *classification* that is *quoted* from the *discourse of another.* When Charles sees her, she is described as "une femme de bonne apparence," "une jeune femme," "Mlle. Emma," "Mlle. Rouault," in fairly quick succession. In the early days of her marriage, with nothing to focus her energies onto except the prescribed functions of her new role as Madame Bovary, she tries to attach some of her aspirations to the name she has acquired. "She would have liked this name of Bovary, that was hers, to be famous, on view at the bookshops, always cropping up in the papers, known all over France" (p. 74). ("Elle aurait voulu que ce nom de Bovary, qui était le sien, fût illustre, le voir étalé chez des libraires, répété dans les journaux, connu par toute la France" [p. 94].) Of course, this ambition is in fact achieved by Flaubert's own book, but within the text of her life Emma finds no satisfactions at all, no meaning to attach herself to, in "ce nom de Bovary, qui était le sien." After her death her father laments her as "Ma fille! Emma! mon enfant!" (p. 438); Charles, wishing to see her corpse, claims "c'est ma femme!" (p. 419); while Lheureux refers to her shamelessly as "cette pauvre petite dame" (p. 434); and Homais adds a piece of his characteristically mindless and empty labeling when he automatically adds "Une si bonne personne." (p. 434). (That she might indeed be regarded as "une si bonne personne" is not in question; the point is that coming from Homais—who is incapable of recognizing real qualities, real things, real people, but only mongers, stereotypes and labels—the words mean nothing, or rather are a mockery of an encomium.) And Berthe—"la petite"—asks for "sa maman." Can we assemble or identify or isolate a "Madame Bovary" from all these names and classifications, roles and descriptions? Can Emma herself? Or is she always adrift under the name—the many names and terms—of *another*?

When she is at the theater, any inclination she may have to criticize the performance vanishes" as the romance of the role took hold of her" (p. 237) ("sous la poésie du rôle qui l'envahissait" [p. 297]). This is, for her, a new depiction of what she has been searching for in her own life—a romantic or poetic role. Of course, we can infer what her notions of what constitutes a romantic role might be from all we have been told about her earlier education and reading. The point is that this need and quest for some such role is precipitated by her inability to recognize or find any of herself in the title-plus-name—Madame Bovary. If she isn't there, she must be somewhere else, in some other name or role. That is what she is looking for. She tries adopting the roles that are prescribed by marriage, at times playing at being the "virtuous wife" (p. 199) ("tout en faisant l'épouse et la vertueuse" [p. 250]), but even at the moment when she is described as doing this, we are also told that for Rodolphe she prepared her room and her person "comme une courtisane" (p. 250). This is not what is now referred to as a matter of "role dissonance," or incompatibility; rather the roles are perversely mutually reinforcing. The more she feels she has to play the virtuous wife, the more resentfully will she play the courtesan; guilt or worry at this will force her back into playing the virtuous wife more plausibly, if possible. And so on. It is an oscillation that is irreversible and uncorrectable and that can only end by making both roles—*épouse* and *courtisane*—indistinguishable and thus meaningless. In a related way we may note that on occasion she tries to play at being the happy mother but reveals her deep disinclination for this role most vividly when she knocks the child away from her and wounds her. "'Oh, leave me alone, will you!' And she pushed her away with her elbow. Berthe fell against the chest of drawers, and cut her cheek on the brass curtain-holder" (p. 128). ("'Eh! laisse-moi donc!' fit-elle en la repoussant du coude. Berthe alla tomber au pied de la commode, contre la patière de cuivre; elle s'y coupa la joue, le sang sortit" [p. 161].) Before this incident Flaubert refers to Emma as "la jeune femme"; immediately after she sees what she has done to the child, she is referred to as "Madame Bovary"—i.e., it is "la jeune femme" who repudiates the child and "Madame Bovary" who picks it up and tries to comfort it. But the gesture of spontaneous repudiation is more powerful than the attempts to enact the maternal role, and once again what we witness is oscillation, not a merging or a discovery of some third term where the oppositions at the lower level might be resolved.

After her visit to the theater, she, in effect, deliberately theatricalizes her life in a desperate simulation of parts and consumption of "roles," and I will return to this visit. But this search effectively leads her into adultery, shortly after the very telling observation of Rodolphe's quoted above. As he increases the pressure on Emma, among other tactics he bemuses her with requests for her to fill various alternative roles in his life, naming different kinds of female figures but excluding the term for what he really wants her to be. Thus he refers to her as a Madonna ("comme une madone") and says, "Oh, be my friend, my sister, my angel!" (p. 173) ("Soyez mon amie, ma soeur, mon ange!" [p. 217]). In this, as in other ways, Rodolphe is loosening her always precarious grasp on her own self-classification and confusing her with a demonstration of the multiplicity and arbitrariness of the names and roles applied and ascribed to women. After she has capitulated (his last appeal is to her first name—"Emma! Emma!"—as though trying to extract the girl from the social context in which she has to be defined), she, at first, regards herself in a new way. Looking in the mirror she feels that something has transfigured her whole person[20] ("Quelque chose de subtil épandu sur sa personne la transfigurait"), and then she thinks about all the heroines and adulteresses in fiction to whom she now feels related: "and that lyrical legion of adulteresses began to sing in her memory with sisterly voices that enchanted her. She was becoming a part of her own imaginings, finding the long dream of her youth come true as she surveyed herself in that amorous role she had so coveted." (p. 175) ("la légion lyrique de ces femmes aldultères se mit à chanter dans sa mémoire avec des voix de soeurs qui la charmaient. Elle devenait elle-même comme une partie véritable de ces imaginations et réalisait la longue rêverie de sa jeunesse, en se considérant dans ce type d'amoureuse qu'elle avait tant envié" [p. 219]). The poignant paradox in this moment is that, in thinking she has now found a role in which she can find and be herself, she is embarking on that long process of loss of differentiation

[20]There are three times of particular significance when Emma looks into her mirror. The first is a period prior to her adultery, when she took joy in saying, "'I am a virtuous woman' and in contemplating her own attitudes of resignation in the mirror" (p. 125) ("la joie de se dire: 'Je suis vertueuse,' et de se regarder dans la glace en prenant des poses résignées" [p. 155]); the second is this moment, after her first adultery; and the third, the moment before her death. "In a clear voice she asked for her mirror, and remained bowed over it for some time, until big tears began to trickle out of her eyes" (p. 336). ("Puis, d'une voix distincte, elle demanda son miroir, et elle resta penchée dessus quelque temps, jusqu'au moment où de grosses larmes lui découlèrent des yeux" [p. 417].) These self-reflexive efforts at self-definition, Emma trying to find herself in the image in the mirror, are solitary "reflections" of her attempts to locate and define herself among others, in what seem to be the available roles and poses offered by marriage and adultery. What she sees in the last mirror is beyond roles and poses and names. The name-bearing body confronts itself in its final disintegration, a disintegration in part brought about by all those names and roles and poses. Emma's searching for herself in the mirror might be considered in connection with Lacan's general comments on what he termed "the mirror stage": "The *mirror stage* is a drama whose internal thrust is precipitated from insufficiency to anticipation and which manufactures for the subject, caught up in the lure of spatial identification, the succession of phantasies that extends from a fragmented body-image to a form of its totality that I shall call orthopaedic" (See Jacques Lacan, *Écrits: A Selection,* trans. Alan Sheridan [London: Tavistock Publications, 1977] p. 4). ("*Le stade du miroir* est un drame dont la poussée interne se précipite de l'insuffisance à l'anticipation et qui pour le sujet, pris au leurre de l'identification spatiale, machine les fantasmes qui se succèdent d'une image morcelée du corps à une forme que nous appellerons orthopédique de sa totalité"). (See "Le stade du miroir comme formateur de la fonction du Je," in *Écrits* [Paris: Editions du Seuil, 1966] pp. 89–97). Emma certainly takes the lure of the identifications she finds in the mirror, as she responds to the hallucinatory images of wholeness—virtuous woman, adulteress—she sees there. And she also constantly oscillates between a growing sense of insufficiency ("D'où venait donc cette insuffisance de la vie?" [p. 368]) and endlessly renewed anticipations. But she never achieves any kind of totality; rather she is increasingly "morcelée" (fragmented). I will return to this process of "morselization" in a later section.

that I have already alluded to. In becoming part of her own imagination, she is starting to merge herself with the stereotypes of human history. It is a "legion" of adulteresses she is joining, an indistinguishable plurality. *Type* carries the connotations of "standard model," and so in her attempt to find some significant identity for herself, Emma has in fact committed herself to a generalization. The classification of "adultery" involves no names, unlike marriage, which is precisely focused on significant changes and adoption of names. Having been unable to find himelf in the names allotted her by marriage, Emma will proceed to lose herself in a category where there are only types. To then discover that there is finally no difference in these two regions of experience is her ultimate despair. Adultery turns out to be something like one of her own little refinements or tricks to keep Charles contented or distracted—"an extraordinary name for some quite ordinary dish which the maid had spoiled" (p. 73) ("le nom extraordinaire d'un mets bien simple, et que la bonne avait manqué" [p. 93]).

Emma's difficulty in locating herself in the names and roles available to her and her desperate oscillations or shifts from one to another is reenacted at the level of the text, where she slips and changes and regresses *in simile and metaphor* in a way that indicates how completely unstable and indefinable is the presence/substance going under the name of Emma. I will give two examples of what I mean. When she has quarreled with her mother-in-law (Mme. Bovary mère), she first of all apologizes to her very patronizingly ("avec une dignité de marquise" [p. 256]) and then flings herself on her bed and cries "comme un enfant" (p. 256). When she enters the theater, she takes great pleasure in pushing open the large doors with her finger, "comme un enfant" (p. 292), and when she is seated in the box, she "draws herself up" "avec une désinvolture de duchesse" (p. 293). The Penguin translation, "she drew herself up in her seat as to the manner born" (p. 233), misses the specific comparison while catching the general meaning. In these two very different situations, within the space of a very few words Emma can be transformed from "enfant" to "duchesse" or revert from "marquise" to "enfant." These rapid metamorphoses of rank and quality—sudden changes, as it were, up and down the scale of both social degree and individual maturity—that take place in similes and metaphors are the textual symptoms of such changes in the putative person of Emma. If she can't discover herself for very long in the names and terms available to her, similarly, the available terms and names find her fleetingly only to lose her again. Perhaps the clearest example of this strange mixture of indefinability within overdefinability (the former in fact caused by the latter) occurs in the description of what Emma means to Léon. "Besides, was she not a lady of style, and a married woman! A real mistress, in fact? . . . She was the 'woman in love' of all the novels, the heroine of all drama, the shadowy 'she' of all poetry books. On her shoulders he saw reproduced the amber colours of the *Odalisque Bathing*. She had the deep bosom of a feudal chatelaine. She bore a resemblance to the *Pale Woman of Barcelona* . . . but she was above all Angels!" (p. 276); the last plural seems to miss an ambiguity present in the French. ("D'ailleurs, n'était-ce pas *une femme du monde*, et une femme mariée! une vraie maîtresse enfin? . . . Elle était l'amoureuse de tous les romans, l'héroine de tous les drames, le vague *elle* de tous les volumes de vers. Il retrouvait sur ses épaules la couleur ambrée de *l'odalisque au bain*; elle avait le corsage long des châtelaines féodales; elle ressemblait aussi à la *femme pâle de Barcelone*, mais elle était par-dessus tout Ange!" [p. 346-67].) Flaubert is here defining very accurately the phenomenon of projection taken to an extreme length, so that the actual being of the other becomes a blank screen on which the lover / voyeur imposes or inscribes particular clusters of associations and memories. But there is another aspect to this phenomenon. The definitions and comparisons change so rapidly—we move from "femme du monde" to "Ange" at a dizzying speed and through a weird confusion of alogical jumps—that "transformation" becomes complete confusion. If Emma is all of these things, she is none of them; she is being smothered in descriptions—identification is becoming annihilation. One of the reasons she "turns" so much is because she is gradually being hemmed in and trapped by an overavailability of terms. She is being fragmented, really cut up into little pieces, not least by the multiplicity of words and names and phrases clustering on her from her environment. The more she seeks for some alternative name / role in and through which to realize a distinct identity (and thus discover what it really is *to be Emma*), the more she loses distinction and distinctness. Of the doomed Macdonwald, Thane of Cawdor, in *Macbeth* it was said, "the multiplying villainies of nature / Do swarm upon him." (Act 1, scene 1) Of Emma we may say, the multiplying terminologies or nomenclatures of bourgeois society swarm upon her. And she too is doomed. It is necessary to comprehend the full pain of this paradox—that she suffers from both a radical insufficiency and a lethal overabundance of "names" of all kinds (I am including comparisons, social ranks, family roles, etc.). Near the end, Léon's mother writes to Léon's employer so that he will warn her son against his involvement with a married woman. She herself has received an anonymous letter about the affair, but she has enough, more than enough, eidetic clichés in her head to imagine what kind of woman her son is involved with, "having visions of that eternal bugbear to family life, the vague pernicious creature, the siren, the monster that dwells fantastically in the deep places of love" (p. 300) ("entrevoyant l'éternel épouvantail des familles, c'est-à-dire la vague créature pernicieuse, la sirène, le monstre, qui habite fantastiquement les profondeurs de l'amour . . . " [p. 375]). She sees sirens and monsters where her son saw odalisques and angels, but they are alike in not seeing Emma Bovary but only a vagueness that they clothe and overclothe with a multiplicity of available images and conceptual garments. In what Saussure calls "the theatre of language," there are too many secondhand (millionthhand) roles and robes, as it were, lying in wait for Emma, yet she cannot find herself in any of them.

To put it simply, it is as if she is at once both starving and being drowned or stupefied (these are all indeed recurring sensations for her, and her death is described as a kind of drowning in a very important manner, to which I will return). And we must remember that in this society the source of all names is the generic Father, i.e., all terms and definitions applied to women derive from the male. Emma is caught and lost, caressed and violated, created and destroyed in and by the language into which she is born—a signal victim of the privileged discourses of the time. This necessarily extends to Flaubert's book as well, as he makes very clear to the reader. In answer to the question—who or what is Emma Bovary? we can ultimately only say "le vague *elle*," a presence dissipated by overdescription, a vagueness beyond all words. Much of the fog in her head may be traced to this; her situation in a language dominated by a confusion of male ascriptions and descriptions and prescriptions. And by a reciprocal paradox, she becomes herself a kind of fog in the head of society—the fog that Flaubert's text so meticulously encloses.

Iron, Mist, and Water—Constriction, Confusion, and Melting

When Emma goes out with Rodolphe on the horse ride that will lead to her first act of adultery, there is a mist on the land that is intimately related to the sort of fog in her head. "A mist lay over the land, swirling away to the horizon between the folds of the hills, or tearing asunder and drifting up into nothingness. . . . From where they were, high up, the whole valley was like a vast white lake melting into the air. Clumps of trees stood out here and there like black rock, and the tall rows of poplars topping the haze reminded one of a wind-swept beach" (p. 171).

("Il y avait du brouillard sur la campagne. Des vapeurs s'allongeaient à l'horizon, entre le contour des collines; et d'autres, se déchirant, montaient, se perdaient. . . . De la hauteur où ils étaient, toute la vallée paraissait un immense lac pâle, s'évaporant à l'air. Les massifs d'arbres, de place en place, saillissaient comme des rochers noirs; et les hautes lignes des peupliers, qui dépassaient la brume, figuraient des grèves que le vent remuait" [p. 214].)

Having considered some of the names and terms that attempted to give Emma some kind of identity or social outline and definition, we should now note that there are a series of words, often repeated, that refer to aspects of her environment that seem to be working to increase her diffusion, dissipation, disintegration, and loss of outline—in a word, her vagueness. These words are characteristically connected with mist (or smoke or vapor) and water, either as phenomena in the terrain and atmosphere around her or in the lexical metaterrain of metaphors and similes. Here, at a crucial moment of her life as she is about to cross the boundary from faithful wife to adulteress, some of these words gather in the terrain around her as if to attend and contribute to this moment when Emma takes a crucial step toward indistinctness (as some of them gather again in the room of her death to be present at the final disintegration of Emma Bovary). Thus "brouillard," "vapeurs" (fog, mists, or vapors), and the activities "s'allongeaient" and "se déchirant" (stretching out, with the sense of extension, thinning, attenuation; and tearing to bits, ripping or rending), here described as climatic phenomena, are, as it were, internalized in Emma; or we may say that she begins to participate in disintegrative and diffusive processes that are operative in the realm of nature. Thus, also, the valley seems like "un immense lac pâle, s'évaporant à l'air"; what in proximity is all too substantial and defined—the town in the valley—now disappears and seems to turn to an immensity of pale water, which in turn seems to evaporate into air. The transformation seems like a rapid ascension through the elements: earth into water into air. By contrast there is the ominous solidity and fixity of those enormous trees, jutting or standing out like black rocks. It would be too easy to say that those menacing upright tree-rocks offer an analogue to the phallic maleness of Rodolphe, while the evaporating water, mist, and air are linked with the elusive femaleness of Emma, but the contrasts in terrain and atmosphere at this crucial moment prior to the episode in which she will, as it were, pass from distinct corporeality to a shimmering vagueness through a kind of diffusive process very like the transformations from earth to water to mist to air noted in the description, become contrasts in the topography and atmosphere of her own life. As the moment of capitulation approaches, she becomes more and more liquid—"through her veil . . . her features were discernible in a haze of blue, as though she were floating beneath azure waves" (p. 172) ("à travers son voile . . . on distinguait son visage dans une transparence bleuâtre, comme si elle eût nagé sous des flots d'azur" [p. 215]). The veil is an object traditionally associated with marriage, but here it becomes a highly significant piece of costume that does not actually hide or conceal or protect the woman's identity, but only makes her features tantalizingly indistinct. It is a garment that blurs, or we could say, it is a blur worn as a garment. Emma is seen again in veils, before disappearing beneath the last veil of her shroud. Under the veil it is as if she is under water although high in the hills, a geographic inversion that evokes the experience she is going through. For she is deliquescing, not only socially but ontologically too. The only words we are given to point out what is about to happen are—"hiding her face, she surrendered" (p. 173) ("et se cachant la figure, elle s'abandonna" [p. 217]). If the face is preeminently the locus of personal and social identity, then this gesture says all we need to know. Emma, canceling the distinctive features of the face, gives herself up, not just to Rodolphe and the hard tree-rocks that will break her but to the mists and waters in which she finally loses both her conscious and her corporeal being. She gives herself up to what is around her, the climate and terrain of her existence.

I have concentrated on this particular description since it is the threshold moment when Emma is about to take that step over a boundary and definition that can never be retraced. It is hardly necessary to quote here all the occasions when fogs and mists and vapors are described in her experience, nor the different kinds of smoke (*fumée* is a recurrent word) that enter her life (coming down to literal cigarette smoke, which on one occasion makes her faint—the fumigation of her consciousness is well along by this point). Nor is it necessary to spell out the many different ways in which her inland life is nonetheless constantly connected to, or associated with, water. Her walks with Léon and her assignations with Rodolphe constantly take her along the river that runs through Yonville, and the river runs constantly ("La rivière coulait toujours" [p. 171]). Her financial troubles likewise take her along the river, as when she goes to visit the lawyer Guillaumin in desperation, and the river continues to run. (There is a subtle relating of the sexual and economic disintegration of Emma in the closing episodes through the use of the word *liquidation,* which of course refers specifically to business affairs ("la liquidation n'est pas finie" [p. 401], she says to Rodolphe, referring to her father's estate), but more generally to that larger process of liquidation in which she is irreversibly involved.) The river continues to run after her death. "Through the darkness came the deep murmur of the river flowing by at the foot of the terrace" (p. 341). ("On entendait le gros murmure de la rivière qui coulait dans les ténèbres, au pied de la terrasse" [p. 423].) While all man-made architecture is ephemeral, the river flows forever. (The fact that there is another "river" in the book, the doctor Larivière, is an important pun to which I will return.) And when she is lying dead in her room, it is as if she finally disappears under water, or the effects of water, and once again a whole vocabulary of indistinctness foregathers, this time around her corpse. "The aromatic herbs still smoked; swirls of bluish vapour mingled with the mist drifting in at the casement. Some stars were shining. It was a mild night.... On Emma's satin dress, white as a moonbeam, the watering shimmered. She disappeared beneath it. It seemed to him as if she were escaping from herself and melting confusedly into everything about her, into the silence, the night, the passing wind, the damp odours rising" (p. 344). ("Les herbes aromatiques fumaient encore, et des tourbillons de vapeur bleuâtre se confondaient au bord de la croisée avec le brouillard qui entrait. Il y avait quelques étoiles, et la nuit était douce.... Des moires frissonnaient sur la robe de satin, blanche comme un clair de lune. Emma disparaissait dessous; et il lui semblait que, s'épandant au dehors d'elle-même, elle se perdait confusément dans l'entourage des choses, dans le silence, dans la nuit, dans le vent qui passait, dans les senteurs humides qui montaient" [p. 427].) It is as though many of the words that have hovered around her in her life here return to pay their obsequies to her, including words that were present just before her first commitment to adultery ("vapeur bleuâtre ... brouillard"), as Emma Bovary abandons herself totally and unreclaimably to the mists and waters that have so often attended on her actions in life. She is indeed spreading out of herself ("s'épandant dehors d'elle-même") and losing herself, or leaking away (se perdre connotes both processes) in "l'entourage des choses." Note that the initial emphasis falls on l'entourage rather than simply the choses—it points not only to the presence of various things around her, but to their "surroundingness"; the word is of course ugly, but I want to point to that quality of their being totally around Emma. Her only possible escape from "l'entourage des choses" is a confused merging with it. Deliverance is obliteration. In the funeral procession the coffin moves forward "in a series of jerks like a boat tossing at every wave" (p. 349) ("comme une chaloupe qui tangue à chaque flot" [p. 433]), indicating that kind of transformation of solid into liquid that was adumbrated in the meteorological description of her first day of adultery, or, as we may say, her first step into a confusion and melting of categories that can only end in the total liquidation of all distinction. I will return to these words.

I have mentioned in an earlier chapter the importance of water as a feature in the narrative topography of the novel of adultery, as when referring to the significance of the "unstable element" in Goethe and to the kind of "thalassic" regression or return experienced by Ottilie in her misadventures on the lake. In Emma's dreams of her fantasy future with Rodolphe, what is soon noted is the loss of specificity and absence of particularity; "no particular phenomenon appeared. The days, all magnificent, were as alike as waves" (p. 208) ("rien de particulier ne surgissait; les jours, tous magnifiques, se ressemblaient comme des flots" [p. 260]). I have discussed Emma's attraction to distance and vagueness in previous sections. In this context it is just worth noting that her fantasies conclude in a way that is similar to the conclusion of her life: her coffin rides on the same waves of simile that had resolved her dreams. The linking word in both cases is *comme,* and the phenomenon being depicted in all this is the way in which apparent extreme differences become almost indistinguishably alike. Depending on how much of life is linked (and thus to some extent merged and mixed) through the process or experience covered by the word *comme,* the participant in life (and the reader of the book) will increasingly feel that everything is starting to run together. This is what happens to Emma. Either way, her destination is water. And at the point at which it seems as if all her experiences have merged into a painful but meaningless blur of equivalence (or nonvalence), *she* merges back into "everything about her" (p. 344) ("l'entourage des choses" [p. 427]). During her lifetime, in contrast with the pure waters of her romantic / erotic fantasies, she is constantly encountering a polluting sediment, indicating that dimension of earth, or mud, or dirt that cannot be eluded in corporeal existence. "The grand passion into which she had plunged seemed to be dwindling around her like a river sinking into its bed; she saw the slime at the bottom" (p. 183). ("Leur grand amour, où elle vivait plongée, parut se diminuer sous elle, comme l'eau d'un fleuve qui s'absorberait dans son lit, et elle aperçut la vase" [299].) And when she is enjoying her "real honeymoon" (p. 267) ("une vraie lune de miel" [p. 335]) with Léon, and they take a boat out to one of the islands, there on the surface of the river are "great oily patches" (p. 267). The French—"de larges gouttes grasses" (p. 335)—carries the connotations of greasy, fatty drops and thus helps to suggest the rich and finally sickening diet to which Emma has desperately turned in her confusion of appetites. The "miel" of this forced and simulated honeymoon soon turns into "gouttes grasses," and the finally totally unpleasant "mixture" of adultery is adumbrated in that description of the greasy blobs floating in the water.

But there is another, contrasting element in the texture of her life and of the book, and that is iron. Again, it would be pointless to list all the references to iron that occur in contexts as various as the description of the box used to cure Hippolyte's deformity and the description of Rouen cathedral with its iron bell, nobleman encased in iron, cast-iron spire, and iron gates. Iron is necessarily a common part of the environment described by Flaubert, and there is no case to be made for saying that it impinges particularly forcefully or directly on Emma. It is occasionally there as a somewhat inexplicably ominous part of her surroundings (rather like the peasant beating the iron in Anna Karenina's nightmare). Thus on one occasion after she has been away from home all night, dancing and finally fainting in a strange café, she wakes up and starts to think about her daughter. "But just then a cart loaded with long iron rods went by, hurling a deafening metallic vibration against the walls of the houses" (p. 303). ("Mais une charrette pleine de longs rubans de fer passa, en jetant contre le mur des maisons une vibration métallique assourdissante" [p. 378].) Iron necessarily suggests what is hard, inflexible, rigid, and by extension, what is cruel, tyrannous, punitive; it is a kind of absolutization of all that is implied by *les règles* and is thus always in latent possible contrast to everything that is pliable, soft, errant, and curvaceous, and all that in implied in *les tournures*. Iron is cast: the body is corporeal. And, for Emma, consciousness is fog (whether the mist of dreams or the vapors of vagueness). The point in isolating these perhaps too obvious oppositions may be justified if we consider part of the account of Emma's journey on the Hirondelle into Rouen at a stage when she is completely committed to her life as an adulteress. Suddenly the town appears "Sweeping down in great tiers, plunged in the mist, it spread out far and wide beyond the bridges, confusedly. . . . The river curved round the green hills, the oblong islands looked like great dark fishes resting on its surface. . . . The roar of the foundries clashed with the clear chimes pealing from the churches that rose up above the mist" (pp. 273–74) ("Descendant tout en amphithéâtre et noyée dans le brouillard, elle s'élargissait au-delà des ponts, confusément. . . . le fleuve arrondissait sa courbe au pied des collines vertes, et les îles, de forme oblongue, semblaient sur l'eau de grands poissons noirs arrêtés. . . . On entendait le ronflement des fonderies avec le carillon clair des églises qui se dressaient dans la brume" [p. 343]). The town has indeed become a "theater" for Emma in another of those transplacements and substitutions that increasingly make up her life, but the confusion has further implications here. This running together of things is hinted at in little details such as the combining of the "courbe" of the river with the "forme oblongue" of the island, but that could be seen as a relation of complementarity that, like female and male, need not necessarily indicate incongruence. However, there is clearly dissonance and disharmony both of substance and sound in the conjunction of the "brouillard" and "le ronflement des fonderies" and "le carillon clair des églises." I am not pointing now to the sufficiently obvious ironic contrast between the "snoring" of the factories and the clear tones of the church bells. It is rather that Flaubert depicts Emma entering an atmosphere in which apparent opposites—such as fog and iron—are becoming indistinguishably, and dangerously, confused. For while the foundries are *making* (*fonder* is to found, base, ground, build), Emma is *melting* (*fondre*, or rather *se fondre*, since it is a reflexive, almost intransitive process). Emma is entering ever deeply into that condition in which she confuses or confounds (*confondre*) these two processes and all the related differences that are indicated by that minute difference in the arranging of letters. Again, the apparently opposite words seem to be moving toward and into each other, for what is the displacement of a single letter? Depending on what state one is in, the answer is everything or nothing, and for Emma the differences between making and melting—and fog and iron—are rapidly becoming indistinguishable and insignificant. Iron retains its hardness, however, and while the fog in Emma's head increases, the cruel and ruthless resolutions of the men around her continue to harden (we must except Charles Bovary here). Her death may finally restore her to the liquid embrace of water, but not before she has undergone atrocious physical pain. "Hardness" is an ineluctable part of her environment, and there is no completely "soft" and easy escape from "l'entourage des choses."

The words *confondre* and *fondre* are constantly occurring in descriptions of what is happening to Emma—the faces of the men at Vaubyessard "blurred in her memory" (p. 69) ("se confondirent dans sa mémoire" [p. 88]); the bitterness she and Rodolphe feel "melted away like snowflakes in the warmth of that embrace" (p. 198) ("se fondit comme une neige sous la chaleur de ce baiser" [p. 248]). Emma "In her longing, she confounded gilded sensuality with heart's delight" (p. 72) ("confondait, dans son désir, les sensualités du luxe avec les joies du coeur" [p. 91])—examples could be multiplied at length, for the process of melting and confusing is continuous in her life in whatever realm she attempts to realize herself. When she attempts to find (i.e., lose) herself in religious feelings, a similar dissolution is at work: "it was as if her soul, ascending to God, were about to be swallowed up in His love like burning incense vanishing in smoke" (p. 224) ("il lui semble que son être, montant vers Dieu, allait s'anéantir dans cet amour comme un encens allumé qui se dissipe en vapeur" [p. 282]). In one way or another her "being" is constantly vapourizing, liquifying, melting: she is a locus of confusion, and while things *con*fuse themselves in her, she *dif*fuses herself in things.

I want to cite just three more examples of this process, all taken from part three, when it is accelerating rapidly. The first is taken from the description of her journey back from Rouen after being with Léon; "At every turn in the road you obtained a fuller view of the lights in the town behind you, forming a broad, luminous vapour above the labyrinth of houses" (p. 277). ("A chaque tournant, on apercevait de plus en plus tous les éclairages de la ville qui faisaient une large vapeur lumineuse au-dessus des maisons confondues" [p. 348].) Emma's mind has been and is moving in a "vapeur lumineuse," while her body has been busy negotiat-ing the claustrophobic labyrinth of the "maisons confondues," and the vapor and confusion reinforce each other and interpermeate both re-alms. At the climax of her despair, when the last possible aid (Rodolphe) has rejected her, she enters into a brief period of madness ("La folie la prenait" [p. 403]) immediately prior to the seeming lucidity of her going to the chemist's shop and eating poison. "All at once it seemed as if the air were bursting with little globes of fire, like bullets, flattening out as they exploded. Round and round they went and finally melted in the snow amid the branches of the trees" (p. 324). ("Il lui sembla tout à coup que des globules couleur de feu éclataient dans l'air comme des balles fulminantes en s'aplatissant, et tournaient, tournaient, pour aller se fondre sur la neige, entre les branches des arbres" [p. 403].) It is the final nightmare of turning and melting and presages her own imminent disso-lution. It is at this moment that her soul effectively makes its escape. "Only in her love did she suffer; through the thought of that she felt her soul escape from her as a wounded man in his last agony feels life flow out through his bleeding gashes" (p. 324). ("Elle ne souffrait que de son amour, et sentait son âme l'abandonner par ce souvenir, comme les blessés, en agonisant, sentent l'existence qui s'en va par leur plaie qui saigne" [p. 403].) Her adultery started when she "s'abandonna"; it ter-minates when she feels her soul "l'abandonner." I have said that Emma lives in the wounds of her life; she also dies, not *of* them, but *through* them.

On her deathbed, as the agony starts, her face is described in this way, "Drops of sweat stood on her blue-veined face, which looked as if it had been petrified by exposure to some metallic vapour" (p. 327). ("Des gouttes suintaient sur sa figure bleuâtre, qui semblait comme figée dans l'exhalaison d'une vapeur métallique" [p. 407].) I have said enough by now concerning the way the same words keep regrouping themselves in different combinations around Emma, as though at the same time both defining and confining her existence in ever more constraining ways. In converging on her, the words are of course converging on, and into, themselves. What is remarkable in this comparison (once again we note that Emma, like the text, is under the ubiquitous sway of *comme*), is how apparent opposites seem finally to have run together—thus Emma is paradoxically *fixed* or solidified—("figée") by a *vapor,* and the vapor is *metallic.* This seemingly contradictory "exhalation" offers a terminal compound image for all the fog and iron that, in different ways, Emma has been "inhaling" all her life, until they have become one as she becomes none. She is now the point at which the confusion of categories, qualities, and substances maximizes itself, and all that is ascertainable about the result may be read in the hideous degenerative metamorphoses her body undergoes as she submits to the final stage in her journey into indistinction. At which point the other "river" in her life makes his appearance.

Dr. Larivière Makes a Joke

Nobody can mistake the significance of the figure of Dr. Larivière, and he has been regarded variously as the one repository of positive values in the book and as Flaubert's version of the position of the artist in society as he saw it.[21] His appearance is literally an apparition, and as I have suggested, he arrives from another level of reality—he is ontogenetically discontinuous with the world he enters. Flaubert marks this quite obviously with the opening of his description. ("The advent of a god could have caused no greater commotion" [p. 331]) ("L'apparition d'un dieu n'eût pas causé plus d'émoi' [p. 411]). He is the ideal model whom all his pupils try to imitate and is utterly contemptuous of all the

---

[21]This is not the place, nor is it part of my intention, to attempt to trace the source or origin of Dr. Larivière. Whether he is a fictional celebration of Flaubert's father, as Harry Levin asserts in *Gates of Horn* (New York: Oxford University Press, 1963), chapter 5, or some more composite figure is beyond the scope of my inquiry. But the words *in the text* concerning his origins should be noted: "He belonged to that great line of surgeons that sprang from Bichat . . ." (p. 331). ("Il appartenait à la grande école chirurgicale sortie du tablier de Bichat . . ." [p. 41].) Flaubert's father was indeed a pupil of Bichat's, and Bichat himself is of course a figure of cardinal importance in the history of nineteenth-century medicine (and biology)—reappearing in English fiction as an influence on George Eliot's Lydgate. Among other things, Bichat contributed significantly to that early nineteenth-century debate concerning just exactly what life is. In Bichat's terse words, worthy of Dr. Larivière, life is "the sum of the functions that oppose death." To quote François Jacob: "Dring the life of an organism, physical properties are, so to speak, 'fettered' by vital properties; consequently, they are prevented from producing the phenomena that their nature leads them to produce. But it is not a lasting alliance, for it is a characteristic of vital properties to become rapidly exhausted. 'Time wears them away,' said Bichat." (See Jacob, *The Logic of Life*, chapter 2, "Organization," and indeed *passim*.) Just so, time wears Emma Bovary's "vital properties" away in the particular way described by Flaubert. The importance of the figure of Bichat is indeed a study in itself. (See not only François Jacob, but chapter 8, "Open up a Few Corpses," in Michel Foucault's *The Birth of the Clinic: An Archaeology of Medical Perception* [trans. A. M. Sheridan; N.Y.: Pantheon, 1973]—from which I cannot resist taking one quotation by Bichat: "for twenty years, from morning to night, you have taken notes at patients' bedsides on affections of the heart, the lungs, and the gastric

currency or titles and decorations and labels that are so slavishly respected by other figures in the book ranging from Homais to Léon. In a
world of copies, duplicates, and triplicates, he is an "original," singular,
inimitable. Which is why Flaubert describes him in such a way as to
make us register him as *entering* this world (book) but not being *of* it. He
might pass for a "saint" or a "demon" but not, in terms of this book, for a
man. Homais is the measure of *homme* in this world. Larivière is only a
hasty, disdainful visitor. His beautiful hands, "always ungloved, as
though to be the readier to plunge to the relief of suffering," (p. 331)
(the French does not specify the intention of relief: "comme pour être
plus promptes à plonger dans les misères" [p. 411]); his lancet eye that
"looked straight into your soul, piercing through all pretence and reticence to dissect the lie beneath" (p. 331) ("Son regard . . . vous descendait droit dans l'âme et désarticulait tout mensonge à travers les alléga-
tions et les pudeurs" [p. 412]); and his practicing goodness without believing in it ("pratiquant la vertu sans y croire" [p. 411])—all can be seen
as attributes that mark him out as the original type, for Flaubert, of what
the artist must try to be in his relationship to the world. Like a god, and
unlike the inhabitants of the world he enters, his attributes are not confused with his accessories; he is an apparently impossible phenomenon,
pure disinterested function ungrounded in belief, an inexplicable presence of gratuitous, autonomous virtue. He is also that absolute point of
reference that would otherwise be missing from the book—for if all the
contrasts have broken down, what point of reference can we invoke in
our assessment of qualities in people and actions? *To* him all the inhabitants of Yonville come for remedies for their various ailments—*by* him
we can suddenly measure with momentary total moral clarity the various
more serious sicknesses of all these inhabitants. He can also be seen as a
reminder of the once all-powerful Father, a figure who has lost much of
his power and authority in the society of Emma Bovary, a power that, no
matter how blindly and tyrannously it was exercised, the Father retains
in *Clarissa* and *La Nouvelle Héloïse.* We may recall that Charles's meeting
with Emma is brought about because her father has broken his leg (the

---

viscera, and all is confusion for you in the symptoms which, refusing to yield up their
meaning, offer you a succession of incoherent phenomena. Open up a few corpses: you
will dissipate at once the darkness that observation alone could not dissipate." Foucault
states that "the great break in the history of Western medicine dates precisely from the
moment clinical experience became the anatomo-clinical gaze," and he regards Bichat as a
key figure in this great change. Flaubert could also be said to be the great novelist of the
anatomo-clinical gaze, and he too opened up a few corpses—not just that of Charles
Bovary.) However, this is not the place, nor do I have the competence, to trace out the
importance of Bichat in relationship to nineteenth-century thought, or even fiction. (I am
indebted to Edward Said for pointing out to me the importance of Bichat for Flaubert,
which I had entirely overlooked.)

number and variety of foot and leg ailments and weaknesses in the book
is a prevalent feature of its symptomatology), which in turn is indicative
of a further-reaching decline in potency and guidance in the figure of
the Father. This decline in potency and decisive authority in the Father
is inextricably linked with the increasing instability of marriage, and with
the growing uncertainty about its status and "binding" power, in the
novel of adultery.[22] Larivière is that father-god whom Emma never had
and cannot name or define.

Two other aspects about his appearance and behavior, which are not
usually commented on but which seem to me to be particularly significant, concern *his* impotence on this specific occasion and his parting joke.
For all his godlike entrance and the list of absolute qualities and virtues
and abilities that Flaubert ascribes to him, even this figure has to admit
that in the case of Emma Bovary, at the point that it has reached, *there is
nothing he can do:* ("Il n'y a plus rien à faire" [p. 412]). This is also the
helplessness of Flaubert over the figure he is describing/creating/
destroying, his beautiful ungloved words plunged deeply and penetrat-
ingly into all her incurable misery. As for his parting joke, this I think is
as important as the secret sign that some painters leave on their canvas to
indicate it is their own work. Mme. Homais stops him in the doorway as

---

[22]The fate of the Father, as depicted in ninteenthand twentieth-century literature,
would make a subject of study in itself. Increasingly the father tends to be either absent,
inefficacious, or simply "asleep"—see Jane Austen's novels, for example. One of the most
memorable works in which he tries to assert his "paternal" rights and powers is
Strindberg's *The Father,* but here the "word of the father" is perversely, and calculatedly,
interpreted as a symptom of insanity. The more he asserts himself *as* the Father, the
madder he is thought to be. The crippling blow to his sanity comes when his wife Laura
manages to infiltrate the doubt into his distracted mind that he is not actually "the Father"
of their daughter, Bertha, at all. This leads to his final breakdown. "Forget I'm a man, a
soldier whose word men—and even beasts—obey. I am nothing but a sick creature in need
of pity. I renounce every vestage of my power and only beg for mercy on my life." He is
finally "dressed" by his old nurse in a straitjacket and becomes a helpless child again. Nearly his final words indicate his loss of any sense of "foundation" for his paternal identity. "A
man has no children. Only women have children. So the future is theirs, while we die child-
less." And he dies as a child. This is an extreme document, but certainly in line with a sense
of the declining power and authority of the Father. (See *Six Plays of Strindberg,* trans. Elizabeth Sprigge [New York: Doubleday Anchor, 1956] pp. 41, 56.) Kafka's famous *Letter to
His Father* reveals an opposite extreme, a sense of the Father so powerful that he over-
shadows any of his son's attempts to establish a life of his own. "But we being what we are,
marrying is barred to me because it is your very own domain. Sometimes I imagine the
map of the world spread out and you stretched diagonally across it. And I feel as if I could
consider living in only those regions that either are not covered by you or are not within
your reach." (See *Letter to His Father,* trans. Ernst Kaiser and Eithne Wilkins New York:
Schocken, 1966, p. 115.) This is the Father who seems totally to pre-empt the map of the
world of possibilities confronting the child. But such a Father is no father at all, in any positive sense. He is the obverse extreme of Strindberg's father—as useless to his children,
and perhaps, in his own way, as mad as him as well.

Joyce, of course, was a writer preeminently preoccupied with the problems of the
father, and paternity in general. They pervade his work, but, as a reminder, here is one

he is about to leave and complains that her husband is "thickening his blood," ("Il s'épaississait le sang"), and Dr. Larivière replies—"Oh, it's not his blood that's thick" (p. 334) (Oh! ce n'est pas le *sens* qui le gêne" [p. 414]). Quite apart from the appropriateness of the joke—for to be sure whatever is hurting or paining Homais, it is not "sens"—it is the *kind* of joke it is that is so important. It is a pun. And it goes unnoticed. It is an "unnoticed witticism" (p. 334) ("calembour inaperçu" [p. 414]) (*Calembour* should be translated as "pun").

There is in fact one *noticed* pun in the book. When Emma, in a period of early crisis when she realizes she is only acting at being the happy wife, goes to the church to seek advice from Lestiboudois, he not only mis-reads her spiritual malaise as some kind of physical upset but wanders off into fatuous irrelevancies; such as the following account of a joke he made, punning on the name of one of the village boys, Boudet. "I some-times call him Riboudet for a joke, you know, like the hill on the way to Marmonne, and sometimes I say "Mon Riboudet"—"Mont Riboudet," you know, ha, ha! I told that to the bishop the other day, and he laughed, he deigned to laugh at it" (p. 125). ("Et moi, quelquefois, par plaisan-terie, je l'appelle donc Riboudet (comme la côte que l'on prend pour aller à Maromme), et je dis même: mon Riboudet. Ah! ah! Mont-Riboudet! L'autre jour, j'ai rapporté ce mot-là à Monseigneur, qui en a ri . . . il a daigné en rire" [p. 158].)

This may seem like a trivial, even pointless, piece of wayward monologizing to isolate for consideration, but in its pointlessness it gives

---

quotation from *Ulysses,* ascribed to Stephen: "Fatherhood, in the sense of conscious beget-ting, is unknown to man. It is a mystical state, an apostolic succession, from only begetter to only begotten. On that mystery and not on the madonna which the cunning Italian intellect flung to the mob of Europe the church is founded and founded irremovably because founded, like the world, macro- and micro-cosm, upon the void . . . Paternity may be a legal fiction. Who is the father of any son that any son should love him or he any son?" (James Joyce, *Ulysses* [New York: The Modern Library-Random House, 1946] pp. 204-5). And *Finnegans Wake* is precisely centered on the giant figure of the father asleep and dreaming, albeit going through all kinds of transformations and condensing with other figures in history and in his own present. For all his sins and degenerations, he is finally a more powerful, majestic, and whole figure than his fragmented, partial sons, Shem and Shaun. But here again a much fuller account of Joyce and "the father" could be written (and of course critics have noted the importance of the theme from different points of view).

The account could continue up to, for example, Donald Barthelme's *The Dead Father.* ("The Dead Father's head. The main thing is, his eyes are open. . . . We *want* the Dead Father to be dead. We sit with tears in our eyes wanting the Dead Father to be dead—meanwhile doing amazing things with our hands.") (See *The Dead Father* [New York: Pocket Books, 1976] pp. 9, 11.) Within the context of this subject, perhaps the most remarkable transformation of the Father occurs in James's *The Golden Bowl,* in which it seems that the father has to be effectively brought-up again by the daughter. Certainly, the figure of the normal, "normative," father is decreasingly in evidence throughout the litera-ture of the period.

us an interesting indirect insight into what Flaubert himself seems to be doing. We can note straight away that Lestiboudois's pun is entirely pointless. That is to say, the connection between the two separate words is purely homophonic. There is no wit involved, in the seventeenth- or eighteenth-century sense of the word, or indeed in any sense of the word. In some puns two apparently disparate meanings, or realms of significance, are suddenly brought together (or condensed) in surprising and sometimes embarrassing propinquity. (Why do we laugh at puns? They are not in themselves funny—are we responding to a sudden recognition of two meanings being in one place where before we had never considered they had any possible connection? Thus punning can be seen as a kind of verbal adultery. I will come to Freud's comments on this subject later.) Lestiboudois's pun is simply an empty echo, and there is a curious kind of linguistic desolation engendered by the totally empty pun that doesn't have in it the slightest trace of any semantic shock. It is a debasement and devaluation of language into mere noise and must necessarily be something of a depressant to any would-be meaning maker or meaning seeker, whether it is Emma Bovary in her quest or us in our readings. We all know how purely empty, pointless puns such as Lestiboudois's can suddenly introduce a dead patch into a conversation, as though language has suddenly gone deaf to its obligations and forgotten its purposes. (I am not referring to the strained pun or what, for the moment, I will refer to as the witty pun; these have very different effects.) Likewise, compulsive punning of this order is not only embarrassing and exhausting but is undoubtedly a symptom of some kind of pathological state—perhaps impotence, or regression, or profound insecurity—but that is not what is in evidence here. As far as we can tell, Lestiboudois's one pun represents the sum total of the community's aspiration to humor!

Not only is it an empty pun, it is, as I said, a noticed one. But the person who makes sure that it is noticed is the person who makes the joke. We have here the doubly embarrassing phenomenon of an empty pun being pointed to by the maker of the pun. The essence of oral humor is that it is generated within a specific context; it is often an indirect comment on that context (and is thus a kind of metamessage in Gregory Bateson's terms—i.e., a message about what kind of context it takes place in), and it is unique to that context and cannot, without considerable loss of significance and point, be transported from that context. Oral humor is thus an activity, a response, a release or an insertion of energy into a specific situation. Decontextualized, it loses nearly all of that energy and becomes as pathetic a thing as a fish out of water. This is not the place to attempt any large-scale theory of humor, but it may be said that oral humor is in fact an extremely important way in which we both explore and seek to convey information about the kind of context (personal, social—cosmic) we believe ourselves to be in; it may be an endless corrective to, and comment on, that context, and through it we maintain an important kind of flexibility within the varying contexts we find ourselves in. We thus avoid becoming slaves of the situation, mere creatures of contexts of which we have no awareness, automatic servants of the unchallenged labels that would tell us what we are. What Lestiboudois's sad little nonjoke reveals is less significant than the manner of its telling—for that bespeaks a complete *loss of the sense of context,* which does in fact pervade the whole community. It is not only a meaningless joke, it is a placeless joke; and in both of these characteristics it is a comment on, or symptom of, the life of the speaker and his society. Lestiboudois has already told it to the bishop, now to Emma—why should he not go on repeating it forever? From the point of view of language and humour Lestiboudois's joke is like one of M. Binet's napkin rings.

Dr. Larivière's pun is very different. It is very precisely engendered by a specific situation, and while it too is a homonym ("sang" "sens"), it carries a real semantic sting and is very much a comment on the particular context. For the context is nothing less than the world of Homais, and the doctor's "calembour inaperçu" is a very condensed but incisive one-word critique of that insidious figure who regards everything as a matter of pills, potions, and prescriptions of all kinds, who seems to address himself to ailments of the body ("sang") but has no real "sense" whatsoever (as in English, the French word, of course, refers both to the five senses and to reason, judgment, intelligence, etc.). The pun passes unnoticed precisely because of that prevailing absence of sense that the doctor has quickly diagnosed. It is unperceived, not just unheard, because the kind of mental attitudes and operations capable of recognizing and responding to this metamessage have been in one way or another eradicated. Coming from outside, the doctor can very quickly recognize and characterize the context (the context, after all, in which Emma is at that very moment dying in unrelievable agony); those within the context have learned not to identify the context but only to operate within it, mechanically, *senselessly.* They have unlearned learning.

So much, it seems to me, is clear enough, and there can be no doubt that Flaubert deliberately juxtaposed the noticed (or rather self-noticing) "empty" pun and the unnoticed "full" one (see the next section). What we now have to consider is where Flaubert's own pun in the naming of Dr. Larivière stands in relation to these two different puns within the text. One could imagine Flaubert writing "et je dis même: la rivière, Ah! ah! Larivière . . . "—this could very easily be another of Lestiboudois's remarkable efforts in the realm of humor. In what way does Flaubert's pun differ? Does it have any of the "point" of the doctor's own pun? And what have all these puns got to do with Emma? In considering these questions, I believe we can recognize some important aspects of Flaubert's own methods and intentions. I have tried to point out how "the river" in an almost generic sense runs through Emma's married life, adultery, and death, reflecting and adumbrating the liquefying process in which she is involved. The doctor would seem to incorporate or stand for qualities and attributes opposed to those implicit in the endless flowing of the river. Firm, distinct, decisive, he is the most clearly defined identity and the most substantial presence in the book. Where *la rivière* may be said to be the realm of the uncontoured, *Larivière* is more firmly in possession of his outline than anyone else depicted in the text. Yet Flaubert "puns" them together. As I have tried to suggest in earlier passages, it seems as if Flaubert is constantly making words of apparent difference turn and recognize their shared similarities (*tour* and *trou*), a procedure that suggests the general tendency to merging and loss of difference that I have described as permeating the book. It enacts a loss of category distinction, thus a loss of meaning, that in experiential terms reaches its climax when Emma discovers that adultery and marriage are effectively the same thing. The most extreme opposites in the lexicon of this book may be said to be marked by *la rivière*, with all that it implies of nature's irresistible endlessly dissolving processes, and *Larivière*, with all that it reveals of the human drive to name, to know, to analyze, to separate, to establish, to identify. Flaubert is reminding us that these too, even these, are inevitably bound finally to merge, just as *règles* and *tournures* ultimately begin to resemble each other. Where the river represents what Conrad (in *Nostromo*, Part 3, chapter 10) called "the immense indifference of things" that finally "absorbs" Emma (and she is always looking for someone, something, anything to "absorb her soul and swallow up her entire being" [p. 123] ["pourvu qu'elle y absorbât son âme et que l'existence entière y disparût." (p. 156)]); the doctor represents the sum of the human—and in that society, more specifically the male—ideal qualities that are powerless to help Emma. Thus we may say that the power of *la rivière* inevitably absorbs and swallows up the skills of *Larivière*. Flaubert's pun is ultimately metaphysical. (It is surely no accident that the doctor's name is characterized by elision; it is made up simply by omitting the gap between *La* and *rivière*. In this it offers an odd echo of *Charbovari*, and Lheureux, though this time it is less an elision prior to full entry into language, or an erosion of values as depicted by the false happiness affected by Lheureux, but rather a reminder of that postlingual condition when the gaps that the human presence introduces into nature are all erased—the condition that Emma is at that moment entering.)

What is involved in such puns is what, following Flaubert, I would call the principle of reciprocal effacement. I take the term from his description of Rodolphe's loss of interest in both Emma and all her mementoes, including a miniature painting of her that she had given him; "As he concentrated on the portrait, trying to visualize the original, Emma's features blurred in his memory, as though the living and the painted face were rubbing together and obliterating each other" (p. 213) ("puis, à force de considérer cette image et d'évoquer le souvenir du modèle, les traits d'Emma peu à peu se confondirent en sa mémoire, comme si la figure vivante et la figure peinte, se frottant l'une contre l'autre, se fussent réciproquement effacées" [pp. 266–67]). This loss of the ability to distinguish the *image* from the *modèle*, the living from the painted face, Emma from other women, and indeed anything from anything else, is, as I have tried to show, a particular feature of the "consciousness" of Rodolphe. In one sense Flaubert's whole text is a visible demonstration of the art of making exquisite distinctions, which is why the words are prompted into hypervisibility so that we may note with what care they have been placed and ordered. But he incorporates within that text many signs of the reverse process, whereby not only do the *image* and the *modèle* become indistinguishable but so do marriage and adultery, wedding rings and napkin rings, holes and lathes, and so on, through a series of apparent opposites and distinctions. It is *as if* (again, *comme*) by running themselves together (or rubbing shoulders, or just associating closely) in the circumscribed area of Flaubert's text, certain important words, concepts, categories, and meanings were obliterating each other through the process of reciprocal effacement. What this can involve on the human level we discover in reading the story of Emma. What it ultimately implies is there in the pun on *la rivière,* for it is not too much to say that man working in and on nature, no matter how intelligently, is involved in a process of reciprocal effacement whereby his name will merge into the environment on which he is trying to leave his mark. Less metaphysically, Flaubert is identifying a process within a particular society; his puns not only *participate* in that process but at the same time they *mark* it, and to that extent they are a comment *on* the context as well as an activity *within* it. They work both inside and outside the frame. Unnoticed within, they are intended to be noted from without by the perceptive reader, who not only wants to read about what happened to Emma, how, when, and where (the context), but about the author's own sense of his material (the comment). Punning works by a, momentary, reciprocal effacement; at the same time it can call attention to other not so momentary reciprocal effacements taking place in the nonlinguistic realm, such as the process whereby Emma is rubbing herself to nothing against everything around her.

Freud and the Duplicity of Language

At this point I want to consider some of Freud's speculations about jokes, and particularly those that involve a play on words. His central document on this matter is of course the work entitled *Jokes and Their Relation to the Unconscious,* and it is from that volume I shall be quoting. His operating speculative idea is that a possibly universal characteristic of jokes is "the process of condensation with substitute-formation" but when he moves on to examine a joke involving a play on the sound of words (*Klangwitz*), he finds this characteristic to be missing. He then offers a new tentative definition of the operative technique in the joke— "the fact that one and the same word—the name—appears in it *used in two ways,* once as a whole, and again cut up into its separate syllables." The joke is based on a play on Rousseau and the words *roux* and *sot*—not so different from *Le Roux* and *Lheureux,* or *la rivière* and *Larivière,* where you have, precisely, the word appearing as a whole as a name, and again in another context it is *zerteilt,* "split up" (the word implies a vigorous parting). The syllables, when they are separated, "give another sense".

As I have said, I think Flaubert realized unsuspected metaphysical possibilities in this splitting up and joining of the word. I will select certain other comments made by Freud concerning the techniques—and satisfactions—involved in the human instinct to play on words (which seems to range from childhood babbling to the most complex and sophisticated utterance, and would seem to be an activity endemic to creatures who are born into language). I hope that the relevance of Freud's comments to the aspects of Flaubert's technique I have described will be self-evident. In some jokes based on sound similarities, "only a single letter is altered," the joke often lies in the fact that "almost the same words" are used, but having different meanings and different purposes, and he cites jokes hinging on "the similarity, amounting almost to identity, of the two words."[23] Consider again, in the context of these comments, the *tour-trou* echo in Flaubert's novel that I discussed. What is important here is the "almost" quality that Freud identifies, the slight modification, the amusing (but potentially worrying) confrontation of an almost identity between words with very dissimilar meanings—the discovery that you can slide from one to the other with surprising ease. This was the quality that Flaubert was, it seems to me, uncannily alert to, and that he exploited for profound artistic purposes.

Freud then moves to an important statement about words that needs

[23]Sigmund Freud, *Jokes and Their Relation to the Unconscious,* pp. 29, 31, 33, 34.

quoting at some length. I will include with the quotation the German for what I consider the key phrases or words.

> Words are a plastic material [*ein plastiches Material*] with which one can do all kinds of things. There are words which, when used in certain connections [*in gewissen Verwendungen*] have lost their original full meaning [*die ursprüngliche volle Bedeutung*], but which regain it in other connections [*in anderem Zusammenhange*]. . . .
>
> There are, too, words in German that can be taken, according as they are "full" or "empty" [*voll und leer*], in a different sense, and, indeed, in more than one. For there can be two different derivatives from the same stem, one of which has developed into a word with a full meaning [*voller Bedeutung*] and the other into a watered-down [*abgeblassten*] final syllable or suffix, both of which, however, are pronounced exactly the same. The identity of sound [*der Gleichlaut—laut* differing from *Klang* in that it carries a reference to phonetics and speech; it implies unstructured sound, whereas *klang* refers to a clear tone] between a full word and a watered-down syllable may also be a chance one. In both cases the joke-technique can take advantage of the conditions thus prevailing in the linguistic material [*Sprachmaterial*].[24]

Freud also notes that the fullness or emptiness of a word may be changed according to connections, i.e., they are qualities (or absences of quality) dependent on context, and, I would add, the speaker's (writer's) *awareness* of context. For the speaker creates the particular environment.

Freud's distinction between full and empty words must have influenced Lacan's meditations on "parole vide et parole plaine,"[25] though I must admit I do not know whether or where Lacan discusses Freud's terms, and he himself makes much more out of the distinction. But Freud's use of the words applies perfectly to the two puns in Flaubert's novel, as I have tried to describe them: that of Lestiboudois is *leer* and that of Larivière is *voll*. Freud's use of *abgeblassten* (which literally means "gone pale" and can be used of faces, photographs, materials, fading colors, etc.) to describe the empty word is also apt, since it implies a kind of bleaching out of language, the semantic etiolation clearly marked in the sort of joke used by Lestiboudois, but also pervasive in the speech of the community. The voluble and authoritative Homais speaks almost entirely in empty words (the notable exception is when he loses his temper, for those words he speaks then, embodying utter confusion, are the fullest ones he ever utters).

Freud cites another joke that I must quote in full; it is, he says, attrib-

[24]Ibid., pp. 34–35.
[25]Jacques Lacan, "Fonction et champ de la parole et du langage en psychanalyse," in *Ecrits I* (Paris: Editions du Seuil, 1966), p. 123. For English translation, see *The Language of the Self: The Function of Language in Psychoanalysis*, trans., with notes and commentary, Anthony Wilden (Baltimore: The Johns Hopkins University Press, 1968).

uted to Schleiermacher: "*Eifersucht* (jealousy) is a *Leidenschaft* (passion) which *mit Eifer sucht* (with eagerness seeks) what *Leiden schafft* (causes pain." He says of this joke, wrongly to my mind, that "the thought expressed in the wording is worthless. . . . There is not a trace of 'sense in nonsense' [*Sinn in Unsinn*], of 'hidden meaning' [*verborgenon Sinn*] or of bewilderment and illumination' [*Verblüffung und Erleuchtung*]. No efforts will reveal a 'contrast of ideas' [*Vorstellungskontrast*]. . . ." The only characteristic that makes it a joke is "the fact that here the same words are put to multiple uses" ("dass hier dieselben Worte eine mehrfache Verwendung erfahren"—the German, interestingly, places the emphasis on the "experience" of the words: they experience or undergo a multiple use). He then adds an observation that has even more potential implications that he pursues. "We find here an unusual state of things established: a kind of 'unification' has taken place, since '*Eifersucht* (jealousy)' is defined by means of its own name—by means of itself, as it were." When language starts to define itself in terms of itself, then we approach a state of affairs that may be called total tautology or solipsism. It is as though words have turned to mirror gazing, or have started to look at each other to establish latent identities. Total "unification," since it would involve total loss of difference, would, by the same token, mean the complete occlusion or erasure of meaning. Such a total unification is unimaginable, but Flaubert's text marks, explores, and enacts a *tendency* toward unification, in both the realm of referend and referent. Here again Freud's comments are strikingly apt. His description of "unification" as "the eliciting of a more intimate connection between the elements of a statement than one would have had a right to expect from their nature," seems to me to describe one aspect of the effect of Flaubert's art very well. He also writes of the "ingenious interlacement" produced by "defining (even if only negatively) two correlative concepts by means of one another," which can be seen as another feature of Flaubert's art. From there Freud goes on to consider jokes of *double entendre* in which words are used having both a prominent and a hidden or covered meaning. He calls all these "double meaning with an allusion." In some jokes multiple use is more noticeable, in others double meaning. In general he proposes to classify what the authorities have identified in jokes as a "kind of 'play' " under the heading of "multiple use."[26]

It is at this point that Freud turns to the subject of puns.

> . . . generally known as "*Kalauer*" (*calembours*) [puns] which pass as the lowest form of verbal joke, probably because they are the "cheapest"—can be made with the least trouble. And they do in fact make the least demand

[26]Freud, *Jokes and Their Relation to the Unconscious*, pp. 35, 39, 41, 36.

on the technique of expression, just as the play upon words proper makes the highest. While in the latter the two meanings should find their expression in identically the same word, which on that account is usually said only once, it is enough for a pun if the two words expressing the two meanings recall each other by some vague similarity, whether they have a general similarity of structure of a rhyming assonance, or whether they share the first few letters, and so on.[27]

Notice that Freud posits a "technique of expression," and then polarizes the bad or empty pun (*Kalauer*—which, like "pun" in English, seems to have no certain etymology) and the "play upon words proper" on an axis, establishing an implicit hierarchy of values in the deployment of words in jokes based on positional (and class) and economic metaphors and an even more interesting metaphor of "demand," or claim. Thus there are the "lowest" and "cheapest," which make the least "demand" on this neutral preexisting entity, the "technique of expression," while the proper, or genuine, play on words makes the "highest" and is thus by implication the most expensive, and occupies the highest rank in the hierarchy. Freud's classification of jokes making play on the sounds or meanings of words quickly takes on the characteristics of class stratification and a free-market economy, with the upper classes making the most demand on this generally available resource, the technique of expression, and thus producing the dearest products. But Freud's attempt to maintain this sharp distinction is not maintained uninterruptedly. We may note that whereas Flaubert's two key puns fitted exactly into the empty and full distinction made by Freud, his more widespread technique falls under the initially derogatory definition of puns in this context. Thus Flaubert uses words of similar assonance (*Léon, de loin*) and words sharing the first few letters (*Rouen, Rouault, roue*), but in a way that, far from being cheap and low, does indeed make the highest demands on the technique of expression and must be considered as the play upon words proper.

At first it would seem that Freud wants to maintain a distinction between jokes based purely on sound similarities and those that operate with meanings. However, he quotes another writer on the subject, Fischer, who seems to hold this opinion, only to disagree with him.

> Fischer has devoted much attention to these forms of joke, and tries to distinguish them sharply from "play upon words." "A pun is bad play upon words, since it plays upon the word not as a word but as a sound." The play upon words, however "passes from the sound of the word to the word itself". . . . I see no necessity for following him in this. In a play upon words, in our view, the word is also only a sound-image, to which one

[27] Ibid., p. 45.

meaning or another is attached. But here, too, linguistic usage makes no sharp distinctions; and if it treats "puns" with contempt and "play upon words" with a certain respect, these judgments of value seem to be determined by considerations other than technical ones.

He then, depressingly enough, gives as an example of a case in which so-called puns can be rated as really high-class and respectable jokes (and thus a proper play upon words), the ability of one of his (very respectable) colleagues and friends who could, "for considerable periods of time, answer every remark addressed to [him] with a pun."[28] This is, to me anyway, a very lowering prospect; but it only serves indirectly to further the point Freud is rather uncertainly making. He is, of course, quite right to resist the rigid distinction offered by Fischer (though he started by making a similar one), and I think the word he needs when he refers to "considerations other than technical ones" is "context," as defined in the work of Gregory Bateson. It is, as I tried to show, the *context* that determines the value of the joke, as Flaubert shows by making *his* most profound pun in exactly the same *form* as the empty pun of Lestiboudois. It is context that determines whether the pun has meaning (and how much) for those both inside and outside the context that is its occasion (it is quite possible to imagine a context in which Larivière's pun on *sang* and *sens* would be quite pointless, though perceived).

Freud establishes a division between "'verbal' and 'conceptual' jokes according to the material handled by their technique" and then moves on to consider "the purposes of jokes." Here he introduces a new division, between what he proposes to call "innocent" and "tendentious" jokes. "In the one case the joke is an end in itself and serves no particular aim, in the other case it does serve such an aim—it becomes *tendentious*. Only jokes that have a purpose run the risk of meeting with people who do not want to listen to them."[29] That last remark is curiously appropriate in the case of Flaubert, whose every joke or play upon words is tendentious to the highest degree. (To the point, it might be noted, that they cease to be funny. There is plenty to laugh at in *Madame Bovary*, but it is not to be found in the puns or in Flaubert's careful manipulation of semantic and phonetic similarities. And the book *Madame Bovary* was a *Witz* ("joke," or "witticism") that did indeed run the risk of meeting with people who had a very strong desire *not* to listen to it! *Tendentious* is a tricky word in English criticism, since there has been a general dislike for literature that has a palpable design on us (albeit the criticism is often tendentious and sententious itself, and sometimes to a degree). Thus *tendentious* has acquired pejorative connotations. On the continent *Ten-*

[28]Ibid., pp. 46, 47.
[29]Ibid., p. 90.

denzlitteratur may either be pejorative or approbative according to where you stand politically, but I have the sense that it can also be used more neutrally as a descriptive term for a discernible mode. Clearly all of **Flaubert's wordplay is tendentious in that it has a *Tendenz* that is not only** a purpose and intention (for which *Absicht* is another word, one also used by Freud) but more generally a moving toward a specific meaning. This meaning could of course include the disappearance of meaning, the discovery not just of sense in nonsense but of nonsense in sense, and this **too is included in the *Tendenz* of Flaubert's work.**

Freud also insists that "with tendentious jokes we are not in a position to distinguish by our feeling what part of the pleasure arises from the sources of their technique and what part from those of their purpose. *Thus, strictly speaking, we do not know what we are laughing at.*" (The editors note that up to 1925 this sentence was always italicized; I have taken the liberty of restoring the emphasis.) He gives the example of an obscene joke that may have wretched "technique" but has "immense success in provoking laughter."[30] We may note the reverse phenomenon, in which Flaubert displays immense skill in the technique but with a purpose and to an end that ultimately provokes no laughter. (*Bouvard et Pécuchet* is, to my mind, one of the funniest books ever written, but it provokes a very particular kind of laughter, stemming from the kind of laughter evoked by, for example, M. Homais and his litanies of noninformation. As I said, we may often laugh during our reading of *Madame Bovary*, but not, surely, by the end.)

Since at this point I seem to be separating Flaubert's novel from the kinds of jokes and their particular attributes that Freud is going on to consider, I should explain why I want to stay with Freud a little longer. It is because of what he has to say about the source of our pleasure in jokes, and their relation to language and the unconscious. He speculates throughout on the "tendency to economy" (*Tendenz zur Ersparnis*) manifested in jokes, asking why indeed this should give "pleasure" (*Lust*), and what exactly is being "saved," since in fact the making of the joke often involves apparently unnecessary trouble. Why not be content to let language go about its usual business in its usual way? And what is this *Lust*? His answer is nothing less than the whole book, but I wish to quote some of his summarizing remarks. He has moved from considering the manifest intentionality of many constructed jokes to those aspects of jokes that "can be referred to their formation in the unconscious."

> In an earlier passage we regarded one of the outcomes of condensation—multiple use of the same material, play upon words, and similarity of sound—as a localized economy, and the pleasure produced by

[30]Ibid., p. 102.

an (innocent) joke as derived from that economy, and later we inferred that the original intention of jokes was to obtain a yield of pleasure of this kind from words—a thing which had been permitted at the stage of play but had been dammed up by rational criticism in the course of intellectual development. We have now adopted the hypote-hsis that condensations of this kind, such as serve the technique of jokes, arise automatically, without any particular intention, during thought-processes in the unconscious.

Notice here the "damming up"—*eindammen*—the blocking and restricting of a word activity comparable to what Freud describes as happening to the sexual drives, so that with "intellectual development" (*intellektuellen Entwicklung*) it would seem that a certain kind of free play with words is blocked just as certain aspects of sexual free play are.

> The thought which, with the intention of constructing a joke, plunges into the unconscious is merely seeking there for the ancient dwelling-place of its former play with words. . . . The effort made by jokes to recover the old pleasure in nonsense or the old pleasure in words [*Lust am Unsinn* and *Wortlust*[[the sexual and the linguistic are brought very close in the latter formulation] finds itself inhibited in normal moods by objections raised by critical reason; and in every individual case this has to be overcome.

He then distinguishes between "dream-work" (*Traumarbeit*) and "joke-work" (*Witzarbeit*).

> For jokes do not, like dreams, create compromises; they do not evade the inhibition, but they insist on maintaining play with words or with nonsense unaltered. They restrict themselves, however, to a choice of occasions in which this play or this nonsense can at the same time appear allowable (in jests) or sensible (in jokes), thanks to the ambiguity of words and the multiplicity of conceptual relations. Nothing distinguishes jokes more clearly from all other psychical structures than this double-sidedness and this duplicity in speech. From this point of view at least the authorities come closest to an understanding of the nature of jokes when they lay stress on "sense in nonsense."[31]

To exploit the "double-sidedness and duplicity of speech," the speaker must perforce be conscious, since from one point of view speech is consciousness, consciousness is speech (silent or uttered). In doing this, the speaker may nevertheless be driven by a complex of intentions that may finally be traceable back to the unconscious in quest of an "*old* pleasure in nonsense" ("*alte* Lust am Unsinn"—my italics). Purposive intention and the processes of the unconscious may then be said to meet or cooperate in "joke-work." This is surely exactly the case in literature, as such a text as Flaubert's novel reveals. And Freud's analysis does away with the

---

[31].Ibid., pp. 44, 169–72.

initial social hierarchy of jokes, since, seen in this way, highest and lowest, most complicated and most silly, most demanding and least demanding on the technique of expression, fullest (and most tendentious) and
emptiest (and most "innocent") are, as it were, democratized into changing aspects of a basic response on the part of man at finding himself
irreversibly involved in language. From this point of view, literature
becomes the most complex kind of *Witzarbeit*. It is the profoundest kind
of play-work.

If all this seems to be too paradoxical and to involve a perverse ignoring of differences in an ambiguous merging of opposites, then we may
say that this is precisely because of what Freud so accurately designates
as "this double-sidedness and this duplicity in speech," which characterizes not only the joke (in which it is briefly foregrounded as a dominant feature for momentary pleasure) but all of literature to some extent
(certainly more in Joyce than Dr. Johnson, but not absent in Johnson
either) precisely because it is a latent characteristic of language in its
entirety. Not that one cannot make unambiguous statements, since the
nature of the rules dominating the code specify that certain formulations
should be taken as intending no ambiguity, excluding other significations that are contextually irrelevant. But "duplicity" is latent in the very
nature of the phenomenon of language. The German words used by
Freud are *Doppelseitigkeit* and *Doppelzüngigkeit,* the latter meaning literally the "two-tongued" quality of speech / language (Freud does not actually specify speech, but it is implicit, as he is discussing spoken jokes). For
language does have two sides, just as it is comprised of both acoustic
images and concepts; it looks at ideas and it looks at itself, turning a side
to things and a side to the speaker. It has referential and "meta" roles; it
is psychological and phonic; it is a map of the world and a serial assemblage of sounds (or signs). Words may not only have dual meanings;
they are dual in their very essence. (This is why, for instance, in discussing Flaubert's novel, it is not only possible but necessary both to refer to
Emma Bovary in the same terms as one would a person with an actual
biography and to scrutinize *Madame Bovary* as a record of a series of
lexical choices, a text: to stress one to the exclusion of the other is simply
to avoid confronting the ineluctable doubleness of language.[32] And all

[32]See Saussure's work passim, but particularly the chapters in *Course in General Linguistics* called "The Immutability and Mutability of the Sign" and "Static and Evolutionary
Linguistics." Here is one of the basic principles he estabilishes:

> The linguistic entity exists only through the associating of the signifier with the
> signified. . . . Whenever only one element is retained, the entity vanishes; instead of
> a concrete object we are faced with a mere abstraction. We constantly risk grasping
> only a part of the entity and thinking that we are embracing it in its totality; this
> would happen, for example, if we divided the spoken chain into syllables, for the

speech is potentially speech with two tongues—the unique physical tongue of the individual giving utterance, and the generally prevailing mother tongue that was outside and prior to the individual, but now takes up residence in his singular tongue. In this way the individual becomes part of the *masse parlante,* speaking both with his own tongue and the tongue of the other. Language is two-tongued in the way Freud describes, so that not only in a joke but in a work of literature and in our own speech one may discern human thought both reaching back to childhood, to the very brink of infancy, "the ancient dwelling-place of its former play with words," and exploring ever further forward, constructing ever more complex and tendentious formulations—such as *Madame Bovary.* And there is always work in the pleasure, and pleasure in the work, as long as the speaker is speaking and not being spoken, the writer writing and not being written. And perhaps all literature that we consider as such offers us, in varying forms, not only the semantic thrust of its conscious intent and *Tendenz* but something of that "euphoria" that, says Freud in his beautiful conclusion, we are always trying to reach in jokes. "For the euphoria which we endeavour to reach by these means is nothing other than the mood of a period of life in which we were accustomed to deal with our physical work in general with a small expenditure of energy—the mood of our childhood, when we were ignorant of the comic, when we were incapable of jokes, and when we had no need of humour to make us feel happy in our life."[33] ("Denn die Euphorie, welche wir auf diesen Wegen zu erreichen streben, ist nichts anderes als die Stimmung einer Lebenszeit, in welcher wir unsere psychische Arbeit überhaupt mit geringem Aufwand zu bestreiten pflegten, die Stimmung unserer Kindheit, in der wir das Komische nicht kannten, des Witzes nicht fähig waren und den Humor nicht brauchten, um uns im Leben glücklich zu fühlen.")

---

syllable has no value except in phonology. A succession of sound is linguistic only if it supports an idea. Considered independently, it is material for a physiological study, and nothing more than that.

The same is true of the signified as soon as it is separated from its signifier. Considered independently, concepts like "house," "white," "see," etc. belong to psychology. They become linguistic entities only when associated with sound-images; in language, a concept is a quality of its phonic substance just as a particular slice of sound is a quality of the concept.

The *two-sided* linguistic unit has often been compared with the human person, made up of the body and the soul. The comparison is hardly satisfactory. A better choice would be a chemical compound like water, a combination of hydrogen and oxygen; taken separately, neither element has any of the properties of water. [My italics.]

[33]Freud, *Jokes and Their Relation to the Unconscious,* p. 236.

Emma in Rouen: She Goes to the Theater and Leaves before the Opera Is Over; She Visits the Cathedral, and Then Agrees to Enter a Carriage

At the theater Emma experiences a range of different kinds of response to the spectacle; it is not simply a matter of her succumbing to the illusion and abandoning herself to the music, and the fact that she leaves before the end is not simply due to the unexpected appearance of Léon, even though he is the occasion of the decision to leave the theater. In one sense Emma experiences a recapitulation of her emotional life in a compressed form. On entering, her pleasure and excitement are specifically described as being that of a child ("comme un enfant" [p. 292]) soon after the opera starts, she finds herself back in the books of her youth ("des lectures de sa jeunesse" [p. 293]); and after Lagardy has made his appearance and cast his spell, Emma seems to run through the gamut of all the emotions and desires and fantasies she has experienced through her marriage, her dreams of Léon, and her adultery with Rodolphe. Just as her cry is "drowned" in the music at the end of the first scene—the French is *se confondit,* which is of course a word in constant attendance on Emma—so all her feelings are merging and intermingling, "confounding," indeed losing, themselves in each other. In particular she thinks back to her marriage day and bitterly regrets not having resisted. But the way in which she thinks about what has happened reveals a rather odd choice of terms. "If only in the freshness of her beauty, before the soilure of marriage and the disillusionment of adultery, she could have grounded her life upon some great, strong heart . . . (p. 236). ("Ah! si, dans la fraîcheur de sa beauté, avant les souillures du mariage et la désillusion de l'adultère, elle avait pu placer sa vie sur quelque grand coeur solide . . . [p. 296].) Soilure is the word for impurity and contamination, and in many primitive societies where pollution fears are still powerful and operative it is adultery that is a source of soilure and as such a danger to the community (so that the touch or glance of an adulterer, or it may be an adulteress, is thought to bring illness). If dirt is "matter out of place," as William James phrased it, then the adulterer or adulteress is "dirty" because he or she has moved out of the socially approved categories, crossed a forbidden boundary, and, in being in the wrong bed, becomes human matter out of place.[34] In orthodox social terms it is impossible to be polluted or stained by marriage, though very possible and unforbidden to become disillusioned with it. Emma is putting the words in the wrong places, she is confusing and confounding terminologies and ascriptions; in this inversion, or "displacement," of the experiences referred to by the labels *souillure* and *désillusion*, Emma reveals that her mental processes are themselves becoming adulterous. It is one thing to step over the boundary between marriage and adultery. It is another, and more disturbing state, not to know the one from the other. This adds to the poignancy of her helpless and hopeless retrospective wish to have grounded her life in a "coeur solide." She is yearning for an impossible solidity just at the time she is committing herself irreversibly to the process of disintegration, in mind as well as body—as later she will think "if somewhere there were a being strong and handsome . . . (p. 295) ("s'il y avait quelque part un être fort et beau . . .[p. 368]) because she thinks she is married to a "néant" and finds a similar insufficiency and absence of substance in her lovers. (If we may speak in Sartrean terms for a moment we may say that Emma yearns toward a dream of Being engendered by the Nothingness of her existence and experience—the vagueness of the terms is itself a part and symptom of her plight.)

At this point in the opera Emma experiences that disillusion that is inseparable from the inevitable unsatisfaction of unspecified desires. Passional happiness, she decides, "must be a fiction, invented to be the despair of all desire" (p. 236) ("un mensonge imaginé pour le désespoir de tout désir" [p. 296]), and here again our reading eyes detect words seeming to confound each other, as though desire contains despair just as the letters do—*dés[espo]ir*. The point is not an idle one, for here again we see a loss of semantic solidity and stability (we might say Being) as vital lines of separation begin to blur. If Emma is here discovering the inextricability of desire and despair, she will finally experience their indistinguishability, a profoundly worrying experience that we reenact at the level of reading. Her momentary recourse is to try to regard the "reproduction of her sorrows" (p. 236) ("reproduction de ses douleurs" [p. 296]) as an "embodied fantasy" (p. 236) ("fantaisie plastique" [p. 296]). But she is soon drawn back into the spectacle by the outraged

[34]Cf. *Purity and Danger* by Mary Douglas, *passim*. In the Introduction, she writes: "I believe that ideas about separating, purifying, demarcating and punishing transgressions have as their main function to impose system on an inherently untidy experience. It is only by exaggerating the difference between within and without, above and below, male and female, with and against, that a semblance of order is created. . . . Reflection on dirt involves reflection on the relation of order to disorder, being to non-being, form to formlessness, life to death." And see, in particular, the remarkable chapter three, "The Abominations of Leviticus."

lover and his "illusion de personnage" (p. 197). *Personnage,* as in English, may denote a person of rank or distinction, or more generally imply a person, any person. Emma, then, is drawn to the illusion that she is in the presence of an actual person—solid, real. Edgar Lagardy is described by Flaubert as "an admirable mountebank type" (p. 235) ("cette admirable nature de charlatan" [p. 295]); fabricated out of ingredients taken from the hairdresser and the toreador, he is another of those synthetic bastard products like Lheureux who, in their composition, look back to Charles Bovary's cap. It would be fatuous to pretend to lay emphasis on the paradox of such a figure giving Emma the illusion of being a real person--such is the very stuff of theater, and Flaubert is never fatuous. Emma is not deceived. She is confused—and more confused than she can know, for she is losing all reference points. It hardly matters that at times she doesn't seem to know where she is; such temporary topographical and temporal displacements are the very promise of that kind of theater. It matters a great deal that she doesn't know *what* she is, nor what, really, is going on. Her plight is ontological even while her experience is physical and emotional. She is in fact becoming untied, undone—*dénouée.* I will return to this word and the condition it denotes.

Before continuing to consider what is happening to Emma in the theater, we might pause for a moment to sympathize with Charles Bovary in his inability to grasp what is supposed to be happening on the stage. From what incoherent and discontinuous fragments Flaubert transcribes, it is impossible to discover even the most inchoate lineaments of a narrative outline. Of course this is because the narrative is just rubbish, an irrelevant vehicle for music and simulations of decontextualized sentiment. But it makes us aware that Emma thinks she is following it, finding narrative and identifiable significant relationships and situations in what is obviously and unabashedly a farrago. Certainly the opera is supposedly based on *The Bride of Lammermoor,* and Emma is providing the narrative from her memory of her readings of Walter Scott—"remembering the novel, she could understand the libretto without difficulty" (p. 234) ("le souvenir du roman facilitant l'intelligence du libretto" [p. 294])—but what she actually does remember of the novel resolves itself into the sound of pipes coming through the mist or fog (again *brouillard* in her head). From Flaubert's method of presenting the fragments of the opera in all its confusion of scenery, costumes, music, and so on, we realize that this is how Emma is perceiving it, except that she accepts the confusion of fragments as a significantly ordered experience. Flaubert is depicting the fragmentation of her consciousness. By contrast, Charles cannot identify rank, role, or situation; he can't tell a lord from a lover and confuses passion and persecution. This is mainly because he is a complete literalist, and when it comes to all the absurd plots and schemes apparently being planned on stage, he is simply lost. In this, if you like, he is completely honest, or completely stupid, but either way he is incapable of being devious or imagining deviousness. He is the man who accepts and follows *les règles* but has no sense of *les tournures,* and the theater is all *tournures.* So that, in a very real sense, he never enters the theater, because he applies to it the rules he has learned to apply to extratheatrical situations. He likes to "get things straight" (p. 236) ("C'est que j'aime . . . à me rendre compte" [p. 296]) where there is nothing straight to get. Emma, by the same token, never leaves the theater, because when she does walk out during the third act, her consciousness has discovered its final mode of operating; it has been definitively theatricalized. When Flaubert writes that a voice tells them to be silent "for the third act was beginning" (p. 238) ("car le troisième acte commençait" [p. 299]), the irony is multiple and ontological. The third act is at once the third act of the opera, the third stage in Emma's life with her third man, and the third section of the novel, which does indeed follow after the end of this chapter—the physical, theatrical, and lexical realms are running together. Emma has entered on the *acte* she will never leave.

One of Charles's confusions in particular suggests the larger confusion in which Emma, unawares, is participating. He mistakes a "faux anneau de fiançailles" (p. 296) ("the supposed wedding ring" [p. 236]—thus the translation, though the French words actually specify an engagement ring) for a "souvenir d'amour" ("love-token"). Emma tries to explain, but when he still cannot understand the function of these deceptive props in the story she says impatiently, "Qu'importe?" (p. 296). You could say that in the context this operates as a piece of instant aesthetic advice (forget the story and submit to the music). But say what she will, either it does matter and can be explained, or it does not and there is nothing to say. If you cannot distinguish—either for the purposes of narrative interpretation or those of social identification—a false engagement ring from a real one, or a deceitful sign from a gift of love, then you are bound to encounter very serious problems of meaning and value. And this of course is what is, and has been, happening to Emma herself. At one stage she could explain (to herself) the difference between marriage and adultery, between what she saw as a meaningless contract and what she felt to be the extreme significance of passionate love, but she is entering the stage where these distinctions are confounding and equivalizing themselves, and her final response is, in effect—"Qu'importe?" That little rhetorical question becomes the question posed by the whole account of Emma's life. What indeed *does* matter or signify? In all this, the ring can easily be seen as an exemplary sign, and to the extent that a recognition of meaning is withheld from the sign, so too is it withheld from the relationships and bonds that it is supposed to signify. Flaubert offers here a potentially puzzling epistemological problem. For even a true ring in the theater would be a false one, inasmuch as it would only be one more prop. Thus this false ring is doubly false, or false in two contexts. There is no need to explore the possibilities of infinite regression hereby implied. But it does underline the problem—what would be a true or "véritable," ring? And how would Emma recognize it? On what would it be grounded; where would it find its sanctions? What ritual would fix its significance? I am spelling out these obvious questions deliberately to underline the fact that when Emma decides that, in effect, her socially ordained and approved wedding ring is meaningless, then *all* other rings can only be false ones, no matter how hard she may strive to invest them with some personal significance, some surrogate authenticity to compensate for the emptiness she found in marriage. Thus she asks Rodolphe for "a ring, a virtual wedding-ring" (p. 182) ("une bague, un véritable anneau de mariage" [p. 229]). But there can be no *véritable* ("true," but also "real," "genuine") wedding ring for Emma after her first act of adultery, which effectively annuls the meaning lodged in her one true wedding ring and thus, as it were, retrospectively falsifies that one as well. It is another disastrous loss of difference, because Emma finds increasingly that there is no way to distinguish the *véritable* from the *faux,* and following the inevitable law that meanings tend rather to deteriorate than to become enhanced, the former disappears in the latter so that finally there is nothing and no one that Emma can experience as "true" as she moves through the proliferating falsities and falsehoods of her theater-world existence. Near the end we are told, "From that moment her existence became nothing but a tissue of lies, in which she hid her love from view" (p. 281) ("A partir de ce moment, son existence ne fut plus qu'un assemblage de mensonges, où elle enveloppait son amour comme dans des voiles" [p. 359]). But there is no love within the veils, and the only reality is precisely the "assemblage de mensonges." By the end, the intolerable paradox is not just that the *véritable* has always turned out to be the *faux,* but also that in her life the *faux is* the *véritable.*

While entering the theater before the play, Emma is "Madame Bovary," as she is when Léon enters their box. While the performance is on, however, she is only "Emma." This indicates clearly enough that she loses her sense of her social title and role as she capitulates to the spectacle. She is just the little girl Emma. After the visit to the theater she gives up any attempt at finding herself in the role and title of Madame Bovary, partly regressing to a childlike condition, partly bringing into her life the intoxicating (and finally stifling) fragmentation and confusion of the theater. Her life does indeed become "une fantaisie plastique." When she does leave the theater there is a "mad" scene being enacted by one of the women. "But the mad scene was little to Emma's taste" (p. 239) ("Mais la scène de la folie n'intéressait point Emma" [p. 300]). The reasons for this lack of interest may be multiple (to talk to Léon, to get out of the air that is stifling her, etc.), but one reason is that, in effect, *la folie* has been transferred from the stage to her head, and when Emma leaves the theater she takes it with her. For at one orgasmic point in the show "une folie la saisit" (p. 298), and it never really lets her go even after the particular fantasy of the moment passes. The *folie* in this case centers on the stage figure of Lagardy, as she starts to imagine the romantic, or operatic, life they might have lived together. This is a sufficiently commonplace fantasy mechanism, but in Emma's case there is a click, a sudden shift in tense that is like a sudden shift in mental gear. She has been imagining their life together in the appropriate tense of the past conditional, in which the impossible not-experienced is forever silently enacting itself. The *folie* is a shift from that tense to the imperfect, so that "would have" and "would" become "was," and fantasy takes over the ontological priority of fact; "he would look up at her . . . he was looking at her now, yes, she was certain he was!" (p. 237) ("il l'aurait regardée . . . il la regardait, c'est sûr!" [p. 298]). The curtain falls, leaving Emma palpitating in the smoky atmosphere (the theater is one of those "stifling" boxes and containers that make up the social architecture and machinery of the book; the box on Hippolyte's foot was another—it was worth remembering that both the theater and the *moteur mécanique* were recommended by M. Homais as cures). But the *folie* remains with her, not in specific details but, we may say, as a technique of displacement, whereby the imagined supplants the given, or the actual may always be diverted into the conditional. The *folie* is inherent in the possibilities of language itself, which can so easily be rearranged and modified, thus rearranging our perceptions of reality. Emma's "cure" results in her succumbing to the infection of a *folie*—really an ontological and epistemological and linguistic *folie*—that is incurable.

None of this touches Charles, for reasons already mentioned. Indeed the text intermittently marks his "bovine" nature by a kind of "*boor*-ish" echo in the words around him, as for example when the angry husband of the wife over whom Charles spills some water mutters in a "ton bourru" (surlily) words about "remboursement" (p. 298) (repayment [p. 238]), or when later, in the café, Charles realizes it is time to pay and takes out his "bourse" (p. 301) (purse [p. 241]). But there is one interesting moment in his reaction to the show; for when Emma wants to go, he suddenly wants to stay. The reason is apparently simple, but touches on a nerve that runs through the whole book. " 'Oh, not yet! Stay a bit!' said Bovary. 'She's got her hair down—looks like being tragic, this does' " (p.

239). ("Ah! pas encore! restons! dit Bovary. Elle a les cheveux dénoués: cela promet d'être tragique" [p. 300]). What suddenly alerts the habitaully impercipient Bovary on the stage—he responds almost automatically to the cliché—has completely escaped his attention in his own house. For when Emma is at the height of her beauty during her affair with Rodolphe this is how her hair ("ses cheveux") is described: "that thick mass rolling carelessly down wherever the daily dishevelments of love might take it" (pp. 206-7) ("ils s'enrouaient en une masse lourde, négligemment, et selon les hasards de l'adultère, qui les dénouait tous les jours" [p. 258]). *Nouer* is "to tie," "to knot." You can knot up hair or, as in English, knot a relationship with somebody. The marriage knot is of course supposed to be the most binding knot of all. As described by Flaubert, Emma's hair is being "untied," or disheveled, by "les hasards de l'adultère." Emma moves first into the knot of marriage and then into the unknotting of adultery, for the more she tries to make something solid and real and whole out of these adulterous illusory bonds, the more she is *un*bound, her whole being becoming as disentangled as was her hair—"selon les hasards de l'adultère." It would be possible to demonstrate in detail how words referring to comparable processes (all with the privative prefix—*dé-*) recur visibly more often around Emma throughout the third "acte" of the book—words such as *déchirer* ("tear" or "rend"), *découper* ("cut up"), *découdre* ("unpick" or "unstitch"), *déclouer* ("unnail," "undo"), *déborder* ("overflow"), *déshabiller* ("undress"), *détourner* ("divert," but it can also imply seducing or alienating someone), *détacher* (detach, untie, unbind, unfasten): many of them appearing in the reflexive and thus contributing to the feeling that Emma is "unstitching" herself, taking herself to bits—but extensive documentation is perhaps not necessary by now. The hints are already gathering on the night at the theater, as when Léon refers to Lagardy's "last act" (p. 240) as "le morceau final" (p. 301) (which can also mean the last morsel, last scrap of food—as I mentioned before, Emma is in one way and another increasingly *morcelée*); or when the tables in the café are said to "se dégarnissaient" (p. 301). This can be translated perfectly well as "the tables were being cleared" (p. 240), but the word carries with it the related meanings of stripping, dismantling, emptying, and turned into a reflexive process this too is a tiny anticipatory sign of what Emma will be doing from this point on: (*se dégarnir* also means "to go bald," another sad inversion and negation of that opulent "cheveux dénoués'!). I do, however, want to refer to one scene when Emma is with Léon in their hotel room and they are pretending it is their own home, reproducing in a kind of parody or theatrical form an improvised domesticity. They have a fireside meal. "Emma carved and served" (p. 275) ("Emma découpait, lui mettait les morceaux dans son assiette" [p. 346]). The first two words, taken as a unit marked off by the comma, indeed mean "Emma cut," and although there is no stated object after the transitive verb, (so that it is not specified what she cut or carved), the context of course allows us to make the necessary inference that it is some kind of food. But in the absence of a specific object, the words also convey a general activity that can spread beyond the context, so that Emma is involved in an ongoing process of cutting up. Furthermore, the two words are homophonically indistinguishable from *Emma découpée,* as though she is *already* all cut up and is serving herself up in bits on Léon's plate, indeed on the plates of all the men she is involved with in one way or another. At the same meal the champagne runs over the rim of her glass ("débordait du verre") onto the rings on her fingers ("sur les bagues de ses doigts" [p. 346]), and she laughs. The rings are now plural, as are her relationships, and the wedding ring is not specified because, indeed, it has lost its specificity and significance in that very plurality. And the wine spilling over the rings is a very suggestive composite image of that increasing liquidation of all bonding and definition that I have mentioned in a previous section. None of those wine-drenched rings has the power or potency to hold Emma together. Indeed, they are the very insignia of her "unknotting" and her "morselization," as she moves ever more quickly to that point when she will spill herself out of herself entirely into "l'entourage des choses."

In the last moments of the second part of the book (it is already "onze heures et demie" (p. 302) in the long-short day of her life), both Léon and Charles are, for different motives, persuading Emma to stay on in Rouen by herself. This is her reaction as she effectively succumbs. " 'It's just,' she faltered with an odd smile, 'that I'm not sure ... ' " (p. 241), ("—C'est que . . . balbutait-elle avec un singulier sourire, je ne sais pas trop ... " [p. 301]). Uncertainty and hesitation in knowledge, inadequacy and faltering in speech, occur together and register themselves physically in that odd "singular" smile (it is the most singular feature of Emma, who for the most part, as I have suggested, is dissolving in repetitions, replications, generalizations, and pluralization). It is the Mona Lisa smile of the adulteress and will reappear on the face of Anna Karenina. It is a totally inscrutable smile and cannot be "disambiguated" (the term, from linguistics, is perhaps ugly, but it emphasizes just the aspect of the smile that I think is most important—a smile cannot mean nothing; it is some kind of expressive signal in no matter what context; but in this case there is no way of ascertaining which of the many possible meanings it might be conveying.) It is the smile with which Emma tries to fill in the gaps that are appearing in her failing articulation (note the dots in the text) and the pockets of uncertainty that are expanding within her knowledge. It is the smile that says what language cannot say and knows what knowledge cannot know. Emma finds herself in an impossible situation. Which is why—being both pushed (unconsciously) by her actual husband and pulled (tentatively) by her would-be lover in the direction of an adultery that will be, not an episode, but an irreversible and inescapable way of life—Emma stutters and smiles that singular smile. In that indecipherable smile may be read for a moment a total, and totally inarticulable, awareness of the actual impossibility of being Emma Bovary.

Nouer can be read as an anagram of *Rouen; Rouen* in turn sounds very like *Rouault* (Emma's "maiden" name); and they both contain *rou[e]*—these transformations of words into one another operate in the first case by what is in effect a mirror image, in the second by echo, and in the third by partial identity (*rou*, the root morpheme, appears in all three words). I have referred to the role played by this kind of deliberate wordplay, or higher-order punning, in the text, and it is indeed in Rouen that Emma embarks on her final transformations—her doings that become undoings and her circlings that are disintegrations. As I have said, the experience in the theater marks the moment when Emma enters into a confused theatricalization of her own existence that is terminal. It is in Rouen that she goes from the theater to her rendezvous with Léon in the cathedral, where her grasp of reality and role is as uncertain as it was in the theater. The confusion of realms—the cathedral is seen as a "gigantic boudoir" (p. 251) "boudoir gigantesque" [p. 316]) by Léon, and is described as a curious atmosphere in which everything is enlarged, distorted, refracted, as if in another kind of theater—is reflected in Emma's uncertainty of how to behave or indeed what to be (devout worshipper, deceiving wife). The very adoption of the cathedral as the location for their meeting is an adulterous mixing of places, functions, and intentions, that foreordains the inevitable physical adultery with which the episode concludes. In the cathedral Emma's "virtue" is said to be "tottering" (p. 252) or staggering ("sa vertu chancelante" [p. 317]), and indeed her innate disposition to dizziness is effectively maximized by her experience in the theater/cathedral (merging confusedly into one) and is exploited to the full by Léon. After their mad coach ride round and round Rouen, Emma will be permanently giddy: vertigo is transformed from an occasional attack to a mode of existence.

The theater/cathedral/coach ride may be said to comprise a kind of wheel of experiences that set Emma spinning off into her final *acte*. It is unnecessary to scrutinize every detail of the sequence in this context, but in view of what I have been selecting for special consideration, certain aspects of the experience in the cathedral and the coach should be alluded to. In the church Emma is, as in the theater, just Emma, until the beadle adds his presence, when she becomes. "Madame Bovary." To

Léon she is just *elle,* and the way he registers her arrival is worth noting. "There was a rustle of silk over the stone slabs, the brim of a hat, a black cape—she had come!" (p. 252) "Mais un froufrou de soie sur les dalles, la bordure d'un chapeau, un camail noire.... C'était elle!" [p. 316]) "She" is composed of certain sounds and colors, textures, edges of clothes, and thus in a certain important way is not seen or heard as herself at all. Even when she kneels to pray, Léon extracts a certain charm from his irritation by "seeing" her as "une marquise andalouse" (p. 316) ("an Andalusian marquesa" [p. 252]). I have discussed this kind of "projection" in a previous section. I mention it again in this context because it is in this sequence of experiences that Emma Bovary is effectively erased. When she leaves the coach at the end of the drive around Rouen she is simply—"une femme" with "le voile baissé" (p. 322) ("a women . . . with her veil lowered" [p. 257]). It is as though she has no more social or familial identity and her very features have been wiped out. After this she can only play roles and think up more roles in the spinning theater of her existence, and it is this process that is so vividly described in the third part of the book. This "erasing" is indirectly adumbrated by the various objects in the cathedral that the beadle singles out for their admiration—a "large circle of black paving stones with no inscription or carving" (p. 252) ("un grand cercle de pavés noirs, sans inscriptions ni ciselures" [p. 317]); "a sort of block that might once have been a crudely carved statue" (p. 253) ("une sorte de bloc, qui pouvait bien avoir été une statue mal faite" [p. 318]); a tomb figure of which "l'éternel guide" (p. 318) (who is indeed a guide into eternity for Emma) says, "It would surely be impossible to find a more perfect representation of death" (p. 253) ("Il n'est point possible, n'est-ce pas, de voir une plus parfaite représentation du néant" [p. 318]). Such objects carry resonant intimations of that condition beyond differentiation, that erosion of distinguishing signs and outlines, that *re*-presentation of nothingness, that in differing ways characterize the remaining part of Emma's experience, both the state that she is dizzily but unerringly approaching and the process by which she arrives at it.

Outside the cathedral Emma is persuaded to step into the carriage, and it is important to note what it is that overcomes her vestigial hesitation. Léon asserts that, "It's done in Paris" (p. 253) ("Cela se fait à Paris!" [p. 320]), and "that word, with its unassailable logic, determined her" (p. 253) ("Et cette parole, comme un irrésistible argument, la détermina" [p. 320]). Determined, not persuaded: here again we see Emma at the mercy of language, the shape of her life fixed by the power of a word. That the *parole* is *Paris* (another notable half echo) adds to our sense of Emma as indeed a figure whose life is hopelessly determined by quoted stereotypes and borrowed patterns that exist only at the level of sign (cf.

Charles's cap), or in this case only at the level of language. (Another indication of the deeply ambiguous power of the *parole* is given in Flaubert's description of Emma and Léon creating in conversation ideal versions of their own past lives; having made clear the vapid and pathetic distortions and exaggerations involved in the process, he comments "Speech acts invariably as an enlarger of sentiments" (p. 246) ("la parole est un laminoir qui allonge toujours les sentiments" [p. 309]). *Un laminoir* is a rolling mill or flattening mill, and the metaphor gives us an image of speech as a kind of mechanical or automatized process for lengthening feelings indefinitely, until it would be impossible to distinguish between what might have been the original emotion (prior to its "extension" into and through language) and the vast enlargements and attenuations that are engendered in the speaking mouth.)

For Emma *Paris* is a completely empty word, though we have some sense of the profusion of imaginary mirages with which she has sought to fill it. Such a word is, to take a phrase from Shakespeare, a "captious and intenible sieve" (*All's Well that Ends Well,* act 1, scene 3): there is no limit to what Emma can pour into it, since it will hold nothing. Thus this word is indeed a hole in her life created, not by the dizzying fullness of an experience (such as her waltz with the Viscount at Vaubyessard), but by the vertiginous emptiness of a word. Yet it is this gap, introduced into her by language alone (I revert to comments made in the first section), that effectively forces or thrusts her into that carriage, which is both a stifling category stereotype and the coffin awaiting her when her suffocation is complete. (Emma steps into an empty cliché and fills her own grave.) It is "sealed tighter than a tomb and being buffeted about like a ship at sea" (p. 256) ("plus close qu'un tombeau et ballottée comme un navire" [p. 322]). Emma is being shaken around in a box (tomb/ship) on water, another composite image of her life. It is the shaking that erases the social and familiar marks of her identity, so that she may be said to step out of the carriage "cured" of her former identity and re-formed or de-formed into an adulteress, worn down into the anonymity of *une femme.* In putting it in these terms, I am deliberately suggesting that the carriage is an odd and disturbing echo of the box in which Charles (but really everyone) tried to cure Hippolyte's foot and only succeeded in wearing away the whole leg. The incidents are neither homologically nor isomorphically symmetrical, but the potency of an unexpected analogy beginning to stir can be registered by the reader. The carriage is described as "la lourde machine" (p. 320) ("lumbering machine" [p. 255]), cf. *machine mécanique.* It goes faster and faster, and the instructions from the interior are always to continue, to accelerate; by contrast the method applied externally to the box holding Hippolyte's foot was to make it tighter, ever tighter. Emma, with and through Léon, has taken over the operation on herself. Thus the bewildered, compulsive, erratic, and finally circular movement of the carriage may be said both to reenact Emma's own mode of motion and also to implant a mode of movement in her confused being, so that—just as I suggested that in one sense she never leaves the theater, since she absorbs its theatricality into her own existence and takes it with her—in one sense she never leaves that carriage, since she follows out its mode of motion throughout the rest of her life. The feminine personal pronoun referring to the errant behavior of the carriage or machine ("la voiture," "la machine") seems also to refer to Emma's own actions, summarizing, defining, and also determining them. "There it turned and came back again, then went roaming at random, without aim or course . . . continually reappearing" (p. 256). ("Elle revint; et alors, sans parti pris ni direction, au hasard, elle vagabonda . . . apparaissait ainsi continuellement" [p. 321].) It is hardly necessary by now to point out how dominant such words as *hasard* and *vagabonder* are in Emma's own life. The bewildered driver cannot understand "what mania for locomotion possessed these individuals that they should want to drive on for ever" (p. 256) ("quelle fureur de la locomotion poussait ces individus à ne vouloir point s'arrêter" [p. 321]). But this "fureur de la locomotion" that ends in going round and round (thus reappearing continually) prior to the final stop, is both Emma's problem and her "determined" temperament; it is her torment, her constituent drive, her destiny. In her person, in the terms available to her, in the forms imposed upon her, she rediscovers the problem of unemployed energy, energy that is emotional, passional, sexual, but an energy that contains all these and is something more—the unique cluster of energies that *is* Emma and that must provide all her motivations and momentums, no matter what socially determined and determining form these may take on. Her problem, and it is also a real part of her pathos, is that having tried different directions, different *tempi*, different ways of moving (running in straight lines, roving at large, proceeding according to volition and intention or simply *au hasard*—which suggests both chance, and hazards and risks), she ends up going round and round in circles. Not only does Emma not know who to *be* or what she *wants*, she does not know what to *do* and where to *go*.[35] It is perhaps the most severe indictment of the society around her as depicted by Flaubert that

---

[35] In this, her experience is directly contrary to Nietzsche's assertions concerning "the dissatisfaction of the will." "The normal dissatisfaction of our drives, e.g., hunger, the sexual drive, the drive to motion, contains in it absolutely nothing depressing; it works rather as an agitation of the feeling of life, as every rhythm of small, painful stimuli strengthens it (whatever pessimists may say). This dissatisfaction, instead of making one disgusted with life, is the great stimulus to life. (One could perhaps describe pleasure in general as a rhythm of little unpleasurable stimuli)" (*The Will to Power*, book 3, section

in Emma's final desperate sexual and financial circlings we begin to hear something of the whirring of M. Binet's lathe and to sense something of its formidable determining power—formidable because mindless and emotionless. It is the very music that presides, one might say, in ignorant triumph over Emma Bovary's accelerating disintegration, fragmentation, liquidation, and obliteration.

The "Morselization" of Emma Bovary:
Cou/Cou-tume—Custom and Costume and Emma's Neck

In this section I want to return to Emma's first appearance in the book. She is first perceived on the threshold ("sur le seuil" [p. 35]), that liminal area of indeterminacy where the Guérin girl languished in a melancholy of transition and uncertainty (see the quotation at the beginning of this chapter). She is wearing a blue dress with three flounces ("trois volants" [p. 35]); as I have said, things in general tend to fall in threes about her (see my comments on triplication, note 2). Her initial environment is the kitchen, where she is surrounded by the usual utensils—but so described as to seem somewhat menacing and disproportionately huge, hard, and shining ("all of colossal size and shone like polished steel" [p. 27]; "tous de proportion colossale, brillaient comme de l'acier poli" [p. 36]), with something potentially percussive and even aggressive about them ("an array of kitchen utensils" [p. 27]; "une abondante batterie de cuisine" [p. 36]—but *batterie* has a harsher aura to it than *array*). There is also a large fire, and some wet clothes drying out. Fire and water produce steam or mist (wet clothes and sheets are referred to more than once in the book), and the softness and moistness of the clothes contrasts with the gleaming polished metallic surfaces of the instruments that are so obtrusively present. In such oppositions and minglings of textures and elements, Emma was, effectively, incubated, and in different forms they will determine the shape of her subsequent life, which is endlessly involved in permutations of clothes, "metallicism" or threatening male "instruments" of various kinds, and water—all exist-

697). In his work Nietzsche was engaged in an attempt to devalue and revalue many of the dominant privileged categories of the nineteenth-century in which he saw people as being imprisoned. But Emma cannot transcend her society and is trapped in a confusion of unexamined, unrevalued categories.

ing in different relationships to the central fire of her urgent and uncertain appetites, her clamorous and indefinable desires.

That is an appearance and a setting: the paragraph contains no mention of any movement on Emma's part. The first time she is described as doing something—so that the static appearance takes on the dimension of activity—occurs when Charles is attending to her father's fracture. She is trying to sew. "Mademoiselle Emma tried to sew some pads. She was so long finding her work-box that her father lost patience with her. She made no answer; but as she sewed she pricked her fingers, and then she put them to her mouth and sucked them" (p. 28). ("Mlle. Emma tâchait de *coudre* des *cous*sinets. Comme elle fut longtemps avant de trouver son étui, son père s'impatienta; elle ne répondit rien; mais tout en cousant, elle se piquait les doigts, qu'elle portait ensuite à sa bouche pour les sucer" [p. 36; my italics]). This is something more than a cameo of harmless domestic incompetence. At this point I just want to stress that the attempt to sew (construct, make up, put together, assemble, etc.) is faulty and results in a slight self-puncturing, a minute but perceptible hint of breaking into or interrupting the smooth continuity of the bodily surface. Emma is indeed a long time in finding her "work-box"—*étui*, a case, box, or cover—and her life is to be paradoxically both a continual encasement and a prolonged uncovering. Her father is impatient but powerless and helpless; she no longer has to speak to the father (her relationship to him may be said to have been fixed at the stage indicated by her drawing of Minerva [sic!] hung in the living room and signed [in Gothic letters] "A mon cher papa" [p. 37]). Instead she puts her fingers to her mouth and sucks them. There is no need to underline the suggestiveness of this self-suckling action, but even though these little aspects of her behavior may pass almost unnoticed as being entirely within the range of average and normal daily behavior in the house, I would suggest that just as the pricking of the fingers carries latent hints of self-piercing, so this sucking of the fingers adumbrates an appetitive drive that will only finally be satisfied by devouring the self (Emma's terminating act is precisely once again to put her fingers to her mouth; this time, of course, carrying poison—but the morphology of the gesture is the same). And the puncturing of Emma's skin is continued after her death by no less an agent than M. Homais, for when Charles asks for a lock of Emma's hair, it is Homais who takes the scissors, but "he was shaking so violently that he punctured the skin in several places" (p. 345) ("il tremblait si fort, qu'il piqua la peau des tempes en plusieurs places" [p. 427]).

So far Emma has been depicted in terms of dress and setting and this activity of attempted sewing. It is then that her physical being begins to emerge, item by item, or, as we say, bit by bit. We may infer that the syntagmatic relationship between one part of the body and the next corresponds to the movements of Charles's attention as his eyes take in one feature after another, but we must also recognize that the sequence (and thus the separation) of features is also an aspect of the text itself. This is the sequence in which Emma's physical presence is preceived/ established, either prefaced by a statement concerning Charles as the perceiver, or simply asserted by the text: her nails, her hands, her finger joints or knuckles (*phalanges* is a fairly technical word and is appropriate to Charles's "medical" perspective—Emma is being anatomized), her eyes, her lips, then her neck, her hair, the curve of her skull ("courbe de crâne," again a rather cold, professional term), the tips of her ears, her temples, her cheekbones ("pommettes"), her shoulder. In the remainder of this first short scene the only other references to her person are to "le front" and "le dos" (forehead, but also more generally, the "front-ing" part, and the back). In the middle of this description/anatomization Charles is invited by Emma's father "to take a bite" (p. 28) ("*à prendre un morceau*" [p. 37]). The italicization of a phrase so that it is visibly discontinuous with the surrounding text is of course a polysemic device; among the different effects it can achieve, one is to mark a phrase, not just as a cliché and a common saying, but as an importation or implantation of a saying from one context to another. Thus *prendre un morceau* is a phrase generally applied not just to taking a bite but to taking a bit, in any one of potentially innumerable contexts. For example, it certainly indicates a similarity of attitude to food and to women. (Homais, we later learn, "in the matter of physical qualities was not averse from a slim morsel" (p. 290) ("quant aux qualités corporelles, ne détestait pas le *morceau*" [p. 364]). Again the word is italicized—it is the commonest currency in that context; it is the accepted word to say. Once again the empty word proclaims itself through the empty man. The phrase thus becomes another borrowed pattern, endlessly duplicating itself in the mouths of differing speakers. Being nonspecific (just "un morceau"), it becomes a general and generalizing activity and thus a homogenizing one. The cliché maps the conduct, and thus one and the same mode of mindless appropriation may be indifferently applied in widely differing contexts. Take a bit—of whatever, or whomsoever.

I have referred already to the process of "morselization" in which Emma seems to get progressively involved, so that by the end she is indeed in every way *morcelée*; I would now suggest that we witness an epitome of this process in this first description of her appearance. She is "morselized" by Charles's eye and by Flaubert's text. Alike, they register the parts with careful and minute attention, but precisely in doing so they miss the whole, which is not to be found in the sum of the separate items. The difference, if I may put it this way, is that Charles does not know this, while Flaubert does. Morselization is inherent in the act of writing. Detailing is dismembering. One might want to make the obvious objection that the breaking up and reassemblage of features that can be practiced in endless permutations at the level of language, is precisely not to be confused with the irreversible corporeal fragmentations of a single body. But I think Flaubert intends us to become aware of the processes by which this apparently neutral activity of language *can* in fact impinge on the body—both as speech and writing—and intrude its dis-integrative and de-structive potentialities into the vulnerable wholeness of the human organism. It is merely a truism to observe that language disintegrates and destructures the continuum of the world, only to reintegrate and restructure it at another level in another medium. Emphasis and context are what matter, and here, it seems to me, Flaubert is revealing Emma Bovary to us as a locus of morselization, a process variously conducted by the author, the men around her, and herself. (Thus, she already reveals a habit of biting her lips in her silent moments, but I want to return to that description.) Something of what I think is present in what Flaubert is doing in this interplay between linguistic and physical atomization may be conveyed by a remarkable passage in one of Lacan's essays, in which he describes the "mystery of the signifier" ("mystère du signifiant") and imagines it making the following statement concerning its own powers. "So runs the signifier's answer, above and beyond all significations: "You think you act when I stir you at the mercy of the bonds through which I knot your desires. Thus do they grow in force and multiply in objects, bringing you back to the fragmentation of your shattered childhood [au morsillement de ton enfance déchirée]. So be it: such will be your feast until the return of the stone guest I shall be for you since you call me forth."[36] One achievement of Flaubert's book is to bring Emma back precisely "au morcellement de [son] enfance déchirée."

The morselizing process is repeated, textually, on Emma's deathbed, when we are given an account of the priest dipping his right thumb in the oil and applying extreme unction, touching the various parts of her body in sequence—first on the eyes, then on the nostrils, then on the mouth, then on the hands, and lastly on the soles of her feet. After the mention of each part Flaubert adds an amplifying comment—e.g., "lastly on the soles of the feet that once had run so swiftly to the assuaging of her desires, and now would walk no more" (p. 335) ("enfin sur la plante des pieds, si rapides autrefois quand elle courait à l'assouvissance de ses désirs, et qui maintenant ne marcheraient plus" [p. 416]). The cumulative effect of these amplifying comments, balanced one with the next, is

---

[36] Jacques Lacan, "Seminar on 'The Purloined Letter.'"

somewhat sententious, even liturgical. But this is appropriate, for while the priest dips his thumb in the oil and touches the parts of Emma's body, intoning the appropriate prayers, Flaubert dips his pen in his ink and likewise touches on the parts of Emma's body and adds his own litany. Author, priest, husband, seducer, lover—all see her partially, in parts, and take her apart, in different ways. Flaubert's itemizing/atomizing continues to the moment of her death, thus also enacting the painful disassembly and disintegration of the body. Near the end her tongue effectly disengages itself from her body completely—"the whole of her tongue protruded from her mouth" (p. 336) ("La langue tout entière lui sortit hors de la bouche" [p. 417]). Earlier her jaws were described as moving "as though she had a heavy weight on her tongue" (p. 327) ("comme si elle eût porté sur la langue quelque chose de très lourd" [p. 407]), and we may say that among other things it is the heavy weight of language itself she has been carrying. Like Charles Bovary and everyone, of course, but Emma's is the exemplary case. She is the figure who is unstable linguistically, as she is domestically and socially; her virtue "totters" in the cathedral as her speech "stutters" in and after the theater, and her attempts at sewing result in pricked fingers. She cannot properly handle what she has to work with. As her tongue leaves her head, Emma effectively disgorges the weight of language that she could never quite carry in a way that would make for a balanced, unvertiginous life. The last parts of her body to be singled out are her hair and eyes, as they were singled out at the beginning. After this her morselization is complete, definitive.

There is one other aspect of the itemization of Emma's features and appearance I wish to note. She is described as carrying a pair of tortoiseshell eyeglasses attached to her bodice "comme un homme" (p. 38) ("in masculine fashion" [p. 29]). The male world is constantly looking at Emma in various kinds of detached, calculating fashions, whether it is Charles's slow examination of her anatomical features, Rodolphe's instant undressing of her in his mind's eye, or Flaubert's "dispassionate" detailing of her life and death. (Justin's adoring gaze is an exception.) Spectacles are often used in literature to imply a particular kind of scrutiny (myopic, unfeeling, ruthlessly analytic, etc.), and we may say that while Emma appears not to use her glasses (indeed from some points of view has exceedingly poor vision and prefers the blurred far to the oppressively clear proximate), she herself is constantly being looked at in different ways by the male world, not only "seen" but "seen not seeing" and even "seen seeing herself not being seen" ("vu ne pas voir," "vu se voyant n'être pas vu"[37]). She is not only under the tyranny of the

---

[37]Lacan, ibid. For French version, see Ecrits I, p. 41.

male word, as I tried to suggest in an early section; she is under the related tyranny of the male eye (a kind of ocular sadism); and she wears, unwittingly, a badge of her bondage as part of her costume.

I now want to quote two other details given us in this first "look" at the front and back of Emma Bovary. The first is while Charles is duly "taking a bite" (though no *food* is mentioned, an unusual absence in this book, perhaps to make us consider what exactly Charles is being invited to take a bit/bite *of*. "The room was chilly, and she shivered as she ate, revealing then something of her full lips, which she had a habit of biting in her silent moments" (p. 28). "Comme la salle était fraiche, elle grelottait tout en mangeant, ce qui *découvrait* un peu ses lèvres charnues, qu'elle avait *coutume* de mordiller à ses moments de silence. Son *cou* sortait d'un col blanc, rabattu" [p. 37; my italics].) The second detail occurs when Charles is about to leave and is looking for his whip. Emma stoops to pick it up, and Charles makes a move to help and a decisive and *determining* contact is made. "He felt his chest brush against the girl's back, bending beneath him. She got up red in the face, and looked at him over her shoulder as she handed him the lash" (p. 29). ("Il sentit sa poitrine effleurer le dos de la jeune fille, *courbée* sous lui. Elle se redressa toute rouge et le regarda par-dessus l'épaule, en lui tendant son nerf de boeuf" [p. 38; my italics].) These bodily responses have their own eloquence, and they seem to foreshadow many of Emma's subsequent actions and reactions, which may be seen as mutations on these early involuntary gestures. Thus her "nibbling" (rather than "biting") of her own lips during her silences adumbrates her ultimately self-devouring attempts to find something to consume to fill up the gaps ("boucher les interstices" [p. 428]) in her conversation, her consciousness, her life. (And note that this was a habit indulged in by Charles's mother—thus, "Mme. Bovary se mordait les lèvres" [p. 27]); it is another repetition, a duplication of habit—not a genetically transmitted quality, but rather a sort of borrowed pattern of response that keeps recurring in that recursive society. As Emma grows up she will graduate from nibbling to biting, as others have before her.) The handing of the whip to the fumbling Charles is a gesture that indeed speaks for itself, and the blush that suffuses Emma's face when her back brushes against Charles's chest is the established signal for the arousal of some latent sexuality (an erection of the head is, I think, how Freud describes the blush). But it is her stance that is, if anything, even more decisive. She is "bending beneath him" ("courbée sous lui"), a position not simply suggesting the sexual dominance of the male (a dominance surely very imperfectly asserted by the meek, compliant Charles), but more generally the inevitable female submission to the matrix of the male world around her. She must and can only "bend" under it to the shapes, postures, and positions that it offers, imposes, or dictates. Thus her bodily curves offer themselves for the curvings (social and sexual) of the men who will form (and deform) her life.

I have so far drawn attention to a series of words in this scene which have a similar root morpheme, or "radical"—*coudre, coussinets, couvrir, coutume, courbée,* and *cou* (for the relationship between roots and radicals see Saussure, *Course in General Linguistics*). Let me add to this group some further instances in the book of words containing the same root or a similar syllable. *Coutume* recurs, as in the phrase "tout rentrait dans la coutume" (p. 205) ("things reverted to normal" [p. 164]), or in the verb *s'accoutumer.* The decisive argument used to persuade Hippolyte to undergo the operation to cure him is "*c'est que ça ne lui coûterait rien*" (p. 236) ("it would not cost him anything" [p. 187]). There are a number of references to both *coups* ("blows," "knocks") and *coudes* ("elbows")— sometimes these are literal, as when a boy knocks Charles's cap to the floor with "un coup de coude" (p. 22), or they may be metaphorical, as when Emma is stunned by Lheureux's threats and sinks back as if from a "coup de massue" (p. 380) ("knock-out blow" [p. 305]). Emma yearns and loves to run ("elle eut envie de courir" [p. 298]), even if it is finally in circles; this in turn produces not only giddiness but exhaustion, "courbature" (p. 377) (at times she feels as if she would like to sleep forever). There is play on the very close assonance of *cour* ("court," "yard") and *coeur* ("heart"), as in the following passage concerning Rodolphe: "car les plaisirs, comme des écoliers dans la cour d'un collège, evaient tellement piétiné sur son coeur, que rien de vert n'y poussait" (p. 267) ("for his pleasures had so trampled over his heart, like schoolboys in a playground, that no green thing grew there" [p. 213]). Where the almost-identity of sound perfectly signals Rodolph's inability to distinguish a common playground from what is traditionally considered the inmost sanctuary of private feelings. It is his *letter* ("ta lettre") that, Emma insists, "tore my heart in two" (p. 323) ("elle m'a déchiré le coeur!" [p. 402]), another indication of the power of the word to penetrate and multilate the body. Inevitably in a book concerning a society so obsessed with clothes there are frequent references to "costume." Emma imagines how she would have embroidered Lagardy's costumes ("brodant elle-même ses costumes" [p. 297]), and the more desperately she commits herself to the final stages of adultery the more recourse she has to "coquetteries du costume" (p. 367). It is, as I have mentioned before, one of the paradoxes of her experience that at the same time as she is getting more and more involved in coquetries of costume and, as it were, pointlessly multiplying her wardrobe, she has an increasing compulsion to throw off all the costumes, as if in quest of some ultimate nakedness. Thus in a famous passage, "She snatched off her dress and tore at the thin laces of her corsets, which whistled down over her hips like a slithering adder . . . then made a single movement and all her clothes fell to the floor" (p. 299). ("Elle se déshabillait brutalement, arrachant le lacet mince de son corset, qui sifflait autour de ses hanches comme une couleuvre qui glisse . . . puis elle faisait d'un seul geste tomber ensemble tous ses vête-ments" [p. 367].) The element of brutality that is entering into Emma's treatment of her own clothes and body is an indication of her accelerat-ing desperation. The simile of the snake is often remarked upon, and it of course has ramifying resonances. Among other things, it introduces a kind of serpentine life to Emma's clothes, an autonomous erotic vitality acquired or displaced from her body. In this connection consider another simile in which she encircles herself (again the ubiquitous *comme*). It is a transcription of her attitude to Charles. "Was not he the very obstacle to all felicity, the cause of all her wretchedness, the pointed buckle, as it were, on the complicated strap that bound her" (p. 121) ("N'était-il pas, lui, l'obstacle à toute félicité, la cause de toute misère, et comme l'ardillon pointu de cette courroie complexe qui la bouclait de tous côtés?" [p. 153]). We may note here again the root echo in *cou*leuvre and *cou*rroie, though this time the simile originates from Emma. That is to say, that just as her life is increasingly permeated with clothes, so clothing per-meates her thinking; Charles is registered as the pointed buckle-tongue, and her situation in general as "cette courroie complexe." She is seeing her life in terms of costume. And if she registers her position as being like a "complex belt" where the circle is rigid, closed, a stifling constraint, then she may well seek to shake and wriggle herself out of it as and when she can, thereby exchanging the dead sign of bondage (*courroie*) for a living, spiraling, sign of release (*couleuvre*). Such moments of release / undress are inevitably temporary, and there is always the return to ever more "costume" and the ever-tightening *courroie complexe*.

It would be possible to point to other words with the *cou* root used in the account of Emma's appearance and behavior (*secouer* and *couper* or *découper* figure among her movements and actions for instance), but I want to return to two of them that occurred in the account of her first appearance and that recur again in the later and final stages of her life. As I said, she is first seen trying, not very successfully, to sew ("tâchait de coudre," "tout en cousant"). In the chapter following what is effectively her complete capitulation to adultery (the carriage ride in Rouen), she is described, back in her home, in an act of un-sewing. "She was unstitch-ing the lining of a dress; bits of stuff lay scattered all around her" (p. 264). ("Elle décousait la doublure d'une robe, dont les bribes s'éparpil-laient autour d'elle" [p. 331].) I have commented before on the ac-cumulating "privatives" in the account of Emma's life, and *décousait* is one of the most significant of all. Emma is unstitching the lining of the garment (covering) of her life. Adultery "unstitches" marriage; Emma is unstitching everything, including herself, and the bits are indeed scattered around her. In unstitching the costume that is her social existence, Emma is at the same time unraveling custom—and she never thinks to count the cost. In a very profound sense custom is costume, and customs are what it costs to be part of a community (hence the importance of The Customs House in Hawthorne's novel of adultery, *The Scarlet Letter*). Custom and costume, both in English and French, derive from *consuescere*, the Latin for "to accustom," just as the English *consuetudinary* and the French *coutumier* can be both adjectives meaning "customary," and nouns referring to a book or collection of customs. "Coudre" is thus a primal activity that both literally and metaphorically creates costumes/customs. By marking her imperfect mastery of this distinctly and distinguishingly human activity from the start, Flaubert can make us aware of a continuity and relatedness between all Emma's uncertainties, instabilities, and incompetencies—in marriage, in money, in language, in love. She cannot sew them together in a coherent way. (Hawthorne's Hester Prynne, by contrast, has a genius for sewing and embroidery.) She is radically not at home in all the customs in which she is born, no matter how hard she tries to accustom herself. She thus, with or without intention, mars what she does, and doing becomes undoing, just as "cousant" gives way to "décousait." Just how serious the implications of this unstitching activity are may be suggested by an abrupt authoritative assertion from one of Shakespeare's heroines, who is particularly notable for being innocent of the adultery that is basely imputed to her and for being a model of married fidelity, Imogen: "the breach of custom/Is breach of all" (*Cymbeline*, act 4, scene 2).

The other word to which I wish to return is *cou*, not as a root but as an independent word. In the first description of her person, Emma's neck is described in active terms—"Son cou sortait d'un col blanc" (p. 37). Her last voluntary act of motion *toward another person or thing* (her very last act is to ask for a look in a mirror, which is an act toward herself), involves another movement of the neck, but this time not, as it were, in repose but in an extreme of desperation. "The priest rose to take the crucifix. Reaching forward like one in thirst, she glued her lips to the body of the Man-God and laid upon it with all her failing strength the most mighty kiss of love she had ever given" (p. 335). ("Le prêtre se releva pour prendre le crucifix; alors elle allongea le cou comme quelqu'un qui a soif, et, collant ses lèvres sur le corps de l'Homme-Dieu, elle y déposa de toute sa force expirante le plus grand baiser d'amour qu'elle eût jamais donné" [p. 416].) The Man-God is the ultimate fusion in the Christian faith, as it is the sign of the confusion in Emma's life since the corporeal and the spiritual realms were, for her, blurred from the outset; a confusion she in part imbibed from the cross she kisses. But it is the stretching out of the neck that conveys so much of Emma's plight, of the particular problem of her existence. At the risk of appearing to rehearse platitudes, let me emphasize some aspects of the role played by the neck in the human body. It is characteristically one of the three points of egress, or exits, at which the body leaves the clothes it wears, the other two being the hands and feet (these are also meticulously observed in Emma's actions). Feet and hands precipitate moving through (toward), and contact with (or manipulation of), the world, and are points at which the body visibly terminates. The neck in itself has no such specific skill (there are very few actions you *do* with your neck) but acts as the connecting link between the exposed head and the covered body; it is a tunnel containing the two-way traffic of words and nourishment, for it is in the neck that we start to swallow and to speak (thus it contains the throat, the vocal cords, the larynx, epiglottis, trachea, esophagus, etc.). It also allows the head its amazing flexibility, so that from birth we can track moving objects and locate differing sound sources. The head turns on the neck, and Emma is continually turning her head and, as we say, having her head turned. In particular, in this final stretching of her neck, she conveys the hopeless hungers, needs, and desires that have impelled her in her life, in her reachings out, turnings, extensions of her self.

If, perhaps somewhat fancifully, we considered the body as a complex word or unit of language, then we could say that the neck operates both as a word in itself and as a syllable in the more complex compound word of the body; by coming between the head and the chest and thus relating and separating them, it plays a crucial part in a larger unit of meaning. I have tried to suggest that something similar may be noted in Flaubert's text, where Emma's neck figures prominently in both her first appearance and her last, but where we also find the syllable *cou* appearing in a large number of longer words describing aspects of her activities and experiences—*coudre, couvrir, coutume, courbée, coûter, coups, couds, cour, coeur, couleuvre, courroie, couper,* etc. I am not trying to suggest any shared etymology, some secret hidden original meaning which we can track down to the source, hoping to experience in its presence an etymic epiphany. I am no more hoping to intimate that all these words can be traced back somehow to the meaning "neck" than one would try to see the different parts of the body as having some common source in the physical neck. My point is literally of the most superficial kind—for I only want to draw attention to a surface phenomenon, namely that the same three letters appear in this cluster of words, modified of course by the other letters they are associated with, just as when spoken the same, or a very similar, sound may be heard, modified of course by the other sounds immediately succeeding or preceding it. (Flaubert, I think, did something similar with *rou* and arguably with *tou,* but I will concentrate on *cou.*) These words, and the many others that could be cited, comprise what Saussure called an "associative series," and I must now quote from his work, *Course in General Linguistics.*

> In a language-state everything is based on relations. How do they function?
>
> Relations and differences between linguistic terms fall into two distinct groups, each of which generates a certain class of values. The opposition between the two classes gives a better understanding of the nature of each class. They correspond to two forms of our mental activity, both indispensable to the life of language.
>
> In discourse, on the one hand, words acquire relations based on the linear nature of language because they are chained together. This rules out the possibility of pronouncing two elements simultaneously. . . . The elements are arranged in sequence on the chain of speaking. Combinations supported by linearity are *syntagms.* . . . In the syntagm a term acquires its value only because it stands in opposition to everything that precedes or follows it, or to both.
>
> Outside discourse, on the other hand, words acquire relations of a different kind. Those that have something in common are associated in the memory, resulting in groups marked by diverse relations. . . .
>
> The coordinations formed outside discourse differ strikingly from those formed inside discourse. Those formed outside discourse are not supported by linearity. Their seat is in the brain; they are a part of the inner storehouse that makes up the language of each speaker. They are *associative relations.*
>
> The syntagmatic relation is *in praesentia.* It is based on two or more terms that occur in an effective series. Against this, the associative relation unites terms *in absentia* in a potential mnemonic series.[38]

He then proceeds to expand on these different relations, and I want to quote from his remarks on "associative relations."

> Mental association creates other groups besides those based on the comparing of terms that have something in common; through its grasp of the nature of the relations that bind the terms together, the mind creates as many associative series as there are diverse relations. For instance, in *enseignement* 'teaching,' *enseigner* 'teach,' *enseignons* '(we) teach,' etc., one element, the radical, is common to every term; the same word may occur in a different series formed around another common element, the suffix (cf. *enseignement, armement, changement,* etc.); or the association may spring from the analogy of the concepts signified (*enseignement, instruction, apprentissage, éducation,* etc.); or again, simply from the similarity of the sound-images (e.g., *enseignement* and *justement* 'precisely').

[38]Ferdinand de Saussure, *Course in General Linguistics,* pp. 122–23.

At this point there is a footnote, to which I will return. Saussure's text continues:

> Thus there is at times a double similarity of meaning and form, at times similarity only of form or of meaning. A word can always evoke everything that can be associated with it in one way or another.
>
> Whereas a syntagm immediately suggests an order of succession and a fixed number of elements, terms in an associative family occur neither in fixed numbers nor in a definite order. . . . We are unable to predict the number of words that the memory will suggest or the order in which they will appear. A particular word is like the center of a constellation; it is the point of convergence of an indefinite number of co-ordinated terms.[39]

In Flaubert's text *cou* operates as just such a word, it seems to me, and it is the center of an indeterminate cluster of other words associated with it in all the ways Saussure lists in the quotation, from identity of appearance with other syllables added, similarities and relatedness of meaning and form, and simple similarity of the sound-images. I must now quote from the footnote concerning this last kind of association, for once again we find what amounts to almost a class attitude of contempt towards the pun. "This last case [i.e., simple similarity of sound images] is rare and can be classed as abnormal, for the mind naturally discards associations that becloud the intelligibility of discourse. But its existence is proved by a lower category of puns based on the ridiculous confusion that can result from pure and simple homonomy. . . . This is distinct from the case where an association, while fortuitous, is supported by a comparison of ideas."[40]

Again it should be pointed out that Flaubert can avail himself of both these ways of relating words, for his own purposes. But what is of particular interest here is Saussure's categorization of a certain kind of punning as abnormal on the grounds—and note the metaphor—that "the mind naturally discards associations that *becloud* the intelligibility of discourse." (My italics.) This follows quite logically from his whole idea of what language is, and again I want to quote from his own statements. "Psychologically our thought—apart from its expression in words—is only a shapeless and indistinct mass. Philosophers and linguists have always agreed in recognizing that without the help of signs we would be unable to make a clear-cut, consistent distinction between two ideas. Without language, thought is a vague, uncharted nebula. There are no pre-existing ideas, and *nothing is distinct before the appearance of language.*" (My italics, and it is worth noting that although that statement might now be accepted as a truism, there is evidence to suggest that there is a good

[39]Ibid., pp. 125–26.
[40]Ibid., pp. 126–27.

deal that is distinct before the appearance of language, and that initially language is a source of confusion and indistinction.) What Saussure stresses is that there are no "predelimited entities" either in the realm of ideas or of sounds. "Phonic substance is neither more fixed nor more rigid than thought; it is not a mold into which thought must of necessity fit but a plastic substance divided in turn into distinct parts to furnish the signifiers needed by thought." As he describes it, there is a mystery in what can only be called the ontology of language, or as he also calls it "the domain of articulations":

> . . . language works out its units while taking shape between two shapeless masses. Visualize the air in contact with a sheet of water; if the atmospheric pressure changes, the surface of the water will be broken up into a series of divisions, waves; the waves resemble the union or coupling of thought with phonic substance. . . .
>
> Linguistics then works in the borderland where the elements of sound and thought combine; *their combination produces a form, not a substance.*

The *source* of distinctions thus appears to be neither exclusively in sound nor in mind, but in their coming together in the linguistic unit ("The unit . . . is *a slice of sound which to the exclusion of everything that precedes and follows it in the spoken chain is the signifier of a certain concept.*") Since language is constantly transforming itself, changing, forgetting, substituting—"Language never stops interpreting and decomposing its units"[41]—this brings into question the whole notion of stability of values (as indeed does his emphasis on the different degrees of arbitrariness operative in the formation or transformation of language). These *are* values but they are a function of difference—hence his stress on the importance of distinction as such, as a crucial phenomenon, and hence too his contempt for the low pun, which "clouds" the "intelligibility of discourse."

His remarks in this area are perhaps too familiar to require much more than allusion but I want to quote from one passage from the section entitled "The Sign Considered in Its Totality".

> Everything that has been said up to this point boils down to this: in language there are only differences. . . . Although both the signified and the signifier are purely differential and negative when considered separately [i.e., "their most precise characteristic is in being what the others are not"—p. 117], their combination is a positive fact. . . .
>
> Any nascent difference will tend invariably to become significant but without always succeeding or being successful on the first trial. Conversely, any conceptual difference perceived by the mind seeks to find expression

---

[41]Ibid., pp. 111–13, 104, 169.

through a distinct signifier, and two ideas that are no longer distinct in the mind tend to merge into the same signifier.

When we compare signs—positive terms—with each other, we can no longer speak of difference; the expression would not be fitting, for it applies only to the comparing of two sound-images, e.g., *father* and *mother,* or two ideas, e.g., the idea "father" the idea "mother"; two signs, each having a signified and signifier, are not different but only distinct. Between them there is only *opposition.* The entire mechanism of language . . . is based on oppositions of this kind and on the phonic and conceptual differences that they imply. . . .

Applied to units, the principle of differentiation can be stated in this way: *the characteristics of the unit blend with the unit itself.* In language, as in any semiological system, whatever distinguishes one sign from the others constitutes it. *Difference makes character just as it makes value and the unit.* (The last italics are mine.)

The precise distinction between "difference" and "distinction" need not concern us here; I want rather to note Saussure's repeated stress on the fact that a word alone is nothing. "Each term present in the grammatical fact . . . consists of the interplay of a number of oppositions within the system. When isolated, neither *Nacht* nor *Nächte* is anything: thus everything is opposition." And again he reverts to the proposition "*language is a form and not a substance.*"[42] Difference makes character and value, and language makes differences (information is, in Gregory Bateson's terms, "any difference which makes a difference in some later event").[43] It is the nonsubstantial form that introduces forms into the world of bodies and substances.

From the outset I have tried to suggest that Emma's problem is in part a crucial problem concerning distinctions and differences (hence the fog in her head), and that in turn this problem reflects a society losing its ability to maintain differences and distinctions (Rodolphe is only an emphasized example). What is it that "constitutes" Emma? She cannot

[42]Ibid., pp. 120–21, 122.

[43]It would perhaps be to invoke unnecessary terminology to attempt to enlist the vocabulary of cybernetics in this context, but a fuller quotation of the passage from Bateson might suggest something of what is going wrong with information that Emma is receiving and of her inability to process it appropriately.

> Information, in the technical sense, is that which *excludes* certain alternatives. The machine with a governor does not elect the steady state; it *prevents* itself from staying in any alternative state; and in all such cybernetic systems, corrective action is brought about by *difference.* . . .
>
> The technical term "information" may be succinctly defined as *any difference which makes a difference in some later event.*

Page 281 in "A Re-examination of 'Bateson's Rule,'" and indeed, see the whole book in which this chapter appears, *Steps to an Ecology of Mind.*

find out, neither in marriage nor adultery nor in any other experience or in any terminology. The crisis of the meaning of marriage, which she experiences, is inextricably involved with, and indistinguishable from, a crisis in the language in and by which she is formed and rent. (It is notable and hardly incidental that Saussure's terms for discussing language overlap with those used in the realm of marriage—"associative family," "relations that bind," etc.) It is well established by now that in all societies marriage is a very important kind of language; it is perhaps worth reminding ourselves that the converse proposition also applies, so that language is a very important kind of marriage, a marriage between sound and concept, and by extension between speaker and listener. The marriage weakens in the case of writing, which, in Saussure's terms, creates "a purely fictitious unity"—"the superficial bond of writing is much easier to grasp than the only true bond, the bond of sound."[44] This bond is the bond between sign and meaning, but it applies just as well to the bond between writer and reader. This is no place to attempt any consideration of a topic as all-embracing as the differences between speaking and writing.[45] My point, a more limited one, is that Flaubert's whole book makes us aware in a new way that the crisis in marriage is also, and not by metaphor but by identity, a crisis in language. To put it very simply, we may recognize four stages in Emma's life: singleness or "daughterhood," marriage, adultery, death (this is indeed a stage or period, for it does not come as an abrupt, sudden event). These may be paralleled by four stages in the life of language (as depicted in the book):

[44]Saussure, *Course in General Linguistics,* p. 25.

[45]It was probably Rousseau who initiated the argument (or debate) in his *Essay on the Origin of Languages,* in which he states:

> Writing, which would seem to crystallize language, is precisely what alters it. It changes not the words but the spirit, substituting exactitude for expressiveness. Feelings are expressed in speaking, ideas in writing. . . . All this tends to confirm the principle that literary languages are naturally bound to undergo changes of character, and to lose in power what they gain in clarity; that the more stress on perfecting of grammar and logic, the faster these changes occur. All that is needed for quickly rendering a language cold and monotonous, is to establish academies among the people who speak it. . . . When the orthography of a language is clearer than its pronunciation, this is a sign that it is written more than it is spoken. (*Essay on the Origin of Languages,* trans. John Moran [New York: Frederick Ungar Publishing Co., 1966], pp. 21, 27–28.)

Saussure (in *Course in General Linguistics*) refers explicitly to "the tyranny of writing" (p. 31) and even asserts that "writing obscures language; it is not a guise for language but a disguise" (p. 30).

Jacques Derrida has opened up this whole problem, scrutinizing Rousseau's essay and challenging the whole idea of the primacy, and privileged nature, of speaking (as opposed to writing), in *Of Grammatology,* trans. Gayatri Spivak (Baltimore: The Johns Hopkins University Press, 1976).

the prelingual stage (singleness); a period when the interplay and relationship of differences *seems* stable and binding, during which time meaning is agreed on and nonproblematical (marriage); a period marked by an accelerating "decomposition" and reinterpretation of "units" (adultery); and the death of this particular phase of language as another one emerges to take its place (Emma's death and the total, ubiquitous triumph of Homais at the end of the book). Emma is caught between, not two languages, but two ways of using language, two different modes of constituting "meaning." Her giddiness and tottering, her confused and desperate searching—in short, the fog in her head—can be attributed to a large extent to her vague and hopeless yearning for a kind of meaning that the existing language into which she is born seems to promise (with its religious and romantic vocabularies, etc.), but that in fact it can no longer deliver or bestow. Before Emma broke her word to Charles, language had broken its word to her. Before Emma committed adultery, meanings had slipped bonds and moved into other beds or disappeared entirely. And when she dies, the death agonies of her final disintegration are the physical registration of the disintegration of an old and superseded kind of language. They are both a long time dying, but by the end they are both utterly dead. Which is, to reiterate a crucial point, why Flaubert abandons the *nous* with which he started his book. All the bonds and ties and contracts and relationships have effectively been broken or are dissolved. "The breach of custom / Is breach of all." Imogen's awesomely succinct formulation applies equally to the marriage that is language and the language that is marriage. Flaubert's book is a study of all those nonlegalized divorces that result from that loss of the sense of difference that makes breaches of custom and all adulterations of relationships possible.

Saussure designated two relationships in a language state, one inside discourse and the other outside. The syntagmatic relationship fixes words in chains; it is based on a linear combination and is characterized by an order of succession and a fixed number of elements. It is a definite order and the constituent parts take on their meaning from their place in the chain. Given this definition, it is hardly inappropriate to regard marriage as a syntagmatic relationship. This is the relationship in discourse in which words are chained together. It is *in praesentia*. The associative relations are unlimited, unfixed, in no definite order, unpredictable, diverse, the convergence of an indefinite number of coordinated terms, terms coordinated not according to the grammatical rules that govern the syntagmatic order, but by a multiplicity of diverse habits of association (similarity of sound, construction, meaning, connotation, etc.). It is a relationship outside discourse and is *in absentia*. Within it, many words come together in unpredictable combinations—such as *cou, coudre, courvrir, coutume, couleuvre, courroie, couper,* etc., etc.—but none of them are chained together in a fixed relationship. This is the equivalent of the realm where adulterous relationships obtain. Inasmuch as we all think in associative relations and speak in syntagms, then we may all be said to participate in these marital/adulterous aspects of language, the condition of being both absent and present, both inside and outside discourse at the same time. Again we must recognize that Emma's is not a unique but an exemplary case. She is inserted into a syntagmatic relationship, but her whole being tends to think and feel in (increasingly confused) associative constellations. Both of these modes of establishing relations are inherent in the language, indeed in *la condition linguistique.* They need not necessarily come into conflict or engender it, but the potential for doing so is always there, and in the figure of Emma Bovary, Flaubert concentrates on just that latent potentiality. Syntagmatic and associative relations are confused and confounded, thus precipitating confoundings in all aspects of Emma's existence: "the appetites of the flesh, the craving for money, the melancholy of passion, all blended together in one general misery" (p. 121) ("les appétits de la chair, les convoitises d'argent et les mélancolies de la passion, tout se confondit dans une même souffrance" [p. 152]). Flaubert's opening description of Charles Bovary's cap depicts it as an associative series or set of relationships gone berserk, not a constellation or coordination, but a chaos. As Charles is ac-costumed so is he ac-customed, and that cap bespeaks a crisis in language in which recognizable families or relationships are being replaced by jumbles of signs that not only make no sense but actively serve to destroy it. (Needless to say, a crisis in language is inseparable from a crisis in customs!) In the particular kind of disintegration and decomposition of language that Flaubert localizes in Emma's consciousness and on her tongue, by a hopeless and lethal paradox the differences that should make the difference instead break the difference, and work to the disestablishment of distinctions (thus when Emma is described both "tout en cousant" and "décousait," she is only doing what language is doing to her). More clearly than ever, Flaubert's careful arrangement of words, maintaining a constant hyperconsciousness of all their differences and similarities, makes us aware to just what an extent the fog in Emma Bovary's head is ultimately language— language in a critical state of malaise that indeed turns out to be fatal. That fog is a sign of the irresolvable difficulty of participating in a pleonastic proliferation of terms that is then compounded by the obligatory but illusory and unstable distinctions imposed by marriage, which, for Emma, confuses where it is supposed to clarify and separates where it joins.

Adultery Triumphant

At the beginning Emma's hair is carefully combed and arranged in an immaculate manner. "Her hair, so smooth that its two black braids seemed each a single piece, was parted in the middle with a fine line that dipped slightly with the curve of her head, and was swept together in a thick bun at the back . . . at the temples was a wavy effect . . . " (p. 29). ("Ses cheveux, dont les deux bandeaux noirs semblaient chacun d'un seul morceau, tant ils étaient lisses, étaient séparés sur le milieu de sa tête par une raie fine, qui s'enfonçait légèrement selon la courbe du crâne, et . . . ils allaient se confondre par-derrière en un chignon abondant, avec un mouvement ondé vers les tempes . . . " [p. 38].) It is hardly necessary to underline the number of premonitive key words in this description, which at this stage are apparently confined to a minute scrutiny of the topography of Emma's hair. But it is notable that while part of the hair is, as it were, "bounded," and parted, at another part of her head these separated *morceaux* come together ("se confondre") in a wavelike movement. It is as though part of her hair is governed by *règles* and another part is given over to *tournures,* discreteness and clearly maintained discriminations giving way to a watery confusion. In one sense her life is in her hair, moving between marriage and adultery. For a period she may be said to hold out against adultery, and then to oscillate between the two states. On her deathbed her hair is totally disheveled, "les cheveux dénoués," and I have said enough about that recurring phrase in a previous section. What has intervened between the two scenes is nothing less than the "triumph" of adultery, and all that I have suggested is implied in that word, adultery. The phrase occurs in the book after Charles has proved himself to be such an utter failure in the attempt to "cure" Hippolyte, and in Emma's eyes he now seems "impossible et anéanti." She looks at him in irritation and fury,—but let us look at Flaubert, looking at her.

"Emma bit her pale lip. Her fingers twisted a piece of coral she had broken off. The blazing points of her pupils were fixed on Charles like two flaming arrows about to be released. . . . She repented her past virtue as though it were a crime; what still remained of it collapsed beneath the savage onslaught of her pride. She reveled in all the malicious ironies of adultery triumphant" (p. 197). ("Emma mordait ses lèvres blêmes, et roulant entre ses doigts un des brins du polypier qu'elle avait cassé, elle fixait sur Charles la pointe ardente de ses prunelles, comme deux flèches de feu prêtes à partir. . . . Elle se repentait, comme d'un crime, de sa vertu passée, et ce qui en restait encore s'écroulait sous les coups furieux de son orgueil. Elle se délectait dans toutes les ironies mauvaises de l'adultère triomphant" [p. 247].) Emma is recognizable in her repetitions, biting her lips, breaking of bits ("brins"); but at this climatic moment in her life everything is inverted or perverted into its opposite. Cupid's shafts have become arrows of hate, virtue has turned into crime, her husband is nothing, her lover everything. But it is not a genuine or lasting transformation of feelings or transvaluation of values. Rather, all these apparent opposites and many others gradually, or rapidly, lose their differential features. The triumph of adultery is the destruction of difference. It is very shortly after this that we read of Rodolphe's failure to distinguish "la dissemblance des sentiments sous la parité des expressions," in the passage I have already analyzed. The effect of this failure on him I have referred to, but what of the effect on Emma? We have seen her looking for herself with her own eyes in the mirror; how does she appear, when she ceases to be a *vertueuse,* to the eyes of the adulterating other? (*To adulterate*—"to make impure by admixture": *adulteratus*—"defiled.") "Rodolphe perceived further pleasures to be exploited in this affair. Refusing to be inconvenienced by a sense of shame, he treated her as he pleased, and turned her into something pliant and corrupt" (p. 203). ("Rodolphe aperçut en cet amour d'autres jouissances à exploiter. Il jugea toute pudeur incommode. Il la traita sans façon. Il en fit quelque chose de souple et de corrompu" [p. 255].) The sexual and orgasmic implications of *jouissance* are clear enough, and to "exploit" them is necessarily to exploit the sexual partner. Nothing, to be sure, very novel in that. But that too is the point. For in the search for *nouveauté* there can only be a loss of the sense of anything *d'original* or significantly different. Rodolphe treats Emma "sans façon"—in an off-handed way, but also "without manner," "unceremoniously"—because adultery *has* no manners or ceremonies. It is defined in their negation and abrogation. In adultery Emma does not become another person, another role, another pose, etc., she becomes a *chose,* a thing devoid of indwelling determinants and thus *pliant* to the handling, shaping forces and figures around her. She enters the realm of interchangeable objects, which is the dehumanized, reified realm of the society and its prevailing currencies, financial and emotional. This is not to say that the implications of adultery as depicted by Flaubert effect a retroactive revalidation of the state of marriage. Marriage as he perceived and depicted it simply offered a different mode of reification and dehumanization. For Emma to "rediscover in adultery all the banality of marriage" (p. 301) ("retrouvait dans l'adultère toutes les platitudes du mariage" [p. 376]) is the ultimate malicious irony of all "les ironies mauvaises de l'adultère triomphant."

5

---•---

CONCLUSION

This study has barely opened up the infinitely complex problems concerning the relations between the family, marriage, adultery, and the novel. In the absence of historical and sociological material in this work, the very close relationship between the novel and the family has not been properly emphasized, yet clearly the genesis of both the modern family and what we call the novel—and their fates—are closely interlinked. The family is, of course, a very different phenomenon from the line (composed of those ties of blood that extended to all the descendants of a single ancestor). According to Philippe Ariès (to whose book *Centuries of Childhood*—particularly part three, "The Family"—I shall be referring) "only the line was capable of exciting the forces of feeling and imagination. That is why so many romances of chivalry treat of it."[1] This raises the important question, What kind of imagination did the *family* stir and nourish? Apparently complicit with the sanctity of the family, the centrality of marriage, and the authority of the Father, the novel has, in fact, in many cases harbored and deviously celebrated quite contrary feelings. Very often the novel writes of contracts but dreams of transgressions, and in reading it, the dream tends to emerge more powerfully.

While the rise of the novel and the emergence of what has been recognized as the modern family[2] are approximately coeval and clearly exerted certain kinds of reciprocal influences on each other (for it would be hard to argue for a one-way determinism operating from family to novel), their relationship has been from the start a strange one. To make the obvious point of basic difference: where the novel necessarily thrived upon *newelty*, no matter how much it appeared to defer to the established middle-class pieties, the family attempted to promote, precisely, familiarity, or perhaps one might say "familiality." Not the familiarity

---

[1]Philippe Ariès, *Centuries of Childhood*, p. 355.
[2]"Between the eighteenth century and the present day, the concept of the family hardly changed at all." Ibid., p. 404. See also Lawrence Stone, *The Family, Sex, and Marriage*.

that breeds contempt, but the familiarity that, it is hoped, will breed more familiarity. Of course, familiality can breed contempt and boredom and rebellion and any number of subversive drives and desires—that, indeed, has been one of the points of some of the books I have looked at. But still, somehow the novel was supposed to work with, or within, the family structure, for all its rogues and vagabonds, and notwithstanding the fact that one of the most famous of all English novels concentrates on a completely desocialized man isolated on an island (though of course he brings his society in his head with him, and the island in due course is colonized and "familied"). The fact is that from the start, the novel had a conservative drive, serving to support what were felt to be the best morals and manners and values of the period, and giving new prominence to that phenomenon only visible so comparatively recently, the family.[3] But in addition to that conservative drive, the novel has also always contained potential feelings for that which breaks up the family—departure, disruption, and other various modes of disintegration.

But then, as we well know, the family itself is an ambiguous institution. For one thing, it has to destroy itself in order to reconstitute itself: continuity involves dissolution. Then again, while for many writers and thinkers the family was the essential unit that held society together and maintained its stability, the family also came to be seen as a refuge *from* society—"the haven in a heartless world" that Christopher Lasch has written about.[4] It would be argued that the novel partook of those ambiguities. Clearly the importance of privacy in all this can hardly be

---

[3]Talking of an earlier period, Ariès says: "But the family existed in silence: it did not awaken feelings strong enough to inspire poet or artist. We must recognize the importance of this silence: not much value was placed on the family" (p. 364). In the eighteenth century, and later, the family precisely *did* awaken feelings in the novelist, ambiguous though they may at times have been.

[4]"Deprivations experienced in the public world had to be compensated in the realm of privacy." See Christopher Lasch, "The Family as a Haven in the Heartless World," *Salmagundi*, no. 35 (fall 1976), pp. 42–55. Ruskin made the same point with characteristic eloquence in *Sesame and Lilies:*

This is the true nature of home—it is the place of Peace; the shelter, not only from all injury, but from all terror, doubt, and division. In so far as it is not this, it is not home; so far as the anxieties of outer life penetrate into it, and the inconsistently-minded, unknown, unloved, or hostile society of the outer world is allowed by either husband or wife to cross the threshold, it ceases to be a home; it is then only a part of that outer world which you have roofed over, and lighted fire in. But so far as it is a sacred place, a vestal temple, a temple of the hearth watched over by Household Gods . . . so far as it is this, and roof and fire are types only of a nobler shade and light,—shade as of the rock in a weary land, and light as of the Pharos in the stormy sea;—so far it vindicates the name, and fulfils the praise, of Home.
(Quoted by Walter Houghton in *The Victorian Frame of Mind* [New Haven and London: Yale University Press, 1957, p. 343.)

overstressed. It is not just that writing and reading novels tend to be private activities, but a whole new desire for privacy seems to have arisen in the eighteenth century. Where the family up until the seventeenth century had been a center of social relations ("until the end of the seventeenth century, nobody was ever left alone"—Ariès), it subsequently tended to be an area of modified and varying secessions. I will run together some quotations from Ariès.

> The progress of the concept of the family followed the progress of private life, of domesticity. For a long time the conditions of everyday life did not allow the essential withdrawal by the household from the outside world. . . . In the eighteenth century, the family began to hold society at a distance, to push it back beyond a steadily extending zone of private life. . . . The modern family . . . cuts itself off from the world and opposes to society the isolated group of parents and children. All the energy of the group is expended on helping the children to rise in the world, individually and without any collective ambition. . . . It is not individualism which has triumphed, but the family. . . . But this family has advanced in proportion as sociability has retreated. It is as if the modern family had sought to take the place of the old social relationships . . . in order to preserve mankind from an unbearable or moral solitude."[5]

The triumph has been a very ambiguous one, as many writers have been at pains to point out.

One rather odd fact worth noting is that for Ariès, as the title of his book implies, the main changes in the family revolve, to a large extent, around the new attitude to children. "This powerful concept [i.e., of the family] was formed around the conjugal family, that of the parents and children. This concept is closely linked to that of childhood. It has less and less to do with problems such as the honour of a line, the integrity of an inheritance, or the age and permanence of a name: it springs simply from the unique relationship between the parents and their children. . . . What counted most of all was the emotion aroused by the child, the living image of his parents."[6] While it would be wrong to say that the novel has showed little interest in the child (though more often it turns to the unplaced or misplaced child rather than to the secure and protected product of a legitimate union), the child does not have anything like that kind of centrality to the novel that it had for the family. Of course there are many novels of childhood, and I am not forgetting our Pips, and Little Nells and David Copperfields, et al. But the child does not seem to engage the imagination of the novelist in quite the same way as it did the family. In a way, this is understandable enough—there is just so much

---

[5]Ariès, *Centuries of Childhood*, pp. 298, 275, 298, 404, 406.
[6]Ibid., p. 364.

you can write about a child: except in their disturbances—or deaths—they are not very rewarding material. Even so, as I have at least intimated in the preceding chapters, children really play a relatively small part in the three novels I have looked at (if not something of a negative one, as in *Madame Bovary*). It is as if the novel has never really been interested in genealogical continuity. It has indeed followed the fortunes, and changes, of the family, and as we all too well know, one of its abiding topics has been the progress toward marriage. Yet is is my contention that its real, if secret, interest has been aroused by the weak points in the family, the possible fissures, the breaches, the breakdowns. Which is why the novel tends to be drawn, all but irresistibly, to the problem of adultery.

Much more could be said about the changes in the family that accompanied, or were reflected by, changes in the novel, one point of particular interest being how marriage ceased to be basically a secular contract and was, in Stone's words, "sanctified" into "holy matrimony,"[7] which of course increases the possibilities for effective blasphemy or desecration, as well as guilt and condemnation. But so much work has been done on the whole change in the history of the family by people like Ariès, Stone, Lasch, and others, that it would be pointless to attempt a condensed recapitulation here. I hope in a subsequent volume to go into detail concerning the relationship between the family and the novel in the nineteenth and early-twentieth centuries. But enough has perhaps been said, or suggested, for the present volume. Another related topic, to which I have alluded, concerns the fate of the father in nineteenth-century fiction. Again, this is something that I wish to examine in more detail, but a paragraph from a recent book on Balzac will perhaps give some emphasis to the importance of the whole topic of the problems and changes involved in the notion of paternal authority.

> The study of the displacement or subversion of the authority of the father in nineteenth-century fiction remains to be written, but Balzac will not only have a central place in it, it will be his melodramatic texts that will attract the greatest attention. For it is here that we encounter one of the most fundamental contradictions of Balzac's work. As we all know, Balzac was not only ideologically committed to the notion of the authoritarian father, he was also obsessed by what has been called "*le mythe de la paternité*," a myth which, in various guises, pervades the whole of the *Comédie Humaine*. Is it therefore a mere accident that in many of the texts I have discussed under the heading of "melodrama," the theme of the father is central, but is articulated in a way completely at odds with the ideological standpoints and the imaginative fantasies? Frequently, they are stories of parental authority and filial obedience falling apart, of absent fathers,

[7]Stone, *The Family, Sex, and Marriage*, p. 136.

rejected fathers, renegade fathers: Hulot betrays his responsibilities and is both resisted and finally usurped by his son; d'Aiglemont is defied by his daughter Hélène; Goriot is humiliated and destroyed by Anastasie and Delphine; Vautrin's quasi-paternal schemes for Lucien come crashing to the ground. At its deepest level, this general spectacle of betrayal, disarray and collapse includes that primary support of the traditional symbolic and social order, the name of the father.[8]

This suggests the importance of the topic in one major novelist, but I think it could and should be examined throughout the whole range of nineteenth-century fiction, bringing in as much social history as seems appropriate. For, among other things, we are dealing here with the major problem of the relationship between author and authority (from another point of view, Edward Said has made many brilliant points about his problem in his book, *Beginnings*).

In this connection I will want to draw on and, where appropriate deploy, the ideas contained in that important essay by Max Horkheimer, "Authority and the Family." As he demonstrates:

Amid all the radical differences between human types from different periods of history, all have in common that their essential characteristics are determined by the power-relationships proper to society at any given time. People have for more than a hundred years abandoned the view that character is to be explained in terms of the completely isolated individual, and they now regard man as at every point a socialized being. But this also means that men's drives and passions, their characteristic dispositions and reaction-patterns are stamped by the power-relationships under which the social life-process unfolds at any time. The class system within which the individual's outward life runs its course is reflected not only in his mind, his ideas, his basic concepts and judgments but also in his inmost life, in his preferences and desires. Authority is therefore a central category for history.

How the nineteenth-century novel actually confronts and dramatizes (or ignores, simplifies, or mystifies) the basic problems of "authority," here sketched by Horkheimer, is another matter that I will want to consider. But as part of the termination of this volume, I cannot resist quoting from the conclusion to his essay, in which he describes "the incongruity of love and its bourgeois form."

However decisive a force in human development monogamous marriage has been in its millennial history, and however long and significant a future it may still have in a higher form of society, it has at any rate served to make very clear the contradiction between life as it unfolds and the circumstances in which it unfolds. In the Renaissance there were two

[8]Christopher Prendergast, *Balzac: Fiction and Melodrama* (London: Edward Arnold, 1978), chapter 9.

legends which both found immortal expression in works of art: Romeo and Juliet, and Don Juan. Both glorify the rebellion of eros against authority ... Such legendary figures manifest the gulf that lies between the individual's claim to happiness and the claim of the family to priority. These artistic creations reflect one of the antagonisms that exist between social forms and vital forces.

And he moves to his conclusion, which by no means forsees the "triumph" of the family, but rather new problems for it.

The means of protecting the cultural totality and developing it further have increasingly come into conflict with the cultural content itself. Even if the form of the family should finally be stabilized by the new measures, yet, as the importance of the whole bourgeois middle class decreases, this form will lose its active power which is grounded in the free vocational activity of the male. In the end everything about the family as we have known it in this age will have to be supported and held together in an ever more artificial fashion. . . .

In the bourgeois golden age there was a fruitful interaction between family and society, because the authority of the father was based on his role in society, while society was renewed by the education for authority which went on in the patriarchal family. Now, however, the admittedly indispensable family is becoming a simple problem of technological manipulation by the government. The totality of relationships in the present age, the universal web of things, was strengthened and stabilized by one particular element, namely, authority, and the process of strengthening and stabilization went on essentially at the particular, concrete level of the family. The family was the "germ cell" of bourgeois culture and it was, like the authority in it, a living reality. This dialectical totality of universality, particularity, and individuality proves now to be a unity of antagonistic forces, and the disruptive element in the culture is making itself more strongly felt than the unitive.

This is perhaps to anticipate a much later development in our study, and yet I trust that the pertinence of Horkheimer's remarks will be readily registered by any reader of this particular volume. Both society and the novel, in their different ways, center on the family, and yet that binding, stabilizing unit turns out to contain potentially antagonistic and disruptive elements that make it a center that cannot hold, an illusory center, or perhaps not a center at all. And this, I think, the novel sensed and discovered at an early stage in its development, no matter how committed it seemed to the contemporary middle-class orthodoxies.

Contracts, pacts, mutual commitments and agreements—these range from the most officially sanctioned and defended to the most private, improvised, and socially nonvalidated. I have not, I am aware, sufficiently differentiated between the socially recognized and ordained contract, marked by signatures and often surrounded by reinforcing symbolic rituals, and those less visible, more metaphoric contracts, such as the contract we enter into when we participate in a language (as Saussure wrote, "Language . . . exists only by virtue of a sort of contract signed by members of a community," *Course in General Linguistics,* chapter 3, p. 15), or the more elusive contract between the writer and reader of a novel. Again, these are matters that I hope can be entered into in more detail in subsequent work. For the moment, it may be enough to suggest the difference in our contemporary sense of the contract from the sense that I suggested obtained at least in the middle of the eighteenth century, by noting that for Roland Barthes, the model of the good contract has become, not marriage—but prostitution! The passage is worth quoting in full:

Ambiguous praise of the contract

His first image of the *contract* (the pact) is more or less objective: sign, language, narrative, society function by contract, but since this contract is generally masked, the critical operation consists in deciphering the confusion of reasons, alibis, appearances, in short, the whole of the social *natural,* in order to make manifest the controlled exchange on which the semantic process and collective life are based. Yet, at another level, the contract is a bad object: a bourgeois value which merely legalizes a kind of economic talion: *nothing for nothing,* says the bourgeois contract: under the praise of bookkeeping, of profit-making, we must therefore read the Base, the Paltry. At the same time, and at yet another level, the contract is ceaselessly desired, as the justice of a world finally "regular": the preference for the contract in human relations, the security once a contract can be interposed between them, the reluctance to receive without giving, etc. At this point—since the body intervenes directly here, the model of the good contract is the contract of Prostitution. For this contract, declared immoral by all societies and by all systems (except the most archaic), liberates in fact from what might be called the *imaginary embarrassments* of the exchange: what am I to count on in the other's desire, in *what I am for him?* The contract eliminates this confusion: it is in fact the only position which the subject can assume without falling into two inverse but equally abhorred images: that of the "egoist" (who demands without caring that he has nothing to give) and that of the "saint" (who gives but forbids himself ever to demand): thus the discourse of the contract eludes two plenitudes: it permits observing the golden rule of any *habitation,* discerned in the Shikidai passageway: *no will-to-seize and yet no oblation.*[9]

The history of the novel is full of the records of the fates of unacceptable egoists and would-be saints, of all kinds of seizures and sacrifices, and it

---

[9]Roland Barthes, *Roland Barthes,* p. 59. More 'perverse' than the 'contract' of Prostitution is the contract signed by Severin and Wanda von Donajew in Sacher-Masoch's *Venus in Furs*—an ultimate travesty of the marriage contract. But that is, indeed, another story.

has, I would contend, shown up all the ambiguities connected with the notion of contract that Barthes, in his own way, alludes to here, showing perhaps, and most worryingly, that the perfect bourgeois contract is an impossibility, and perhaps an undesirable impossibility at that. Which would seem to leave us, in Barthes' terms, with the perverse ideal of the good contract of prostitution (the reverse mirror image of the bourgeois ideal of a good contract, but arguably the very structure of its bad conscience)—or that something in between contract and prostitution, which I have called adultery or transgression—for an adulteress is a wife who is not a wife, a prostitute who is not a prostitute, the keeper and breaker of the insecure security of the contract of marriage.

One of the basic problems about marriage is that its security depends upon repetition—"le mariage implique l'habitude"—and that repetition and habit diminish the feelings, particularly the erotic intensity, upon which the marriage was founded. Hence, and only apparently paradoxically, marriage can breed the need for "irrégularité," "des explosions capricieuses," "désordre et l'infraction." The quotations are from Georges Bataille's book *L'Erotisme,* in which he also writes:

> What makes it difficult to speak about the forbidden is not only the variability of its objects, but also its illogical character. With reference to the same object, it is never impossible to make a directly contrary proposition. There is nothing that is forbidden that may not be transgressed. *Often transgression is admitted, often it is even prescribed.* [my italics] . . . In the realm of the irrational, where our reflections effectively enclose us, we must say: "Occasionally an intangible prohibition is violated—that doesn't mean it has ceased to be intangible." We could even go so far as to putting forward the absurd proposition: "*the forbidden is there to be violated.*" This proposition is not, as it at first seems, outrageously risky, but *the correct statement of an inevitable relation between emotions pulling us in contrary directions.* [My italics]
>
> *Ce qui rend malaisé de parler d'interdit n'est pas seulement la variabilité des objets, mais un caractère illogique. Jamais, à propos du même objet, une proposition opposée n'est impossible. Il n'est pas d'interdit qui ne puisse être transgressé. Souvent la transgression est admise, souvent même elle est prescrite.*
>
> *. . . Dans le domaine irrationnel, où nos considérations nous enferment, nous devons dire: "Parfois un interdit intangible est violé, cela ne veut pas dire qu'il ait cessé d'être intangible." Nous pouvons même aller jusqu'à la proposition absurde: "l'interdit est là pour être violé." Cette proposition n'est pas, comme il semble d'abord, une gageure, mais l'énoncé correct d'un rapport inévitable entre des émotions de sens contraire.*[10]

The relevance of these observations, particularly the words I have italicized, for the study of this book should be amply clear by now; for

[10]Georges Bataille, *L'Erotisme*, pp. 122, 123, 70–71. See in particular chapter 5, "La Transgression," from which the final quotation above is taken.

the novel, despite—or in addition to—no matter how much surface facticity and material mimesis, does much of its work in that *domaine irrationel* of which Bataille writes, and has brought to light and laid bare many of the strange connections and rapports between apparently opposed or contradictory feelings. In particular, as I have tried to suggest, it does not show a simple *contest* between marital fidelity and adultery; rather, contracts and transgressions are inseparable, the one generating the other. Or, in Bataille's words, interdictions are there to be at once respected and violated. This deep and troubling paradox is one that, I have been suggesting, the novel has known, perhaps from the beginning, and much of its power comes from its awareness of it.

Foucault makes a point related to Bataille's ideas, and my attempts to intimate the complex relationship between contract and transgression. "Transgression is neither violence in a divided world (in an ethical world) nor a victory over limits (in a dialectical or revolutionary world); and exactly for this reason, its role is to measure the excessive distance that it opens at the heart of the limit and to trace the flashing line that causes the limit to arise. Transgression contains nothing negative, but affirms limited being—affirms the limitlessness into which it leaps as it opens this zone to existence for the first time." For the social world of the novel in the period I have been referring to, adultery is precisely such a leap into limitlessness, with the result that the whole ambiguous problematics of limits are brought into the open. And Foucault sees an even more important aspect to transgression. "Profanation in a world which no longer recognizes any positive meaning in the sacred—is this not more or less what we may call transgression? In that zone which our culture affords for our gestures and speech, transgression prescribes not only the sole manner of discovering the sacred in its unmediated substance, but also a way of recomposing its empty form, its absence, through which it becomes all the more scintillating."[11] It would be misleading to say that every heroine who commits adultery finds a devious way back to an experience of the sacred, but profanation *can* be for her an entry into a world of meaning, at least temporarily. The problem is that by definition you cannot transform transgression and profanation into a regular way of life, for then, as Emma found, you are back into the vicious downward spiral of devaluation through repetition, and the loss of difference engendered by habit. Which is why, for Emma to rediscover in adultery all the banality of marriage, is one of the most disturbing discoveries in the history of the novel. For, once in that condition, nothing, literally, makes any difference. And that is death.

[11]Michel Foucault, "Preface to Transgression," in *Language, Counter-Memory, Practice,* pp. 35, 30.

But since this volume has attempted to trace out some of the connections between adultery and the novel, I should end with a note stressing the importance of this connection. Barthes writes:

Marriage

The relation to Narrative (representation, to *mimesis*) has something to do with the Oedipus complex, as we know. But it also has something to do, in our mass societies, with marriage. Even more than the number of plays and films of which adultery is the subject, I see a sign of this in that (painful) moment of a TV interview: the actor J.D. is being questioned, "roasted," as to his relations with his wife (herself an actress); the interviewer *wants* the good husband to be unfaithful: this excites him, he *demands* an ambiguous phrase, the seed of a story. Thus marriage affords great collective excitations; if we managed to suppress the Oedipus complex and marriage, what would be left for us to *tell*? With them gone, our popular arts would be transformed entirely.[12]

This opens up more questions than I wish to go into here and is, in any case, a comment aimed in particular at contemporary mass entertainment. But it is clear that the connection between adultery and narration is a close and important one. Just as one could say that by entering into an adulterous relationship, a person introduces a new element of narrative into his or her life, initiates a new living "story," so for the novelist it is often not really marriage that initiates and inspires his narrative, but adultery. That *does* offer something to tell. (Just as, perhaps, the adulterer or adulteress, effectively "renarrativizes" a life that has become devoid of story.) It would be tempting to suggest that without adultery, or the persistent possibility of adultery, the novel would have been bereft of much of its narrational urge. But that, perhaps, would be to conclude too much. What is certain is that without the subject of adultery, the history of the novel would, indeed, have been very different—and much poorer.

[12]Barthes, *Roland Barthes*, p. 121.

SELECTED BIBLIOGRAPHY

Ariès, Phillippe. *Centuries of Childhood: A Social History of Family Life.* Translated by Robert Baldick. New York: Alfred A. Knopf, 1962.

Barthes, Roland. *Roland Barthes.* Translated by Richard Howard. New York: Hill and Wang, 1976.

––––––. *Sade, Fourier, Loyola.* Translated by Richard Miller. New York: Hill and Wang, 1976.

Bataille, Georges. *L'Erotisme.* Paris: Union Générale d'Editions, 1965.

Bateson, Gregory. *Steps to an Ecology of Mind.* New York: Ballantine Books, 1975.

Douglas, Mary. *Purity and Danger: An Analysis of Concepts of Pollution and Taboo.* New York: Praeger Publishers, 1966.

Flaubert, Gustave. *Madame Bovary.* Paris: Gallimard, 1972.

––––––. *Madame Bovary.* Translated by Alan Russell. Harmondsworth, Middlesex: Penguin, 1950.

Foucault, Michel. *Language, Counter-Memory, Practice: Selected Essays and Interviews.* Edited by Donald F. Bouchard. Translated by Donald F. Bouchard and Sherry Simon. Ithaca, N.Y.: Cornell University Press, 1977.

Freud, Sigmund. "Antithetical Sense of Primal Words." In *Collected Papers,* edited by James Strachey, vol. 4. London: Hogarth Press, 1950.

––––––. "Family Romances." In *Collected Papers,* edited by James Strachey, vol. 5. London: Hogarth Press, 1959.

––––––. "Femininity." In *The Standard Edition of the Complete Psychological Works of Sigmund Freud,* edited by James Strachey, vol. 22. London: Hogarth Press, 1964.

––––––. "Fetischismus." In *The Standard Edition of the Complete Psychological Works of Sigmund Freud,* edited by James Strachey, vol. 21. London: Hogarth Press, 1964.

––––––. *Jokes and Their Relation to the Unconscious.* In *The Standard Edition of the Complete Psychological Works of Sigmund Freud,* edited by James Strachey, vol. 8. London: Hogarth Press, 1960.

––––––. "The Most Prevalent Form of Degradation in Erotic Life." In *Collected Papers,* edited by James Strachey, vol. 4. London: Hogarth Press, 1950.

Girard, René. *Deceit, Desire, and the Novel: Self and Other in Literary Structure.* Translated by Yvonne Freccero. Baltimore: The Johns Hopkins Press, 1966.

Goethe, Johann Wolfgang. *Kindred by Choice.* Translated by H. M. Waidson. London: John Calder, 1960.

———. *Die Wahlverwandtschaften*. Munich: Deutscher Taschenbuch Verlag, 1972.

Herder, Johann Gottfried. "Essay on the Origin of Language." In *On the Origin of Language,* translated by Alexander Gode. New York: Frederick Ungar Publishing Company, 1966.

Horkheimer, Max. "Authority and the Family." In *Critical Theory,* translated by Matthew J. O'Connell et al. New York: Herder and Herder, 1972.

Jacob, François. *The Logic of Life: A History of Heredity.* Translated by Betty E. Spillman. New York: Pantheon Books, 1973.

Lacan, Jacques. "The Insistence of the Letter in the Unconscious." *Yale French Review,* no. 36/37 (1966), pp. 112–47.

———. *The Language of the Self.* Translated with notes and commentary by Anthony Wilden. Baltimore: The Johns Hopkins Press, 1968.

———. "Seminar on 'The Purloined Letter.'" *Yale French Review,* no. 48 (1972), pp. 39–72.

———. "Le stade du miroir comme formateur de la fonction du Je." In *Ecrits I.* Paris: Editions du Seuil, 1966.

Lefebvre, Henri. *Everyday Life in the Modern World.* New York: Henri Lefebvre-Harper Torch Books, 1971.

Lévi-Strauss, Claude. *The Savage Mind.* Chicago: University of Chicago Press, 1966.

Mann, Thomas. *Last Essays.* Edited by Richard Winston et al. New York: Alfred A. Knopf, 1959.

Marx, Karl. *Selected Writings.* Edited by David McLellan. Oxford: Oxford University Press, 1977.

Mead, George Herbert. *Mind, Self, and Society: From the Standpoint of a Social Behaviorist.* Edited by Charles W. Morris. Chicago: University of Chicago Press, 1934.

Nietzsche, Friedrich. *The Genealogy of Morals.* Translated by Francis Golffing. New York: Anchor Books, 1956.

———. *The Will to Power.* Translated by Walter Kaufmann. New York: Vintage, 1968.

Rougement, Denis de. *Love in the Western World.* New York: Anchor Books, 1957.

Rousseau, Jean Jacques, *Julie, or The New Eloise.* Translated and abridged by Judith H. McDowell. University Park: Pennsylvania State University Press, 1968.

———. *Julie ou La Nouvelle Héloïse.* Paris: Garnier-Flammarion, 1967.

Said, Edward. *Beginnings: Introduction and Method.* New York: Basic Books, 1975.

Saussure, Ferdinand de. *Course in General Linguistics.* Edited by Charles Bally et al. Translated by Wade Baskin. London: Peter Owen, 1959.

Scheffler, Harold W. "Structuralism in Anthropology." *Yale French Review,* no. 36/37 (1966), pp. 66–88.

Stone, Lawrence. *The Family, Sex, and Marriage: In England, 1500–1800.* London: Weidenfeld and Nicolson, 1977.

Wilden, Anthony. *System and Structure: Essays in Communication.* New York: Barnes and Noble, 1972.

INDEX